D0081097

Diversity in Organizations

Myrtle P. Bell
UNIVERSITY OF TEXAS, ARLINGTON

SOUTH-WESTERN
CENGAGE Learning™

Australia • Brazil • Japan • Korea • Mexico • Singapore • Spain • United Kingdom • United States

Diversity in Organizations
Myrtle P. Bell

VP/Editorial Director:
Jack W. Calhoun

Director of Development/ Sr. Publisher:
Melissa S. Acunã

Executive Editor:
John Szilagyi

Sr. Developmental Editor:
Mardell Glinski Schultz

Sr. Marketing Manager:
Kimberly Kanakes

Sr. Marketing Communications Manager:
Jim Overly

Production Project Manager:
Robert Dreas

Manager of Technology, Editorial:
Vicky True

Technology Project Editor:
Kristen Meere

Web Coordinator:
Karen Schaffer

Manufacturing Coordinator:
Doug Wilke

Production House:
International Typesetting and Composition

Printer:
R.R. Donnelley
Crawfordsville, Indiana

Art Director:
Tippy McIntosh

Internal and Cover Designer:
Kim Torbeck, Imbue Design

Cover Images:
Leon Zernitsky/Images.com

Printed in the United States of America

5 6 10 09

Student Edition:
ISBN-13: 978-0-324-30257-8
ISBN-10: 0-324-30257-6

Library of Congress Control Number:
2005934424

For more information about our products, contact us at:
Cengage Learning
Customer & Sales Support,
1-800-354-9706

South-Western Cengage Learning
5191 Natorp Boulevard
Mason, OH 45040
USA

This book is dedicated to my great-great-grandmother,
Laura Ratcliff Lenoir (1835–1948), born enslaved, but died free,
and to my grandfather, Geylon Johnson.

Brief Contents

Table of Contents

Chapter 3 *Theories and Thinking about Diversity* 65

Section II Examining Specific Groups and Categories 87

Chapter 4 *Blacks/African Americans* 89

Chapter 5 *Latinos/Hispanics* 127

PREFACE

My goal in writing *Diversity in Organizations* is to provide readers with a comprehensive source of information about diversity issues relevant to work, workers, and organizations. This book combines research from management, sociology, psychology, and other disciplines pertinent to "diversity in organizations" into one cohesive, understandable, engaging, and thought-provoking whole. The audience for the book is everyone who has worked, currently works, or intends to work in any organization. Those who teach and study diversity and those who wish to be better employees and managers in organizations having diverse applicants, employees, and customers should find this book useful in their pursuits. *Diversity in Organizations* fills a void for (1) undergraduate and graduate students in every discipline, (2) researchers seeking a source of information on a wide variety of diversity topics, and (3) employees, managers, and executives who have a commitment to diversity that goes beyond short-term training efforts.

It is my opinion, and increasingly that of many other researchers, that diversity is no less important than more established fields. As with other disciplines, there are theories and empirical research, along with centuries of related history. In a critical contrast to some other disciplines, diversity is relevant to everyone's educational and employment experiences, regardless of their primary field of study or of their career paths.

BACKGROUND, RATIONALE, AND APPROACH OF THE BOOK

In the two decades since *Workforce 2000*[1] focused the attention of the media, managers, executives, and researchers on the increasing diversity in the workplace, the diversity industry has burgeoned. Countless diversity training books and diversity articles (empirical and otherwise) have been published, and hundreds of Web sites, skills-building courses, and training programs have appeared. Management and human resources research suggest that training is short term and with an immediate focus. Education and development, on the other hand, have a long-term focus.[2] While diversity training and skills-building programs are useful in many ways, in-depth education (including theory, research, and data) is vital to long-term success.

A major barrier to providing or obtaining education about diversity in organizations has been that there are relatively few inclusive scholarly books or texts that use a data-based approach. Those who teach or want to learn about diversity have often done so through "readings"—bringing together a compendium of articles, cases, and focused books (e.g., on race, gender, or discrimination at work). Lacking one comprehensive research-based book that covered many diversity issues, I too have used the readings approach in the past.

Over several years of teaching diversity to hundreds of undergraduate and graduate

---

[1] Johnston, W. B., & Packer, A. E. (1997). *Workforce 2000,* Indianapolis, IN: Hudson Institute.

[2] Bohlander, G. W., & Snell, S. (2004). *Managing Human Resources* (13th edition), Mason, OH: South-Western Publishers.

students, I have gathered valuable information that is reflected in *Diversity in Organizations*. I have asked my students what they learned, what was most meaningful to them, what surprised them most, and how they could use this information to make their organizations best deal with the inevitable fact of diversity. I have asked how they would use the information personally to improve their careers and experiences and treatment of others.

Students from all backgrounds have said that the course upon which this book is designed should be mandatory for everyone who will ever work in a diverse environment. It is my hope that many will find it useful in making diversity in organizations a positive attribute, in dispelling many myths and misperceptions about diversity issues, and in sharing data-based knowledge about diversity. The question is not whether one's organization will be affected by diversity, but rather whether it will be a positive or negative factor in the organization's existence and whether the organization will embrace and seek it, or reluctantly tolerate it. *Diversity in Organizations* is written to help those who wish to develop a greater understanding of diversity and to make it a positive force in our existence. Most importantly, I hope it will contribute to pursuit of fairness, equity, and opportunity for all workers, regardless of race, ethnicity, gender, religion, age, physical and mental ability, sexual orientation, weight and appearance, and other diversity factors.

Acknowledgements

My department chair, Jeffrey McGee, Dean Dan Himarios, and the University of Texas at Arlington's Faculty Development Leave Program have generously supported this project and my diversity work. My colleagues at UTA created an open and encouraging environment. Jim Quick has offered moral and tangible support, and I thank him for being a trusted, valued ally. I am deeply grateful to Gary McMahan for providing consistent, humorous friendship, for gathering unorthodox and empirical research, and for teaching me some important things about diversity that I otherwise would never have learned. Eileen Kwesiga located countless articles and books, and regularly reminded me to think on the good and lovely—reminders that were often sorely needed. I am fortunate to have had Eileen as my student and friend. Mary McLaughlin (Pennsylvania State University) was a constant source of research, ideas, and compassion. I thank Mary and her students at Penn State who provided useful comments and suggestions that helped strengthen the book. I sincerely appreciate Debra Nelson's (Oklahoma State University) early advice and encouragement. The librarians and support staff at my university were immensely helpful, fast, and generous in their research support. I am deeply indebted to the many students in my *Diversity in Organizations* courses, too many to name, who provided several semesters of detailed explanations of what they learned, asking insightful questions, and sharing their experiences; the book is much better for their diversity and candor.

Dave Harrison (Pennsylvania State University), my major professor and friend, collaborated with me on my first formal diversity research and provided incomparable support, guidance, and training in my quest to be a professor, researcher, and scholar. I strive to pass it on. I am very grateful to Jean Ramsey (Texas Southern University), to Alison Konrad (University of Western

Ontario), to my colleagues in the Gender and Diversity in Organizations Division of the Academy of Management, who are too numerous to name, and to all who teach diversity. Thank you for your commitment to the field as we continue this worthwhile work.

Many thanks to Beth Patterson, of Deloitte Consulting, for introducing me to Deloitte's Women's Initiatives Network and to Deloitte's purposeful diversity efforts. I thank Moira P. Baker for so modeling genuine diversity supportive leader behaviors some 30 years ago at Notre Dame that they remain fresh in my mind.

The team at South-Western, a part of Cengage Learning, was incredible from the start to the completion of this book. Michele Progransky's initial and subsequent patient queries about my readiness to write this book were perfectly timed. Mardell Glinski Schultz was an invaluable source of encouragement, advice, and support throughout the process. I am indebted to John Szilagyi, for pairing me with Mardell, and for his confidence about this project and patience to see it to fruition. I thank Michele, Mardell, John, Bob Dreas, Mona Tiwary, and so many others at South-Western whose contributions to the project made it a reality.

I thank my husband, Earnest, for believing in me continually, for participating in the second shift, and for rejecting stereotypes. My mother-in-law, Vera Jefferson, shaped Earnest's views of work, family, and working women. Joy and Josh clarified the need to write this book and are constant sources of inspiration to continue diversity work. Daphne Berry provided me with a motivational prod when I really needed it and kept prodding and helping in countless ways throughout the process. I appreciate Sonia Jefferson and Carol Washington for supporting me in ways that cannot be verbalized, and Ken Johnson, for his lifelong, single-minded commitment to civil rights and justice.

I am grateful for my mother, Iris Johnson, for being an ideal model of a working mother, and for providing countless opportunities to learn about diversity, and to learn to love differences in people from the neighborhood and from around the world. I thank her for instilling in me a clear understanding of our common humanity. I am especially grateful to God, for setting before me an open door and for providing me with a lifetime of diversity learning experiences and a passion for the work. Lastly, I am very grateful to countless unknown others who have done this work for a very long time, and to Dr. George C. Wright (President, Prairie View A&M University), for helping me find the courage to go through the open door.

The author and publishing team would like to thank the following individuals whose review of individual chapters of this text helped shape the final text. Thank you so much for your valuable insights.

Jeanne Aurelio
Bridgewater University

Dawn D. Bennett-Alexander
University of Georgia

Gwendolyn M. Combs
University of Nebraska-Lincoln

Beverly DeMarr
Ferris State University

Jeanie M. Forray
Western New England College

Thomas E. Harris
University of Alabama

Linda M. Hite
Indiana University-Purdue University

Helen J. Muller
University of New Mexico

Laura Morgan Roberts
Harvard Business School

Janet Romaine
Saint Anselm College

Ashleigh Shelby Rosette
Duke University

Ancillaries

Instructor's Resource CD-ROM (0-324-36460-1) Includes instructor's manual with chapter outlines, teaching notes, and suggested testing options along with complete PowerPoint presentation that covers each chapter's main concepts.

Section I

Introduction, Legislation, and Theories

1 Chapter

Introduction

Chapter Objectives

After completing this chapter, readers should have a firm understanding of the importance of diversity in organizations. They should specifically be able to:

- *explain recent and projected changes in the demographic makeup of the U.S. population.*
- *explain what "diversity" encompasses.*
- *discuss research supportive of the individual and organizational benefits of diversity.*
- *understand the rationale and structure behind the organization of the book.*

Key Facts

After more than two decades of diversity research, four decades of antidiscrimination legislation, and extraordinary media attention to diversity, discrimination and exclusion in organizations persist.

Valuing diversity can benefit organizations in the areas of cost, resource acquisition, marketing, creativity, problem solving, and system flexibility, and individuals through intellectual engagement, perspective taking, and greater understanding of the implications and benefits of diversity.

Despite the amount of media attention focusing on lawsuits and damage settlements, an organization's likelihood of being sued is relatively small.

If an organization develops a reputation for valuing all types of employees, it will become known as an employer of choice, increasing its ability to attract and retain workers from a variety of backgrounds.

Introduction and Overview

What is Diversity?

Diversity is defined as real or perceived differences among people that affect their interactions and relationships.[1] Drawn from more than two decades of theoretical and empirical research in management, psychology, social psychology, sociology, and economics, this book focuses on real or perceived differences among people in race, ethnicity, sex, religion, age, physical and mental ability, sexual orientation, work and family status, and weight and appearance. These areas are differences that are based on power or dominance relations between groups, particularly "identity groups," which are the collectivities people use to categorize themselves and others.[2] They are often readily apparent, strong sources of personal identity, and stem from historical disparities in treatment, opportunities, and outcomes. Some diversity research has considered diversity in functional area, education, tenure, values, and attitudes as they affect people's organizational experiences. While these areas may also be sources of real or perceived differences among people that affect their interactions and relationships, they are rarely readily apparent or strong sources of personal identity and generally do not stem from historical disparities in treatment, opportunities, or outcomes. Focusing on *any* individual difference, rather than differences having strong personal meaning and stemming from or coinciding with significant power differences among groups, would make all groups diverse, and would therefore make the entire concept of workplace diversity meaningless.[3]

Multiple Group Memberships and Permeability of Boundaries

People have different outcomes, opportunities, and experiences in organizations based on their group memberships. In the United States, those who are White, male, and do not have a disability generally earn higher wages and have higher organizational status than persons who are non-White, female, or have a disability.[4] Whites are more likely to work in the primary labor market, which includes jobs in large organizations, with more opportunities for advancement and retirement, vacation, and medical benefits. People of color are more likely to work in the secondary labor market of low-skilled, low-paid, insecure jobs. Secondary labor market jobs, often service-sector jobs, offer little or no opportunities for advancement, or health, vacation, or retirement benefits.[5]

[1] Dobbs, M. F. (1996). "Managing diversity: Lessons from the private sector." *Public Personnel Management*, 25 (Sept), p. 351–368.

[2] Konrad, A. M. (2003). "Defining the domain of workplace diversity scholarship." *Group and Organization Management,* 28(1), 4–17.

[3] Ibid., p. 7.

[4] See, for example, *U.S. Department of Labor, Women's Bureau*. "Earnings differences between women and men." In D. Dunn & P. Dubeck (Eds.). (2002). *Workplace/Women's Place: An Anthology*. Los Angeles: Roxbury Publishing Company. Braddock, D. & Bachelder, L. (1994). The glass ceiling and persons with disabilities. Washington, DC: Department of Labor.

[5] For a discussion of dual labor markets, see Healey, J. F. (2004). *Diversity and Society: Race, Ethnicity, and Gender*. Thousand Oaks, CA: Pine Forge Press.

The categories of race, ethnicity, sex, religion, age, physical and mental ability, and sexual orientation are not mutually exclusive, however. Men and women have a race and ethnic background, an age, a sexual orientation, and possibly a religion. Further, some of the categories are immutable, but others are not, and may change over one's lifetime. People may be born with or acquire disabilities, and everyone ages. A person who is dominant in one group may not be in another, for example, White and female or male and Latino. A White man may have a disability, be an older worker, or a member of another nondominant group and personally experience job-related discrimination. He may also have a working wife, mother, or sister who has faced sex-based salary inequity or harassment or a daughter or granddaughter whom he would prefer did not have to face such discrimination at work. In addition, diversity research consistently suggests that top management commitment is required to effect change. White men are considerably more likely to occupy leadership positions (executives, board members, or managers) than others. As such, they are more likely to have the power to implement important changes at the organizational level and influence behaviors and perspectives about the overall benefits of diversity; their commitment to diversity is essential.

Misperception: Diversity is beneficial only to minorities and women.

Reality: Diversity benefits everyone.

Although we emphasize and data clearly show that some groups (people of color, women, and people with disabilities) face more barriers and organizational discrimination, the value of diversity to *everyone* is stressed in this book. As does Roosevelt Thomas, a pioneer in diversity work, we suggest that "managing diversity is a comprehensive managerial process for developing an environment that works for all employees."[6] At the same time, it is naïve to ignore the fact that membership in some groups or that some combinations of memberships (e.g., woman of color) have more negative ramifications for job-related opportunities and success than others.[7] Commitment to diversity requires concerted measures to recognize, acknowledge, and address historical discrimination and differential treatment, rather than undermining diversity programs or efforts to address inequities in the name of inclusiveness. The research and recommendations in this book make apparent the need to consider the past and present while working toward a more diversity-friendly future.

---

[6] Thomas, Roosevelt. (1991). *Beyond Race and Gender: Unleashing the Power of Your Total Work Force by Managing Diversity*. P. 10. New York: AMACOM.

[7] For a discussion of the intersection of race and sex discrimination and the need to consider both in research, see Reskin, B. F., & Charles, C. Z. (1999). "Now you see 'em, now you don't." In I. Browne (Ed.) *Latinas and African American Women at Work: Race, Gender, and Economic Inequality*. New York: Russell Sage Foundation.

The organizations for which this book is relevant include large and small companies covered by federal legislation, colleges and universities, religious organizations (e.g., churches), military organizations, and any others in which people work, wish to work, or that have clients, customers or constituents. Although some organizations are allowed to prefer certain types of people as employees (e.g., churches, private clubs), many of the concepts in this book are also relevant to such organizations and can benefit their leaders. For example, a religious organization may legally require that employees be members of a particular faith, yet such an organization will still likely have employees who have work and family issues or may wrestle with ordination of women or sexual minorities. Similarly, the U.S. military is a unique, historically male organization, yet its issues with sexual harassment and sexual orientation diversity can provide information that is helpful to other types of organizations. As will be apparent from the breadth of organizations included in the book, some aspect of diversity affects all organizations at some point in time.

Terminology

In this book, when referring to the U.S. population, the following terms are used somewhat interchangeably: sex/gender, Blacks/African Americans, Latinos/Hispanics, Asians/Asian Americans/Asians and Pacific Islanders, Whites/Anglos/European Americans/Caucasians, and people of color/minorities.[8] Although the linked terms are not exactly the same (e.g., sex is biological while gender is socially constructed), they are widely recognized, their meanings are generally well understood, and they are often used interchangeably.

Despite the common and often interchanged use of these terms, there are important differences among them. Indeed, some researchers have persuasively argued that the ambiguity and fluidity of terminology render "race" and "ethnicity" almost meaningless.[9] Ethnicity refers to a shared national origin or a shared cultural heritage among people. On the other hand, like gender, "race is socially constructed to denote boundaries between the powerful and less powerful," and is often defined by the more powerful, dominant group.[10] The social constructions of race are reflected in the changes in terminology of categories used by the U.S. Census Bureau over the years.

[8] Terminology is discussed further in Chapters 4, 5, 6, 7, 8, and 14. Individuals' different preferences for particular terms are respected and acknowledged. See Jordan, Jeffrey. (2001), September 11. "Racial or Ethnic Labels Make Little Difference to Blacks, Hispanics." http://www.gallup.com., and Tatum, B. D. (1997). *Why Are All the Black Kids Sitting Together in the Cafeteria?* New York. Basic Books.

[9] See Wright, L. (1997). "One drop of blood." In C. Hartman (Ed.). *Double Exposure: Poverty and Race in America*. Armonk, NY: M. E. Sharpe.

[10] Healey, J. F., & O'Brien, E. (2004). p. 282. *Race, Ethnicity, and Gender*. Thousand Oaks, CA: Pine Forge Press.

Latinos may be of any race, and people may be of more than one racial or ethnic background. There are also considerable differences between Asians who are from Korea and those from India or Vietnam and between Black Americans and South African Blacks. Although all are categorized as Latinos, there are substantial differences in the diversity-related experiences of Mexican Americans and Puerto Ricans and between Black Nicaraguans and White Colombians. Ambiguity also surrounds the term "Asian." Is it an ethnicity, since ethnicity refers to a shared national origin, or is it a race? We explore these and other complexities related to race, ethnicity, sex, and gender and their effects on individuals in organizations in the relevant chapters.

The Stimulus: Workforce 2000

In 1987, the Hudson Institute published Johnston and Packer's research on the changes in the nature of work and in the demographic background of workers in the twenty-first century.[11] Their research sent shock waves into organizations and the media and the book became a best seller. Johnston and Packer noted that by the year 2000, 85% of the *net new entrants* to the U.S. workforce would be women and minorities. This statement was often quoted, and was widely misunderstood to mean that by 2000, White men would only constitute 15% of the workforce. However, White men were then and still remain the largest single group in the labor force. It was the *net new entrants* who were increasingly women and people of color. The term "net new entrants" refers to the difference between those who entered the workforce (newcomers to the workforce) and those who left the workforce (e.g., via retirements, death, etc.). Although women and people of color would comprise 85% of the net new entrants, because of the immense size of the workforce and the single majority of White men in the workforce, it will be a very long time before White men are no longer the largest single group. This misunderstanding or misinterpretation of terminology and projections about the increasing diversity of the workforce fueled interest in the topic and prompted concerns about the organizational ramifications of these changing demographics.

In 1997, the Hudson Institute published *Workforce 2020,* which again predicted changes in work and in workforce demographics, but for the year 2020, and attempted to clarify some of the misunderstandings about their earlier publication.[12] Importantly, they emphasized that about 66% of the workforce would continue to be non-Hispanic White men and women, 14% would be Latinos, 11% non-Hispanic Blacks, and 6% Asians. Most important to the demographics of *Workforce 2020,* they suggested, would be the aging of the baby boomers.

[11] Johnston, W. B. and Packer, A. E. (1987) *Workforce 2000: Work and Workers for the 21st century.* Indianapolis, IN: Hudson Institute.

[12] Judy, R. W., & D'Amico, C. (1997). *Workforce 2020*. Indianapolis, IN: Hudson Institute.

Table 1.1. ***Highlights from the Census 2000 Demographic Profiles (United States)***

	Number	Percent
General Characteristics		
Total population	281,421,906	100.0
Male	138,053,563	49.1
Female	143,368,343	50.9
Median age (years)	35.3	
Under 5 years	19,175,798	6.8
18 years and over	209,128,094	74.3
65 years and over	34,991,753	12.4
One race	274,595,678	97.6
White	211,460,626	75.1
Black	34,658,190	12.3
American Indian and Alaska Native	2,475,956	0.9
Asian	10,242,998	3.6
Native Hawaiian and other Pacific Islander	398,835	0.1
Some other race	15,359,073	5.5
Two or more races	6,826,228	2.4
Hispanic or Latino (of any race)	35,305,818	12.5
Average household size	2.59	
Average family size	3.14	
Social Characteristics		
Population 25 years and over	182,211,639	100.0
High school graduate or higher	146,496,014	80.4
Bachelor's degree or higher	44,462,605	24.4
Civilian veterans	26,403,703	12.7
With a disability (population 5 years and over)	49,746,248	19.3
Foreign born	31,107,889	11.1
Now married (population 15 years and over)	120,231,273	54.4
Speak a language other than English at home (population 5 years and over)	46,951,595	17.9
Economic Characteristics		
In labor force (population 16 years and over)	138,820,935	63.9
Median household income in 1999 (dollars)	41,994	
Per capita income in 1999 (dollars)	21,587	
Families below poverty level	6,620,945	9.2
Individuals below poverty level	33,899,812	12.4

Source: Adapted from U.S. Census Bureau, American FactFinder, http://factfinder.census.gov/servlet/SAFFFacts?_see+on, accessed 12/20/04.

Because the baby boomers would be retiring in large numbers then, worker age would plateau.

What has happened now that the year 2000 has come and gone and we are proceeding toward the year 2020? White men and women are about 75% of the workforce (men and women are 41% and 34%, respectively). Latinos (of all races) and non-Hispanic Blacks are both about 12% of the population, and Asians are about 4%. There are nearly 53 million workers aged 45 and over in the workforce. It appears that the current workforce is indeed more diverse than it was in the prior century, but Whites remain the largest numerical group.

In addition to the changes in the demographic makeup of employees, as the Hudson Institute predicted, economic changes and globalization have resulted in more service-oriented jobs and more international customers and business relationships. The loss of manufacturing jobs, where there is less opportunity for contact with dissimilar others, and the growth of service industry jobs, which involve considerable person-to-person interaction with dissimilar others, make awareness of and efforts to understand dissimilar others more critical than ever. Similarly, increasing globalization results in greater interaction among people from diverse backgrounds than in the past. Not only do employees work with peers in their local environment, they also work and travel around the world, interacting with people from different cultures and belief systems, and who often speak different languages.

Similar changes are occurring in many countries around the world. In the United States and Canada, workforce growth is slowing; aging workers are retiring and fewer younger workers are being added. In some European countries, Japan, and China the workforce is actually shrinking, and more people are leaving than joining the workforce. Developing nations are increasingly being seen as sources of new workers for many countries, many of which had historically resisted immigration.

Diversity and Organizational Competitiveness

What is the meaning of this increasing diversity for individuals and organizations? In their often-cited article on the implications of cultural diversity for organizational competitiveness, Taylor Cox and Stacy Blake proposed that there are six specific reasons that organizations should value diversity. They explained that effective management of diversity could benefit organizations in the areas of cost, resource acquisition, marketing, creativity, problem solving, and system flexibility.[13,14] These areas have been cited in numerous management, marketing,

[13] Cox, T., & Blake, S. (1991). "Managing cultural diversity: Implications for organizational competitiveness." Academy of Management Executive, 5(3): 45–56.

[14] Ibid., note 3. Cox and Blake's focus on those six advantages associated with valuing diversity was not meant to undermine the social, moral, and legal reasons for doing so but to investigate areas that had previously received little research attention. Along with the advantages proposed by Cox and Blake, in this book, we also discuss some of the social, moral, and legal reasons for valuing diversity.

FIGURE 1.1 ***Organizational and Individual Benefits of Diversity***

Organizational and Individual Benefits of Diversity

Organizational	Individual
• Cost	• Preparation for democratic citizenship
• Resource acquisition	• Intellectual engagement
• Marketing	• Perspective taking
• Creativity	• Support for diversity initiatives
• Problem solving	• Interest in poverty
• System flexibility	• Tolerance for sexual minorities
• Cooperative behaviors	• Perceiving common values with those from different racial/ethnic backgrounds
• Stock prices	
• Organizational performance	
• Reductions of lost business	

Sources: Cox, T., & Blake, S. (1991). "Managing cultural diversity: Implications for organizational competitiveness." *Academy of Management Executive*, 5(3): 45–56. Gurin, P., Dey, E. L., Gurin, G., & Hurtado, S. (2003). "How does racial/ethnic diversity promote education?" *The Western Journal of Black Studies,* 27(1): 20–29. Gurin, P. Dey E. L., Hurtado, S., & Gurin, G. (2002). "Diversity and higher education: Theory and impact on educational outcomes." *Harvard Educational* Review, 71(3): 332–366. Gurin, P., Nagda, B. A., & Lopez, G. E. (2004). "The benefits of diversity in education for democratic citizenship." *Journal of Social* Issues, 60(1): 17–34. Hurtado, S. (2005). "The next generation of diversity and intergroup relations research." *Journal of Social Issues,* 61: 595–610. Richard, O. C. (2000). "Racial diversity, business strategy, and firm performance: A resource based view." *Academy of Management Journal,* 43: 164–178.

and organizational behavior textbooks, as well as news magazines and the popular press, and continue to shape thinking about the value of diversity. Although Cox and Blake focused their suggestions on diversity brought by women and people of color, their suggestions are also applicable to the effects of different aspects of diversity—such as age, religion, sexual orientation, and others considered in this book—on an organization's competitiveness.

Figure 1.1 presents organizational and individual benefits of diversity identified by theoretical and empirical research. We consider these benefits in the following sections.

Cost

Costs associated with doing a poor job in integrating workers from different backgrounds can be extremely high. These costs are related to lower job satisfaction and subsequent turnover of women, minorities, and, we suggest, people of various religious faiths, gays and lesbians, and others whose contributions are devalued in organizations. Cox and Blake and other researchers have reported lower satisfaction and higher turnover of women and minorities when compared to men and Whites. This is an important organizational concern, particularly as the number of women and minorities in the workforce increases. If, along with women and minorities, workers from other devalued groups (such as those with child and/or elder care responsibilities or people with disabilities) are dissatisfied and quit in response to negative organizational treatment, organizational costs related to turnover may be tremendous. Although the majority of research focuses on the turnover of women and minorities, Tsui, Egan, and O'Reilly found that increasing organizational diversity was associated with lowered attachment for Whites and males but not for women and minorities.[15] It is possible that Whites and men in the study associated increasing sex and racial diversity with a lowering of the status of their organization, and thus felt less attachment to the organization. The possibility that increases in diversity may be associated with lower attachment and turnover for people of different backgrounds (e.g., Whites, people of color, men, and women) suggests that organizations should take proactive measures to address and circumvent these negative outcomes while maximizing the positive outcomes.

Costs associated with turnover include exit interviews, lost productivity while positions are unfilled, and recruiting costs for replacement employees. Average recruiting costs for professional positions are about $12,000 per hire.[16] Organizations may find replacement more expensive than retaining current employees. This is particularly true when the learning curve and training costs of replacements are also considered. Specific organizational efforts to address needs of specific workers may minimize turnover. For example, research indicates that workers with child care responsibilities (women, and increasingly, men) have more organizational commitment and lower turnover when companies provide child care subsidies, on-site day care, or other child care support.[17] In addition, education for all workers about the benefits of increasing diversity may reduce dissatisfaction and lowered attachment among employees.

Lastly, although many people think of the costs associated with doing a poor job of integrating workers as being largely related to discrimination lawsuits, Cox and Blake did not specifically include litigation expenses in their costs. Texaco's $176 million class action racial discrimination settlement, Mitsubishi's $34.5 million sexual harassment settlement, and other large discrimination damage awards were widely reported in the 1990s, striking fear in the minds of many organizational leaders. Despite the amount of media attention focusing on lawsuits and damage settlements, an organization's likelihood of being sued is relatively small when compared with the continuing costs associated with low job satisfaction and high turnover. For example, the number of discrimination-related charges filed with the U.S. Equal Employment Opportunity Commission (EEOC) between 1992 and 2002 averaged about 80,000 per year. Although 80,000 is a substantial number of claims, it is very small relative to the number of firms

[15] Tsui, A. S., Egan, T. D., & O'Reilly, C. A. (1992). "Being different: Relational demography and organizational attachment." *Administrative Science Quarterly,* 37: 549–579.

[16] Prizinsky, D. (2000). *Crain's Cleveland Business,* 21(50): 3–5.

[17] Youngblood, S. A., & Chambers-Cook, K. (1984, February). "Child Care assistance can improve employee attitudes and behavior." *Personnel Administrator,* 93–95.

in the United States and relative to the 139 million people in the workforce. The majority of workers who feel they are treated unfairly, not valued, or discriminated against do not sue. Instead, they may simply leave the organization and tell their family and friends about their experiences, affecting the organization's ability to attract other workers (e.g., resource acquisition).

Misperception: The risk of being sued for discrimination is fairly high.

Reality: An organization's likelihood of being sued is very small.

Resource Acquisition

Cox and Blake described an organization's ability to attract and retain employees from different backgrounds as resource acquisition. Employees from diverse backgrounds may include women, people of color, older workers, workers with disabilities, sexual minorities, and people from various religious faiths—workers who have often been overlooked as potential employees. As members of these groups represent an increasing proportion of the workforce, the need to consider them and to be able to attract and retain workers from nontraditional pools becomes more important. Cox and Blake proposed that if an organization develops a reputation for valuing all types of workers, it will become known as an employer of choice, increasing its ability to compete in tight labor markets. Empirical research provides support for the positive effects of heterogeneous recruitment ads on minorities' desire to work for organizations.[18] Conversely, if an organization develops a reputation for valuing only a subset of workers, it may miss the opportunity to hire excellent workers who do not fall into that subset. Other researchers have similarly argued that "talented people may be predisposed to avoid companies that discriminate."[19] We suggest that such an organization may also have higher compensation costs because of drawing from a smaller pool of workers (e.g., supply would be lower, making demand costs higher). As discussed in Case 1.1, such an organization may also have lower productivity from both the preferred subset of workers and those who are not preferred.

In addition to *Fortune's* annual issue of the best companies for minorities, *Working Mother, Latina Style, Catalyst, American Association of Retired Persons* (AARP), *Hispanic Today, DiversityInc,* and other entities routinely publish lists of best companies for women, minorities, parents, and other groups. These reports are widely read and provide substantial publicity for the companies that make or

---

[18] Avery, D. R., Hernandez, M., & Hebl, M. R. (2004). "Who's watching the race? Racial salience in recruitment advertising." *Journal of Applied Social Psychology,* 34(1): 146–161. Perkins, L. A., Thomas, K. M., & Taylor, G. A. (2000). "Advertising and recruitment: Marketing to minorities." *Psychology and Marketing,* 17: 235–255.

[19] Wright, P., Ferris, S. P., Hiller, J. S., & Kroll, M. (1995). "Competitiveness through management of diversity: Effects on stock price valuation." *Academy of Management Journal,* 38: 272–288.

Case 1.1 *Case Study of Fictitious Company, Inc. and Fictitious Savvy Company, Inc.*

Assume that people from demographic groups A and B are employed at Fictitious Company, Inc. Both Workers A and Workers B have similar numbers of excellent performers and poor performers in their group. Workers from both groups expect fair performance evaluations, pay raises, and promotions based on their performance. After a period of working for and excelling in performance, high performing Workers B realize that despite their high qualifications and strong performance, their performance is rated lower than Workers A, their pay raises are lower, and they are not likely to be promoted. This perception is validated when Workers B consider the management and executive levels of Fictitious Company, and see very few people from Workers B category in those levels. What is the expected result of motivation and future performance for high performing Workers B? Low and average performing Workers B are observing. They realize that high performing Workers B, despite their high performance, receive low performance ratings and few to no raises and promotions. What is the expected effect on motivation to work harder and future performance of low performing Workers B?

After a period of employment at Fictitious Company, Workers A realize that they are continually rated highly, and receive pay raises and promotions, regardless of their performance. If they make their sales and quality goals, they receive high raises and are promoted. If they miss their sales and quality goals, remarkably, they receive high raises and are promoted. If they are chronically late or absent on Mondays and Fridays, there are few to no negative consequences. What is the expected result of future performance and motivation for Workers A who are truly good performers but observe Workers A who miss sales and quality goals still being promoted and rewarded? What is the expected result of future performance and motivation to improve for Workers A who are low performers but receive rewards nonetheless?

To summarize, at Fictitious Company, high performing Workers B receive clear messages that their high performance is not valued. Low performing Workers B receive messages that there is no reason to strive for high performance because people like them receive no reward for high performance. Workers A receive messages that low and high performance for Workers A are valued and rewarded similarly, so there is no need to strive for excellence. What is the result of this scenario for the overall performance of Fictitious Company, Inc.?

Contrast this scenario to that of Fictitious Savvy Company, Inc., in which members of Workers A and Workers B expect, and receive, fair performance evaluations, promotions, and raises. What is the expected result of future motivation and performance for high, average, and low performance of Workers A and Workers B in Fictitious Savvy Company, Inc.? What is the result of this scenario for the overall performance of Fictitious Savvy Company, Inc.?

fail to make the lists. Despite methodological problems with data collection in some of the reports, the companies that make, fail to make, or fall off these lists receive considerable media attention. This high level of attention from the media may affect applicants' interest in companies as well as companies' ability to market to diverse consumer groups, as explored in the following section.

Marketing

Cox and Blake proposed that an organization's reputation for valuing all types of workers will also affect its ability to market to different types of consumers. This is accomplished in multiple ways. First, consumers who appreciate fair treatment for everyone will be more likely to patronize an organization known to value diversity and to treat all workers fairly. Employers that are known for supporting particular organizations (e.g., the United Negro College Fund or the Human Rights Campaign) receive recognition from those organizations and their patrons. This recognition may translate into purchases and customer loyalty.

Second, having employees who are from various backgrounds improves a company's marketing ability because such organizations will be better able to develop products that meet the needs of and appeal to diverse consumers. In the 1990s, after a period of declining sales and profits, Avon Products was able to successfully market to African Americans and Latinas by increasing the representation of African Americans and Latinas as marketing managers.

Third, organizations with employees from various backgrounds may also be more likely to avoid expensive marketing blunders associated with having homogeneous advertising or marketing teams. In the early history of Frito-Lay's Frito's corn chips, the major focus of its advertising was the *Frito Bandito*. This character was known for stealing Fritos because they were so good that he was unable to resist. The character had a heavy accent, his appearance was stereotypical, and the portrayal of Latinos as stealing was insulting. Complaints from Latinos resulted in Frito-Lay's discontinuation of the use of the Frito Bandito.[20]

Though not an advertising blunder per se, in the 1990s, American Airlines' Latin America Pilot Reference Guide, an internal document, caused the company negative publicity that could have affected its ability to market to Latino consumers (and those of other racial and ethnic backgrounds). The guide reportedly warned pilots that Latin American customers would call in false bomb threats to delay flights when they were running late and that they sometimes became unruly after drinking too much on flights. When news of the statements in the reference guide hit the press, the airline apologized and stated it would revise the manual.[21]

Creativity and Problem Solving

Research indicates that groups composed of people from different backgrounds bring with them different experiences that result in greater creativity and problem-solving ability. These abilities stem from different life experiences, language abilities, and education that groups composed of diverse members have.

[20] "Justice for My People, the Hector Garcia story." http://justiceformypeople.org, accessed 10/08/03.

[21] Hetter, K., & Mallory, M. (1997). "American: More Apologies." *U.S. News & World Report,* 123(8): 57.

Empirical research supports the idea that diversity positively affects group performance, creativity, and innovation. In longitudinal research, Watson, Kumar, and Michaelsen investigated the effects of diversity (in race, ethnicity, and nationality) on group performance. Following diverse and homogeneous groups of students over the course of a semester, these authors found that initially, the homogeneous groups outperformed the diverse groups. By the end of the semester, however, the performance of the diverse groups exceeded the performance of the homogeneous groups. After learning to interact with each other, the diverse groups developed more and higher-quality solutions to problems than homogenous groups, exhibiting greater creativity and problem-solving skills.[22]

Poppy McLeod, Sharon Lobel, and Taylor Cox have empirically investigated the effects of racial diversity on idea-generation in small groups. Using brainstorming techniques (which are commonly used in developing new ideas in organizations), they found that groups composed of diverse members produced higher-quality ideas than groups composed of homogenous members. The ability to generate superior ideas is vital to success as global competition increases.[23]

System Flexibility

System flexibility is the final way that Cox and Blake proposed that valuing diversity provides organizations with a competitive advantage. They argued that women have a higher tolerance for ambiguity than men. Tolerance for ambiguity is associated with cognitive complexity and success in uncertain situations. Other researchers have pointed out women's ability to "multitask," successfully handling multiple tasks concurrently. Successful multitasking is valuable in complex work environments.

Bilingualism and biculturalism are indicative of cognitive flexibility and openness to experience.[24] Latinos and Asian Americans are often bilingual and bicultural. African Americans tend to be bicultural.[25] Although not traditionally perceived as bicultural, we suggest that the life experiences of some people with disabilities, gay males, and lesbians may provide them cognitive flexibility and openness to experience similar to bicultural individuals. Exposure to other cultures, languages, or having experienced challenges of being different from those in the majority may help individuals develop cognitive flexibility and openness to experience not possessed by others.

---

[22] Watson, W. E., Kumar, K., & Michaelsen, L. K. (1993). "Cultural diversity's impact on interaction process and performance: Comparing homogeneous and diverse task groups." *Academy of Management Journal,* 36: 590–603.

[23] McLeod, P., Lobel, S. A., & Cox, T., Jr. (1996). "Ethnic diversity and creativity in small groups." *Small Group Research,* 27(2): 248–264.

[24] Bell, M. P., & Harrison, D. A. (1996). "Using intra-national diversity for international assignments." *Human Resources Management Review,* 6: 47–73; Cox & Blake. (1991); LaFromboise, T., Coleman, H. L. K., & Gerton, J. (1993). "Psychological impact of biculturalism: Evidence and theory." *Psychological Bulletin,* 114: 395–412.

[25] Cox & Blake. (1991).

Other Areas Where Diversity Is Advantageous

Cooperative behaviors. Researchers have found that groups composed of members from collectivist (such as Asians, Blacks, and Latinos) instead of individualist backgrounds (such as Whites/European Americans) displayed more cooperative behavior on group tasks.[26] Where cooperation is important to business success, for example, in an increasingly global and diverse environment, and where teamwork is vital, organizational diversity will be an asset.

Stock prices. Effective management of diversity has been associated with stock prices. Using six years of data, Wright and colleagues assessed the effect of positive publicity from affirmative action programs (which they used as evidence of valuing diversity) and negative publicity from damage awards in discrimination lawsuits on the stock returns of major corporations. They found positive influences on stock valuation for firms that received awards from the U.S. Department of Labor regarding their affirmative action programs. In contrast, announcements of discrimination settlements were associated with negative stock price changes for the affected companies.[27]

Organizational performance. Orlando Richard's study of the relationship between racial diversity and firm performance found a complex interaction effect.[28] Firms with a growth strategy (which would require innovation, idea generation, and creativity) were more successful when employees were diverse. Richard suggested that when firms have a growth strategy, racial diversity increases productivity, which increases firm performance. Thus, organizations might wish to actively seek out diversity as a source of competitiveness when pursuing a growth strategy. Although Richard did not test other aspects of diversity, diversity in gender, age, and other areas may also be advantageous for high-growth firms.

Reductions of lost business. Lastly, we suggest that costs associated with lost business should be added to the costs of absence, turnover, and discrimination lawsuits that are commonly associated with mismanagement of diversity. These costs can be minimized through commitment to diversity. When employees or customers learn of or personally experience unfair treatment towards their group by an organization, they are less likely to patronize the organization. In addition, other groups who were not personally affected may find overt discrimination or other negative behaviors offensive and choose to spend their dollars elsewhere. Organized and informal boycotts can be extremely expensive for organizations. Instances of such boycotts will be discussed in later chapters.

---

[26] Cox, T., Lobel, S. A., & McLeod, P. L. (1991). "Effects of ethnic group cultural differences on cooperative and competitive behavior on a group task." *Academy of Management Journal,* 4: 827–847.

[27] Wright et al. (1995).

[28] Richard, O. C. (2000). "Racial diversity, business strategy, and firm performance: A resource based view." *Academy of Management Journal,* 43: 164–178.

Difficulties Resulting from Increased Diversity and Organizational Responses

Although Cox and Blake's positive perspective of diversity sets the stage for many of the perspectives on valuing diversity that are presented in this book, it is important to also consider some of the negative outcomes that may be consequences of increased diversity. Some of these negative outcomes include dysfunctional communication processes between different group members, discrimination, harassment, perceptions that nontraditional workers are unqualified, and lowered attachment, commitment, and satisfaction.[29] As mentioned earlier, researchers have found that increasing organizational diversity was associated with lowered attachment for Whites and males but not for women and minorities.[30] On the other hand, multiple studies have indicated that although increased diversity was associated with negative outcomes initially, this lessened over time.[31] Researchers suggest that as employees get to know one another and exchange job-relevant information, negative effects of surface-level differences are reduced.

Organizational leaders should facilitate interactions between people of diverse backgrounds at work, providing communication training if necessary, and monitoring dysfunctional behaviors. Managers should directly confront and dispel the common perceptions that minorities and women are unqualified while only Whites and males are qualified. As with an important organizational change, proactive steps should be taken to minimize negative outcomes resulting from increasing diversity while maximizing the positive ones. Inevitable changes in population demographics make doing so critical to organizational success.

Organizations that are supportive of diversity have faced boycotts and negative publicity from those who are resistant to diversity. *Fortune* magazine reports that in 1962, when Harvey C. Russell, a Black man, was named a vice-president at Pepsi, the Ku Klux Klan called for a boycott of Pepsi products, flooding the country with handbills that read: "Don't buy Pepsi-Cola and make a nigger rich."[32] Undeterred, Pepsi continued in its diversity efforts. In 2005, PepsiCo was ranked number four in *DiversityInc's* fifth annual "Top 50 Companies for Diversity Survey," including number one rankings for Blacks and Latinos,

---

[29] See, for example, Jackson, S. E., Brett, J. F., Sessa, V. I., Cooper, D. M., Julin, J. A., & Peyronnin, K. (1991). "Some differences make a difference: Interpersonal dissimilarity and group heterogeneity as correlates of recruitment, promotion, and turnover." *Journal of Applied Psychology,* 76: 675–689; Konrad, A. M., Winter, S., & Gutek, B. A. (1992). "Diversity in work group sex composition: Implications for majority and minority members." In P. Tolbert & S. B. Bacharach (Eds.), *Research in the Sociology of Organizations,* Vol. 10: 115–140. Greenwich, CT: JAI Press; Harrison, D. E., Price, K., & Bell, M. P. (1998). "Beyond relational demography: Time and the effects of surface- and deep-level diversity on work group cohesion." *Academy of Management Journal,* 41: 96–107.

[30] Tsui et al. (1992).

[31] Harrison et al. (1998); Watson et al. (1993).

[32] Daniels, C., Neering, P., & Soehendro, M. (2005). "Pioneers." *Fortune,* 8/22/2005, Vol 152 (4), pp. 72–88.

number four for Asians, and number five for gay, lesbian, bisexual, and transgender employees.[33] In the more recent past, the Southern Baptist Convention led an 8-year boycott of Disney because of its inclusive policies toward gay and lesbian employees and customers.[34] The Convention ended its boycott in 2005, having had little apparent effect on Disney.

Individual Benefits of Diversity

In addition to the organizational benefits of diversity, longitudinal research provides evidence of the value of diversity to individuals. Research conducted by Patricia Gurin and her colleagues identifying the benefits of a diverse learning environment for students was used by the U.S. Supreme Court in its 2003 decision in favor of the University of Michigan's diversity programs.[35] Gurin found that students whose classmates were diverse and who interacted with each other in meaningful ways and learned from each other were more likely to see diversity as not being necessarily divisive, to see commonality in values, and to be able to take the perspective of others.

In another longitudinal study, Sylvia Hurtado also found evidence of the benefits of diversity among college students.[36] Hurtado's study involved 4,403 students from nine public universities across the United States. She found that when students interacted with diverse peers during their first year of college, changes in cognitive, social, and democratic social outcomes followed. By the second year of college, students expressed more interest in poverty, support for diversity initiatives, perspective-taking, and tolerance for sexual minorities. Students who had taken diversity courses and participated in campus-sponsored diversity learning programs experienced the greatest number of positive benefits. Hurtado proposed that "These results suggest that campus efforts to integrate the curriculum, or adopt a diversity requirement, have far-reaching effects on a host of educational outcomes that prepare students as participants in a diverse economy".[37] Continued predictions for increased diversity in the future make preparation for such diversity an invaluable asset.

---

[33] "PepsiCo ranks number four on DiversityInc's Fifth Annual Top 50 Companies for Diversity." At http://www.pepsico.com/diversitywork/20050411-b.shtml, accessed 09/18/05.

[34] Mills, K. (1997). Religious wrong. HRC Quarterly, Summer. At http://www.hrc.org/Content/ContentGroups/Publications1/HRC_Quarterly/1997/Religious_Wrong.htm, accessed 09/18/05. See also Southern Baptists end Disney boycott. At http://www.cnn.com/2005/US/06/23/baptists.disney.ap/, accessed 07/04/05.

[35] Gurin, P., Nagda, B. A., & Lopez, G. E. (2004). "The benefits of diversity in education for democratic citizenship." *Journal of Social Issues,* 60(1): 17–34. See also Gurin, P., Dey, E. L., Hurtado, S., & Gurin, G. 2002. "Diversity and higher education: Theory and impact on educational outcomes." *Harvard Educational Review,* 71, 3: 332–366; Gurin, P., Y., Dey, E. L., Gurin, G., & Hurtado, S. (2003). "How does racial/ethnic diversity promote education?" *The Western Journal of Black Studies,* 27(1): 20–29.

[36] Hurtado, S. (2005). "The next generation of diversity and intergroup relations research." *Journal of Social Issues,* 61: 595–610.

[37] Ibid., p. 605.

Organization of the Book

In the preceding part of Chapter 1, we introduced the concept of diversity and discussed Cox and Blake's proposals about the six areas in which diversity is beneficial for organizations and other researchers' empirical findings on the relationships between diversity and group and organizational performance. In the remainder of the book, we refer to these areas and to other ways in which diversity is valuable and inevitable. As much as possible, for each group or topic (race and ethnicity, sex, age, workers with disabilities, sexual orientation), we cover the same standard areas, as well as areas unique to the particular topic. Although the uniqueness of the topics prevents identical coverage and topics, the standardization provides cohesion and improves readers' ability to consider and compare similarities and differences across groups. Each chapter begins with key facts relevant to the topic, along with chapter objectives. Where appropriate, the standard areas covered for each group are: introduction and overview, population (including percentages and growth rates), education, and employment (including participation rates, unemployment rates, income levels, and employment types). Different chapters combine some of the standard areas when doing so creates a more cohesive picture of the topic or group being discussed. Within the standard areas, points of particular relevance to diversity in organizations are highlighted, for example, the role of gender role socialization in women's and men's choices of occupation, and the long-term effects of the gender wage gap on women's retirement and poverty.

The use of the standard topical areas, unique information, and topical highlights provides a distinct picture of the status and experiences of group members. These areas are important to being able to critically think and learn about diversity issues. They also provide readers with a cohesive foundation for understanding the aspects of diversity considered in this book and other aspects of diversity that they may encounter in the future in the United States and worldwide. For example, although specific minority or nondominant groups may be different in different areas (e.g., in the United States and in India), readers can use the same standard approach to learn about and develop an understanding of them. The standard areas utilized in each chapter are discussed further in the following sections.

Introduction and Overview of Chapters

Each chapter or subchapter that focuses on a particular group (e.g., racial and ethnic groups, workers with disabilities, etc.) begins with an introduction and overview of the group, including information that is unique for each group that helps to explain their diversity-related status in the United States but may be unknown to readers. For example, in the United States, only Blacks have experienced the historical background of slavery and subsequent discrimination that continues to shape their position in organizations and in society. Latinos are unique in their diverse backgrounds (e.g., Cuba, Puerto Rico, Mexico, Central America, etc.), races, language ability, and youthfulness of population. It is not widely known that although they were considerably more accepted than Blacks, Mexican Americans experienced extreme discrimination, segregation, and lynching in parts of California and Texas during the early 1900s to the 1970s. Mexican Americans fought for their civil rights during the same period African Americans fought for their civil rights, at times along with African Americans and Asians.[38]

The experiences of Asian Americans as immigrants, refugees, or native-born Americans—being perceived as the "model minority," while at the same time experiencing the glass ceiling and other forms of discrimination[39]—are unique to them. As we will see, however, Asians have distinct experiences in the United States, representing a bimodal distribution of education, wealth, and success versus lack of education, extreme poverty, and welfare dependency.[40] In addition, many perceive that Asians choose self-employment as a means of earning high wages; however, research indicates some Asian entrepreneurs are self-employed as a result of discrimination, a lack of opportunities in formal organizations, and the glass ceiling. As with small businesses in general, many Asian businesses fail and others are only profitable because of long hours and unpaid labor of family members.[41] Similar to others of color in different cities, in some parts of the United States, Asian Americans comprise the bulk of the hotel housekeepers and janitorial staffs, neighborhood gardeners, garment workers, and other low-wage, low-status occupations. These jobs are quite different in occupation and earnings from the model minority stereotype.

Population

The number of people in a particular group is critical for many different reasons. Large groups have more voice in democratic governmental processes, more consumer buying power, and strength in other areas. These benefits may positively affect their treatment in organizations and result in organizations being more attentive to their needs. In addition, as "minority" groups grow in size, they may appear to be more threatening to those in the majority, which may negatively affect their organizational status and treatment.[42] Positively, as minority groups grow in numbers, majority group members may have more personal experiences with and knowledge of particular individuals, and may therefore learn to rely on

---

[38] See Acuna, R. (1988). *Occupied America: A History of Chicanos*. 3rd Edition. New York: Harper Collins Publishers. See also "Justice for My People," (2003).

[39] Wood, D. (2000). *Glass Ceilings and Asian Americans: The New Face of Workplace Barriers*. Walnut Creek, CA: AltaMira Press.

[40] Espiritu, Y. L. (1999). "The refugees and the refuge: Southeast Asians in the United States." In A. G. Dworkin and R. J. Dworkin (Eds.), *The Minority Report*. Orlando, FL: Harcourt Brace.

[41] Espiritu, Y. L. (1999).

[42] Kanter, R. M. (1977). *Men and Women of the Corporation*. New York: Basic Books.

this personal knowledge, rather than stereotypical information, particularly if given organizational stimuli and support for doing so.

Similar to population numbers, as the relative size of a group increases and the group becomes a greater percentage of the overall population, its voice, buying power, and other strengths increase. As an example, 30 million may be construed as a large number; however, 30 million of a population of 60 million is considerably different from 30 million of a population of 300 million.

Population growth rates of a particular group are notable in that growth rates affect both sheer numbers and percentages. When a minority group is growing at a faster rate than the majority, over time, the minority group will grow in percentage of population, as well as in raw numbers. Population growth occurs through births and immigration and warrants attention from persons interested in diversity issues. When a minority group has both a higher birth rate and greater immigration than the majority group, as do Latinos and some Asians in the United States, this leads to a faster shift in the numbers and percentages of the minority group compared with the majority group. These shifts in population require different strategies and perspectives for addressing needs of diverse consumers, applicants, and employees. As an example, as Latinos have become a larger percentage of the population, some organizations have begun to actively recruit bilingual employees in human resources, customer service, marketing, and management positions.

Education

Education levels for each group affect whether and where people are employed, income levels, and opportunities for and actual advancement. Thus, this book provides details on the numbers of people in each group of working age with and without high school, college, and advanced degrees. Comparisons of education levels within (between men and women) and across groups provide insights into other factors (e.g., the glass ceiling and walls) that may be influencing the employment, income, and organizational advancement of different groups. For example, are White men and women receiving similar levels of education? If so, are they receiving similar returns (e.g., income, status, advancement) on their educational investment? What are the education levels of immigrants? How does this affect their employment? We investigate these and similar questions as relevant for each demographic group.

Employment, Unemployment, and Participation Rates

Employment levels and participation rates of a group are closely tied to educational levels and provide information about a group's position in organizations. The percentages of people in a group who are employed, unemployed, underemployed, and not seeking work, when compared with those of other groups are important in understanding group status and other diversity factors. We seek to answer questions such as the following:

- Are Blacks with similar education levels more, less, or equally likely to be employed as are Whites?
- When laid off, how long do minority and majority group members, such as older and younger workers, remain unemployed before finding similar employment?
- Are men more likely to be participating in the workforce than women in each racial and ethnic group?
- Are women from some racial groups more likely to be in the workforce than women from other groups?
- Why are people with disabilities consistently less likely to be employed than are people without disabilities, even when similarly qualified and able to work?

We investigate what can be done about these issues and why organizations should be concerned about them. We consider what employment levels actually mean, compared with what is commonly reported, and how these figures differ across groups, emphasizing that for certain groups, the unemployment levels are often understated and deceptive. In periods of apparent economic success (as in the mid-through-late 1990s), or more difficult economic periods (as in the early 2000s), the job-related status of people of color, women, and people with disabilities may be more negative than is apparent. Because Whites are the majority of the population, White unemployment levels heavily weight the reported unemployment rates. Unemployment for African Americans has consistently been about twice the unemployment rate for Whites, but this is not commonly known. In 2003, the overall unemployment rate was about 6%. For Whites, Blacks, Latinos, Asians, and American Indians the rates were about 5%, 10%, 8%, 6%, and 15% respectively. These differences in unemployment rates are not completely explained by differences in education. Asian Americans have higher average education levels than Whites, yet Asians have higher unemployment rates. Blacks have higher average education levels than Latinos, yet Blacks have higher unemployment rates. What diversity dynamics are affecting these unusual relationships?

Many people do not know about other distortions in reported unemployment levels. People who have given up actively seeking work in their field (e.g., "discouraged" workers), those working at lower levels appropriate for their education (e.g., underemployment), or people who work part-time because they are unable to find full-time work are not included in the unemployment rate. We discuss discouraged, unemployed, and part-time workers and their relationships to diversity in organizations.

Employment Types and Income Levels

Employment types and income levels provide great insights into the status of different groups. Comparisons between people of similar qualifications but different group memberships provide even greater insights into diversity-related factors at work (e.g., discrimination, equal opportunity, the glass ceiling, etc.). We investigate questions such as the following:

- In what types of occupations and industries do most members of a group work?
- What percentages of the group occupy executive, managerial, professional and administrative, or other positions?
- Are similarly qualified women less likely to be in managerial or executive positions than men?
- Are women and people of color more likely to be clustered into certain jobs and industries?
- How do the pay and advancement potential of the jobs and industries in which women and people of color are clustered compare with the pay and advancement potential of jobs and industries in which Whites and men tend to be clustered?

Education, employment levels, and employment types lead logically to income. The more education one has, the more likely one is to be employed, and earning higher wages. This is theoretically and practically true; however, returns on education vary by race, ethnicity, gender, physical ability, and other factors. Education does not translate to higher income at similar rates for all racial and ethnic groups. Asian Americans have higher average education levels than other groups; however, their returns on educational investment are lower than the returns Whites receive. Specifically, although wide variations exist for U.S.-born versus immigrant Asians and vary by country of birth, the average educational level of Asian American men is higher than that of White men, but the average earnings of Asian men are lower than the earnings of White men. For Asian Americans, then, the education to income relationship is different than the relationship for Whites. The chapters explore relationships between education, employment, and income for different groups, providing some startling insights into the dynamics of discrimination, stereotyping, and other diversity issues.

Focal Issues

Where appropriate, each chapter provides details on one or more issues of particular relevance to the chapter's focal area or group. For example, for Chapter 9, one focal area is the relationship between socialization and women's lower likelihood of successfully negotiating salaries (and its impact upon the wage gap).

Focal investigations for African Americans consider negative effects of discrimination on African Americans' health and the persistent effects of slavery and discrimination on their social and financial progress. Chapter 13 considers "the second shift"—the extra shift of housework and child care that employed women perform after leaving work, its effects on organizations, why organizations should be concerned, and what can be done about it. These investigations provide details on some of the many diversity-related concerns unique to specific groups that may be unfamiliar to readers as diversity concerns, but which are quite familiar on a day-to-day basis. Many people "know" how much more housework wives generally perform compared with husbands, but giving such phenomena a name and presenting empirical evidence about them will help readers see everyday influences of diversity on individuals and organizations.

Individual and Organizational Recommendations

Each chapter provides recommendations for individuals and for organizations relevant to the specific chapter focus. These recommendations are related to the concerns raised for the particular groups as well as to improving the organization's overall climate for diversity. Although organizational, societal, and systemic factors underlie much of the extant discrimination and resistance to diversity, some individual actions that people may take can influence individual outcomes. What can one person do? As an example, Chapter 4 provides recommendations for African American women to reduce the double-whammy of disadvantage associated with membership in two nondominant groups. Chapter 9 includes specific recommendations on how organizations can prevent sexual harassment and how individual women can reduce or address individual discrimination. Chapter 11 suggests ways in which older workers can avoid pre-interview exclusion based on high school or college completion dates on a resume.

International Feature

Many chapters include an international feature, which considers some aspect of the subject matter from an international perspective. Chapter 11 explores recently passed legislation in Australia that prohibits age discrimination against younger, as well as older workers. Chapter 13 compares family policies in the United States with those of other developed nations. Inclusion of these international features clarifies the importance of diversity around the world and demonstrates ways in which readers and organizations may learn from and improve diversity issues in different regions. Chapter 16 further considers the international relevance of diversity issues, including factors that are common worldwide and ways to assess the key diversity factors in a particular region.

Other Items in Each Chapter

Each chapter includes at least one case study, individual or organizational feature, research translation, or discrimination charge and analysis (e.g., apparent name-based discrimination against Black applicants and applicant and employee discrimination charges against Abercrombie and Fitch retail stores). Translations of research from a variety of disciplines provide understandable discussions of rigorous empirical research, bringing credibility to the chapter material. Litigation or discrimination charges drawn from the EEOC or media provide realistic reports with which the reader may be familiar and encourage in-depth analysis and critiquing. Rather than being critical of these organizations, many of which have long-standing diversity programs, inclusion of these charges and settlements emphasizes the importance of continued, vigilant commitment to diversity. Organizations must make the commitment to diversity widely known to every employee in every location through repeated training, communication, and monitoring. Our inclusion of positive reports coupled with discrimination charges, settlements, or other problems (e.g., L'Oreal and DuPont, discussed in Chapters 11 and 12, respectively), also demonstrates the need to avoid making blanket assumptions or judgments about an organization based on limited information.

Suggested "actions and exercises" enhance readers' understanding of the subject matter and help make abstract concepts and discussion more legitimate. Some actions and exercises include interviewing a person working in a sex atypical job, documenting the race and ethnic makeup of cashiers at discount stores, or constructing an organization chart of a company with which one is familiar (for possible evidence of glass ceilings, walls, and escalators). Thought-provoking and memorable misperceptions and reality points interspersed throughout the chapters provide common misperceptions about the topic and then contrast them with more accurate information.[43]

Because diversity issues are related to each other, an important feature of the book is cross-references and discussion of relevant interrelationships between topics. For example, in Chapter 11's consideration of age diversity, an EEOC case against Babies "R" Us, Inc. reflects harassment of a young worker who did not fit gender role stereotypes of how a male should act—relevant to Chapter 9's coverage of sex and gender. Chapter 13 includes a section on same-sex families that is also referenced in Chapter 15. Chapter 13 also refers to the effect of part-time work and women's lower lifetime earnings on the feminization of poverty that was considered in Chapter 9. Although separate examination of the individual groups and topics (e.g., separate chapters on racial groups) is important, cross-references to and discussions of these interrelationships within chapters bring a holistic view of diversity in organizations. Diversity issues are relevant to everyone and to each other.

[43] Not every reader will be familiar with every misperception.

Summary

This chapter has introduced the concept of diversity and provided details of the organization of the book and of what readers may expect. In conceptualizing diversity, areas that are prohibited from employment discrimination by federal regulations (e.g., race, ethnicity, sex, national origin, religion, age, and ability) as well as those that are not (e.g., sexual orientation, weight, and appearance) are included. Although some groups are clearly devalued and underutilized in organizations more than others are, this book emphasizes the idea that everyone has multiple group memberships, and that group boundaries are permeable, *making diversity of importance to everyone*. The overriding premise of this book is that diversity is valuable to individuals and to organizations and that people with various group memberships should be afforded employment opportunities and allowed to reach their potential as employees, managers, executives, and leaders. Research indicates that job applicants, employees, customers, and constituents will respond positively when organizations value diversity and negatively when they do not. From this perspective, the book continues its consideration of the past, present, and future of diversity in organizations.

Key Terms

Diversity — real or perceived differences among people that affect their interactions and relationships, often viewed in terms of race, ethnicity, sex, national origin, and other demographic and identity-based factors.

Identity group — the collectivities people use to categorize themselves and others.

Labor force — all persons age 16 and over working or looking for work.

Participation rate — the ratio of persons age 16 and over who are working or looking for work divided by the population of persons age 16 and over.

Primary labor market — jobs in large, bureaucratic organizations that have opportunities for advancement and include lucrative retirement, medical, and vacation benefits.

Secondary labor market — jobs, often in the service sector, that offer few or no opportunities for advancement, nor medical, retirement, or vacation benefits.

Questions to Consider

1. What is diversity?
2. List and discuss the six areas that Cox and Blake proposed as reasons for valuing diversity. What else can be added to this list as reasons for valuing diversity?
3. What are some negative outcomes of increasing diversity and, given the inevitability of increasing diversity, what can organizations do to reduce these negative outcomes?
4. Why is diversity important to everyone?
5. What is one thing you learned from this chapter that is most surprising to you?

Actions and Exercises

1. Begin observing diversity in your work, school, neighborhood, religious, and/or entertainment environments. What is the racial, ethnic, gender, and age distribution of the people in each of these environments? What do you observe

that you may not have noticed were you not investigating diversity in organizations? Explain.

2. Locate the Web site of a major corporation of your choice. What statements about diversity are included? Is there a nondiscrimination policy? If so, which areas are included (e.g., race, sex, etc.). If possible, determine the race, ethnicity, and sex of the CEO, board members, and other top executives of the organization.
3. Locate the Web site of a large university and a small university. What statements about diversity are included? Is there a nondiscrimination policy? If so, which areas are included (e.g., race, sex, etc.). What clubs or organizations at the universities appear to be related to diversity? What is the racial, ethnic, gender, and other demographic composition of the student body at each school and of the communities in which they are located?
4. Prepare a PowerPoint presentation for the CEO of a medium-sized company (less than 1000 employees) who is considering implementing diversity initiatives but is unsure of the benefits for companies that are not very large. Make a presentation to convince the CEO of the benefits to such a company.

2 Chapter

Legislation

Chapter Objectives

After completing this chapter, readers should have a firm understanding of U.S. laws and executive orders as they relate to diversity in organizations. They should specifically be able to:

- *explain the historical background of and rationale behind specific diversity-related legislation.*
- *describe components and limitations of such legislation and understand why legislation alone is an insufficient incentive to cause organizations to value diversity.*
- *discuss events in several egregious diversity-related lawsuits against companies in the United States and speculate on reasons for the persistence of discrimination.*
- *consider reasons that companies may be charged with, and found liable for discriminatory acts, even though discrimination is at odds with the company's stated policies and beliefs.*
- *discuss ways to minimize the likelihood of discrimination and maximize the benefits of diversity in organizations.*
- *speculate on what other laws may be passed in the future.*

Key Facts

Although the Equal Pay Act has existed for more than 40 years, women in the United States still earn about 76 cents for each dollar that men earn. Sex-segregation limits the effectiveness of the Equal Pay Act.

Title VII of the Civil Rights Act is the most comprehensive civil rights legislation in the United States, prohibiting race, sex, religion, and national origin discrimination.

White women have benefited more from affirmative action more than people of color.[1]

Affirmative action does not mean quotas. Quotas are generally illegal.

Employment discrimination against people over 40 is generally prohibited. Discrimination against younger workers is not illegal except in a few states.

[1] For a discussion, see Reskin, B. F. (2000). "From the Realities of Affirmative Action in Employment." In F. J. Crosby & C. VanDeVeer (Eds.), *Sex, Race, and Merit: Debating Affirmative Action in Education and Employment,* Ann Arbor: University of Michigan Press, pp. 103–113.

Introduction and Overview

A brief review of the listing of settlements on the U.S. Equal Employment Opportunity Commission (EEOC) Web site for the past several years provides astonishing accounts of charges of discrimination, harassment, and retaliation against employees based on race, sex, age, national origin, disability, and religion. Organizations involved include Fortune 100, 500, and 1000 companies, universities, not-for-profit organizations, minority-owned businesses, churches, and other reputable organizations. Some of the organizations involved are recognized as being diversity leaders, having mentoring programs, affinity groups for people from diverse backgrounds, broad nondiscrimination policies, or other diversity-supportive programs, yet somehow these discriminatory actions were reported. Descriptions of the organizations involved include "a global diversified technology business," "one of the nation's largest specialty retailers of automotive aftermarket parts, tools, and supplies," "a fast food chain," "the largest minority-owned business in the state," "a leading manufacturer of custom cabinets," "the largest manufacturer of flexible packaging material in North America," and a company that "operates 122 auto paint and body shops in more than 100 cities nationwide." Many of the illegal acts, particularly sexual harassment, are against young workers, often teenagers in their first jobs, who are unaware of the relevant laws, who may not receive diversity training at work, and who may think they have no recourse. Consider the following offensive reports taken directly from the EEOC Web site.[2,3]

Sexual Harassment, Retaliation, and Termination

- **EEOC v. Jack in the Box, Inc.**
  No. CV03-814P (W. D. Wash. June 6, 2004)

  The Seattle District Office brought this Title VII suit, alleging that defendant, a fast food chain, subjected five female charging parties working at a location in Everett, Washington (store 8438) to a sexually hostile working environment and retaliated against two of them for their complaints about the discrimination. A male store manager, who directly supervised the CPs, made derogatory and insulting statements, such as constant comments about wanting to get into the women's pants, called the women bitches, sluts and whores, and remarked on the attractiveness of the women's breasts and buttocks. Unwilling to discipline the store manager despite CPs' complaints, defendant's Area Manager transferred one CP, causing her to resign because of the undesirable new location. The store manager was eventually terminated for reasons unrelated to the discrimination complaints, but his replacement retaliated against another CP who had complained by disciplining her for cash shortages for which she was not responsible.[4]

Race Discrimination and Sex Segregation

- **EEOC v. Carl Buddig & Co.**
  No. 02-C-2240 (N.D. Ill. September 7, 2004)

  The Chicago District Office filed this Title VII case alleging that the defendant, which processes and packages meat and deli products in South Holland, Illinois, a Chicago suburb, denied employment to African American applicants because of their race and segregated female applicants into lower paying jobs. Defendant's hiring practices included reliance on referrals of its almost all white workforce, many of whom were Eastern European immigrants, and physically segregating the employment applications of women, considering them only for packing line

[2] The offensive language used in some of the case summaries in this and other chapters was retained to demonstrate the egregious nature of the discrimination and harassment and the vile nature of behaviors endured by employees at work.

[3] CP refers to charging party, or the aggrieved person who brought forth the complaint.

[4] EEOC Litigation Settlements—June 2004, http://www.eeoc.gov/litigation/settlements/settlement06-04.html, accessed 07/08/05. Offensive language drawn verbatim from EEOC Web site.

jobs in which periodic raises were characteristically lower than in other unskilled jobs.[5]

National Origin Discrimination

- **EEOC v. Amycel**

  No. 04-cv-3295 (WY) (E.D. Pa. September 14, 2004)

  The Philadelphia District Office filed this Title VII action alleging that defendant, a mushroom production and distribution company, subjected Charging Party, who is of Mediterranean/Middle Eastern descent, to harassment because of his national origin, and discharged him for complaining of the harassment. CP has an olive complexion and had a long full beard at the time of his employment. He had worked for defendant since 1985 and been promoted into several management positions when, in September 2002, defendant's Sales Director became his supervisor. The Sales Director made a number of comments insinuating, with references to Charging Party's appearance, that CP was associated with terrorists. The Sales Director also called CP 'Osama Bin Laden' whenever he saw him at defendant's plant. CP complained to the Human Resources Manager by phone about the harassment, sent her e-mails documenting the harassment incidents, and advised two company vice presidents by phone of his complaints. The Human Resources Manager conducted an investigation consisting of nine brief telephone interviews with staff and concluded that CP had not been harassed on the basis of his national origin. Approximately a month after issuance of the Human Resources Manager's report, the Sales Manager summoned CP back three days early from a vacation and told him his position was being eliminated and he was discharged.[6]

- **EEOC v. Pesce, Ltd.**

  No. H-03-2503 (S.D. Tex. March 5, 2005)

  In this Title VII suit, the Houston District Office alleged that Pesce, an upscale seafood restaurant in Houston, discharged an Egyptian-born General Manager due to his national origin following the 9/11 terrorist attacks. Defendant hired charging party as General Manager in May 2001. In an August 2001 performance review, defendant told charging party that he was doing very well. After the terrorist attacks, one of defendant's co-owners said that charging party's name and appearance might scare customers and might be the reason for a decline in earnings in the weeks following the terrorist attacks. The co-owner repeatedly suggested that charging party could "pass for Hispanic" and should change his name to "something Latin." The co-owner discharged charging party on November 2, 2001, telling him that "things just weren't working out." Defendant claimed that charging party's management style made it difficult for him to supervise and lead others; however, on November 14, 2001, defendant gave charging party a letter of reference stating that charging party "showed great knowledge of his trade, dedication and was diligent in accomplishing all he set out to do," and that he "would be an asset to any service establishment."[7]

Disability Discrimination

- **EEOC v. Ft. Austin Limited Partnership dba Broadway Plaza at Cityview & American Retirement Corp.**

  No. 3:02-CV-2090-M (N.D. Tex. June 8, 2004)

  The Dallas District Office brought this ADA retaliation suit, alleging that a Fort Worth retirement home and its parent company fired charging party, an assistant nursing director, because she refused to fire a nurse's assistant who tested positive for HIV. According to the suit, CP was hired to supervise certified nurse assistants (CNAs), who attend to residents by helping them groom themselves, make their beds, and feed themselves. When management learned that one of the CNAs was HIV-positive, CP was ordered to fire him. She refused, citing her knowledge of the ADA and was fired.[8]

---

[5] EEOC Litigation Settlements—September 2004, http://www.eeoc.gov/litigation/settlements/settlement09-04.html, accessed 07/08/05.

[6] Ibid.

[7] EEOC Litigation Settlements—March 2005, http://www.eeoc.gov/litigation/settlements/settlement03-05.html, accessed 11/11/05.

[8] EEOC Litigation Settlements—June 2004, http://www.eeoc.gov/litigation/settlements/settlement06-04.html, accessed 06/15/05.

Sex-Based Pay Discrimination

- **EEOC v. R.E. Michel Co.**
  (EPA and Title VII - Sex)

  A female purchasing agent for a major heating, ventilation, and air-conditioning wholesaler, was paid less than half of what her male colleagues were paid. After ten years of employment, she complained to her supervisor, the company owner, about her low salary and requested to be paid what her male colleagues were being paid. Within a few weeks of her complaint, she was terminated and told that the company was downsizing. Nine months later, she was replaced by a higher paid male who assumed all her accounts.[9]

Age Discrimination

- **EEOC v. Family Dollar Operations, Inc., dba Family Dollar Store**
  No. 3:02-CV153-JAD (N.D. Miss. Apr. 29, 2004)

  In this ADEA action, the Birmingham District Office brought suit against a leading discount retail store chain alleging that charging party, a 61-year-old District Manager, was constructively discharged because of his age. According to the suit, defendant's Regional Vice President (RVP) told CP that he had been instructed by his superior to discharge CP or harass him into resigning. The RVP stated that his superior felt CP 'was just too old' and told the RVP to find a way to get rid of CP. The RVP said that the same superior told him to get rid of two other managers who were in their 50s because they were too old. When CP learned of the superior's instructions he felt compelled to resign.[10]

These cases are representative of numerous others that appear on the EEOC Web site, and likely of countless situations that were unaddressed because the applicant or employee did not have time, knowledge, or resources to do so. From an employer's perspective, aside from the risk of litigation, many performance and, ultimately, profit-related issues exist. In some cases, the applicant met all qualifications for an open position, with the exception of a non-job-related demographic factor (e.g., preferred race, sex, or physical ability). In other situations, the complaining party was an employee whose performance had merited multiple promotions in the past. Coworkers and managers who were not themselves targeted by harassment or discrimination, but refused to participate, were fired.

Clearly, termination or constructively discharging valuable workers and failing to follow the organization's guidelines on harassment and discrimination are simply poor management practices. Excluding qualified applicants and continuing to search for similarly qualified applicants wastes organizational resources. Customers who hear managers calling employees derogatory names may choose to do business elsewhere. Recruiting and training expenses for those hired, but terminated, are expensive, as are the resulting recruitment and training costs for their replacements. Lowered productivity for affected workers and their peers and increased medical costs and absence related to discrimination are just a few of the negative consequences of discriminatory practices.

Are the perpetrators of the kinds of egregious behaviors described just a few outliers or are they examples of many others who hold erroneous, stereotypical, or discriminatory beliefs? Is it unethical for an employer to be concerned about the organization's escalating medical costs? Is it illegal to discriminate against a qualified person with a disability because of trying to control medical costs? Using referrals for new applicants is an easy, reliable means of sourcing employees. Is doing so wrong if the referrals tend to be homogeneous

[9] Recent Examples of EEOC's Enforcement of Equal Pay in Litigation, http://www.eeoc.gov/epa/litigation.html, accessed 06/15/05.

[10] EEOC Litigation Settlements—May 2004, http://www.eeoc.gov/litigation/settlements/settlement05-04.html, accessed 12/18/04.

and workers who are different in race, ethnicity, or sex are excluded? Does stereotyping play a role in discrimination at work? After almost two decades of diversity research, four decades of antidiscrimination legislation, and extraordinary media attention to diversity, why do individuals within companies and organizational practices persist in overt discrimination and exclusion? What can be done to help organizations avoid these costly, counterproductive practices?

Chapter 1 considered some of the reasons that organizations should value diversity, for example, cost and marketing advantages, the increasing diversity of the workforce, and performance benefits. These reasons remain the major emphasis and foci of this book. Even so, the laws, executive orders, and court decisions surrounding and, for some, propelling interest in diversity issues, are critical to diversity in organizations. Without such stimuli, many of the diversity-related decisions that organizations have made within the last four decades would not have been made. Further, it is important to understand the rationale behind such legislation, their specific areas of coverage and prohibitions, and their limitations. We reiterate, however, that to focus on avoidance of litigation is a shallow approach that is unlikely to reap the benefits associated with truly valuing diversity or to encourage managers to sincerely pursue diversity. In addition, despite the media and managerial attention generated by large damage awards, relative to the numbers of applicants and employees, few people litigate each year, for various reasons. First, many discrimination claims must be filed within 180 days after the perceived discrimination occurred. In addition, people may be unaware that discrimination, which may be covert, has occurred. Others may simply not have the resources required to sue and the Equal Employment Opportunity Commission (EEOC)—the governmental agency that enforces many laws—may be unwilling to litigate individual cases. The EEOC is attempting to "strategically concentrate its limited resources on resolving systemic discrimination issues through class-based litigation,"[11] which makes litigation of individual claims less likely than class-based cases. Despite the relatively low likelihood of an organization being sued, the increasing diversity, globalization, and international competition faced by organizations make abiding by laws a necessary, but not sufficient, goal.

Historical Background

The majority of the primary legislative, judicial, and executive branch decisions that have affected diversity in organizations in the United States began occurring in the early 1960s and continued through the end of the twentieth century. Stimuli for these acts included important societal issues, such as overt social and employment discrimination against women and Blacks, as well as against other people of color, people of different religions, older workers, and people with disabilities. This discrimination prevented people from these groups from obtaining or maintaining employment or from being treated fairly once employed, contributing to large wage, income, and quality of life disparities between people of color

[11] Comment made by EEOC General Counsel C. Gregory Stewart, regarding settlement of a class-action pregnancy discrimination claim against Cincinnati Bell. EEOC and Cincinnati Bell Settle Class Pregnancy Bias Suit, http://www.eeoc.gov/press/6-15-00-a.html.

and Whites.[12] Resistance against this discrimination, in the form of marches, boycotts, and sit-ins, resulted in passage of Title VII of the Civil Rights Act in 1964 and numerous subsequent acts. As societal issues have evolved, appropriately, so too has legislation, responding to the increasing diversity among applicants and employees. In this chapter, we consider these acts in a chronological order, because their effective dates provide insights into societal recognition of the need to address significant diversity issues of the time. We also provide brief references to EEOC litigation and settlements regarding the specific areas. After completing this chapter, readers should have a firm and broad understanding of U.S. legislation related to diversity in organizations and the continued need for such laws. Later chapters provide more details on specific legislation related to the chapter topic.

Major Federal Acts Related to Diversity in Organizations

The areas covered in our discussion of federal legislation and diversity include laws, executive orders, and judicial decisions, which, for brevity, we refer to as "legislation" or "acts." The specific acts considered in this chapter are the Equal Pay Act, Title VII of the Civil Rights Act, executive orders for affirmative action, the Age Discrimination in Employment Act, the Rehabilitation Act, the Vietnam Veterans Reform Act, the Americans with Disabilities Act, the Civil Rights Act of 1991, and the Family and Medical Leave Act. Although the Emancipation Proclamation and Executive Order 8802 are not considered in detail, it is important to acknowledge that without them, the other acts that were pivotal to diversity in organizations would likely not exist at all or as they do currently. In the following sections, we consider these acts, providing key information relevant to diversity in organizations. For mechanical details (e.g., on implementation of affirmative action plans or calculation of the four-fifths rule), readers are referred to human resources management books or EEOC resources.

Title VII of the Civil Rights Act (Title VII), the Age Discrimination in Employment Act (ADEA), and the Americans with Disabilities Act (ADA) are the primary acts under which most litigation occurs. Prohibiting discrimination or harassment on the basis of race, color, religion, sex, national origin, age (at least 40), and physical and mental ability, these acts have the potential to protect every employee from illegal employment-related discrimination. Under these acts, most employers, labor unions, and employment agencies must not discriminate in hiring and firing; compensation, assignment, or classification of employees; transfer, promotion, layoff, or recall; job advertisements; recruitment; testing; use of company facilities; training and apprenticeship programs; fringe benefits; pay,

[12] Because of common family income, White women married to White men suffered fewer negative economic effects of employment-related discrimination. Never married, divorced, and widowed White women suffered more of the negative effects of employment discrimination.

retirement plans, and disability leave; or other terms and conditions of employment. Also prohibited are harassment on the basis of one's group memberships (e.g., race, color, religion, sex, national origin, age, and disability); employment decisions based on stereotypes about one's ability because of one's group memberships; retaliation for filing a claim of discrimination or complaining about it, or marriage to or affiliation with individuals of a particular group.[13]

Figure 2.1 lists major federal acts and their provisions regarding diversity issues.

The Equal Pay Act of 1963

The Equal Pay Act of 1963, an amendment to the Fair Labor Standards Act (FLSA) of 1938, is the first major legislation included as a key act relevant to diversity in organizations. The Equal Pay Act is now enforced by the Equal Employment Opportunity Commission (see discussion of the EEOC in the following section), but was enforced by the U.S. Department of Labor between 1963 and 1979. Because it covers employers who are covered by the FLSA, virtually all employers are subject to the provisions of the Equal Pay Act. The Equal Pay Act attempted to address pay inequities between men and women, requiring equal pay for equal work for men and women. In 1963, at the time the act went into effect, women earned about 59 cents to the dollar that men earned. Forty years later, in 2003, women working full-time, year-round earned about 76 cents to the dollar that men earned, a substantial improvement, but a significant difference nonetheless.

Jobs are considered to be equivalent, or substantially similar, when they require similar skill, effort, and responsibility, are in the same organization, and are performed under similar conditions. These requirements for "equivalence" severely limit the effectiveness of the Equal Pay Act. Men typically work with other men, and women typically work with other women. This phenomenon is termed "sex-segregation," and exists when at least 70% of incumbents in a particular job are male or female.

Employer preferences and illegal discrimination alone do not exclusively control sex segregation. Many factors contribute to the sex segregation of jobs, including **socialization,** which is the process by which social institutions, including families, friends, organizations, and the media, form and shape expectations of acceptable behaviors (and jobs) for men and women. People are socialized to view certain jobs as appropriate for women and others as appropriate for men. Unfortunately, "women's jobs" (such as receptionist and elementary school teacher) typically pay substantially less than men's jobs (such as manager and high school principal). In Chapter 9, more details about gender role socialization and its role in pay inequity and gender-based opportunities are provided.

Seemingly valid exceptions due to merit and seniority that disadvantage women have also limited the effectiveness of the Equal Pay Act. Exceptions to

[13] http://www.eeoc.gov/abouteeo/overview_practices.html, accessed 02/22/04.

Figure 2.1 ***Major Federal Acts Affecting Diversity in Organizations***

ACT	PROVISIONS
Emancipation Proclamation (1863)	By freeing slaves, allowed Blacks the opportunity to work for wages rather than as slaves.
Executive Order 8802 (1941)	Required equal employment opportunities for all American citizens, regardless of race, creed, color, or national origin.
Equal Pay Act of 1963	Requires women and men to be paid equally for equal work.
Title VII of the Civil Rights Act of 1964	Prohibits discrimination on the basis of race, color, religion, sex, or national origin in employment-related matters.
Executive Orders for Affirmative Action (EO 11246 in 1965 and 11375 in 1966)	Require employers to take affirmative steps to prevent discrimination in employment, including taking proactive measures to ensure hiring and promotion of minorities (men and women) and women (White and women of color).
The Age Discrimination in Employment Act of 1967	Prohibits employment-related discrimination against persons aged 40 or older. Exceptions can be made for bona fide occupational qualifications.
Rehabilitation Act of 1973	Prohibits discrimination against federal employees with disabilities, requires federal government and contractors to take affirmative action for the hiring, placement, and advancement of people with disabilities, and to make reasonable accommodations to allow them to work.
Vietnam Veterans Readjustment Assistance Act of 1974	Prohibits discrimination against Vietnam Era and other veterans and requires affirmative action for them.
Pregnancy Discrimination Act of 1978	An amendment to Title VII, clarified that Title VII's prohibition against discrimination on the basis of sex included pregnancy, childbirth, and related medical conditions. Requires employers to treat pregnancy similarly to other temporary disabilities for medical and benefits-related purposes.
EEOC Guidelines on Sexual Harassment 1980	Defines sexual harassment, formally acknowledging it as a form of sex discrimination prohibited by Section 703 of Title VII and suggests affirmative steps employers may take to prevent sexual harassment. The EEOC uses these guidelines in enforcement and many courts rely on them in decisions.
Older Workers Benefit Protection Act of 1990	An amendment to the ADEA of 1967. Prohibits employers from denying benefits to older workers, but allows reductions in benefits based on age, as long as the employer's costs of providing benefits to older workers are the same as their costs for providing benefits to younger workers.
Americans with Disabilities Act of 1990	Prohibits employment-related discrimination against people with physical and mental disabilities for employers of 15 or more people in the private sector and in state and local government. Requires employers to make reasonable accommodation for those otherwise qualified to work, but does not require affirmative action for people with disabilities.
Civil Rights Act of 1991	An amendment to Title VII of the CRA of 1964. Provides for compensatory and punitive damages (limited to 300k) in cases of intentional discrimination and harassment; allows for jury trials; extends coverage of act to U.S. citizens working abroad for U.S. companies; established Glass Ceiling Commission.
Family and Medical Leave Act of 1993	Allows certain employees to take up to 12 weeks unpaid leave to care for a spouse, child, or parent, or for a personal illness. Employers must maintain employees' benefits and the same or a substantially similar job upon employees' return from leave.

the equal pay requirement are allowed when there are differences based on the employees' job seniority, merit (e.g., skill, education), or performance. These exceptions are generally accepted as legitimate by employers, employees, and unions, but may serve to reduce the effectiveness of the Equal Pay Act. That an employee who has worked for the company longer, who has more job-related skill, and better performance would earn more than one who has less tenure, skill, and lower performance, appears logical to most people. For a variety of reasons, however, on average, men have longer seniority than women do. Some of those reasons are "voluntary," such as intermittent work due to child and eldercare responsibilities. Other reasons include past sex discrimination of unions and employers that kept women out of jobs, reserving them instead for (White) men. Although such discrimination is now illegal, discrimination that occurred in the past has resulted in men having longer tenure and being able to enjoy the benefits of such tenure. These benefits include higher seniority-based pay, more vacation accruals, and, perhaps most importantly, longer protections from lay-offs, as the last hired are often the first fired when downsizing occurs.

In addition to the problems with the apparently neutral practice of favoring those who have more seniority, judgments of merit and ratings of performance are not always objective. This subjectivity, and people's propensity to prefer those who are similar, may disadvantage members of nondominant groups, including women.

Effectiveness of the equal pay act. Although the effectiveness of the Equal Pay Act has been limited by sex segregation and seemingly legitimate exceptions, it is still credited with helping to reduce the pay gap between men and women. In the early 1960s, pay disparities between men and women were considerably more than they are now. Women working full-time earned less than 60 cents to each dollar that men earned.[14] The wage gap remained about the same until the early 1980s when women's wages reached about 75 cents to the dollar that men earned. Women's wages then plateaued, and by the year 2002 were at 76.3 cents to the dollar that men earned.[15] Some researchers express concern that the stagnating reduction in the gap and evidence of declines in the gap followed by increases in the size of the gap in the 1990s bring into question women's likelihood of ever achieving earnings parity with men.[16] Other researchers argue convincingly that the wage gap is largely due to women's "choices" of careers, fields of study, time spent out of the workforce, and number of hours worked.[17] Chapter 9 considers

---

[14] U.S. Census Bureau, 2003.

[15] Reported male to female earnings ratio varies depending on whether mean or median, full-time, year-round workers or all workers earning income for any portion of the year.

[16] "The Gender Wage Gap: Progress of the 1980's Fails to Carry Through," Publication # C353. Institute for Women's Policy Research, November, 2003. http://www.iwpr.org/paf/C353.pdf, accessed 02/15/04.

[17] Hattiagadi, A. U. (1997). "'Where's My 26 Cents?': Choices Explain Gender Wage Gap," http://www.epf.org/ff/ff4-6.htm, accessed 02/15/04.

the role of "choice" in women's and men's careers, fields of study, workforce participation, and hours worked in more detail, providing evidence that gender role socialization and employer and societal expectations affect these "choices" more than is commonly acknowledged.

Litigation under the equal pay act. Sex segregation does not negate the need for the Equal Pay Act, however. Considerable litigation under the Equal Pay Act provides evidence of sex-based pay disparities for men and women performing substantially similar work. In the 14 years between 1979 (when enforcement powers were transferred to the EEOC) and 2003, the EEOC filed 364 lawsuits under the Equal Pay Act. Settlements resulted in over $28 million in monetary relief for charging parties.[18] Several significant cases resolved in the complaining parties' favor include those in which women working in male-dominated fields were paid less than similarly situated men. Settlements ranged from $25,000 to $4.5 million (class action) for women engineers, controllers, truckers, machine operators, teachers, university professors, and jail guards in a few of such cases.

In *EEOC v. Baltimore Cable Access Corporation (BCA),* BCA was charged with discrimination against a woman executive director.[19] She was continually promised salary increases, but remained at her starting salary throughout her 3 years of employment at BCA. After complaining to the board of directors, the executive director was fired, and replaced with a less qualified man, whom BCA paid a 20% higher salary than the fired woman had earned. After the EEOC filed suit, BCA entered into a consent degree, providing for a $45,000 payment to the terminated executive director. Other sex-based compensation cases are presented in Chapters 9 and 13.

Title VII of the Civil Rights Act of 1964

Title VII is considered to be the most comprehensive act related to diversity and civil rights.[20] It prohibits discrimination on the basis of race, color, religion, sex (including sexual harassment or pregnancy discrimination), and national origin in employment-related matters. Title VII covers the great majority of employers, including:

1. all private employers, state and local governments, and education institutions that employ 15 or more individuals for 20 or more weeks per year
2. private and public employment agencies
3. labor organizations

[18] http://www.eeoc.gov/epa/anniversary/epa-highlights.html, accessed 12/05/04.

[19] http://www.eeoc.gov/press/4-28-00.html, accessed 12/05/04.

[20] Wolkinson, B. (2000). "EEO in the Workplace, Employment Law Challenges," Module 8. In E. E. Kossek & R. Block, *Managing Human Resources in the 21st Century,* p. 75. Cincinnati, OH: South-Western Publishing.

4. joint labor management committees controlling apprenticeship and training
5. employers that are incorporated or based in the United States or controlled by U.S. companies that employ U.S. citizens outside the United States or its territories

Certain employers are excluded from coverage under Title VII, including private membership clubs, religious organizations, schools, associations, or organizations hiring American Indians on or near reservations. For those organizations operating solely within the confines of the exclusion, certain discrimination is not illegal.

Disparate treatment occurs when an applicant or employee is treated differently because of membership in a protected class, such as refusing to hire Blacks as restaurant servers or men as childcare workers. Disparate treatment is also referred to as "intentional discrimination," and evidence of such treatment would include such things as statements by employers or written policies—items that are often difficult to verify or obtain. Common stereotypes about abilities, traits, or performance of people belonging to certain groups may lead to disparate treatment. An example of a stereotype that could lead to disparate treatment is the assumption that women have limited math skills that could result in their purposely not being assigned to jobs requiring math skills. Assuming applicants who have Hispanic names will have limited English skills and refusing to interview them is another way that stereotypes could lead to disparate treatment.

Disparate or adverse impact occurs when an apparently neutral, evenly applied, job policy or employment practice has a negative effect on the employment of people belonging to protected classes. Adverse impact is demonstrated by statistical evidence showing that the number of people in a protected class were disproportionately affected by a particular "neutral" practice. This type of discrimination, also referred to as "unintentional discrimination," might occur with educational requirements or height and weight restrictions that may exclude large numbers of certain groups.

Neutral practices that disproportionately exclude members of certain groups should be carefully scrutinized. Are the requirements legitimately required for successful job performance? Are there no other nondiscriminatory alternatives that would still allow for successful performance? Title VII does not require employers to hire, promote, or retain people who do not meet job requirements. Title VII, instead, requires employers to pay careful attention to job requirements and employment decisions to ensure that members of certain groups are not excluded by factors that are not clearly related to successful job performance. Such a case is described next.

- **EEOC v. STI Holdings, Inc., f/k/a Stoughton Trailers, Inc.**

  No. 03-C-543-S (W.D. Wis. October 6, 2003)

  In this Title VII action, the Milwaukee District Office alleged that defendant, a semi-trailer manufacturer, engaged in unlawful discrimination by using a written

> preemployment test for entry-level assembler positions that had a disparate impact on African American and female applicants. By a two-year consent decree, defendant is enjoined from using the challenged test or any other pre-employment selection procedure which has or may have a disparate impact on African Americans or women without providing EEOC an opportunity to review information on its validity and raise objections with the court.[21]

The equal employment opportunity commission. Title VII created the Equal Employment Opportunity Commission (EEOC), which began operating on July 2, 1965. The EEOC's stated mission is to "eradicate employment discrimination."[22] During the first year it was opened, the EEOC received 9,000 charges—four times the number expected, demonstrating the gravity and pervasiveness of discrimination in the United States.[23] The primary role of the EEOC is to enforce Title VII, which involves investigating complaints of discrimination, conciliating when complaints are deemed meritorious, and, in some cases, litigating when efforts to resolve complaints through conciliation are unsuccessful. Instead of litigating, the EEOC may also issue complainants a "Right-to-Sue-Notice" allowing them to file individual actions in court (without the EEOC's involvement). The EEOC also enforces the Equal Pay Act (as described earlier), the ADEA, parts of the ADA, the Rehabilitation Act, and the Civil Rights Act of 1991, which are discussed later in the chapter.

Although about 80,000 claims are filed with the EEOC annually, relatively few claims result in EEOC lawsuits. Between 1992 and 2002, the number of lawsuits filed by the EEOC on behalf of plaintiffs averaged only 383 per year, less than one half of 1% of all claims.[24] In some cases, plaintiffs may litigate without EEOC assistance, but doing so can be quite costly to individuals. As shown in Table 2.1, the percentage of all charges resolved by the EEOC in favor of the charging party in 2003 ranged from a low of about 15% (age) to a high of 29% (sexual harassment). These "merit resolutions" include settlements, withdrawals with benefits, and conciliations. On the other hand, charges closed for administrative reasons or because they were deemed to have no reasonable cause ranged from a high of 85% to a low of 71%. These figures indicate that despite media attention and managers' fears, EEOC charges, litigation, settlements, or damage awards are unlikely events for individual employers. Even so, the EEOC plays a vital role in enforcing various laws, issuing guidelines to assist employers in interpreting and complying with laws, and providing individuals with voice in employment-related treatment.

---

[21] EEOC Litigation Settlements—October 2003, http://www.eeoc.gov/litigation/settlements/settlement10-03.html, accessed 06/15/05.

[22] http://www.eeoc.gov/abouteeoc/plan/strategic-2000.html, accessed 03/05/04.

[23] Ibid.

[24] http://www.eeoc.gov/abouteeoc/overview.html, accessed 02/21/04.

TABLE 2.1 ***EEOC Charges and Resolutions by Area for 2003***

	Race	Sex	Sexual Harassment	Pregnancy	National Origin	Religion	Age	Disability
Receipts of charges	28,526	24,362	13,566	4,649	8,450	2,532	19,124	15,377
Resolutions of charges*	30,702	27,146	14,534	4,847	9,172	2,690	17,352	16,915
Resolutions by type:								
Settlements	2,890	2,877	1,783	685	839	221	1,285	1,748
%	9.4%	10.6%	12.3%	14.1%	9.1%	8.2%	7.4%	10.3%
Withdrawals w/benefits	1,125	1,329	1,300	429	333	86	710	750
%	3.7%	4.9%	8.9%	8.9%	3.6%	3.2%	4.1%	4.4%
Administrative closures	4,759	5,484	3,600	901	1,353	434	2,824	2,995
%	15.5%	20.2%	24.8%	18.6%	14.8%	16.1%	16.3%	17.7%
No reasonable cause	20,506	15,506	6,703	2,629	6,117	1,744	11,976	10,251
%	66.8%	57.1%	46.1%	54.2%	66.7%	64.8%	69.0%	60.6%
Admin. closures + no reasonable cause	25,265	20,990	10,303	3,530	7,470	2,178	14,800	13,246
%	82.3%	77.3%	70.9%	72.8%	81.4%	81.0%	85.3%	78.3%
Reasonable cause	1,422	1,950	1,148	203	530	205	557	1,171
%	4.6%	7.2%	7.9%	4.2%	5.8%	7.6%	3.2%	6.9%
Successful conciliations	392	520	350	75	112	67	166	487
%	1.3%	1.9%	2.4%	1.5%	1.2%	2.5%	1.0%	2.9%
Unsuccessful conciliations	1,030	1,430	798	128	418	138	391	684
%	3.4%	5.3%	5.5%	2.6%	4.6%	5.1%	2.3%	4.0%
Merit resolutions†	5,437	6,156	4,231	1,317	1,702	512	2,552	3,669
%	17.7%	22.7%	29.1%	27.2%	18.6%	19.0%	14.7%	21.7%
Monetary benefits in millions	$69.6	$98.4	$50.0	$12.4	$21.3	$6.6	$48.9	$45.3

*Resolutions include charges from previous years.

†Merit resolutions include settlements, withdrawals with benefits, and reasonable cause claims.

As with many understaffed and underfunded federal agencies, many of the EEOC's resources are allocated to helping organizations comply with the law rather than solely focusing on penalizing them for violations. One helpful employer guideline issued by the EEOC is the 1980 guideline on sexual harassment, discussed later in the chapter. The EEOC defines harassment in employment settings as "bothering, tormenting, troubling, ridiculing, or coercing a person because of race, color, religion, sex, national origin, disability, or age."[25] Harassment guidelines issued by the EEOC now include prohibitions against racial, religious, national origin, age, and disability-based harassment, which are increasing in frequency.[26]

Race and national origin. Under Title VII, it is illegal to discriminate against someone because of his or her race, color, birthplace, ancestry, culture, or linguistic characteristics common to a particular ethnic group. The extreme and pervasive discrimination against African Americans in the United States resulted in their being the primary racial group for whom the protections of Title VII were originally intended. Other racial and ethnic groups, including Latinos, Asian Americans, American Indians, and Arab Americans have also benefited significantly from the provisions of Title VII. Recently, national-origin discrimination has been increasing; many charges involve low wage earners and immigrants in fishing, poultry, and agricultural industries, many of whom have limited English proficiency and few other employment options.

In addition to prohibiting disparate treatment based on race, color, birthplace, and the other covered factors, apparently neutral practices, such as English-only rules, can be in violation of Title VII, unless the employer has a business necessity for them. Some of the companies affected by recent EEOC litigation or settlements involving race and national origin discrimination include Salomon-Smith Barney, Commonwealth Edison, American-Seafoods, and Prudential Insurance, involving African American and African, Hispanic, Vietnamese American, and Haitian employees, respectively.[27] In a disturbing case, in September of 2004, the Cracker Barrel restaurant chain agreed to pay $8.7 million to settle lawsuits filed by Black employees and customers alleging discrimination in job assignments against employees and denial of service, placing customers in segregated seating areas and serving them food taken from the trash.[28] Cracker Barrel has dealt with charges of sexual harassment and sexual orientation discrimination (see Chapter 15) as well.[29]

[25] Equal Employment Opportunity Commission, Office of Public Affairs (1992). *Issue Codes.* Washington, DC: Author, p. 68.

[26] http://www.eeoc.gov/abouteeoc/plan/strategic-2000.html, accessed 03/14/04.

[27] Recent Examples of EEOC Litigation Alleging National Origin Discrimination, http://www.eeoc.gov/origin/lit_examples.html, accessed 02/21/04.

[28] "Cracker Barrel to pay $8.7 million to end suits." *Dallas Morning News,* September 10, 2004, p. 2D (U.S. and World Briefs).

[29] EEOC Sues Cracker Barrel for Sex Bias and Racial Harassment, August 11, 2004, http://www.eeoc.gov/press/8-11-04.html, accessed 03/4/05.

Sex. Along with prohibitions against sex discrimination in hiring, firing, promotions, and other commonly recognized areas of employment, Title VII prohibits sex discrimination in the form of sexual harassment and pregnancy discrimination. It has been reported that the inclusion of prohibitions against sex discrimination in Title VII was a last ditch effort by conservative Southern legislators to ensure that the act did not pass. Some research contradicts this claim, noting that feminists had been fighting for such legislation for a long time. Regardless of different beliefs about why prohibitions against sex discrimination were included in Title VII, it is clear that some aspects of discrimination against women were stronger than discrimination against Black men, who obtained the right to vote (in theory, if not in practice) before White women. Despite persistent sex discrimination, harassment, and gender-based pay differences, Title VII has been very beneficial to working women in the United States.

Title VII has also been used when sex-based discrimination against men occurs. In 1996, the EEOC filed a notable case against Hooters restaurant alleging discrimination against men. Hooters restaurants are known for scantily clad servers (waitresses), which called into question the need for such a lawsuit. As an example, in the *EEOC v. Parmalat* sexual harassment case discussed later in the chapter, one complaint from the charging party was having been forced to attend business meetings at Hooters and a transvestite bar.

In another case, Jillian's—a nationwide chain of family dining/entertainment facilities with headquarters in Louisville, Kentucky—agreed to settle a class-action lawsuit in which at least 100 men alleged sex discrimination. Jillian's operates in about 25 states and employs over 5,000 employees. The lawsuit alleged that Jillian's maintained sex-segregated job classifications and failed to hire and/or transfer men to more lucrative server positions because they were men. Jillian's agreed to pay $350,000 in damages to men in Indianapolis, to hire and place employees at all its facilities without regard to sex, to train its managers on Title VII's regulations against sex discrimination, and to post nondiscrimination notices at all facilities and on its employment applications.[30]

Religion. The inclusion of religion in Title VII provides people of different or no religious beliefs with protection from employment-related discrimination. Employers are prohibited from treating applicants or employees more or less favorably because of their religious beliefs or practices. Employers are also required to reasonably accommodate employees' sincerely held religious beliefs or practices, using flexible scheduling, job reassignments, lateral transfers, and other accommodations that do not impose undue hardship. Employers are encouraged to have antiharassment policies that include religious harassment.

[30] http://www.eeoc.gov/press/index.html, accessed 09/16/04.

Title VII has been helpful to many Muslims who faced overt discrimination and harassment after the terrorist attacks in the United States on September 11, 2001. Recent cases involving religious discrimination have also been brought by employees who were terminated for harassment of those who do not share their religious beliefs or who were terminated because their religious beliefs conflicted with their company's diversity program. Two of such cases, involving Hewlett-Packard and AT&T Broadband, are discussed in Chapter 10.

As shown in Table 2.1, in 2003, the EEOC received 2,532 charges of religious discrimination and recovered $6.6 million in monetary benefits for complainants and other aggrieved parties.[31] However, 81% of the charges resolved that year were deemed to have no reasonable cause or were closed for administrative reasons.

In 1966, the EEOC issued its "Guidelines on Discrimination Because of Religion," to help employers avoid discriminating against employees and applicants. In 1997, "Guidelines on Religious Exercise and Religious Expression" in the federal workplace were issued by the Clinton administration.[32] Although intended for the federal workplace, these guidelines provide useful suggestions for employers wishing to address religious exercise and expression in the workplace. These guidelines and recommendations for employers are discussed further in Chapter 10.

Exceptions: Bona fide occupational qualifications and business necessity. In a limited number of situations, discrimination on the basis of sex, religion, and age is not illegal. Bona Fide Occupational Qualifications (BFOQs) refer to certain situations in which employers may require that all employees hold a certain characteristic. For sex as a BFOQ, for example, an employer could legitimately require that women model evening gowns, that a male be hired to play a leading man in a movie, or that women work in dressing or changing rooms in a lingerie shop. Age may be a BFOQ in certain circumstances when it is "reasonably necessary to the normal operation of the business." Mandatory retirement of pilots and age limits for hiring of public safety officers are examples of the narrow legal use of age limits. Religion could be a BFOQ for particular religious organizations.

An organization may claim that a particular practice that results in disparate impact is a "business necessity." For business necessity to be a valid defense, the employer must demonstrate that there is no alternative practice that would serve the same purpose without having the discriminatory effect.

Although the aforementioned situations are those in which discrimination may not be illegal, organizations should emphasize using legitimate job-related qualifications, and attending to what is actually mandatory, rather than eagerly discriminating when it is not illegal to do so. In addition, customer preferences

[31] http://www.eeoc.gov/stats/religion.html, accessed 02/22/04.

[32] http://clinton4.nara.gov/textonly/WH/New/html/19970819-3275.html.

for certain types of workers do not qualify as BFOQs or business necessity. When organizations are able to remove obstacles to employment for larger proportions of the population, organizations, individuals, and society all benefit.

Executive Orders for Affirmative Action in Employment

In 1965 and 1966, President Lyndon Johnson issued key executive orders for affirmative action in employment. These orders are administered and enforced by the U.S. Department of Labor's Office of Federal Contract Compliance Programs (OFCCP). Executive Orders (EO) 11246 and 11375, as amended, prohibit federal contractors with over $10,000 in government business per year from discriminating in employment decisions on the basis of race, color, religion, sex, or national origin. In addition to prohibiting discrimination, these orders require proactive measures, affirmative action, to help ensure equality of employment opportunities for women (EO 11375) and minorities (EO 11246). Government contractors having 50 or more employees and at least $50,000 in government contracts are required to develop an affirmative action plan for each of their establishments.[33]

Affirmative action programs. Affirmative action programs are written programs or plans that help employers identify areas in which women, minorities, persons with disabilities, and covered veterans are underutilized in the employers' workforce. A utilization analysis is a comparison of the numbers of underrepresented groups in the surrounding or relevant (for recruiting purposes) labor market as compared with the numbers of those groups in the organization, in particular job categories. For example, if there are fewer women and minorities employed by the organization than in the relevant labor market, underutilization is indicated, and the organization should implement plans to correct this. While Title VII is passive, prohibiting discrimination, affirmative action means taking action—taking steps to correct or reduce underutilization.

Legitimate plans to correct underutilization might include additional training programs or different recruitment measures, not such things as "quotas," which are generally illegal. Employers may not legally implement quotas and only in unique cases of blatant discrimination may a judge impose quotas on an offending employer. Judges are reluctant to impose quotas, however. Even in cases of egregious discrimination, rather than imposing quotas, judges recommend that employers pay careful attention to recruiting practices and have hiring **goals** for the group that experienced discrimination.[34]

---

[33] http://www.dol.gov/esa/regs/compliance/ofccp/fs11246.htm.

[34] For an example, in *EEOC v. Bazaar del Mundo* in Chapter 4, defendant agreed to "actively recruit black job applicants with a goal of 5% black employees in each 12 month period" of the three year decree.

Misperception: Affirmative action programs require employers to have hiring "quotas" if minorities or women are underutilized.

Reality: Employers should have goals and timetables for correcting underutilization; employer-imposed quotas are illegal and judges are reluctant to impose them.

As discussed in Research Translation 2.1, research on perceptions of the characteristics of affirmative action plans indicates that few people associate them with recruitment efforts, even though recruitment is an important and accepted means of increasing numbers of qualified applicants from diverse backgrounds.[35] If an organization is underutilizing women, for example, it might alter recruitment efforts to include universities with large percentages of women students, such as Smith College, Texas Woman's University, or St. Mary's College in Indiana. Organizations wishing to increase representation of people of color might include recruiting at the University of Texas at El Paso, St. Mary's University in San Antonio, University of California at San Diego, which have high percentages of Latinos, historically Black schools such as Southern University, Prairie View A&M University, North Carolina A&T, Tuskegee Institute, or Wilberforce College, or Haskell Indian Nations University, the University of New Mexico, and other schools with high representation of American Indians. Advertising in media that target specific groups, such as *Essence* or *Ebony* magazine (Blacks), or *Univision* or *Latina Style* (Hispanics) are simple, easy means of increasing the diversity of the applicant pool. By changing recruiting venues or methods, people from diverse backgrounds have more opportunities to compete for job openings.

Misperception: Affirmative action programs are only for minorities.

Reality: Affirmative action programs typically include men and women of color, White women, and in some cases, people with disabilities, and Vietnam Era and other veterans (typically, White men and men of color).

Periodic compliance reviews by the Office of Federal Contract Compliance Programs (OFCCP—the monitoring agency) can help employers identify problem areas and corrective action. Persistent or unaddressed underutilization may result in conciliation agreements, which may include back pay, promotions, or other forms of relief for affected parties. When attempts to conciliate are unsuccessful, sanctions, including loss of government contracts, may be imposed upon employers. As with other diversity efforts, avoidance of sanctions or penalties should not be an organization's primary goal in compliance. Nor should the relationship

[35] See Bell, M. P., Harrison, D. E., & McLaughlin, M. E. (2000). "Forming, Changing, and Acting on Attitude toward Affirmative Action in Employment: A Theory Based Approach." *Journal of Applied Psychology,* 85: 784–798, and Kravitz, D. A. & Platania, J. (1993), "Attitudes and Beliefs about Affirmative Action: Effects of Target and of Respondent Sex and Ethnicity." Journal of Applied Psychology, 78: 928–938.

Research Translation 2.1 *Focus on: Affirmative Action*

Numerous researchers have investigated the often negative perceptions and attitudes people have about affirmative action programs (AAPs) in employment. Many of these perceptions are obtained from news media and political advertisements, which frequently contain inaccuracies or intentional misrepresentations about the content, requirements, and function of affirmative action. Some of these misperceptions include: erroneous beliefs about the requirements of and processes required by affirmative action programs (for example, quotas) and beliefs that those hired under affirmative action are less competent and qualified than others.[36] Madeline Heilman and her colleagues have conducted extensive research on stigmatization and presumptions of incompetence about women hired under AAPs. In field and laboratory studies, women hired under AAPs were *perceived to be* less competent than persons not hired under AAPs. These findings occurred when the raters were White men and also White women, Black men, and Black women—those who are from groups who are likely to be helped by AAPs. These findings are likely to be related to people's general perceptions that affirmative action results in organizations passing over more qualified workers for less qualified or unqualified workers and other inaccuracies that have been identified by researchers.[37] These perceptions are starkly contrasted with the actual requirements of AAPs that applicants must first be qualified to be considered, and findings of other research that indicate preferences for equally qualified or, at times, even unqualified Whites over persons of color. Art Brief, a professor at Tulane University, and his colleagues found that when instructed to discriminate under the guise of a "business justification," research subjects did so, rating Black applicants lower than similarly qualified White applicants. Most disturbing, when given this justification to discriminate, some respondents chose *unqualified Whites* over qualified Blacks.[38,39] A similar study replicated these findings of discrimination against minorities in Germany.[40] Years of covert and overt discrimination against minorities and women have been called "affirmative action for White males," as by excluding other candidates, White males have been advantaged in many contexts.[41]

To reduce misperceptions about affirmative action and assumptions that women and people of color are hired solely because of AAPs, and White males are hired because of discrimination against others, it is important for organizations to publicize the qualifications of new hires of

[36] See Heilman, M. E., Block, C. J., & Lucas, J. A. (1992). "Presumed Incompetent? Stigmatization and Affirmative Action Efforts." *Journal of Applied Psychology,* 77: 536–544; Bell, et al. (2000) 85: 784–798. Kravitz & Platania (1993). "Further Development of a Test of Knowledge of Affirmative Action." Paper presented at the Academy of Management meeting, Honolulu HI. Crosby, F. J. (2004). *Affirmative Action is Dead: Long Live Affirmative Action,* Cambridge, MA: Yale University Press.

[37] For example, Bell et al. (2000); Kravitz, D., & Yun, G. (2005).

[38] Brief, A. P., Buttram, R. T., Reizenstein, R. M., Pugh, S. D., Callahan, J. D., McCline, R. L., & Vaslow, J. B. (1997). "Beyond Good Intentions: The Next Steps toward Racial Equality in the American Workplace." *Academy of Management Executive,* 11(4): 59–72. See also Brief, A. P., Dietz, J., Cohen, R. R., Pugh, S. D., & Vaslow, J. B. (2000). "Just Doing Business: Modern Racism and Obedience to Authority as Explanations for Employment Discrimination." *Organizational Behavior and Human Decision Processes,* 81: 72–97.

[39] More details on this study are provided in Chapter 4.

[40] Petersen, L., & Dietz, J. (2005). "Prejudice and Enforcement of Workforce Homogeneity as Explanations for Employment Discrimination." *Journal of Applied Social Psychology,* 35(1): 144–159.

[41] For example, Brodkin, K. (2004). "How Jews Became White." In J. F. Healey & E. O'Brien (Eds.), *Race, Ethnicity, and Gender,* Thousand Oaks, CA: Pine Forge Press, pp. 283–293. "Dedicated Lives." (1997). *Emerge,* July/August, pp. 35–38.

all backgrounds. Publicizing the background and qualifications of new hires of all races, ethnic groups, men, and women would help demonstrate that all employees are hired because of job-related qualifications. Make crystal clear that women and people of color are not hired solely because of affirmative action and White males are not hired because of the good old boys' network and discrimination against women and people of color.

Employees should also be educated about the affirmative practices that the organization employs (such as broader recruitment methods) and the benefits of diversity for all employees. Education is an important tool in increasing support for diversity efforts. Brief and colleagues also recommend that employees be encouraged to engage in **principled disobedience** when faced with discrimination against and exclusion of certain groups. Principled disobedience against all forms of discrimination (racism, sexism, ageism, etc.) and refusal to accept stereotypes about people based on their group memberships can be beneficial for organizations pursuing diversity and for people from all backgrounds.

Questions to Consider

1. *What factors likely contribute to common, erroneous beliefs about affirmative action, even among intended beneficiaries?*
2. *How do perceptions that minorities and women hired are unqualified contrast with research indicating that unqualified Whites are sometimes chosen over qualified Blacks?*
3. *Had you considered the discrimination against women and minorities as "affirmative action for White males" prior to reading this selection?*
4. *The assistant nursing director in the* EEOC v. Ft. Austin Limited Partnership *case discussed in the chapter engaged in "principled disobedience" by refusing to fire someone who was HIV positive and was fired herself. What is the likely role of beliefs about true organizational commitment to diversity in people's willingness to engage in principled disobedience?*

between employers and the OFCCP be assumed to be solely an adversarial one. The OFCCP can assist employers in developing AAPs by offering company seminars and individual consultations on company policies and procedures. When used correctly, affirmative action can be a valuable tool in increasing the representation of underutilized groups in an organization, providing opportunities to benefit from their inclusion and contributions.

On the other hand, when incidents occur in which a person hired under affirmative action or a diversity program is unsuccessful, a media storm emphasizing the issue and blaming the program, rather than the individual, can occur. One highly publicized case about the hiring and firing of Jayson Blair is such a case. Blair is an African American man who was hired by *The New York Times* under an internship designed to increase the diversity in newsrooms and media organizations, which are extremely dominated by White males. After a few years at the newspaper, Blair was fired in the spring of 2003 for fabricating stories and sources. This brought about a hailstorm of negative commentary that often emphasized that Blair was hired under a program designed to increase diversity. In an interesting contrast, in early 2004, Jack Kelley, a White male reporter for *USA Today* was fired for the same reasons Blair had been fired: fabricating stories and sources.

As pointed out by Leonard Pitts, a well-known African American journalist, the many white journalists who spoke vehemently about Blair's failures and emphasized race rather than ethics, were conspicously silent on the Jack Kelley episode.[42] As with other undesirable events (e.g., dishonesty, theft, sabotage, etc.) individual behaviors (by a particular person) should not be attributed to groups of people or used to denigrate entire programs, such as diversity or affirmative action efforts.

Relationships between affirmative action in education and employment. Many newspaper and magazine articles and academic publications refer to issues related to affirmative action in education, contracts with the government, or employment. Because the terminology "affirmative action" alone does not specify what type of affirmative action is being discussed, people's views of affirmative action may be based on misunderstandings of its focus or goals (e.g., increasing representation in elite schools or in jobs). Indeed, research indicates that opposition to affirmative action is related to lack of knowledge about it.[43] The focus of affirmative action in this chapter and book is primarily affirmative action in employment, but the two are clearly related. Professor Patricia Gurin's longitudinal research on the benefits of diversity in the learning environment to students in the long-term can help clarify these relationships. As discussed in Chapter 1, in several studies, Gurin and colleagues found that many students' experiences with diversity at the University of Michigan were related to an increased sense of commonality with those from different racial and ethnic backgrounds, to increased ability to take the perspective of other groups, and to perspectives that differences are not necessarily divisive.[44] The more purposeful contact that students had with people from other racial and ethnic backgrounds, the more they engaged in active, critical thinking, and the more they embraced democratic values. These benefits occurred for both White students (the majority of the samples of thousands of students) and students of color.

The amicus briefs (friend of the court) filed by numerous Fortune 500 companies in support of the University of Michigan's (UM) programs to increase diversity of its students indicate that major corporations are aware of the important relationships between diversity in educational institutions and the subsequent benefits of a diverse workforce. As shown in Table 2.2, some of the companies in favor of UM's programs include General Motors, Johnson & Johnson, Intel, Microsoft, Boeing, Kodak, and American Airlines. Competitors (e.g., Coke and Pepsi,

[42] Pitts, L., Jr. (2004, April 27). "Scandal Tainting White Journalists." *Dallas Morning News*. p. 11A.

[43] Kravitz & Yun (2005, August). Honolulu, HI. Kravitz and Yun found that opposition to affirmative action in employment is related to lack of knowledge about the law.

[44] Gurin, P., Nagda, B. A., & Lopez, G. E. (2004). "The Benefits of Diversity in Education for Democratic Citizenship." *Journal of Social Issues,* 60(1): 17–34. See also Gurin, P., Dey, E. L., Hurtado, S., & Gurin, G. (2002). "Diversity and Higher Education: Theory and Impact on Educational Outcomes." *Harvard Educational Review,* 71(3): 332–366; Gurin, P., Y., Dey, E. L., Gurin, G., & Hurtado, S. (2003). "How Does Racial/Ethnic Diversity Promote Education?" *The Western Journal of Black Studies,* 27(1): 20–29.

TABLE 2.2 ***Limited List of Companies Filing Amicus Brief in Support of the University of Michigan's Admission Program***

3M	Intel Corporation
Abbott Laboratories	Johnson & Johnson
Alcoa, Inc.	Kaiser Found. Health Plan, Inc.
Alliant Energy Corporation	Kellogg Company
Altria Group, Inc.	KPMG Int'l for KPMG LLP
American Airlines, Inc.	Kraft Foods Inc.
American Express Company	Lockheed Martin Corporation
Amgen Corporation	Lucent Technologies, Inc.
Ashland Inc.	Medtronic, Inc.
Bank One Corporation	Merck & Co., Inc.
Baxter Healthcare Corporation	Microsoft Corporation
The Boeing Company	Mitsubishi Motors North America
Charter One Financial, Inc.	MSC.Software Corporation
ChevronTexaco Corporation	Nationwide Mutual Insurance Co.
The Coca-Cola Company	NetCom Solutions International
Coca-Cola Enterprises Inc.	Nike Inc.
DaimlerChrysler Corporation	Northrop Grumman Corporation
Deloitte Consulting LLP	Pepsi Bottling Group, Inc.
Deloitte & Touche LLP	PepsiCo Inc.
The Dow Chemical Company	Pfizer Inc.
Eastman Kodak Company	PPG Industries, Inc.
Eaton Corporation	PricewaterhouseCoopers LLP
Eli Lilly & Company	The Procter & Gamble Company
Ernst & Young LLP	Reebok International
Exelon Corporation	Sara Lee Corporation
Fannie Mae	Schering-Plough Corporation
General Dynamics Corporation	Shell Oil Company
General Electric Company	Steelcase Inc.
General Mills, Inc.	Sterling Financial Group of Cos.
John Hancock Financial Services	United Airlines, Inc.
Harris Bankcorp, Inc.	Whirlpool Corporation
Hewlett-Packard Company	Xerox Corporation
Illinois Tool Works Inc.	

Source: http://www.umich.edu/~urel/admissions/legal/gru_amicus-ussc/um/Fortune500-both.pdf.

Chevron/Texaco and Shell, General Mills and Kellogg, Nike and Reebok, DaimlerChrysler and Mitsubishi) also joined forces to support the university's diversity efforts. "The rich variety of ideas, perspectives and experiences to which both nonminority and minority students are exposed in a diverse university setting, and the cross-cultural interactions they experience, are essential to the students' ability to function and contribute to this increasingly diverse community" expresses the views of 65 Fortune 500 companies that filed one brief on the importance of diversity in educational settings.[45]

In the early 1980s during the Reagan administration's efforts to curtail affirmative action programs, 122 of 128 heads of major corporations stated they would continue their voluntary AAPs even if requirements for such plans were ended by the federal government.[46] Similarly strong corporate support for affirmative action was indicated in a 1996 study in which 94% of CEOs reported perceptions that affirmative action had improved their hiring and marketing programs.[47] Affirmative action has clearly been helpful to its intended beneficiaries as well. In 1973, firefighters in the Los Angeles fire department were 94% White and 100% male. By 1995, 55% of the LA firefighters were White, 26% were Latino, 13% were Black, 6% were Asian, and 4% were women.[48] In addition to greater representation of targeted groups, employees (regardless of race or sex) of affirmative action companies have higher earnings than people employed at nonaffirmative action companies.[49]

The Age Discrimination in Employment Act of 1967

The Age Discrimination in Employment Act (ADEA) prohibits employment-related discrimination against persons who are aged 40 and older, which is an important issue for the millions of aging baby boomers in the United States. Under the ADEA, employers of 20 or more people, including state and local governments, employment agencies, and labor organizations are prohibited from discrimination on the basis of age in employment-related matters. This act also prohibits age-based harassment, retaliation for filing a claim of discrimination or complaining about it, and employment decisions based on stereotypes about one's ability based on age. Employers should not intentionally target older workers for layoffs or termination, or deny them training because they are believed to be close to retirement or unwilling or unable to learn.

Nearly 20,000 age discrimination claims are filed each year. In 2003, $48.9 million was recovered by the EEOC for claimants.[50] Well-known companies involved in age discrimination charges have included Martin Marietta, the L'Oreal cosmetics company, GulfStream Aerospace, and Woolworth Stores. Some of the many benefits of hiring and retaining older workers are discussed in Chapter 11.

---

[45] Source: http://www.umich.edu/~urel/admissions/legal/gru_amicus-ussc/um/Fortune500-both.pdf, accessed 09/15/04.

[46] Reskin, B. et al. (2000).

[47] Crosby, F. J., & Herzberger, S. D. (1996). "For Affirmative Action." In R. J. Simon (Ed.), *Affirmative Action: Pros and Cons of Policy and Practice,* Washington, DC: American University Press, pp. 3–109.

[48] Rosenthal, S. J. (1997). "Affirm Equality, Oppose Racist Scapegoating: Myths and Realities of Affirmative Action." In C. Herring (Ed.), *African Americans and the Public Agenda,* Thousand Oaks, CA: Sage Publications, pp. 105–125.

[49] Ibid.

[50] http://www.eeoc.gov/stats/adea.html, accessed 09/22/04.

The Rehabilitation Act of 1973

The Rehabilitation Act of 1973 (RA) prohibits discrimination against employees and applicants with disabilities when they work for or apply to the federal government or government contractors. The RA also requires the federal government to take affirmative action for the hiring, placement, and advancement of people with disabilities, similar to affirmative action for women and minorities.

An individual with a disability is a person who has a physical or mental impairment that substantially limits one or more of his or her life activities, has a record of such an impairment, or is regarded as having such an impairment. The covered impairments, notably, do not include current drug users, persons having "sexual behavior disorders," kleptomaniacs, compulsive gamblers, and certain specific other issues.[51]

Vietnam Era Veterans Readjustment Assistance Act of 1974

The Vietnam Era Veterans Readjustment Assistance Act requires federal contractors take affirmative action for disabled veterans and Vietnam Era and other veterans.[52] It is included as diversity-related legislation because despite the common misperceptions of affirmative action benefiting only minorities and women, about 80% of all veterans, targets of this affirmative action legislation, are White men.[53]

The Pregnancy Discrimination Act of 1978

The Pregnancy Discrimination Act (PDA), an amendment to Title VII, clarified that Title VII's regulations against discrimination because of sex included discrimination on the basis of pregnancy, childbirth, and related medical conditions. Despite laws prohibiting it, as discussed in Feature Case 2.1, overt pregnancy discrimination still occurs. The PDA prohibits discrimination in hiring, leave, health insurance, and fringe benefits. Prior to 1978, in some organizations pregnant women were required to resign or take leave and could be denied medical benefits that others receive. The PDA does not require employers to provide benefits or leave for pregnancy or related conditions. However, if benefits or leave are provided for other temporary medical conditions, the PDA requires that employers provide the same benefits for pregnancy and related conditions. As with employees with other conditions, if pregnant women can still work, they cannot be forced to go on leave. If other employees who are temporarily unable to work because of illness are entitled to return to work once they have recovered, the

[51] http://www.eeoc.gov/policy/ada.html, accessed 11/26/04.

[52] http://www.dol.gov/esa/regs/statutes/ofccp/4212.htm, accessed 09/15/04.

[53] Wilson, M., Perry, S., Helba, C., Hintze, W., Wright, M., Lee, K., Greenlees, J., Rockwell, D., & Deak, M. A. *National Survey of Veterans (NSV) Final Report, 2001,* http://www.va.gov/vetdata/SurveyResults/nsv/final/NSV%20Final%20Report.pdf.

Featured Case 2.1 *Pregnancy Discrimination at Wal-Mart—Case Settled When the Baby is 10 Years Old!*

Although the Pregnancy Discrimination Act has existed for many years, and employers should be well aware of it, overt pregnancy discrimination still occurs. One such case began in November of 1991, when Jamey Stern applied for a job at Wal-Mart. Stern had worked at Wal-Mart before, as a clothing clerk, and was applying for rehire. When Stern told the Assistant Manager that she was pregnant, the Assistant Manager told her to "come back after she had the baby." Stern did not know that refusing to hire someone because of pregnancy was illegal until later when she read a magazine article about pregnancy discrimination while in her doctor's waiting room. Stern then filed a discrimination charge with the EEOC, which filed a lawsuit in 1994 after attempts to settle the case with Wal-Mart were unsuccessful.

In 1997, a jury found that Wal-Mart had intentionally discriminated against Stern, awarding her $1,700 in back pay, but the issue of punitive damages (available in cases of intentional discrimination) was not addressed in the award. Punitive damages are "money damages designed to punish the wrong-doing employer and deter other employers" from discriminating. The EEOC appealed, given the jury's finding that the discrimination was indeed intentional. After multiple setbacks, appeals, and the revelation that Wal-Mart had "fabricated a number of facts during the investigation and the trial," Wal-Mart settled the case. In December 2002, 11 years after the incident, Wal-Mart agreed to pay $220,000 in damages to Stern, and to provide comprehensive training on pregnancy discrimination to managers.

After the settlement, Ms. Stern noted that "one person can truly make a difference . . . even in the face of such an adversary as Wal-Mart." Stern also expressed confidence that others would benefit, become educated about their rights, and about resources, such as the EEOC, available to protect those rights.

Source: Wal-Mart to pay $220,000 for rejecting pregnant applicant, in EEOC settlement, http://www.eeoc.gov/press/12-23-02.html, accessed 11/25/04, and Litigation Settlement report—December 2002, http://www.eeoc.gov/litigation/settlements/settlement12-02.html, accessed 11/25/04.

Questions to Consider

1. ***Although the Pregnancy Discrimination Act had been in existence for 13 years when Jamey Stern applied for the job at Wal-Mart, the Assistant Manager still refused to hire Stern and did not attempt to hide the reason. What might explain the Assistant Manager's actions?***

2. ***Jamey Stern was unaware that pregnancy discrimination is illegal.***
   a. ***Speculate on the proportion of the population that is also unaware of this and other areas covered under discrimination legislation. Estimate the proportion of employees in hiring positions at Wal-Mart and other organizations who are not aware that pregnancy discrimination is illegal.***
   b. ***What is the average education level of the U.S. population? Estimate the average education level of Wal-Mart employees and managers.***
   c. ***What might have been Jamey Stern's response to being hired at Wal-Mart while being pregnant, with regard to loyalty and goodwill?***

3. ***What is the average family income of people who work in low-wage jobs? Without the resources of the EEOC, how likely is it***
   a. ***that someone like Jamey could have personally brought this case against Wal-Mart,***
   b. ***that the case would have gone to trial and,***
   c. ***that Jamey could have engaged in an 11-year litigation?***

4. Had Jamey Stern applied to work for a lesser-known company, speculate on how likely is it that the case would have been taken on by the EEOC. What, if any, effects might publicity about lawsuits and judgments against large companies have on the actions of managers in smaller companies that may be less likely to be sued?

same opportunities are required for women who are unable to work because of pregnancy or related conditions.[54]

In 2003, the EEOC received 4,649 charges of pregnancy discrimination and resolved 4,847 (including some from previous years). Of those, 72.8% were deemed to have no reasonable cause and 27.2% were resolved with merit, resulting in $12.4 million in monetary benefits for the charging parties and other aggrieved individuals. As with other charges of discrimination, charging parties in pregnancy discrimination cases are unlikely to prevail.

Another case involving pregnancy discrimination involved pension plans, rather than overt pregnancy discrimination (such as a refusal to hire pregnant women). The case was brought by the EEOC against Cincinnati Bell on behalf of 458 employees who took maternity leave that was deducted from their service credit. The service credit reductions negatively affected certain employees' pensions and benefits under early retirement plans.[55] The company agreed to provide service credit adjustments for the majority of the affected women and monetary relief to about 40 of them. Such a case clearly demonstrates the need to understand and attempt to comply with intentions and goals behind diversity-related legislation rather than simplistically agreeing not to discriminate.

The Pregnancy Discrimination Act also protects male workers whose wives or covered female partners become pregnant. In 1983, the U.S. Supreme Court ruled that companies could not limit insurance benefits for pregnancy and related medical conditions of employees' covered spouses.

Misperception: The Pregnancy Discrimination Act requires employers to provide maternity leave and benefits for pregnant women.

Reality: The Pregnancy Discrimination Act requires employers to treat pregnancy as other temporary disabilities are treated for leave and benefits purposes.

EEOC Guidelines on Sexual Harassment (1980)

Although Title VII had improved women's opportunities to work in the 16 years since it had been passed between 1964 and 1980, during that time, many women were being negatively affected by sexual harassment at work. Requests (or demands)

[54] Code of Federal Regulations, Title 29, Volume 4. Revised as of July 1, 2001. From the U.S. Government Printing Office via GPO Access, [CITE: 29CFR1604.11].

[55] http://www.eeoc.gov/press/6-15-00-a.html, accessed 03/14/04.

for sex in exchange for jobs or promotions, sexual comments, and inappropriate touching were just a few of the discriminatory behaviors experienced by working women. Sexual harassment results in numerous negative physical and psychological outcomes for those who are harassed and is expensive for harassment targets and employers.[56] Therefore, in 1980, the EEOC issued its first formal guidelines on sexual harassment, providing direction for employers in addressing and curbing this specific form of sex discrimination. The EEOC described sexually harassing behaviors as including unwelcome sexual advances, requests for sexual favors, and other verbal or physical conduct of a sexual nature that explicitly or implicitly interferes with a person's employment, unreasonably interferes with her or his work performance, or creates an intimidating, hostile, or offensive work environment.[57]

Two forms of sexual harassment are: quid pro quo (this for that) or hostile environment harassment. In *quid pro quo* harassment, managers, supervisors, or others with authority make sexual demands and submission to or rejection of those demands is used as a basis for employment decisions (such as promotion, termination, etc.). In *hostile environment* harassment (by managers, coworkers, customers, or clients), unwelcome sexual conduct has the "purpose or effect of unreasonably interfering with job performance, or creating an intimidating, hostile, or offensive working environment."[58] Lewd jokes, sexually explicit posters, sexual comments could constitute hostile environment sexual harassment. Research indicates that men and women differ in their perceptions of what behaviors constitute hostile environment harassment or innocuous behavior; therefore, clear organizational policies prohibiting sexual harassment and education about what constitutes harassment are imperative.

EEOC charges of sexual harassment. It is estimated that up to 75% of working women have already experienced or will experience sexual harassment at some point during their work lives; however, most women who are harassed do not file complaints.[59] In 2003, the EEOC received 13,566 new charges of sexual harassment, 85% of which were filed by women. During that year, the EEOC resolved 14,534 charges of sexual harassment (including charges from previous years). Importantly, resolved claims include those that were deemed to have no reasonable cause or closed for administrative reasons, and these were 71% of all resolutions. Only 29% of complaints were resolved in the charging parties' favor.

[56] Schneider, K. T., Swan, S., & Fitzgerald, L. F. (1997). "Job-Related and Psychological Effects of Sexual Harassment in the Workplace: Empirical Evidence from Two Organizations," *Journal of Applied Psychology,* 82: 401–415.

[57] "Sexual Harassment," The U.S. Equal Employment Opportunity Commission, http://www.eeoc.gov/types/sexual_harassment.html, accessed 02/22/04.

[58] Guidelines on Discrimination Because of Sex, 29, C. F. R. Section 1604. 11(a). 1995.

[59] See Fitzgerald, L. F., & Ormerod, A. J. (1993). "Breaking Silence: The Sexual Harassment of Women in Academia and the Workplace." In F. Denmark & M. Paludi (Eds.), *Psychology of Women: A Handbook of Issues and Theories,* Westport, CT: Greenwood Press, pp. 553–582; Gutek, B. A. (1985). *Sex and the Workplace.* San Francisco: Jossey-Bass; Martindale, M. (1990). *Sexual Harassment in the Military: 1988.* Arlington, VA: Defense Manpower Data Center.

However, $50 million was recovered for complainants and other aggrieved parties.[60] As with other types of equal employment opportunity issues, these figures indicate that, for individual parties, filing a complaint is considerably more likely to result in an unsuccessful claim than in a successful claim. Even so, because of the large collective amount of damage awards and negative publicity associated with such cases, employers are motivated to avoid being one of the companies charged in a high profile case. In addition to those companies discussed in Chapter 1, other companies involved in recent sexual harassment settlements include Mitsubishi Motors, Asta Pharmaceuticals, Federal Express, and South Beach Beverage Company (a division of PepsiCo).[61, 62]

Following is a particularly offensive case of sexual harassment and retaliation described on the EEOC's Web site.[63]

- **EEOC v. Parmalat Bakery Div. of North Am.**
  No. 03-4026 (D.N.J. March 31, 2004)

  The Philadelphia District Office brought this Title VII action, alleging sexual harassment, retaliation and constructive discharge against defendant, a New Jersey division of an international company headquartered in Italy that produces and distributes snacks, bread, pasta and similar products. Charging party, a sales division manager and the only woman in an office of four male executives, was subjected to unwelcome sexual advances, sexually explicit comments, the showing of a pornographic video, and unwelcome touching by her supervisor and other male executives during her employment at the New Jersey facility. Her supervisor asked her to attend sales meetings—at his apartment, a topless bar, and a swingers club—invitations which she refused; and required her to attend work-related dinners at Hooters and a transvestite karaoke bar where the entertainment included lap dances and striptease contests. While charging party initially did not complain about the harassment because she believed her supervisor and the human resources manager condoned it, she eventually complained to her supervisor about a coworker slapping her on the buttocks. In response, her supervisor told her if she reported the incident, he would fire her. CP complained anyway to the vice president of sales and vice president of human resources, and her supervisor instructed her peers to ostracize her. He also threatened to suspend her, and made derogatory comments about her performance and gave her a low rating. Suffering from posttraumatic stress and depression, CP took a leave of absence and never returned.

[60] EEOC, Sexual Harassment.

[61] EEOC, SOBE and PepsiCo Settle Harassment Suit for 1.79 million, http://www.eeoc.gov/press/12-23-02-a.html, accessed 02/21/04.

[62] Federal Express to Pay over $3.2 Million to Female Truck Driver for Sex Discrimination, Retaliation, http://www.eeoc.gov/press/2-25-04.html, accessed 05/13/04.

[63] EEOC Litigation Settlements—March 2004, http:/.www.eeoc.gov/litigation/settlements/settlement03-04.html.

Prevention of sexual harassment. As discussed earlier, the likelihood that an organization will be sued for sexual harassment is relatively small. Even so, the many negative individual and organizational outcomes of sexual harassment should provide sufficient stimuli for organizations to try to prevent sexual harassment. The EEOC recommends that organizations take proactive steps against sexual harassment. These steps include having and widely disseminating the organization's policy on harassment, educating employees about sexual harassment and their rights to a harassment-free environment, and having multiple ways to complain if harassment occurs. When a complaint of harassment is made, the employer should investigate promptly and thoroughly, and if harassment is found, take immediate action to end the harassment and prevent future harassment. Disciplinary actions against the harasser should be directly related to the severity of the harassment. A warning may be appropriate for some harassment and immediate termination may be appropriate for other acts of harassment. If the complainant experienced any negative employment benefits or opportunities as a result of failure to comply with sexual demands, those benefits or opportunities should be restored.[64]

The EEOC issues updates to its guidelines on sexual harassment (and other areas enforced by the EEOC) when appropriate. These updates are readily available on the EEOC's Web site: http://www.eeoc.gov. Organizations should pay careful attention to these updates, as they provide invaluable assistance to organizations interested in a discrimination-free environment. That the courts also rely on EEOC guidelines should provide additional reasons to attend to them.

Older Workers Benefit Protection Act of 1990

The Older Workers Benefit Protection Act (OWBPA) is an amendment to the ADEA of 1967. It prohibits employers from denying benefits to older workers, but recognizes that it is more expensive to provide some benefits, such as life or disability insurance, to older workers. Thus, this act allows employers to reduce benefits based on age, as long as the employers' costs of providing benefits to older workers are the same as the costs of providing benefits to younger workers.[65] An example of this would be an employer providing an older employee with $50,000 of life insurance coverage at an employer cost of $100 per month and a younger employee with $75,000 of life insurance coverage at an employer cost of

[64] http://www.eeoc.gov/policy/docs/currentissues.html, accessed 02/29/04. See also Bell, M. P., Cycyota, C., & Quick, J. C. (2002). "Affirmative Defense: The Prevention of Sexual Harassment," In D. L. Nelson & R. J. Burke (Eds.), *Gender, Work Stress, and Health: Current Research Issues,* Washington, DC: American Psychological Association, pp. 191–210.

[65] http://www.eeoc.gov/types/age.html, accessed 09/15/04.

$100 per month. Although the younger employee has more insurance, because the employer contribution is the same, there is no illegal discrimination.

The Americans with Disabilities Act of 1990

Although discrimination against persons with disabilities by the federal government and its contractors was prohibited by the Rehabilitation Act of 1973, the persistent unemployment or underemployment of people with disabilities and employment discrimination against them led to the passage of the Americans with Disabilities Act (ADA) in 1990, which affects more employers. The stated purpose of the ADA is to "establish a clear and comprehensive prohibition of discrimination on the basis of disability."[66] As with Title VII and the ADEA, under the ADA, employers having 15 or more employees, employment agencies, labor unions, and state and local governments are prohibited from discrimination against workers with disabilities in employment matters. These areas include: hiring and firing; compensation, assignment, or classification of applicants or employees; transfer, promotion, layoff, or recall; job advertisements; recruitment; testing; use of company facilities; training and apprenticeship programs; fringe benefits; pay, retirement plans, and disability leave; or other terms and conditions of employment. Unlike the RA, the ADA does not require affirmative action.

As with the RA, an individual with a disability is defined as a person who currently has, has a record of, or who is regarded as having a physical or mental impairment that substantially limits one or more major life activities. To be covered by the ADA, individuals (employees or applicants) must be qualified to perform the essential (but not marginal) functions of the job in question, with or without reasonable accommodation. Reasonable accommodation includes such things as job restructuring, modifying work schedules, providing readers or interpreters, or other accommodations. Importantly, research indicates that accommodations are usually free or cost less than $100.[67]

Misperception: Complying with the ADA is very costly to employers.

Reality: Most accommodations cost less than $100.

Employers are also prohibited from asking job applicants about the existence, nature, or severity of a disability; instead, they may only ask about applicants' ability to perform specific job functions. These questions should be asked of all applicants, not only those with visible disabilities.

[66] http://www.eeoc.gov/policy/ada.html, accessed 11/22/04.

[67] Job Accommodation Network (1999). *Accommodation Benefit/Cost Data,* Morgantown, WV: Job Accommodation Network of the President's Committee on Employment of People with Disabilities.

EEOC charges of disability discrimination. The ADA is enforced by the EEOC, and between 1993 and 2002, the number of charges filed under the ADA ranged from about 15,000 to 20,000. In 2003, the EEOC received 15,377 new charges of disability discrimination and resolved 16,915 charges. Of the resolved claims, 60.6% were deemed to have no reasonable cause and 17.7% were closed for administrative reasons. Although a small percentage of the resolved claims, the complaints resolved in the charging parties' favor resulted recovery of $45.3 million for complainants and other aggrieved parties.[68]

The Civil Rights Act of 1991

The 27 years between the passage of Title VII of the Civil Rights Act of 1964 and the Civil Rights Act (CRA) of 1991 brought numerous and significant changes for employees, employers, and applicants. More people knew what was considered illegal and the demographic composition of the workforce and employees was changing. Even so, several issues remained, prompting the passage of the CRA of 1991, the stated purpose of which was "to strengthen and improve Federal civil rights laws, to provide for damages in cases of intentional employment discrimination, to clarify provisions regarding disparate impact actions, and for other purposes."[69]

Some of the changes were viewed as favorable to employees and applicants, but others were viewed as favorable to employers. Most commonly discussed as an employee-favorable change, with the CRA of 1991, federal law now provided for compensatory and punitive damages in cases of intentional race, sex, religious, national origin, or disability discrimination or harassment. The damages any one person can receive, however, are limited to maximums of

- $50,000 for employers having between 15 and 100 employees
- $100,000 for employers having between 101 and 200 employees
- $200,000 for employers having between 201 and 500 employees
- $300,000 for employers having over 500 employees.

While the addition of compensatory and punitive damages seems like a major victory, close scrutiny of these amounts makes them appear small, particularly given charging parties' relatively low likelihood of prevailing in any single claim.

Other changes from the CRA are allowing for jury trials; awarding of attorney's fees to the prevailing party; clarifying the concept of "business necessity" and "job-related"; extending protection to U.S. citizens working abroad for U.S. companies; and establishment of the Glass Ceiling Commission to study and

[68] http://www.eeoc.gov/stats/ada-charges.html, accessed 02/29/04.

[69] http://www.eeoc.gov/policy/cra91.html, accessed 03/13/04.

report on the status of women and minorities in upper-level jobs. The Glass Ceiling Commission issued compelling, widely distributed reports on the existence of the glass ceiling, sparking numerous changes in organizations. The Commission has now been disbanded.

The Family and Medical Leave Act of 1993

The passage of the Family and Medical Leave Act in 1993 (FMLA) was indicative of the changing needs of workers in the United States. Most couples now consisted of dual-earners, many had minor children, and many families were headed by single, working women. The need to allow employees to take time off from work, with continuance of benefits and assurance of a job upon one's return, was clear. Enforced by the U.S. Department of Labor, the FMLA requires employers having at least 50 employees for at least 20 weeks per year to grant eligible employees up to 12 weeks of unpaid leave per year to care for personal or family medical needs. Eligible employees may take leave for the birth and care of their newborn child, for adoption or foster child placement, to care for a seriously ill spouse, child, or parent, or for their own serious health condition.[70] Eligible employees are those who have worked for the employer for at least 1,250 hours during the past 12 months at a worksite where 50 or more employees work within 75 miles of the worksite. Importantly, teachers (who may be off during the summers and who are disproportionately women) are also deemed to meet the hourly and weekly requirements.

Criticisms surrounding the FMLA include its lack of pay and its failure to include employers of fewer than 50 people, parents-in-law, other family members, and nonmarital partners. Personal or family illness may increase the need for income—how many employees can afford much time without pay when illness strikes? Further, because many U.S. workers are employed in small organizations, the requirement for 50 or more employees excludes many people. Another important criticism is related to gender and family roles; many argue that couples should be able to decide which spouse takes leave and the exclusion of parents-in-law does not allow for this. On a family income basis, it would appear logical that the person who earned the least would take leave without pay. Because only 15% of married women earn more than their husbands, in most cases, the lower earning partner would be the woman. Allowing leave for parents-in-law could have positive and negative consequences—potentially helpful to individual families' income, but reinforcing women's gender role of caretaker, and potentially disruptive for employers of large numbers of women. Finally, many people have relational ties that include those who are not immediate (grandparents, aunts, uncles, etc.) or

[70] http://www.dol.gov/esa/whd/fmla/, accessed 03/01/04.

biological (godparents, fictive kin) family, and committed, but not marital, partners are common.

In summary, although the FMLA is indeed helpful to many families who need it, limitations and exclusions make it of little use to many employees. As a result, research indicates that people who most need family leave do not take it.[71]

Other Relevant State, Local, and City Ordinances

In addition to the key federal acts discussed in the previous section, several state, local, and city ordinances relevant to diversity in organizations exist. Although the multitude of such legislation makes it impossible to consider them all, some of the specific ordinances that prohibit employment-related discrimination on the basis of sexual orientation, weight, and/or appearance will be discussed later in the book. Where no federal acts prohibit discrimination on the basis of those factors, other ordinances may. Therefore, it is imperative that managers be aware of laws that exist in their particular location, especially when the organization has multiple sites of operation. In such cases, implementing company specific guidelines for nondiscrimination that apply to the entire organization would provide proactive diversity support as well as helping to avoid violation of a state, local, or city ordinance.

Future Federal Acts: What's Ahead?

The extant laws, executive orders, and EEOC guidelines were passed because of recognized discrimination and inequitable treatment against certain groups. Although these laws have been somewhat successful in improving employment and opportunities for nondominant groups, many inequities remain. In addition, egregious behaviors, such as placing condoms in the lockers of women or nooses on the desks of African Americans still occur and may even be on the rise.[72] These behaviors must still be addressed using existing or additional legislation as appropriate. Perhaps most importantly, however, these egregious acts must be prevented by a genuine organizational stance of inclusion and zero tolerance for harassment and discrimination.

Some emerging areas of increasing interest are related to existing legislation, including genetic testing and changes in the definition of family. Genetic testing is ostensibly used by employers attempting to avoid placing people with propensities for certain illnesses or preexisting conditions in certain jobs. Depending on

[71] Gerstel, N., & McGonagle K. (2002). "Job Leaves and the Limits of the Family and Medical Leave Act." In D. Dunn & P. Dubeck (Eds.), *Workplace, Women's Place,* Los Angeles: Roxbury Publishers, pp. 205–215; American Association of University Women, http://www.aauw.org/takeaction/policyissues/familymedical_leave.cfm, accessed 05/10/04.

[72] http://www.eeoc.gov/abouteeoc/plan/strategic-2000.html, accessed 03/05/04.

the type of testing, doing so may disadvantage women, men, people of color, people with existing disabilities, and other groups. For example, certain cancers are solely or predominantly found in women (e.g., ovarian, breast) or men (prostate). Certain diseases are predominantly found in different ethnic groups, for example, Blacks, Jews, and Caucasians are most likely to have sickle cell anemia, Tay Sachs disease, and cystic fibrosis, respectively. Any efforts to implement genetic testing must be very carefully scrutinized.

As discussed earlier, the FMLA currently defines family as the natural, adopted, or foster children, spouse, or parent of an employee. Not included are same sex partners, parents-in-law, grandparents, aunts, uncles, siblings, and informal family who may have no biological relationships with the employee. As family relationships change, so too must relevant legislation; some states are ahead of federal legislation regarding who constitutes family. At the time of this writing, 11 states have enacted statutes that are similar to the FMLA, including California, Connecticut, Hawaii, Maine, Minnesota, New Jersey, Oregon, Rhode Island, Vermont, Washington, and Wisconsin. Some of these state statutes differ in the definition of "family," with some including parents-in-law and other kin.[73]

As we consider in later chapters, people who are gay, lesbian, bisexual, transgendered, overweight, or obese face considerable employment-related discrimination, and discrimination against people from these groups is not currently illegal under broad federal legislation. Similar to laws regarding discrimination on race, sex, age, national origin, religion, and disability, activism and public outcry are drawing attention to these areas of concern; more regional laws will probably address these areas in the future. Given the current political climate and volatility of such issues, it is unlikely that any new protected classes will be added to major federal laws in the near future, yet individual states may continue to make changes that affect organizations. As an example, in the spring of 2004, the state of Massachusetts passed legislation recognizing marriage between persons of the same sex. Because same-sex partners were then able to marry in Massachusetts, some companies discontinued offering domestic partner benefits. Domestic partner benefits and other issues related to sexual orientation are discussed further in Chapter 15.

Summary

This chapter has considered the history behind and details of several key laws and executive orders related to diversity in organizations. These acts formally provide employees with rights to nondiscrimination and organizations with guidelines for fairness in these areas of diversity. Title VII of the Civil Rights Act as amended, the ADEA, and the ADA, which prohibit discrimination on the basis of race, sex,

[73] U.S. Department of Labor, Federal vs. State Family and Medical Leave Laws, http://www.dol.gov/esa/programs/whd/state/fmla/index.htm, accessed 05/10/04.

national origin, religion, age, and disability protect workers of all backgrounds. Because they cover a broad range of employment matters and provide recourse for affected applicants and employees, these acts have been somewhat effective in increasing opportunities, income, and employment for various groups. Many issues remain, however. As diversity in organizations continues to evolve, and needs are identified, other legislation, judicial decisions, and executive orders will continue to address them. Despite the existing laws and likelihood of future acts, when compared with the number of workers, relatively few people bring charges with the EEOC, fewer charges are deemed meritorious, and even fewer charges result in settlements or judgments for plaintiffs. Avoidance of lawsuits is a shallow impetus for compliance with laws; organizations should, instead, use compliance with laws as one of many methods and means to pursue diversity.

Key Terms

Constructive discharge — making working conditions so unpleasant that an employee is forced to quit.

The glass ceiling — an invisible barrier that prevents women, minorities, and people with disabilities from advancing in organizations.

Retaliation — responding to an employee's complaint about mistreatment (e.g., discrimination or harassment) by treating them more negatively.

Sexual harassment — unwelcome sexual advances, requests for sexual favors, and other verbal or physical conduct of a sexual nature that explicitly or implicitly interferes with a person's employment, unreasonably interferes with her or his work performance, or creates an intimidating, hostile, or offensive work environment.

Principled disobedience — refusal to obey a superior's commands to discriminate against applicants or employees based on non-job-related factors.

Punitive damages — money damages awarded in cases of intentional discrimination that are designed to punish the employer and deter other employers from discriminating.

Questions to Consider

1. What is the relationship between compliance with legislative acts and valuing diversity? Explain.
2. Why do you think that many Fortune 500 companies were supportive of the University of Michigan's programs to increase diversity among its student body? What does the companies' support signal to their employees, customers, and constituents?
3. Some of the companies listed in Table 2.2 as supporting the University of Michigan's diversity programs have faced discrimination lawsuits alleging racial, ethnic, age, or disability discrimination or sexual harassment. Choose several of such companies and document these apparent contrasts. What might explain the charges, judgments, and settlements (if appropriate) given their stated support for diversity in higher education?
4. Are the EEOC cases described in this chapter surprising? Do you personally

know anyone who has engaged in an employment discrimination lawsuit against an employer and prevailed?

5. Many of the EEOC cases presented in the chapter are egregious, offensive, and obviously illegal. Choose several cases and for each case, speculate on the organizational factors that existed that would allow such practices to happen, and in some cases, to persist for extended periods. In multiple cases, more than one person (e.g., assistant manager, manager, HR manager, district or area manager, etc.) was involved. Why do you think no one in the management chain intervened?
6. What have you learned from this chapter that is most surprising to you?

Actions and Exercises

1. Access the Equal Employment Opportunity Commission's Web site: http://eeoc.gov/. Document a recent lawsuit or settlement involving race, ethnic, sex, age, disability, national origin, or religious discrimination that was likely to have been covered by the media. Describe the allegations, plaintiffs, and resolution of the cases. Document the time periods between the incidents and final resolution of the cases. Search the Web for newspaper articles or other media presentations relevant to each case. Are there different perspectives in the EEOC's presentation and the media's presentation? Discuss.
2. Access the EEOC Web site again. Document a lawsuit that involved particularly egregious actions but that likely did not receive any significant media attention. What happened? Describe the allegations and resolution of the cases. Discuss.
3. The EEOC sued Hooters for employment discrimination against men, yet Hooters is known for having scantily clad waitresses and could be perceived as a sex-oriented business, rather than a family restaurant. Investigate what happened in this case from reputable sources and form your own opinions.
4. Consider issues discussed as possibilities for coverage under federal law in the future. Pick one issue, then list and discuss the elements that would be included in such legislation. What steps should employers take after such legislation to ensure equal treatment of the affected parties?

3 Chapter

Theories and Thinking about Diversity

Chapter Objectives

After completing this chapter, readers should have a greater understanding of what constitutes minority groups and the processes surrounding people's thinking about and treatment of those who are dissimilar to them. Readers can expect to:

- *examine the meaning of the terms* minority *group and* nondominant *group.*
- *understand characteristics used to identify minority groups and be able to use these characteristics to identify the nondominant groups in one's particular environment.*
- *discuss thought processes related to stereotyping, prejudice, and discrimination.*
- *understand in-group favoritism and out-group bias and how they disadvantage nondominant group members and impede diversity efforts.*
- *understand ways to avoid automatic stereotyping.*
- *have a better foundation for synthesizing the material in the remaining chapters.*

Key Facts

Characteristics of minority or nondominant groups often include identifiability, differential power, discrimination, and group awareness.

Minority, or nondominant, groups are not necessarily fewer in number than majority, or dominant, groups.

Categorization and stereotyping are often unconscious processes, but the propensity to automatically stereotype can be reduced through deliberate measures.

People tend to attribute positive characteristics to members of their in-groups, and negative characteristics to members of groups to which they do not belong.

In-group favoritism and out-group bias disadvantage nondominant groups and impede diversity.

Introduction and Overview

This chapter considers some of the many theories and research related to psychological processes affecting diversity in organizations. What are prejudice, stereotyping, and discrimination and how do they work to impede diversity? Why is it that the diversity among people is at times a negative attribute of organizational functioning and what can be done to change this? What factors are associated with people's preferences for similar others and hostility and discrimination toward dissimilar others? Knowledge of these factors will provide a foundation for understanding the material in the remaining chapters of the book, for resisting factors that make one prone to stereotyping and discrimination, and for fostering diversity in organizations.

We begin with a discussion of the characteristics associated with minority groups. What defines minority groups? How does one tell who is the majority and who is the minority in a society? After discussion of some of these characteristics, we consider factors that affect people's treatment, exploring research on stereotyping and social categorization as they specifically relate to diversity in organizations. We then consider how aversive racism (and other "isms") affects individuals' behavior toward others. We conclude with suggestions to reduce stereotyping and the propensity to make job-related decisions on the basis of stereotypes.

WHAT IS A MINORITY?[1]

In Chapters 4 through 15 we consider history, population, education, employment, earnings, and organizational experiences of members of several minority groups in the United States (primarily, but not exclusively), along with those of the relevant majority groups. Although the term *minority* is generally understood to mean fewer in number, it does not necessarily refer to groups that are numerically fewer than majority group members. What, then, *is* a minority?[2] Minority or nondominant groups are those subordinated to majority or dominant group members in terms of power, prestige, and privilege.[3] Although the term *minority* formally means fewer in number, not all nondominant groups are fewer in number than the dominant groups. In South Africa, for example, Whites are the dominant group, although they are outnumbered by people of color. In the United States, women outnumber men, but men are the dominant group. *Nondominant,* then, is a more accurate term than *minority* although we use both in this book.

For many of the topics we cover, there are clearly dominant and nondominant groups. In other chapters, the distinction is ambiguous. Of the racial and ethnic groups discussed in this book, Blacks, Latinos, Asian Americans,

[1] Dworkin, A. G., & Dworkin, R. J. (1999). *The Minority Report* (3rd edition), Orlando, FL: Harcourt Brace Publishers, pp. 11–27.

[2] Ibid.

[3] Schaefer, R. T. (1989). *Racial and Ethnic Groups* (4th edition), New York: Harper Collins Publishers.

American Indians, and multiracial group members represent nondominant groups, while Whites are the dominant group. Men are the dominant sex, although women outnumber men. In the United States, Christians are members of the dominant religious group, and heterosexual is the dominant sexual orientation. People without disabilities are clearly the dominant group. Attractive people are dominant to unattractive people, and thinner people are dominant to overweight people. Whether younger or older workers are the dominant group is ambiguous. While older workers are more likely to occupy high-status, high-paid organizational positions, stereotypes and misperceptions pervade the workplace experiences of many older workers. At times younger workers are clearly preferred over older workers, but at other times younger people are viewed as irresponsible, not dependable, and having no organizational commitment. The question of whether people with or without families are dominant is illogical. Even so, for men, having a family contributes to being viewed positively in organizations, to higher wages, and to greater advancement. For women, having a family contributes to perceptions of divided loyalties, lower wages, and fewer promotions.

Social scientists propose that nondominant group members have distinguishing characteristics across societies and time. Factors included as distinguishing have varied somewhat, but four common ones remain fairly stable and appear to well-differentiate dominant groups from nondominant groups. Drawing from the seminal work of a group of noted social scientists, Anthony and Rosalind Dworkin propose that minority group members have four common characteristics: identifiability, differential power, the experience of discrimination,[4] and group awareness. These characteristics are considered in the following sections.

Identifiability

For subordinating systems to work, distinguishing physical or cultural traits between minority and majority group members must exist. Identifiability of a nondominant group is required to single them out for differential treatment, such as discrimination and segregation. If members of nondominant groups were not recognizable, differential treatment would be difficult or impossible. Historical records suggest that dominant groups devise means to identify nondominant groups if the members have no distinguishing features. As an example, in Nazi Germany, Jews were required to wear yellow armbands to distinguish them from non-Jews.[5] In the United States, women, Blacks, Latinos, Asians, and American Indians are generally fairly easily identified, making differential treatment easier than if they were difficult to distinguish.

[4] Dworkin and Dworkin used the term differential and pejorative treatment as well as discrimination. For brevity and clarity, we use discrimination only.

[5] Dworkin & Dworkin. (1999).

In the past as in the present, many individual members of nondominant racial groups have been difficult to identify, however. Some who self-identify as being members of a minority group are identified as belonging to another group by independent observers. If a person's Black, Hispanic, Asian, or American Indian heritage is clearly visible, however, differential treatment from prejudiced employers, businesses (e.g., banks, stores, hotels, restaurants), and even the police (e.g., racial profiling) are potential consequences. On the other hand, as we discuss in later chapters, the lack of identifiability of some nondominant group members creates some problems as well. Identities of gays and lesbians, some multiracial group members, and some people with disabilities are invisible and they may face stress and guilt associated with this invisibility and, at times, fear of disclosure.

Differential Power

Dworkin and Dworkin define power as the "actual use of resources to influence and control others."[6] Differential power allows those who have more power to control those who have less power. Although power is associated with numerical dominance, those larger in number are not always the most powerful. As examples, American Indians in the United States were originally more in number but were less powerful than Europeans, and thus they were able to be dominated. There are more women in the United States than men, but women as a group are less powerful than men. In their control of resources, the powerful also control access to education, employment, food, health care, and other things that affect the life chances and futures of those without power. Thus, power and control also help the dominant remain dominant.

Discrimination

Discrimination has been defined as differential and pejorative actions that serve to limit the social, political, or economic opportunities of members of particular groups.[7] Although prejudice and discrimination are sometimes viewed as synonymous, they are not. Prejudice is "irrationally based, negative attitudes" about certain groups and their members.[8] Prejudice is an attitude, while discrimination is behavior based on the attitude. Given power to act on it and the absence of sanctions for doing so, discriminatory acts may result from prejudice.

---

[6] Ibid., p. 19.

[7] Ibid., p. 98; Frederickson, G. M., & Knobel, D. T. (1980). "A History of Discrimination." In T. F. Pettigrew, G. M. Fredrickson, D. T. Knobel, N. Glazer, & R. Ueda (Eds.), *Prejudice,* Cambridge, MA: The Belknap Press of Harvard University, pp. 30–37.

[8] Pettigrew, T. (1980). "Prejudice." In T. F. Pettigrew, G. M. Fredrickson, D. T. Knobel, N. Glazer, & R. Ueda (Eds.), *Prejudice,* Cambridge, MA: The Belknap Press of Harvard University, pp. 1–29.

When experienced, discrimination leads to group awareness and becomes the focus of protests and activism against it.[9]

With ideas similar to those of Dworkin and Dworkin, Edward Sampson suggests the following relationships between identifiability, power, and discrimination:

> ...which types of differences are emphasized and which are ignored is usually a choice made by the social groups that occupy positions of dominance within a society. These are the groups that have the power to make their definitions of who is one of them and who is different stick. Dominant groups not only select the qualities of difference that will be emphasized but also develop the rationale to explain why those differences mean one group should be treated differently from another. (p. 22.)[10]

Group Awareness

Group awareness is proposed as the final characteristic of minority groups. Group awareness among minorities is one consequence of their subordination and discrimination by the majority. As minority groups experience unfair treatment, they begin to identify themselves as being subjected to differential treatment simply because of their group membership. Subordinated group members begin to realize that the differential treatment they experience is a result of the definitions and evaluations of their group by the majority, rather than to any intrinsic qualities or actions of their group. They may also realize that they can achieve certain goals (e.g., better education, jobs), through cooperative resistance (such as protests, boycotts, and participation in the political process).

Analysis of the Characteristics

Although the criteria of identifiability, differential power, discrimination, and group awareness in many cases do help clarify which groups are minority groups, they are by no means unequivocal. Table 3.1 presents a framework of the groups considered in this book as they seem to fit using Dworkin and Dworkin's criteria for determining what is a minority or nondominant group. In the appropriate chapters, we further analyze the applicability of some of these characteristics to the particular groups.

Of particular interest are areas in which the characterizations fail to identify nondominant groups or are otherwise insufficient, such as with invisible identities and powerful nondominant group members (e.g., woman of color executive). In other situations, there are disconnects between the group to which one appears to belong and one's self-identity. Taylor Cox describes such events as incongruence

[9] Dworkin & Dworkin. (1999).

[10] Sampson, E. E. (1999). *Dealing with Differences,* Orlando, FL: Harcourt Brace.

TABLE 3.1 ***Typology of Nondominant Groups in Relation to the Relevant Dominant Group*** *,†

Group	Identifiability (Visibility)	Power	Discrimination	Group Awareness
Blacks	High	Little, but increasing	Significant	Significant
Mexican Americans	Varies	Little, but increasing	Significant, but varies by race and identifiability	Some, increasing
Puerto Ricans	Varies	Little, but varies by location	Significant, but varies by race	Some, increasing
Cuban Americans	Varies	Some, but varies by location	Little, but varies by location and identifiability	Significant
Asian Americans	High	Varies by country of origin	Significant, but varies by country of origin	Significant
Whites	High	Significant, but varies by sex	Little	Little, increasing‡
American Indians	Varies	Little, but varies by location and identifiability	Significant, but varies by location and identifiability	Significant, but varies by location and identifiability
Multiracials	Varies	Little, but varies by visibility and self-identification	Some, but varies by identifiability and racial or ethnic background	Little
Women	High	Some, but varies by race and ethnicity	Some, but varies by race and ethnicity	Significant, but varies by race and ethnicity
Men	High	Significant, but varies by race and ethnicity	Significant for men of color	Significant for men of color, but varies by race
People with disabilities	Varies	Varies by visibility and type of disability	Varies by visibility and type of disability	Some, but varies by visibility and type of disability
Overweight, obese	High	Little, but varies	Significant	Increasing
Gays and lesbians	None	Some, increasing	Significant, when sexual orientation is known	Significant, increasing

*Although the table is adapted from Dworkin and Dworkin, some categories were added and others were deleted. The ratings of the levels of appropriateness of the group to the criteria are the author's.

†Aside from Whites and men, all groups are nondominant groups.

‡Dworkin and Dworkin's definition of group awareness as resulting from discrimination makes this less relevant for Whites, although White ethnic identity is increasing—see Chapter 7. Group awareness for men of color varies by race but would not result from discrimination by women because women are not "dominant" to men.

Source: Adapted from Dworkin, A. G., & Dworkin, R. J. (1999). *The Minority Report* (3rd edition), Orlando, FL: Harcourt Brace, p. 178.

of phenotype (e.g., visible) and culture identities.[11] He describes a situation in which a Mexican American with Caucasian physical features identifies with the Mexican American culture and this creates cognitive dissonance among observers. This dissonance may cause discomfort or even negative reactions from others.

Categorization and Identity

As discussed in the previous section, Dworkin and Dworkin's first defining criterion for minority groups is identifiability. Once identified, what factors make groups single out others for discrimination? What factors make otherwise rational people prone to believe stereotypes? Why do prejudicial attitudes sometimes result in discrimination and not in other times?

Negative stereotypes about minority groups are key building blocks for prejudice and discrimination. Stereotypes are the overgeneralization of characteristics to large human groups. Fairly common job-related stereotypes about the groups we consider in the chapters can be easily listed even by those who do not believe them or who are themselves members of the targeted groups.[12] Blacks, Latinos, American Indians, and overweight people (Chapters 4, 5, 8, and 14, respectively) are often stereotyped as being lazy. Asians (Chapter 6) are viewed as technically skilled, but unable to speak English well. Whites (Chapter 7) are stereotyped as racist and self-seeking. White women are often viewed as uncommitted workers while (White) men are viewed as providers for their families (Chapter 9). Religious (Chapter 10) stereotypes vary by religion, and common stereotypes of Jews, Christians, Muslims, and other religious groups are widely recognized. Older workers and those with disabilities (Chapters 11 and 12) are often stereotyped as less competent than younger workers and those without disabilities.

Some stereotypes reflect interactions between race, ethnicity, gender, and, at times, parental status. Black men's assumed criminal tendencies and background (see Chapter 4) are particularly harmful job-related stereotypes. Relevant to Chapter 13, White women with children are perceived as uncommitted workers, eagerly anticipating leaving the workforce (e.g., to be "stay-at-home moms") when children arrive. Black women with children are seen as unreliable workers because of inadequate child care (see Chapter 4). White men with children are viewed as being more committed because of being fathers, with stay-at-home wives to support (Chapter 9). In a job-related context, stereotyping can prevent individuals who would be capable, committed workers from being hired, promoted, or trained. Negative organizational outcomes follow from the individual outcomes.

---

[11] Cox, T. (1993). *Cultural Diversity in Organizations: Theory, Research, and Practice,* San Francisco: Berrett-Koehler Publishers.

[12] Although the stereotypes are fairly well known, not every reader will be familiar with the listed stereotypes of each group. See Cox, (1993), p. 91 for a detailed list of stereotypes about various groups.

Although common stereotypes can be easily identified, many readers know of a person from each group who does not fit the stereotype, when prompted to think of such a person. Even so, people attend to evidence that supports the stereotypes they hold, but ignore evidence that disconfirms stereotypes. Further, stereotypes can lead to prejudice—irrationally based, negative evaluations of a group—which can lead to discrimination, given the right circumstances.

Social Categorization and Stereotyping

Social cognitive theory suggests that people use categorization to simplify and cope with the large volumes of information to which they are continually exposed. Categories allow us to quickly and easily compartmentalize data. Consistent with Dworkin and Dworkin's proposals that minority group members must be identifiable, people often use visible characteristics, such as race, sex, and age, to categorize others. Thus, when one sees a person of a particular race, the automatic processing occurs, and beliefs about this particular race are activated. When the person is not seen, but his or her name is known (perhaps on a resume), this provides information on the person's sex, which allows categorization: male or female. Mental models of a person suited to a particular job (e.g., bank teller) are often associated with sex, and sorting of candidates by sex occurs as a result of such models. A name may also provide evidence of a person's race or ethnic background, which could also allow categorization and discrimination (see Chapter 4). People's propensity to categorize, coupled with the need to then *evaluate* the person categorized, leads to stereotyping.[13]

Along with the tendency to categorize, people have a tendency to perceive themselves and others as belonging to particular groups. This part of categorization, referred to as social categorization, involves ordering one's social environment by groupings of persons.[14] Social categorization helps create and define one's place in society. Groups define one's place by separating people—where we belong or do not belong, and where others belong and do not belong. A person's in-group is the group to which he or she belongs, while out-groups are groups to which he or she does not belong. Depending on the situation, and what factor is salient, or distinctive, a person's in-group may be based on his or her race, sex, age, or other factor of importance. Salient characteristics are important to an individual at a particular time, or at all times, depending on how critical the characteristic to the individual's experiences and life chances. For example, in a department with 3 women and 10 men, the in-group for the women would be women, and the out-group would be men. If the department is comprised of

---

[13] Nelson, T. (2002). *The Psychology of Prejudice,* Boston: Allyn & Bacon.

[14] Tajfel, H. (1978). "Social Categorization, Social Identity and Social Comparison." In H. Tajfel (Ed.), *Differentiation Between Social Groups,* London: Academic Press, pp. 61–76.

2 Blacks (1 man and 1 woman) and 11 White men and women, in-groups and out-groups could instead be determined using racial categories. Which category would be salient would depend on the situation (e.g., if the men were all sitting together on one side of the room, or if the conversation were about racial profiling) and the extent to which people *identified* themselves by their race or sex. For a Black person in the United States, race may be salient in an organization in which there are few Blacks, or in an organization in which everyone is Black (if being in such an organization is unusual). Beverly Daniel Tatum's book *Why Are All the Black Kids Sitting Together in the Cafeteria?* explains that the clustering of Blacks in the cafeterias of predominantly White educational institutions is obvious and disturbing to some observers.[15] The similar clustering of Whites is less obvious or disturbing.

Social identity refers to the part of an individual's self-concept that derives from his or her membership in a particular social group and the value and emotional significance attached to that group membership.[16] Using race as an example, social identity describes how much a person identifies as a member of a certain race and how strongly and passionately he or she feels about belonging to that race. Is being Black integral to one's life, experiences, and being? For sex as a characteristic, social identity describes how much a person identifies as a man or woman, and how strongly and passionately he or she feels about being a man or woman. Is being a man integral to one's life, experiences, and being? Social identity is similar to Dworkin and Dworkin's conceptualization of group awareness for nondominant group members. Those who see that they belong to a particular group and that the group receives pejorative treatment by others (out-groups) become aware of their group membership as a collective body able to take resistive action.

Consequences of Social Categorization and Social Identity

As noted earlier, when we first come into contact with others, we categorize them as belonging to an in-group, or an out-group. We tend to see members of our in-group as being heterogeneous, but out-group members as being homogeneous—having similar attitudes, behaviors, and characteristics (e.g., fitting stereotypes). Researchers suggest that this may occur because of the breadth of interactions we have with people from our in-group as compared with those from out-groups. There also is often strong in-group favoritism, and, at times, derogation of out-group members. Favoritism and viewing members of one's group positively bolster one's self-esteem, as does viewing other groups negatively. Alone, favoritism for one's particular group is not necessarily negative. When coupled with power,

[15] Tatum, B. D. (1997). *Why Are All the Black Kids Sitting Together in the Cafeteria?,* New York: Basic Books.
[16] Ibid., p. 63.

however, favoritism is associated with negative opportunities and outcomes for the out-group.

In-group favoritism and out-group biases. A likely result of in-group favoritism in a work-setting is when those in power (e.g., dominant groups) hire, promote, and reward members of their in-group. Even if no overt derogation of out-group members is involved, by favoring the dominant in-group, one disadvantages the nondominant out-group. Because women and people of color are typically nondominant in organizations, social categorization and in-group favoritism work against them, negatively affecting their chances for employment, high-status positions, promotion, and other opportunities. Women and people of color generally have little power (see Table 3.1), thus, any favoritism they may have toward women and people of color is less likely to disadvantage men and Whites. The documented existence of the similarity effect, or similarity bias, in which people are more likely to select or hire demographically similar others is also a manifestation of in-group favoritism.

In addition to favoring the in-group and derogating the out-group, similar behaviors exhibited by members of the in-group and the out-group are judged differently.[17] A man who exhibits a "take charge" attitude is viewed as assertive (a positive attribute), but a woman who does so is "aggressive" (a negative attribute; see also the Ann Hopkins case in Chapter 9). Again, because men are in positions of power, their propensity is to see men as having certain positive attributes, but to judge these same attributes as negative when they are held or exhibited by women disadvantages women.

Fundamental attribution error. The *fundamental attribution error,* the tendency to underestimate the influence of external factors (e.g., situations or circumstances) and overestimate the influence of internal factors (e.g., personal qualities) when evaluating the behavior of others, also occurs during in-group and out-group evaluations. Thus, when in-group members behave positively or are successful, this behavior is attributed to the character (or personal attributes) of in-group members. When they behave negatively (such as screaming at a subordinate), this behavior is attributed to the circumstances (e.g., being upset because the computer system crashed and records were lost). When out-group members exhibit desirable behaviors, this behavior is attributed to luck, chance, or circumstances. When they behave negatively (such as screaming at a subordinate), this behavior is attributed to the character of the out-group member (e.g., rude, inconsiderate). The entire out-group is also then viewed as being rude, rather than as having one member who behaved rudely at a

[17] Dworkin & Dworkin. (1999).

particular point in time. Future interactions with out-group members will be shaped by perceptions that they are rude. Ironically, expecting that someone will be rude may lead to treating that person rudely, to which they may respond rudely, confirming the expectation that they (and people like them) are rude.

When confronted with information about an out-group member that is contradictory to stereotypes, people tend to see this is as "unique" rather than using it to question and discard their beliefs. When confronted with behavior that confirms a stereotype about an out-group member, people attend to such information and then hold faster to the stereotypes. From a diversity perspective, let us consider stereotypes about Asians being lacking in communication skills and thus preferring to work in technical jobs rather than managerial jobs. Let us assume that a decision maker who is making promotion and succession plans holds this stereotype about Asians. If this decision maker knows an Asian American who was born and reared in the United States (and who speaks English as well or poorly as any other American), the decision maker is still likely to think Asians as a group do not speak English well and will not make good managers. Rather than using the known individual Asian with good communication skills as a reason to question and discard the stereotype that Asians have poor language skills, the decision maker is likely to discard the information as being unique to this particular Asian. Were that decision maker to encounter an Asian who preferred the technical promotion track over the managerial path, he or she would attribute this to the Asian's lack of communication skills (rather than to a genuine personal strength or interest), confirming an existing stereotype.

Using women as an example, if a decision maker holds to the stereotype of women as not having requisite managerial skills (e.g., think manager, think male), a woman who expresses interest in advancing in organizations, and is highly successful in assessment center exercises will still be disadvantaged by those perceptions. Such a successful woman will be viewed as an anomaly, and her success would be attributed to external factors (the organization's desire to increase representation of women in management, or affirmative action), rather than to her personal qualities and motivation. Were she to enter management and fail, this confirmatory failure would be attributed to her (and women) not having the requisite skills for managers. In actuality, this failure may be related to failure of management to provide training, mentoring, and encouragement because of stereotypes about women managers.[18] Feature 3.1 describes how media portrayals contribute to stereotyping and distorted perceptions of group members.

[18] Featured Case 9.4, in Chapter 9, describes a case in which a woman was used as a test case, to see how women drivers would fare—expectations for her success were low, however. The woman's failure as a delivery driver resulted in the company's decision not to hire any more women drivers, because it was clear that they would not work out.

ASSIGNMENT #1

FEATURE 3.1 *The Media and Promulgation of Stereotypes*

The media play a critical role in promulgation of stereotypes.[19] News reports, television and movies, and commercials communicate stereotypes about perpetrators and victims of crime, gender roles, age groups, and numerous other diversity issues. People tend to believe what they see on television and read in the paper, implicitly trusting writers and reporters as objective conveyors of what is actually occurring. Yet, those who write and choose stories are not unbiased. Instead, they are products of a society that views certain groups as more likely to commit crimes, to have large families they are unable to support, be illegal immigrants, and other negative biases reflecting racial, ethnic, gender, and other stereotypes. Although Whites commit a greater proportion of drug-related crimes, Blacks and Latinos are more likely to be shown on television being arrested for such crimes. Although most crime is intraracial (e.g., Black on Black or White on White), news reports are more likely to portray Black on White crime.[20] People of color are also more highly portrayed as perpetrators of crime in the news. One study found that over 14 weeks, people of color were shown as crime perpetrators in 20% more cases than would be predicted based on FBI statistics.[21]

Misperception: Blacks and Latinos commit more crimes than Whites.

Reality: Blacks and Latinos are more likely to be arrested than Whites and to be depicted on television being arrested than their actual representation among arrests.

In addition to biased reporting of crimes, use of divisive or misleading terminology by the media causes resistance to diversity. Affirmative action does not mean quotas, for example, but if the news media equate them, people will be more likely to equate them also. Women are working at some of the highest participation rates in history, but if *60 Minutes* reports that large numbers of executive women are leaving the workforce to stay at home, people will believe this is true. During the aftermath of the 2005 Hurricane Katrina, Yahoo! news (online) displayed photos of the flooding in New Orleans and people wading through the water with food, drawing the ire of many people of all racial and ethnic backgrounds. Whites were reported to be wading after *finding* food, while a young Black male was reported to be wading after *looting* a store. Explanations that the photos were taken by two different reporters and that the descriptive bylines were the reporters' words did little to reduce the perceptions of bias. After complaints, at the request of the photo owner, Yahoo! removed the photo of the Whites, while the one showing the Black man remained.

QUESTIONS TO CONSIDER

1. ***In addition to racial, ethnic, and gender stereotyping, what other kinds of stereotypes have you seen in the media? How do frequent portrayals of such stereotypes affect people's perceptions of their veracity?***

2. ***Choose one weeknight and one weekend night during prime time to watch television. Document***

[19] Nelson. (2002). See also Anastasio, P. A., Rose, K. C., & Chapman, K. C. (1999). "Can the Media Create Public Opinion? A Social-Identity Approach." *Current Directions in Psychological Science,* 8(5): 152–155.

[20] For a discussion of intraracial crime compared with interracial crime, see Gross, S. R., Jacoby, K., Matheson, D., Montgomery, N., & Patil, S. (2005). "Exonerations in the United States: 1989 through 2003." *The Journal of Criminal Law and Criminology,* 95: 524–560.

[21] Romer, D., Jamieson, K. H., & deCouteau, N. J. (1998). "The Treatment of Persons of Color in Local Television News: Ethnic Blame Discourse or Realistic Group Conflict?" *Communication Research,* 25(3): 286–305, cited in Nelson. (2002).

the programs watched. Who are the main characters? Describe their race, sex, approximate age, and other notable factors. What diversity-related factors do you observe?

3. One commercial that has attempted to change what was a stereotypical statement is the revised "Jif®" peanut butter commercial. While previous commercials said "Choosy Moms choose Jif®," the newer one says "Choosy Moms . . . and Dads choose Jif®." What other stereotype-resistant commercials have you observed? What stereotype-supportive commercials have you observed? What messages are being conveyed?

Again turning to how these attribution errors disadvantage nondominant groups, imagine that those in positions of power—the dominant group—attribute their own failures to circumstances, but their successes to personal strengths and character (e.g., merit). Imagine also that they see the failures of nondominant groups as resulting from lack of strength and moral character, but the successes of those groups as due to luck, accident, or chance. A likely consequence, then, is to tend to hire, promote, and reward the in-groups, because they deserve those advantages, and not to hire, promote, and reward out-groups, because they clearly do not deserve those advantages. Chapter 4 examines how the contribution of slavery and the legacy of discrimination have contributed to wealth disparities between Whites and Blacks. Chapter 7 considers how privileges enjoyed by Whites as "normal" aspects of everyday life contribute to the "myth of meritocracy." For example, when Whites believe that Blacks do not have as much wealth as Whites have because of failing to invest, to become entrepreneurs, or to work hard, and that Whites have greater wealth because of hard work, this is an example of the fundamental attribution error. Making such an error does not allow Whites to see how their personal, unearned advantages (such as networks in organizations that hire them because of in-group referrals, legacy admissions to prestigious universities, inheritance from ancestors, and preferences in selection) also disadvantage nondominant group members.

Multiple group memberships. Multiple group memberships make relationships between in-groups and out-groups and social identities quite complex. A White male has a racial identity and a sex or gender identity. Depending on the circumstances and particular stereotypes, Whites or men may be perceived as the in-group with non-Whites and women perceived as the out-groups as appropriate. In some cases, his Whiteness may be most salient, and he may display favoritism toward White women. In other cases his maleness may be more salient, and he may favor a Black man. When stereotyping is included as a factor, different decisions may be made. If Blacks are not reliable, for example, the White male manager may prefer to hire a White woman. If he views women as likely to quit work to stay at home with children, he may favor a man of color.

Add religion, sexual orientation, and disability to that White male's social identities and the situation becomes even more complex: imagine the White man is also Jewish, gay, and has a disability. In some circumstances, being Jewish or having a disability may be salient. In other circumstances, his White maleness may be overshadowed by his having a disability or being gay. These factors would reduce his power and the perception that he was a member of the in-group of White heterosexual males without a disability. Being gay or having a disability would likely also affect his perceptions of and actions toward (other) nondominant group members. If his identity as a nondominant group is salient, this may increase the likelihood he will see other nondominant group members less negatively as well. The experience of heterosexism, for example, may cause him to see women as individuals with a variety of characteristics, rather than as a monolithic group. Being Jewish may make him see Blacks as experiencing unfair discrimination and to be supportive of Blacks' pursuit of equality.

Nondominant groups as the in-group. The results of the social categorization of people into in-groups and out-groups are significantly different for nondominant group members as in-groups. Women, for example, may view other women as having positive attributes and prefer them to men. They may attribute positive behaviors to the characteristics of women, and negative behaviors to circumstances in which women find themselves. They may attribute negative behaviors to the characteristics of men, and positive behaviors to circumstances. Similarly, Blacks, Hispanics, Asians, and American Indians may see themselves as belonging to their group and attribute positive characteristics to themselves and negative characteristics to Whites. As discussed earlier, a key difference in women, people of color, people with disabilities, and other nondominant group members as in-groups, however, is their access to power over scarce resources. Because they are less likely to be in positions of power, they are less likely to be able to control resources, and to be able to discriminate against men, Whites, people without disabilities, and other dominant group members.

It is also important to note that nondominant group members may also adhere to stereotypes against members of their own groups. Instead of favoring their group members as members of their in-groups, they may also stereotype them and view the dominant group as being more likely to have positive attributes than their own group. In research conducted using real teams (rather than those formed in the laboratory), Jennifer Boldry and Deborah Kashy found that status of the group affected perceptions of the homogeneity of out-groups and the heterogeneity of in-groups.[22] Lower-status groups viewed themselves and high-status groups (their out-groups) as having variation in member characteristics.

[22] Boldry, J. G., & Kashy, D. A. (1999). "Intergroup Perception in Naturally Occurring Groups of Differential Status: A Social Relations Perspective." *Journal of Personality and Social Psychology,* 77(6): 1200–1212.

In contrast, high-status group members saw themselves and their group as having heterogeneous characteristics, but saw the out-group members as having homogenous characteristics. In interesting findings, the lower-status group members rated the high-status group members more favorably in terms of leadership, motivation, and character than the high-status group members rated themselves.

Boldry and Kashy's sample comprised undergraduate freshmen and juniors participating in a campus Corps of Cadets. Although the Corps of Cadets were a legitimate group, the sample was composed of 90% males. The race and ethnicity of the sample was not reported, but it is expected that more diversity in status characteristics (e.g., race, ethnicity, or sex) would result in different perceptions of the variance in qualities of in- and out-groups. In addition, the out-group members were striving to become official in-group members as they moved up the status hierarchy (e.g., become senior members of the Corps), which is not likely for those different in race, ethnicity, or sex. It is possible, however, that other non-dominant group members (e.g., Blacks, Latinos, women) may to a certain extent "buy-in" to the negative stereotypes about their group members and also prefer members of the dominant group. As products of a society in which stereotypes and socialization are common, this is indeed a possibility and may come with a host of negative consequences (e.g., depression, hopelessness, and low aspirations).

Aversive Racism and Other Contradictions

Demonstration of overt, intentional discrimination is considerably less likely in the twenty-first century than it has been in the past. However, researchers have identified contemporary, different forms of racism, including aversive, symbolic, and new racism. Aversive racism occurs when those who ostensibly adhere to egalitarian values and believe themselves to be unprejudiced still possess negative feelings and beliefs about racial issues and minority group members. Different from traditional, overt racist behavior, those who hold aversive racist beliefs do not openly discriminate, but when their actions can be justified by some other factor (e.g., lack of "fit" or some other factor other than race), they are likely to exhibit aversive racist behaviors. The existence of this form of racism has been documented in multiple studies, across times and settings, and could be considered more troublesome than traditional racism. While those who hold traditional racist beliefs might openly state them, aversive racists state their espousal of egalitarian beliefs, making efforts to identify and change their true beliefs more difficult.

In one study, John Dovidio and Samuel Gaertner documented the change in White participants' expressed espousal of prejudiced beliefs between 1989 and 1999, finding significantly fewer expressions of such beliefs in 1999.[23] Even so,

[23] Dovidio, J. F., & Gaertner, S. L. (2000). "Aversive Racism and Selection Decisions." *Psychological Science,* 11(4): 315–319.

the researchers did find that participants who expressed prejudicial beliefs (e.g., traditional racism) in both times were less likely to recommend Blacks for selection decisions, regardless of the qualifications of the Black candidates. For those who did not express prejudicial beliefs, there were no differences in rates of recommendations for selection when qualifications for either Blacks or Whites were particularly high. When qualifications were ambiguous—neither particularly strong, nor particularly weak, Whites were more frequently recommended than similarly qualified Blacks. Thus, when qualifications were strong and discrimination could be easily identified, aversive racists made similar recommendations for Blacks and Whites. When qualifications were ambiguous and decisions could be attributed to factors other than discrimination (e.g., "fit" or "personality"), aversive racists made fewer selection recommendations for Blacks. Dovidio and Gaertner suggested that this behavior may be based in part on the fundamental attribution error (discussed earlier) and reflective of Whites' tendency to give the benefit of the doubt to ambiguously qualified in-group members, but not to out-group members. As we discuss in Chapter 4, Blacks with similar financial qualifications are less likely to be approved for credit (e.g., loans, mortgages) than Whites, which may also indicate in-group favoritism and out-group bias.

In another complex study, Eduardo Bonilla-Silva and Tyrone Forman investigated changes in Whites' reported racial attitudes, hypothesizing that recent changes overstate the amount of positive change in racial attitudes.[24] Using qualitative and quantitative data drawn from 732 students at three universities, Bonilla-Silva and Forman found that students avoided the appearance of holding discriminatory beliefs in surveys, but interview data presented a different picture. "I'm not a racist . . . but . . ." preceded statements expressing hostile attitudes toward racial minorities, beliefs that minorities, rather than systematic discrimination, were responsible for their own situations, and belief in the existence of reverse discrimination, among other things. The researchers urged caution in concluding that racial attitudes were improving, suggesting that "racetalk" and "colorblind racism" were replacing expression of traditionally racist attitudes that are no longer widely acceptable.

Symbolic racists use symbols, rather than race, to attempt to explain their resistance to equality.[25] Symbolic racists, for example, are not against integrated schooling, but think forced busing is unfair. Symbolic racists may argue that they are not against affirmative action, per se, but they think it provides unqualified people with unearned advantages. "New" and "modern" racism are similar to

[24] Bonilla-Silva, E., & Forman, T. (2000). "'I'm Not a Racist, But . . .' 'Mapping White College Students' Racial Ideology in the USA." *Discourse and Society,* 11: 50–85.

[25] Kinder, D. R., & Sears, D. O. (1981). "Symbolic Racism versus Racial Threats to the Good Life." *Journal of Personality and Social Psychology,* 40: 414–431.

other contemporary forms of racism, and reflect people's decreasing willingness to express overtly racist beliefs, but their propensity is to behave in discriminatory manners when provided a rationale or justification for doing so.[26]

Neosexism is similar to aversive racism, and occurs when people's reported egalitarian values conflict with negative attitudes toward women.[27] The existence of neosexism has been documented in studies conducted in the United States, Croatia, and Slovenia, among other areas.[28] It could be argued that similar aversive attitudes exist for other nondominant groups. Reporting egalitarian attitudes toward gays and lesbians, but resisting equitable work-related benefits for them, or reporting egalitarian attitudes toward people with disabilities, but resisting accommodations for them as expensive or unfair to people without disabilities are possible examples.

Individual and Organizational Recommendations

Stereotype reduction must be purposeful. As we have discussed, when confronted with information that is contradictory to stereotypes, people tend to see this is as "unique" rather than using it to question and discard their beliefs. When faced with behavior that confirms stereotypes, people attend to such information instead of recognizing that there is variation among members of all groups. Indeed, it is likely that every stereotype could legitimately be applied to an individual from many different groups. With concerted efforts, stereotypes can be deactivated and automatic categorization can be stopped. Kerry Kawakami and colleagues have empirically investigated the effects of training on stereotype reduction, finding that practice in negating stereotypes results in reduced stereotype activation.[29] Adam Galinsky and Gordon Moskowitz have also found that perspective taking helps to reduce stereotyping and some of its negative consequences.[30]

Even without formal training, as individuals, we can and should work consciously to resist stereotyping, in-group favoritism, and out-group biases. Awareness of these processes is an important step, as is organizational support of equity. Question oneself and one's beliefs, behaviors, and attitudes toward others.

---

[26] See Chapter 4 for a discussion of research by Art Brief and his colleagues on new racism and recommendations for hiring.

[27] Tougas, F., Brown, R., Beaton, A. M., & Joly, S. (1995). "Neosexism: Plus ca change, plus c'est pareil." *Personality and Social Psychology Bulletin,* 21(8): 842–849.

[28] Frieze, I. H., Ferligoj, A., Kogovsek, J., Rener, T., Hovat, J., & Sarlija, N. (2003). "Gender-Role Attitudes in University Students in the Untied States, Slovenia, and Croatia." *Psychology of Women Quarterly,* 27: 256–261.

[29] Kawakami, K., Dovidio, J. F., Moll, J., Hermsen, S., & Russin, A. (2000). "Just Say No (to Stereotyping): Effects of Training in the Negation of Stereotypic Association on Stereotype Activation." *Journal of Personality and Social Psychology,* 78(5): 871–888.

[30] Galinsky, A., & Moskowitz, G. (2000). "Perspective Taking: Decreasing Stereotype Expression, Stereotype Accessibility, and In-Group Favoritism." *Journal of Personality and Social Psychology,* 78(4): 708–724.

Table 3.2 ***Questioning Stereotypes***

Is it logical to believe that

- there is considerable variation among my in-group, but all ______ are just alike?
- most Mexican Americans are undocumented immigrants, when people of Mexican descent have been in the United States for hundreds of years?
- all Whites are racist when White allies to diversity have worked as abolitionists, resisted discrimination, participated in boycotts, and risked their lives along with Blacks in the fight for equality?
- most women are uncommitted workers, when the great majority of women are employed and contribute substantially (or, for single women, completely) to their family income?
- Whites and men are not advantaged by systematic discrimination against minorities and women?
- all Arabs are terrorists when Arabs have lived and worked among Americans for years?
- older workers are less competent than younger workers, but CEOs and executives should be older, rather than younger, people?
- experiences of immigrant Jews, Italians, Germans, and Irish would be the same as those of Blacks, for whom identifiability is high and discrimination persists?
- most Black men are criminals when they are represented among various levels of educational and occupational attainment?
- most people with disabilities are incapable of being good performers, when many people with invisible disabilities successfully work among us?

As considered in Table 3.2, some fairly common stereotypical beliefs appear ridiculous upon analysis and can cause significant employee and customer concerns and generate considerable negative publicity.

The appearance of having made decisions on the basis of stereotypical beliefs generated considerable negative publicity for Wal-Mart in December 2005.[31] Reginald Pitts, a Black man, and the human resources manager at GAF materials went to a Tampa area Wal-Mart to purchase 520 gift cards for company employees and appears to have been assumed to be engaging in criminal activity. GAF is the biggest roofing systems maker in the United States, with $1.6 billion in revenues in 2004 and had been purchasing about $50,000 worth of gift cards at Wal-Mart for several years without incident. The gift cards were typically picked up by a White female administrator, but in 2005, she was on vacation, and Pitts decided to get the gift cards himself. He phoned in the order and went to Wal-Mart with a $13,600 company check, his driver's license and his GAF business card. When called, a GAF accounting supervisor assured store managers the check was good, but the managers still told Pitts they were having trouble verifying the check. While he waited more than two hours at the customer service desk, two Black

[31] Albright, M. (December 2, 2005). "Racial profiling feared at Wal-Mart". *St. Petersburg Times.* http://www.sptimes.com/2005/12/02/news_pf/Tampabay/Racial_profiling_fear.shtml, accessed 12/08/05.

Wal-Mart employees told Pitts that similarly large transactions by other customers had been processed without delay and suggested he was being closely scrutinized because he is Black. When Pitts asked for the check to be returned so he could purchase the cards elsewhere, the store managers refused to return the check and continued stalling. They had called the Hillsborough County sheriff. When the deputies arrived, one grabbed Pitts, telling him they needed to talk with him about the "forged check" and that Wal-Mart had called to report a felony. Pitts said he thought he was going to prison and that the experience was "totally humiliating".

After 19 minutes of reviewing the "evidence," the deputies concluded there were no grounds for a criminal charge returned the check to Pitts. Pitts said that the Wal-Mart store manager told him he 'did what he had to do,' and 'have a great day, sir'. GAF and Pitts lodged complaints with Wal-Mart, which opened its own investigation. Wal-Mart conceded the situation was 'handled very poorly' but that Wal-Mart does not tolerate racial profiling or discrimination. Four Wal-Mart officials have called Pitts to apologize for the incident, which received considerable media attention. GAF purchased the employees' gift cards at Target instead.

Because aversive racists are unaware that they hold prejudiced attitudes and genuinely think they are unbiased, efforts to change their attitudes are necessarily different from attempts to change those who openly acknowledge and express overt prejudice. Dovidio and Gaertner suggest several strategies that may be employed to help people reduce their propensities to stereotype and reduce the in-group–out-group categorizations that people seem to automatically make.[32] Their analyses suggest the following measures may be effective:

- Lead aversive racists to see the inconsistencies in their behaviors and their stated values, thereby developing cognitive dissonance and the desire to reduce it. Active efforts to reduce dissonance will help aversive racists reduce and ultimately eliminate automatic activation of stereotypes in interactions with out-group members.
- Engage group members in activities to achieve common, superordinate goals. Doing so will reduce perceptions of competition among in-groups and out-groups while increasing perceptions of cooperation.
- Encourage groups to perceive themselves as members of a single, superordinate group, rather than as two separate groups. Doing so will help create a common identity and result in in-group favoritism that includes both groups.

In an organizational setting, group members who view themselves as part of the organization working for the same employer, pursuing the organization's vision and mission, and competing against others in the industry will be more likely to see their diverse group as the in-group working toward the same goal. In organizations

[32] Dovidio, J. F., & Gaertner, S. L. (1999). "Reducing Prejudice: Combating Intergroup Biases." *Current Directions in Psychological Science,* 8(4): 101–105.

in which diversity is embraced and valued and discrimination and exclusion are not tolerated, those who would exclude and limit based on characteristics such as race, sex, age, religion, sexual orientation, ability, and other irrelevant factors at work should be viewed as undesirable out-groups working against the important organizational goal of inclusion and equity.

In addition to working to reduce discrimination based on stereotyping and social categorization processes, organizational monitoring and control measures should be implemented. Diverse recruitment and selection teams, supervisors and managers, and legitimate selection criteria would be helpful at organizational entry. Salary decisions should be made based on job requirements as should training, development, promotion, and termination decisions. Organizational leaders must be willing to implement strong policies and monitoring and control measures supportive of diversity throughout their organizations and among their customers and constituents.

SUMMARY

In this chapter, we have considered factors that characterize minority, or nondominant, groups and provided a rationale for determining "What is a minority?" yet we have acknowledged that identifiability, power, discrimination, and group awareness vary among nondominant groups. We have incorporated literature from social psychology to help understand prejudice, stereotyping, and social categorization. These social processes were linked to behaviors that support or hinder diversity in organizations, and to some specific examples that will be discussed further in subsequent chapters. Stereotyping and social categorization processes are problematic when customers are treated unfairly or job-related decisions (e.g., hiring, firing, compensation, promotion and advancement, training, and job placement) are made on the basis of them. Measures to reduce stereotyping, aversive racism, and other aversions were presented.

Although it is impossible to consider every theory and psychological process related to diversity, readers should now be aware that along with deliberate, overt categorization of different others, underlying, unconscious processes also occur. Behaviors in some of the lawsuits and settlements presented in Chapter 2, along with many from the chapters to follow, are indicative of overt, conscious differential treatment. Both the overt and the unconscious discrimination often result from people's propensity to stereotype and see members of certain groups as being more or less appropriate for certain jobs (e.g., woman as secretary vs. truck driver). In Featured Case 9.4 mentioned earlier, licensed women delivery drivers were not hired because of stereotypical perceptions about "women drivers." One woman was told that she looked more like a secretary and was encouraged to apply for a secretarial position, and the company then hired a man who did not meet the minimum job qualifications. It is these unconscious propensities that are most insidious and difficult to eradicate. As some EEOC cases show, some employers verbalize their stereotypical perceptions, but most would simply act on them, and the affected individual would have little or no concrete evidence of discrimination.

In taking the perspective that diversity is valuable to individuals and organizations, individuals should be aware of both overt discrimination and the unconscious processes that result in discrimination. Willingness to listen, think, understand, and grow in diversity learning will be helpful in improving positive outcomes of diversity. From that perspective, we begin our investigation into the history and current status of various groups in the United States, with goals of reducing misperceptions, stereotypes, and biases, increasing awareness and understanding, and fostering diversity in organizations.

Key Terms

Aversive racism — when those who adhere to egalitarian values and believe themselves to be unprejudiced still possess negative feelings and beliefs about racial issues and minority group members.

Discrimination — negative behavior toward a person based on his or her group membership.

Egalitarian — one who believes in human equality, particularly regarding social, political, and economic rights and privileges.

Fundamental attribution error — the tendency to underestimate the influence of external factors (e.g., situations or circumstances) and overestimate the influence of internal factors (e.g., personal qualities) when evaluating the behavior of others.

Neosexism — when people's reported egalitarian values conflict with negative attitudes toward women.

Prejudice — irrational, negative evaluations of a group.

Social identity — the part of an individual's self-concept that derives from his or her membership in a social group and the value and emotional significance attached to that group membership.

Stereotypes — overgeneralizations of characteristics to large human groups.

Questions to Consider

1. The chapter discusses many identities and multiple group memberships that people have. If you were to describe the important parts of your identity, what would be on your list? Make a list, then rank the most to least important aspects of your identity.
2. Common stereotypes about the groups considered in this book were listed in this chapter. For each group, were you aware of the listed stereotype? Do you know of someone who is a member of that group who does not fit the stereotype? Do you know someone who is not a member of that group who nonetheless exhibits the stereotyped characteristic? For example, one stereotype is that Blacks are lazy. Do you know a Black person who is not lazy? Do you know a White person who is lazy? Another stereotype is that Asians are smart and hardworking. Do you know an Asian who is neither? Do you know a Black person who is smart and hardworking? Continue the process for the stereotypes listed, and for others that you are aware of that exist for different groups.

3. Review Table 3.1. Do you agree with the description of where each group falls with respect to identifiability, power, discrimination, and group awareness? What, if anything, would you change, and why?
4. In addition to the "is it logical to believe that . . ." statements listed in Table 3.2, what other illogical beliefs about particular groups can you think of? How could they be harmful in a diversity context?
5. Researchers have found that people are less willing to express "traditionally" prejudiced beliefs than in the past, but their behavior does not agree with espoused beliefs. How can such disparities in expressed beliefs and actions undermine diversity in organizations? What organizational measures can be implemented to investigate whether there are inconsistencies in expressed beliefs, behaviors, and outcomes related to diversity in organizations?
6. If you are White, have you experienced being the minority in a situation (for example, among many Blacks, Asians, or others of color)? If you are a person of color, have you experienced being a minority among others of color (for example, Asian among many Blacks; Latino among many Asians) rather than among Whites? If you are a man, have you experienced being the minority at work in a meeting or at school in a class? If you are a woman, have you experienced being the minority in a meeting at work or at school in a class? What were these experiences being a "minority" like?
7. What have you learned from this chapter that is most surprising to you?

Actions and Exercises

1. Investigate the projected 2050 population by race, ethnicity, gender, and median ages. Reconstruct Table 3.1 using the 2050 population and your perceptions of the groups' identifiability, power, discrimination, and group awareness then.
2. Discuss stereotypes with a trusted friend or family member. What kinds of job-related stereotypes is he or she aware of? (Note that awareness of stereotypes does not mean belief in the veracity of the stereotype.) Discuss how these stereotypes can negatively affect individuals' job opportunities and advancement.
3. Using physical copies of a local newspaper (e.g., *San Francisco Chronicle, Chicago Tribune,* and *Dallas Morning News*), a campus or university newspaper, and a community or city newspaper, locate stories that include photos of people in the story. Make a table of the type of story (e.g., human interest, business news, and crime), and the race, ethnicity, sex, and estimated age of the subject. What diversity-related observations can be made from the table?
4. Locate a newspaper that has an Executive or Business section that includes promotions, executive changes, or other career moves. If there are photos of the people involved, list their race, ethnicity, and sex. If names only are provided, where possible, determine the sex of the person. What observations can you make from your list?

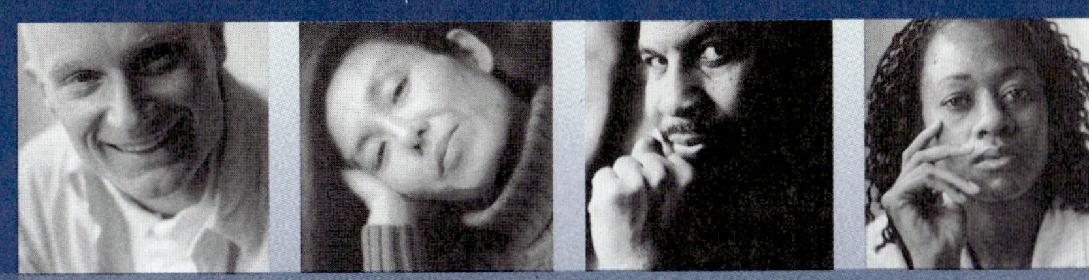

Section II

Examining Specific Groups and Categories

4 Chapter

Blacks/African Americans

Chapter Objectives

After completing this chapter, readers should have a greater understanding of African Americans and diversity in organizations. Readers can expect to:

- *be aware of the historical background and current status of Blacks in the United States.*
- *be able to discuss participation rates, employment, and income levels of Blacks in the United States.*
- *examine racial differences in educational return on investment for Blacks and other racial and ethnic groups.*
- *understand research evidence of access and treatment discrimination experienced by Blacks.*
- *be able to discuss similarities and differences between employment experiences of Black men and women.*
- *understand individual and organizational measures that can be used to improve organizational experiences of Blacks.*

Key Facts

Blacks who are high school graduates are about twice as likely to be unemployed as White high school graduates.

Black men with college degrees earn over $20,000 less than White men with college degrees; but over $20,000 more than Black men with only high school degrees.

Black women have higher workforce participation rates than White women, but White men have higher participation rates than Black men.

Disparities in wealth between Blacks and Whites are largely the result of differences in inheritance due to slavery and the legacy of discrimination since slavery ended.

In 2004, 24.7% of Blacks and 8.6% of Whites lived in poverty.

Introduction and Overview

We begin our discussion of racial and ethnic groups with African Americans because of their unique position as descendants of slaves in the United States and the legacy of societal and organizational discrimination that Blacks continue to face.[1] The current status of Blacks in the United States is strongly influenced by the conditions under which most Blacks originally came to the United States. In contrast to immigrants who came seeking opportunities or fleeing their homeland (refugees), most of the first Blacks arrived in the United States as slaves, with no options or opportunities for status improvement. Indeed, their status as American slaves was markedly lower than was their status as free Africans. Although many other immigrants (for example, Irish, Italians, and Germans) faced hostility, overt discrimination, and even periods as indentured servants, no other people were enslaved. In addition, though significant, the discrimination and segregation experienced by and among European immigrants was less pervasive, less vehement, and considerably shorter lived when compared with that experienced by African slaves and their descendants.[2] Researchers have documented how people of color, including "African Americans, Latinos and Latinas, and Asian immigrants have faced and continue to encounter substantial barriers to assimilating into and full participation in mainstream American society relative to *all* White ethnic groups"[3] (emphasis in original). The Declaration of Independence stated that all men were created equal and endowed with inalienable rights of life, liberty, and the pursuit of happiness; however, these rights clearly did not apply to Blacks, women, American Indians, or immigrants of color.[4] The Naturalization Law of 1790, the first federal law regarding citizenship of immigrants, specifically allowed only *White men* to become citizens. The racial restrictions on citizenship were not repealed until 1952, with the McCarran-Walter Act. The 162-year life of the Naturalization Act of 1790 negatively affected the rights and opportunities of many immigrants of color, and highlights the importance of race-based ethnic differences.[5]

The absence of clear physical distinctions, such as skin color, to provide knowledge of whether one is of Irish, German, Italian, or English descent, is one impediment to immediate overt discrimination against members of those groups. Dworkin and Dworkin have proposed that one characteristic of minority groups is visibility, which allows for immediate categorization and stereotyping.[6] For the most part, European Americans' country of origin is invisible, which makes discrimination on that basis very difficult. High rates of intermarriage between Whites of different ethnic backgrounds and less legal segregation and

[1] The introduction and history sections refer to the experiences of non-Hispanic Blacks, as descendants of slaves, in the United States. Blacks who came to the United States after slavery face similar discriminatory barriers in organizations and society. The terms "Black" and "African American" are used interchangeably.

[2] Johnson, C., & Smith, P. (1998). *Africans in America: America's Journey through Slavery,* Orlando, FL: Harcourt Brace; Williams, J. (1987). *Eyes on the Prize: America's Civil Rights Years, 1954–1965,* New York: Viking Penguin.

[3] Reskin, B. F., & Charles, C. Z. (1999). "Now You See 'em, Now You Don't." In I. Browne (Ed.), *Latinas and African-American Women at Work: Race, Gender, and Economic Inequality,* New York: Russell Sage Foundation, pp. 380–407. See also Takaki, R. (Ed.) . . . (1987). *From Different Shores,* New York: Oxford University Press, p. 390.

[4] Herring, C. (1999). "African Americans in Contemporary America: Progress and Retrenchment." In A. G. Dworkin & R. J. Dworkin (Eds.), *The Minority Report,* Fort Worth: Harcourt Brace Publishers, pp. 181–208; Takaki, R. (1987). "Reflections on Racial Patterns in America." In R. Takaki (Ed.), *From Different Shores, Perspectives on Race and Ethnicity in America,* New York: Oxford University Press, pp. 26–37.

[5] Takaki. (1987).

[6] Dworkin, A. G., & Dworkin, A. (1999). "What is a Minority?" In A. G. Dworkin & R. J. Dworkin (Eds.), *The Minority Report,* Fort Worth: Harcourt Brace Publishers, pp. 11–27.

exclusion also reduced the overt and lasting discrimination against White ethnic minority groups when compared with Blacks. Segregation, exclusion, and discrimination against Blacks in the United States have proven to be formidable foes, shaping the lives and opportunities of African Americans for generations.

Terminology

In this chapter, consistent with U.S. Census Bureau terminology, we use "Black" or "African American" interchangeably, to refer to people having origins in any of the Black racial groups from Africa. Individuals with different preferences for different terms are acknowledged, however.

History of Blacks in the United States

Historical records indicate that Africans were first sold in what is now known as the United States in about 1619. During the same period, Whites were also held as indentured servants. Over time, White servitude of any sort ended, while African servitude continued as slavery, and a "complete deprivation of civil and personal rights" for the next 146 years.[7] The formal institution of slavery ended by decree in 1863 with the Emancipation Proclamation, but even the end of the Civil War in 1865 did not provide Blacks with the rights and opportunities provided to Whites in the United States at the end of the American Revolution. Between 1865 and 1964, formal, legally sanctioned segregation in many parts of the country severely impeded the progress of Blacks, particularly in the South, where most Blacks resided. "Jim Crow" laws required "separate but equal" accommodations, transportation, education, and even burial, for Whites and Blacks.[8] Instead of equality, however, separate meant unequal, inferior, and often substandard facilities for Blacks.

Misperception: Legalized discrimination and segregation ended with the end of slavery.

Reality: Legally sanctioned (or mandated) discrimination and segregation persisted for decades after the end of slavery, including "separate but equal" schools and other facilities for Blacks and Whites.

Extremely hostile attitudes toward Blacks in the South and greater employment opportunities elsewhere contributed to large-scale migration of Blacks to cities such as Chicago, Boston, Detroit, and New York. Employment at steel mills, automakers, and railroads provided Black men with higher earnings than sharecropping, picking cotton, and other low-wage jobs in the South, but better paying, safer, and more prestigious jobs were still reserved for Whites. Housing,

[7] Jordan, W. D. (1962). *Journal of Southern History,* 28 (Feb.): 18–30. See also Jordan, W. D. (1968). *White over Black: American Attitudes toward the Negro, 1550-1812,* Chapel Hill, NC: The University of North Carolina Press, p. 107; from Rose, P. I. (1970). *Slavery and Its Aftermath,* New York: Atherton Press.

[8] Herring. (1999).

education, and other overt racial discrimination existed in the North as well. See Chapter 7 for a discussion of how Black migration from the South to the North improved lower and working class White immigrants' position in the North.

Focal Issue 4.1 considers differences in accumulation of wealth between Blacks and Whites, focusing on slavery, subsequent pervasive discrimination against Blacks, and inheritance.

Blacks in the Military

Segregation and discrimination extended to the armed forces, where Black servicemen faced open hostility from fellow White military personnel and nonmilitary personnel alike. Black men served in the military in the French and Indian War, the American Revolution, the War of 1812, the Civil War, and the wars of the twentieth century, although with many restrictions. Blacks fighting in the American Revolution helped gain freedom from British rule, but freedom from slavery was still elusive. Through World War II, Blacks were denied the right to carry arms and commonly experienced sanctioned segregation and discrimination, as did their nonservice counterparts.[9] Denying Blacks the dubious privilege of engaging in combat resulted in part from fears of arming Blacks (especially during the slavery years), and in part from beliefs that Blacks were intellectually incapable of or lacked the skills to adequately perform in combat. This denial was a mixed blessing; although Blacks avoided being directly fired upon, they held menial roles, such as janitors, clerks, cafeteria workers, and laborers, even when aptly qualified for higher roles.[10] Once Blacks were allowed to fill combat positions, they remained segregated, and for a time, reported solely to White officers, as Blacks were not allowed to be officers.[11]

Other overt discrimination against Black soldiers included accusations of theft, insubordination, and, the most life-threatening for the accused, rape and harassment of White women. These accusations were often followed by biased court martials and punishments that were far harsher than similarly charged and convicted Whites would face, including significantly more imprisonments for life and dishonorable discharges.[12] On some military bases in the South, Black soldiers had to drink from separate water fountains for "colored" people while White soldiers and *German prisoners of war* drank from the fountains for Whites.[13] In some areas of the country, children of Blacks in the military were

[9] Astor, G. (2001). *The Right to Fight: A History of African Americans in the Military,* Cambridge, MA: DaCapo Press.

[10] Astor. (2001).

[11] Blacks remain significantly less likely to be officers than enlisted men. For details, see Population Representation in the Military Services, http://www.dod.mil/prhome/poprep2001/chapter4/chapter4_5.htm, accessed 03/18/05; Segal, D. R., & Segal, M. W. (2004). *America's Military Population.* Population Reference Bureau.

[12] Astor. (2001).

[13] Ibid.

Focal Issue 4.1 *Differences in Black/White Accumulation of Wealth: Effects of Slavery and Generations of Discrimination*

Many researchers in various disciplines (e.g., sociology, economics, and finance) have investigated differences in accumulation of wealth between Blacks and Whites. Some suggest that these differences in wealth are primarily due to differences in inheritance, rather than differences in saving or spending habits.[14] For the first 250 years of their existence in what is now the United States, Blacks *were* property, rather than *owning* property. For decades after being freed in 1865, Blacks were still legally denied the right to own property, through various laws across the United States. Whereas Whites had property and wealth to pass on to heirs, Blacks generally did not.[15] Systematic and legal discrimination in employment and earnings exacerbated these disparities for nearly 100 more years until passage of the Civil Rights Act in 1964, which prohibited race-based discrimination in employment and helped narrow the White/Black earnings gap to some extent. "Put simply, long after legalized discrimination and segregation ceased, their intergenerational impacts persist."[16] Not only was there little or no inheritance to pass on wealth due to slavery and its aftermath, Blacks' wages still suffer effects of discrimination, which limits their ability to acquire and, thus, pass on wealth.

Black/White differences in wealth have also been partially attributed to discrimination in access to credit, which results in Blacks being less likely to be homeowners or to start their own businesses, both of which contribute strongly to accumulation of wealth.[17] In an analysis of access to business loans, Ando found that Blacks were significantly less likely to obtain credit than were Whites, Asians, and Latinos. Ando controlled for differences that might have explained Blacks' lower acceptance rates, and still found significant differences.[18] Similar disparities in mortgage loan approvals and rates for comparably credit-worthy Blacks and Whites also exist.[19] As with employment discrimination, it appears that Blacks with marginal qualifications are rejected, while Whites with marginal qualifications are given the benefit of the doubt.[20]

Compared with 76.2% of non-Hispanic Whites, 49.7% of Blacks owned their own homes in 2004.[21] In the 1940s–1960s, while White (male) veterans capitalized on education, employment, and housing benefits after their service, Black veterans were systematically and purposefully denied such benefits even though they had earned them.[22] The Federal Housing Authority believed in racial segregation of neighborhoods, publicly promoted

[14] Darity, W. A., Jr., & Myers, S. L., Jr. (2000). "Languishing in Inequality: Racial Disparities in Wealth and Earnings in the New Millenium." In J. S. Jackson (Ed.), *New Directions: African Americans in a Diversifying Nation,* Washington, DC: National Policy Association, pp. 86–118; Black American's Wealth Increases—They Still Lag, Reuters, 10/29/03.

[15] Blau, F. D., & Graham, J. W. (1990). "Black/White Differences in Wealth and Asset Composition." *Quarterly Journal of Economics,* 105: 321–339.

[16] Darity & Myers. (2000). p. 104.

[17] Ibid.

[18] Ando, F. (1988). *An Analysis of Access to Bank Credit,* Los Angeles: UCLA Center for Afro-American Studies.

[19] Yinger, J. (1995). *Closed Doors, Opportunities Lost: The Continuing Costs of Housing Discrimination,* New York: Russell Sage Foundation.

[20] See George, C. G. (1991). "Use of Testers in Investigating Discrimination in Mortgage Lending and Insurance." In M. Fix & R. J. Struyk (Eds.), *Clear and Convincing Evidence,* Washington, DC: Urban Institute Press, pp. 257–306.

[21] U.S. Department of Commerce News. Bureau of the Census. Table 7. Homeownership Rates by Race and Ethnicity of Householder: 2002 to 2004, http://www.census.gov/hhes/www/housing/hvs/q204prss.pdf, accessed 12/07/04.

[22] Brodkin, K. (2004). "How Jews Became White." In J. F. Healy & E. O'Brien (Eds.), *Race, Ethnicity, and Gender,* Thousand Oaks, CA: Pine Forge Press, pp. 282–294.

segregation, and often denied Blacks loans. Renting instead of owning also contributed to Blacks having less property to leave to subsequent generations; renters do not will homes to heirs. For Blacks who were able to purchase homes, residential segregation and steering by realtors contributed to continued stratification.[23] Evidence of residential segregation and steering continues to be documented.[24] Homes in predominantly Black neighborhoods are worth less and appreciate more slowly than homes in neighborhoods that are not predominantly Black. In addition, school systems tend to be worse, opportunities for employment are less, and services are lower in such neighborhoods, also contributing to persistent, enduring gaps in income and opportunities for wealth.[25]

QUESTIONS TO CONSIDER

1. *Prior to reading this section, had you considered the roles of slavery and subsequent continued discrimination in the ability of (a) Blacks and (b) Whites to inherit and earn wealth, savings, and property?*
2. *What factors may affect the higher rejection rates of equally credit-worthy Blacks for business and home loans?*
3. *Why might realtors steer Blacks to "Black" neighborhoods?*
4. *What organizational steps can banks, mortgage companies, and realties take to ensure they do not perpetrate credit and housing discrimination?*

bussed to Black schools in town, because the on-base schools were reserved for White children. Outside military bases, Blacks had to ride in the back of trolleys and busses and in the "colored" sections of trains, with new draftees reporting to duty after long rides on the back of segregated busses.[26] Soldiers were denied service in restaurants, theaters, and bars in many cities; at times facing open hostility, assault, and lynching from townspeople.[27] Understandably, Black soldiers serving the United States, often supporting democratic beliefs in foreign countries, opposed and resisted such hypocritical treatment within the United States.

Individual Feature 4.1 considers the successful military career of Vincent Brooks, Brigadier General, an African American and West Point graduate.

The Civil Rights Movement

Although Blacks had resisted discrimination and segregation for many years, the civil rights movement of the 1950s and 1960s was more successful than previous efforts in bringing about social and legal change and in obtaining rights previously

[23] Ibid.

[24] Oliver, M. L., & Shapiro, T. M. (1995). *Black Wealth/White Wealth: A New Perspective on Racial Inequality,* New York: Routledge; Turner, M. A. (1992). "Limits on Neighborhood Choice: Evidence of Racial and Ethnic Steering in Urban Housing Markets." In M. Fix & R. J. Struyk (Eds.), *Clear and Convincing Evidence,* Washington, DC: Urban Institute Press, pp. 95–130.

[25] Massey, D., & Denton, N. A. (1993). *American Apartheid: Segregation and the Making of the Underclass,* Cambridge, MA: Harvard University Press.

[26] Johnson, K. L. (Ret. Judge), Feb. 4, 2004, personal communication.

[27] Astor. (2001).

INDIVIDUAL FEATURE 4.1 *Vincent Brooks, U.S. Army Brigadier General*

Vincent Brooks comes from a family of brigadier generals. His father, Leo A. Brooks, Sr., and his brother, Leo, also earned the title of brigadier general. Vincent was educated at West Point, where he became the first Black in West Point history to be named cadet brigade commander, a position similar to class president. In addition to leading his class, Brooks also graduated first in the class of 4,000 students. He went on to study at the U.S. Army Command and General Staff College in Kansas and at Harvard.

Brooks has served in the Army around the world, including Iraq, South Korea, Panama, Kosovo, and Kuwait, moving through the ranks of the Army. A recognized leader, he served as the spokesperson for the U.S. Army Central Command during early 2003. As spokesperson, Brooks was diplomatic and respectful of the media, earning their confidence and respect in return. In late 2004, Brooks was named deputy chief of public affairs for the U.S. Army, responsible for projecting a positive image of the Army around the world, and the highest communications position in the U.S. Army.

QUESTIONS TO CONSIDER

1. ***What is the racial and ethnic composition of the U.S. Army?***
2. ***How many Blacks as a proportion of the entire Army are in officer positions?***
3. ***Blacks are sometimes stereotyped as being poor communicators, yet Vincent Brooks has served as spokesperson for the Army and occupies the highest communications position in the U.S. Army. Is seeing and hearing Vincent Brooks in his role as spokesperson likely to affect people's perceptions of Blacks as poor communicators? Why or why not?***

Source: Curry, G. E. (2005, March, 18). "Gen. Vincent Brooks is 'Drafted' into Another Top Job," http://www.blackpressusa.com/news/Article.asp?SID=3&Title=National+News&NewsID=3602, accessed 03/18/05.

Current Biography, 2003: 64(6). Vincent Brooks, U.S. Army Brigadier General.

denied to Blacks but available to Whites. Well-known activists and organizers included Medgar Evers, Fannie Lou Hamer, Dr. Martin Luther King, Jr., Rosa Parks, legendary baseball player Jackie Robinson, Dorothy Height, and Malcolm X. Many unknown Blacks participated in boycotts, demonstrations, and "sit-ins" as well. In the early 1960s, college students organized sit-ins at lunch counters in stores in the South that refused service to Blacks, mirroring sit-ins that college students had organized during the 1940s. Students were often arrested and jailed, but on the immediately following days, other student protesters again sat at lunch counters requesting service. Although most of the sit-ins occurred in the South, Northern stores also faced negative consequences from the discriminatory actions of their Southern locations. When Northern stores had Southern counterparts that refused service to Blacks (for example, Woolworth's, a large discount store that had locations in both the North and South), many Black and White Northerners refused to patronize those stores in both locations, putting economic pressure on the entire company.

As early as 1938, Black leaders had called for boycotts and picketing against organizations that refused to hire Blacks. The "Don't buy where you can't work," slogan used in many effective boycotts exemplifies the costs of lost business when an organization becomes known for not valuing diversity.[28]

Many Whites also participated in battles for equality for Blacks, before, during, and after the civil rights movement. Whites who fought for equal treatment included Alabaman Virginia Durr, and New Yorkers, Michael Schwerner and Andrew Goodman. Schwerner and Goodman were murdered in Mississippi along with James Chaney (a Black activist) while fighting for Blacks' civil rights. Despite past and present periods of enmity between Blacks and Jews, estimates suggest that two-thirds of the Whites who participated in the civil rights movement were Jewish, including Schwerner and Goodman.[29] Whites who supported Black causes in the South risked ostracism, harassment, and death.

When coupled with greater societal and governmental pressure, the sit-ins, boycotts, and picketing of the 1960s were more successful than earlier ones had been in achieving results in customer service and hiring for Blacks. The combined efforts of many fighting for justice in the United States during this time resulted in the passage of the Civil Rights Act of 1964, and executive orders for affirmative action, discussed in Chapter 2. In large part due to those laws and legislative acts, the 1960s, 1970s, 1980s, and 1990s brought about conflict, change, and some progress for African Americans and diversity in the United States. Table 4.1 depicts some of the changes in population and status of Blacks between 1964 and 2003.

Relevant Legislation

Perhaps the most important legislative act relevant to the organizational experiences of Blacks in the United States is Title VII of the Civil Rights Act. Given the existence of overt racial discrimination and civil rights activities of the 1950s and 1960s preceding passage of Title VII, Blacks were the primary targets of Title VII. As presented in Chapter 2, Title VII, as amended, prohibits discrimination on the basis of race in employment matters, including prohibitions against racial harassment. Executive orders for affirmative action are also particularly relevant to employment experiences of African Americans because of their active nondiscrimination measures, rather than passive ones such as in Title VII. As we discuss later in the chapter, Blacks and women who work for affirmative action employers earn more than those who work for non-affirmative action employers. Despite the more than 40 years that Title VII and executive orders

---

[28] Sewell, S. K. (2004). "The 'Not Buying Power' of the Black Community: Urban Boycotts and Equal Employment Opportunity." *Journal of African American History,* 89(2): 135–152.

[29] Schoenfeld, E. (1999). "Jewish Americans: A Religio-Ethnic Community." In A. G. Dworkin & R. J. Dworkin (Eds.), *The Minority Report,* Orlando, FL: Harcourt Brace, pp. 364–394; Takaki, R. (1993). *A Different Mirror: A History of Multicultural America,* Boston: Back Bay Books, Little Brown and Company. See also, J. Salzman, A. Back, & G. S. Sorin (Eds.). *Bridges and Boundaries: African Americans and American Jews,* New York: George Braziller.

TABLE 4.1 ***Civil Rights Act of 1964: 40th Anniversary Key Facts for African Americans***

Factor	1964	2002/2003*
Population	20.7 million	38.7 million
Median family income	$18,859 (inflation adjusted)	$33,634
Median income for men working full-time, year-round	$20,805 (inflation adjusted)	$31,966
Median income for women working full-time year round	$13,085 (inflation adjusted)	$27,703
Poverty rate	41.8% (1966 rate)	23.9%
High school graduates age 25 and over	26%, 2.4 million	80%, 16.4 million
College students	306,000	2.3 million
College graduates age 25 and over	4%, 365,000	17%, 3.6 million

*Population and education data are from 2003. Income and poverty data are from 2002. The median income is the income at which half the population is above and half the population is below.

Source: "Facts for Features." U.S. Census Bureau. Special Edition. Civil Rights Act of 1964: Fortieth Anniversary, http://www.census.gov/Press-Release/www/releases/archives/facts_for_features_special_editions/001800.html, accessed 12/06/04.

have existed, however, the employment status, earnings, and income of African Americans continue to lag that of Whites. While slavery and sanctioned discrimination existed for more than 300 years in the United States, Title VII and affirmative action have existed less than 50 years.

Misperception: The playing field is now level; affirmative action is no longer needed.

Reality: Affirmative action is still needed to combat persistent, pervasive discrimination in hiring, placement, promotions, and advancement.

Selected EEOC Cases Involving Race Discrimination

The cases that follow, drawn verbatim from the EEOC Web site document, are charges of discrimination against Blacks in a variety of organizations. Settlements included financial payments to Charging Parties (CPs), revision of selection criteria, promotion of aggrieved party or other remedies.

Race discrimination, retaliation, and constructive discharge

- **EEOC v. Earl Scheib, Inc., d/b/a Earl Scheib Paint**[30]

  No. 03-cv-1934-BTM/BLM (S.D. Cal. Aug. 30, 2004)

  The Los Angeles District Office filed this Title VII class suit, alleging race discrimination and retaliation at defendant's San Diego-area auto paint and body shop stores. Defendant operates 122 auto paint and body shops in more than

[30] EEOC Litigation Settlements—August 2004, offensive language retained from original material, http://www.eeoc.gov/litigation/settlements/settlement08-04.html, accessed 12/08/04.

100 cities nationwide, including 50 shops in Southern California. The district office asserted that two black CPs endured racial harassment by white coworkers, including the wife of a white district manager. Los Angeles alleged that another white district manager used racial slurs such as "nigger" and "boy" when referring to African American employees and led a campaign of race-based discrimination and retaliation, that included disparate discipline, placement in less desirable stores, and forced demotions and reassignments, especially after the two CPs filed complaints with the EEOC. One of the CPs was discharged and the other was constructively discharged. Lastly, the district office alleged that defendant retaliated against a white store manager and an Hispanic employee by disciplining them, demoting them, cutting the Hispanic employee's wages, and then forcing them out because they complained about or refused to participate in the racial harassment and discrimination directed at black employees.

- **EEOC v. Charapp Ford South**[31]

  No. 03-0171 (W.D. Pa. November 12, 2003)

  In this Title VII race discrimination suit, the Philadelphia District Office alleged that defendant, a car dealership, created a racially hostile environment for four African American salespeople and then constructively discharged them when they quit their jobs to escape the harassment. The harassment included offensive jokes, racial epithets, displays of the Confederate flag on cars, racist cartoons, and threats such as a list of '10 ways to kill a black man.

- **EEOC v. Bazaar Del Mundo (BDM)**[32]

  No. 02 CV 01908 W (S.D. Cal. August 5, 2003)

  The Los Angeles District Office alleged in this Title VII lawsuit that defendant, a Mexican-themed tourist attraction with shops and restaurants in Old Town San Diego which employs over 500 workers, refused to hire black job applicants because of their race. The black claimants applied for various jobs with defendant, including cashier, salesperson, line cook/food prep, and customer service positions, and though qualified for the positions for which they applied, were not hired. Instead, defendant continued soliciting applications and hired less qualified non-black applicants.

- **EEOC v. Home Depot**[33]

  No. CV-S-02-12668-KJD-LRL (D. Nev. August 12, 2003)

  The Los Angeles District Office alleged in this Title VII lawsuit that defendant, a nationwide retailer of home improvement products, discriminated against

[31] EEOC Litigation Settlements—November 2003, http://www.eeoc.gov/litigation/settlements/settlement11-03.html, accessed 06/15/05.

[32] EEOC Litigation Settlements—August 2003, http://www.eeoc.gov/litigation/settlements/settlement08-03.html, accessed 06/15/05.

[33] Ibid.

charging party, a black department manager, when it refused to promote him to an Assistant Store Manager position at one of its Las Vegas, Nevada stores. Charging party applied for the promotion on three separate occasions between April 2001 and August 2001 and despite his qualifications (four years of experience as department manager in five different departments) and a recommendation for promotion from his supervisor, he was rejected each time. Defendant instead selected three white candidates for Assistant Manager positions.

- **EEOC v. Wal-Mart Stores, Inc.**[34]
  No. H-02-2404 (S.D. Tex. August 21, 2003)

  In this Title VII lawsuit, the Houston District Office alleged that defendant, the nationwide discount retailer, discriminated against charging party, a black Unloader, when it denied him a promotion to a Receiving Team Supervisor position and instead promoted a less qualified non-black employee. The suit further alleged that defendant discriminated against a group of black Unloaders by denying them pay raises and paying them lower wages than comparable non-black Unloaders.

Population

The 38.7 million Blacks in the United States comprise 13% of the population. Of these, 52% are women and 48% are men.[35, 36] Blacks are relatively young; 80% of Blacks are under age 50, and 32% are age 18 or younger. This youthfulness of the population reflects the slightly higher than average birthrates and the shorter life expectancy of Blacks, both of which are related to diversity in organizations. First, the larger proportion of young Blacks means a larger proportion of Blacks will enter the workforce in the future. To fully utilize the assets possessed by this large segment of the population, organizations must create environments that welcome and provide opportunities for Blacks rather than fostering discrimination, segregation, and exclusion. Second, although there are many contributions to the shorter life expectancies of Blacks (such as lower access to health care, crime, and poverty), researchers have suggested that stress related to discrimination, low responsibility and autonomy, and underutilization of Blacks' skills at work also contribute to illness and early death.[37] Organizational pursuit of fairness and

---

[34] Ibid.

[35] McKinnon, J. (2003). "The Black Population in the United States: March 2002." U.S. Census Bureau, Current Population Reports, Series P20-541. Washington, DC.

[36] Ibid.

[37] Sagrestano, L. M. (2004). "Health Implications of Workplace Diversity." In M. S. Stockdale & F. J. Crosby (Eds.), *The Psychology and Management of Workplace Diversity,* Malden, MA: Blackwell Publishing, pp. 122–143; Keita, G. P., & Jones, J. M. (1990). "Reducing Adverse Reaction to Stress in the Workplace: Psychology's Expanding Role." *American Psychologist,* 45(10): 1137–1141; James, K. (1994). "Social Identity, Work Stress, and Minority Workers' Health." In G. P. Keita & J. J. Hurrell (Eds.), *Job Stress in a Changing Workforce: Investigating Gender, Diversity, and Family Issues,* Washington, DC: American Psychological Association, pp. 127–145.

equity can reduce discrimination-related stress. Lastly, Blacks and other people of color are also often concentrated in occupations with higher risks of injury and death than Whites (e.g., convenience store clerk, construction worker), which contributes somewhat to shorter life expectancies.[38]

EDUCATION, EMPLOYMENT, AND EARNINGS

Education

During slavery, laws in many states prohibited teaching slaves to read or otherwise providing them with education,[39] although some Whites and many literate Blacks still did so. When slavery ended, as Blacks were faced with trying to find subsistence, they also continued trying to obtain education. For nearly 90 years after the Civil War, laws and many communities required Blacks to be educated separately from Whites. At times, no facilities for Blacks were available. Since the 1954 Supreme Court decision in *Brown v. the Board of Education of Topeka,* which outlawed the "separate but equal" educational system, marked increases in Black education have occurred. In 1940, 7.7% of Blacks and 26.1% of Whites had completed high school or college, but by 2002, 80% of Blacks and 89% of Whites had done so.[40] As shown in Figure 4.1, at the lowest education levels there are higher percentages of Blacks than Whites, while there are higher percentages of Whites than Blacks at higher education levels. These different educational levels contribute some explanation to the Black/White earnings and employment gap, but do not completely explain it.[41]

Misperception: Earnings and employment differences between Blacks and Whites are due to the lower educational attainment of Blacks.

Reality: Blacks with the same level of education as Whites are more likely to be unemployed than Whites and earn less when employed than Whites.

A comparison of education levels of Black men to Black women shows that more Black men have high school education alone (34.8%) than women (33.3%). Black women are more likely to have some college credits (28.3%) than Black men (27.3%) and to have bachelor's degrees (18% vs. 16%).[42] Black women's higher

---

[38] Sagrestano. (2004). p. 127.

[39] Pollack, B. H. (2001). "An Act Prohibiting the Teaching of Slaves to Read," *Zamani to Sasa: Readings on the Black Quest for Freedom, Identity and Power in America.* Dubuque, Iowa: Kendall/Hunt Publishing Company, pp. 107–108.

[40] http://www.census.gov/population/socdemo/education/tabA-2.pdf, accessed 11/6/04.

[41] Herring. (1999). p. 187. See also Reskin & Charles (1999) for a discussion of how and why the relationship between education and earnings and other labor market outcomes differs between Whites and other groups.

[42] Ibid.

FIGURE 4.1 ***Educational Attainment by Sex and Race (2002)***

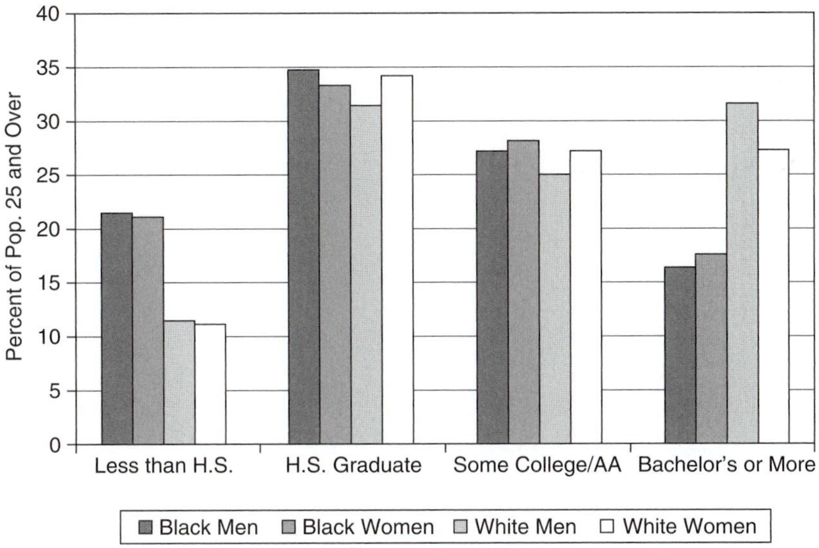

Source: McKinnon, J. (2003). "The Black Population in the United States: March 2002." U.S. Census Bureau, Current Population Reports, Series P20-541. Washington, DC.

education levels do not translate into higher earnings than those of Black men, however. Black women have higher educational levels, but still earn less, calling into question the relationship between education and earnings and the applicability of models derived using only White men as subjects. Sex, race, and ethnicity affect labor market outcomes differently for different groups; clearly Black women (as well as White women, Black men, and others of color) receive different returns to education than White men receive.[43]

Participation Rates

How likely are African Americans to be in the labor force? Table 4.2 presents actual (2002) and projected (2012) participation rates (e.g., those who are employed or seeking employment) for men and women, by race. White men have slightly higher participation rates than Black men, while Black women have slightly higher participation rates than White women. By 2012, the gap in participation between White men and Black men is projected to decrease by more than half, from 7.4 to 3.3 percentage points. On the other hand, the gap in participation between Black women and White women is projected to increase, with Black women's participation growing from 2.4 to 4.6 percentage points more than

[43] Reskin & Charles. (1999).

TABLE 4.2 ***Projected Participation Rates***

	2002 Actual		2012 Projection	
	Men	**Women**	**Men**	**Women**
All Groups	74.1	59.6	73.1	61.6
White, non-Hispanic	73.8	59.6	72.4	59.4
Black	66.4	62.0	69.1	64.0
Hispanic	80.2	57.1	79.0	58.6
Asian	75.6	57.9	77.3	61.3

Source: Civilian Labor Force Participation Rates by Sex, Age, Race, and Hispanic Origin, 1982, 1992, 2002, and Projected 2012. U.S. Department of Labor, Bureau of Labor Statistics, http://www.bls.gov/emp/emplab2002-03.htm, accessed 08/27/05.

White women. In all, relative to non-Hispanic Whites, Black men and women's workforce participation is expected to grow.

The increasing participation rate of Blacks is partially the result of gains in Blacks' attainment of higher education during the last half of the twentieth century, discussed earlier in the chapter. Increases in the relative employment and earnings of Blacks have not proportionately followed their increasing educational levels, however. For the twentieth century and in the twenty-first century thus far, unemployment levels of Blacks have been considerably higher than those of Whites.[44, 45] As shown in Table 4.3, in every category, Black unemployment is higher than those of every other racial/ethnic group at the same educational level. Black/White comparisons are most striking; Blacks are considerably more likely to be unemployed than Whites with one and sometimes two fewer levels of education. Blacks who are high school graduates are nearly twice as likely to be unemployed as White high school graduates. Blacks with at least a college degree have the same unemployment as Whites who have some college, but no degree. Blacks with some college, but no degree are more likely to be unemployed than Whites who dropped out of high school.

Earnings by educational attainment are also different for people of different racial or ethnic backgrounds. As shown in Table 4.4, for year-round, full-time workers, non-Hispanic White men, Asian men, Asian women,[46] non-Hispanic White women, Black men, Hispanic men, Black women, and Hispanic women, respectively, have the highest to the least annual earnings. The racial and gender makeup of most to least varies by educational level, but at all levels non-Hispanic White men receive the highest returns to their education. When earnings for "all males" and "all females" are combined, important earnings differences by race

[44] McKinnon. (2003).

[45] Herring. (1999).

[46] As discussed in Chapter 6, Asians' higher earnings are also partly reflective of their greater propensity to live in areas with high costs of living, such as New York, California, and Hawaii.

TABLE 4.3 ***Unemployment Level by Educational Attainment by Race (Percent of Population 25 and Over): 2003***

	Total	Men	Women	White	Black	Asian	Hispanic*
Less than H.S.	8.8	8.2	9.8	7.8	13.9	9.5	8.2
H.S. graduate	5.5	5.7	5.2	4.8	9.3	5.6	5.9
Some college, no degree	5.2	5.4	4.9	4.5	8.6	6.4	5.8
Associate degree	4.0	4.4	3.7	3.6	6.2	5.2	5.3
Bachelor's and higher†	3.1	3.2	2.9	2.8	4.5	4.4	4.1

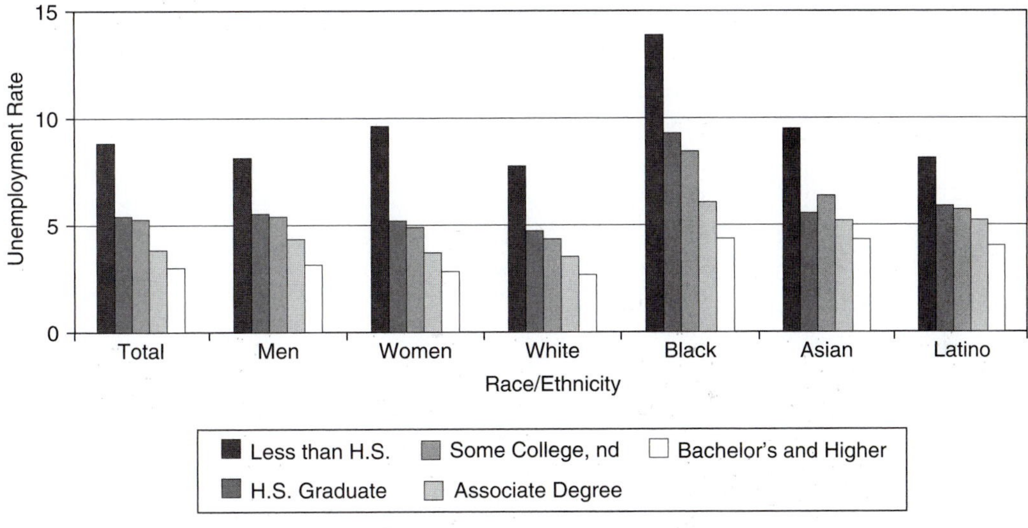

*Persons whose ethnicity is Hispanic are classified by ethnicity as well as by race.

†Bachelor's and higher includes persons with bachelor's, master's, professional, and doctoral degree.

Source: http://www.bls.gov/cps/cpsaat7.pdf, accessed 10/22/04.

and ethnicity are obscured, further supporting the need to pay attention to differences by race and ethnicity in organizational assessments. In addition, because men and Whites are more likely to be working full-time, year-round than women and minorities, annual earnings differences between men and Whites and women and minorities are greater than they appear.

RESEARCH ON THE EMPLOYMENT EXPERIENCES OF AFRICAN AMERICANS

As discussed in Focal Issue 4.2, un- and underemployment have long-term negative effects on people's outcomes. Although they are more likely to experience un- and underemployment, clearly, education, employment, and earnings of Blacks have increased markedly in the past decades. However, their returns to education, higher un- and underemployment and lower earnings suggest that Blacks still experience discrimination in organizations. In this section, we

TABLE 4.4 ***Mean Income in 2002 by Educational Attainment of Population 18 Years and Over***

		High School				Bachelor's or More	
Year-round, full-time workers	**Total**	**Not High School Graduate (<H.S.)**	**Graduate, Including GED (H.S. Grad)**	**Some College No Degree (Some Coll.)**	**Associate's Degree (AA Deg)**	**Bachelor's Degree (B.S./B.A.)**	**Master's Degree (Master's)**
All races male	$54,572	$28,350	$38,841	$47,947	$50,150	$73,139	$85,574
All races female	$37,624	$20,673	$28,496	$33,243	$35,544	$49,909	$58,914
Women's % of men's	69%	73%	73%	69%	71%	68%	69%
Non-Hispanic White male	$60,169	$32,441	$41,439	$50,558	$51,683	$76,832	$88,234
Non-Hispanic White female	$39,844	$23,016	$29,675	$35,045	$36,231	$51,283	$58,800
Women's % of men's	66%	71%	72%	69%	70%	67%	67%
Black male	$40,289	$28,073	$31,008	$40,978	$44,938	$54,655	$71,470
Black female	$32,843	$19,719	$27,111	$29,663	$32,951	$45,367	$54,844
Women's % of men's	82%	70%	87%	72%	73%	83%	77%
Asian male	$57,862	$21,937	$35,209	$44,625	$41,939	$64,336	$79,389
Asian female	$41,006	$20,793	$24,657	$31,751	$35,292	$47,692	$59,890
Women's % of men's	71%	95%	70%	71%	84%	74%	75%
Hispanic male (any race)	$34,822	$25,374	$32,794	$39,659	$46,018	$53,067	$66,781
Hispanic female (any race)	$28,062	$18,889	$24,058	$27,938	$32,668	$44,475	$65,953*
Women's % of men's	81%	74%	73%	70%	71%	84%	99%
Income as a Percent of Non-Hispanic White Men's Income							
Non-Hispanic White male	100%	100%	100%	100%	100%	100%	100%
All males	91%	87%	94%	95%	97%	95%	97%
Non-Hispanic White females	66%	71%	72%	69%	70%	67%	67%
All females	63%	64%	69%	66%	69%	65%	67%
Black males	67%	87%	75%	81%	87%	71%	81%
Black females	55%	61%	65%	59%	64%	59%	62%
Asian males	96%	68%	85%	88%	81%	84%	90%
Asian females	68%	64%	60%	63%	68%	62%	68%
Hispanic males	58%	78%	79%	78%	89%	69%	76%
Hispanic females	47%	58%	58%	55%	63%	58%	75%

Table 4.4 ***Continued***

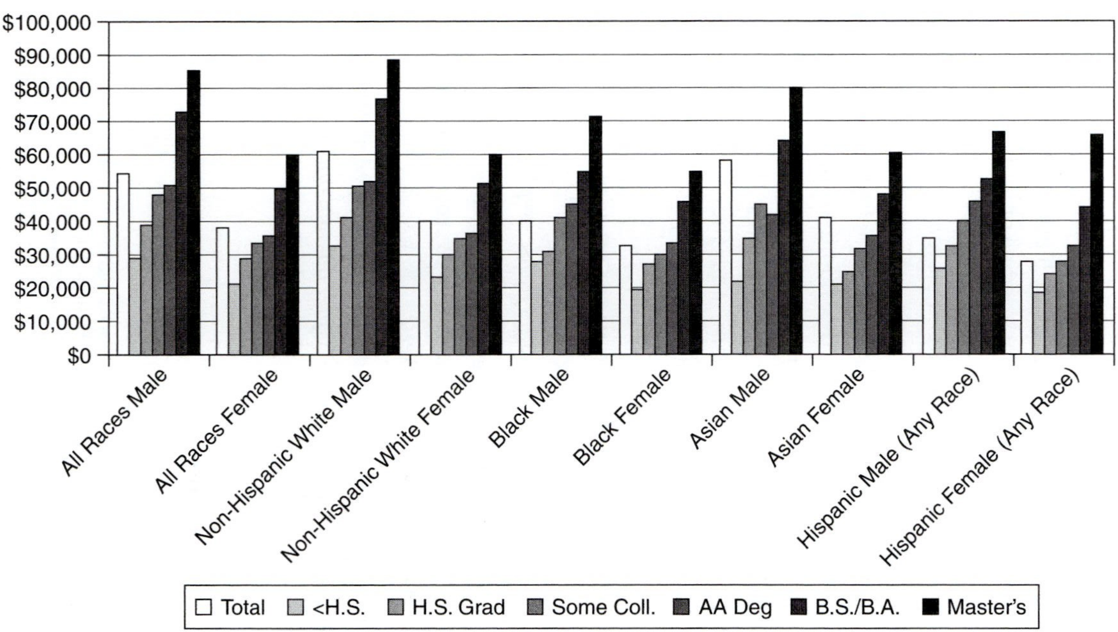

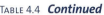

*Large standard error ($13,004) explains high mean wage for Hispanic woman with master's degree. Median of $46,255 is more representative.

Note: Percentage calculations are the author's.

Source: Table 8. Income in 2002 by Educational Attainment of the Population 18 Years and Over, by Age, Sex, Race Alone, And Hispanic Origin: 2003. U.S. Census Bureau, Men's data: http://www.census.gov/population/socdemo/education/CPS2003/tab08-2.xls, accessed 10/05/05. Women's data: http://www.census.gov/population/socdemo/education/CPS2003/tab08-3.xls, accessed 10/05/05.

Focal Issue 4.2 *Un- and Underemployment, What Do They Really Mean?*

Unemployment levels published by the U.S. government understate the true levels of employment and completely exclude people who are "underemployed." Using the official definition, an individual must be actively seeking work and receiving unemployment benefits to be included in the "official" unemployment rate. Thus, workers who "have been discouraged to the point of having given up searching for employment" or who have run out of unemployment benefits are not included in the official rates.[47] This presents a more positive political picture, but belies true employment levels.

Researchers have described the underemployed as: discouraged workers; those working part-time, temporary, or intermittent employment but desiring regular full-time work; those working for lower wages than their skills would imply, or in positions requiring considerably lower skills than they possess; and those involuntarily working outside their fields (e.g., "occupational mismatch"). Underemployment negatively affects workers in a variety of ways. Earnings and benefits are lower when working part-time, temporary, or intermittent employment; health benefits, retirement, vacation, and other benefits are less likely and, if they exist, less lucrative in such jobs. Working for lower wages than one's skills would negatively affect workers immediately, as well as resulting in receipt of lower employer contributions to their retirements, 401k, or other salary-driven benefits. Involuntarily working outside one's field can erode skills and decrease competitiveness for future opportunities. In addition to the aforementioned negative effects, those who are underemployed experience decrements to their self-esteem, job attitudes, and likelihood of appropriate later employment.[48]

As discussed earlier in the chapter, for most of the twentieth century and continuing into the present, unemployment rates of Blacks have been considerably more than those of Whites. In 2003, 4.5% of Blacks and 2.8% of Whites with a Bachelor's degree or more were considered "officially" unemployed. Blacks are also more likely to be underemployed than Whites are.[49] Given the discouraging effects of employment discrimination and underemployment, one could speculate about the numbers of underemployed, well-educated Blacks who are missing from the official employment figures, the negative ramifications for them, and the opportunities missed for prospective employers.

Questions to Consider

1. ***How can underemployment affect the quality of a person's future employment? Explain.***
2. ***Why might organizations wish to seek appropriate skills and educational placement for all workers?***
3. ***In addition to Blacks, what other groups experience higher un- and underemployment than dominant groups?***

---

[47] Herring, C., & Fasenfest, D. (1999); Tipps, H. C., & Gordon, H. A. (1985). "Inequality at Work: Race, Sex, and Underemployment." *Social Indicators Research*, 16: 35–49; Ullah, P. (1987). "Unemployed Black Youths in a Northern City." In D. Fryer & P. Ullah (Eds.), *Unemployed People*, Milton Keynes, UK: Open University Press, pp. 110–147; Winefield, A. H., Winefield, H. R., Tiggemann, M., & Goldney, R. D. (1991). "A Longitudinal Study of the Psychological Effects of Unemployment and Unsatisfactory Employment on Young Adults." *Journal of Applied Psychology*, 76: 424–431. See also "How the Government Measures Unemployment," http:///www.bls.gov/cps/cps_htgm.htm, accessed 11/29/05.

[48] Ibid. See also Tipps & Gordon. (1985); Ullah. (1987); Winefield et al. (1991).

[49] Herring & Fasenfelt. (1999); Tipps & Gordon. (1985); Ullah. (1987).

consider empirical research evidence of access and treatment discrimination, name-based discrimination (a form of access discrimination), and other overt racial discrimination in organizations. **Access discrimination** occurs when people are denied employment opportunities, or "access" to jobs, based on their race, sex, age, or other factors. **Treatment discrimination** occurs when people are employed, but are treated differently once employed, receiving fewer job-related rewards, resources, or opportunities than they should receive based on job-related criteria.[50] As discussed in Chapter 2, both access and treatment discrimination are prohibited by Title VII of the Civil Rights Act; however, research and discrimination settlements indicate both still occur.

Access Discrimination

African Americans frequently experience access discrimination based on stereotypes, prejudice, stated instructions to discriminate, or even because their names "sound Black." Several recent field studies using equally matched Black and White applicants have found evidence of access discrimination in a variety of settings. Multiple audit studies using Black, Latino, and White job seekers with matched educational credentials (fields of study, degrees, schools attended, and grade point averages) found that Blacks and Latinos fared worse than White applicants about 20% of the time.[51] In another study using well-matched applicants, Marianne Bertrand and Sendhil Mullainathan from the University of Chicago and MIT, respectively, found that applicants with names that are common to Blacks, such as Lakisha and Jamal, were 50% less likely to be called for interviews than were applicants with names that are common to Whites, such as Emily and Greg. Additional "Black-sounding" names used in the study were Aisha, Keisha, Tamika, Tanisha, LaToya, Kenya, LaTonya, Ebony, Darnell, Hakim, Jermaine, Kareem, Leroy, Rasheed, Tremayne, and Tyrone. Other "White-sounding" names used were Allison, Anne, Carrie, Jill, Laurie, Kristen, Meredith, Sarah, Brad, Brendan, Geoffrey, Brett, Jay, Matthew, Neil, and Todd.

Applicants with "White-sounding" names needed to send out 10 resumes to receive one callback, while those with "Black-sounding" names had to send out 15 resumes; a 50% gap in callbacks. Having higher quality resumes (e.g., more credentials) improved Whites' likelihood of being called, but did not increase callbacks for Blacks. In other words, increasing credentials did not matter if the applicant had a "Black-sounding" name. Having a White-sounding name resulted

---

[50] Greenhaus, J. H., Parasuraman, S., & Wormley, W. M. (1990). "Effects of Race on Organizational Experiences, Job Performance Evaluations, and Career Outcomes" *Academy of Management Journal,* 33:64–86.

[51] Bendick, M., Jr., Jackson, C., & Reinoso, V. (1994). "Measuring Employment Discrimination through Controlled Experiments." *Review of Black Political Economy,* 23: 25–48; Bendick, M., Jr., Jackson, C., Reinoso V., & Hodges L. (1991). "Discrimination against Latino Job Applicants: A Controlled Experiment." *Human Resource Management,* 30: 469–484; Fix, M., & Struyk, R. (Eds.) (1991). *Clear and Convincing Evidence*. Washington, DC: The Urban Institute.

in as many additional callbacks as having 8 more years of experience on a resume.[52] Along with the Bertrand and Mullainathan research described above, several other audit studies have found evidence that people with distinctively Black names were less likely to be called for interviews.

Roland Fryer and Steven Levitt of Harvard University investigated patterns in naming among Blacks in California between 1961 and 2000.[53] During that time, the appearance of "distinctively Black" names increased markedly and Fryer and Levitt sought to investigate factors associated with such naming practices. In a carefully constructed study, in addition to the distinctiveness of the name, Fryer and Levitt found that those with distinctively Black names are more likely to come from low socio-economic backgrounds.[54] Fryer and Levitt proposed that employers may be exercising **statistical discrimination,** using distinctiveness of names as proxies for potential productivity or skills of applicants with such names. Although they were unable to empirically assess that possibility, the relationship between having a "Black name" and low socioeconomic status was clearly indicated by their data. Because the resumes in Bertrand and Mullainathan's study were identical (e.g. in credentials) aside from the applicants' names, statistical discrimination based on the names would result in increased recruitment and selection costs along with unfair treatment of applicants with "Black names."

In one of the few investigations that have focused on the effects of firm size and applicant race on hiring practices, Harry Holzer, former chief economist with the U.S. Department of Labor, investigated employers in four large cities across the United States: Atlanta, Boston, Detroit, and Los Angeles.[55] Size of companies was broken into categories of 1–14, 15–49, 50–99, and 100–499, and over 500 employees. Holzer found that small companies hire much smaller percentages of Black employees than larger companies do, and that they hire a significantly smaller percentage of the Blacks who apply. Holzer, now a professor at Georgetown University, suggested that large firms are more likely to have affirmative action programs and to have experienced compliance reviews, which may account for some of these differences. Larger firms are also more likely to have formal hiring practices, which leave less room for subjective and possibly discriminatory employment decisions. Holzer noted that the demand for Black labor in the United States would be at least 40% higher if Blacks' hiring rates in small companies were similar to their hiring rates in large firms. Recall that Blacks'

---

[52] Bertrand, M., & Mullainathan, S. (2004, June). "Are Emily and Greg More Employable than Lakisha and Jamal? A Field Experiment on Labor Market Discrimination." Working paper. http://post.economics.harvard.edu/faculty/mullainathan/papers/emilygreg.pdf, accessed 11/13/04.

[53] Fryer, R. G., & Levitt, S. D. (2004). "The Causes and Consequences of Distinctively Black Names." *Quarterly Journal of Economics,* 119(3): 767–804.

[54] Ibid., p. 787.

[55] Holzer, H. (1998). "Why Do Small Establishments Hire Fewer Blacks Than Larger Ones?" *Journal of Human Resources,* 33(4): 896–915.

unemployment levels are consistently about two times those for Whites; employer hiring practices may provide some explanations for these differences.

In neither of the studies using testers, mailed in resumes, nor analyses of other data would applicants be aware that access discrimination had occurred. All that applicants would know is they were not called for an interview or were not hired. This reinforces the idea noted in Chapter 2 that those who experience discrimination do not generally sue—many times they do not even know that discrimination has occurred. Research Translation 4.1 reports on a study of access discrimination documenting employers' preferences for White convicted felons over Blacks with no criminal record.

Treatment Discrimination

Even though there is considerable evidence of access discrimination, and Blacks have higher unemployment than comparably educated Whites, clearly many Blacks are employed and have stable employment histories. How do Blacks fare once they have obtained employment? Does equal opportunity step in after employment and result in fairness in earnings, promotions, job placement, and other rewards?

To stringently examine race effects in performance ratings, Kraiger and Ford performed a meta-analysis of research conducted over a 15-year period. A *meta-analysis* is a statistical method of integrating results of findings from multiple studies that address similar hypotheses. There were 74 studies conducted in the field and in the laboratory included in the meta-analysis. All of the studies had White managers, but only 14 had Black managers. Results indicated that being the same race as one's supervisor resulted in higher ratings for employees; both Black and White raters gave significantly higher ratings to employees who were similar to them in race. As Whites are significantly more likely to be managers than Blacks are, the "similarity" effect tends to advantage White employees and disadvantage Black employees. Kraiger and Ford also found that these race effects were substantial in the field, but not in the lab. Training had no effect in reducing same-race bias, but race effects did decline as the percentage of Blacks in the workgroup increased.[56]

In another study that included several work-related outcome variables, Greenhaus, Parasuraman, and Wormley investigated whether treatment discrimination negatively affects the job satisfaction, career progress, performance evaluations, and organizational experiences of Blacks.[57] Greenhaus and his colleagues surveyed 828 Black and White managers and their immediate supervisors from the communications, banking, and electronics industries. The sample

[56] Kraiger, K., & Ford, J. K. (1985). "A Meta-Analysis of Ratee Race Effects in Performance Ratings." *Journal of Applied Psychology,* 70: 56–65.

[57] Greenhaus et al. (1990).

Research Translation 4.1 *Which Do Employers Prefer—a White Convicted Felon or a Black Person with a Clean Record?*

In her dissertation, Dr. Devah Pager, now a professor at Princeton University, investigated the effects of a criminal record and race on job search outcomes. Using an audit study methodology, Dr. Pager sent pairs of well-matched applicants to apply for 350 real entry-level advertised jobs in Milwaukee, Wisconsin. There were two teams of Black "applicants" and two teams of White "applicants" who were all well-groomed, well-spoken, college-educated men with identical resumes. The only difference was that one member of each pair said that he had served an 18 month prison sentence for possession of cocaine.

Numerous other studies have reported racial disparities between equally qualified Blacks and Whites (or more qualified Blacks) in access to credit, insurance, and employment, so Dr. Pager expected some disparities. The callback rate for Blacks with a criminal record was 5%, and for Blacks with no record, the callback rate was 14%. The callback rate for Whites without a record was 34%, more than twice the rate for Blacks without a record—a disturbing, but not surprising result. In what surprised even Dr. Pager, although the differences did not reach statistical significance, the callback rate for Whites with a criminal record was 17%—more than the 14% callback rates for Blacks without a criminal record. Because one would expect Blacks without a record to be preferred over ex-criminals of any race, although statistically not different, these findings do speak volumes.

Whites without a criminal record, Whites with a criminal record, Blacks without a criminal record, and Blacks with a criminal record were most to least likely to be called back. Differences were most pronounced between Whites without a criminal record and Blacks with a criminal record. Within group differences indicate that the ratio of callbacks for nonoffenders relative to ex-offenders is 2 to 1 for Whites and nearly 3 to 1 for Blacks; the negative effect of having a criminal record on employment opportunities is 40% larger for Blacks than for Whites.

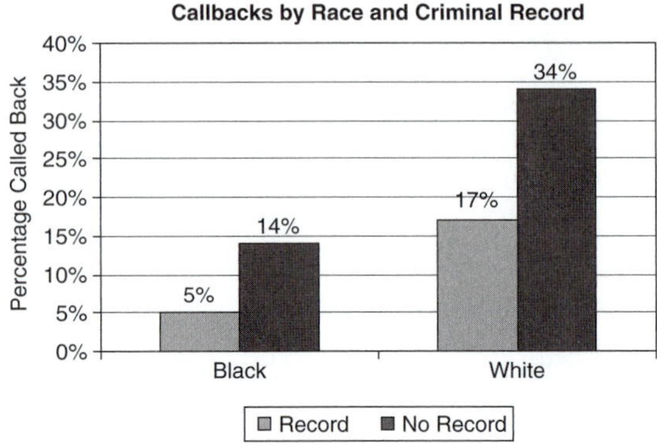

Detailed reports about the testers' interactions with the managers provide interesting insights. In one case, the hiring manager told the White tester with a record that he liked hiring people who had just been released from prison as they tended to be harder workers and motivated to avoid returning to prison. Another employer discouraged the White tester without a record from applying for a cleaning job because of the "dirty work" required, but offered the job to the White tester with the criminal record on the spot. In three cases, Black testers were asked before even submitting their applications whether they had a criminal history, but no Whites were asked whether they had a criminal history up front.

Questions to Consider

1. ***The order of most to least preferred were Whites without a record (34%), Whites with a record (17%), Blacks without a record (14%), and Blacks with a record (5%). What are the callback rates***

for each group that you would have estimated prior to reading this case?

2. The testers in these studies were well-educated, well-spoken applicants. Speculate on what results would be for applicants with less education and lower communication abilities.

Source: Pager, D. (2003). "The Mark of a Criminal Record." *American Journal of Sociology,* 108: 937–975.

of managers was matched in terms of age, company tenure, job function, and organizational level; 45% of the managers were Black and 55% were White. More than 93% of the supervisors to whom the managers reported were White. Managers responded to questions about their job and career satisfaction, job discretion, perceived organizational acceptance or isolation, supervisory support, and mentoring. Their supervisors responded to questions about the managers' promotability and job performance. Results indicated that Black managers were more likely to have reached a career plateau (e.g., to have stayed in one position without being promoted), to report less job discretion and less organizational acceptance, and were more likely to receive less favorable assessments of promotability from their supervisors. Overall, supervisors rated the performance of Blacks lower than the performance of Whites—4% of the variance in performance ratings was explained by the race of the manager. Because wages are closely tied to performance evaluations (as they should be when the evaluations are accurate and unbiased), lower performance evaluations of Blacks may help explain their lower wages, particularly when differences accumulate over time.

In addition to the treatment discrimination identified by researchers, discrimination in actual companies has resulted in formal lawsuits against many well-known companies. In November 2000, the Coca-Cola Company settled a lawsuit that alleged systematic discrimination against Black employees, agreeing to a record $192.5 million settlement. Black employees alleged that Blacks were consistently at the bottom of pay scales, earning $26,000 per year less than Whites in comparable jobs, and that Blacks were denied promotions they deserved.[58] In another major settlement, Texaco agreed to a $140 million cash settlement to compensate Black plaintiffs in a class action lawsuit. The Texaco case was particularly hard to defend because Texaco executives made disparaging racial comments that were recorded on tape and released to the public during the lawsuit. Some other well-known companies that have been involved in race discrimination lawsuits include: IBM, Southwestern Bell, CBS, Ford Motor Company, Anheuser Busch, Du Pont, and Lucky Stores.[59]

[58] Winter, G. (2000, November 17). "Coke Bias Settlement Sets Record." *The Dallas Morning News,* New York Times News Service.

[59] Wright, P., Ferris, S. P., Hiller, J. S., & Kroll, M. (1995). "Competitiveness through Management of Diversity: Effects on Stock Price Valuation." *Academy of Management Journal,* 38: 272–288.

Although these cases are cited for informational purposes, we reiterate that most employees who experience discrimination do not sue.[60] As discussed in Chapter 2, obtaining a "right to sue" letter or EEOC support in litigation is unlikely except for those claims most likely to have a large impact, such as class action cases against large corporations. Further, most employees who feel they have experienced treatment discrimination may have little or no concrete data to substantiate such discrimination, nor resources to support a lengthy litigation, even if they had evidence of discrimination. The negative outcomes resulting from access and treatment discrimination, including lowered individual and organizational performance and productivity, should provide a greater impetus to avoid discrimination than fears of litigation.

Since Title VII has been in effect for more than 40 years, a legitimate question is why overt discrimination, along with disparities in occupational attainment, employment, and income between Blacks and Whites remain. What explanations exist for such persistent discrimination? New forms of racism may help explain these issues.

New racism. As discussed in Chapter 2, Art Brief, a professor at Tulane University, uses the term "new racism" to describe beliefs that racism is a thing of the past and that Blacks have attained excessive, unfair gains through programs such as affirmative action. New racists, according to Brief, do not display overt racism, but, when provided with a rationale, use business justifications as excuses to deny employment to Blacks. In a laboratory study, Brief and his colleagues investigated whether explicit instructions from "company officials" to discriminate against Blacks would be followed. The business justifications provided were that the company president believed it was important to 1) continue the good relationships built by the previous (White) job incumbent, 2) keep the marketing teams as homogeneous as possible, or 3) match the newly hired employee to the race of the majority of clients in the assigned territory base. Study participants who had high scores on the new racism scale were likely to avoid hiring qualified Blacks when provided with this "business justification." In nearly 40% of the cases, those participants chose an *unqualified White* instead of a *qualified Black*.

These findings contrast sharply with perceptions that Blacks who are not qualified obtain jobs via affirmative action. In contrast, African Americans often perceive they must be clearly more qualified than Whites to obtain a job or a promotion. Consider the use of the term "qualified minorities," compared to the use of the term "qualified Whites." How frequently, if ever, is the latter

[60] That an organization has been sued for discrimination does not indicate that discrimination and resistance to diversity is an organization-wide pervasive problem; many of the organizations listed have recognized diversity programs.

term used? Whereas Whites are often assumed to be qualified, Blacks are often assumed not to be qualified.[61]

The glass ceiling and walls. The **glass ceiling** is an invisible barrier that prevents women, people of color, and people with disabilities from progressing beyond a certain level in organizations.[62] Although many perceive that the glass ceiling begins near top management or at executive levels, empirical evidence shows the ceiling is actually quite low, beginning in first line management and supervisory levels and continuing to the top.[63] At the chief executive officer level, African Americans are almost nonexistent, ranging between three and six individuals (men only) within the last decade.

Glass walls are horizontal barriers that confine minorities and women to certain positions within organizations. Blacks are often concentrated in positions such as communications, community relations, and human resources, rather than marketing, finance, and operations, which are more likely to lead to higher level executive jobs. Typically staff instead of line positions, these positions do not involve finance or key decision making, and thus prevent Blacks from obtaining the breadth of skills needed to advance past certain levels.[64]

Negative health effects of discrimination. In the previous section, we reported research findings indicating that Blacks may have more negative organizational experiences and lower job satisfaction than Whites. Egregious racial harassment at work can also negatively affect the health of Blacks. Reports of nooses (i.e., for lynching), racist graffiti, being called "boy" or asked if they eat "monkey meat," and other harassment at such reputable companies as Lockheed Martin, Northwest Airlines, Bemis, and Earl Schieb have been documented.[65] These negative experiences affect Blacks' health through hypertension and greater risks of heart attacks. Lack of autonomy and advancement, job segregation, negative stereotyping, and perceived discrimination have been associated with stress and

---

[61] For a discussion of how Blacks and women who are "equally qualified" as Whites and men are less likely to be hired, see Browne, I. (Ed.) (1999), "Latinas and African American Women in the Labor Market," *Latinas and African American Women at Work: Race, Gender, and Economic Inequality,* New York: Russell Sage Foundation, p. 17.

[62] This chapter considers the effects of the glass ceiling on Blacks; see other chapters for its effects on different groups.

[63] Hurley, A. E., Fagenson-Eland, E. A., & Sonnenfeld, J. A. (1997). "Does Cream Always Rise to the Top? An Investigation of Career Attainment Determinants." *Organizational Dynamics,* 26(2): 65–71; Maume, D. J., Jr. (1999, November). "Glass Ceilings and Glass Escalators: Occupational Segregation and Race and Sex Differences in Managerial Promotions." *Work and Occupations,* 26(4): 483–509; Maume, D. A., Jr. (2004). "Is the Glass Ceiling a Unique Form of Inequality?" *Work and Occupations,* 31(2): 250–274.

[64] Collins, S. M. (1997). "Race Up the Corporate Ladder: The Dilemmas and Contradictions of First-Wave Black Executives." In C. Herring (Ed.), *African Americans and the Public Agenda,* Thousand Oaks, CA: Sage Publications, pp 87–101.

[65] Bernstein, A. (2001, July 31). "Racism in the Workplace." *Business Week Online;* The U.S. Equal Employment Opportunity Commission, Litigation Settlements—August 2004, http://www.eeoc.gov/litigation/settlements/settlement08-04.html, accessed 12/08/04; The U.S. Equal Employment Opportunity Commission Litigation Settlements, September—2004, http://www.eeoc.gov/litigation/settlements/settlement09-04.html.

high blood pressure for Blacks. These health factors make diversity issues even more important for African Americans and their employers.[66]

African American Women at Work: Negative Perceptions and Erroneous Stereotypes

Misperceptions about employment experiences of women of color, particularly Black women, abound. On one hand, Black women are often perceived as being unwilling to work, preferring instead to draw welfare to support their many children. On the other hand, some perceive that Black women are more highly desired by employers than White women or Black men because they are counted under affirmative action programs as being minority and female (e.g., "two-fers"). Analyses of participation rates and income of Black women shed some light on the inaccuracies of both views of Black women and work.

Black women in the United States have been more likely to work outside the home than women of all other groups virtually throughout history, sharply contrasting perceptions that they do not work. Black women are 7.6% of the total workforce.[67] As we have discussed, Black women have the highest rates of participation (followed by White, Asian, and Hispanic women). In part, Black women's higher participation rates reflect their greater likelihood to be unmarried than other women and their greater likelihood of being dependent upon their own earnings for subsistence than married women. In addition, when Black women are married, they are more likely to be employed because of the lower earnings of their husbands when compared with White men.

Misperceptions about Black women's propensity to miss work because of being "single mothers" of many children also disadvantage Black women. Irene Browne and Ivy Kennelly's investigation of the effects of stereotypes on Black women's employment experiences found that employers' negative perceptions about Black women persisted despite evidence contradicting those perceptions. They found that employers expected Black women to miss work more because of their children. When they did not and were reliable workers, employers attributed this to being "desperate" for income rather than to their having a "true work ethic."[68]

---

[66] Mays, V. M., Coleman, L. M., & Jackson, J. S. (1996). "Perceived Race-Based Discrimination, Employment Status, and Job Stress in a National Sample of Black Women: Implications for Health Outcomes." *Journal of Occupational Health Psychology,* 1: 319–329.

[67] Women of color make gains in employment and job status: Stubborn patterns persist among African American, Hispanic, Asian, and Native American Women, http://www.eeoc.gov/press/7-31-03a.html, accessed 06/17/05.

[68] Browne, I., & Kennelly, I. (1999). "Stereotypes and Realities: Images of Black Women in the Labor Market." In I. Browne (Ed.), *Latinas and African American Women at Work: Race, Gender, and Economic Inequality,* New York: Russell Sage Foundation, pp. 302–326.

Misperception: Blacks have considerably more children than Whites have.

Reality: Birth rates for Black and White women are 2.1 and 1.7, respectively; individual Black and White women are likely to both have about 2 children.

A contrasting perception about Black women is that they are preferred by employers because of their double-minority status. If accurate, one might expect income and occupational status advantages for Black women when compared with White women and men of color. Data do not support such advantages, however. As shown in Table 4.4, Black women (who are more likely to work than other women), along with Latinas (who are least likely to be employed), have the lowest earnings among women. Black women's earnings range from 70% to 87% of Black men's earnings, depending on the education level.

What is a Black woman to do about these disparities? Several individual strategies and occupational decisions can help Black women increase their individual earnings. First, because sex and race segregation combine to lower Black women's wages,[69] actively seeking a male-dominated job and avoiding a racially segregated position or firm would likely increase educational return on investment (EROI). Next, additional education itself will not increase EROI, but earnings themselves clearly increase with additional education. For an individual Black woman, the more than $28,000 average additional dollars earned for a Master's degree compared with a high school degree would double her income. Any degree past the high school degree would increase earnings. Although additional years of schooling may be costly, a lifetime of considerably higher earnings would make it a good investment. Choose the best school affordable and make the best grades possible.

Black women should also consider working for unionized and/or affirmative action firms. In 2000, Black women who worked for unionized firms earned nearly 40% more than Black women who worked for nonunionized firms.[70] Blacks and women who work for affirmative action firms have higher earnings and are more likely to work in higher status positions (e.g., professional, managerial, or technical) than those who work for non-affirmative action firms.[71] Finally, negotiate salary offers, rather than accepting the first offer made[72]; even a modest increase in one's starting salary builds over time. Use federal,

[69] Reskin, B. F. (1999). "Occupational Segregation by Race and Ethnicity among Women Workers." In I. Browne (Ed.), *Latinas and African American Women at Work: Race, Gender, and Economic Inequality,* New York: Russell Sage Foundation, pp. 183–204.

[70] National Committee on Pay Equity, http://www.pay_equity.org/PDFs/BLACKWMN2000d.pdf, accessed 10/22/04.

[71] Herring, C. (1997). "African Americans, the Public Agenda, and the Paradoxes of Public Policy: A Focus on the Controversies Surrounding Affirmative Action." In C. Herring (Ed.), *African Americans and the Public Agenda: The Paradoxes of Public Policy,* Thousand Oaks: Sage, pp. 3–26.

[72] See Chapter 9 for evidence of women's reluctance to negotiate salary offers compared to men and their lower success rates when negotiating.

state, and local governments, professional organizations, and Web sites such as http://www.salary.com for information on salary ranges by education and experience. Be well aware of and confident about your abilities and worth, and do not be afraid to negotiate. While these measures would not address systemic issues associated with race and sex-based employment inequities, increases in earnings would make a difference for individual women and their families as well as providing greater opportunities to effect broader changes.

Entrepreneurship is also an option that many women and people of color are pursuing in the face of limited opportunities and discrimination. Entrepreneurship allows for flexibility, leadership, autonomy, and the ability to provide a diversity-friendly workplace for others. Cathy Hughes, founder of Radio One, is a successful Black female entrepreneur, as discussed in Individual Feature 4.2.

Discrimination against Customers

The previous sections document applicant and employee discrimination that have negative organizational implications for diversity, including decrements to creativity, resource acquisition, problem solving, and flexibility. Clearly, unemployment and low earnings have negative effects on individual Blacks as well. If such employee discrimination becomes widely known, it may also have negative implications for an organization's ability to market to diverse customer groups through negative publicity and boycotts. A more direct negative effect on organizations' ability to market to Blacks occurs when discrimination against customers exists. The Adams Mark hotels, Dillard's, Denny's, Shoney's, Cracker Barrel, Bloomingdale's, and Eddie Bauer have been charged with discrimination against Black customers. Allegations include making unfounded accusations of theft, unauthorized physical searches, being ignored, refusals of service, and/or inordinate wait times for service.[73]

Two beliefs appear to be driving discrimination against Black customers: (1) that Blacks are more likely to be shoplifters, and (2) that Blacks are less likely to have money to spend. Profiling potential shoplifters using demographic characteristics is simply not a good practice; there is no "typical" shoplifter.[74] Shoplifters vary in race, sex, age, and socio-economic status (as is apparent when successful actors are convicted of shoplifting). Rather than watching Blacks and ignoring everyone else, a more effective approach would be to monitor suspicious behavior, such as wearing heavy clothing when it is warm, looking around quickly, or having a baby stroller, but no baby. Lastly, Blacks in the United States earn more

[73] See Harris, A., Henderson, G., & Williams, J. (2005). "Courting Customers: Assessing Consumer Racial Profiling and Other Marketplace Discrimination." *Journal of Public Policy & Marketing,* 24(1): 163–171.

[74] Klemke, L. (1982). "Exploring Juvenile Shoplifting." *Sociology and Social Research,* 67: 59–75; Lo, L. (1994). "Exploring Teenage Shoplifting Behavior." *Environment and Behavior,* 26(5): 613–639.

Individual Feature 4.2 *Cathy Hughes, Successful Entrepreneur*

Catherine Liggins Hughes, founder of Radio One, has been called "Ms. Radio," and is referred to as "the most powerful woman in the industry." Her passion for radio, persistence, and creativity have all contributed to her tremendous success. During her lengthy career in the radio industry, Ms. Hughes has performed a variety of jobs, including hiring disc jockeys, hosting a talk show, selling advertising, and answering the phones.

At 22, Hughes took her first job in radio at KOWH, a Black radio station in Omaha, Nebraska, her hometown. In 1972, Hughes began working at Howard University, in Washington, D.C., where she headed sales at WHUR radio station. In her first year, the station's revenues increased more than ten-fold, from $250,000 to $3 million. The once ailing WHUR rose from number 38 to number 3 in the market. In 1978, Hughes began transforming another D.C. station, WYCB-AM. Although WYCB had been off the air for 12 years, Hughes' work made it succeed as the first 24-hour gospel station in the country; a format that is now widely emulated.

In 1980, after her achievements with those two stations, Hughes began trying to buy WOL-AM, a station that was in trouble with the Federal Communications Commission. Her first 32 attempts to obtain financing were unsuccessful until a woman newly hired at Chemical Bank as a loan officer agreed to lend Hughes $600,000 of the $1,500,000 she needed. Venture capitalists provided the rest of the funding, and Cathy's ownership of radio stations had begun.

As with many successful entrepreneurs, the road to success for Hughes was paved with financial difficulties, including losing her home and car, selling personal possessions to meet the company's debt payments, and, of course, very hard work. For a while, Hughes and her son, Alfred C. Liggins, III, lived in the radio station, adding a shower to one of the offices and cooking on a hot plate. She eventually turned one of the station's offices into an apartment, making her available 24 hours per day.

Her work at WOL paid off, and once the station was profitable, Hughes began buying more stations in the Baltimore-Washington area. Between 1987 and 1995 she acquired WMMJ-FM, WWIN-AM and FM, and WKYS-FM. Hughes continued buying radio stations, while also still working as a talk-show host. In May 1999, Radio One raised $172 in an initial public offering, and Hughes became the first African American woman to head a publicly traded company. Shares opened at $24 and have traded as high as $97 in what is now the 16th largest media company in the United States. With personal wealth near $300 million, Hughes and her son retain 71% of Radio One voting stock.

Hughes is also a leader in the Black community, addressing social, political, and financial issues, providing employment opportunities, and mentoring others. She considers providing opportunities for others an important aspect of her profession as a broadcast entrepreneur. Radio One has over 1,500 Black broadcasters. *Fortune Magazine* has rated Radio One as one of the 100 Best Companies to Work.

Questions to Consider

1. ***What factors do you think most strongly contributed to Hughes' success in radio?***
2. ***Why do you think the loan officer at Chemical Bank took a chance on Hughes?***
3. ***In addition to rating Radio One highly, what else does*** Fortune Magazine ***have to say about working at Radio One? Investigate.***

Source: Norment, L. (1999). "Cathy Hughes, Ms. Radio." *Ebony Magazine*, 55(7): 100, 4 p, 7c; Cathy Hughes, http://www.mddailyrecord.com/top100w/hughes.html, accessed 03/17/05; Soul of the City, Cathy Hughes Radio Empire Brings Sound with Spirit to Urban Listeners, http://www.blackperspective.com/pages/mag_articles/sum01_soulofthecity.html, accessed 03/17/05; "Catherine Elizabeth 'Cathy' Hughes." *Infoplease*, http://www.infoplease.com/ipea/A0880022.html, accessed 03/17/05.

than over $600 billion each year, and spend nearly $23 billion on clothes and $3 billion on electronics. Blacks treated as potential shoplifters rather than customers may choose to spend their money elsewhere.

Research Translation 4.2 describes an empirical study detailing discrimination against Blacks in new car pricing, a form of discrimination that treats Blacks as less knowledgeable customers.

Individual and Organizational Recommendations

The education, employment, EROI, and other types of discrimination presented in this chapter are discouraging but efforts to combat them do exist. Access discrimination *before* employment and treatment discrimination *after* Blacks are employed emphasize the need for organizational leaders to make diversity paramount in the post as well as pre-employment stages. Not only are efforts to recruit and hire people from diverse backgrounds important, efforts to ensure that they are treated fairly after employment are also critical to successful diversity programs. In this section, recommendations are presented for individuals and for organizations from employer/employee and customer service/sales perspectives. The recommendations presented encourage readers to make what changes they can, in whatever level and position they occupy.

Employer/Employee Perspectives

What are some successful strategies that individual Blacks control that may be employed to increase their positive employment outcomes? Suggestions made for Black women earlier in the chapter also apply to Black men. First, obtain as much education as possible. Education increases earnings and decreases the likelihood of being unemployed, across racial and ethnic groups.[75] Second, seeking employment in an affirmative action firm appears helpful. In a similar vein, given Holzer's findings about the negative relationships between establishment size and hiring of Blacks, one strategy might be to seek employment in larger firms. Larger firms are also more likely to have formal hiring programs, which are more likely to include recruiter training on attending to job-related criteria in selection processes. Avoiding race (and, for women, gender) segregated firms should also help increase earnings.

Given research evidence of access discrimination, Blacks may have to search harder, longer, and smarter for an appropriate position. While data on access, treatment, and earnings discrimination are discouraging, knowing of their existence

[75] Day, J. C., & Newburger, E. C. (2002, July). *The Big Payoff, Educational Attainment and Synthetic Estimates of Work-Life Earnings,* Washington, DC: U.S. Census Bureau.

RESEARCH TRANSLATION 4.2 *Why Pay More? Race (and Gender) Discrimination in New Car Pricing*

Do Blacks and White women pay more for cars? Many newspaper articles and hidden television investigations have suggested that they do. What does sound empirical research suggest? Ian Ayres and Peter Siegelman's study published in *The American Economic Review,* "Race and Gender Discrimination in Bargaining for a New Car," provides empirical evidence that indeed Blacks and White women are asked to pay more for new cars than White men are.

Three hundred testers who were matched in terms of age, educational level, attire attractiveness, and were trained to negotiate similarly went to Chicago-area car dealerships ostensibly to buy a car. White male, White female, Black male, and Black female testers used identical bargaining strategies after having received two days of formal training, where they memorized the bargaining script, and participated in negotiation role plays. To avoid biasing the study, the testers were told only that the study involved how sellers negotiate for cars, and did not know that other testers would also visit the same dealerships.

Findings strongly support race bias in initial pricing and negotiations. Initial offers to White male testers were about $1,000 over dealer costs. Initial offers to Black males were over $900 greater than those to White males. Initial offers to Black women and White women were $320 and $110 over initial offers to White men. Differences between initial offers for White men and Black men and women were significant at the 0.05 level; however, differences between White women and White men were not statistically significant.

Prices for all testers were lowered during negotiations, but dealer concessions exacerbated the advantages already present in White males' offers. When these concessions were factored in, a stronger pattern of discrimination in the final offers when compared with the initial offers resulted. Specifically, Black men, Black women, and White women were offered final prices of $1,100, $410, and $92, respectively, more than White men. Ayres and Siegelman point out that although Black men were quoted the highest initial offer, they received the lowest average concession. In all, testers' race and sex were strongly related to both their initial offer and the final price offered. Perhaps most disturbing, in almost 44% of cases, the *initial offers* made to White men were lower than the *final offers* made to other testers.

It is impossible to unequivocally explain why these results were found. Some suggest that sellers may expect White men to be more serious, sophisticated customers and non-Whites and White women to be less savvy customers. Others suggest that dealers may believe the latter groups have a lower average reservation price, and are willing to pay higher markups than White men. Regardless of the theoretical explanations for the disparate treatment, Blacks were offered significantly higher prices, while White women were offered higher prices that did not reach statistical significance.

Source: Ayres, I., & Siegelman, P. (1995). "Race and Gender Discrimination in Bargaining for a New Car." *The American Economic Review,* 85 (3): 304–321.

QUESTIONS TO CONSIDER

1. ***If results of this study, with dealers' names and identification, were to be released to the public, what would the likely outcome be for those dealers? How might competing dealerships capitalize on such a disclosure?***

2. ***What can individual dealers do to avoid customer discrimination, given the need to maximize profit? Is a profit maximization strategy***

consistent with discriminatory dealer behavior in the long term?

3. What are some specific steps that individual new car purchasers can take to avoid dealer discrimination in pricing?

4. If such discrimination in large purchases is common, what short and long-term economic effects are likely for Blacks and White women, who earn less than White men and for Black families, which earn less than White families?

provides understandable explanations for lack of callbacks that are not related to individual qualifications. Instead of internalizing the rejection, which may be demoralizing and result in dropping out of the labor market,[76] persistence and strategy in searching are required. Both are also completely under one's control.

Individuals of any race and ethnic background in positions of power and at any other levels can also take steps to eliminate discrimination against African Americans (and others). Knowledge of the phenomena described (access and treatment discrimination), preferences for Whites (even those with lower qualifications or for those with criminal backgrounds, etc.) that contradict popular perceptions, differential returns to education and other issues detailing inequitable treatment should provide strong impetus and information to effect change. One can view these efforts to avoid discrimination against Black employees and customers as bottom line issues. Some specific suggestions are:

- Be aware of one's own stereotypes and biases, making conscious efforts to challenge and address them.
- As a manager or supervisor with hiring or performance management authority, pay careful attention to relevant information and ignore irrelevant, race-based stereotypes.
- Remove name and sex-identifying information (e.g., use initials or numbers) from resumes and applicants in the initial stages of selection. Guard carefully for fairness afterwards.
- Question one's own decision making at all times.
- Challenge unfair behavior when it is exhibited by others. People may be intentionally discriminating, but it is also possible they are unaware of the roles of stereotypes and misperceptions in behavior and would be receptive to learn of these influences and how to combat them.

Organizational strategies may also be implemented by organizations seeking to avoid discriminating against a large portion of the population that is growing in employment participation. Organizational decision makers are subject to the same stereotypes and misperceptions as the general population. In one case, the Denver EEOC office alleged that the plant manager at Milgard Manufacturing,

[76] See Focal Issue 4.2 for information about "discouraged" workers.

a window and sliding glass company, directed the human resources staff not to hire Black workers on the production line because "Black people are lazy and move too slowly."[77] When the human resources employee responsible for screening and interviewing job applicants reported the plant manager's comments, she was harassed, taunted, and denied a full bonus. Settlement of the case cost Milgard over $3 million, including $750,000 in back pay to the human resources representative who complained and $2.35 million for Black applicants who had applied to work at Milgard's Denver facility but were not hired.

What training, control, and monitoring procedures exist to minimize the costly effects of stereotypes on organizational practices? Having formal hiring programs may reduce reliance on and attending to non-job factors in the hiring process. If a firm is not officially an affirmative action employer, investigating measures (e.g., benchmarking) used by affirmative action employers may be helpful. Where appropriate, recruitment, training and development, and other human resources programs that are used by affirmative action firms may be modeled. Internal analysis of hiring, promotion, compensation, and termination figures should be conducted regularly. Is there evidence of access or treatment discrimination? Are procedures in place and monitored to avoid selection of Whites with lower qualifications than Blacks? Attention to such a question requires careful, deliberate measures, given common views that Blacks are not as qualified as Whites.

Multiple people, from diverse backgrounds, should be involved in the selection process. From empirical research, we have learned that heterogeneous groups generate more, and better, solutions to problems; a heterogeneous selection team could be expected to do so as well. It could also be expected to be less likely to fall prey to discrimination and more likely to have members who would resist and reject stereotypes.

What are the performance evaluation, promotion, and advancement rates of employees by race, ethnicity, and sex? Do these rates appear to coincide with qualifications (education, tenure, and other attributes) of employees? Is there evidence of a glass ceiling or walls in the organization? Where are Blacks (and other non-dominant groups) employed? Are there barriers to entry of minorities and women in line positions? Are there differences among employees in rates of turnover? If so, are organizational factors, such as treatment discrimination, partly responsible for such turnover? According to Cox and Blake, this is a distinct possibility. Exit interviews may provide invaluable information. Attention to these matters may allow firms to capitalize on the advantages of having a diverse workforce while avoiding the (however unlikely) possibility of being charged with discrimination.

[77] The U.S. Equal Employment Opportunity Commission. EEOC Litigation Settlements—May 2004, http://www.eeoc.gov/litigation/settlements/settlement05-04.html, accessed 12/19/04.

Consumer/Customer Service Perspectives

From a consumer perspective, African Americans (and all consumers) would be well-advised to be savvy shoppers. Conducting thorough online and in-person searches for negotiable, high-cost consumer goods, loan rates, etc., is simply good practice. Having knowledge of fair prices and seeking out reputable organizations or those known to be diversity-friendly dealers can help decrease the likelihood of experiencing discrimination as customers. Posted, flat-price dealerships that charge the same price to all customers may be preferable. African Americans, women, and others ignored or overcharged should choose to do business elsewhere. Others with a distaste for discrimination from any racial or ethnic group may also choose to do so.

Organizational leaders should make concerted efforts to ensure all customers are treated fairly. Sales people should be trained to avoid discriminating against and stereotyping of customers. Take customer surveys (from purchasers as well as from those who shop but do not buy), and pay attention to the data gathered from them. Internal audits can determine if evidence exists of disparate treatment of customers based on demographic factors. Mystery shoppers of different races can provide valuable information. Customer complaints should also be investigated and addressed. By prioritizing and attending to these matters before problems arise, organizations can build customer loyalty, generate future business, and avoid a host of negative outcomes.

Summary

This chapter has focused on the diversity-related experiences of African Americans, who have a unique background of slavery and discrimination in the United States. African Americans in the United States vary in education, employment, and work, but share many negative employment experiences. Fewer Blacks obtain college degrees than Whites and Asians, but more than Latinos. Blacks at all education levels receive lower returns on their educational investment than Whites, particularly Black women. Blacks experience access and treatment discrimination in organizations as applicants and employees along with discrimination as customers. Negative organizational experiences are associated with negative health effects for Blacks, providing personal and organizational stimuli for continued emphasis on fairness and equity in employment for Blacks. Finally, we considered individual and organizational strategies to reduce discrimination, increase fairness and equity, and improve the climate for diversity in organizations.

Key Terms

Access discrimination — employment discrimination in which certain group are denied "access" or initial positions into organizations.

Discouraged workers — a type of underemployed workers, people who have become so discouraged about the lack of employment opportunities that they have stopped looking for jobs and dropped out of the workforce.

Glass ceiling — an invisible barrier that prevents women, minorities, and people with disabilities from advancing in organizations.

Glass walls — are horizontal barriers that confine minorities and women to certain positions within organizations.

New racism — describes beliefs that racism no longer exists and that Blacks (or other racial groups) have attained excessive, unfair gains through programs such as affirmative action, resulting in discrimination against them when opportunity or rationale to do so is provided.

Statistical discrimination — using observable characteristics (e.g., race, sex, or age, etc.) as proxies for information about the productivity of workers.

Treatment discrimination — employment discrimination that occurs after employment. Certain groups are treated differently, such as in salary growth, promotions, performance evaluations, and awards, when compared with other groups.

Underemployment — workers, who for some reason are not achieving or earning to their full potential, including discouraged workers; those working part-time, temporary, or intermittent employment but desiring regular full-time work; those working for lower wages than their skills would imply, or in positions requiring considerably lower skills than they possess; and those involuntarily working outside their fields (e.g., "occupational mismatch").

Questions to Consider

1. What factor(s) caused the experiences of European and African newcomers to the United States during the 1600s through the 1800s to be so different?
2. What does empirical research say about access and treatment discrimination against Blacks?

3a. In Brief's empirical study of "new racism," unqualified Whites were preferred over qualified Blacks. In three of the EEOC cases presented, clearly qualified Blacks were rejected for hiring or promotions (e.g., access and treatment discrimination). Bazaar Del Mundo "hired less qualified non-black applicants." The Home Depot would not promote the charging party "despite his qualifications." In the Wal-Mart case, a "less qualified non-Black employee" was promoted instead of a more qualified Black employee. What might the role of pervasive stereotypes of Blacks as unqualified play in decision makers' failure to promote clearly qualified Blacks, even those who have been working for organizations for a period and have clearly demonstrated their competencies? What can be done about this?

3b. Blacks often feel they must be considerably more qualified than Whites to obtain a job or promotion. Based on empirical research and the EEOC cases described, it appears these perceptions are accurate in some cases. What proportions of Blacks, Whites, Latinos, and Asians would you estimate to believe that Blacks have to be more qualified than Whites to obtain a promotion?

4a. In the Bertrand and Mullainathan study of name-based discrimination, applicants with "Black-sounding" names were called for interviews significantly less than those with "White-sounding" names. Speculate on what might happen to a Black applicant who had a "White-sounding" name (for example, Laurie) and was called for an interview. At what point(s) might prejudice and discrimination eliminate her from the selection process? What benefit(s) to such an applicant might accrue from being called for the interview? What might organizations do to reduce the likelihood of name-based discrimination in the selection process?

4b. Do you know any Blacks with any of the "White-sounding" names used in the study or others more commonly associated with Whites?

4c. Do you know of any Whites with any of the "Black-sounding" names used in the study or others more commonly associated with Blacks?

5a. How do you think most African American customers respond when treated unfairly in a store (for example, being passed over for service)? If an African American customer were to complain to store management about disparate treatment by an employee, what would you suggest the manager should do to retain the customer? How should the manager respond to the employee?

5b. How do you think most White customers would respond if they were served before Black customers who had arrived first in a store or restaurant? Would the White customers notice that the Black customers had been skipped? What would they do? How would they react if the Black customer complained? Have you observed (or experienced) such an event?

6. What have you learned from this chapter that is most surprising to you?

Actions and Exercises

1. Observe employment of African Americans in your community in a particular place (such as a store, restaurant, office, etc.) in which there are White employees also. What do you observe of interest to diversity in organizations?
2. Conduct library or Internet research on the negative effects of discrimination on the health and well-being of African Americans. What does this research say about this relationship? What can individual Blacks do to minimize these health effects?
3. Use a calculator to make a chart projecting the effects of discrimination in initial salaries offered to Blacks and Whites and annual salary increases for two equally qualified, college-educated new hires.
   a. Make columns for starting salaries of $30,000 and $33,000, respectively, for the Black and White new employees. Assume the Black employee earns a 4% increase per year, and the White employee earns a 6% increase per year, based on their evaluated performance.[78] What are the salary differences after 10 years? After 20 years?

[78] Recall from Greenhaus et al. (1990) and Kraiger and Ford (1985) that Blacks receive lower performance evaluations and are rated as less promotable.

b. Make another column, with the assumption that the White applicant receives promotions every 3 years, and the Black applicant is promoted every 5 years. For promotions, assume an increase of an additional 10%. What are the salary differences after 10 and 20 years given the differences in initial salaries, in increases, and in promotion rates?

c. What effects would such salary disparities have on each employee's and the employer's contributions to the employees' Social Security, tax-deferred savings plans, and retirement plans?

d. Research Translation 4.2 "Why pay more? Race (and gender) discrimination in buying a new car" considers effects of discrimination in car pricing on Blacks. Speculate on the effects of lower initial starting salaries, lower salary increases, and fewer promotions, combined with high prices for consumer goods, mortgages, and insurance on one's ability to increase wealth.

4. For your own consideration (this does not have to be shared), make a list of at least 5 common stereotypes about African Americans.

   a. Beside each stereotype, write the name of a real person who is an African American who does not fit this stereotype. Look first for a friend, family member, or yourself if applicable. If you cannot think of a person whom you know, use a public figure or celebrity.

   b. Beside each stereotype common to African Americans, write the name of a real person, preferably one whom you know, who is *not African American* who has exhibited the stereotyped characteristic.

   c. How many times did you use a friend, family member, or yourself if applicable instead of a public figure or celebrity? What is the effect of knowing someone personally, and somewhat well, who is African American in addressing stereotypes? How conscious of an effort would one have to make to avoid behaving on the basis of these stereotypes?

5. For Table 4.1, use U.S. Census Bureau data to update the most currently available population, median family income, median income for men and women working full-time year-round, poverty rate, and relevant school attendance and graduation rates for Blacks and Whites. How different are the figures for the two groups?

5 Chapter

Latinos/Hispanics

Chapter Objectives

After completing this chapter, readers should have a greater understanding of Hispanics and diversity in organizations. Readers can expect to:

- *understand the historical background and current status of Hispanics in the United States.*
- *understand the effects of higher population growth rates among Hispanics on diversity issues.*
- *examine diversity in education, participation rates, employment, and income levels among Cuban, Puerto Rican, and Mexican Hispanics in the United States.*
- *be able to discuss employment experiences of Hispanics, focusing on those of Latinas, immigrants, and managers and professionals.*
- *examine the experiences of Hispanics with police misconduct and racial profiling.*
- *discuss aspects of the growing Latino consumer market.*
- *understand individual and organizational measures that can be used to improve organizational experiences of Hispanics.*

Key Facts

The category Hispanic *includes people with different origins and those who have distinct education, income, and employment experiences in the United States.*

About 50% of Mexican Americans, 67% of Puerto Ricans, and 71% of Cubans have at least a high school diploma.

According to the U.S. census categories, Hispanics can be White, Black, Asian, American Indian, or other races.

Sixty percent of the Hispanic population in the United States is native-born. Many Hispanics are second, third, and fourth generation Americans.

Strict "English-only" rules are generally not defensible under Title VII of the Civil Rights Act.

Introduction and Overview

Hispanics are one of the fastest growing groups in the United States, and, as of July 1, 2004, there were 41.3 million Hispanics in the country. Hispanics include people from various races, such as Blacks, Whites, American Indians, and Asians whose ancestors have resided in Central and South America for generations and who are native Spanish speakers. Although many are White, Hispanics are included in the "people of color" category, further confounding race, ethnicity, color, and minority group status. Many Latinos view their race as being cultural, often variable, and contextual.[1] The fluid continuum of race for Hispanics is different from race in the United States, which may cause confusion and identity issues for Hispanic immigrants. In addition, the confounding of race with ethnicity among Hispanics sometimes creates double jeopardy, in which they experience discrimination based on skin color as well as ethnicity.

In this chapter, we consider the unique perspectives of Hispanics in the United States, recognizing their long history in the country, their struggles for civil rights, misperceptions and stereotypes about them, and their numerous contributions to diversity in organizations. As we will see, the diversity-related experiences of Hispanics vary by race, country of birth, English language fluency, and education.

Terminology

The U.S. Census Bureau describes *Hispanics* as people who identify themselves as having Mexican, Puerto Rican, Cuban, or other Spanish origin or culture, regardless of race. In this chapter, we interchange use of the Census term *Hispanic*, with *Latino* and when referring to women, we use the term *Latinas*. When reporting research or historical events, we may use the terms in the referenced publication or during the historical period, including Chicano or Chicana, Puerto Rican, Mexican or Mexican American, Cuban, or Peruvian. As much as possible, we strive for accuracy, acknowledging the great diversity among this group and people's preferences for different terms.[2] Space constraints prevent the coverage of Hispanics from all backgrounds; readers are encouraged to continue their own investigations.

History of Hispanics in the United States

This section considers the history of Mexicans, Puerto Ricans, and Cubans in the United States. These three groups, respectively, represent the largest group of Hispanic Americans (who also have the longest history in the United States), those with a clear dual-homeland and identity, and those who have been most economically successful after arriving in the United States.

Mexicans

The earliest known ancestors of Mexican Americans have a long history in what is now the United States, as indigenous people residing in the Southwest and large parts of Mexico long before the arrival of European Americans.[3] When Spaniards

[1] Rodriguez, C. (2000). *Changing Race: Latinos, the Census, and the History of Ethnicity in the United States,* New York: New York University Press.

[2] See, for example, Gutierrez, Jr., O. R. (2005). "'Hispanic' Vs. 'Latino': Why It Matters." *DiversityInc.com,* accessed 08/17/05.

[3] Saenz, R. (1999). "Mexican Americans." In A. G. Dworkin & R. J. Dworkin (Eds.), *The Minority Report* (3rd edition), Fort Worth: Harcourt Brace Publishers, pp. 209–229.

arrived in the area in 1519, the colonization of "New Spain" and conquest of the indigenous people began.[4] Intermarriages between Spaniards and indigenous women occurred, and many Mestizos were born. Cultures and religions blended over the next centuries, as New Spain fought for freedom from Spanish rule. During the same time, the Louisiana Purchase and other treaties regarding land ownership were signed with Spain. New Spain won its freedom from Spain in 1821 but disputes with the United States over Texas boundaries and rule continued. After the Mexican-American War, Mexicans residing in Texas were given the option to remain on their now U.S. land and become Americans. Many chose to remain in the country, becoming *Mexican Americans* instead of Mexicans alone.[5]

Being declared Mexican Americans did not guarantee them equal rights, however. Early on, Mexicans were classified as White for census purposes, yet they were sometimes barred from restaurants and other businesses, harassed, and lynched.[6] Between 1929 and 1939, many Mexican Americans were *repatriated,* under a program authorized by President Herbert Hoover. Estimates of the numbers of people repatriated range between 500,000 and 2 million, including many legal immigrants and U.S. citizens, who were sent to Mexico in an effort to free up jobs during the Depression. Some went voluntarily, while others were forced to go by police and other authorities, leaving homes and possessions because of the sudden and forced nature of the repatriation. Ironically, many of those repatriated had never even been to Mexico, having been born and reared in the United States.[7]

Mexicans began large-scale migration to the United States again during World War II, and many who returned learned then that they were already U.S. citizens, by birth.[8] As with many Japanese who were interned (see Chapter 6), Mexicans often did not speak of the repatriation, but continued to distrust police and government authorities. Some purposely did not speak Spanish to help avoid identification, which may explain why many of that generation still do not speak the language.[9]

Mexican children attended segregated schools and at times, they were severely punished by teachers for speaking Spanish. The well-known 1954 case of *Brown v. Topeka Board of Education* that declared segregated schools illegal was preceded, in 1946, by *Mendez v. Westminster School District in Orange County, California.*[10] In *Mendez v. Westminster,* the segregation of Mexican children into

[4] Ibid.

[5] Ibid.

[6] McLemore, D. (2004). "The Forgotten Carnage." *Dallas Morning News,* November 28. Cover story.

[7] Fox, B. (2004). "Hispanics Deported in 1931 Seek Reparations." *Dallas Morning News,* September 12, p. 33A. (Associated Press story).

[8] http://www.losrepatriados.org, accessed 08/16/05.

[9] Ibid.

[10] Wollenberg, C. (1976). *All Deliberate Speed: Segregation and Exclusion in California Schools, 1855–1975,* Berkeley, CA: University of California Press.

Mexican schools was declared illegal. The judge ruled in favor of the Mexican plaintiffs because the separate education codes in California specifically called for separation of children of Chinese, Japanese, and American Indian descent, but made no reference to Mexican children.

Despite the favorable ruling in California, many schools there remained segregated. Texas schools were also segregated, as part of the 1876 constitution. In Texas, the segregation was purposely to exclude Blacks, but resulted in the separation of Mexican children as well. In some communities, there were White, Black, and Mexican schools with the latter two being clearly "unequal."[11]

Mexicans in the United States also experienced residential segregation and segregation in public accommodations and businesses (e.g., theaters, pools). During World War II, Mexican American soldiers served valiantly, but returned to their "second-class" citizenship status on returning to the United States.[12] As did Blacks returning from war (see Chapter 4), Mexican American soldiers grew increasingly unwilling to accept such disparate treatment. A Mexican American physician, Dr. Hector Garcia, founded the G.I. Forum in an attempt to gain rights for Mexicans. The G.I. Forum worked against poll taxes (required for voting), to enroll Mexican children in schools, and to obtain medical benefits for Mexican veterans. When Felix Longoria, a soldier who had been killed in the war, was denied burial in the White cemetery in Three Rivers, Texas, the Mexican community was outraged. In response to protests of the G.I. Forum, then Senator Lyndon Baines Johnson arranged for Longoria to be buried in Arlington National Cemetery.[13]

In addition to rights of veterans, many involved in the Chicanos' quest for equality were pursuing workers' rights. Cesar Chavez (founder of the United Farm Workers' Union), Corky Gonzalez, Jose Angel Gutierrez, Dolores Huerta, and Eliseo Medina are some of the people who worked for farm workers' rights, using strikes and boycotts to reduce wage discrimination, among other benefits. The Chicano Movement emerged during the same time that strong and vocal Black, American Indian, and women's movements emerged in the 1960s and 1970s. The Chicano movement took pride in the group's culture and emphasized members' Indian and Mexican heritage, no longer viewing Chicano as having a negative connotation.[14] As we will discuss, Mexican Americans have obtained many rights, but some remain elusive, particularly for recent immigrants.

---

[11] Valencia, R. R. (2000). "Inequalities and the Schooling of Minority Students in Texas: Historical and Contemporary Conditions." *Hispanic Journal of Behavioral Sciences,* 22: 445–459.

[12] Saenz, R. (1999).

[13] Saenz, R. (1999). See also Justice for My People, the Hector Garcia story, https://justiceformypeople.org, accessed 10/8/03.

[14] Saenz, R. (1999).

Individual Feature 5.1 *Ida Castro, New Jersey Commissioner of Personnel*

Ida Castro, a native of Puerto Rico, is the New Jersey Commissioner of Personnel, the first Latina to serve in this position. She formerly served as the chair of the U.S. Equal Opportunity Commission, from 1998 to 2001, and was responsible for many accomplishments during her tenure. Castro's accomplishments as EEOC chair included: reducing the backlog of charges to a 15-year low, cutting the average processing time in half, obtaining record monetary benefits for discrimination victims, increasing litigation of systemic and egregious discrimination and harassment cases, and establishing a field office in San Juan to serve Puerto Rico and the U.S. Virgin Islands, among other notable accomplishments.[15]

Castro received her undergraduate degree from the University of Puerto Rico, and M.A. and law degrees from the Rutgers Law School in Newark. In addition to her work with the New Jersey Commissioner of Personnel and the EEOC, Castro has also served as the acting director of the Women's Bureau and deputy assistant secretary and director of the office of Workers' Compensation at the U.S. Department of Labor, where she managed an $8 billion budget.[16] She was a tenured professor at the Institute for Management and Labor Relations (IMLR) at Rutgers, where she developed and taught courses on sexual harassment, equal opportunity law, and alternative dispute resolution methods. Castro was the first Latina to earn tenure at the IMLR at Rutgers.[17]

Puerto Ricans

Puerto Ricans are Hispanics with a unique dual homeland on the U.S. mainland and Puerto Rico. Puerto Rico was seized by the United States in 1898 during the Spanish-American War. The Jones Act of 1917 extended citizenship to Puerto Ricans, who are citizens at birth, whether born in the United States or in Puerto Rico. Outside of the island, most Puerto Ricans reside in New York City, and many spend time in New York and in Puerto Rico easily navigating between the two. Puerto Ricans are diverse in race, including White, Black, and mixed race people and many are bilingual—Puerto Rico's official languages are English and Spanish. Puerto Rico has a history of slavery (abolished in 1873), racial segregation, and classism, which remain concerns for Puerto Ricans on the island and in the states today. Despite being U.S. citizens at birth, Puerto Ricans have low education and occupational attainment and high rates of unemployment and poverty. Average rates do not apply to every individual, however. As described in Individual Feature 5.1, Ida Castro, a native of Puerto Rico, is high in educational and occupational attainment. She has served as chair of the Equal Opportunity Commission, assistant director of the Women's Bureau, and the New Jersey Commissioner of Personnel.

[15] "Ida Castro Resigns from Commission." (2001). http://www.eeoc.gov/press/8-13-01.html, accessed 09/19/05.

[16] "Ida L. Castro Takes Oath as EEOC Chairwoman." (1998). http://www.eeoc.gov/press/10-23-98.html, accessed 09/19/05.

[17] "EEOC Chairwoman Castro to Deliver Commencement Address at Touro College School of General Studies". (1999). http://www.eeoc.gov/press/6-3-99-a.html, accessed 09/19/05.

Cubans

Cubans began arriving in the United States in large numbers beginning in January 1959, when Fidel Castro's government obtained power by force. Castro had promised democracy and other freedoms, but the promised benefits did not materialize. During the remainder of 1959 through the mid-1970s, Cubans began to flee political and economic instability in Cuba, and what appeared to be the beginnings of communist rule. During 1960, an estimated 60,000 Cubans fled to the United States, with at least 50% arriving in Miami.[18] By the mid-1970s, more than 500,000 Cubans had fled to the United States.[19]

Early émigrés were often wealthy or middle class and able to bring wealth and property with them as they fled. Later ones were often destitute as Castro began limiting what could be taken out of the country. Although they arrived without money or possessions, many of them were professionals, including physicians, lawyers, teachers, and engineers. Most of the Cuban refugees were White Cubans, as some Afro-Cubans feared racial unrest and discrimination that was rampant in the United States during that time. Of the relatively few Afro-Cubans who did flee Cuba, instead of remaining in Florida, most of them headed north attempting to avoid racism and unrest in the South.[20]

The U.S. government helped Cubans find a place in the U.S. society, assisting professionals with retraining and recertification, scholarships, business loans, and permanent resident status.[21] Cubans have capitalized on these unprecedented and unparalleled benefits for immigrants, becoming more financially and economically successful than all other Hispanic immigrants and than many other immigrants in U.S. history. As we will discuss, Cuban Americans have higher incomes and education levels than other Latinos and other minority group members.

Relevant Legislation

Executive orders for affirmative action apply to Hispanics, as does Title VII of the Civil Rights Act. Title VII is relevant to them because of its prohibition against race and national origin discrimination. Hispanics may be of any race, and many U.S. Hispanics are immigrants. English-only rules sometimes specifically target Hispanics, some of whom speak only Spanish. As is apparent in the selected EEOC cases below, Hispanics experience multiple forms of sometimes virulent workplace discrimination and harassment.

[18] Gay, K. (2000). *Leaving Cuba: From Pedro Pan to Elian,* Brookfield, CT: Twenty-first Century Books.

[19] Ibid.

[20] Ibid.

[21] Ibid.

Selected EEOC Settlements

English-only rules

- **EEOC v. Anchor Coin d/b/a Colorado Central Station Casino, Inc.**[22]
  No. 01-B-0564 (D. Colo. July 21, 2003)

  The Denver District Office alleged in this Title VII lawsuit that defendant, a casino located in Black Hawk, Colorado, subjected a group of Hispanic employees working in its housekeeping department to a hostile working environment based on their national origin and imposed unlawful English-only rules on Hispanic workers. In 1998, defendant's Human Resources Director instructed the Chief of Engineering, the Housekeeping Manager and other housekeeping supervisors to implement a blanket English-only language policy in the housekeeping department and to discipline any housekeeping employee, some of whom only spoke Spanish, who violated the policy. Managers chastised employees for speaking Spanish at any time and would shout "English-English-English" or "English-only" at them in the halls.

Stereotyping and retaliation

- **EEOC v. Campbell Concrete of Nevada, Inc.**[23]
  No. CV-S-03-1104-KJD-PAL (D. Nev. May 18, 2004)

  The Los Angeles District Office filed a Title VII action alleging that defendant, a concrete business, retaliated against charging party, a Hispanic female dispatcher, after she opposed practices she believed to be discriminatory against Latinos. CP and other Hispanic employees were told by their respective managers not to speak Spanish on the work premises. This directive was often accompanied by the statement, "This is America and they should learn to speak English." Other derogatory comments and actions included a supervisor's cattle call yells and whistles at Hispanic employees over a loudspeaker; asking CP whether she missed getting up late and having siestas; and asking CP if she would be having burritos for Thanksgiving. After CP complained to the HR department about the derogatory comments made to her and other Hispanic employees, she was written up for disparaging the company by making allegations of racism. Defendant then moved CP to a small, windowless office in another building, which was isolated from other workers and lacked air conditioning. CP's work received more scrutiny and, for the first time, was audited. Based on a single discrepancy, which CP claimed was the fault of information provided by a third party, defendant gave CP a negative performance evaluation and fired her the same day.

---

[22] EEOC Litigation Settlements—July 2003, http://www.eeoc.gov/litigation/settlements/settlement07-03.html, accessed 06/15/05.

[23] EEOC Litigation Settlements—May 2004, http://www.eeoc.gov/litigation/settlements/settlement05-04.html, accessed 06/15/05.

Discriminatory working conditions, disparagement, and termination

- **EEOC v. Phase 2 Co.**[24]

  No. 03-N-1911 (D. Col. June 1, 2004)

  The Denver District Office brought this Title VII class suit alleging that a drywall and steel framing firm headquartered in Fort Collins, Colorado that specializes in large industrial and commercial projects, subjected Mexican workers to ethnic slurs, national origin harassment, and retaliation at the site of a multimillion-dollar hospital construction project. According to the suit, 10 charging parties and a class of similarly situated individuals were called "lazy," "stupid," "(expletive deleted) wetbacks," and "damn wetbacks" on a daily basis. Mexican workers also were subjected to discriminatory working conditions. They were not permitted to use the cleaner ground floor restrooms or to use the elevators even when carrying heavy items. Further, they were not permitted to enter the supervisor's trailer to drink water, and were told they must bring their own water to the worksite. Following a one-hour peaceful protest of the discriminatory conduct, held on September 15, 2000, several Mexican workers, including six of the charging parties, were given layoff notices.

When are English-only rules legal? The EEOC regards such rules as being justified when needed for employers to operate safely or efficiently. Some situations in which English-only rules are justified include

- for communications with customers, coworkers, or supervisors who only speak English
- in emergencies or other situations in which employees must speak a common language for safety reasons
- for cooperative work assignments in which speaking English promotes efficiency
- to enable supervisors who only speak English to monitor the performance of employees who speak with coworkers or customers as part of their job duties[25]

English-only rules are not generally acceptable for break or lunch times, or other nonwork periods. We discuss additional considerations relevant to language at work later in the chapter.

---

[24] EEOC Litigation Settlements—June 2004, at http://www.eeoc.gov/litgation/settlements/settlement06-04.html. As in other chapters, most of the offensive language was retained from original EEOC Web site quotations of actual language.

[25] http://www.eeoc.gov/policy/docs/national-origin.html#VC, accessed 08/31/05.

FIGURE 5.1 *Hispanics by Origin: 2002*

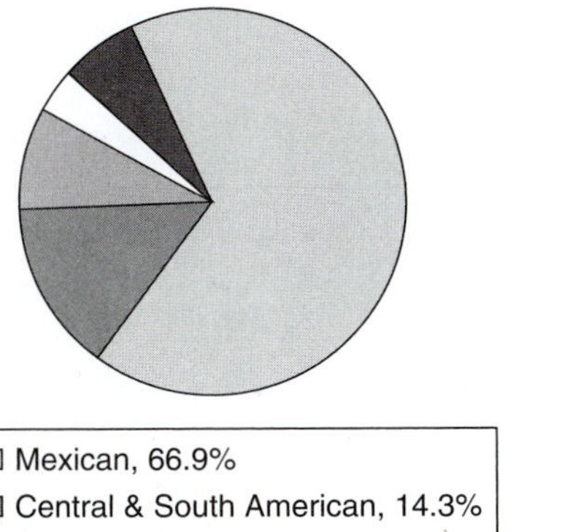

- Mexican, 66.9%
- Central & South American, 14.3%
- Puerto Rican, 8.6%
- Cuban, 3.7%
- Other Hisp, 6.5%

Source: Adapted from U.S. Census Bureau, Annual Demographic Supplement to the March 2002 Current Population Survey.

POPULATION

In 2004, there were 41.3 million Hispanics in the U.S. population, representing about 14% of the total population. Hispanics vary by race, with White, Black, American Indian, Asian, Native Hawaiian, respectively, comprising 47.9%, 2.0%, 1.2%, 0.3%, and 0.1% of the Hispanic population who reported one race alone in the 2000 full census. Reflecting the failure of the categorization used by the U.S. Census bureau to reflect the identity of many Latinos, 42.2% of the Hispanic population identified as "some other race" and 6.3% reported two or more races.[26] For nearly half the Latino population, simplistic racial categories do not fit their complex sense of identity.[27]

As shown in Figure 5.1, the great majority of Hispanics in the United States are of Mexican origin; nearly five times as many as Central and South Americans, who are the next largest group of Hispanics in the United States. Fifty percent of U.S. Hispanics live in California and Texas, where they make up 34% of each state's population.[28] Overall, over 75% of Hispanics live in California, Texas, New York, Florida, Illinois, Arizona, and New Jersey.[29]

[26] Griego, E. M. & Cassidy, R. C. (2001). Overview of Race and Hispanic Origin 2000. http://www.census.gov/prod/2001pubs/cenbr01-1.pdf, accessed 1/3/06.

[27] For a thorough discussion of Latinos and racial identity development, see Ferdman, B. M. & Gallegos, P. I. (2001). "Racial Identity Development and Latinos in the United States." In C. L. Wijeyesinghe & B. W. Jackson (Eds.), *New Perspectives on Racial Identity Development: A Theoretical and Practical Anthology*. New York: New York University Press, pp. 32–67.

[28] Hispanic Heritage Month 2004. Facts for Features. http://www.census.gov/Press-Release/www/releases/archives/facts_for_features_special_editions/002270.html, accessed 08/20/05.

[29] Ibid.

TABLE 5.1 ***Population Growth* for Hispanics by Race***

	April 2000 (Census)	July 2000	July 2001	July 2002	July 2003	July 2004
Hispanic	35.31	35.65	37.06	38.48	39.90	41.32
White alone	32.53	32.85	34.19	35.53	36.87	38.22
Black alone	1.39	1.40	1.44	1.47	1.50	1.54
American Indian/Alaska Native	0.57	0.57	0.58	0.59	0.61	0.62
Asian	0.23	0.23	0.24	0.25	0.25	0.26
Native Hawaiian/Pacific Islander	0.10	0.10	0.10	0.10	0.10	0.11
Two or more races	0.49	0.50	0.52	0.54	0.56	0.58

*Population estimates in millions.

Source: Annual Estimates of the Population by Sex, Race, and Hispanic or Latino origin for the United States: April 1, 2000, to July 1, 2004 (NC-EST 2004-03). U.S. Census Bureau. National Population Estimates Characteristics, http://www.census.gov/popest/national/asrh/NC-EST2004/NC-EST2004-03.xls, accessed 08/15/05.

Hispanics are a youthful population, with 34.4% under 18, compared with 22.8% of non-Hispanic Whites. Considerably fewer Hispanics are 65 years and older (5.1%) compared with Whites (14.4%). In the 18- to 64-year-old age range, there are 60.5% and 62.9% of Hispanics and non-Hispanic Whites, respectively. Having disproportionately fewer Hispanics at younger ages has important meaning for diversity in organizations. As the youthful population ages, there will be increasingly more Hispanics compared with non-Hispanic Whites as potential workers. Organizational efforts to attract and retain Hispanic workers (e.g., Cox and Blake's resource acquisition) will become increasingly important. In addition, more than 40% of Hispanics are foreign-born, which has implications for English-only rules at work and the need for bilingual managers and employees. Twenty-nine million Latinos in the United States speak Spanish at home—20% of U.S. residents. More than half of those who speak Spanish at home report speaking English "very well," however.[30]

Population Growth Rates by Race

The proportion of Hispanics in the United States is growing rapidly as a result of more immigration and higher birth rates of Hispanics when compared with other groups. As shown in Table 5.1, Hispanics increased from 35.3 million in the 2000 census to 41.3 million in July 2004. Estimates suggest

[30] Ibid.

FIGURE 5.2 ***Population by Hispanic Origin and Educational Attainment: 2002***

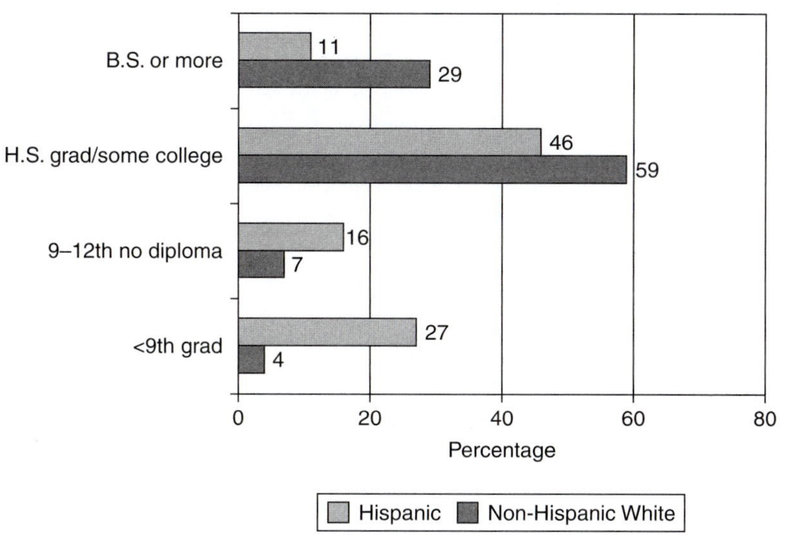

Source: Adapted from Ramirez, R., & de la Cruz, G. P. (2003). "The Hispanic Population in the United States: March 2002." Current Population Reports, p. 20–545, U.S. Census Bureau, Washington, DC. http://www.census.gov/prod/2003pubs/p20-545.pdf, accessed 08/14/05.

that by 2050 the Hispanic population will reach 102.6 million or 24% of the U.S. population.

EDUCATION, EMPLOYMENT, AND EARNINGS

Education

As shown in Figure 5.2, Hispanics lag non-Hispanic Whites in educational attainment. At the lowest education levels there are higher percentages of Hispanics, while there are more non-Hispanic Whites at higher education levels. Most striking is that 43% of Hispanics aged 25 and older did not complete high school. In comparison, 20% of Blacks aged 25 and older did not complete high school (not shown in Figure 5.2; see Chapter 4).

At higher educational levels, Asians, non-Hispanic Whites, Blacks, and Hispanics have most to least representation, with nearly 50% of Asians holding at least a college degree, compared with 11.4% of Hispanics. At the lowest educational levels, 57% of Hispanics, 80.0% of Blacks, 87.6% of Asians, and 89.4% of non-Hispanic Whites had at least a high school diploma in 2003.

As we have discussed, there are many differences within the Hispanic population, including in level of educational attainment. As shown in Table 5.2, while about half of Mexicans have at least a high school diploma, 67% of Puerto Ricans

TABLE 5.2 ***Population with At Least a High School Education by Detailed Hispanic Origin: 2002***

	Percent
Mexican	50.6
Central and South American	64.7
Puerto Rican	66.8
Cuban	70.8
Other Hispanic	74.0
All Hispanic	57.0
Non-Hispanic White	88.7

Source: Data adapted from Ramirez, R., & de la Cruz, G. P. (2003). Figure 8. "The Hispanic Population in the United States: March 2002." Current Population Reports, p. 20–545, U.S. Census Bureau, Washington, DC. http://www.census.gov/prod/2003pubs/p20-545.pdf, accessed 08/14/05.

and 71% of Cubans do. Nearly 19% of Cubans have at least a college degree, compared with less than 8% of Mexicans (not shown in Table 5.2).[31] These educational differences contribute to lower employment and wages for Mexican Hispanics compared with Cubans.

Misperception: Hispanics have low education levels.

Reality: Education levels of Hispanics differ by country of origin.

The PhD Project is an organization designed to increase the educational competitiveness of Latinos (and other underrepresented minorities), as described in Organizational Feature 5.1. Through increasing the numbers of Latinos and others of color who are business professors, the PhD Project contributes to the higher representation of Latinos as business students and potential employees.

Employment

Hispanic men have the highest participation rates of all men, with more than 80% participating in the workforce. In contrast, Latinas are least likely to be participating in the workforce relative to other women, with a 57.1% participation rate. As shown in Table 5.3 (page 140), the unemployment rates at all educational levels of Whites are lowest of all, followed by those of Hispanics, Asians, and Blacks. At the lowest educational level, Latinos and Whites are more likely to be working than Blacks and Asians.

[31] Ramirez, R., & de la Cruz, G. P. (2003). "The Hispanic Population in the United States: March 2002." Current Population Reports, U.S. Census Bureau, Washington, DC, pp. 20–545. http://www.census.gov/prod/2003pubs/p.20-545.pdf, accessed 08/04/05.

Organizational Feature 5.1 *The PhD Project: Increasing Diversity through Holistic Means*

As their proportions in the workforce increase, lower educational levels among Latinos, Blacks, and American Indians compared with non-Hispanic Whites are an important diversity concern. The PhD Project is an organization designed to improve workforce diversity by improving the diversity of business school faculties. It was started in 1994, with the goal of increasing diversity in business schools by attracting underrepresented minorities to doctoral programs, recognizing that having more diversity at the front of classrooms would increase the amount of diversity among students in the classroom.

In 1994, the PhD Project estimated that less than 300 of the 22,000 business school faculties in the United States were from underrepresented minority groups. With the help of the PhD Project, between 1994 and 2004, the number of Latinos, Blacks, and American Indians on certain business school faculties increased from 294 to 686.

The PhD Project believes that increasing the diversity of business school faculty will

a. encourage more underrepresented minorities to pursue business degrees.
b. improve the performance and completion rate of underrepresented minorities by providing role models and more natural mentors.
c. better prepare all business students for today's multicultural society and work environment.

Recognizing the importance of diversity to organizational success, many universities and well-known corporations have joined in supporting the PhD Project. Included sponsors are PhD Project founder KPMG Foundation, the Graduate Management Admission Council, Citigroup Foundation, Ford Motor Company, Daimler/Chrysler Corporation Fund, GE Foundation, Abbott Labs, JP Morgan Chase, Hewlett-Packard, and numerous other companies. These sponsors believe that participating in the PhD Project signals commitment to diversity in the workforce to their employees and to universities.

The PhD Project provides peer support and assists selected students with obtaining scholarships and funding to obtain a PhD. Doctoral students involved in the PhD Project have higher rates of completion of their degrees and are more likely to work in academic positions than other students are. There are currently more than 400 PhD Project students in doctoral programs around the nation.

Source: http://phdproject.com/index.html, accessed 01/01/05; "In Just 10 Years, the PhD Project Has More Than Doubled the Corps of Minority Business School Faculty." Press Releases, Ned Steele Communications. http://phdproject.com/10thanniversary.pdf, accessed 01/01/05.

Questions to Consider

1. *The PhD Project estimates that on average, less than one Black, Latino, or Native American faculty in business exists at universities around the United States. If you are a university student, or have studied at that level, how many Black, Latino, or American Indian faculty do/did you have? Estimate or investigate the actual proportion of Black, Latino, or American Indians faculty at a university (that is not a historically Black university) with which you are familiar.*

2. *What are potential effects on White students and students of color of severe underrepresentation of Blacks, Latino, or American Indians as university-level faculty?*

3. *What are the benefits for White students and students of color of having minority faculty members?*

4. *The PhD Project assumes that having more faculty of color will increase the probability that students of color will attend and complete college, reducing the education gap between Whites and Blacks, Latinos, and American Indians. Investigate the changes in college completion rates for these groups between 1995 and the present.*

TABLE 5.3 ***Unemployment Level by Educational Attainment and Race (Percent of Population 25 Years and Over): 2003***

	Total	White	Black	Asian	Hispanic*
Less than H.S.	8.8	7.8	13.9	9.5	8.2
H.S. graduate	5.5	4.8	9.3	5.6	5.9
Some college, no degree	5.2	4.5	8.6	6.4	5.8
Associate degree	4.0	3.6	6.2	5.2	5.3
Bachelor's and higher†	3.1	2.8	4.5	4.4	4.1

*Persons whose ethnicity is Hispanic are classified by ethnicity as well as by race.

†Bachelor's and higher includes persons with bachelor's, master's, professional, and doctoral degrees.

Source: http://www.bls.gov/cps/cpsaat7.pdf, accessed 10/22/04.

Earnings

Table 4.4 (Chapter 4) presents 2002 earnings by educational attainment, sex, race, and Hispanic origin. As shown in the table, for each individual education category, earnings of non-Hispanic White men are higher than those of every racial and ethnic group. Depending on the educational level, the earnings of Hispanics are at or near the lowest. Even so, Hispanic men and women with college degrees earn about $20,000 more than those with only high school degrees.

Organizational Experiences of Hispanics

The earnings and employment experiences of Latinos are strongly affected by their education, language fluency, nativity, sex, race, and skin color. Research on the organizational experiences of Hispanics indicates they sometimes face treatment and access discrimination by employers, customer discrimination, racial profiling, and police misconduct. We consider some of these factors in the following sections.

Race, Hispanic Ethnicity, and Employment Outcomes

As we have discussed, Hispanics can be of any race: There are Black Hispanics, White Hispanics, those who self-report as "some other race," and others. A research report by the Lewis Mumford Center for Comparative Urban and Regional Research in Albany, New York, suggests that race divides U.S. Hispanics, similar to ways in which it divides non-Hispanics.[32] Hispanics who

[32] Logan, J. R. (2003). *How Race Counts for Hispanics,* Lewis Mumford Center, University of Albany. http://mumford1.dyndns.org/cen2000/BlackLatinoReport/BlackLatinoReport.pdf, accessed 08/20/05. For additional research on race and Hispanic origin, see Gomez, C. (2000). "The Continual Significance of Skin Color: An Exploratory Study of Latinos in the Northeast." *Hispanic Journal of Behavioral Sciences,* 22: 94–103; Telles, E. E., & Murguia, E. (1990). "Phenotype Discrimination and Income Differences among Mexican Americans." *Social Science Quarterly,* 73: 120–122.

are White have higher incomes and lower unemployment and poverty rates than Black and other-race Hispanics. The median household income of White Hispanics is nearly $40,000, compared with about $35,000 for Black Hispanics and about $38,000 for Hispanics who are some other race. Unemployment for White, Black, and Hispanics who are some other race is 8%, 10%, and 12%, respectively. White Hispanics are also less residentially segregated than other Hispanics—they are more likely to live among White non-Hispanics and to marry non-Hispanic Whites. Levels of intermarriage with Whites are one measure test of the strength of discrimination against particular groups.[33]

Although they have higher education than White Hispanics, Black Hispanics fare considerably worse than White Hispanics in terms of income, poverty, unemployment, and residential segregation. Black Hispanics have about 12 years of education, compared with 11 and 10 years, respectively, for White and other race Hispanics.[34] Those interested in race, ethnicity, and diversity in organizations are advised to consider race when investigating the experiences and opportunities of U.S. Hispanics.

Hispanic Immigrants at Work

There are more Hispanic immigrants in the United States than any other group; 40% of the Hispanic population is foreign-born. The majority of the foreign-born Hispanics in the United States (52%) entered the United States between 1990 and 2002, making them very recent immigrants.[35] Nearly 10 million of the foreign-born in the United States were born in Mexico, and another 7.3 million are from other Latin American countries.[36] For Latinos, being an immigrant is associated with lower education and lower wages, but, ironically, not with lower employment levels. Immigrants' relatively high employment levels in part reflects their willingness to work in jobs viewed as undesirable by other workers. These jobs are often low wage, dangerous jobs, with little or no opportunity for advancement and other negative attributes.

Misperception: Immigrant workers are preferred because they have a stronger work ethic than native-born Americans.

Reality: Immigrants are often preferred because they will work for lower wages and are less likely to complain about mistreatment than native-born Americans.

---

[33] See Dworkin, A. G., & Dworkin, A. (1999). "What is a Minority." In A. G. Dworkin & R. J. Dworkin (Eds.), *The Minority Report* (3rd edition), Fort Worth, TX: Harcourt Brace Publishers, pp. 11–27; Herring, C. (1999). "African Americans in Contemporary America: Progress and Retrenchment." In A. G. Dworkin & R. J. Dworkin (Eds.), *The Minority Report* (3rd edition), Fort Worth, TX: Harcourt Brace Publishers, pp. 181–208.

[34] Logan, J. (2003).

[35] Hispanic Heritage Month 2004.

[36] Ibid.

Exploitation of immigrant workers is a common phenomenon. Research documents exploitation through low wages, excessive hours with no overtime, sexual harassment and assault, and various other abuses endured by immigrants, particularly illegal ones. Denise Segura has documented the experiences of Chicanas, noting the particular issues that undocumented workers face, which make them susceptible to threats of deportation or being reported to the Immigration and Naturalization Service if they complain about abuse.[37] An egregious case involving exploitation and abuse of Latinas follows.

- **EEOC v. Rivera Vineyards, Inc., d/b/a Blas Rivera Vineyards, et al.**[38]
  No. EDCV 03-01117 RT (C.D. Cal. June 15, 2005)

  In this Title VII suit, the Los Angeles District Office alleged that Rivera Vineyards one of the largest vineyards in Coachella Valley, California and its affiliates engaged in a pattern or practice of sexually harassing female workers and making job assignments based on sex; defendants also retaliated against women who complained about harassment. A Rivera Vineyard supervisor, assistant supervisor, and some of the crew leaders (male) harassed female migrant workers, most of whom were Spanish-speaking (although one crew leader targeted women who spoke neither English nor Spanish, only their indigenous languages). The harassment consisted of sexual comments, unwelcome rubbing and touching, offers of better assignments in exchange for sex, and in at least one case, forced submission to sexual intercourse. Also, Rivera Vineyard admitted that only men had been hired into the more desirable year-round positions (including pruning, girdling, irrigation, and vine tying). Women were employed only in seasonal positions (including picking and packing) available from about February to June or July.

  Rivera Vineyard retaliated against women who resisted or reported sexual harassment. For instance, two charging parties (a crew leader and a woman on the crew) complained to the owner that the assistant supervisor had grabbed one of the women's breasts and had engaged in other objectionable conduct. The same day, the assistant supervisor sent the whole crew home. He laid off the two women in May 2000 before the end of the harvest season and in subsequent seasons refused to recall them.

In their book *Stories Employers Tell,* Philip Moss and Chris Tilly describe employers' stated preferences for Latino workers and their praise of the "immigrant work ethic." One employer specifically explained that he viewed hiring

[37] Segura, D.A. (1992). "Chicanas in White-Collar Jobs: 'You Have to Prove Yourself More.' " *Sociological Perspectives,* 35: 163–182.

[38] EEOC Litigation Settlements—June 2005, http://www.eeoc.gov/litigation/settlements/settlement06-05.html, accessed 10/19/05.

Latinos as contributing to his organization's competitive advantage: "We have to have a competitive edge, and our edge is that our prices are lower . . . All of my guys, practically, start at five dollars an hour." He went on to say, "Some of the competitors that we deal with pay $15 per hour."[39]

Some of employers' preferences for immigrant workers are clearly related to immigrants' tolerance of lower wages. Moss and Tilly's findings indicated that overall, employers who stated preferences for Hispanic or Asian immigrants over native-born American workers paid noticeably lower wages. In organizations where at least one manager praised the immigrant work ethic, the wage penalty was 39 cents per hour. When half or more managers praised immigrant workers, the wage penalty was 96 cents per hour.

Small and large employers are able to exploit immigrant workers easily because of workers' fears of deportation and little government attention to the matter.[40] In 2005, Wal-Mart Stores Inc. agreed to settle the largest case to date involving immigrant labor. The U.S. government alleged that Wal-Mart knowingly hired illegal immigrants from Mexico, Eastern Europe, and other countries, even though the employment was done through contractors rather than through Wal-Mart directly. The $11 million settlement was almost four times as large as the largest prior settlement involving hiring illegal immigrants, but still allegedly amounted to less than 1 hour's sales at Wal-Mart.[41] An additional civil suit filed by some former workers alleges the workers, illegal immigrants, were not paid for overtime, even though they often worked 7 days per week.

Joseph Healey assesses the conflict between concern over immigration and willingness to benefit from and participate in it.

> Two points seem clear in the midst of the frequently intense and continuing debate over immigration. First, prejudice and racism are part of what motivates people to oppose immigration, and second, immigrants, legal and illegal, continue to find work with Anglo employers and niches in American society in which they can survive. The networks that have delivered cheap immigrant labor for the low-wage sector continue to operate as they have for more than a century. Frequently, the primary beneficiaries of this long-established system are not the immigrants, but employers who benefit from a cheaper, more easily exploited workforce and American consumers who benefit from lower prices in the marketplace.[42] (p. 174).

---

[39] Moss, P., & Tilly, C. (2001). *Stories Employers Tell: Race, Skill, and Hiring in America,* New York: Russell Sage Foundation, p. 117.

[40] Solis, D., & Mittelstadt, M. (2005). "Wal-Mart to Settle Immigrant Case." *Dallas Morning News*. March 19. Section D, p. 1.

[41] Ibid.

[42] Healey, J. F. (2004). *Diversity and Society: Race, Ethnicity, and Gender.* Thousand Oaks, CA: Pine Forge Press, pp. 157–188.

Latinas at Work

Some researchers have proposed that the criminalization of working "without papers" by the Immigration Reform and Control Act of 1986 serves as a motivation for some immigrants to work for private individuals to decrease their likelihood of being detected.[43] Many Latinas who are illegal immigrants opt for household domestic work as it reduces likelihood of detection and deportation when compared with public work. Ironically, this also subjects them to greater likelihood of exploitation as such employers are considerably less likely to be audited or penalized for abuses. Private work and public work as illegal immigrants also provide no benefits, no contributions to retirement programs, and no contributions to Social Security.

Whether immigrants or U.S. natives, participation and wage rates of Latinas are lower than those of other women. As discussed earlier, participation rates of Latinas are lowest among non-Hispanic White, Black, Asian, and Hispanic women. Although Latinas are less likely to be in the workforce than other women are, the majority of Latinas (57%) are indeed in the workforce.

Misperception: Due to strong cultural traditions, Latinas are unlikely to work outside the home.

Reality: Nearly as many Latinas (57%) work outside the home as Asian women (58%) and non-Hispanic White women (60%). Five percent more African American women participate in the workforce than Latinas.

As women and as women of color, Latinas are subject to multiple forms of disadvantage in formal organizations and this contributes to their experience of employment hardship, as discussed in Research Translation 5.1. Latinas lag non-Hispanic White women, and often Black women, in occupational status and earnings. Latinas tend to work in female-dominated positions with other women of color, and the larger the proportion of women of color, the lower the wages overall.[44]

Between 1990 and 2001, the employment of Latinas in the private sector increased from 2.9% to 4.7%, an increase of 104%. Crop production employs 18.5% of Hispanic women (and 61.8% of all Hispanics).[45] In the Southwest, Latinas (primarily Mexican Americans) work in agriculture and food processing,

[43] Hondagneu-Sotelo, P. (1997). "Working 'without Papers' in the United States: Toward the Integration of Legal Status in Frameworks of Race, Class, and Gender." In E. Higginbotham & M. Romero (Eds.), *Women and Work: Exploring Race, Ethnicity, and Class,* Thousand Oaks, CA: Sage, pp. 101–125.

[44] Baker, S. G. (1999). "Mexican-Origin Women in Southwestern Labor Markets." In I. Browne (Ed.), *Latinas and African-American Women at Work,* New York: Russell Sage Foundation, pp. 244–269.

[45] Women of Color: Their Employment in the Private Sector, http://www.eeoc.gov/stats/reports/womenofcolor/#Section_1.1.3, accessed 06/17/05.

Research Translation 5.1 *Employment Hardship among Mexican-Origin Women*

"Employment hardship" includes joblessness, involuntary part-time work, and working poverty. Underemployment is also an aspect of employment hardship, and is associated with low wages, and nonexistent medical and pension benefits. In a longitudinal study, Roberto De Anda, of Portland State University, investigated the prevalence of employment hardship among Mexican-origin women, compared with non-Hispanic White women. The sample included 60,000 households, of which 3,000 were of Mexican origin and data were collected in 1992, 1996, 2000, during a period of economic expansion.

De Anda controlled for factors that could contribute to employment hardship, including length of residence in the United States and characteristics of the jobs themselves. After controlling for those factors, De Anda found that Mexican-origin women were 1.7 more likely than non-Hispanic White women to experience employment hardship. These disparities existed at lower (e.g., less than high school), and higher (some college, or college degree) educational levels and varied by job sector. For women in the least skilled occupations, Mexican-origin women were 3.1 times as likely as White women to experience employment hardship. De Anda also found that 20% of the Mexican-origin women in his sample were in poverty, despite working and one-third experienced employment hardship.

Young Mexican women (16 to 29 years old) were more likely to be participating in the labor force than young White women, but faced a higher risk of employment hardship. Because employment hardship works to reduce one's likelihood of future adequate employment, De Anda expressed concern about young Mexican women's prospects for improvement in the future. De Anda found that Mexican-origin women who had been in the United States for more than 10 years had similar employment outcomes as did Mexican-origin women who were born in the United States. Both fared better than did women who more recently arrived in the country.

Source: De Anda, R. M. (2005). "Employment Hardship among Mexican-Origin Women." *Hispanic Journal of Behavioral Sciences,* 27: 43–59.

in housekeeping departments of hotels and motels, and in other service jobs. In the Northeast, Latinas (primarily Puerto Ricans) often work in the garment industry, although these jobs are declining and displacing many workers. As shown in Table 4.4 (Chapter 4), at the high school level (where most Hispanics fall), Latinas earn 73% of the earnings of Hispanic men.

Despite multiple disadvantages faced by Latinas in the workplace, Latinas are represented in high-level and executive positions in several large organizations, including Fortune 500 companies. The *Hispanic Business Magazine* identified the 25 Hispanic women in business in 2004, including chief executive officers, directors, vice presidents, and other executives.[46] Selection criteria included job responsibilities and position, involvement in promoting advancement or favorable

[46] "2004 Elite Hispanic Women." *Hispanic Business*. http://www.hispanicbusiness.com/news/news_print.asp?id=15146, accessed 09/17/05.

Research Translation 5.2 *Causes of Hispanic Underrepresentation in Managerial and Professional Occupations*

Hispanics are underrepresented in managerial and professional occupations relative to their representation in the United States' population. Although Hispanics are increasing as a proportion of the population, their representation in management and professional occupations has not kept pace. In fact, between 1990 and 2000, Hispanic underrepresentation in management increased from 3.9% to 5.0% and in professional occupations, the underrepresentation increased from 4.0% to 6.1%.

Kusum Mundra and her colleagues sought to investigate causes for this underrepresentation and included possible contributions of human capital barriers (e.g., education, language proficiency, and work experience) and economic and spatial barriers (e.g., travel time to work). Data analyses indicated that education, age, sex, English proficiency, marital status, type of employer, travel time to work, and year of entry in to the United States affected one's likelihood of being in a managerial or professional occupation, regardless of race or ethnicity. Education was the strongest factor for Whites and the second strongest factor for Hispanics. Language proficiency was the strongest predictor of working in a managerial or professional job for Hispanics, and the third strongest predictor for Whites, reflecting the importance to every one of communications skills in obtaining higher positions.

The underrepresentation of Hispanics in managerial and professional occupations is increasingly problematic as Hispanics' share of the population increases. Because fluency in English and education most strongly contributed to having a managerial or professional position for Hispanics, the authors recommended organizations become involved in increasing and expanding educational opportunities for Hispanics. They also suggested English as a second-language training and tuition reimbursement and time off for pursuit of a college degree as possible mechanisms to do so.

Source: Mundra, K., Moellmer, A., & Lopez-Aqueres, W. (2003). "Investigating Hispanic Underrepresentation in Managerial and Professional Occupations." *Hispanic Journal of Behavioral Sciences*, 25: 513–529.

perception of the Hispanic community, and size of the organization. Included were: Maria Elena Lagomasino (Chairman and CEO of J.P. Morgan Private Bank), Maria Martinez (Corporate Vice President, Communications and Mobile Solutions Unit, Microsoft Corporation), Carmen Nava (President, Consumer Markets, SBC Communications), Gloria Santona (Executive Vice President, General Counsel, McDonald's Corporation), Graciela Eleta de Cacho (Vice President, Multicultural Development Organization, Proctor & Gamble), and Mercy Jimenez (Senior Vice President, Business and Product Development, Fannie Mae).

Bilingualism: An Uncompensated Skill

As discussed in Research Translation 5.2, communication proficiency and education are the strongest predictors of the representation of Latinas in managerial and professional occupations. Twenty-nine million Latinos in the United States speak

Spanish at home, but more than half of them report speaking English very well, as discussed earlier.[47] In two of the EEOC cases presented in this chapter, employers' English-only language policies violated Title VII of the Civil Rights Act. In one case, the English-only directive was accompanied by the statement that "This is America and they should learn to speak English".[48] Such statements are employed and discarded when convenient. Bilingual employees are often called upon to assist monolingual English speakers with their work tasks. In her analysis of this irony for Latinos, Mary Romero aptly describes the situation for bilingual employees:

> Bilingual employees are frequently pulled away from their regular jobs to translate conversations between monolingual English-speaking employees and non-English-speaking clients/customers. Yet the English-speaking employees' need for assistance does not lead to questions about their ability to do their jobs, and the bilingual abilities of racial/ethnic [employees] are rarely considered criteria for higher salary or promotion. Generally, the need for bilingual skills is ignored as a job criterion. The deficiencies of monolingual employees are simply covered up by the availability of bilingual employees to translate. Employers have refused to recognize language as a marketable skill and have refused to provide wage differentials to compensate for the skill. Instead, bilingual employees find themselves in a double bind: They must take on the additional work of translators, yet they are evaluated poorly because they cannot accomplish as much of their regular work as expected because they are constantly called away to serve as translators.[49] (p. 244.)

The rapid growth of the Hispanic population makes the need for more bilingual employees and the need to recognize bilingualism as a compensable skill increasingly important. Rather than resisting bi- and multilingualism as un-American, employers should recognize its existence and attempt to address it positively. Encouraging multilingualism among all workers (not just Latinos) and hiring and compensating multilingual workers are positive steps.

Misperception: Hispanics should learn English, since English is the "official" language in most of the United States.

Reality: Multiple language fluency is an asset for everyone.

Compared with many other nations, the monolingual nature of the majority of the U.S. population is less common in other parts of the world. Multilingual countries

---

47 Ibid.

48 EEOC Litigation Settlements—May 2004, http://www.eeoc.gov/litigation/settlements/settlement05-04.html, accessed 06/15/05.

49 Romero, M. (1997). "Epilogue." In E. Higginbotham & M. Romero (Eds.), *Women and Work: Exploring Race, Ethnicity, and Class,* Thousand Oaks, CA: Sage, pp. 235–248.

include Canada, China, India, Ireland, South Africa, and New Zealand, among others. In areas that have no official multilingual policy, many of the population is nonetheless multilingual. For example, many Swiss speak English, French, Spanish, and German. Although there is no official language for the United States as a whole, in 23 states English has been identified as the official language. In three states, there are two official languages: New Mexico (English, Spanish), Louisiana (English, French), and Hawaii (English, Hawaiian).

Racial Profiling and Police Misconduct against Hispanics

Racial profiling by law enforcement officers has received considerable media attention and 22 million people in the United States report that they have experienced profiling.[50] Profiling occurs most frequently against people of color, including Latinos, Blacks, Asians, and American Indians, and more recently, Arabs in the United States.[51] Other forms of police misconduct, including dishonest police officers and informants, planting real and fake drugs and guns, and assaulting innocent people have also been documented. Many of those victimized by police misconduct are Latino immigrants.

In Los Angeles, in 1999, Rafael Perez, a police officer facing trial for stealing 6 pounds of impounded cocaine, agreed to a plea deal to reduce his sentence. He would expose criminal activity among the Los Angeles police in exchange for a reduced sentence. Over 9 months, Perez revealed how Los Angeles police "routinely lied in arrest reports, shot and killed or wounded unarmed suspects and innocent bystanders, planted guns on suspects after shooting them, fabricated evidence, and framed defendants," the majority of whom were young Hispanic men.[52] Because of the information provided by Perez, more than 100 defendants had their convictions vacated and dismissed.

In 2002, another form of police misconduct came under the microscope when rumors of a "fake-drug scandal" began to surface in the city of Dallas, Texas.[53] Paid "informants" targeted innocent Latinos and then the undercover officers, Mark De La Paz and Eddie Herrera, planted what appeared to be cocaine in the targets' vehicles. What appeared to be cocaine was gypsum, commonly used in making sheetrock, and could easily have been identified had drug testing taken place. Because drug testing did not occur until the trials, those targeted were jailed for months and years or, as occurred in several cases, deported.

---

[50] Amnesty International. (2004). *Threat and Humiliation: Racial Profiling, Domestic Security, and Human Rights in the U.S.*, New York: Amnesty International USA.

[51] Ibid.

[52] Gross, S. R., Jacoby, K., Matheson, D., Montgomery, N., & Patil, S. (2005). "Exonerations in the United States: 1989 through 2003." *The Journal of Criminal Law and Criminology,* 95: 524–560.

[53] See Gross et al. (2005); Donald, M. (2002). "Dirty or Duped? Who's to Blame for the Fake-Drug Scandal Rocking Dallas Police?" *Dallasobserver.com*. http://www.dallasobserver.com/issues/2002-05-02/news/feature_6.html, accessed 09/19/05.

Many of those arrested were auto mechanics, day laborers, and construction workers, with no prior criminal records, who spoke little English and had little money to mount a defense.[54] Yvonne Gwyn, a 52-year-old grandmother from Honduras, who is a naturalized U.S. citizen and was running her own auto detail shop, was one of those arrested and jailed.[55] When investigations revealed that the cocaine was gypsum, more than 80 innocent people were released.

One informant in the Dallas case had earned $210,000 in 2001, making him the highest paid informant that year.[56] In April 2005, former officer De La Paz was convicted of lying in a search warrant and sentenced to 5 years in prison. He and Herrera face additional charges. Poor management procedures, lack of supervision, and considerable professional incentives to make drug busts set the stage for the abuses that occurred in both Los Angeles and Dallas. Vulnerability and devaluation of Latino immigrants also facilitated the abuse. These examples are relevant to diversity in organizations in that they reflect the role of organizations in facilitating unequal treatment of people based on their ethnicity and class. These examples also raise questions about the veracity and fairness of other arrests and convictions. As discussed in Research Translation 5.3, Latinos and Blacks in Florida are less likely to receive withheld adjudication, a legal benefit that would allow them to avoid the stigma of being convicted felons and the associated negative employment and social costs.

LATINOS AS CUSTOMERS

The Marketing Advantage

As we have discussed so far, Latinos are a large and rapidly growing proportion of the U.S. population. As potential employees and customers, Latinos are a growing force to be reckoned with. Hispanic buying power increased from $504 to $686 billion between 2000 and 2004 and estimates suggest it will reach $992 billion by 2009.[57] *People en Español's* fourth annual Hispanic Opinion Tracker (HOT) reported important differences in the consumption behavior of Hispanics and the general population.[58] Phone interviews were conducted with 6,000 Hispanics and 2,000 non-Hispanics aged 18 and over. Of the 6,000 Hispanics, 55% are Hispanic dominant—those who prefer to speak Spanish and have a strong desire to maintain their Hispanic culture. Of the remaining 45%, 23% are bicultural and bilingual, but are culturally more Hispanic. Another 22% identify

[54] Donald, M. (2002).
[55] Ibid.
[56] Ibid.
[57] *Marketing News*. 7/15/2005, 39(12): 23.
[58] Wentz, L. (2005, July 18). "Survey: Hispanics 'Passionate' about Shopping." *Advertising Age,* 76(29): 29.

RESEARCH TRANSLATION 5.3 ***Convicted Felon, or Not? Differences by Race and Ethnicity***

Considerable research in criminology documents the existence of disparate arrests, convictions, and sentencing for Latinos and Blacks when compared with Whites allegedly involved in criminal activity, particularly drug activity. After describing results from numerous studies, for different types of crimes, Stephanie Bontrager and her colleagues at Florida State University concluded that Latinos and Blacks "are sentenced more severely for drug crimes and certain crimes of violence."[59] Under certain circumstances, Florida law allows judges to use their discretion and withhold adjudication, which frees those involved in criminal activity from being labeled a convicted felon. Through a plea agreement, those charged plead guilty and receive probation, thus avoiding the stigma associated with being convicted of a felony. A felony conviction is associated with many negative consequences—even after serving time and being released such a conviction often prevents people from obtaining employment, voting, serving on juries, and holding political office.

Given the documented disparities in sentencing by race and ethnicity, Bontrager and her colleagues set out to investigate possible disparities in withholding adjudication based on race and ethnicity. Between 1999 and 2002, 91,477 men were sentenced to probation. Overall, 57% received withheld adjudication, with Hispanics, Whites, and Blacks receiving it in 62%, 58%, and 48% of cases. The perceived advantages of Hispanics in sentencing changed after researchers controlled for individual-level factors, contextual variables, and "concentrated disadvantage." These factors included the person's age, case seriousness, legal residency, prior supervision violation, seriousness of crime, rates of drug arrests, crime rates, and overall arrest rates in the county, and population percent Black and percent Hispanic, among other factors. Prior research supported inclusion of these factors as predictors in research on crime and sentencing. After controlling for these factors, Blacks remained least likely to have adjudication withheld, followed by Hispanics and then Whites. The lower likelihood of receiving this benefit was strongest for drug and violent crimes, for both Blacks and Hispanics. This is consistent with perceptions of threat of drug or violent crimes associated with Blacks and Hispanics. Because they are less likely to have adjudication withheld, Hispanics and Blacks have less opportunity to retain certain civil rights, gain citizenship, or obtain employment when compared with Whites. Avoiding the stigma of a felony conviction could—all other things being equal—diminish the prospects of recidivism, and increase the prospects of a successful return to life.

Source: Bontrager, S., Bales, W., & Chiricos, T. (2005). "Race, Ethnicity, Threat and the Labeling of Convicted Felons." *Criminology,* 43: 589–622

with their Latino heritage, but are more similar in market attitudes to the general population. In all, over three-fourths of the Hispanic population reported being bilingual, bicultural, and identifying with their Hispanic heritage.

In the HOT survey, Hispanics reported spending an average of $1,992 on clothing and accessories compared to $1,153 for general market customers in the

[59] Bontrager, S., Bales, W., & Chiricos, T. (2005). "Race, Ethnicity, Threat and the Labeling of Convicted Felons." *Criminology,* 43: 589–622.

12 months prior to the survey data collection. Hispanics were also more likely to report strong enthusiasm about shopping (56%) than was the general population (39%). About 75% of the Hispanics reported preferring to pay cash for their purchases, and only 15% use credit cards, which is significantly lower than the 40% who use credit cards in the general market. The survey also indicated that Hispanics are affected much more by advertising and marketing than general market consumers.

With strong and growing buying power, nearly 75% more annual spending on clothing and accessories, and a preference for paying cash, Latinos are indeed a valuable market segment. Organizations wishing to tap into the market are using such sources as *People en Español* and Univision to reach the market. Univision saw a 26% increase in viewership in 2005. On its Web site Univision is referred to as "the leading Spanish-language media company serving the rapidly growing Hispanic population in the United States"[60] In a key and noteworthy accomplishment, for the week of June 27–July 3, 2005, for the first time, Univision was the top ranked network in prime time ratings for the week among all 18- to 34-year-old viewers—regardless of language.[61] By focusing on Latinos, Univision has been able to capitalize on the growing market and become a top-ranked network, even though Latinos are currently a relatively small proportion of the population.

In September of 2005, ABC viewers began offering prime time shows in Spanish and English, an acknowledgment of the growing proportion of Latinos in the United States.[62] Prior to then, only "George Lopez," a sitcom featuring the comedian of the same name, was broadcast in both English and Spanish. ABC's entertainment chief, Stephen McPherson, noted that the company wanted to "move beyond toe-dipping and really dive in" the market for Latino customers. Both dubbing and closed captioning will be provided for some of the most popular shows. In test screenings, ABC found enthusiasm among Latinos who did not speak English and who had previously been unable to view prime time shows.

Discrimination against Hispanic Customers

In contrast to welcoming and pursuing Hispanic customers, researchers have also documented discrimination that sometimes targets Hispanics as undesirable customers or potential shoplifters. In their article on customer racial profiling and other marketplace discrimination, Ann-Marie Harris, Geraldine Henderson, and Jerome Williams describe one egregious case of discrimination that occurred

[60] http://www.univision.com, accessed 08/21/05.

[61] Wentz, L. (2005).

[62] "ABC to Offer Primetime Shows in Spanish." *DiversityInc.com*. Accessed 09/18/05.

in a Conoco convenience store and gas station in Fort Worth, Texas.[63] The store employee cursed the Hispanic customers and referred to one as an "Iranian Mexican bitch, whatever you are."[64] The employee then shoved the customers' purchases on the floor and, over the store loudspeaker, told the customers to "go back to where you came from you poor Mexicans . . ." in an escalating verbal assault. When the customers complained to Conoco, their complaints were ignored, even though the clerk admitted she had done what the customers alleged. Although the courts are often unfriendly to customer complaints of discrimination, costs related to negative publicity and lost business may be potentially higher than those of a lawsuit or damage award may be. As discussed in Chapter 1, discrimination against customers can result in lost business from customers personally targeted by unfair treatment or from other customers when they learn of discriminatory treatment based on race or ethnicity. Both members of the targeted group and members of other racial and ethnic groups may find such behavior unacceptable and choose to do business elsewhere.

Individual Recommendations

As with other groups, individual Latinos should obtain as much education as possible. Although returns on educational investment differ by race and national origin, for everyone, education increases earnings and the likelihood of employment. Latinos should also carefully investigate prospective employers. What is the demographic composition of the employees? Are Hispanics and other nondominant group members represented in management, supervisory positions, or other positions of power? Who are potential role models and mentors? As Solomon Trujillo, CEO of Telstra, learned, at one time, Latino role models were hard to find. Trujillo himself is a role model now, as considered in Individual Feature 5.2.

For Latinos for whom English is a second language, personal efforts to ensure English fluency are critical. As discussed earlier, bilingualism is increasingly valuable in today's workplace, for both Hispanics and non-Hispanics. Those who are bilingual should actively pursue positions in which bilingualism is valued and compensated. In addition, people who are monolingual should consider learning another language, recognizing that bilingualism is a valuable skill, certain to increase in market value.

Because of the large proportion of Latino immigrants and their relatively low education levels, it is possible that those most in need of these individual recommendations will not encounter them. As such, readers interested in workplace fairness

[63] See Harris, A., Henderson, G., & Williams, J. (2005). "Courting Customers: Assessing Consumer Racial Profiling and Other Marketplace Discrimination." *Journal of Public Policy & Marketing,* 24(1), Spring: 163–171.

[64] Ibid, p. 168.

Individual Feature 5.2 *Solomon Trujillo, CEO of Telstra*

Solomon Trujillo was named CEO of Telstra, Australia's largest telecommunications and information services company, effective July 1, 2005. Born in 1952, Trujillo has an MBA and a bachelor of business degree from the University of Wyoming. Trujillo worked his way through school playing trumpet in his family's mariachi band. His current compensation package at Telstra is reportedly $10 million, including $3 million in salary.

Trujillo's resume includes positions at some of the largest and most successful communications companies around the world. At age 32, Trujillo became the youngest vice president ever at US West. At that time, Trujillo says there were no Hispanic role models for him to follow. Trujillo was named CEO in 1998, and served as quite a role model for other Hispanics himself. As CEO, he named seven Latinos as vice presidents, including five women. He also transformed US West from being perceived as "US Worst" to one of the most successful, customer friendly, innovative communications companies.

Under Trujillo's leadership, the merger of US West with Qwest Communications occurred in 2000. After retiring from Qwest, Trujillo became CEO of Orange CA, one of the leading wireless companies in Europe. In addition to his positions with US West, Orange CA, and Telstra, Trujillo has served on the boards of directors of EDS, PepsiCo, Target, and Gannett.

Sources: "Leading the Way: These Latinos are Setting New Trends in America." (1999). *Hispanic Magazine.* http://www.hispanicmagazine.com/1999/nov/CoverStory/, accessed 08/20/05.

Telstra Appoints New CEO, http://www.telstra.com.au/abouttelstra/media/mediareleases_article.cfm?ObjectID=34035, accessed 08/20/05.

and equity are encouraged to pursue it for those who are not able to pursue it for themselves. Serving as a mentor, an ESL tutor, or friend and advocate for those who are devalued is beneficial to recipients as well as to those who serve.

Organizational Recommendations

Zero tolerance for discrimination and harassment based on race and ethnicity should specifically include unfair treatment of Latinos. Because discrimination often targets Blacks, Latinos are sometimes overlooked. Further, because Latinos may be immigrants or may speak little English, they are sometimes singled out for virulent discrimination and harassment. Proactive fairness policies would help eliminate or reduce such discrimination. Thorough investigation and discipline as appropriate are important to curb harassment.

Along with prohibiting against unfair treatment based on ethnicity, organizational leaders should take proactive measures to ensure fairness for Latino applicants and employees. Recruitment at high schools and universities with large Latino populations, referrals from Latino employees, and targeted advertising in Latino media should be helpful in increasing representation of Latino employees.

Organizational leaders should consider providing ESL classes for non-English speaking workers. One such program is Sed de Saber (thirst to know), offered through a partnership of The MultiCultural Foodservice and Hospitality Alliance and Coca-Cola, Inc. Sed de Saber is an English as a second language program designed specifically for adults. Vocational ESL classes have also been suggested as important ways to help non-English-speaking workers obtain job-related skills while also learning English.[65] These programs have also been argued to reduce turnover and improve safety and customer satisfaction while also improving workers' skills, self-esteem, and loyalty.

Along with helping employees to learn English, leaders should encourage English-speaking managers, supervisors, and employees to learn Spanish, a measure that employers of large numbers of Latinos are finding productive, relatively simple, rewarding, and positive for employee relations.[66] Employers in the restaurant industry are learning Spanish as a means to help reduce turnover, improve training, and connect with employees, many of whom do not speak English. While offering English as a second language classes is useful for employees, high turnover in certain industries makes having managers and supervisors who speak Spanish (and who have lower turnover) far more effective. Organizations should provide incentives and opportunities for managers to learn Spanish. In addition, reward those who already speak Spanish, rather than taking it for granted. Being bilingual is a job-related compensable skill; treat it as such.

As discussed in the chapter, managers' stated preferences for Latinos because of their strong "work ethic" are sometimes instead preferences for workers who are more likely to accept low wages and unfair treatment. As legal and ethical considerations, employers should provide no less than minimum wages, appropriate payment for overtime, Social Security contributions, and safe working consideration for all workers, period. Organizations will likely find that fair treatment of all workers is a good investment, even when wage rates are low. For low-wage, low-skilled workers, fair treatment, efforts to help them improve their language skills, and efforts to learn their language may translate into resource acquisition and cost advantages, reducing turnover, improving recruitment, and increasing productivity.

Employers should be aware that Hispanics are diverse in education, language fluency, background, and experiences. Although many Hispanics are recent immigrants and some have limited language fluency, many are native-born, fluent in English, and some do not even speak Spanish. As with any group, it is important to avoid making assumptions and job-related decisions about individuals based on their group membership rather than on their individual qualifications.

---

[65] See Huerta-Macias, A. (2002). *Workforce Education for Latinos,* Westport, CT: Greenwood Publishing Group.

[66] Berta, D. (2005, June 6). "English-Speaking Managers Learn to Use Spanish in Workplace." *Nation's Restaurant News,* 39(26): 6–22.

Summary

In this chapter, we have considered the diverse backgrounds, language fluency, educational levels, and experiences of Hispanics in the United States. Readers are encouraged to remember that organizational experiences of Hispanics are based in part on their race and ethnicity, but also on their immigrant or native status, education, occupation, industry, and geographic location. Hispanics are far from being a monolithic group, as is apparent in the diversity in population, education, earnings, and unemployment among Hispanics.

Individual recommendations centered on education, careful selection of employers, and English language fluency. Bilingualism was suggested as a positive attribute for Hispanics and non-Hispanics as well, and organizations should encourage and compensate it among employees. Organizational recommendations were provided to assist organizations in including Hispanic workers, valuing them as customers, and reducing workplace discrimination against them.

Key Term

Employment hardship — joblessness, involuntary part-time work, and working poverty.

Questions to Consider

1. Prior to reading this chapter, were you aware of the repatriation of Mexicans during the 1930s, lynching, and the fight for civil rights by Latinos?
2. Given the Hispanic buying power discussed in this chapter, what might retailers do to capitalize on the Hispanic consumer market?
3. What would your recommendations be for dealing with the behavior of the Conoco clerk in the incident in Fort Worth, Texas? What measures would you recommend to prevent such discrimination against Hispanic customers in the future?
4. What specific steps can organizations take to ensure that bilingual workers' skills are compensated when these skills are job-relevant, to encourage bilingualism among employees, and to reduce resistance against Spanish speakers?
5. In the *EEOC v. Campbell Concrete of Nevada, Inc.* case described, the supervisor asked the Hispanic employee if she missed getting up late and having siestas, reflecting negative job-related stereotypes about Hispanics. In addition to derogatory comments such as these, in what other ways may stereotypes and biases negatively affect Hispanic applicants and employees?
6. What can organizations that pay low wages for low-skill work do to ensure that workers are treated fairly? What is the role of perceptions that immigrant workers are "better off than if they were in __________" in justifying paying them low wages?
7. What should law enforcement agencies do to curb discrimination against minorities? What can the public do?
8. What have you learned from this chapter that you did not know previously?

Actions and Exercises

1. Observe employment of Hispanics in your community in a particular place (such as a store, restaurant, and office) in

which there are also non-Hispanic White, Black, Asian, and employees of other backgrounds. What do you observe of interest to diversity in organizations?

2. If you are not Hispanic, do you know someone well who is Hispanic? In what capacity do you know him or her (e.g., personal friend, manager, classmate, neighbor, etc.)? Do you know his or her ethnic origin (e.g., Mexico, Cuba, Central America, etc.)? Is he or she bilingual? Have you discussed race, ethnicity, or other diversity issues with him or her? Explain.
3. Investigate the repatriation of Mexican Americans. Have efforts to secure reparations for those affected been successful?
4. Conduct research to find several Hispanics in positions of power in corporations, politics, or universities. Describe their positions, educational background, experience, and other relevant factors that have contributed to their successes.
5. Investigate current instances of racial profiling and police misconduct against people of color. What are your findings?
6. See Table 3.1 in Chapter 3. After reading this chapter, do you agree with levels of identifiability, power, discrimination, and group awareness that Mexicans, Cubans, and Puerto Ricans are described as having? What, if anything, would you change?
7. In Chapter 4, Devah Pager's research documented employers' preferences for Whites with criminal records over Blacks without criminal records. Are these preferences also likely for Latinos? How might the failure of Latinos and Blacks to obtain withheld adjudication or similar benefits in other states exacerbate employers' existing preferences for Whites? How might questionable arrests and convictions, coupled with lower likelihoods to obtain withheld adjudication, have on the employment levels and earnings of Latinos and Blacks?

6 Chapter

Asians and Asian Americans

Chapter Objectives

After completing this chapter, readers should have a greater understanding of the roles of Asian Americans in diversity in organizations. Readers should expect to:

- *have increased awareness of the history of and diversity among Asians in the United States.*
- *be able to discuss participation rates, employment, and income levels of Asians.*
- *examine differences in educational return on investment for Asians when compared with other groups.*
- *be aware of research regarding Asians' attitudes toward affirmative action and their experiences with the glass ceiling and with individual and organizational discrimination.*
- *understand the "model minority myth" and similarities and differences among Asian Americans and between Asians and other minority groups.*

Key Facts

The category Asian American *includes people from many different backgrounds who have disparate education, income, and employment experiences in the United States.*

Asians with college degrees earn about 15% less per year than Whites with college degrees.

About 64% of Asian Indians, 50% of Chinese, and 14% of Vietnamese have completed college.

Although Asians are overrepresented in technical fields, they are less likely to be in management in such fields than other minority group members.

Many Asian-owned small businesses succeed only through long hours and unpaid labor of family members; many others fail despite the long hours and unpaid labor of family members.

Introduction and Overview

Asians are perhaps the most understudied, yet most diverse minority group in the United States. There are differences in culture, languages, experiences, and background among Asian Americans, particularly between some recent immigrants and those who are American born. Despite these differences, Asian Americans are often perceived as the "model minority" group, having come to the United States and, through hard work, determination, and strong cultural values, were able to achieve educational and financial success. These perceptions are contrasted with perceptions of other minority groups, who are portrayed as having done little to improve themselves when compared with Asians. At times, promulgation of such ideas has served to pit minority groups against each other, detracting from more accurate and important issues for all people of color. What is accurate about Asians in America? How much in common do Asians share with each other and with other minority group members in terms of education, income, and occupation? In what ways are they different? We consider these and other questions in this chapter.

We begin with a historical review of Asians in the United States, which, as with other racial and ethnic groups, provides important, often unknown insights into their status in the United States today. The remainder of the chapter covers standard topic areas, research translations, and focal issues for Asian Americans, including sections on Chinese, Indians, and Southeast Asians. Although space constraints prevent detailed coverage of all Asian groups, readers are encouraged to conduct their own investigations.

Terminology

The term *Asian American* refers to a heterogeneous group of people having origins in the Asia Pacific region. According to the current classifications of the U.S. Census Bureau, the category of Asians includes people from the Far East, Southeast Asia, or the Indian subcontinent, including Cambodia, China, India, Japan, Korea, Malaysia, Pakistan, the Philippine Islands, Thailand, and Vietnam, among many other areas. Reflecting the fluidity of "race" as discussed in previous chapters, racial classifications in the U.S. census of people of Asian descent have changed multiple times. In 1860, a category for Chinese was first included, and one for Japanese was added in 1870. Between 1910 and 1970, data for other Asian groups were collected periodically. In 1970, Asian Indians were classified as White and Vietnamese were included in the "other" racial category.

In the past, the U.S. Census Bureau has used the broad category "Asians and Pacific Islanders," which included Native Hawaiians and other Pacific Islanders along with Chinese, Koreans, and many other Asian groups. Due to the small numbers of Native Hawaiians, in 1997, the categories were separated into "Asians" and "Native Hawaiians or other Pacific Islanders." In some cases prior to this change, specific data were collected for Asian and Pacific Islanders, thus, in this book, the term *Asians and Pacific Islanders* (API) is sometimes used for accuracy of data reported. *Asian* and *Asian American* are generally used as interchangeable. Where possible and appropriate, specific references to the ethnic origin help clarify differences among this diverse category of people and in respect of preferences of members of the group.

Researchers have found that when given a choice to identify oneself as Asian American, Asian, ethnic American (e.g., Chinese American, Korean American), or as one's own ethnic origin alone (e.g., Chinese, Korean), 34% and 33% of respondents chose the latter two categories (e.g., ethnic American or ethnic origin alone).[1] Fully 67% preferred these categories over Asian or Asian American. However, when probed, 60% of respondents indicated acceptance of the term Asian American, reflecting the fluidity and malleability of ethnic identity and the influence of others on one's self-perceptions.

History of Asians in the United States

Asian Americans have long been part of U.S. history, contributing to its development in many ways. Many Americans of Filipino, Japanese, and Chinese ancestry have been in the United States for several generations, while most Southeast Asians are considerably more recent immigrants or refugees who have fled their country in the face of war and fear for their lives. Because entrance criteria (e.g., education, occupation) for refugees are less stringent than requirements for immigrants, Southeast Asian refugees often enter the country with fewer skills and assets, which has long-term effects on their future in the United States.[2]

Filipinos first arrived in what is now the United States around 1763, when Filipino crewmen who had been forced into service jumped ship in Louisiana and escaped into the bayous. They settled there, making their homes and developing Filipino communities. By the late nineteenth century, Filipinos had become thoroughly incorporated into Louisiana life.[3] Chinese immigrants began arriving in the United States in the 1850s, seeking work and opportunity. Early migrants worked as laborers in agriculture, fishery, domestic and laundry work, mines during the California gold rush, and as railroad workers. Some researchers suggest that Chinese laborers replaced the African slave trade that had become illegal in the 1840s.[4] One major contribution of Chinese railroad workers was in the completion of the first transcontinental railroad in May 1869, although Chinese workers were paid less than White European American workers. Once the railroad was completed, East Coast laborers were able to more easily move westward, fostering stiff labor market competition and fueling anti-Chinese rioting and lynching during the 1870s and 1880s.[5] The Chinese Exclusion Act of 1882 was the first federal legislation to bar immigrants based on national origin and severely and purposefully restricted entry of Chinese laborers into the United States for many decades.

[1] Lien, P., Conway, M., Wong, J. (2003). "The Contours and Sources of Ethnic Identity Choices among Asian Americans." *Social Science Quarterly,* 84: 461–482.

[2] Gold, S., & Kibria, N. (1993). "Vietnamese Refugees and Blocked Mobility." *Asian and Pacific Migration Journal,* 2(1): 27–56.

[3] Espina, M. (1988). *Filipinos in Louisiana,* New Orleans, LA: LaBorde & Sons.

[4] Lin, J. (1999). "Chinese Americans: From Exclusion to Prosperity?" In A. G. Dworkin & R. J. Dworkin (Eds.), *The Minority Report* (3rd edition), Fort Worth, TX: Harcourt Brace, pp. 321–342.

[5] Lin, J. (1999); Takaki, R. (1993). *A Different Mirror,* Boston: Back Bay Books; Zia, H. (2000). *Asian American Dreams: The Emergence of an American People,* New York: Farrar, Straus, and Giroux.

Although the first Japanese immigrants arrived in May 1843, the years between 1884 through 1924 are recognized as the period in which the ancestors of most present day Japanese Americans began arriving in the United States. Economic and political unrest in Japan, coupled with labor shortage and Western expansion, led to migration from Japan to Hawaii and California during the late nineteenth century.[6] Between 1884 and 1908, more than 150,000 Japanese laborers migrated to Hawaii. The migration of Japanese workers increased after the Chinese Exclusion Act, and many Japanese workers labored long hours for low pay on Hawaiian sugar plantations. Many workers exchanged their passage to Hawaii for a 3-year period of work with little or no pay, similar to indentured servants.

As were the Chinese, Japanese people were faced with hostility and exclusionary legislation. The 1908 Gentleman's Agreement and the 1924 National Origins Act were aimed at limiting Japanese worker immigration.[7] In 1922, the U.S. Supreme Court ruled that Japanese, along with others of Asian descent, were ineligible for naturalized citizenship.

The internment of more than 120,000 Japanese Americans during World War II is recognized as an historical act of devastating proportions. After the December 1941 Japanese attack on Pearl Harbor, panic and paranoia ensued about Japanese Americans who were living in the United States. In February 1942, President Franklin Roosevelt signed Executive Order 9066 authorizing the evacuation and internment of anyone considered a threat to national security. Included were all who had at least one-eighth Japanese ancestry, more than 100,000 Japanese Americans. Many of the evacuees were native-born American citizens; two-thirds of those evacuated were citizens and three-quarters were under age 25.[8] Branded as "enemy aliens" in 10 camps throughout the United States, the detainees' privacy, possessions, and freedom were gone. Ironically, while Japanese American U.S. soldiers fought in the war, some had family members being detained in the "relocation centers," which have also been referred to as concentration camps. One battalion included Japanese soldiers who were drafted out of the relocation centers to serve in the war.[9] Researchers have argued that racism was a key factor in the rationale to order the evacuation of 90% of Japanese Americans, but very few German or Italian Americans, in relocation centers.[10]

After 3 years, the centers closed, and Japanese Americans were allowed to return home, although many homes and considerable property had been lost,

---

[6] Fujiwara, J. H., & Takagi, D. Y. (1999). "Japanese Americans: Stories about Race in America." In A. G. Dworkin & R. J. Dworkin (Eds.), *The Minority Report* (3rd edition), Fort Worth, TX: Harcourt Brace, pp. 297–320.

[7] Fujiwara & Takagi. (1999).

[8] Schaefer, R. T. (2002). *Racial and Ethnic Groups. Census 2000 Update* (8th edition), Upper Saddle River, NJ: Pearson Education.

[9] Fujiwara & Takagi. (1999).

[10] See Schaefer. (2002). p. 370.

stolen, or destroyed during their internment. Estimates suggest that Japanese Americans lost $3.7 billion (1995 dollars) during that time. In 1988, the Civil Liberties Act authorized payments of $20,000 tax free to each of the 66,000 surviving internees. The payments were deemed too little and too late for many survivors, yet they were more than has been paid to some other groups that have suffered injustice sanctioned by the U.S. government.

People from Southeast Asia began coming to the United States in large numbers as a result of the Vietnam War. Many spoke no English and arrived with few possessions, making their transition extremely difficult. Initially, the U.S. government carefully orchestrated the settlement of Southeast Asian refugees, placing them in disparate cities across the country. Many refugees resettled to warmer climates, to areas in which family members had been settled, or to areas with stronger mechanisms in place (such as public assistance and language training) to assist them in making their transitions. As a result, many Southeast Asians, along with Asians from other areas, are significantly represented in California, Texas, and Washington, primarily in large urban cities.

Relevant Legislation

Restrictive immigration laws in the past affected entry of Asians who were not born in the United States. The Chinese Exclusion Act, discussed earlier, severely restricted Chinese immigration between 1882 and 1943, when it was repealed. It was replaced with a quota system, which allowed only 105 Chinese to enter the United States each year. Other restrictions and quotas, including the National Origins Act of 1924, severely limited other Asians' entry or ability to become naturalized citizens. Many such laws were enacted specifically to limit the number of Asian workers who were competing with European-born laborers. The Immigration and Nationality Act of 1965 eliminated race, national origin, or ancestry quotas for immigration into the United States, leading to a substantial increase in immigration in the years since then.[11]

As discussed in previous chapters, Title VII of the Civil Rights Act of 1964, as amended, is the key legislation relevant to people of color and their employment-related experiences. Although race and national origin limits have been eliminated, Asians still experience race and national origin discrimination, both of which are prohibited by Title VII. Executive orders for affirmative action also apply to people of Asian descent. As we will discuss, Asians are often confined to certain job categories, experience the glass ceiling, and receive lower returns on their educational investments than Whites. These factors reiterate Asians' need for Title VII and affirmative action, along with other nondominant groups.

[11] Mosisa, A. T. (2002). "The Role of Foreign-Born Workers in the U.S. Economy." *Monthly Labor Review,* 125(2): 3–14.

Asians and the Civil Rights Movement

Although the civil rights movement in the United States is primarily associated with Blacks, discrimination in employment, education, housing, and other areas led some Asians (specifically, Japanese, Chinese, and Filipinos), Latinos, and American Indians to participate in the civil rights movement.[12] In many cases, people of color (and Whites) often worked side by side to advance common civil rights. One Chinese man noted that "What Martin Luther King, Jr., is doing is going to benefit Chinese Americans," while others picketed with signs saying: "Minorities unite! Fight for Democratic rights!"[13] More recent issues with employment discrimination, hate crimes, racial profiling by police, and customer discrimination continue to underscore and reiterate similarities in experiences between Asians and other people of color and the need to include Asians in any study of diversity. Helen Zia, a Chinese American writer and activist discussed in Individual Feature 6.1, works tirelessly in the pursuit of fairness and equity for Asian Americans and other nondominant groups.

Selected EEOC Cases

Recent cases drawn from the EEOC Web site detail charges and settlements involving employment discrimination against Asians from various backgrounds and in distinct occupations.

- **EEOC v. QPM Aerospace, Inc.**

  No. 04-677-P (W.D. Wash. July 30, 2004)

  The Seattle District Office brought a Title VII suit alleging that a sheet metal fabrication and machining company retaliated against a Vietnamese-American machinist when it fired him for complaining about a manager's derogatory comments about Asians. Two other employees of Asian national origins (Laotian and Korean) intervened in the Commission's case alleging federal and state claims.[14]

- **EEOC v. Pacific Micronesia Corp.**

  No. 02-0015 (D. N. Mar. I. Mar. 3, 2004)

  The San Francisco District Office filed this Title VII action against defendants, the current and former owners of the Dai-Ichi Hotel, Saipan, alleging that the former

---

[12] Louie, S. (2001). "When We Wanted It Done, We Did It Ourselves." In S. Louie & G. Omatsu (Eds.), *Asian Americans: The Movement and the Moment,* Los Angeles: UCLA Asian American Studies Center Press, pp. xv–xxv. See also Widener, D. (2003). "Perhaps the Japanese Are to Be Thanked? Asia, Asian Americans, and the Construction of Black California." *Positions,* 11(1): 135–182. For an investigation of housing discrimination against Asians, see Turner, M. A., Ross, S. L., Bednarz, B. A., Herbig, C., & Lee, S. J. (2003). *Discrimination in Metropolitan Housing Markets: Phase 2—Asians and Pacific Islanders,* Washington, DC: The Urban Institute, http://www.huduser.org/publications/pdf/phase2_final.pdf, accessed 07/27/05.

[13] Lee, C. (2001). "Untitled Photo Essay." In S. Louie & G. Omatsu (Eds.), *Asian Americans: The Movement and the Moment,* Los Angeles: UCLA Asian American Studies Center Press, pp. 130, 131.

[14] Litigation Settlements—July 2004, http://www.eeoc.gov/litigation/settlements/settlement07-04.html, accessed 06/15/05.

Individual Feature 6.1 *Helen Zia*

Helen Zia is a Chinese American journalist and activist who has made a difference in the lives of countless people by her tireless commitment to equity and justice. Zia was born in New Jersey in 1952, educated at Princeton, and has worked as an autoworker, executive editor of *Ms.* magazine, a writer, and a civil rights and community activist.

As a member of one of the earliest classes that included women, Zia attributes her admission to Princeton both to graduating at the top of her high school class and to the civil rights movement. While at Princeton, Zia worked for equality for oppressed groups. There she joined a multiracial coalition to denounce racism and the Vietnam War. She also worked on Asian women's issues and became painfully aware of the focus on race as Black and White, while neglecting Asians.

Zia first came onto the media radar after Vincent Chin's brutal murder in Detroit in June of 1982. Chin, a second-generation Chinese American, was attacked by two unemployed White autoworkers who ostensibly blamed the Japanese for taking away Americans' auto jobs. The men supposedly thought Chin was Japanese, beat him into a coma with a baseball bat, and he died 4 days later. The assailants were sentenced to 3 years' probation and a $3,780 fine, but served no jail time. Outraged at the injustice, Zia and other activists formed a coalition, American Citizens for Justice (ACJ), to seek justice for the heinous crime and sentencing insult to the Chinese American community.

In addition to her work with ACJ, Zia has been an outspoken voice about other issues involving race, sex, and sexual orientation. Her work has been widely published in numerous respected magazines, including *The Nation, Essence, The New York Times, The San Francisco Chronicle*, among others. Her book, *Asian American Dreams: The Emergence of an American People*, is a compelling account of the history of Asian Americans in the United States and of Zia's own discovery of what it meant to be an Asian American and a feminist in a patriarchal society.[15]

Questions to Consider

1. ***Prior to reading this selection, had you heard of Helen Zia? With what famous Asian Americans are you familiar?***

2. ***Zia learned that many people see race as Black and White, while neglecting Asians. How prevalent is that perspective today? How does this perspective affect Asians in the United States? How prevalent is the perspective of diversity issues as being primarily race issues? How does this perspective affect other diversity issues?***

Source: Chinese American Forum. (2002, January). "Helen Zia: A Dedicated Civil Rights Advocate for Chinese/Asian Americans." 17(3), 5–8; Wang, A. L. (2002). "Eight Greats: Helen Zia." *Political Circus.com*, republished on Model Minority.com, http://modelminority.com/article794.html, accessed 06/20/05.

owner terminated over 40 employees in 1998 and 1999, following a union organizing campaign, due to their Filipino national origin. The former owner had replaced the Filipino workers with employees from countries other than the Phillippines because it believed they would be less likely to support unions. The complaint further alleged that the former owner denied promotions to Assistant

[15] Zia, H. (2000).

Executive Chef to non-Japanese employees, and retaliated against charging party, a Filipino hotel cook, by terminating him because he filed a charge with EEOC.[16]

- EEOC Settles National Origin Lawsuit for $1.25 million on behalf of Vietnamese American Fishing Crew Members

  SEATTLE — The U.S. Equal Employment Opportunity Commission (EEOC) today settled a lawsuit alleging that American Seafoods Company, a Seattle-based operation and a dominant force in the U.S. fishing industry, subjected 18 Vietnamese American at-sea workers to discriminatory conditions because of their national origin. Under terms of the settlement, the workers will be awarded $1,250,000 for the discrimination they suffered.

  The class action lawsuit, the first of its kind filed by the Commission which involves a class of Vietnamese Americans, alleged that American Seafoods created a hostile work environment for the crew members, denied training and promotional opportunities, subjected members to undesirable living and working conditions (housing, meals and medical treatment), demoted them, and reduced pay rates and terminated crewmen for requesting time off due to illness.[17]

- **EEOC v. The Herrick Corporation d/b/a Stockton Steel**
  No. S-00-0102-MCE-DAD (E.D. Cal. March 18, 2003)[18]

  In this Title VII lawsuit, the San Francisco District Office alleged that defendant, a steel fabrication plant, denied equal employment opportunities to and subjected four Pakistani-American and Muslim employees to a hostile working environment based on their national origin (Pakistani) and religion (Islam). Over an extended period of time, the employees, who were primarily machine operators, were hassled during their daily Muslim prayer obligations, mocked because of their traditional dress and repeatedly called 'camel jockey' and 'raghead.'

In view of the volume of discrimination involving Asian Americans, in August 2003, the EEOC announced a program called The Information Group for Asian American Rights (TIGAAR) that is designed to help educate Asian American employers and employees who may be unfamiliar with employment laws, rights, and responsibilities. TIGAAR is a partnership between the EEOC, the U.S. Department of Labor, local government entities, and numerous community

[16] Litigation Settlements—March 2004, http://www.eeoc.gov/litigation/settlements/settlement03-04.html, accessed 06/16/05.

[17] EEOC Settles National Origin Lawsuit for $1.25 Million on Behalf of Vietnamese American Fishing Crew Members, http://www.eeoc.gov/press/9-22-99-b.html, accessed 06/17/05.

[18] Litigation Settlement Report—March 2003, http://www.eeoc.gov/litigation/settlements/settlement03-03.html, accessed 07/08/05.

and advocacy groups. It uses radio, television, billboards, and videos to encourage employers to voluntarily comply with employment laws and to educate employees about their rights in the workplace. Inclusion of both Asian American employers and employees helps spread the word to affected parties. A 2005 Gallup Poll study conducted conjunction with the 40th anniversary of the U.S. Equal Opportunity Commission indicated that 31% of Asians, 26% of African Americans, 12% of Whites, and 18% of Hispanics reported experiencing workplace discrimination within the past year. Although Asians were most likely to report discrimination, only 3% of race discrimination claims were filed by Asians,[19] indicating continued need to inform Asians of their rights and responsibilities at work.

Population

There are 13.5 million U.S. residents of Asian descent reporting Asian alone or Asian in combination with some other race(s). Now comprising 5% of the U.S. population, the Asian population increased more than 9% between the 2000 census and 2004. Asians and Latinos are now the fastest growing groups in the United States, with both growing more rapidly than other racial and ethnic groups due to higher birth and immigration rates than other groups. High birth rates result in a young population; 26% of Asians are under 18, compared with 23% of Whites. In contrast, 14% of Whites are over 65, compared with 7% of Asians. As discussed in previous chapters, groups with younger average ages will make up proportionately more of the new entrants to the workforce in the future.

Almost 9 million of the 13.5 million Asian U.S. residents were born in Asia, making Asians 25% of the total foreign-born population in the United States. The majority of foreign-born Asians, 1.7 million, were born in China. More than half (52%) of the Asians who were born outside the United States have been naturalized. This contrasts with 38% of people born elsewhere.[20]

Misperception: Asian Americans are "perpetual outsiders."

Reality: Asians are more likely to be naturalized citizens than other immigrants.

As shown in Figure 6.1, Chinese, Filipinos, Japanese, Indians, Koreans, and Vietnamese, are the largest groups of people with Asian ancestry. At 3.6 million, California has the largest population of Asian Americans. Hawaii has the largest

[19] "New Gallup Poll on Employment Discrimination Shows Progress, Problems 40 Years After Founding of EEOC." http://www.eeoc.gov/press/12-8-05.html, accessed 12/09/05. Yen, H. (2005, December 8). "Poll: Nearly 1 out of 6 Workers Claim Bias." *The Associated Press.*

[20] Facts for Features, Asian/Pacific Heritage Month, May 2005, http://www.census.gov/Press-Release/www/releases/archives/facts_for_features_special_editions/004522.html, accessed 05/26/05.

FIGURE 6.1 ***Asian Population by Detailed Group: 2000***

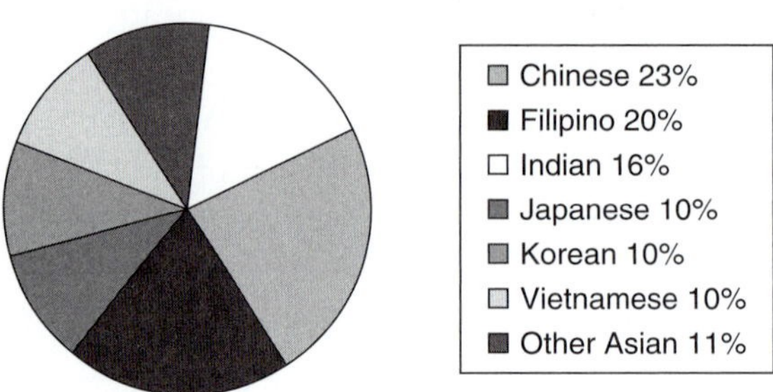

Note: Includes those who report "Asian alone" or Asian in combination with any other group.

Source: Barnes, J., & Bennett, C. (2002). *The Asian Population: 2000,* Washington, DC: U.S. Census Bureau, http://www.census.gov/prod/2002pubs/c2kbr01-16.pdf.

proportion of Asian American residents, where 58% of the population is of Asian descent.[21] The largest groups of Asians reside in New York City, Los Angeles, San Jose, San Francisco, and Honolulu. These cities have high costs of living, which, as we discuss later, affects Asians' earnings relative to other groups that are more geographically dispersed.

Education, Employment, and Earnings

As a group, Asian Americans have more education than other racial/ethnic groups in the United States. As shown in Table 6.1, nearly 50% of Asians have bachelor's degrees, compared with about 30%, 17%, and 11%, respectively, of Whites, Blacks, and Hispanics. On the other hand, Asians are also more likely not to have completed high school than Whites (13.2 vs. 10.0), which is additional evidence of the great diversity of experiences among people of Asian backgrounds. Immigrants generally fall into two educational categories—highly educated and poorly educated, with relatively few with moderate levels of education.[22]

Misperception: Asian Americans are well-educated.

Reality: Some Asians are well-educated, while others are poorly educated, representing a bimodal distribution of educational attainment.

Asian Indians are significantly more likely than members of all other groups, including other Asians, to have at least a college degree. Many well-educated

[21] Hawaii is the only state in which the majority group is of Asian descent.

[22] Mosisa. (2002).

TABLE 6.1 ***Educational Attainment by Race and Ethnicity for Population 25 Years and Older (in Percentages): 2003***

	Less than High School Graduate	High School Graduate or More	Some College or More	B.S. or More
Asian	13.2	87.6	67.4	49.8
White	10.0	89.4	56.4	30.0
Black	19.4	80.0	44.7	17.3
Hispanic (any race)	41.6	57.0	29.6	11.4

Source: Stoops, N. (2004). "Educational Attainment in the United States: 2003." Washington, DC: U.S. Census Bureau, http://www.census.gov/prod/2004pubs/p20-550.pdf, accessed 06/19/05.

Asian immigrants arrived in the United States with educations, reflecting what is termed as "brain drain," in which those who are well-educated leave one country to seek greater opportunities and income in other countries. Being well-educated and skilled generally increases the likelihood of gaining entry into and employment in the United States.

The distribution of education among Asians is bimodal, with 64.4% of Asian Indians, but 13.8% of Vietnamese and 9.2% of Cambodians/Hmongs/Laotians having completed college.[23] Fewer of the latter groups have college degrees than Blacks and Latinos. In support of affirmative action in education, in 2003 Asian Americans from various ancestries filed a "friend of the court" brief in support of the University of Michigan's admission program that included consideration of being an underrepresented minority, along with other factors. Included signers of the brief were the Asian American Legal Defense and Education Fund, Chinese for Affirmative Action, Filipinos for Affirmative Action, the Southeast Asia Resource Action Center, and the National Association for the Education and Advancement of Cambodian, Laotian, and Vietnamese Americans, among many others, in support of diversity in higher education. In contrast to the view that such programs harm Asians, the brief stated:

> The reality is that Asian Pacific Americans continue to suffer from racial discrimination in many aspects of life. In certain contexts, such as employment or public contracting, the effects of such discrimination are sufficiently egregious that Asian Pacific Americans should be specifically included in affirmative action programs to ensure diversity. In other contexts. . . . Asian Pacific Americans will receive fair treatment even if not expressly included in affirmative action programs because the flexibility of programs such as Michigan's

[23] Le, C. N. (2005). "Socioeconomic Statistics and Demographics." *Asian-Nation: The Landscape of Asian America,* http://www.asian-nation.org/demographics.shtml, accessed 07/10/05.

TABLE 6.2 ***Socioeconomic Statistics and Demographics for Selected Racial/Ethnic Groups (2000 Census)***

	Asian Indians	Cambodians, Hmongs, or Laotians	Chinese	Koreans	Vietnamese
Less than high school	12.6	52.7	23.6	13.8	40.4
College degree	64.4	9.2	46.3	43.6	13.8
Median family income in 000s*	$69.5	$43.9	$58.3	$48.5	$51.5
Living in poverty	8.2	22.5	13.1	15.5	13.8

*The median income is the income at which half the population in a category is below and half the population is above. Median incomes are generally lower than mean incomes.

Note: All measures are percentages except income.

Source: Adapted from Le, C. N. (2005). "Socioeconomic Statistics & Demographics." *Asian-Nation: The Landscape of Asian America,* http://www.asian-nation.org/demographics.shtml, accessed 05/29/05.

takes into account the unique backgrounds and distinctive experiences of Asian Pacific American applicants."[24]

For many Asians, education levels are related to their country of birth; U.S. natives or voluntary immigrants tend to have more education, while refugees (fleeing their homelands) are more likely to have low levels of education. Asians who are native-born and some immigrants are more likely to have advanced degrees and to speak English fluently, while refugees are more likely to be uneducated and have limited language skills. As shown in Table 6.2, significant differences among Asians exist in education, income, and likelihood of being in poverty or of receiving public assistance. While Asian Indians are generally quite successful, the experiences of Cambodians, Hmongs, Laotians, and Vietnamese are quite different.

Participation and Occupations

As of 2002, Asian men were slightly more likely to be participating in the workforce than White men, while Asian women were slightly less likely to participate than White women. By 2012, it is projected that 5% more Asian men will participate in the workforce than White men, and Asian women's participation rates will exceed those of White women by nearly 2% (Table 6.3). Estimates suggest that by 2012 Asian women's participation rates will exceed those of all women but African American women.

As shown in Figure 6.2, Asians are concentrated in managerial and professional specialty occupations, which include job titles such as managers, executives,

[24] Brief of Amici Curiae National Asian Pacific American Legal Consortium, Asian Law Caucus, Asian Pacific American Legal Center, Et al., In support of Respondents, http://www.napaba.org/uploads/napaba/02-14-2003_Grutter_&_Gratz_Brief.pdf, accessed 07/05/05.

TABLE 6.3 ***Projected Participation Rates (in Percent)***

	2002 Actual		2012 Projection	
	Men	**Women**	**Men**	**Women**
All groups	74.1	59.6	73.1	61.6
White, non-Hispanic	73.8	59.6	72.4	59.4
Black	66.4	62.0	69.1	64.0
Hispanic (any race)	80.2	57.1	79.0	58.6
Asian	75.6	57.9	77.3	61.3

Source: Table 4. Civilian labor force by age, sex, race, and Hispanic origin, 1992, 2002, and projected 2012, http://www.bls.gov/news.release/ecopro.t06.htm, accessed 06/01/05.

FIGURE 6.2 ***Occupation Distribution of the White and API Employed Civilian Labor Force 2002***

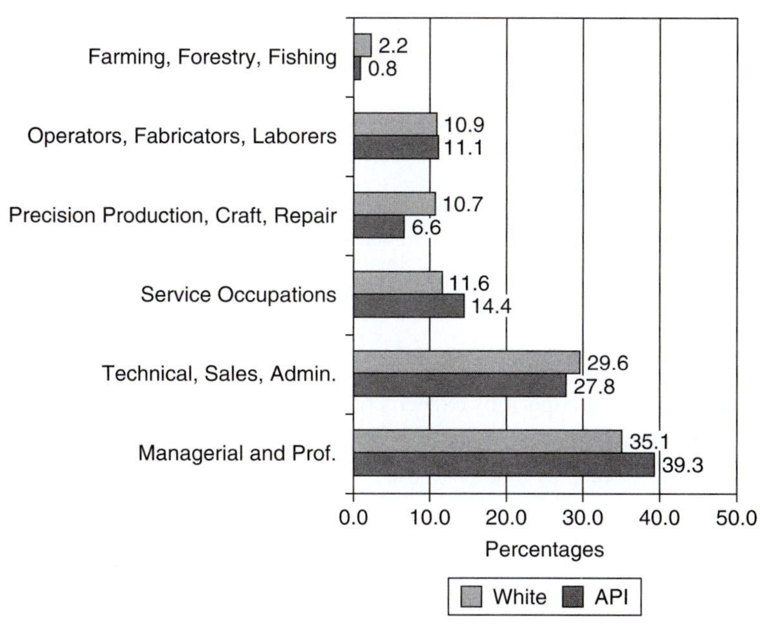

Source: The Asian and Pacific Islander Population in the United States: March 2002 (PPL-163), Table 11. Major Occupation Group of the Employed Civilian Population 16 Years and Over by Sex, and Race and Hispanic Origin: March 2002, http://www.census.gov/population/www/socdemo/race/api.html, accessed 07/09/05.

administrators, physicians, nurses, lawyers, architects, engineers, scientists, and teachers. Asian Americans represent 15% of the nation's physicians and surgeons but about 5% of the nation's population.[25] At 39.3%, Asian representation in the managerial and professional specialty occupations exceeds that of Whites by 4.2 percentage points. On the other hand, the representation of Whites in precision

[25] Asian Pacific American Population Census Facts for Heritage Month May 2004, http://www.imdiversity.com/villages/asian/reference/census_apa_stats_2004.asp.

FIGURE 6.3 ***Earnings of Full-Time, Year-Round Workers 15 Years and Over, 2001***

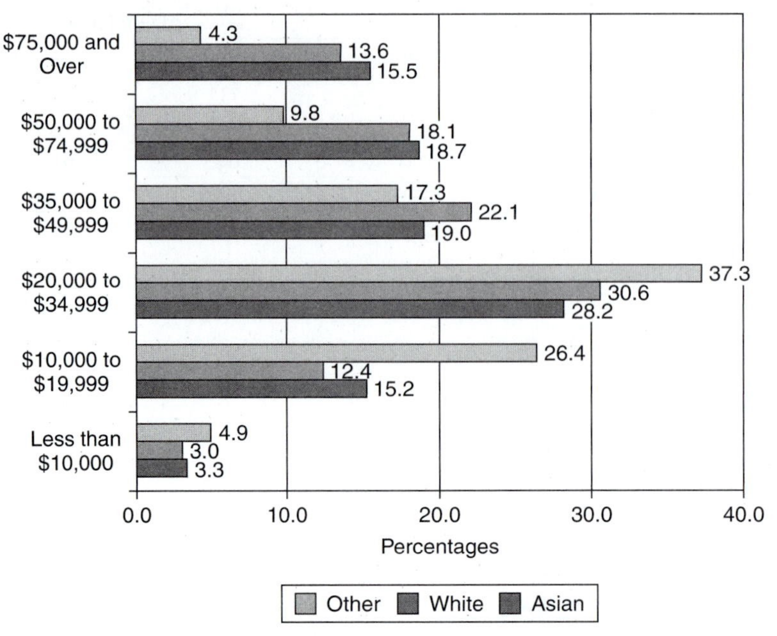

Note: Other includes all groups who are not Asian or non-Hispanic White.

Source: Author's calculations based on Current Population Survey, Asian and Pacific Islander Populations. Table 13. Earnings of Full-Time, Year-Round Workers 15 Years and Over in 2001 by Sex and Race and Hispanic Origin: March 2002, http://www.census.gov/population/www/socdemo/race/api.html, accessed 07/09/05.

production, craft, and repair occupations exceeds that of Asians by 4.1 percentage points. Asians are slightly more likely than Whites to work in service occupations (14.4% compared with 11.6%).

Earnings

In terms of income, in 2001, 40% of API families had incomes of $75,000 or more, compared with 35% of White families. On the other end of the income spectrum, about 17% of API families earned less than $25,000, compared with less than 15% of White families. Similarly, 2% more API families than White families lived in poverty in 2001.[26] Individual earnings of Asians, Whites, and others are presented in Figure 6.3. Again, when compared with Whites, more Asians are at the highest and the lowest ends of the spectrum.

[26] Reeves, T., & Bennett, C. (2003). "The Asian and Pacific Islander Population in the United States: March 2002." Current Population Reports, P20–540. U.S. Census Bureau, Washington, DC, http://www.census.gov/prod/2003pubs/p20–540.pdf, accessed 07/09/05.

Asians as the Model Minority

Despite many authors' concerted efforts to refute the stereotyped perception of Asians as "model minorities," the perception remains enduring and fairly widely held. As "model minorities," Asians are viewed as succeeding through hard work and determination, in contrast to Blacks, Latinos, and American Indians. One author suggested that Asians were "outwhiting the whites," excelling even more than Whites in education and income.[27] These distorted portrayals often fuel animosity toward Asians from other minority groups and Whites, while ignoring differences among Asians in education, income, and employment along with understating barriers and discrimination Asians face. As discussed in Focal Issue 6.1, Asians face overt racist behavior and recognize and resist being portrayed as a "voiceless model minority."

As it does other minority groups, underemployment affects educated Asian Americans. Despite their often having higher education than Whites, Asians are underrepresented in senior management and executive ranks. Asians comprise less than 0.5% of senior management positions in the United States.[28] Asians are frequently perceived as being technically astute and good at math, which are "positive" stereotypes but which likely also contribute to Asians' underrepresentation in higher-level organizational positions. Asians are also often stereotyped as being passive, nonconfrontational, and lacking in communication and language skills—regardless of whether they are native English speakers. These common misperceptions work to prevent Asians from advancing in organizations and often confine them to positions in which little communication, leadership, and decision making are required. These positions also often have few advancement opportunities, resulting in a glass ceiling for Asians.[29] For example, although Asians are overrepresented in technical fields, they are less likely to be in management in such fields than other minority group members.[30]

Although Asians have higher earnings than Whites, many Asians live in high-cost areas (Los Angeles, San Francisco, Honolulu, and New York); 95% of all API live in metropolitan areas, compared with 78% of Whites.[31] In addition, Asian family incomes are based on more workers than White family incomes.

---

[27] "Success Story: Outwhiting the Whites." (1971, June 21). *Newsweek*, pp. 24–25.

[28] Minami, D. (1995). *Perspectives on Affirmative Action*, Los Angeles: Asian Pacific American Public Policy Institute, p. 11; See Korn/Ferry International, *Executive Profile: A Decade of Change in Corporate Leadership*, 23, (1990). See also Brief of Amici Curiae National Asian Pacific American Legal Consortium, Asian Law Caucus, Asian Pacific American Legal Center, Et al., In support of Respondents.

[29] Woo, D. (2000). *Glass Ceiling and Asian Americans: New Face of Workface Barriers*, Walnut Creek, CA: Alta Mira Press.

[30] National Science Foundation, Division of Science Resource Statistics, *Women, Minorities, and Persons with Disabilities in Science and Engineering*, NSF 04-317 (Arlington, VA 2004), http://www.nsf.gov/statistics/wmpd/pdf/front.pdf, accessed 07/05/05.

[31] Reeves & Bennett. (2003).

Focal Issue 6.1 *Jersey Guys Disc Jockeys Make Racist Anti-Asian Statements on Air*

On April 25, 2005, two disc jockeys for New Jersey radio station NJ 101.5, Craig Carton and Ray Rossi, astounded and offended many listeners by making anti-Asian remarks on air. The discussion began with negative comments about a Korean American named Jun Choi who was running for mayor of Edison, NJ. Carton asked, "Would you really vote for someone named Jun Choi?" One DJ noted that concern about the Asian vote from both Choi and his opponent in the election, Jim Spadoro, was "part of a larger problem ... forgetting that we're Americans." The on-air show deteriorated from there, with derogatory comments about Chinese, Asians, Indians, and referrals to their previous negative comments about Arabs. Carton and Rossi complained that there were too many Asians in New Jersey casinos, suggesting that there should be "Asian-only" rooms there because of Asians' lack of knowledge of the games and their "little beady pocketbooks" stuffed with wads of $100 bills. "Ching chong, ching chong, ching chong," was interspersed with laughter and comments that the DJs had "nothing against them" (Asians), who were "very good people ... very nice people ..."[32]

Many people were outraged by the anti-Asian comments, and complaints poured in to the radio station, which was reportedly caught off guard by the volume of complaints. Both the NAACP and the Anti-Defamation League joined Asian groups in expressing outrage at the broadcast. Hyundai Motors America indefinitely suspended its advertisements from the station. Cingular Wireless withdrew advertising from the Jersey Guys' afternoon programming spots. In commenting on the vocal response from the Asian American community, Veronica Jung, executive director of the Korean American League for Civic Action, stated that "... we will no longer be the voiceless model minority. We represent significant buying power and a large consumer base, and we'll use that weight." The radio station refused to comment on the amount lost in advertising revenues.

Questions to Consider

1. *When Michelle Kwan, Chinese American Olympic skater (native of Torrance, California), came in second place in an Olympic event, a major news headline read "American Beats Kwan." Four years later, after another skating loss, other news source reported that Kwan had been beaten by an "American," repeating the earlier terminology and again alienating and aggravating Asian Americans. As is evident in comments of the Jersey Guys, Asian Americans are often seen as outsiders, even when they are native-born or naturalized citizens. Why might this perception persist?*
2. *Aside from apologies, what specific responses are appropriate from organizations when actions such as those of the Jersey Guys occur?*
3. *What specific preventive actions should organizations take to avoid such offensive actions by employees?*
4. *Jun Choi won the June 2005 primary election, defeating the three-term incumbent. Did Choi win in the November election? Investigate.*

[32] Quotes taken from: "Transcript of the Jersey Guys on the Edison Mayoral Race NJ 101.5," http://www.sepiamutiny.com/sepia/archives/TranscripttheJerseyGuys.pdf, accessed 06/08/05.

In metropolitan areas, API are eight times more likely to live in crowded household conditions than Whites.[33]

Misperception: Asians have higher incomes than Whites.

Reality: Asians tend to live in high-cost areas and have more family members contributing to family income, making their earnings appear higher than they actually are.

Yen Espiritu has described the idea of Asians as model minorities as telling "only half-truths, masking the plight of disadvantaged subgroups and glossing over the problems of underemployment, misemployment, and unemployment" that Asians face.[34] Many others echo Espiritu's sentiments about the inaccuracies and questionable motivations behind the idea of Asians as "model minorities."[35] If Asians are held up as a successful model, other minority groups can be viewed as failures who blame racism for their plight instead of working hard, as Asians do.

One important factor in determining how well people have avoided discrimination and how successful they are is to measure their returns on educational investment. As discussed earlier, overall, Asian Americans are the most highly educated group in the United States. As such, one might expect their earnings to also exceed those of every other racial and ethnic group, but this is not always the case. As shown in Table 6.4, earnings of Whites exceed those of every other group except where Asian women earn more than White women at the master's level and in the total of all categories. Asians with professional degrees (e.g., MD, JD) earn about 15% less than Whites with these degrees (not shown).

Unemployment and occupation are other indicators of a group's success. As shown in Table 6.5, at all levels, White unemployment is lowest while Black unemployment is generally highest. Asian unemployment is more similar to that of Blacks and Latinos than to that of Whites. Well-educated Asian Americans are likely to be employed, while those with less education often work for low wages or are unemployed, in poverty, and often on welfare.[36] As an example, one study investigating changes in immigrant receipt of public assistance found that

---

[33] Ro, M. (2000). Overview of Asians and Pacific Islanders in the United States and California, http://www.communityvoices.org/Uploads/om3gfk55hhzyvrn00n4nerbf_20020828090003.pdf.

[34] Espiritu, Y. L. (1999). "The Refugees and the Refuge: Southeast Asians in the United States." In A. G. Dworkin & R. J. Dworkin (Eds.), *The Minority Report* (3rd edition), Fort Worth, TX: Harcourt Brace, pp. 343–363.

[35] For discussions of the model minority myth, see Le, C. N. (2005). "The Model Minority Image." *Asian-Nation: The Landscape of Asian America,* http://www.asian-nation.org/model-minority.shtml, accessed 07/10/05; Takaki. (1993); Gold & Kibria. (1993); Hurh, W. M., & Kim, K. C. (1989). "The Success Image of Asian Americans—Its Validity, and Its Practical and Theoretical Implications." *Ethnic and Racial Studies,* 12(4): 512–538.

[36] Borjas, G. J., & Trejo, S. J. (1991). "Immigrant Participation in the Welfare System." *Industrial and Labor Relations Review,* 44(2): 195–211; Jensen, L. (1988). "Patterns of Immigration in Public Assistance Utilization, 1970–1980." *International Migration Review,* 22(1): 51–83. See also Bean, F. D., Van Hook, J. V. W., & Glick, J. E. (1997). "Country of Origin, Type of Public Assistance, and Patterns of Welfare Recipiency among U.S. Immigrants and Natives." *Social Science Quarterly,* 78: 432–451.

TABLE 6.4 ***Mean Income in 2002 for Full-Time, Year-Round Workers by Race, Sex, and Hispanic Origin***

	Total	<H.S.	H.S. Graduate	Some College	Associate's Degree	Bachelor's Degree	Master's Degree
Asian male	$57,862	$21,937	$35,209	$44,625	$41,939	$64,336	$79,389
Asian female	$41,006	$20,793	$24,657	$31,751	$35,292	$47,692	$59,890
% Asian female/ male earnings	71%	95%	70%	71%	84%	74%	75%
White male	$60,169	$32,441	$41,439	$50,558	$51,683	$76,832	$88,234
White female	$39,844	$23,016	$29,675	$35,045	$36,231	$51,283	$58,800
Black male	$40,289	$28,073	$31,008	$40,978	$44,938	$54,655	$71,470
Black female	$32,843	$19,719	$27,111	$29,663	$32,951	$45,367	$54,844
Hispanic male	$34,822	$25,374	$32,794	$39,659	$46,018	$53,067	$66,781
Hispanic female	$28,062	$18,889	$24,058	$27,938	$32,668	$44,475	$65,953*

*Large standard error ($13,004) explains high mean wage for Hispanic women with master's degree. Median of $46,255 is more representative.

Source: U.S. Census Bureau, Internet Release Date: June 29, 2004. Table 8. Income in 2002 by Educational Attainment of the Population 18 Years and Over by Age, Sex, Race, and Hispanic Origin, http://www.census.gov/population/socdemo/education/cps2003/tab08-2.xls, accessed 10/29/05.

TABLE 6.5 ***Unemployment Level by Educational Attainment and Race (Percent of Population 25 Years and Over): 2003***

	Total	White	Black	Asian	Hispanic*
Less than H.S.	8.8	7.8	13.9	9.5	8.2
H.S. graduate	5.5	4.8	9.3	5.6	5.9
Some college, no degree	5.2	4.5	8.6	6.4	5.8
Associate's degree	4.0	3.6	6.2	5.2	5.3
Bachelor's and higher	3.1	2.8	4.5	4.4	4.1

*Persons whose ethnicity is Hispanic are classified by ethnicity as well as by race.

Source: http://www.bls.gov/cps/cpsaat7.pdf, accessed 10/22/04.

of Japanese, Chinese, Filipino, and Vietnamese immigrant families, 8.7%, 5.1%, 10.6%, and 29.3%, respectively, were receiving public assistance. Rates were even higher for female-headed households—39.1% of Vietnamese female-headed households were receiving public assistance during the period studied.[37] When employed, many immigrant women work in the garment industries, while men often work in restaurants, often at substandard wages under poor working conditions, and with excessive hours. Without education and language skills, Asian immigrants may be locked in these dead end positions.

Asian American Entrepreneurs

One accurate perception of Asian Americans is that they are more likely to start their own businesses than other minority groups. Some researchers suggest that higher entrepreneurship among Asians is in part due to their having

[37] Borjas & Trejo. (1991).

FIGURE 6.4 ***Distribution of Asian and Pacific Islander Owned Firms***

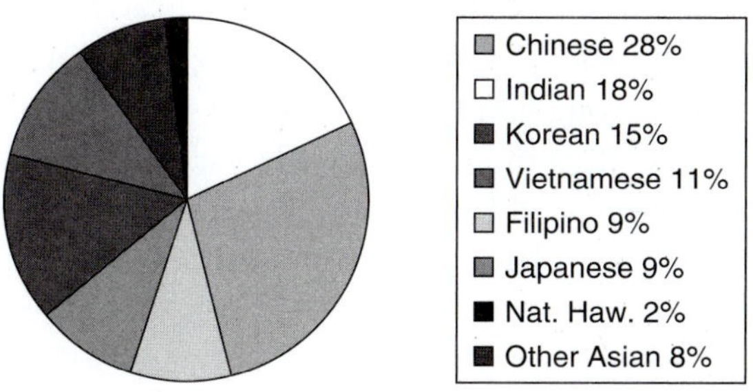

Source: U.S. Census Bureau. (2001). "Asian- and Pacific Islander-Owned Businesses: 1997." http://www.census.gov/prod/2001pubs/cenbr01-7.pdf.

encountered the glass ceiling in other organizations. Others propose that limited skills and informal networks among some Asian immigrants make them more likely to start small businesses, but that they suffer numerous and expensive social costs as a result of entrepreneurship. It is likely that both perspectives have some merit and that the theories apply to different groups of Asians with different skills.[38] Well-educated, more highly skilled Asian entrepreneurs may start their own businesses in response to discrimination or they may be professionals who originally intended to start professional businesses in the United States (e.g., consulting, technical, medical, or legal). Asian entrepreneurs with few language skills, low education, and few other opportunities may also start small businesses.

There are nearly a million Asian owned businesses in the United States, employing more than 2 million people and generating over $300 billion in revenues in a wide variety of industries. As shown in Figure 6.4, among Asians, those from Chinese, Indian, Korean, and Vietnamese ancestry are most likely to have their own firms. For example, three of four API-owned hotels and motels are owned by Asian Indians, two in three API-owned fishing, hunting, and trapping firms are owned by Vietnamese, and Koreans own half of the API-owned apparel and accessory stores.[39]

Most Asian-owned firms are in the service industries (44%), and 21% are in the retail trade industry. Although there are more than twice as many firms in service industries as compared with retail trade industries, both generate 22% of total receipts of API-owned firms. Asians from different backgrounds tend to own different kinds of businesses. As with small businesses in general, many

[38] For a detailed discussion of theories about Asian entrepreneurship, see Le, C. N. (2005). "Asian Small Businesses." *Asian-Nation: The Landscape of Asian America,* http://www.asian-nation.org/small-business.shtml, accessed 06/09/05.

[39] "Asian- and Pacific-Islander owned businesses: 1997." (2001). U.S. Census Bureau, http://www.census.gov/prod/2001pubs/cenbr01-7.pdf, accessed 06/09/05.

Asian-owned firms struggle for survival and many fail within the first few years. While 5% of Asian-owned firms have receipts of $1 million or more, nearly 30% have receipts under $10,000 each year. Researchers have documented long hours of unpaid or extremely low wage labor among family members of Asian business owners as part of their ability to survive.[40] In a thought-provoking article, Edna Bonacich has argued that many immigrant small business owners are pawns in a capitalistic society, discussed in Research Translation 6.1.

Misperception: Asian business owners are highly successful.

Reality: Some Asian business owners are highly successful, while others marginally succeed due to long hours and unpaid labor of family members.

Research on Experiences of Asian Americans at Work

Along with the "positive" stereotypes about Asian Americans (e.g., good at math, technically astute, hardworking, highly educated, wealthy), negative stereotypes also exist such as that Asians lack leadership qualities and communication skills and are arrogant. Many of these critical perspectives are partially due to animosity about Asians' perceived success in educational and business arenas.[41] Researchers have found that when Asians are portrayed in the media, they are likely to be depicted as affluent, highly educated, and proficient with technology.[42] Because many Americans say they do not know any Asians, stereotypes and media representations are the bases for many of their perceptions.

Compared with Blacks, little empirical research has investigated the organizational experiences of Asian Americans. What research exists indicates that Asians' report experiences with discrimination and the glass ceiling that are similar to those of other minority groups. This differential treatment takes the form of access and treatment discrimination. For example, treatment discrimination faced by Asians sometimes occurs when they are steered to particular jobs deemed appropriate for people who are technically strong but have limited English skills, and when they are denied management positions due to perceptions of lack of leadership skills. Evidence of the glass ceiling for Asians has been found in state, local, and federal government positions, college and university

[40] Espiritu. (1999).

[41] For example, see "Committee of 100: American Attitudes toward Chinese Americans and Asian Americans." (2004, Summer). *The Diversity Factor,* 12(3): 38–44.

[42] Paek, H. J., & Shah, H. (2003). "Racial Ideology, Model Minorities, and the 'Not-so-Silent Partner:' Stereotyping of Asian Americans in U.S. Magazine Advertising." *Howard Journal of Communications,* 14(4): 225–244.

Research Translation 6.1 *Successful Small Business Owners or Unsuspecting Pawns?*

Edna Bonacich is a professor of sociology and ethnic studies at the University of California, Riverside. Based on her considerable research on experiences of Korean immigrant entrepreneurs, Bonacich documents the expensive individual and social costs of immigrant entrepreneurship that often go unreported and unrecognized.

Small businesses are often concentrated in areas that major retailers (and employers) have abandoned,[43] employ workers (often other immigrants or minority group members) at below minimum wages, and are often unregulated by government entities. Capitalist producers of goods sold or made in small businesses earn profits from those entities without investing in them. Low wage workers do not organize to demand higher wages because of familial relationships, lack of knowledge, and lack of other opportunities. The small sizes of most entities keep them from government oversight that would help protect workers. Ethnic small business owners whose businesses are in minority communities are referred to as *middlemen*, minorities who serve communities that White business owners have abandoned. As middlemen, these business owners at times experience hostility and frustration from African American and Latino customers as well as conflicts with their White suppliers and landlords.[44]

Bonacich and her colleague Ivan Light studied Korean immigrant entrepreneurs in Los Angeles, carefully investigating the reasons behind their entrepreneurship and their personal and professional experiences as a result of entrepreneurship. Bonacich concluded that immigrant entrepreneurship comes at high costs to the immigrants and to society at large. These costs include

a. family breakdown, including neglected children, due to excessive hours spent working, spousal (wife) abuse, and marital discord, due to wives having to contribute long (unpaid) hours in support of the business, yet still being expected to maintain the home.
b. anti-immigrant expression and hostility from customers and clients (e.g., by Black and Latino customers against Korean entrepreneurs, although all three are victims), and other immigrant competitors.
c. lowered labor standards for society as a whole because of labor exploitation that includes long hours at very low wages and unpaid child and family labor in immigrant businesses.

"Large corporations such as supermarkets have abandoned these neighborhoods, but the producers of the goods sold by immigrant shops continue to get the profits out of the ghetto and the barrio through immigrant firms," says Bonacich (p. 121).[45] She further states that when firms are small and dispersed, this limits employees' ability to unionize and the ability of government agencies to enforce labor standards,[46] making abuses more likely.

Pyong Gap Min and other researchers have echoed Bonacich's concerns about entrepreneurship in the Korean community. Min's research indicates that 67% of husbands and 59% of wives who work in Korean businesses work 6 or 7 days

---

[43] See also Wilson, W. J. (1996). *When Work Disappears: The World of the New Urban Poor,* New York: Knopf.
[44] Min, P. G. (1996). *Caught in the Middle: Korean Communities in New York and Los Angeles,* Berkeley, CA: University of California Press.
[45] Bonacich, E. (1988). "The Social Costs of Immigrant Entrepreneurship." *Amerasia Journal,* 14(1): 119–128.
[46] Ibid.

per week.[47] Steven Gold and Nazli Kibria have documented experiences of Vietnamese small business owners that are similar to those reported by Bonacich.[48] They report extremely low wages of small business owners, family members, and other employees, no benefits, high rates of business failure, and stiff competition from other ethnic-owned small businesses.

Questions to Consider

1. ***How familiar are you with small businesses owned by Asian immigrants? If you are familiar with such businesses, how does what you perceive about their level of profitability, hours worked, and employees compare with what Bonacich reports?***
2. ***Many small businesses are staffed entirely or almost entirely by people of the same race or ethnicity of the owners—indeed they are very homogeneous. Is such homogeneity of employees in violation of Title VII of the Civil Rights Act? Why or why not?***
3. ***What does the most recently available U.S. Census Bureau data say about the ownership, numbers, types, size, and profitability of Asian-owned businesses?***

Source: Bonacich, E. (1988). "The Social Costs of Immigrant Entrepreneurship." *Amerasia Journal*, 14(1): 119–128.

administration and professional school faculty positions, the judiciary system, and corporations.[49]

In the study described in Research Translation 6.2, Asians reported experience with workplace discrimination that was similar to that reported by Blacks and Latinos. Asians' attitudes toward affirmative action in employment were also more similar to the attitudes of Blacks and Latinos than Whites.

A study conducted in New Zealand investigated the effects of having a Chinese, Indian, or Anglo-Saxon name found effects similar to those found in the study of effects of having a Black or White sounding names in Chapter 4.[50] Study participants, primarily practicing managers, chose applicants to be placed on a short list of candidates and rated them in terms of suitability for the position. Applicants were all highly qualified for the positions in question, but Chinese applicants were least likely to be placed on a short list and received lowest suitability ratings, followed by Indian, and Anglo-Saxon applicants. Applicants with Anglo-Saxon names received more favorable ratings than candidates with ethnic names. Chinese applicants with anglicized names (such as Polly Wong) received lower ratings from European raters than they did from Asian

[47] Min, P. G. (1997). "Korean Immigrant Wives' Labor Force Participation, Marital Power, and Status." In E. Higginbotham & M. Romero (Eds.), *Women and Work: Exploring Race, Ethnicity, and Class,* Thousand Oaks, CA: Sage, pp. 176–191.

[48] Gold & Kibria. (1993).

[49] For a discussion, see Brief of Amici Curiae National Asian Pacific American Legal Consortium, Asian Law Caucus, Asian Pacific American Legal Center, Et al., In support of Respondents.

[50] Gee-Wilson, M., Gahlout, P., Liu, L., & Mouly, S. (2005). "A Rose by Any Other Name . . . : The Effect of Ethnicity and Name on Access to Employment." *The University of Auckland Business Review,* 7(2): 55–68; Wilson, M., Mouly, S., Gahlout, P., & Liu, L. (2005). "The Effects of Ethnicity, Ethnicity of Name, and Immigration Status on Employment Short-listing." *Paper presented at the Academy of Management Meeting,* Honolulu, HI.

Research Translation 6.2 *Asian Americans, Discrimination, and Attitudes toward Affirmative Action in Employment: Empirical Research Evidence*

Asian Americans' attitudes about affirmative action are common topics in the debate about affirmative action with some authors arguing that Asians support it, and others that Asians are against it. Still others present both sides of the story, for example, Michael Fletcher's article published in the *Washington Post* debated whether affirmative action was a "barrier or a boon" for Asian Americans.[51] Fletcher's and many popular press articles confound affirmative action in education with affirmative action in employment, both of which strive to help underrepresented groups, but which do so by very different mechanisms. Even so, it is clear that some Asians are supportive of affirmative action measures, while others are against it. For example, 61% of Asian Americans voted against California's Proposition 209, an anti-affirmative action effort. Many Asians supported Washington State's Initiative 200, which was modeled after Proposition 209. One Seattle physician felt that "Asian Americans lose their competitive edge because of affirmative action," while another stated that "there has been an attempt to use us (Asians) as a wedge, but the fact is that we are direct beneficiaries of affirmative action."[52]

As with other issues confounded by different articles in the media, empirical research may help clarify inconsistencies. The majority of research assessing employees' experiences with workplace discrimination and attitudes toward affirmative action has focused on Whites and Blacks, however. A lesser amount of research had Latino samples, and even fewer studies have included Asian Americans. Although some studies have included Asians in their "minorities" category, this prevents separate analysis of each group's perspective and masks differences between them.

One study, "Asian American Attitudes toward Affirmative Action in Employment: Implications for the Model Minority Myth," specifically assessed Asians' attitudes and compared them with those of Whites, Blacks, and Latinos. The researchers also compared attitudes of Asian U.S. citizens with those of Asian noncitizens, recognizing the potential for differences in experiences, perspectives, and beliefs between these groups.

The survey asked questions about the specific attributes commonly associated with affirmative action programs, such as whether they improve job opportunities of women and minorities, reduce discrimination in historically segregated jobs, and create a lot of paperwork for employers. Overall, Asians (both groups) held significantly more positive beliefs about the attributes of affirmative action than Whites, in every instance. In addition, for some attributes, Asian noncitizens held significantly more positive attitudes than Asian U. S. citizens. The former were more likely to think that affirmative action in employment helps to give everyone qualified an equal chance, create greater awareness of discrimination, and produce a more diverse workforce. They were also less likely to have negative views about attributes of affirmative action programs than Asian citizens, such as that they frequently operate as quotas or cause employers to hire people who are less qualified.

Study participants' overall impression of affirmative action and their experiences with

[51] Fletcher, M. A. (1998). "For Asian Americans, a Barrier or a Boon?" *Washington Post,* June 20, 1998. Reprinted in Crosby, F. J., & VanDeVeer, C. (Eds.), *Sex, Race, and Merit: Debating Affirmative Action in Education and Employment,* Ann Arbor: The University of Michigan Press.

[52] Ibid.

discrimination were also measured. In all, Whites' attitudes toward affirmative action were most negative, Blacks' attitudes were most favorable, followed by Asians and Latinos, whose attitudes were statistically similar and moderately favorable. Asians reported experiencing workplace discrimination at similar rates to other Latinos and Blacks and significantly less than Whites reported.

As Asians grow as a percentage of the population, it is expected that more research will investigate their workplace experiences. In addition to distinctions between Asian citizens and those who are not citizens, differences among Asians of different ancestry (e.g., Filipino, Chinese, Korean, and Indian) and various educational and occupational levels should also be investigated.

Source: Bell, M. P., Harrison, D. A., & McLaughlin, M. E. (1997). "Asian American Attitudes toward Affirmative Action: Implication for the Model Minority Myth." *Journal of Applied Behavioral Science*, 33: 356–377.

Questions to Consider

1. ***Why have attitudes of Asian Americans toward affirmative action in employment been studied so little?***
2. ***What issues likely contribute to attitudinal differences between Asian U.S. citizens and Asian immigrants?***
3. ***What factors may influence differences in experiences with discrimination between minority groups?***
4. ***As discussed earlier in the chapter, many Asian Americans also support affirmative action in education. Why might perceptions that Asians do not benefit from affirmative action in employment and that they are harmed by affirmative action in education be so prevalent?***

raters. Overall, ethnic candidates were significantly underrepresented in the final short lists and received significantly lower suitability ratings, despite equal qualifications. International Feature 6.1 considers the population, employment, and workplace experiences of Asians in the United Kingdom.

Asian American Women at Work

As discussed in previous chapters, women of color face unique obstacles in their organizational experiences related to their sex and race or ethnicity. Asian American women are no exception to the "double-whammy" resulting from multiple minority group statuses, earning less than Asian men in every earnings category. As discussed earlier, Asian women's participation in the workforce is increasing. By 2012, it is projected that more Asian women will work outside the home than all women except African American women. Between 1990 and 2001, Asian women's share of the total workforce grew from 1.3% to 2.1%; nearly twice as many Asian women were working in 2001 as in 1990.[53]

[53] Women of Color: Their Employment in the Private Sector, http://www.eeoc.gov/stats/reports/womenofcolor/#Section_1.1.3, accessed 06/17/05.

International Feature 6.1 *Asians in the United Kingdom*

Asians have resided in the United Kingdom for centuries and are significant contributors to its history and successes. The United Kingdom has historically placed stringent limitations on immigration, although records document that Asian merchants, politicians, suffragettes, teachers, students, military personnel, and others have resided there for many years. England's deliberate effort to restrict entry of Asian seamen through the Special Restriction Order of 1925 is viewed as a precursor to the area's current demographic and social conditions, including "institutional racism" against Asians in Britain today.[54]

As of the 2001 census, there are about 60 million people in the United Kingdom, and 92.1% are White, 2% Black, 1.8% Indian, 1.3% Pakistani, 1.2% mixed, and 1.6% other (Chinese, Bangladeshi, and other Asian, etc.).[55] The Race Relations Act in 1968, as amended in 1976, prohibits "open and direct" and indirect race-based discrimination in employment, housing, and public services in the UK.

Educational levels and employment experiences of Asians in the UK vary greatly, and education and employment of Indians and Chinese are significantly different from the experiences of Pakistanis and Bangladeshis. In some cases, Chinese and Indian earnings, employment levels, and occupational status approach those of Whites. In contrast, Pakistanis and Bangladeshis have lower earnings and higher unemployment. Whereas Indians and Chinese in the UK are likely to be from established immigrant communities, Pakistanis and Bangladeshis are more recent immigrants and are less established. The latter often work in low-wage positions in declining industries and are residentially segregated.

The experiences of Asians and other ethnic minorities with discrimination in employment, harassment, exclusion, hate crimes, and racial profiling by police are gaining increased attention in the British media, among the public, and among lawmakers. Overall, unemployment for Asians is considerably more than for Whites, although unemployment levels ranged between 13% for Indians and 33% for Bangladeshis compared with 8.8% for Whites in one study. In addition, at comparable education levels, Asian unemployment is significantly higher than that of Whites, indicating a lower return on educational investment for Asians. Asians are more likely to be in declining industries or those involving manual labor, such as manufacturing, or to be self-employed.[56]

As in other areas, some women of color in the UK are particularly marginalized in employment. White, Black, Indian, and Chinese women have similar rates of workforce participation (about 60%), compared with less than 30% for Pakistani and Bangladeshi women. When employed, Pakistani or Bangladeshi women earn 56 cents to the dollar earned by White men.[57]

Sources: Jones, T. (1993). *Britain's Ethnic Minorities,* London: Policy Studies Institute; Muhammad, A. (1998). *Between Cultures: Continuity and Change in the Lives of Young Asians,* London: Routledge.

[54] See Visram, R. (2002). *Asians in Britain: 400 Years of History,* London: Pluto Publishers.

[55] The World FactBook. United Kingdom. http://www.cia.gov/cia/publications/factbook/geos/uk.html, accessed 07/11/05.

[56] Muhammad, A. (1998). *Between Cultures: Continuity and Change in the Lives of Young Asians,* London: Routledge.

[57] "UK Blacks, Asian women being ostracized: Report." *Hindustan Times*. February 17, 2005.

More Asian women work in the computer and electronic product manufacturing industry than in any other single industry. Many Asian women also work in retail industries, including clothing and health and personal care stores, often family-owned or immigrant businesses. Hospitals, nursing, and residential care facilities employ 6.9% of Asian women.[58] Featured Case 6.1 presents a case of egregious discrimination against Asian registered nurses in a nursing and residential care facility.

Asian immigrant women are particularly likely to work in family-owned businesses, computer manufacturing, or garment industries, often working long hours, at low wages, and with no benefits. Such work is often piece work, and workers may have difficulty keeping up with production rates. Some workers assemble circuit boards and cables for one penny per component.[59] Despite the possibility of facing race and sex discrimination, many Asian women have successful careers.

Focus on Selected Asian Americans: Chinese, Indians, and Southeast Asians

Chinese

China has the largest population in the world, and people from China make up the largest subgroup of people with Asian ancestry in the United States. As discussed earlier in the chapter, the Chinese Exclusion Act and later, quotas, severely and purposely restricted Chinese immigration. Since 1965, however, Chinese immigration to the United States has increased tremendously. There now are 2.7 Chinese Americans in the United States, including 1.5 million who were born in China. About 2.0 million people speak a Chinese language at home.

Chinese Americans have disparate incomes, education levels, and occupational success. On one hand, many immigrants are well-educated and often wealthy professionals or business owners. On the other hand, many immigrants have low incomes, are uneducated, impoverished, and often work long hours in poor conditions. Tourist meccas of Chinatowns in major metropolitan cities obscure the poverty and substandard housing and working conditions of some Chinese immigrants.[60] Many Chinese immigrant women work in garment industries (e.g., sweatshops), restaurants, or those with strong English language skills, at clerical positions while men work in the low-wage restaurant market.[61] Exploitation of Asian immigrant workers is associated with low wages and long

[58] Ibid.

[59] See Ro, M. (2000) for a discussion of manufacturing and garment work among Asian immigrants.

[60] See Loo, C., & Ong, P. (1987). "Slaying Demons with a Sewing Needle: Feminist Issues for Chinatown's Women." In. R. Takaki (Ed.), *From Different Shores: Perspectives on Race and Ethnicity in America,* New York: Oxford University Press, pp.186–191.

[61] Takaki. (1993).

FEATURED CASE 6.1 *Woodbine Healthcare Center's Treatment of Filipino Registered Nurses*

The EEOC headline reads "EEOC Announces $2.1 Million Settlement of Wage Discrimination Suit for Class of Filipino Nurses," and the text details a case against Woodbine Healthcare Center, a nursing home in Gladstone, Missouri. The lawsuit alleged that Woodbine discriminated against 65 Filipino registered nurses (RNs) in multiple ways, including wages, job assignment, and other terms and conditions of employment.

Woodbine had petitioned the Immigration and Naturalization Service (INS) to be allowed to employ foreign RNs because of a shortage of RNs in the local area. In its petition, Woodbine gave the INS assurances that the Filipinos would be hired as RNs and paid the same wages as U.S. RNs were paid. After receiving permission to hire the Filipino nurses, however, Woodbine did not do as agreed. The Filipino nurses were paid about $6.00 per hour less than U.S. nurses and many were assigned to work as aides and technicians instead of RNs. Two Filipino nurses filed discrimination lawsuits, and the EEOC found their claims to be meritorious and to be of "general public importance," and certified it as a class action suit. Woodbine agreed to a $2.1 million settlement, including $1.2 million in back pay and $470,000 in interest to the nurses and $430,000 in fees and expenses to the women's attorneys. Woodbine sent each nurse a letter of apology for "being misassigned into a lower-paying and less responsible position than that of a registered nurse, and being treated differently from the U.S. employees in other ways."

During the same time of the EEOC lawsuit, Woodbine also had problems with the U.S. Department of Labor, who had investigated them for prevailing wage discrimination violations against the Filipino nurses. As a result of the DOL investigation, Woodbine had to pay $700,000 in back pay and penalties for those violations. In all, the discrimination against the Filipino nurses cost Woodbine $2.8 million.

Source: EEOC Announces $2.1 Million Settlement of Wage Discrimination Suit for Class of Filipino Nurses, http://www.eeoc.gov/press/3-2-99.html, accessed 06/18/05.

QUESTIONS TO CONSIDER

1. *Woodbine had petitioned the INS to allow Filipinos as RNs, committing to pay them the same wages, but did not do so. What factors may have led to this failure?*

2. *Some of the Filipino RNs were assigned to work as nursing aides and technicians instead of RNs. Shortages of RNs are widely reported in U.S. media. Are there comparable shortages of nursing aides and technicians? What skills are required for the latter jobs?*

3. *Woodbine had trouble with the EEOC and the Department of Labor. In the American Seafoods case discussed earlier in the chapter, American Seafoods had trouble with the EEOC and U.S. maritime laws. What factors cause organizations to fail to comply with multiple types of employment-related laws? What can organizations do to avoid this?*

4. *One common issue in discrimination against nonnative English speakers is claims of language problems. If the Filipino nurses were unable to adequately communicate in English, what could Woodbine have done to avoid illegal discrimination? What safeguards should an organization put in place to ensure any communication difficulties are real rather than imagined?*

5. *Researchers have documented discrimination against medical professionals by patients who*

wish to be treated only by Whites.[62] In a case of discrimination charges against Georgetown Place senior community, the former general manager was found to have used elaborate markings to identify Black and other applicants of color to avoid hiring them. She claimed that residents "preferred White employees, and did not want minorities to come in their rooms."[63] In another case, management at Linden Grove Health Care Center complied with a family's request that no "colored girls" work with the resident, did not address frequent use of racial slurs by residents and employees, assigned nursing staff to work shifts, lunch times, and lunch rooms by race, and denied promotions to experienced, highly qualified Blacks.[64]

a. Could patient discrimination have played a role in what happened to the Filipino at Woodbine nurses? If so, what should Woodbine management have done? Explain.

b. What proportion of RNs, LPNs, LVNs, and nursing aides in nursing homes and hospitals are women of color?

c. Speculate on the turnover and morale costs associated with discrimination against women of color in nursing homes that organizations incur. Contrast these estimates with costs of losing a patient who only wishes to have White attendants.

hours. A respondent in one study stated that "Asians are very good workers," especially compared with Blacks and Whites, who "wouldn't do the type of job" he offered, due to lack of "stamina" or "humility to do that type of job."[65]

As shown in Table 6.2, nearly 50% of Chinese in the United States have a college degree, which is considerably more education than most people in the country have obtained. The median family income for Chinese families is $58,300, which exceeds the median family income of Whites. It should be noted that Chinese Americans are concentrated in the West and the Northeast, which contributes to their higher incomes than other groups. Representative of the diversity of experiences among Asian Americans, 13.1% of Chinese live in poverty, compared with 9.4% of Whites.[66]

Asian Indians

In the United States, Asian Indians were once categorized as "White" in the census, again providing evidence of the fluidity of racial categories. Asian Indians have a wide variety of skin tones, and as with Blacks, among Indians, skin tone has historically held significance within and outside the community.

[62] For example, see Diamond, T. (1992). *Making Gray Gold: Narratives of Nursing Home Care,* Chicago: University of Chicago Press; DasGupta, T. (1996). *Racism and Paid Work,* Toronto: Garamond.

[63] Georgetown Place to Pay $650,000 to Settle EEOC Race Discrimination Lawsuit. June 22, 2005. http://www.eeoc.gov/press/6-23-05.html, accessed 07/05/05.

[64] EEOC Litigation Settlement Reports, May 2005. *EEOC v. Central Park Lodges Long Term Care, Inc., d/b/a Linden Grove Health Care Center,* NO. 04-5627 RBL (W. D. Wash. May 13, 2005).

[65] Moss, P., & Tilly, C. (2001). *Stories Employers Tell: Race, Skill, and Hiring in America,* New York: Russell Sage Foundation, p. 119.

[66] Le, C. N. (2005). "Socioeconomic Statistics and Demographics." *Asian-Nation: The Landscape of Asian America,* http://www.asian-nation.org/demographics.shtml, accessed 07/10/05.

INDIVIDUAL FEATURE 6.2 ***Indra Nooyi, President and Chief Financial Officer, PepsiCo***

Indra Nooyi was named president and chief financial officer of PepsiCo in May 2001. PepsiCo is one of the largest producers of convenience foods and beverages, having revenues of over $29 billion and 153,000 employees in 2004. PepsiCo includes Frito-Lay North America, PepsiCo Beverages North America, PepsiCo International, and Quaker Foods North America. Nooyi is responsible for PepsiCo's corporate functions, including finance, strategy, procurement, and information technology, among other responsibilities. *Fortune* magazine has described Nooyi as a "skilled strategist" responsible for engineering "billions of dollars in acquisition deals." She was integral in the purchase of Tropicana and the merger with Quaker Foods.

Prior to joining PepsiCo in 1994, Nooyi held positions at the Boston Consulting Group, where she directed international corporate strategy projects, and in senior management at Motorola. She holds a master's degree in public and private management from Yale, a master's degree in finance and marketing from the Indian Institute of Management in Calcutta, and a degree in chemistry, physics, and mathematics from Madras Christian College in India.

Fortune credits Pepsi with having the most diverse team of top leaders. PepsiCo consistently rates in lists of top companies for minorities, African American women, Latinas, women executives, and supplier diversity as rated by various entities.

Sources: Allers, K. L., Hira, N. A., Tkaczyk, C., Mero, J., Forte, T., & Soehendro, M. (2005, August 22). "From Business and Academia to Hollywood and the Beltway, Meet the People with the Most Clout." *Fortune*, 152(4): 89–99; PepsiCo Corporate Overview, http://www.pepsico.com/company/overview.shtml, accessed 09/17/05; Profile of a SAJA (South Asian Journalists Association) Speaker, Indra Nooyi, http://www.saja.org/nooyi.html, accessed 09/17/05.

Before 1965, when the Immigration and Nationality Act was passed, few Asian Indians resided in the United States. Since then, the U.S. population of Asian Indians has grown significantly; between 1980 and 2000, the number of Asian Indians in the country increased from less than 400,000 to nearly 2 million. Asian Indians are now 16% of the Asian population in the United States.

Higher earnings and education of Asian Indians contribute strongly to the high average earnings of Asians overall. Asian Indians have considerably more education than all other racial and ethnic groups in the United States, including Whites. As discussed earlier, more than 64% of Asian Indians have at least a college degree, compared with about 30% of Whites. At one point, 11% of Asian Indian men and 8% of women in the United States were physicians.[67] As discussed in Individual Feature 6.2, Indra Nooyi is president and chief financial officer of PepsiCo.

Greater opportunities in the United States help fuel the migration of well-educated or affluent people from India, China, and other less developed countries to the United States. However, even highly educated Indians face discrimination and exclusion, making their returns on educational investment lower than the returns of highly educated Whites. In addition, in the aftermath of the 2001 terrorist

[67] Healey, J. F. (2004). *Diversity and Society,* Thousand Oaks, CA: Pine Forge Press.

attacks in the United States, Asian Indians and other Asians have faced severe religious and national origin discrimination and harassment at work (see Chapter 10).

Southeast Asians

Southeast Asians, including Vietnamese, Laotians, Hmongs, Cambodians, and others from the area, began arriving in the United States in the mid-1970s.[68] As the newest groups of Asians in the United States, Southeast Asians are the least established. They are more likely to have limited English proficiency than other Asians and non-Asians; over 40% of Vietnamese, Cambodians, Laotians, and Hmongs report having limited English proficiency. Southeast Asians are slightly less likely to have completed college than Blacks and Latinos and have similar individual earnings, which are lower than those of other Asian Americans and Whites. C. N. Le's analyses of 2000 census data indicate that 13.8% of Vietnamese have college degrees, compared with 13.6% of Blacks, 40.8% of Japanese, and 25.3% of Whites.[69] In the 2000 census, twice as many Cambodians, Hmongs, and Laotians reported being on public assistance than Blacks.

As a result of low education and lack of opportunities in other organizations, many immigrants open small businesses. Readers may be familiar with doughnut shops, dry cleaners, and "mom-and-pop" stores owned by Southeast Asians. As discussed in Research Translation 6.1 (presented earlier), many of the businesses owned by ethnic immigrant entrepreneurs are "profitable" at high personal and social costs, yet are the only source of income for immigrant families.

Individual and Organizational Recommendations

Because Asian Americans are often viewed as being well-educated, successful, and free from discrimination, both they and organizations are faced with an unusual situation. The "positive" stereotypes contribute to Asians being overlooked as minority group members and being seen as not needing assistance and efforts to ensure fairness for them. Stereotypes of Asians as passive contribute to their overrepresentation in technical positions and underrepresentation in management, particularly when compared to their educational levels. Individuals should make their desire to be considered for management and other promotional opportunities known. If one indeed has the tendency to avoid being vocal, recognize that this may be required to advance.[70] As with women (see Chapter 9),

[68] Espiritu. (1999).

[69] Le. (2005).

[70] Hyun, J. (2005). *Breaking the Bamboo Ceiling: Career Strategies for Asians,* New York: HarperCollins.

it is possible to learn to exhibit behaviors that do not come naturally or, more likely, that were not learned throughout life. As with everyone, it is important to obtain as much education as possible, in your preferred field, rather than being steered to a technical or mathematical field because of expectations of others.

Organizational leaders, management, and human resources should acknowledge that not all Asian Americans are well-educated, and all may be subject to exclusion and differential organizational treatment. When underrepresented in particular job categories, or when evidence of the glass ceiling for Asians exists, make concerted efforts to include Asians in nondiscrimination policies and affirmative action programs. If Asians do not express interest in advancement or managerial positions, recognize that this may reflect cultural differences in self-promotion. Approach them about interest, include them in assessment center activities, and provide them with mentors, along with other high performing employees.

Be aware that some discrimination against Asians occurs because of perceptions they have done too well. Perceptions of language barriers also impede Asians' progress. Organizational leaders should work to ensure that these barriers are real rather than imagined; many Asians who were born in the United States and are native English speakers experience differential treatment based on imagined lack of English fluency. A culture of inclusion, rather than exclusion, and zero tolerance for unfair treatment would be beneficial to Asians as well as to other nondominant groups.

Summary

In this chapter, we have considered the diversity among Asians, the perceptions of Asians as a "model minority" group, and the similarities and differences between Asians, other minority group members, and Whites. Asian Americans are a large and diverse group of people with distinct organizational experiences, education levels, opportunities, and incomes. As have many other minority group members, Asians have contributed to the United States in many ways, while experiencing individual, organizational, and societal racism, discrimination, and exclusion.

Although Asians have the highest education levels of any racial/ethnic group, their returns to their educational investment are lower than the returns of Whites. In addition, some groups of Asians are poorly educated and suffer the poverty and low earnings typical of minorities with limited education and skills. This bimodal distribution is partly a consequence of the large variation within the category of Asian American. Indeed, this categorization obscures important differences among the people who make up this group.

Many of the organizational experiences of Asian Americans vary by country of origin and education level. U.S. natives and a subset of immigrants are well-educated and have high earnings. As with others of color, they still receive lower returns on their educational investments than Whites.

Another subset of immigrants, particularly recent immigrants, have little education and very low earnings.

This chapter provided individual and organizational recommendations for addressing the unique diversity issues faced by Asian Americans. Because Asians are one of the fastest growing populations in the United States, and more than half the world's population, it is imperative that they be recognized as important contributors to the future of diversity in organizations around the world.

Key Term

Model minority — a nondominant group whose members have achieved success through hard work and determination and who should be used as the *model* or *ideal* for other nondominant groups to emulate.

Questions to Consider

1. Japanese Americans served in World War II while their family members were held in relocation centers. As discussed in Chapter 4, African Americans served in World War II but rode in the back of busses and drank from separate "colored only" water fountains while German prisoners of war drank from "Whites only" fountains and Latinos returning from war faced considerable hostility and violence. What ironies exist for people of color in the U.S. military in the present?
2. Prior to reading this chapter, were you aware of the Chinese Exclusion Act and the internment of Japanese Americans? If yes, which? What was your level of knowledge?
3. What are some potential negative organizational consequences of being perceived as a "model minority" for Asian Americans?
4. Prior to reading this chapter, what would your estimates have been for the distribution of education, earnings, and poverty for Asian Americans? Were you aware of the wide variety in Asians' education, earnings, and poverty?
5. If you are not Asian American, do you know someone well who is Asian American? In what capacity do you know him or her (e.g., personal friend, manager, classmate, neighbor, etc.)? Where in Asia are his or her roots (e.g., Japan, China, India)? How much time have you spent with him or her? Have you discussed race, ethnicity, or other diversity issues with him or her? Explain.
6. What have you learned from this chapter that is most surprising to you?

Actions and Exercises

1. Go to U.S. government Web sites (e.g., http://www.census.gov, http://www.dol.gov, and others) to investigate the most current earnings, education, and poverty for Asian Americans from five different backgrounds of your choice (e.g., India, Korea, Thailand, Vietnam, and Japan). Document your findings. What would be the result of viewing any one of these groups as representative of all Asian Americans?
2. Search the EEOC Web site (http://www.eeoc.gov) for recent cases of

discrimination charges and settlements against Asian Americans. What are the details of the cases (e.g., who was involved, what happened, and what was the outcome, etc.)?

3a. Chapter 14 describes the case and settlement of charges that Abercrombie and Fitch (ANF) retail store discriminated against Asian American applicants and employees (and other people of color). If there is an ANF near where you live, visit and document the race and ethnicity of the employees there. If there is no ANF near where you live, conduct this exercise at another high-end specialty store. Compare this with the population of Asians in your area—this is available from the U.S. Census Bureau Web site.

3b. Conduct an informal census of employees in several places: fast food restaurant, sit-down restaurant, discount store (e.g., Target, Wal-Mart), department store (e.g., Macy's, Filene's, Marshall Fields), government office, bank, or other locations in which many employees are visible. Document the number of employees overall and the number of Asian American employees visible. Compare your findings with the population of Asians in your area.

3c. Choose two nights to watch television for 30 minutes to 1 hour each. Document the program, commerical type, and the numbers of Asian American characters on the programs and commercials.

3d. What similarities and differences are apparent between the people in 2, 3a, 3b and 3c above?

4. Research from Housing and Urban Development using paired testers indicates that at times Asian Americans experience housing discrimination (renting and homebuying) that is similar to that experienced by Blacks, Hispanics, and American Indians. Search the HUD Web site for such studies to review them. Speculate on reasons for this discrimination.

5. Conduct research to find several Asian Americans in positions of power in corporations, politics, or universities. Describe their positions, educational background, experience, and other relevant factors that have contributed to their successes.

7 Chapter

Whites/European Americans

Chapter Objectives

After completing this chapter, readers should have a greater understanding of White Americans as they relate to diversity in organizations. Readers can expect to:

- *have an awareness of the historical background of White ethnic groups in the United States.*
- *be able to discuss participation rates, employment, and income levels of White men and women.*
- *examine racial differences in educational return on investment for Whites and other racial and ethnic groups.*
- *be able to discuss similarities and differences between employment experiences of White men and women.*
- *discuss the fluidity in groups deemed "White" in the United States and aspects of "White privilege" and the "myth of meritocracy."*
- *understand individual and organizational measures that can be employed to include Whites in the study of diversity and to obtain their commitment to diversity in organizations.*

Key Facts

Whites are 75% of the U.S. population, but occupy more than 90% of the highest level positions.

When working full time, year round, White men with college degrees earn about $22,000 more than Black men with college degrees.

When working full time, year round, White women with college degrees earn about $25,000 less than White men with college degrees.

White women have higher workforce participation rates than Asian and Hispanic women but lower participation than Black women.

Even Whites who have neither owned slaves nor practiced discrimination have benefited from slavery of Blacks and systemic discrimination against people of color.

Introduction and Overview

In this chapter, we consider the experiences of non-Hispanic Whites as they relate to diversity in organizations.[1] Whites are the largest and most dominant racial group, yet they are often overlooked in discussions of diversity and in diversity research. Despite this oversight, Whites have unique and significant diversity-related experiences that warrant inclusion in the study of diversity. White women benefit considerably from affirmative action yet face the glass ceiling and walls and lower return on their educations, as do other nondominant group members. They also face sex segregation and sexual harassment and the resulting negative consequences for their careers. As mothers, wives, sisters, and other relatives of White men (who are most likely to be in positions of power in organizations), White women have the opportunity to relate credible perspectives of their experiences as nondominant group members. As members of the most dominant group, White men who value diversity are most likely to be in positions to effect change. Having multiple group memberships (e.g., race, sex, age, sexual orientation, and religion) themselves, they may also have personal stakes in pursuit of diversity. Often sharing family incomes with White women, many White men also experience negative effects of sex discrimination on their family incomes.

Also relevant to the study of diversity in organizations, the history of White ethnic groups in the United States provides interesting insights into the differences between their experiences and those of people of color in the United States. Differences in the organizational experiences between White men and women and between White men and people of color are also worthy of exploration.

Terminology

The U.S. Census Bureau describes "White" as persons having origins in any of the original people of Europe, the Middle East, or North Africa, including those who indicate their race as "White" or report entries, such as Irish, German, Italian, Lebanese, Near Easterner, Arab, or Polish. In this book we primarily use the term *White*, but at times we use Anglo, Caucasian, European American, or non-Hispanic White as interchangeable.

History of Whites in the United States

In contrast to the majority of other racial and ethnic groups profiled in this chapter, anyone who was educated in the United States has likely had some exposure to Whites in an "American history" course. Indeed a common complaint about such courses for a while was that they effectively, and at times, purposely excluded or represented people of color in a derogatory manner. Recent decades have seen changes in the content of such courses to include more and more accurate representations of American Indians, Blacks, Latinos, and Asians in the United States, but discussion of the experiences of different White ethnic groups remains limited. In this chapter, we consider some of those ethnic groups, comparisons of their

[1] We use the term "Whites" throughout the chapter to mean Whites not of Hispanic origin.

experiences with people of color, and the racial and ethnic identity of Whites in the present.

As we discuss in other chapters, some White ethnic groups faced considerable overt discrimination and exclusion in their early years in the United States. Nearly 40 million Europeans (including Irish, Greek, Germans, Italians, Polish, and other Europeans) migrated to the United States between the 1820s and 1920s. Clashes between Irish, German, Polish, and Italian immigrants, conflicts over work, and residential segregation were common. There was a pecking order of Whites, with the earliest entrants, the English, at the top, followed by Germans, Irish, Italians, and Polish. The English viewed later White immigrants as dirty, immoral, unintelligent, and dishonest (terms quite similar to those used for Blacks and immigrants of color), and sought to avoid interactions with them at work and at home.

As Blacks migrated from the South to the North seeking better jobs and greater opportunities, many of the European ethnic groups perceived Blacks as a threat to their status and livelihoods. Sociologist Joseph Healey states that

> Ironically, however, the newly arriving African Americans helped White ethnic groups to become upwardly mobile . . . the arrival of African Americans from the South actually *aided* the European immigrants and their descendants in their rise up the social class structure. Whites in the dominant group became less vocal about their contempt for the White ethnic groups as their alarm over the presence of Blacks increased. The greater antipathy of the White community toward African Americans made the immigrants less undesirable and thus hastened their admittance to the institutions of the larger society (p. 79).[2]

White ethnic groups encouraged and capitalized on the fear and antipathy of high status Whites toward Blacks, using it to "become insiders, or Americans, by claiming their membership as Whites" using Blacks as the "other."[3] Because the ethnicity of White ethnic groups is largely invisible, it was considerably easier for White immigrants and their descendants to become insiders than it was for native-born Blacks.

The Past Transience and Current Meaning of "Race" for Whites

In a thought-provoking book, Karen Brodkin considers the transformation of Jews in America from a separate race to White and in the process provides interesting insights into the social constructions of race in America.[4] Brodkin documents the

---

[2] Healey, J. F. (2004). *Diversity and Society,* Thousand Oaks, CA: Pine Forge Press.

[3] Takaki, R. (1993). *A Different Mirror,* Boston: Back Bay Books, p. 151.

[4] Brodkin, K. (1998). *How Jews Became White Folks & What That Says About Race in America,* New Brunswick, NJ: Rutgers University Press; Ignatiev, N. (1995). *How the Irish Became White,* New York: Routledge.

initial employment discrimination by the original Whites to come to America (English and Northern Europeans) against White ethnic groups who arrived in the United States later, including Irish, Italians, Poles, Greeks, French, and Jews. White ethnic groups were segregated from one another, with certain jobs reserved for members of one ethnic group and other jobs designated for other groups. Italians were perceived as engaging in criminal activity, and this stereotype remains to some extent (e.g., mobsters).[5] Irish Catholics, many of whom had fled Ireland in the face of religious persecution, faced open hostility and exclusion in the United States. In response, Catholics formed social, political, and labor organizations to resist the discrimination they faced and played key roles in formation of the American Federation of Labor.[6] The exclusion and discrimination faced by Irish Catholics in the United States was instrumental in their efforts to shape, innovate, and change "ethnic politics" in the United States.[7]

Although they also were fleeing persecution elsewhere, Jews were excluded from many jobs and denied service in some organizations in the United States. Albert Einstein's views on race and racism in America, discussed in Individual Feature 7.1, were reportedly influenced by his experiences with racism as a Jewish person in Germany.

As does Robert Healey, Brodkin suggests that White ethnic groups "became White" through overt actions of the government, their own recognition that the way to become American was to assert their Whiteness (in contrast to Blacks), intermarrying among other Whites that diluted the strength of differences among groups, and the invisibility of their ethnicity. Healey, Brodkin and other researchers have documented the inconsistency in categorizations of White and non-White groups over time and entity.[8] Prior to the 1850 census, categorizations included "free Whites." After 1850, the category was changed to Whites, because all Whites were indeed free.[9] The 1930 census distinguished immigrant Whites from native Whites and recorded their country of origin.[10] By the 1940 census, however, distinctions between native Whites and immigrant Whites were no longer recorded, allowing immigrants' further incorporation into the "White" category, although some overt discrimination against certain ethnic groups remained.

Feature 7.1 discusses the largely unknown internment of Italians and Germans in World War II, an aspect of discrimination against certain ethnic groups that remained during that period.

---

[5] Schaefer, R. T. (2002). *Racial and Ethnic Groups: Census 2000 Update* (8th edition), Upper Saddle River, NJ: Pearson Education.

[6] Kennedy, R. E., Jr. (1999). "Irish Catholic Americans: A Successful Case of Pluralism." In A. G. Dworkin & R. J. Dworkin (Eds.), *The Minority Report* (3rd edition), Fort Worth: Harcourt Brace Publishers, pp. 395–414.

[7] Ibid.

[8] Lopez, I. F. H. (1996). *White by Law: The Legal Construction of Race,* New York: New York University Press.

[9] Rodriguez, C. (2000). *Changing Race: Latinos, the Census, and the History of Ethnicity in the United States,* New York: New York University Press, p. 71.

[10] Brodkin, K. (2004). "How Jews Became White." In J. F. Healey & E. O'Brien (Eds.), *Race, Ethnicity, and Gender,* Thousand Oaks, CA: Pine Forge Press, pp. 283–294; Brodkin, K. (1998).

INDIVIDUAL FEATURE 7.1 *Albert Einstein, Genius and Antiracist*

Albert Einstein, 1879–1955, is viewed by many as perhaps the smartest person to ever live, with the name "Einstein" often used instead of "genius." Winner of the 1921 Nobel Prize in physics, Einstein is widely known for his theory of relativity and for his contributions to the study of quantum physics. In 2000, *Time* magazine named Einstein the person of the century for his intellectual contributions. His passionate resistance to racism and civil rights activism, however, are virtually unknown. References to his antiracist stance and activism are virtually absent in nearly all books and publications about his life and work. This absence is attributed to the media and biographers' desire to avoid controversy, to avoid tarnishing Einstein's "feel-good" image, and to the strength of his views about what he called the "worst disease" in America, a "disease of White people," which he did not "intend to be quiet about."[11] Since his death, the silence surrounding his views on racism has been deafening.

In a recent book, however, *Einstein on Race and Racism,* Fred Jerome and Rodger Taylor detail some of Einstein's close relationships with key Black activists, his cochairing the American Crusade to End Lynching (ACEL), the FBI's files on him, and the peculiar void about this aspect of Einstein's life and work. Jerome and Taylor cite a 1932 letter from Einstein published in *The Crisis* magazine written "to American Negroes."[12] In part, the letter stated that "It seems to be a universal fact that minorities, especially when their individuals are recognizable because of physical differences, are treated by majorities among whom they live as an inferior class." Einstein encouraged Blacks to engage in purposeful activism, educational enlightenment, and to work toward emancipation, and encouraged others to recognize and assist Blacks in their work.

Einstein perceived the treatment of Blacks in the United States as making mockery of the principle that "all men are created equal." He referred to Blacks as the "stepchildren" of the United States, a country that "still has a heavy debt to discharge for all the troubles and disabilities it has laid on the Negro's shoulders, for all that his fellow-citizens have done and to some extent still are doing to him."[13]

Einstein also discouraged discrimination against and restriction of immigrants. He argued that unemployment is "*not* decreased by restricting immigration" (emphasis in original), but that it "depends on faulty distribution of work among those capable of work. Immigration increases consumption as much as it does demand on labor . . ."[14] Some who oppose immigration today continue to argue that immigrants take jobs from "Americans."

Einstein believed that the only remedies to racism are "enlightenment and education" and did his part to help with both. Authors Jerome and Taylor's insightful book contributes to our knowledge about Albert Einstein's other, virtually ignored, work of a genius.

QUESTIONS TO CONSIDER

1. ***Prior to reading this section, were you aware of Albert Einstein's strong antiracist stance?***
2. ***Some have suggested that because Einstein was Jewish and also experienced discrimination, he was more antiracist than he otherwise might have been. Is this a likely cause of Einstein's perspective? Explain.***

Source: Jerome, F., & Taylor, F. (2005). *Einstein on Race and Racism,* Piscataway, NJ: Rutgers University Press.

[11] Jerome, F., & Taylor, R. (2005). *Einstein on Race and Racism,* Piscataway, NJ: Rutgers University Press, p. 91.

[12] Ibid., p. 136.

[13] Ibid., p. 73.

[14] Ibid.

Feature 7.1 *The Internment of Italians and Germans in World War II*

Many people are unaware of the internment of more than 100,000 Japanese Americans during World II under Executive Order 9066. Even fewer are aware that Italians and Germans were also evacuated and held in relocation centers during the same time. Estimates suggest that 2,100 Italians were interred and between 10,000 and 14,000 Italians and Germans were arrested for being "enemy aliens" during the war.[15] Although far fewer Americans of Italian and German descent were interred than Japanese, their story is no less important to those who suffered and their descendants. In the past two decades, the internment of Italian Americans has gone from being told primarily through word of mouth in the Italian community to one more widely known and shared. An exhibit called "Una Storia Segreta" documents surprise evacuations to unknown cities, sons in the military returning home to find their parents had been evacuated, having to change the Italian family name to avoid being recognized as Italian, and other humiliations.

In New York City, San Francisco, Washington, DC, and other major cities in which many Italians resided, mandatory curfews were imposed and Italians were forced to carry bright pink enemy alien passbooks, and searched almost at will. Property that was deemed dangerous (e.g., flashlights, radios, cameras, and firearms) was seized. On the West Coast, Italian, German, and Japanese aliens were removed from "prohibited zones."

Geoffrey Dunn, whose great grandmother, at 78, was relocated in Santa Cruz, CA, details some of the events of evacuations and internments in the Santa Cruz area. He and others propose that the Japanese (but not Italians and Germans) were singled out for large-scale, mass evacuations due to racism, economics, and comparative lack of strength of the Japanese. Because people of German and Italian descent were more widely assimilated, more involved in politics (e.g., mayors of large cities), and had widespread public recognition (e.g., baseball's Joe DiMaggio) this also limited the internment of Germans and Italians. According to Dunn, then California Attorney General, Earl Warren (who went on to become chief justice of the Supreme Court), stated that "when we are dealing with the Caucasian race we have methods that will test the loyalty of them . . . but when we deal with the Japanese, we are on an entirely different field."[16]

In October 1942, Italians were removed from the "enemy aliens" classification and allowed to return to prohibited zones. Restrictions for Germans were lifted in January 1943. As they returned to their homes and resumed their businesses, life for the Italian and German Americans returned to some semblance of normalcy.

Questions to Consider

1. ***Prior to reading this selection, were you aware that Italians and Germans had been evacuated and relocated as enemy aliens during World War II?***

2. ***Aside from differences in the numbers of people affected, why do you think that the Italian and***

[15] Fox, S. C. (1988). "General John DeWitt and the Proposed Internment of German and Italian Aliens during World War II." *Pacific Historical Review,* 57 (November): 407–438. Exhibition announcement for "Prisoners in Our Own Home: The Italian American experience as America's Enemy Aliens." 2004. Exhibition on view at the Garibaldi-Meucci Museum March 6 through March 13, 2004, http://www.garibaldimeuccimuseum.org/Resources/PRMarEnemyAliens2004.pdf, accessed 07/29/05; Dunn, G. (1996). "Male Notte: The Untold Story of Italian Relocation during World War II," http://www.santacruzpl.org/history/ww2/male.shtml, accessed 07/30/05.

[16] Dunn. (1996).

German relocation experience has received such little focus when compared with that of the Japanese?

3. ***Why might Caucasians have been perceived to be more loyal than the Japanese?***

Sources: Fox, S. (1990). *The Unknown Internment: An Oral History of the Relocation of Italian Americans during World War II,* Boston: Twayne; Scherini, R. D. (1991/1992). "Executive Order 9066 and Italian Americans: The San Francisco Story." *California History,* Winter, 367–377; Una Storia Segreta: When Italian-Americans Were 'Enemy Aliens,' http://hcom.csumb.edu/segreta/, accessed 07/29/05.

More recently, the racial categories used in the U.S. census shuttled Mexicans, Middle Easterners, and East Indians (Asian Indians) between White and non-White.[17] Berkeley Law Professor Ian Haney Lopez provides details of how court rulings based on "common knowledge" and "legal precedent" wavered in their judgments of who was White or not.[18] Syrians are White, Syrians are not White; Asian Indians are not White, Asian Indians are White; Arabians are White, Arabians are not White; and other irrational decisions were rendered in cases in which people tried to "prove" their Whiteness in order to become U.S. citizens.

Misperception: White racial categorizations are inerrant and stable.

Reality: White racial categorizations have varied considerably in the United States.

In addition to allowing immigrants to become citizens through much of the 1900s, being White is associated with many other unrecognized advantages. Some of those advantages are considered in Research Translation 7.1. One of the advantages refers to Whites' ability to behave badly without such behavior being attributed to all Whites. Because Whites are the dominant and majority group, they are less likely to be viewed as homogenous (e.g., in-group heterogeneity and out-group homogeneity—see Chapter 3). As an example, Timothy McVeigh, a young White man, was convicted for the 1995 bombing of the U.S. federal building in Oklahoma City. Eric Rudolph, responsible for the 1996 Olympic Park bombing in Atlanta and bombings of an abortion clinic and a gay nightclub was a young White man at the time of his crimes. These two high-profile cases did not result in young White men as a group being widely believed to be terrorists.

History of Whites as Diversity Allies

As discussed in previous chapters, throughout the history of the United States, Whites have participated in the quests for equality of Blacks, American Indians, Latinos, and Asians. As abolitionists, hosts and workers in the underground

[17] Brodkin. (1998). p. 74.

[18] Lopez. (1996). p. 203, Table 1: The racial prerequisite cases, 1878–1909.

ASSIGNMENT #2

Research Translation 7.1 *"White Privilege" and the "Myth of Meritocracy"*

Dr. Peggy McIntosh is associate director of the Wellesley College Center for Research on Women. Through her work in women's studies, and her awareness of male privilege as a result of women's disadvantages, Dr. McIntosh began thinking about the privilege that Whites experience at the expense of non-Whites. Although men may acknowledge that women are *disadvantaged* in society, most men are unwilling to acknowledge that men are *advantaged* at women's expense. She argues that while some men may concede that male privilege exists in broad institutional and societal forms, those same men will deny any *personal* advantages stemming from male privilege.

As she considered the strength of men's denial of unearned privileges, McIntosh began to recognize the existence of her own advantages, as a White woman, at the expense of non-Whites. Similar to men's unwillingness to accept unearned privilege, McIntosh notes the difficulty in acknowledging unearned advantages based on White skin color: "I think Whites are carefully taught not to recognize White privilege, as males are taught not to recognize male privilege."[19] (p. 297) Part of her (and men's) unwillingness to deny privilege is that to acknowledge privilege would make plain the "myth of meritocracy . . . one's life is not what one makes it; many doors open for certain people through no virtues of their own."[20] (p. 298)

In their book on the subject, Professors Stephen McNamee and Robert Miller include several nonmerit factors that strongly influence people's success in life. They include "the effects of inheritance as unequal starting points in the race to get ahead," knowing the right people and being able to fit in with them (social and cultural capital), unequal access to educational opportunities, and discrimination. According to McNamee and Miller, "by excluding entire categories of people from equal access to opportunity, discrimination has reduced competition and increased the chances of others to get ahead who mistakenly conclude that their success is based exclusively on their own individual 'merit.'"[21] The concept of "affirmative action for White males" refers to historical preferences for Whites, in particular White men, by organizational decision makers that have systematically advantaged them at the expense of others.[22] By excluding women and minorities from union membership, training programs, certain (or any) jobs, employer discrimination provided systematic advantages for White men and allowed for perceptions that only they were qualified for those positions.

McIntosh began documenting and analyzing her every day experiences that were part of the unearned advantages she experienced as a consequence of being White. She amassed 46 unearned advantages that have been widely reported in women's studies and gender and

---

[19] McIntosh, P. (2004). "White Privilege and Male Privilege: A Personal Account of Coming to See Correspondences through Work in Women's Studies (1988)." In J. F. Healey & E. O'Brien (Eds.), *Race, Ethnicity, and Gender,* Thousand Oaks, CA: Pine Forge Press, pp. 294–301.

[20] Ibid.

[21] McNamee, S. J., & Miller, R. K., Jr. (2004). *The Meritocracy Myth,* Lanham, MD: Rowman & Littlefield Publishing Group, p. 17.

[22] Brodkin, K. (2004). See also, Jacques, R. (1997). "The Unbearable Whiteness of Being: Reflections of a Pale, Stale Male." In P. Prasad, A. Mills, M. Elmes, & A. Prasad (Eds.), *Managing the Organizational Melting Pot; Dilemmas of Workplace Diversity,* Thousand Oaks, CA: Sage, pp. 80–106; "Dedicated Lives." (1997). *Emerge,* 8(9): 35–38.

diversity literatures. The following have specific, clear relevance to diversity in organizations.[23]

- I can go shopping alone most of the time, fairly well assured that I will not be followed or harassed by store detectives.
- I can be pretty sure that my children's teachers and employers will tolerate them if they fit school and workplace norms; my chief worries about them do not concern others' attitudes toward their race.
- I can be reasonably sure that if I ask to talk to "the person in charge," I will be facing a person of my race.
- I can go home from most meetings of organizations I belong to feeling somewhat tied in, rather than isolated, out of place, outnumbered, unheard, held at a distance, or feared.
- I can be pretty sure that an argument with a colleague of another race is more likely to jeopardize her chances for advancement than to jeopardize mine.
- I can take a job with an affirmative action employer without having co-workers on the job suspect that I got it because of my race.
- I can be pretty sure of finding people who would be willing to talk with me and advise me about my next steps, professionally.
- I can be late to a meeting without having the lateness reflect on my race.
- I can choose public accommodation without fearing that people of my race cannot get in or will be mistreated in the places I have chosen.
- If I have low credibility as a leader, I can be sure that my race is not the problem.

These privileges touch upon many of the factors discussed in *Diversity in Organizations,* including discrimination against customers, racial profiling, stereotyping, perceptions that people of color are unqualified, and others that are familiar to many non-Whites but generally unfamiliar to Whites. These and the remaining privileges McIntosh compiled provide a thought-provoking view of everyday life and events through different lenses. Although she used the term "privilege" to describe these unearned advantages, Dr. McIntosh views this term as misleading. Privilege is generally seen as a positive term, yet what she describes "simply *confers dominance,* gives permission to control, because of one's race or sex" (emphasis in original).[24] McIntosh further notes that being White in the United States opens many doors for Whites, whether or not individual Whites personally approve of the way that dominance is conferred on members of their group. When Whites remain oblivious about White advantage, the myth of meritocracy is allowed to continue, thus perpetuating the system of White privilege. In discussing White, heterosexual, male privilege, Roy Jacques (a White, heterosexual male) similarly notes that passively receiving privileges does not make one a bad person, but failing to question and resist privileges are "moral and ethical" issues.[25]

McIntosh argues that racism not only involves "individual acts of meanness" but also "invisible systems conferring racial dominance." Whites are taught not to recognize these invisible systems of privilege that advantage Whites in the same way that men are taught not to recognize systems that advantage men. Because of the role of systems (e.g., institutional discrimination) in promoting advantages for one group over others, focusing on one's own attitudes (e.g., deciding not to behave in a racist manner) is but one aspect of addressing inequality. Those in power can continue to ignore systemic influences on inequality or they can work to weaken and reconstruct power systems so that the "normal" privileges can also be enjoyed by other groups.

[23] Privileges are quoted from McIntosh (2004), pp. 296–298. Original numbers for the privileges presented are: 5, 16, 24, 27, 28, 35, 37, 39, 40, and 43.

[24] McIntosh. (2004). p. 299.

[25] Jacques. (1997).

Sources: McIntosh, P. (2004). "White Privilege and Male Privilege: A Personal Account of Coming to See Correspondences through Work in Women's Studies (1988)." In J. F. Healey & E. O'Brien (Eds.), *Race, Ethnicity, and Gender,* Thousand Oaks, CA: Pine Forge Press, pp. 294–312; McNamee, S. J., & Miller, R. K., Jr. (2004). *The Meritocracy Myth,* Lanham, MD: Rowman & Littlefield Publishers. See also Jacques, R. (1997). "The Unbearable Whiteness of Being: Reflections of a Pale, Stale Male." In P. Prasad, A. Mills, M. Elmes, & A. Prasad (Eds.), *Managing the Organizational Melting Pot; Dilemmas of Workplace Diversity,* Thousand Oaks, CA: Sage, pp. 80–106; Wildman, S. M. (Ed.) (1996). *Privilege Revealed: How Invisible Preference Undermines America,* New York: New York University Press; Scheurich, J. J. (1993). "Toward a White Discourse on White Racism." *Educational Researcher,* 22(8): 5–10.

Questions to Consider

1. ***What other White privileges can you think of that have specific relevance to diversity in organizations?***
2. ***If you are a member of a nondominant racial or ethnic group, how many of the privileges listed resonate with you? Which ones?***
3. ***If you are White, how many of the privileges listed had you recognized prior to reading this selection? Which ones are most sobering or surprising to you?***
4. ***Had you considered "the myth of meritocracy" prior to reading this selection? What do you think of the possibility that by discriminating against people of color, a society and organizations provide advantages for Whites? In what ways does failure to acknowledge the consequences of discrimination contribute to Whites' feelings of their own individual qualifications and "merit?"***

railroad for runaway slaves, participants in boycotts, marches, and sit-ins, educators, and researchers, Whites have played many roles as diversity allies. From John Brown, Henry David Thoreau, and Harriet Beecher Stowe, to Michael Schwerner and Andrew Goodman, Whites worked (and sometimes died) along with people of color. White female suffragists, such as Susan B. Anthony, Elizabeth Cady Stanton, Lucretia Mott, and many others pursued rights for Blacks along with pursuing women's rights to vote. Currently, many White diversity allies support equality of racial, sexual, religious, ability, and other minorities. As discussed in Chapter 1, because White men are more likely to occupy decision-making positions in organizations, and have more authority and credibility in many areas, their commitment to equity and fairness is vital. The lifelong commitment to justice of Morris Dees, of the Southern Poverty Law Center, is described in Individual Feature 7.2.

Relevant Legislation

As with the other racial and ethnic groups covered thus far in this book, the primary legislation protecting Whites from discrimination in employment is Title VII of the Civil Rights Act. Title VII is often thought of as being solely for people of color, but it prohibits discrimination on the basis of race and national origin, and thus is applicable to Whites as well as to people of color. Title VII is indeed used considerably less by Whites than by people of color, simply because Whites are far less likely to be targeted by intentional employment discrimination (e.g., disparate treatment). Whites are considerably more likely to be in positions

Individual Feature 7.2 *Morris Dees, Southern Poverty Law Center*

Morris Dees is a White man with sandy-blonde hair and blue eyes, and a passion for justice. Dees was born in 1936 in Alabama, where he lived during his formative years, witnessing the consequences of prejudice and racial injustice. Trained as a lawyer, Dees had founded a successful book publishing company, when, in 1967, after much soul searching, he acknowledged that working for justice and equality was his appointed path. "I was a good lawyer wasting my time trying to make a few more million dollars," Dees said, and decided instead to specialize in civil rights law.

In 1969, Dees sold his publishing company to Times Mirror (the parent company of *The Los Angeles Times*), and began to take on controversial cases important to civil rights and justice. He sued to integrate the all White, Young Men's Christian Association (YMCA) in Montgomery, Alabama, and to prevent the state of Alabama from building another university in an Alabama city that already had a predominantly Black university. Dees soon recognized the need for a nonprofit organization that would seek justice for minorities and the poor, and along with his law partner, Joseph Levin, Jr., and civil rights activist, Julian Bond, founded the Southern Poverty Law Center (SPLC) in 1971.

The SPLC has been instrumental in many cases of importance to people in the United States, including cases involving challenges to segregation, employment discrimination, the death penalty, hate groups, and the confederate flag. The SPLC has pursued worker safety, tax equity, medical services for the poor, improved prison conditions, parity in education for the poor, and equity for immigrants. Some of the cases involved employer abuses of workers and detriments to their health, government sanctioned abuse and neglect of mentally ill patients, charges of murder against people who killed in self-defense, and denial of public education to homeless children. In one case, SPLC defended an inmate charged with murdering a prison guard who was found dead in her cell partially undressed (e.g., without his pants). The inmate said the guard had tried to rape her and semen and an ice pick were found on his body. In another death row case, SPLC won an acquittal for a 16-year-old boy who had been convicted of rape and sentenced to die in Louisiana's electric chair. Scientific evidence, available at the time he was first convicted, but withheld, helped in his later acquittal. The SPLC was instrumental in gaining equitable rights for women in the military and their dependents, and for women in law enforcement. In some of its most highly recognized cases, the SPLC was successful in gaining judgments against various groups that had targeted Blacks, Vietnamese fishermen, Jews, and nonviolent Black and White protesters. Some of the SPLC's most influential cases have been heard by the U.S. Supreme Court.

A quarter-century after it was founded, the Southern Poverty Law Center continues to work for justice for disenfranchised groups of all backgrounds. Organizations around the United States recognize the role Dees plays in seeking and obtaining justice for the disenfranchised. He has received The American Bar Association's Young Lawyers Distinguished Service Award and the Roger Baldwin Award from the American Civil Liberties Union. The Trial Lawyers for Public Justice named him Trial Lawyer of the Year in 1987. In 1990, Dees received the Martin Luther King Jr. Memorial Award from the National Education Association. In 1993, Dees received the Humanitarian Award from the University of Alabama. He has been awarded at least 25 honorary degrees, and speaks at colleges and universities around the country, exhorting others to seek justice.

Sources: http://www.splcenter.org/center/history/dees.jsp; Dees, M. (1991). *A Season for Justice*, New York: Charles Scribner's Sons.

of power (e.g., managers, executives, supervisors, and others with hiring, firing, promotional, and other responsibilities), than are members of other groups, and making disparate treatment by non-Whites against Whites unlikely. In addition, although Whites are often underrepresented in jobs primarily occupied by people of color, such jobs are likely to be lower paid, less desirable jobs than those commonly occupied by Whites. Claims of disparate impact or underutilization of Whites in such jobs would seem illogical—why would Whites generally aspire to work in jobs that are lower paid, less desirable, with fewer opportunities for advancement? Lastly, despite resistance to affirmative action often expressed among Whites, executive orders for affirmative action have benefitted White women more than other groups, as discussed in Chapter 2.

Misperception: Title VII protects only minorities from racial discrimination.

Reality: Title VII prohibits discrimination against Whites, including White males.

The EEOC case presented below represents a Title VII case of discrimination by a Black manager against a White person in which the White male plaintiff prevailed. For the EEOC settlements available for the 34 consecutive months between December 2002 and September 2005, this case was the only case involving this form of discrimination.

- **EEOC v. Horizon/Mercy Health Plan of Trenton, N.J.[26]**
  No. 03-cv-4402(GEB) (D.N.J. May 14, 2004)

  The Philadelphia District Office resolved a Title VII race discrimination suit against an independent licensee of Blue Cross/Blue Shield of New Jersey, Inc., alleging that defendant denied a promotion to charging party, defendant's medical director, because he is Caucasian, and discharged him because of his race. In August 2001, an African American female CEO promoted CP to Acting Chief Medical Officer (CMO). When CP applied for the permanent CMO position, the CEO hired a less qualified, less experienced African American candidate. The suit alleged that during the selection process, the CEO kept commenting that defendant company was "too White" and directed defendant's officials to recruit applicants from organizations with numerous Black medical directors. When discussing qualifications for the CMO job, the CEO purportedly stated that she "did not want any more White boys hired." Thereafter, in February 2000, CP was named Vice President of Health Services and he reported to the new CMO. Without warning or documentation justifying the action, the new CMO eliminated CP's job and fired CP in June 2002.

[26] EEOC Litigation Settlements—May 2004, http://www.eeoc.gov/litigation/settlements/settlement05-04.html, accessed 07/15/05.

Despite the low likelihood of discrimination against Whites by nondominant group members in positions of power, some overt discrimination against Whites still occurs. The race and national origin of the perpetrators was not disclosed in the following EEOC reports, but it appears that the perpetrators were U.S. native-born Whites rather than people of color.

- **EEOC v. Control Building Services, Inc.**
  No. 01-CV-3822 (D. N.J. September 9, 2003)

  The Philadelphia District Office alleged in this Title VII lawsuit that defendant, a cleaning contractor, subjected two female maintenance employees to a hostile working environment based on their sex and national origin (Polish), and that the women were given extra cleaning assignments in retaliation for rejecting their supervisor's sexual advances. The supervisor repeatedly called the two women derogatory names which emphasized their Polish heritage and requested sexual intercourse and other sexual acts with them. On one occasion, the supervisor pushed one of the women to the floor and kicked her after she rejected his sexual advances. One of the female claimants was forced to quit her job due to the harassment. In addition to the sexual harassment, a male maintenance employee was harassed because of his national origin (Peruvian) and race (dark-skinned Hispanic).[27]

- **EEOC v. Pinnacle Nissan, Inc., and ABC Nissan, d/b/a Automotive Investment Group, Inc.**
  No. CIV 00-1872 PHX MHM (D. Ariz. February 20, 2003)

  The Phoenix District Office alleged in this Title VII lawsuit that defendant, a car dealership, subjected employees to a hostile working environment based upon their national origin (Middle- Eastern and Hispanic) and religion (Jewish) and retaliated against those employees who opposed discrimination.[28]

- **EEOC v. Creative Playthings, Inc.**
  No. 04-3243 (AB) (E.D. Pa. Sept. 13, 2005)

  The Philadelphia District Office claimed that defendant, the nation's largest manufacturer of wooden play sets and outdoor gyms, violated Title VII by (1) discharging charging party, the District Manager of its stores in New Jersey, Delaware, Pennsylvania, and Maryland, in retaliation for opposing discrimination; (2) failing to hire and promote blacks and Hispanics into available positions; and (3) subjecting black and Hispanic employees to a hostile work environment. When defendant offered to promote charging party

[27] EEOC Litigation Settlements—September 2003, http://www.eeoc.gov/litigation/settlements/settlement09-03.html, accessed 07/15/05.

[28] EEOC Litigation Settlement Report—February 2003, http://www.eeoc.gov/litigation/settlements/settlement02-03.html, accessed 07/11/05.

(white) into a new VP position, he recommended his two top performers, both black, to replace him and fill another anticipated District Manager opening. Defendant's owner and another senior manager refused to consider the two black employees for promotion and fired charging party 3 weeks later. According to charging party, the owner expressed discomfort with minority managers and believed that white customers could not relate to them, and directed charging party to fire a Hispanic employee because she had an accent. Witnesses stated that the owner referred to minorities as "those people," and said that employees should dress, act, and speak white to be successful.[29]

- **EEOC v. G.F.B. Enterprises, LLC d/b/a Lexus of Kendall**
  No. 01-4035-CIV-MARTINEZ/GARBER (S.D. Fla. September 3, 2003)

  In this Title VII lawsuit, the Miami District Office alleged that defendant, a car dealership, subjected a group of employees to a hostile working environment on the basis of national origin (Hispanic), race (Black) and religion (Jewish). The harassment consisted of derogatory comments ("America is for Whites only") and name-calling ("spic," "nigger") made by the Director of Fixed Operations and the son of the dealership's owner. One of the charging parties was forced to quit his job due to the harassment.[30]

Along with discrimination and retaliation against Whites, these cases involved sexual harassment, national origin discrimination against Middle Easterners and Hispanics, religious discrimination, and race discrimination against Blacks. As discussed in other chapters, discrimination against members of one group is commonly accompanied by discrimination against members of other groups, including nondominant Whites (e.g., White women, gays and lesbians, or Whites from religious minority groups).

Recall from Chapters 5 and 6 the exploitation and abuse of Latino and Asian immigrant workers. White immigrant workers also experience exploitation and abuse. In some of the Wal-Mart cases, along with Mexican immigrants, immigrants came from Russia, Poland, Lithuania, Uzbekistan, and other Eastern European countries. The *New York Times* reports the story of one man from Prague who worked every night for 8 months with no overtime pay, no contributions to Social Security, and no health insurance. The man was arrested on October 23, 2003, during a raid of Wal-Mart stores along with 250 other janitors and deported.[31] In *Nickel and Dimed* investigating work and living experiences of

---

[29] EEOC Litigation Settlement Report—September 2005, http://www.eeoc.gov/litigation/settlements/settlement09-05.html, accessed 11/11/05.

[30] EEOC Litigation Settlement Report—September 2003, http://www.eeoc.gov/litigation/settlements/settlement09-03.html, accessed 07/11/05. Offensive terms from original document were retained.

[31] Greenhouse, S. (2003, November 5). "Illegally in the U.S., and Never a Day Off at Wal-Mart." *New York Times,* Section A, Page 1, Column 2.

FIGURE 7.1 ***White Ethnic Groups in the United States: 2003***

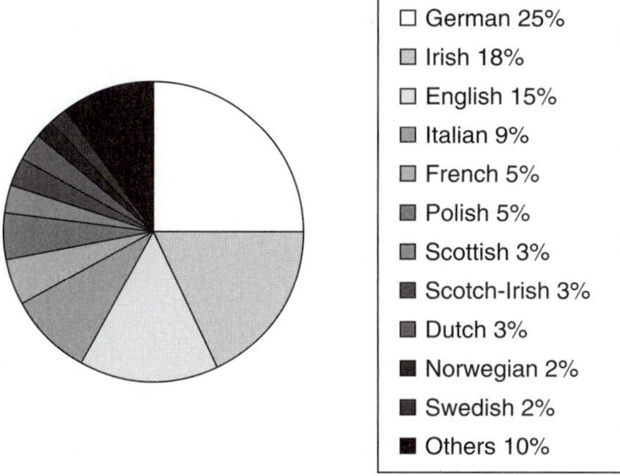

Note: Others include Lithuanian, Slovak, Ukrainian, Swiss, Greek, Arab, Czech, Danish, Hungarian, Welsh, French Canadian, Portuguese, and Russian; each was less than 1% of the U.S. population.

Source: U.S. Census Bureau, 2003 American Community Survey. Table 2. Selected Social Characteristics, http://www.census.gov/acs/www/Products/Profiles/Single/2003/ACS/Tabular/010/01000US2.htm, accessed 07/15/05.

low wage workers, Barbara Ehnrenreich describes a young Polish immigrant's exploitation as a dishwasher in a restaurant.[32]

POPULATION

In the most recent full U.S. census (2000), 75.1% of the population (about 217 million people) reported being White alone, and another 1.9% reported being White in combination with some other race. The White population is declining as a percentage of the total U.S. population. When the census data collection first began in 1790, 80.7% of the population was White and 19.3% was Black (92% were slaves). In 1930 and 1940, the White population was the largest proportion, 89.8%, and although Whites are still the largest, this proportion has declined to the current 75.1%.[33] As discussed in Chapter 1, Johnston and Packer's reports of the changing racial and ethnic composition of the U.S. population, particularly the declining proportion of non-Hispanic Whites in the workforce, stimulated considerable interest in diversity in organizations.

According to the U.S. Census Bureau, the term *White* refers to those having origins in any of the original peoples of Europe, the Middle East, or North Africa, and includes those who wrote Irish, German, Italian, Lebanese, Arab, and Polish, among other areas. As shown in Figure 7.1, as of 2003, 25% of the

[32] Ehrenreich, B. (2001). *Nickel and Dimed: On (not) Getting by in America,* New York: Metropolitan Books.

[33] Gibson, C., & Jung, K. (2002). *Historical Census Statistics on Population Totals By Race, 1790 to 1990, and by Hispanic Origin 1970 to 1990 for the United States, Regions, Divisions and States*. Table 1. United States Race and Hispanic Origin. 1790 to 1990, http://www.census.gov/population/documentation/twps0056/tab01.pdf, accessed 07/16/05.

TABLE 7.1 ***Mean Income in 2002 for Full-Time, Year-Round Workers by Race, Sex, and Hispanic Origin***

	Total	<H.S.	H.S. Graduate	Some College	Associate's Degree	Bachelor's Degree	Master's Degree
White male	$60,169	$32,441	$41,439	$50,558	$51,683	$76,832	$88,234
White female	$39,844	$23,016	$29,675	$35,045	$36,231	$51,283	$58,800
Asian male	$57,862	$21,937	$35,209	$44,625	$41,939	$64,336	$79,389
Asian female	$41,006	$20,793	$24,657	$31,751	$35,292	$47,692	$59,890
Black male	$40,289	$28,073	$31,008	$40,978	$44,938	$54,655	$71,470
Black female	$32,843	$19,719	$27,111	$29,663	$32,951	$45,367	$54,844
Hispanic male	$34,822	$25,374	$32,794	$39,659	$46,018	$53,067	$66,781
Hispanic female	$28,062	$18,889	$24,058	$27,938	$32,668	$44,475	$65,953*

*Large standard error ($13,004) explains high mean wage for Hispanic women with master's degree. Median of $46,255 is more representative.

Source: U.S. Census Bureau, Internet Release Date: June 29, 2004. Table 8. Income in 2002 by Educational Attainment of the Population 18 Years and Over By Age, Sex, Race, and Hispanic Origin, http://www.census.gov/population/socdemo/education/cps2003/tab08-2.xls, accessed 10/29/05.

Whites reporting an ethnicity were German, 18% were Irish, 15% were English, and 9% were Italian. People from other groups represented 5% of less of the White population reporting an ethnicity. Perhaps reflecting lack of knowledge of their original ancestry, 7% of Whites who reported an ethnicity reported "United States or American."

Education, Earnings, and Employment

As discussed in previous chapters, the educational levels of non-Hispanic Whites are higher than those of Blacks and Hispanics but generally lower than those of Asians. As of 2002, the percentage of Whites with a high school education or more, some college or more, or at least a bachelor's degree were 89.4%, 56.4%, and 30.0%, respectively (see Table 6.1 in Chapter 6). At the college level or above, 49.8% of Asians, 17.3% of Blacks, and 11.4% of Hispanics had completed such education.

By now, readers are aware that the earnings and employment of Whites, particularly White males, generally exceed those of others. As indicated in Table 7.1, in 2002, the average income of all non-Hispanic White men (working full time, year round) was $60,169, followed by Asian men, who earned $57,862, and Black men, who earned $40,289. When comparing educational return on investment (EROI), White men's higher returns than others' are quite apparent. At the high school level, White men earned $41,439 while Asian men earned $35,209, and Black men earned $31,008. Disparities in EROI for White men compared with all others exist at every educational level. In addition, because nondominant groups

FIGURE 7.2 ***Mean Income for White Men and Women Working Full Time, Year Round, 2002***

	Total	<H.S.	H.S. Graduate	Some College	Associate's Degree	Bachelor's Degree	Master's Degree
White men	$60,169	$32,441	$41,439	$50,558	$51,683	$76,832	$88,234
White women	$39,844	$23,016	$29,675	$35,045	$36,231	$51,283	$58,800
Women's percentage of men's	66%	71%	72%	69%	70%	67%	67%

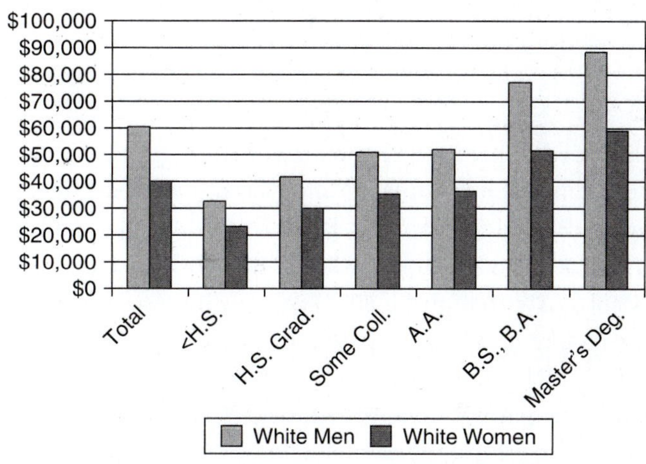

Source: U.S. Census Bureau, Internet Release Date: June 29, 2004. Table 8. Income in 2002 by Educational Attainment of the Population 18 Years and Over By Age, Sex, Race, and Hispanic Origin, http://www.census.gov/population/socdemo/education/cps2003/tab08-2.xls, accessed 10/29/05.

are less likely to work full time, year round than others, differences between earnings of members of dominant groups and others are even more extreme than shown in Table 7.1. In other words, the average White woman or Black man is more likely to work intermittently or part time than the average White man. Thus, earnings differences for most of the population in these groups are more extreme than depicted.

Income differences between White men and White women reveal gender-based disparities that are present across racial and ethnic groups, but that are exaggerated because White men's incomes are generally higher than the incomes of men of color. For White men and women at all educational levels, women's earnings are 69% of men's, as indicated in Figure 7.2. At the master's degree level, White men working full time, year round, averaged $88,234 in income in 2002, while White women averaged $58,800. Because White women work fewer hours even when working full time, and have shorter tenure than White men, this contributes to the male/female earnings gap in that group (see also Chapter 9).

TABLE 7.2 ***Unemployment Level by Educational Attainment by Race (Percent of Population 25 and Over): 2003***

	Total	Men	Women	White	Black	Asian	Hispanic*
Less than high school	8.8	8.2	9.8	7.8	13.9	9.5	8.2
High school graduate	5.5	5.7	5.2	4.8	9.3	5.6	5.9
Some college, no degree	5.2	5.4	4.9	4.5	8.6	6.4	5.8
Associate's degree	4.0	4.4	3.7	3.6	6.2	5.2	5.3
Bachelor's and higher†	3.1	3.2	2.9	2.8	4.5	4.4	4.1

*Persons whose ethnicity is Hispanic are classified by ethnicity as well as by race.

†Bachelor's and higher includes persons with bachelor's, master's, professional, and doctoral degree.

Source: http://www.bls.gov/cps/cpsaat7.pdf, accessed 10/22/04.

As discussed in previous chapters, workforce participation rates indicate that Hispanic, Asian, White, and Black men are most to least likely to be participating in the workforce. For women, Black, Asian, White, and Hispanic women are most to least likely to be participating in the workforce (see Table 4.2). Ranging from lows of 57.1% to highs of 80.2%, clearly most adults participate in the workforce. White men's participation rates exceeded those of White women by about 14.2% in 2002, and are projected to exceed them by 13% in 2012.

When participating in the workforce, Whites are less likely to be unemployed than all other groups, at each educational level. As shown in Table 7.2, White unemployment levels are lower than the levels that are widely reported—those for the entire population. At the highest educational levels, 2.8% of Whites are unemployed, compared with 4.1% of Hispanics, 4.4% of Asians, and 4.5% of Blacks. Differences are most extreme at the lowest educational levels, where 7.8%, 8.2%, 9.5%, and 13.9% of Whites, Hispanics, Asians, and Blacks, respectively, are unemployed.

RESEARCH ON WHITES AND DIVERSITY

In contrast to other racial and ethnic groups, the majority of research in management, psychology, and sociology has, by default, focused on the experiences of Whites. Whites are the numerical majority, and race differences in experiences, outcomes, and opportunities were thus not generally specifically considered by most researchers for a long time. Consequently, as a much smaller proportion of the population, minority experiences were simply subsumed in the data for all workers. Cox and Nkomo emphasized the absence of race as a variable in organizational behavior research in a 1990 publication, noting the invisibility of men and women of color (as contrasted with the unspoken visibility of Whites).[34]

[34] Cox, T., & Nkomo, S. (1990). "Invisible Men and Women: A Status Report on Race as a Variable in Organization Behavior Research." *Journal of Organizational Behavior,* 11: 419–431.

Since Cox and Nkomo's call for more research on the subject, hundreds of articles in management (e.g., organizational behavior, human resources, strategy) have included race and ethnicity as variables. Most of this research has focused on people of color, using Whites as the "norm" and comparing minorities to Whites. Researchers have reported differences between Whites and minorities in terms of income, promotions, performance evaluations, training, opportunities for mentoring, and job-related attitudes (e.g., job satisfaction, attitudes toward affirmative action programs, and organizational commitment). In previous chapters we have considered some of that research, Whites' advantages in most job-related outcomes, and many of the differences between Whites and minorities in job-related attitudes. In the following sections we focus on differences between White men and women and the meaning of ethnicity for Whites.

Similarities and Differences in the Experiences of White Women and Men

As we have discussed in previous chapters, race and sex affect one's opportunities, experiences, and outcomes in organizations. Patriarchal systems disadvantage White women as they do other women. Despite early discrimination among White immigrants against other White ethnics, the Naturalization Law of 1790 specifically allowed only White men to become citizens. Male immigrants of color were denied citizenship and White women experienced differential treatment as well. In many cases, White women were unable to own property, enter into agreements, or make decisions about themselves, or if married, about their children. Although they were White, they were also women, and subject to patriarchal systems and ideals. As a result, Black men, at least in theory, obtained the right to vote in 1870, 50 years before White women did.[35]

Because White women generally marry White men, married White women's current economic status benefits from White men's higher earnings and occupational status, making their individual disadvantages less obvious than those of women of color. When viewed as individuals, however, White women's earnings and occupational status indicate similarities of White women's experiences to those of other nondominant groups. See Figure 7.2 for the earnings disparities between White men and women. Currently, as do women of color, White women work in female-dominated jobs, and experience the glass ceiling and glass walls. When compared with White men, White women are more likely to work part time, and to work fewer hours when working full time. Women have been called the "51% minority" and "the oppressed majority" in reflection of their lower status in organizations and society.

[35] The theoretical right to vote did not guarantee Black men the actual right to vote, however; property requirements, poll taxes, literacy requirements, lynching, and other obstacles prevented Blacks from voting well into the 1900s with the passage of the Voting Rights Act of 1965.

As discussed in Chapter 6, a 2005 Gallup Poll study found 12% of Whites reported experiencing some form of discrimination within the prior year. Women were considerably more likely to report discrimination—22% compared to 3% of men.[36]

Misperception: Because they are White, White women experience few disadvantages at work.

Reality: Although White women are the least disadvantaged of all women, they are disadvantaged relative to White men, occupying lower level, status, and paid occupations and having lower returns to their educational investments.

The Meaning of Ethnicity for Whites

Research on ethnic identity development indicates that those with high identity development have positive attitudes toward their own and others' ethnic group members. One study found that Whites with high racial identity development, measured as having acceptance, appreciation, and respect for racial differences, and active involvement in cross-racial interactions, were most comfortable with Blacks.[37]

Donna Chrobot-Mason and others have found support for the relationship between White ethnic identity development and ability to work with and fairly manage dissimilar others.[38] Chrobot-Mason hypothesized that Whites who perceived themselves as being a member of a White ethnic group would be better at managing diverse employee groups due to having developed higher ethnic identity. In her study investigating the role of White managers' identity development on minority employees' perceptions of support, 20% of the White managers reported their ethnicity as something other than White/American, such as *Italian American* or *German American*. Importantly, these reports were responses to an open-ended question, in which the managers wrote in their ethnicity. Chrobot-Mason found that when White managers and minority employees both had high ethnic identity development, the managers were perceived to be more supportive, through listening, encouraging, guiding, being a role model, and fostering a relationship of mutual trust.

The difference between those who genuinely hold an ethnic identity and those whose ethnic ties are symbolic is worth noting. Herbert Gans has described the latter as "symbolic ethnicity," which is invoked at will, but has little meaning on a person's everyday life. An example of symbolic ethnicity is when those from

[36] Yen, H. (2005, December 8). "Poll: Nearly 1 Out of 6 Workers Claim Bias." *The Associated Press.*

[37] Claney, D., & Parker, W. M. (1989). "Assessing White Racial Consciousness and Perceived Comfort with Black Individuals: A Preliminary Study." *Journal of Counseling and Development,* 67: 449–451.

[38] Chrobot-Mason, D. (2004). "Managing Racial Differences: The Role of Majority Managers' Ethnic Identity Development on Minority Employee Perceptions of Support." *Group and Organization Management,* 29(1): 5–31.

Irish backgrounds emphasize and celebrate St. Patrick's Day, but their ethnicity has little meaning to them at other times.[39] For symbolic ethnics, the diversity-related benefits identified by Chrobot-Mason are probably less likely to be experienced. In addition, it is important to emphasize that in contrast to the positive outcomes of White ethnicity identified by researchers (e.g., listening, encouraging, guiding, being a role model, fostering a relationship of mutual trust, acceptance, appreciation, respect for racial differences, and active involvement in cross-racial interactions), some forms of White identity are associated with negative outcomes. Such outcomes can include hatred and hostility toward people of color, religious minorities, immigrants, Whites who are antiracist, and sexual minorities, and resistance to equality.

Caryn Block, Loriann Roberson, and Debra Neuger investigated the racial identity development of White adults, and found a complex relationship between levels of racial identity and attitudes toward interracial situations at work.[40] Participants' levels of identity development were related to their beliefs in the existence of discrimination against Blacks, the need for affirmative action and the existence of reverse discrimination against Whites, and to their support for or resistance to measures to increase equity and levels of comfort interacting with Blacks at work or in work-related social settings. Block and her colleagues emphasized the importance of measuring Whites' levels of identity development prior to implementing diversity training, as the type of training needed (e.g., awareness of the existence of inequities and the need for efforts to reduce them vs. skills training) would vary based on employees' level of identity.

Perceptions of "Quotas" and "Reverse Discrimination"

The terms "reverse discrimination" and "angry White male" are often used in discussions of diversity in organizations.[41] These terms refer to the idea that White men experience discrimination as a result of efforts to include and reduce discrimination against people of color and women in organizations. Research consistently shows that attitudes of White men and women are most negative toward affirmative action programs, which are valuable to increasing diversity in organizations. Faye Crosby's book, "Affirmative Actions is Dead: Long Live Affirmative Action" thoroughly discusses research on resistance to affirmative action and the continued need for such programs in the United States.[42] Frequent use of the term "quotas" by the media, politicians, and even some

[39] Rubin, L. B. (2004). "Is This a White Country, or What?" In J. F. Healey & E. O'Brien, *Race, Ethnicity, and Gender,* Thousand Oaks, CA: Pine Forge Press, pp. 301–310.

[40] Block, C. J., Roberson, L., & Neuger, D. A. (1995). "White Racial Identity Theory: A Framework for Understanding Reactions toward Interracial Situations in Organizations." *Journal of Vocational Behavior,* 46: 71–88.

[41] See Bonilla-Silva, E., & Forman, T. A. (2000). "'I Am Not a Racist but . . .': Mapping White College Students' Racial Ideology in the USA." *Discourse & Society,* 11(1): 50–85.

[42] Corsby, F. (2004). *Affirmative Action is Dead: Long Live Affirmative Action.* New Haven, CT: Yale University Press.

researchers in reference to affirmative action and other diversity efforts contributes to misperceptions that quotas are legal and commonly used.

Misperception: Affirmative action frequently results in quotas and reverse discrimination.

Reality: Quotas are largely illegal and reverse discrimination is uncommon.

As discussed in previous chapters, instead of "quotas," through affirmative action, employers use flexible goals and timetables to reduce imbalances in representation of underrepresented groups (for example, women, Blacks, Latinos, or Asians). These efforts may include increasing the pool of applicants by using different recruitment sources, through training and development of current employees, or through other legal means. These goals and timetables are flexible, and if not met after legitimate efforts, there is no penalty.

Whites also tend to think that reverse discrimination is far more common than minorities do. Reverse discrimination is the act of giving preference to members of protected classes to the extent that others feel they are experiencing discrimination. How likely and common is "reverse discrimination" in organizations? Although we have reiterated that most people do not sue when they feel they have experienced discrimination, one gauge of the prevalence of reverse discrimination would be the relative prevalence of lawsuits in which reverse discrimination was alleged. Richard Schaefer reports that "fewer than 100 of the more than 3,000 discrimination opinions in federal courts from 1990 to 1994 even raised the issue of reverse discrimination, and reverse discrimination was actually established in only six cases."[43] The EEOC litigation settlement reports available online for the period between December 2002 and September 2005 included only one case involving reverse discrimination, *EEOC v. Horizon/Mercy Health Plan of Trenton, N.J.,* presented earlier.[44] As discussed in previous chapters, multiple audit studies conducted in major U.S. cities confirm the greater likelihood of Whites to be preferred over similarly qualified Blacks and Latinos.[45]

Another gauge of the existence of reverse discrimination would be disproportionate changes in the representation of Whites in positions of power, status, and high earnings, compared with minorities and women. As we have discussed, White men's representation in those positions far exceeds their representation in the population. High-level executives in Fortune 500 companies, university

---

[43] Schaefer, R. T. (2002). p. 96. See original article: "Reverse Discrimination Complaints Rare, a Labor Study Reports," 1995, March 31. *New York Times,* A 10.

[44] EEOC Litigation Settlements—May 2004, http://www.eeoc.gov/litigation/settlements/settlement05-04.html, accessed 07/15/05.

[45] See Bendick, M., Jr., Jackson, C., & Reinoso, V. (1994). "Measuring employment discrimination through controlled experiments." *Review of Black Political Economy,* 23: 25–48; Bendick, M., Jr., Jackson, C., Reinoso V., & Hodges L. (1991). "Discrimination against Latino Job Applicants: A Controlled Experiment." *Human Resource Management,* 30: 469–484; Fix, M., & Struyk, R. (Eds.) (1991). *Clear and Convincing Evidence,* Washington, DC: The Urban Institute.

administrators and professors, physicians and surgeons, politicians, and many other positions involving high status, power, and earnings are disproportionately occupied by White males. Although White men make up less than 40% of the population, more than 90% of the highest level corporate executives, for example, are White men. It is irrational to assume that these disproportionate figures exist because White men are more meritorious than other groups or that these differences would remain so persistent after 40 years of reverse discrimination. It is more rational to assume that at least some of the disproportionate figures exist because of discrimination against other candidates for positions, as proposed by Stephen McNamee and Robert Miller in Research Translation 7.1, presented earlier. The following EEOC case describes a situation in which young Whites were promoted into management instead of a more qualified, older Black man.

- **EEOC v. Bancroft Neurohealth d/b/a Bancroft Brain Injury Services**[46]
  No. 03-4225 (JHR) (D.N.J. Aug. 11, 2005)

  The Philadelphia District Office alleged in this ADEA/Title VII suit that defendant, a healthcare provider headquartered in Haddonfield, New Jersey, failed to promote charging party into a Brain Injury Services (BIS) Program Manager position because of his race (black) and age (47). Charging party, who had worked for about 7 years as an Educator/Residential Rehabilitation Associate at defendant's Mullica Hill, New Jersey facility, applied for a Program Manager position in March 2002. Qualifications for the position included 3 to 4 years of experience, a bachelor's degree or related experience in lieu of the degree, and 1 year of supervisory experience. The charging party met the qualifications for the position and had received good performance evaluations. Defendant rejected charging party and promoted a 19-year-old white individual, with a high school diploma and 1 year of experience, whom charging party had trained. On three earlier occasions, defendant had passed over charging party and selected younger white candidates for Program Manager positions.

Race, quality of education and grades, and "fit". Evidence from empirical research also questions the veracity of claims that minorities and women are now advantaged over Whites and males. In one study of the near absence of Blacks in corporate law firms, researchers found that Blacks with average grades were significantly less likely to be hired than Whites with the same grades.[47] To be hired and to excel at elite firms was far easier for Whites who attended average schools than for Blacks who attended such schools. Whites with average performance at average schools had substitutes for educational qualifications,

---

[46] EEOC Litigation Settlements—August 2005, http://www.eeoc.gov/litigation/settlements/settlement08-05.html, accessed 10/29/05.

[47] Wilkins, D. B., & Gulati, G. M. (1996). "Why Are There So Few Black Lawyers in Corporate Law Firms? An Institutional Analysis." *California Law Review,* 84: 496–625.

such as "personality," and "fit." The authors proposed that stereotypes and unconscious biases in such firms advantage Whites over equally qualified Blacks.

Race, sex, interview assessments, and offer decisions. In a study involving 311 pairs of recruiters and applicants, Caren Goldberg assessed the effects of similarity in race and sex on interview assessments and offer decisions.[48] The recruiters were managers and human resources professionals for a variety of industries, including banking, telecommunications, manufacturing, services, and retail. Goldberg found that White recruiters preferred White applicants, rating them higher in interview assessments and making more job offers to them. Black recruiters did not favor Black applicants, however. Goldberg suggested that her findings regarding Whites, but not Blacks preferring similar others are consistent with high-status group members seeking to maintain their status, thus overvaluing in-group members (see also Chapter 3). The results for sex similarity indicated that male recruiters preferred female candidates, but female recruiters showed no preference for male or female applicants. Data analyses indicated that physical attractiveness of female applicants affected male recruiters' ratings of them.[49]

Race, sex, performance ratings, and salary increases. In a study of the relationships between performance ratings and salary increases, Professor Emilio Castilla of Massachusetts Institute of Technology found that women and minorities received lower salary increases than White men even with the same performance.[50] Because Castilla controlled for factors other than race, ethnicity, and sex that could contribute to differences in salary increases, any differences could then be attributed to race, ethnicity, and sex (e.g., discrimination). Castilla's sample of nearly 9,000 employees worked between 1996 and 2003 in a large service organization in the United States and received performance evaluations at least once per year by their immediate supervisor. There were no differences in starting salaries based on race, sex, or other ascriptive characteristics (e.g., age and nationality); comparably skilled employees, regardless of their demographic characteristics, received similar initial salaries. Over time, however, employees who were carefully matched in terms of human capital characteristics, job experience and performance, job class, work unit, and supervisor, but different in demographic characteristics earned different dollar amounts of salary increases. These differences resulted in significantly smaller salary growth for women and minorities. Professor Castilla speculated that this "performance-reward"

[48] Goldberg, C. (2005). "Relational Demography and Similarity-Attraction in Interview Assessments: Are We Missing Something?" *Group and Organization Management,* 30: 597–624. Goldberg also assessed effects of age similarity on interview assessments and offer decisions, but found no differences.

[49] Chapter 14 considers the effects of appearance on organizational outcomes.

[50] Castilla, E. J. (2005). "Gender, Race, and Meritocracy in Organizational Careers." *Academy of Management Best Papers,* Honolulu, HI.

discrimination occurred when employers consciously or unconsciously underweigh the work of minorities in reward situations.

Effects of Increasing Diversity on Dominant Group Members

In a field study of more than 1,700 people working in 151 groups, Tsui, Egan, and O'Reilly found that increasing organizational diversity was associated with lowered psychological attachment for Whites and males but not for women and minorities.[51] They speculated that increasing diversity may require changes in behavioral norms, such as in language or behavior (for example, in cases of the presence of more women, this could require changes in sexist language or behavior that may be offensive to women). Such changes could be taxing, stressful to, or resisted by the dominant group. Tsui and her colleagues also suggested that increased numbers of women and minorities in formerly homogenous groups may signal a lowering of job status to Whites and males. This lowering of status may result in decreased attachment to the organization. The researchers suggested that future research should more closely examine the effects of increasing diversity on majority group members, rather than solely focusing on minority group members.

Misperception: Women and minorities have difficulty fitting in when organizations become more diverse.

Reality: In some ways, increasing diversity can be more difficult for Whites and males—members of higher status groups—than for women and minorities.

Individual Recommendations

Whites play distinctive roles in diversity in organizations. As members of the dominant racial group, Whites have more interpersonal power to make changes than do people of color. As members of the dominant group, they may also erroneously view increasing diversity as lowering their individual power, although diversity is beneficial to everyone in the large scheme. Along with other groups, Whites should view diversity as a potential source of competitive advantage, to be embraced, rather than feared. Through proactively working toward diversity, organizations will be able to increase competitiveness through gains in costs, resource acquisition, system flexibility, marketing, creativity, and problem-solving, among others. This increased competitiveness will result in more opportunities for all, rather than in fewer opportunities and advantages for Whites.

As recipients of discrimination and disadvantage while also being members of the dominant group, White women are in a particularly unique situation.

[51] Tsui, A. S., Egan, T. D., & O'Reilly, C. A. (1992). "Being Different: Relational Demography and Organizational Attachment." *Administrative Science Quarterly,* 37: 549–579.

White women in positions of power have an opportunity to effect changes through their own positional and organizational power. In addition, because their spouses, fathers, and other male relatives are generally White men, White women have the power to influence beliefs and behaviors of White men. As credible spouses, mothers, daughters, and other relatives of White men, White women have the opportunity to share experiences with White men that may help them view discrimination, the glass ceiling, and at-work harassment and exclusion as real and pervasive problems, rather than a few isolated and unique incidents. White women may be viewed as more believable and trusted sources of invaluable diversity-related information than people of color. White women should also acknowledge their advantages when compared with women of color, rather than expecting women of color to see themselves only as women working for women's equality. Many women of color view their race, rather than their sex, as being their primary impediment to fairness.

White men and women should recognize the privileges associated with Whiteness. Denial of privilege and support of the myth of meritocracy serves to limit Whites' opportunities for growth. Acknowledge and work to dismantle systems of unfair advantage and to share the advantages construed as "normal" for Whites among other racial groups. Whites should also actively work to dispel myths and stereotypes about nondominant group members. When working for equality, Whites, particularly White men, are viewed as more credible than people of color.

Whites are members of the dominant racial and ethnic group, but they may also belong to nondominant groups at some points in their lives. White men may be older, gay, Jewish, overweight, or have a disability. White women experience sex discrimination and harassment and may also be older, lesbian, members of a nondominant religious group, have a disability, or other nondominant group status. Although Whites' racial dominance likely pervades their diversity learning and understanding, active efforts to apply learning from any nondominant group membership to their racial privileges would be worthwhile.

Because Whites are more likely to be executives, managers, and organizational leaders than others, they are in influential positions to create climates favorable to diversity.[52] The favorable environment and the diversity-supportive behaviors they model are likely to be modeled by subordinates, contributing to a positive diversity climate. Bill Proudman and Michael Welp joined forces in running "The White Men's Caucus," which presents "White Men as Full Diversity Partners" workshops that are specifically designed to engage White men in diversity initiatives. Employees at clients such as Shell Oil and Detroit Edison report being enlightened about White male privilege, the dominance of White male cultures in organizations, and other diversity issues to which they were previously oblivious. One client realized the need for White men "to get more

[52] See the focus of Chapter 9 on Sharon Allen, Chairman of the Board of Deloitte Touche, USA.

involved in diversity. We tend to think of it as other people's issues," rather than being relevant to White men as well as to minorities, women, and other non-dominant groups.[53]

One effective way that Whites in positions of power can "get more involved in diversity" is by serving as mentors for nondominant group members. Mentoring is a clear way to facilitate entry of nondominant group members into positions of power, providing access to resources and insights, information on power systems and organizational dynamics, and a host of other benefits. Historically, White men have been advantaged by mentoring and networking systems (e.g., "the good old boy network"), while women and people of color have been excluded. Active mentoring by Whites in power can open access doors to more employees and more widely distribute some of the many benefits of mentoring both to the mentors and to those who are mentored.

Organizational Recommendations

As we have discussed, for organizational diversity efforts to be successful, it is imperative that Whites be actively included. As those most likely to be in positions of power, Whites who are allies in diversity efforts are vital resources. Organizational leaders must recognize that Whites may resist diversity efforts because they feel excluded, that focusing on diversity efforts is a waste of resources, or that the organization is already diverse and supportive to people of color and women. Including Whites as active participants in the diversity process is a key step to reducing some resistance. Education about the advantages to everyone of increased diversity and about the existence of the glass ceiling and walls, sexual harassment, and other barriers to diversity is also important. Whites should be assured that diversity is not an "us or them" situation, but is valuable to everyone.

In the individual recommendations section, mentoring was suggested as a means that individual Whites in power can assist with diversity efforts. Institutions should facilitate mentoring of nondominant group members through organizationally sanctioned mentoring programs, mentoring training, and recognition for mentors.

Goldberg's finding that White managers and human resources professionals serving as recruiters rated racially similar others more highly and were more likely to make job offers to them indicate that interviewer ratings and job offers should be carefully monitored and scrutinized. Castilla's findings of similar starting salaries for women and minorities but differential salary increases for women and minorities than White males despite the same performance underscore the need for organizational attention to the outcomes of processes designed to be meritocratic. Not only should employers pay attention to initial salaries and to biases in

[53] Atkinson, W. (2001). "Bringing Diversity to White men." *HR Magazine,* 46(9): 76–83.

performance evaluation ratings for different demographic groups, they should also monitor salary increases and promotions based on equivalent ratings. Because research indicates that formalization of human resource practices reduces gender and race discrimination in earnings, as much as possible, practices should be formalized and monitored.[54]

Summary

In this chapter, we have considered the contributions of Whites to diversity in organizations. The history of Whites in the United States, including hostility and exclusion among White ethnic groups and the transition from non-White to Whites of some of those groups was discussed. Research was presented on the relationship between Whites' perceptions of themselves as having an ethnicity and their ability to effectively manage diversity. Differences in the experiences of White women and White men, and Whites who belong to other nondominant groups (such as religious minorities, sexual minorities, or people with disabilities) were considered.

Whites are often overlooked in diversity research, training, and efforts, yet, as the dominant group, they play a key role in organizational diversity efforts. Historically, many Whites have served as diversity allies and they continue to do so. Suggestions for individual Whites to participate and contribute to diversity in organizations and for organizations to facilitate Whites' inclusion were provided.

Key Terms

Myth of meritocracy — the idea that societal resources are distributed exclusively or primarily on the basis of individual merit.

Performance-reward discrimination — the act of giving different amounts of rewards (e.g., salary increases) to members of different groups who have similar performance evaluations.

Reverse discrimination — the act of giving preference to members of protected classes to the extent that others feel they are experiencing discrimination.

Symbolic ethnicity — a form of ethnicity that has little impact on one's daily life and is invoked at will.

Questions to Consider

1. Many Whites argue that their resistance to affirmative action and diversity programs is due in part to their not having had slaves or practiced discrimination.[55] What are some ways in which

[54] Anderson, C. D., & Tomaskovic-Devey, D. (1995). "Patriarchal Pressures: An Exploration of Organizational Processes That Exacerbate and Erode Gender Earnings Inequality." *Work and Occupations,* 22(3): 328–357; Elvira, M. M., & Graham, M. E. (2002). "Not Just a Formality: Pay System Formalization and Sex-Related Earnings Effects." *Organization Science,* 13(6): 601–617; Konrad, A. M., & Linnehan, F. (1995). "Formalized HRM Structures: Coordinating Equal Employment Opportunity or Concealing Organizational Practices?" *Academy of Management Journal,* 38: 787–820; Reskin, B. (2000). "The Proximate Causes of Employment Discrimination." *Contemporary Sociology,* 29(2): 319–328.

[55] For discussions of advantages, disadvantages, oblivion, and consciousness of privilege versus discrimination, see McIntosh (2004).

Whites who have not owned slaves and have not practiced discrimination in employment nonetheless benefitted from and been advantaged by slavery and discrimination?

2. How does the visibility (identifiability) of groups such as Blacks and Asians contrast with the invisibility of White ethnics in shaping their organizational experiences?
3. Recall from Chapter 4 that many of the Whites who participated in Blacks' struggle for civil rights were Jewish. How were the organizational experiences of Jews and Blacks in the United States similar and dissimilar?
4. Is the transition of Jews and Irish from being viewed as non-White to White surprising to you? Brodkin also discusses the transformations of Mexicans to White then back again. Were you aware of these changes? In addition to those listed in this chapter, what other changes in race occurred within the U.S. census categorizations?
5. Prior to reading this chapter, what would your estimates have been for the differences between earnings of White men and White women?
6. Recall the study by Dr. Castilla that found similar starting salaries but differential salary growth for women and minorities compared with White men even with the same performance. What are some possible negative consequences for the organization if these salary differences were widely known? What specific, detailed steps would you recommend be taken to avoid "performance-reward" discrimination?

7a. If you are not White, do you know someone well who is White? In what capacity do you know him or her (e.g., personal friend, manager, classmate, neighbor, etc.)? Do you know his or her ethnic origin (e.g., Italy, Ireland, Germany, etc.)? How much time have you spent with him or her? Have you thought about him or her as having a race or ethnicity? Have you discussed race, ethnicity, or other diversity issues with him or her? Explain.

7b. If you are White, do you know your ethnic origin? How much of a role does your ethnic origin play in your everyday life, experiences, and opportunities?

7c. How is ethnicity of Whites different from visible differences in affecting one's experiences and opportunities?

8. In the case *EEOC v. Bancroft Neurohealth d/b/a Bancroft Brain Injury Services* discussed in the chapter, the 47-year-old Black man (charging party) was passed over for promotion four times before bringing suit. In each case, young Whites with fewer qualifications were promoted, one of whom the charging party had trained. What are (a) possible morale issues in the workplace, (b) perspectives of the Whites selected about what happened, (c) possible reasons the employer would give for not promoting the charging party and promoting the young White men instead, and (d) reasons the charging party did not bring suit until the fourth incident or turn over during the 7 years he worked there?
9. What have you learned from this chapter that is most surprising to you?

Actions and Exercises

1. Search EEOC Web site (http://www.eeoc.gov) litigation settlement report for the most recent 3 or 6 months for cases of discrimination charges and settlements against Whites. In any month that you find a case involving discrimination against Whites, document the events surrounding this case. What proportion of cases involved race-based discrimination against Whites?
2. Although "quotas" are illegal, many people believe they are legal and common. What is the role of the media and politicians on promulgating this misperception? Prepare an argument to dispel the idea of reverse discrimination using education and earnings and representation in senior and executive management of White men, White women, and people of color.

3a. Conduct an informal census of employees in several places: fast food restaurant, sit-down restaurant, discount store (e.g., Target, Wal-Mart), department store (e.g., Macy's, Filene's, Marshall Fields), government office, bank, or other locations in which many employees are visible. Document the number of employees overall and the number of White employees visible. What is the race and sex of the store manager? Estimate the proportion of the employees who are White in each place. How many managers and assistant managers are White? How many are White and male?

3b. Choose two nights to watch television for 30 minutes to 1 hour each. Document the program, commerical type, and the numbers of White characters on the programs and commercials. In what roles are they portrayed?

3c. What similarities and differences are apparent between the people in 3a and 3b above?

4. In your exercises 3a and b above, speculate on the ethnicity of the White employees (3a) or characters (3b). What factors did you use in your speculation? Compare the difficulty in speculating on ethnicity for the Whites with identifying them by race and sex.
5. Use a calculator to make a chart projecting the effects of "performance-reward" disparities (discussed in Dr. Castilla's study in the chapter) in salary growth of White men, White women, and people of color.
   a. Make columns for starting salaries of $30,000 for the new employees. Use different annual salary increase estimates (e.g., 1%, 3%, 5%, or other estimates) for each demographic group. What are the salary differences after 10 years? After 20 years?
   b. What effects would such salary growth disparities have on each employee's and the employer's contributions to the employees' Social Security, tax-deferred savings plans, and retirement plans?
   c. What effects would such salary growth disparities have on other outcomes for these groups (e.g., housing opportunities, investment, and children's education)?

8 Chapter

American Indians, Alaska Natives, and Multiracial Group Members

Chapter Objectives

After completing this chapter, readers should have a greater understanding of American Indians, Alaska Natives, and multiracial group members in the United States. Readers can expect to:

- *be aware of the historical background and current status of American Indians, Alaska Natives, and multiracial group members in the United States.*
- *be able to discuss education, participation rates, employment, and income levels of American Indians and Alaska Natives in the United States.*
- *have an increased understanding of the diversity among multiracial group members and issues unique to them.*
- *understand legislation related to employment experiences of American Indians, Alaska Natives, and multiracial group members.*
- *be able to make recommendations for inclusion of these groups in diversity efforts.*

Key Facts

The 4.4 million people who are American Indians and Alaska Natives make up 1.5% of the U.S. population.

Fourteen percent of American Indians and Alaska Natives have at least a bachelor's degree—fewer than all racial and ethnic groups except Hispanics.

AI/AN have the worst or nearly the worst unemployment, poverty, and health insurance rates in the United States.

In the 2000 census, for the first time, people could report belonging to two or more races, and 6.8 million people did so.

Ninety-three percent of multiracial people are two races and 6% are three races.

Multirace people are younger than single race people; 42% of multiracials are under 18, compared with 25% of single race people.

Introduction and Overview

This chapter considers American Indians and Alaska Natives (AI/AN) and multiracial group members and their experiences relevant to diversity in organizations. This combination is done for several reasons. First, as the original inhabitants of the United States, American Indians preceded any *diversity* to speak of in the country. Because they are a relatively small portion of the population, AI/AN are often overlooked in studies of diversity in organizations, yet their role in the history and diversity of the United States should not be ignored. Next, multiracial group members—people who reported belonging to two or more racial backgrounds—could perhaps be considered the "newest" groups in the United States, at least in their ability to identify themselves as such in the U.S. census records. In the 2000 census, respondents had the option to self-identify using two or more races for the first time since census data collection began. This change reflects a previously unacknowledged (at least formally) aspect of the racial diversity of the U.S. population. Allowing multiracial group members to indicate their multiracial heritage, rather than having to choose one, provides more information about the increasing racial diversity and the recognition of different identities of the population.

The chapter begins with a brief discussion of the history, population, education, earnings, and employment of American Indians and Alaska Natives, with a primary focus on American Indians. We next discuss the limited extant research on the organizational experiences of AI/AN in the United States. Next, the history and population of multiracial group members in the United States are considered.[1]

Terminology

In this chapter, we use the term *American Indian* in reference to the descendants of the people indigenous to what is now the mainland (lower 48) United States. This usage is consistent with that of many other researchers, the Office of American Indian Trust, and the U.S. Census Bureau when referring to that specific population. Although *Native American* is often construed as more appropriate, American Indian is more commonly used by members of the group themselves and is considered broadly acceptable.[2] Further, the term Native Americans has been used to include American Indians, Alaska Natives, Native Hawaiians, and sometimes Chamorros and American Samoans, but the latter three groups are not the targets of this chapter.[3] Thus, in this chapter, we use the term American Indians or American Indians and Alaska Natives (AI/AN) as appropriate. Much of the research investigates experiences of American Indians alone, and in those cases we refer only to American Indians. At times, data for American Indians and Alaska Natives are included in an "other" category, as described. Lastly, we use the term *nation* as well as *tribe* in referring to different groups of American Indians, respecting variations in the preferred terminology among Indians themselves and among researchers.[4]

When referring to persons of more than one racial background, we use the term *multiracial* to mean people with two or more (identified) racial backgrounds. This term includes biracial people

[1] The diversity of people included in the multiracial group category prevents coherent discussions of their earnings, education, and unemployment so we do not attempt to discuss them.

[2] Wildenthal, B. H. (2003). *Native American Sovereignty on Trial,* Santa Barbara, CA: ABC-CLIO.

[3] Ibid.

[4] See Massey, G. M. (2004). "Making Sense of Work on the Wind River Indian Reservation." *American Indian Quarterly,* 28(3/4): 786–816, footnote 1.

along with those with more than two identified racial backgrounds. Although some researchers have limited their focus to people with White/ Black heritage,[5] we do not limit our discussion to White/ Black multiracial group members. However, we acknowledge the importance of the specific combination of multiracial categories (and their visibility) to one's diversity-related outcomes.

HISTORY OF AMERICAN INDIANS IN NORTH AMERICA

Many people in the United States are familiar with American Indians only through media images, including television shows (e.g., *The Lone Ranger,* with Tonto), movies (e.g., *Dances with Wolves, Windtalkers*), and sports teams (e.g., Florida State Seminoles, Atlanta Braves, Washington Redskins, and Cleveland Indians). Perceptions of Indians as savage enemies are often reinforced by these images, although recent media attempt to portray Indians more accurately and fairly. Feature 8.1 considers stereotyping, insensitivity, and debate around organizations using American Indians as mascots and sports symbols.

American Indians were the original inhabitants of North America, already present when Columbus is credited with discovering America. After an initial period of what appeared to be peaceful coexistence, relations between American Indians and Europeans began to decline. Historical records document the violence, conquest, and near extermination of American Indians. In 1830, the Indian Removal Act, passed under President Andrew Jackson, authorized the expulsion of 14,000 Indians from lands in the southeastern portion of the country to Arkansas and Oklahoma. Thousands of Indians died on the "Trail of Tears" westward, continuing the decline in population begun by war, disease, and annihilation of buffalo.

The U.S. census did not include American Indians until 1860, and then only if they were not living on reservations. With the 1890 census, all American Indians, both on reservations and outside reservations were included in the census figures.[6] Estimates of the number of American Indians at first European contact range from 1 million in the United States to 8 million,[7] a very wide range of estimates. In 1890, with the first census count, 248,000 American Indians were recorded, far less than even the lowest end of the original estimated Indian population.[8]

After conquest and near extermination, European Americans focused attention on assimilating Indians into American society. Many American Indian

[5] Rockquemore, K. A., & Brunsmir, D. L. (2002). *Beyond Black,* Thousand Oaks, CA: Sage.

[6] U.S. Census Bureau. (1993). *We the . . . first Americans,* Washington, DC: U.S. Department of Commerce.

[7] Thornton, R. (2004). "Trends among American Indians in the United States." In J. F. Healey & E. O'Brien (Eds.), *Race, Ethnicity, and Gender,* Thousand Oaks, CA: Pine Forge Press, pp. 195–210.

[8] U.S. Census Bureau. (1993).

FEATURE 8.1 ***American Indians as Sports Symbols and Mascots***

In the 1970s, Oklahoma, Marquette, Stanford, Dartmouth, and Syracuse discontinued using Indian mascots.[9] Debate over the use of American Indians as mascots has waxed and waned since then, with some viewing such usage as insensitive and offensive while others viewing it as harmless. In 2001, the U.S. Civil Rights Commission issued a statement on the use of American Indian images and nicknames as sports symbols.[10] The Commission opined that the use of such symbols is insensitive and implies that stereotyping is acceptable, a "dangerous lesson in a diverse society." Arguing that the use of stereotypical images of American Indians could create a hostile educational environment for Indian students, the Commission cited the low high school and college graduation rates of Indians. The Commission rejected arguments that such images honor American Indians and stimulate interest in Indian cultures. Instead, according to the Commission, such images prevent people from learning about real American Indians and their current issues.

When the National Collegiate Athletic Association (NCAA) voted to penalize 18 schools if they continued using inappropriate American Indian nicknames, mascots, or images, the controversy generated heated debates, threats, and considerable media attention. The NCAA's proposed bans included the use of American Indian imagery and nicknames, performance of mascots at NCAA tournament games, and, by 2008, cheerleaders and band members would not be allowed to use Indian images on their uniforms.[11] The Florida State University Seminoles was one mascot deemed culturally "hostile and abusive." University administrators, alumni, supporters, and politicians from Florida were outraged at the proposed sanctions and vowed to pursue all legal avenues available to fight the NCAA's decision.

The NCAA's decision may have been partially based on media reports that the Seminole Nation of Oklahoma had voted to denounce the use of American Indian names and images in sports and other events.[12] While the Seminole Nation did vote on such a motion, and some media reported it was passed, the motion failed by an overwhelming majority. One member of the NCAA executive committee stated that committee members had discussed reports that the Oklahoma Nation had condemned FSU's use of the Seminole mascot.[13] The Oklahoma Seminole Nation sent a letter to various media outlets to clarify the misunderstanding. In addition, the Tribal Council of the Seminole Tribe of Florida voiced its unequivocal support of FSU's use of the Seminole mascot.

After review of appeals and statements of support, the NCAA decided to allow FSU to use the Seminoles nickname, removing FSU from the list of restricted schools. Along with FSU, the Illinois Fighting Illini, the North Dakota Fighting Sioux, and the University of Utah Utes were among the original list of 18 schools, although these schools received considerably less media and political attention. Utah also appealed its inclusion on the list, arguing they had a "close and mutually respectful relationship" with the Utes. The university's

---

[9] Saraceno, J. (2005, August 10). "Some Colleges Have a Lot to Learn about Racism." *USA Today,* p. 2C.

[10] United States Commission on Civil Rights, http://aistm.org/2001usccr.htm, accessed 09/05/05.

[11] "NCAA: Tribes Must OK Use of Their Names." 2005, August 19. *The Associated Press,* http://www.msnbc.msn.com/id/8838557/, accessed 09/05/05.

[12] D'Angelo, T. (2005, August 12). "Seminole Tribe: NCAA Mistaken." *Palm Beach Post,* p. 1C.

[13] Ibid.

appeal was accompanied by a letter of support from the Northern Ute Indian Tribal Business Committee. The NCAA accepted Utah's appeal, agreeing that approval from the Ute Nation should keep the university from facing sanctions.[14]

The NCAA has said that it will handle reviews from other schools on a case by case basis, according to NCAA Senior Vice President Bernard Franklin. Franklin noted that "The decision of a namesake sovereign tribe, regarding when and how its name and imagery can be used, must be respected even when others may not agree."[15] He further stated that the NCAA remains committed to ensuring an atmosphere of respect and sensitivity for those participating in and attending its championships.

Although the appeals by FSU and Utah have been granted, the debate about the use of American Indians as mascots is far from over. Some American Indians continue to protest the use of such images, focusing on the political pressures placed on the Florida Seminoles to grant their approval of the use of the mascot.[16] In late August 2005, the Spirit Lake Sioux tribe withdrew its "already tepid" support of the University of North Dakota's use of the "Fighting Sioux" and "Sioux" as nicknames, even as the university prepared its appeal to the NCAA for being included on the list of schools marked for sanctions.[17]

Questions to Consider

1. ***Colleges and schools are unique organizations, with diverse students, alumni, faculty, and the public as customers and constituents. How might the use of an American Indian name and mascot affect individuals from the groups of customers and constituents? What should be done to address disputes that will inevitably arise when a decision is made to use or to discontinue use of a particular mascot?***
2. ***Why is the use of the Seminoles and other American Indians as mascots different from the "Fighting Irish" mascot at the University of Notre Dame?***
3. ***In its decision to penalize the 18 schools, the NCAA may have relied, in part, on faulty information they received from the media. Prior to acting upon such information, what should the NCAA have done?***

children were forced to attend American schools, where they were forbidden to speak their native languages as part of attempts to "civilize" them. Lost language and religions, through attempts to convert American Indians to Christianity, resulted in the loss of many cultural values and practices.[18]

Through the nineteenth and twentieth centuries, laws were passed and court decisions were rendered regarding the rights and fates of American Indians in the United States. Assimilation, termination, and self-determination were stated purposes of various decisions.[19] The 1924 Indian Citizenship Act gave citizenship to Indians born in the United States.[20] In 1953, laws were passed to terminate

---

[14] Lewis, M. C. (2005, September 3). "NCAA Allows Utah to Keep Being 'Utes.'" *The Salt Lake Tribune.*

[15] "Florida State Threatened to Sue over Postseason Ban." 2005, August 23. *Associated Press,* http://sports.espn.go.com/ncaa/news/story?id=2141197, accessed 08/05/05.

[16] American Indian Sports Team Mascots, http://aistm.org/1indexpage.htm, accessed 08/05/05.

[17] Dodds, D. (2005, August 31). "Spirit Lake Withdraws Support for Nickname. GrandForksHerald," http://www.grandforks.com/mld/grandforks/news/12519481.htm, accessed 08/05/05.

[18] Wildenthal. (2003).

[19] Deloria, V., Jr., & Lytle, C. M. (1983). *American Indians, American Justice,* Austin, TX: University of Texas Press.

[20] Recall that for long period of time, only White men in the United States were allowed to become citizens.

Indian tribes, causing more than 100 tribes to cease to be recognized. Most recently, the pendulum has swung again to the goal of self-determination, with American Indians being again allowed certain rights of self-governance and decision making. The 1978 Indian Child Welfare Act (restricting the removal of Indian children from their families by the courts), the American Indian Religious Freedom Act (1978) and the Tribal Self Governance Act of 1994 were significant steps in this self-determination.

Population

After being decimated in the 1700s and 1800s, the American Indian population began to recover during the 1900s due to declining mortality rates and increasing fertility rates. Changes in self-identification have also contributed to increases in this population.[21] As of July 1, 2003, there were 4.4 million people in the United States who were American Indians and Alaska Natives alone or in combination with one or more other races, comprising 1.5% of the U.S. population. Although they are counted as a single group for census purposes, the AI/AN population is diverse in language, religions, culture, beliefs, values, and geographic backgrounds.[22] In addition, estimates suggest that 60% of American Indians marry those who are not American Indians,[23] which contributes to the diversity among those with AI ancestry and to increases in the multiracial category.

The self-report data collection of the U.S. census allows for more flexibility in recognition of who is American Indian. If a respondent reports that he or she is American Indian, this reporting is counted as valid, even though this reporting may change, even within the same year. As an example, only 42% of the people who identified as American Indian did so on both the 1990 census and the follow-up reinterview survey later that year. In comparison, 96% of Whites and 91% of Blacks reported the same racial identity in both surveys. For recognition by the Bureau of Indian Affairs, one-quarter American Indian ancestry and/or tribal membership has generally been required. Among Indian nations, there is wide variation in the amount of Indian ancestry required for people to be officially recognized as being American Indian.[24] Table 8.1 presents numbers and proportions of people identifying as AI/AN alone or in combination with one or more other races, as of the 2000 census (the first time one could self-identify with more than one race, as previously noted).

---

[21] Deloria, V., Jr., & Lytle, C. M. (1983). See also Eschbach, K., Supple, K., & Snipp, C. M. (1998). "Changes in Racial Identification and the Educational Attainment of American Indians, 1970–1990." *Demography,* 35(1): 35–43.

[22] Green, D. E. (1999). "Native Americans." In A. G. Dworkin & R. J. Dworkin (Eds.), *The Minority Report* (3rd edition), Fort Worth: Harcourt Brace Publishers, pp. 255–277; Wildenthal. (2003).

[23] Thornton, R. (2004). "Trends among American Indians in the United States." In J. F. Healey & E. O'Brien (Eds.), *Race, Ethnicity, and Gender,* Thousand Oaks, CA: Pine Forge Press, pp. 195–225.

[24] Ibid.

TABLE 8.1 ***Ten Largest American Indian or Alaska Native Tribes Alone or in Combination with One or More Race According to Number of Self-Identified Members, by Tribe: 2000***

	AI/AN in Combination*	AI/AN Alone†	Total AI/AN	% AI/AN in Combination	% AI/AN Alone
American Indian Tribes					
Cherokee	429,671	299,862	729,533	59%	41%
Navajo	22,206	275,991	298,197	7%	93%
Latin American Indian‡	74,736	106,204	180,940	41%	59%
Choctaw	61,873	96,901	158,774	39%	61%
Sioux	40,294	113,066	153,360	26%	74%
Chippewa	41,032	108,637	149,669	27%	73%
Apache	31,856	64,977	96,833	33%	67%
Blackfeet	54,288	31,462	85,750	63%	37%
Iroquois§	33,292	47,530	80,822	41%	59%
Pueblo	11,025	63,060	74,085	15%	85%
Alaska Native Tribes					
Eskimo	7,424	47,337	54,761	14%	86%
Tlingit-Haida	6,481	15,884	22,365	29%	71%
Alaska Athabascan	3,503	15,335	18,838	19%	81%
Aleut	4,205	12,773	16,978	25%	75%

**In combination* refers to people who selected American Indian/Alaska Native and one or more other race categories. Includes American Indians/Alaska Natives of Hispanic origin. Tribal groupings compiled by the Census Bureau do not necessarily correspond with federally recognized tribes. Self-identified membership does not necessarily correspond with official membership in a federally recognized tribe.

†*Alone* refers to respondents who selected American Indian/Alaska Native and not any other race category.

‡Latin American Indian includes people who listed any of a number of Latin American tribes (e.g., the Maya or Yanomamo).

§Iroquois is a language group that includes six federally recognized tribes.

Source: Adapted from "Status and Trends in the Education of American Indians and Alaska Natives." National Center for Education Statistics. NCES 2005-108. Table 1.3. Largest American Indian and Alaska Native tribes according to number of self-identified members, by tribe: 2000, http://nces.ed.gov/pubs2005/nativetrends/ShowTable.asp?table=tables/table_1_3.asp&indicator=1.3&excel=xls/table_1_3.xls&excelsize=20, accessed 10/15/05.

[Original source: U.S. Department of Commerce, Census Bureau, *Census 2000 Brief: The American Indian and Alaska Native Population, 2000,* 2002.]

In 2003, there were 562 federally recognized American Indian tribes in the United States. "Recognized" tribes have certain rights and privileges, including funding and services from the Bureau of Indian Affairs and the power of self-government (e.g., rights to make and enforce laws, tax, establish membership, license and regulate activities, and exclude people from tribal territories).[25]

[25] "Status and Trends in the Education of American Indians and Alaska Natives." National Center for Education Statistics. NCES 2005-108, http://nces.ed.gov/pubs2005/nativetrends/ind_1_3.asp, accessed 10/15/05.

As of July 1, 2004, the largest American Indian nations are Cherokee, with 234,000, and Navajo, with 204,000 members. The Apache, Chippewa, Choctaw, Lumbe, Pueblo, and Sioux all have at least 50,000 members.[26] With 37,000 members, Eskimo is the largest Alaska Native tribal group. Approximately 381,000 American Indians speak an Indian language. The most commonly spoken language is Navajo, spoken by 178,014 people.[27]

More than half a million American Indians live on reservations or trust lands, including 175,200 residing on Navajo lands in Arizona, New Mexico, and Utah. California has the most American Indian residents—687,400—followed by Oklahoma, with 398,200, and Arizona, with 322,200.

Misperception: The majority of American Indians live on reservations.

Reality: About 538,300 Indians (12%) live on reservations.

American Indians and Alaska Natives are a youthful people, significantly younger than the general population, and thus will compose a larger portion of the workforce as these youth age. Nearly one-third of the 4.4 million AI/AN are under age 18. Eight percent of the AI/AN population are in the 14 to 17 age range, which is the largest proportion of all racial and ethnic groups in this age category. As examples, 6% of Latinos and 5% of Whites fall into the 14 to 17 year old age group. Indigenous people in various countries are younger than other groups, including the Maori of New Zealand, as discussed in International Feature 8.1.

Fifty-seven percent of AI/AN now live in metropolitan areas, which is a smaller proportion than any other racial group, but a larger proportion than any time in the past. Until 1990, more than half of the AI/AN population lived outside metropolitan areas.[28] The growth of American Indians in metropolitan areas reflects concerted efforts to move American Indians to places having more employment opportunities than rural or reservation lands. Specifically, in the 1950s, U.S. government relocation programs contributed to the large-scale migration of American Indians from reservations that had few economic opportunities to cities which had greater opportunities for employment.[29] This migration resulted in more job opportunities, but less cohesion, fewer relationships with other American Indians and family members, discrimination, and other problems for American Indians.

[26] Facts for Features. "Native Indian and Alaska Native Heritage Month: November 2005," http://www.census.gov/Press-Release/www/releases/archives/facts_for_features_special_editions/005684.html, accessed 10/15/05.

[27] Ibid.

[28] Ibid.

[29] Green. (1999). p. 265.

International Feature 8.1 *Maori: Native New Zealanders*

Maori are the indigenous people to New Zealand who inhabited New Zealand prior to any other racial or ethnic group. At the time of their first European contact, in 1769, an estimated 100,000 Maori lived in New Zealand. By 1896, the population of Maori had declined to about 42,000. Presently, there are more than 600,000 Maori in New Zealand, comprising nearly 15% of its total population. Maori are growing faster than the general population and are projected to make up 17% of New Zealand's population by 2021. Between 1991 and 2001, the New Zealand European population (Pakeha) grew by 2.1%, while the New Zealand Maori population grew by 21.1%.[30]

The higher Maori growth rates are due to higher fertility rates, births between non-Maori and Maori, and to a younger population (who are in childbearing ages) than the general population.[31] In 2001, Maori children under age 15 comprised one quarter of all New Zealand children, and this is projected to grow to 28% by 2021. When compared with the proportion of Maori in the general population (15%), the proportion of Maori children indicates the importance of full inclusion of Maori in educational and employment opportunities in New Zealand.

Maori have lower education, employment, and income than non-Maori and higher levels of poverty, incarceration, and unemployment rates than the dominant group. Maori are two to three times as likely to be unemployed as are Pakeha and are more likely to be long-term unemployed than non-Maori.[32] As are minorities in the United States, Maori tend to be residentially segregated, which contributes further to polarization and disadvantage of nondominant groups.[33]

The 1977 Human Rights Act in New Zealand prohibits discrimination in organizational policies and practices against minorities and indigenous people, women, people with disabilities, sexual minorities, religious minorities, and other nondominant group members.[34] Diversity issues, including discrimination against nondominant groups, changing demographics, equity in employment, and other issues are of importance to New Zealand researchers as well as those in other areas. The importance of attention to differences in key issues among various nations must not be ignored, however.[35]

Questions to Consider

1. *The Maori, as indigenous people to New Zealand, experienced severe population declines after their first contact with Europeans in New Zealand. How do the current experiences (birth rates, education, employment, etc.) of Maori in New Zealand compare with those of American Indians in the United States?*

2. *The New Zealand Human Rights Act prohibits discrimination against Maori and other racial and ethnic minorities. How effective has it been?*

---

[30] Johnston, R. J., Poulsen, M. F., & Forrest, J. (2003). "The Ethnic Geography of New Zealand: A Decade of Growth and Change, 1991–2001." *Asia Pacific Viewpoint,* 44(2): 109–130.

[31] "Maori Population: Looking out to 2021." Hui Taumata 2005, http://www.huitaumata.maori.nz/pdf/population.pdf, accessed 09/03/05.

[32] Te Puni Kokiri: Maori in New Zealand—Maori Population, http://www.tpk.govt.nz/maori/population/rural.asp#key, accessed 09/03/2005.

[33] Johnston et al. (2003).

[34] The Human Rights Commission, http://www.hrc.co.nz/index.php?p=13814, accessed 09/04/05; Jones, D., Pringle, J., & Shepherd, D. (2000). "'Managing Diversity' Meets Aotearoa/New Zealand." *Personnel Review,* 29: 364–380.

[35] Jones, D. et al. (2000).

Table 8.2 ***Educational Attainment of Population 25 Years and Over: 2003***

	High School Graduate or More (%)	College Degree or More (%)
Non-Hispanic White	89.4	30.0
Black	80.0	17.3
Asian	87.6	49.8
Hispanic	57.0	11.4
American Indian/Alaska Native	75.0	14.0

Figure 8.1 ***Educational Attainment by Race and Ethnicity***

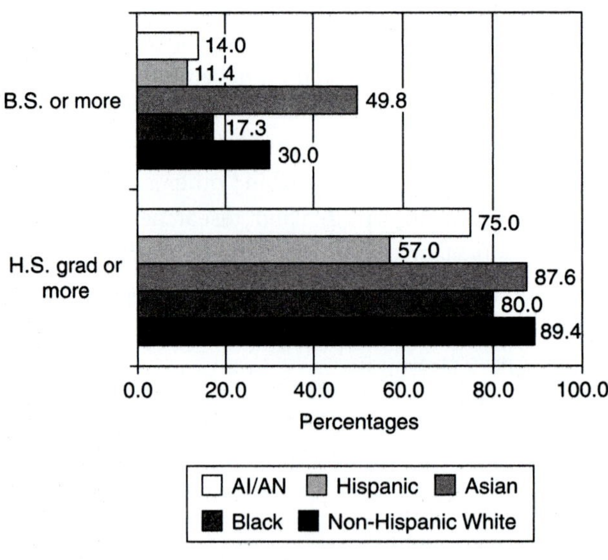

Sources: Facts for Features. "American Indian and Alaska Native Heritage Month: November 2004," http://www.census.gov/Press-Release/www/releases/archives/facts_for_features_special_editions/002950.html, accessed 08/26/05.

Education, Employment, and Earnings

Fourteen percent of American Indians aged 25 and older have a college degree, and 75% have at least a high school diploma (Table 8.2). As shown in Figure 8.1, these education levels are higher than persons of Hispanic ethnicity, but lower than those of Asians, Whites, and Blacks. Workforce participation rates of American Indians are about 3% lower than those of the total population. American Indian men participate about 5% less than rates for all men, while American Indian women participate at about 2% less than rates for all women.[36]

[36] U.S. Census Bureau. (1993). *We the . . . first Americans,* Washington, DC: U.S. Department of Commerce; "American Indians and Alaska Natives." (1999). Office of American Indian Trust. Department of the Interior. Washington, DC.

TABLE 8.3 ***Unemployment, Poverty, and Lack of Health Insurance by Race and Hispanic Origin 2003/2004***

	Unemployment Rate (2003)	Poverty (2004)	Without Health Insurance (2004)
Non-Hispanic White	4.9%	8.6%	11.3%
Black	9.8%	24.7%	19.7%
Hispanic (any race)	7.8%	21.9%	32.7%
Asian	6.3%	9.8%	16.8%
American Indian/ Alaska Native	15.1%	24.5%	29.0%

Sources: Non-Hispanic White, Black, Hispanic, and Asian data drawn from U.S. Census Bureau. 2005; Income Stable, Poverty Rate Increases, Percentage of Americans without Health Insurance Unchanged, http://www.census.gov/Press-Release/www/releases/archives/income_wealth/005647.html, accessed 10/15/05; AI/AN data from "Status and Trends in the Education of American Indians and Alaska Natives," http://nces.ed.gov/pubs2005/nativetrends/ShowTable.asp? table=tables/table_1_6a.asp&indicator=1.6&excel=xls/table_1_6a.xls&excelsize=17&excelse=xls/table_S_1_6a.xls&excelsesize=18, accessed 10/15/05; Unemployment rates for all groups taken from Indicator 8.2 (Unemployment Rates) of "Status and Trends in the Education of American Indians and Alaska Natives," http://nces.ed.gov/pubs2005/nativetrends/ ShowTable.asp?table=tables/table_8_2.asp&indicator=8.2&excel=xls/table_8_2.xls&excelsize=16&excelse=xls/table_S_8_2.xls&excelsesize=16, accessed 10/15/05.

Overall, employment and earnings for AI/AN are significantly lower than those of Whites and similar to those of Blacks and Hispanics, while the poverty rates for AI/AN are higher than for all groups except Blacks.[37] Of people who are AI/AN alone (one race), 24.5% live in poverty, compared with 8.6% of non-Hispanic Whites. The poverty threshold for a family of four in 2004 was $19,307.[38] As shown in Table 8.3, AI/AN have the worst or nearly the worst unemployment, poverty, and health insurance rates in the United States. An Urban Institute study investigating the status of American families concluded that overall, AI/AN "seem to fare the worst of all the racial and ethnic groups."[39]

As shown in Table 8.4, the proportion of the labor force comprised of members of the "other" category (which includes American Indians and Alaska Natives) is projected to grow at a 3.7% rate by 2012 to 3.2 million workers.[40] This rate is second only to Asians and higher than the growth rates for Latinos, Blacks, and non-Hispanic Whites. Although those in this category will still only comprise 2% of the workforce (not shown), their size (3.2 million) and growth in proportion to people from other backgrounds are significant.

[37] Ibid.

[38] U.S. Census Bureau. (2005). "Income Stable, Poverty Rate Increases, Percentage of Americans without Health Insurance Unchanged," http://www.census.gov/Press-Release/www/releases/archives/income_wealth/005647.html, accessed 10/15/05.

[39] Staveteig, S., & Wigton, A. (2000). *Racial and Ethnic Disparities: Key Findings from the National Survey of America's Families,* Washington, DC: The Urban Institute, p. 4.

[40] Due to small numbers, the "other" category comprises (1) American Indians and Alaska Natives or Native Hawaiians and other Pacific Islanders and (2) multi-racial group members (two or more races).

TABLE 8.4 ***Labor Force Growth Rates by Race and Hispanic Origin***

	1992–2002	2012 Projection
White, non-Hispanic	0.5	0.3
Black	1.7	1.8
Hispanic (any race)	3.6	2.9
Asian	3.4	4.2
Other*	n/a	3.7

*Other includes American Indian and Alaska Natives, but not separately identified.

Source: Table 4. Civilian labor force by age, sex, race, and Hispanic origin, 1992, 2002, and projected 2012. Bureau of Labor Statistics. U.S. Department of Labor. Washington, DC, http://www.bls.gov/news.release/ecopro.t06.htm, accessed 09/01/05.

We emphasize that although U.S. census and much other data present summary figures for AI/AN as a group, there are important differences among AI/AN members in terms of education, employment, earnings, values, beliefs, and traditions. When working with, recruiting, or employing American Indians and Alaska Natives, readers are encouraged to investigate the attributes of the specific population, and, more importantly, the individual applicant or employee. Further, persons who have lived primarily on reservation or trust lands will have extremely different experiences, expectations, and backgrounds than those who have primarily (or totally) lived elsewhere.[41] Education, employment, and earnings of AI/AN differ depending on residence, appearance, and language, among other things. Those who live on or near reservations, closely identify with their culture, speak a native language, and participate in religious and cultural traditions may have experiences similar to those of others of color.[42]

Debates surround determinations of members of the AI/AN population, fluidity and motivations for self-identifying, and the variation among experiences between AI/AN living on reservations and elsewhere. A common perception about AI/AN is that their share of gaming wealth associated with casinos on or near reservations is significant. In actuality, such wealth is an important source of revenue for a very small proportion of tribes. In those cases, gaming operations have increased employment opportunities and economic development for the associated nations. For reservations in rural, isolated places (which are the majority), casinos and gaming revenues and associated financial benefits are nonexistent.[43] In addition, some tribes view gaming as contrary to their values and refuse to participate in it, even given prospects of financial gain.[44]

[41] Massey. (2004).

[42] See Eschbach et al. (1998) for a discussion of race as an ascribed characteristic or a reflection of situational ethnicity and how changes in racial identification affected changes in the reported outcomes of American Indians.

[43] Ibid.

[44] Thornton. (2004).

Misperception: American Indians reap significant benefits from tribal casino operations.

Reality: Some Indian nations have benefited significantly from gaming revenues, but many have not. American Indians and Alaska Natives have some of the highest poverty rates in the United States.

Relevant Legislation

Legislation regarding employment of AI/AN on reservation or trust lands is generally governed by tribal regulations rather than federal, state, or local laws. Some federal laws specifically exclude reservations and trust lands. To ensure compliance, with appropriate laws, readers are encouraged to consult labor law experts in the local area about tribal regulations and governance.

Outside reservation or trust property, American Indians and Alaska Natives are covered under federal legislation prohibiting race and national origin-based employment discrimination, specifically Title VII of the Civil Rights Act of 1964. As apparent in the case below, AI/AN do experience such discrimination in employment. In September 2002, the first ever English-only case was filed by the EEOC on behalf of American Indians.[45] As of this writing, the case does not appear to have been resolved, but the EEOC alleged that employees were prohibited from speaking Navajo in the workplace and terminated for refusal to speak English only.

> EEOC SUES ARIZONA DINER FOR NATIONAL ORIGIN BIAS AGAINST NAVAJOS AND OTHER NATIVE AMERICANS[46]
>
> *First-Ever English-Only Lawsuit by Commission on Behalf of Native Americans*
>
> PHOENIX - The U.S. Equal Employment Opportunity Commission (EEOC) announced that it filed a national origin discrimination lawsuit under Title VII of the Civil Rights Act of 1964 on behalf of Native American employees who were subjected to an unlawful English-only policy precluding them from speaking Navajo in the workplace and terminating them for refusing to sign an agreement to abide by the restrictive language policy. The lawsuit, the first-ever English-only suit by the Commission on behalf of Native Americans, was filed by the EEOC's Phoenix District Office against RD's Drive-In, a diner located in Page, Arizona—a community adjacent to the Navajo reservation.

---

[45] As of this writing, we were unable to ascertain whether the case had been resolved. Given the long time to settlement or resolution of other EEOC cases, it is possible that the case is still in process.

[46] EEOC sues Arizona Diner for National Origin Bias against Navajos and other Native Americans, http://www.eeoc.gov/press/9-30-02-c.html, accessed 08/31/05.

> ... The suit, *EEOC v RD's Drive In*, CIV 02 1911 PHX LOA, states that in approximately June 2000, RD's posted a policy stating: "*The owner of this business can speak and understand only English. While the owner is paying you as an employee, you are required to use English at all times. The only exception is when the customer can not understand English. If you feel unable to comply with this requirement, you may find another job.*"
>
> ... This policy, in an early form, prohibited employees from speaking "Navajo" in the workplace. Two employees, Roxanne Cahoon and Freda Douglas, refused to agree to the policy because they believed it to be discriminatory. As a result, they were asked to leave their employment by RD's. In addition, at least two other employees resigned prior to being terminated because they could not agree to the policy. The vast majority of the employees working at the time spoke Navajo.

Also of specific relevance to American Indians is Title VII's prohibition against discrimination based on religion and requirements for reasonable accommodations of the religious practices of applicants and employees. American Indian religious beliefs are different from the dominant beliefs in the United States. Some American Indian practices are long in duration and may necessitate time off from work. As discussed in Chapter 10, allowing personal holidays for all employees, rather than limiting holidays to Christmas, Thanksgiving, and others preferred by the dominant groups, flexible holidays allow people to celebrate and worship as when it is appropriate for them. In addition, for certain Indians, wearing their hair uncut is also spiritual and should be accommodated (see Chapters 10 and 14 for discussions of hair length and diversity concerns). Reasonable accommodation of strongly held religious beliefs or practices should be made for AI/AN, as for the practices of those who hold other belief systems.

Research on American Indians at Work

Compared with other groups, little research has investigated the organizational experiences of American Indians. This lack of research may be partly attributed to the relatively small proportion of American Indians in the population and therefore working in formal organizations, and to the invisibility of some American Indians' ancestry. In one of the few studies relevant to diversity in organizations, researchers found that perceived discrimination and depressive symptoms were correlated. For nearly 300 adult American Indians living in the U.S. Midwest, perceived social support and participation in traditional cultural practices served as buffer against discrimination, however.[47] In an analysis of

[47] Whitbeck, L. B., McMorris, B. J., Hoyt, D. R., Stubben, J. D., & LaFromboise, T. (2002). "Perceived Discrimination, Traditional Practices, and Depressive Symptoms." *Journal of Health and Social Behavior,* 43(4): 400–418.

data from the General Social Surveys, Charles Weaver found that American Indians were less likely to feel secure in their jobs and were less satisfied with their present financial situation than Whites. Although Weaver had numerous other hypotheses about differences in job satisfaction, preferred job attributes, and perceptions about opportunities for advancement, no differences were found.[48]

American Indian and Alaska Native Women

Researchers have detailed many disadvantages experienced by American Indian and Alaska Native women that are directly correlated with their race and gender status. These include high infant mortality, high rates of victimization by violence, involuntary sterilization, and questionable removal of children from their homes.[49] As with other women of color, the approximately 1.2 million AI/AN women do not fare well in terms of education, participation, unemployment, and income. These factors severely limit the self-sufficiency and constrain the life chances of AI/AN women. AI/AN women earn less and are more likely to be in poverty than Black, Asian, and White women, particularly when they live on reservations.[50] In comparison to White men, AI/AN women earn 57.8% of the median annual earnings for full-time workers. Researchers suggest that AI/AN women are "systematically paid less than their male counterparts under similar circumstances."[51] AI/AN women are most likely to be employed as sales, clerical, or service workers; as managers, they are most likely to work in gas stations, general merchandise stores, and in social assistance positions.[52]

Although their average participation rates, unemployment levels, and incomes are worse than those of many other women, many American Indian women are well-educated and have successful careers. Wilma Mankiller, discussed in Individual Feature 8.1, became the first woman chief of the Cherokee Nation in 1985, a position she held until 1995. Mankiller encourages other American Indian women to assume leadership roles in tribal communities.

In an award-winning study, Helen Juliette Muller reported the distinct experiences of American Indian women managers from several different tribes in the southwestern United States.[53] All of the women in the sample of 20 managers

[48] Weaver, C. (2003). "Work Attitudes of American Indians." *Journal of Applied Social Psychology,* 33(2): 432–443.

[49] Allen, P. G. (2004). "Angry Women are Building: Issues and Struggles Facing American Indian Women Today." In J. F. Healey & E. O'Brien (Eds.), *Race, Ethnicity, and Gender,* Thousand Oaks, CA: Pine Forge Press, pp. 217–220.

[50] Caiazza, A., Shaw, A., & Werschkul, M. (2004). "The Status of Women in the United States." Institute for Women's Policy Research, Washington, DC, http://www.iwpr.org/States2004/PDFs/National.pdf, accessed 09/05/05.

[51] Snipp, C. M. (1992). "Sociological Perspectives on American Indians." *Annual Review of Sociology,* 18: 351–371.

[52] "Women of Color: Their Employment in the Private Sector." EEOC. 2003, http://www.eeoc.gov/stats/reports/womenofcolor/#Section_1.1.4, accessed 09/05/05.

[53] Muller, H. J. (1998). "American Indian Women Managers: Living in Two Worlds." *Journal of Management Inquiry,* 7(1): 4–28.

INDIVIDUAL FEATURE 8.1 ***Wilma Mankiller, Chief of the Cherokee Nation, 1985–1995***

Wilma Mankiller was born in 1945 in Tahlequah, Oklahoma. Her father was a full-blood Cherokee and her mother was Caucasian, of Dutch and Irish heritage. As chief of the Cherokee Nation, Mankiller managed a $75 million budget, comparable to budgets of major corporations. The Cherokee Nation is the second largest Indian nation in the United States.

Mankiller spent her formative years in San Francisco, where her family moved in 1956 as part of the U.S. government relocation program for American Indians. Adjustment to life in San Francisco was hard for the Mankiller family. Wilma and her siblings were teased about their last name, their accent, and their clothing. Both her father and elder brother had to work to earn enough money to support the family. Wilma noted that Blacks, Latinos, and American Indians were targets of prejudice and discrimination. It was in San Francisco that Mankiller's quest for and pursuit of justice began.

Mankiller learned from the actions of Black and Mexican Americans, including Huey Newton, Bobby Seale, and Cesar Chavez, who worked for change and resisted oppression in California during her youth. In what was a life-changing event, Mankiller participated in the lengthy occupation of Alcatraz prison in 1969. American Indians from numerous tribes, along with celebrities and activists, participated in the occupation of Alcatraz, drawing attention to the history of abuses, broken treaties, and continued discrimination and inequity faced by American Indians.

Mankiller's management experiences began with her position as the acting director of the Native American Youth Center in East Oakland, California. In 1977, she returned to live in Oklahoma and began working for the Cherokee Nation, first working as an economic stimulus coordinator. As such, Mankiller worked to help American Indians obtain education and be reintegrated into their communities. Her next position was as a program development specialist, and Mankiller excelled in writing grants and obtaining revenue for the tribe.

At the same time, Mankiller returned to college to finish her degree in social work at the University of Arkansas at Fayetteville, a short drive from where she lived in Oklahoma. In 1983, Mankiller agreed to run for deputy chief of the Cherokee Nation, the second person in command. Thinking the community would question her democratic beliefs and history of grassroots activism, Mankiller was surprised that her most vociferous opposition was based purely on sexism. Some claimed her running for office was an "affront to God," while others said that having a woman run the tribe would make the "Cherokees the laughingstock of the tribal world."[54] With every outrageous comment, Mankiller became more certain her decision to run for office was the right one to make.

Mankiller was elected, and took office as deputy chief in August 1983. In 1985 Mankiller became chief of the Cherokee Nation, the first woman in modern history to serve as chief of an American Indian tribe. In 1991, Mankiller was elected to her third term in office, winning 82% of the votes.

During her terms as chief, Mankiller focused on education, health care, and economic development for the Cherokee Nation. She acknowledges the tremendous responsibility of the role of chief and encourages young women to "take risks, to

[54] Mankiller, W., & Wallis, M. (1993). *Mankiller: A Chief and Her People,* New York: St. Martin's Press.

stand up for the things they believe in, and to step up and accept the challenge of serving in leadership roles."[55] Now having a role model who has done so, Mankiller expects other Cherokee women to assume leadership roles in tribal communities, "returning the balance to the role of women in our tribe." A recognized model for many, Mankiller has been awarded an honorary doctorate from Yale University.

Sources: Mankiller, W., & Wallis, M. (1993). *Mankiller: A Chief and Her People,* New York: St. Martin's Press; Wilma Mankiller Former Principal Chief of Cherokee Nation, http://www.powersource.com/gallery/people/wilma.html, accessed 11/05/05.

spoke English, and all but one were bilingual or had some level of fluency in a tribal language (e.g., subordinate bilingualism). Fifteen of the women in the sample had at least a bachelor's degree. The women worked in a variety of jobs, including industrial development manager, education specialist, director of human services agency, tribal administrator, and materials manager, among others, and they managed between 1 and 800 people. The women reported living in two worlds, which required them to be able to navigate between "distinctive yet interconnected worlds." Interactions in these "two worlds" included those with customers, employees, peers, supervisors, and competitors. Because the traditional Navajo culture (which was used as the comparison culture) differed from Anglo culture in ways of interacting and learning, association, and authority, importance of work, time-orientation, spirituality, and natural resources, the AI women managers developed complex strategies and "switching techniques" to work successfully in both worlds. Recall that flexibility, biculturalism, and bilingualism are positive attributes and consequences of diversity among employees.[56]

Multiracial Group Members

We now turn to the investigation of multiracial group members in the United States. We begin with an introduction and history of the population, and then discuss relevant legislation. We conclude with a focus on Amerasians, a distinct group of multiracial group members with a unique history.

Introduction and History

As we will discuss, in the 2000 census, more than 6 million people said they belong to two or more races. Being allowed to self-identify in this manner was a first ever, although one's race could and did change between census counts. Previous chapters on African Americans, Latinos, Whites, and Asian Americans

[55] Ibid., p. 250.

[56] Cox, T., & Blake, S. (1991). "Managing Cultural Diversity: Implications for Organizational Competitiveness." *Academy of Management Executive,* 5(3): 45–56.

have considered some of the fluidity regarding race and ethnicity in the United States. Since the U.S. Census Bureau began collecting such data, different groups have been included or excluded from certain racial categories but the option of being included in more than one category at the same time did not exist until 2000. Indeed, miscegenation was formally illegal in the country until 1967, when the U.S. Supreme Court ruled that state laws prohibiting interracial marriages were unlawful. Despite laws prohibiting it, mixing of races occurred long before the Supreme Court's decision or the addition of the option to identify as being multiracial in the U.S. census. Most of the debate around miscegenation has focused on White and Black unions, and such unions still remain less likely to occur than those among Whites and other groups.

In her article on legal trials involving racial determination, Ariela Gross described historical cases in which people of mixed racial ancestry were attempting to prove or disprove their race. In some cases, issues of inheritance (Blacks could not own property), freedom (Whites could not be held as slaves), or ability to serve as witnesses (Blacks could not be witnesses) were at stake. The presence of American Indians in the population during slavery times further confused attempts to determine who was Black when dark skin and wiry hair could be attributed to being Indian rather than Black.[57] Although afforded few rights, Indians were free. Historical records indicate that some Indian tribes allowed slave ownership and some specifically forbade it.[58] Many Blacks who escaped slavery found refuge among Indians who refused to return them to slavery. In some cases, the presence of Black Indians on Indian reservations threatened the tax-exempt status of reservations, and was viewed suspiciously and nervously among Whites.[59]

Racial Determination and the "One-Drop" Rule

The *one-drop rule* was used throughout much of U.S. history in deciding who was Black. That is, anyone with one known Black ancestor was usually deemed to be Black (rather than another race or multiracial) regardless of the number or proportion of non-Black ancestors. During certain periods, mulatto, quadroon, and octoroon referred to people who were one-half, one-quarter, or one-eighth Black. Unless their Black ancestry was invisible and, importantly, they chose to let it remain so (e.g., passing), such people were deemed to be, and treated as being Black.

Children that White slave owners and their sons conceived with slaves were considered slaves rather than family members.[60] Pulitzer nominee and

---

[57] Gross, A. J. (1998). "Litigating Whiteness: Trials of Racial Determination in the Nineteenth-Century South." *Yale Law Journal,* 108(1): 109–188.

[58] Katz, W. L. (1997). *Black Indians,* New York: Aladdin Paperbacks.

[59] Ibid.

[60] See Ball, E. (1998). *Slaves in the Family,* New York: Farrar, Straus, and Giroux.

sociologist Joe Feagin of the University of Texas painfully describes the rapes of Black women and molestation of Black children that contributed to the physical appearance of Blacks today.[61] Feagin cites the story of the lineage of Patricia Williams, a Black law professor at Columbia University. Her great great grandmother, Sophie, was purchased at age 11 by her great great grandfather, 35-year-old Austin Miller, a lawyer. The next year, 12-year-old Sophie, a child, bore Miller's daughter, Mary—who was Patricia Williams's great-grandmother. Mary became a house servant to Miller's White children, who were her siblings.[62]

Evidence suggests that Thomas Jefferson, third president of the United States, and Sally Hemings, one of Jefferson's slaves, had a lengthy "relationship"[63] and conceived several children who lived as slaves at Monticello.[64] Jefferson freed three of those believed to be his children, and Hemings was freed by Jefferson's White daughter after his death. More recently, one-time arch segregationist South Carolina Senator Strom Thurmond is reported to have fathered a child at age 22 with a 16-year old who worked in his parents' home.[65] In late 2003, after Thurmond's death, his family acknowledged Essie Mae Washington-Williams as the Thurmond's daughter.[66] Washington-Williams lived life as Black as do her children and grandchildren, despite their identifiable multiracial ancestry.

In a case involving a man whose great-grandfather was Black, the U.S. Supreme Court agreed that "separate but equal" facilities for Whites and Blacks were not unconstitutional.[67] The plaintiff in the case was Homer Plessy, and aside from his great-grandfather, Plessy's other ancestors were all known to be White. In some states, Plessy would also have been White by law because of the preponderance of White ancestors. At seven-eighths White, Plessy looked White, but lived as Black, and volunteered to test the *separate but equal law* in Louisiana. Having been advised that Plessy would be entering and sitting in the "White" section of the train (otherwise, Plessy would have gone unnoticed), the conductor had him ejected, arrested, and fined. In what became a landmark case with lasting, devastating consequences, the courts ruled that separate, but ostensibly equal, facilities did not violate the Constitution.

---

[61] Feagin, J. R. (2004). "Slavery Unwilling to Die: The Historical Development of Systemic Racism." In J. F. Healey & E. O'Brien (Eds.), *Race, Ethnicity, and Gender,* Thousand Oaks: Pine Forge Press, pp. 92–108.

[62] Ibid., pp. 97–98.

[63] Researchers note the difficulty Black females faced in resisting sexual advances or rape by slave-owners or employers. See, for example, Feagin (2004).

[64] See Gordon-Reed, A. (1997). *Thomas Jefferson and Sally Hemings: An American Controversy,* Charlottesville, VA: University of Virginia Press.

[65] Washington-Williams, E., & Stadiem, W. (2005). *Dear Senator,* New York: HarperCollins Publishers.

[66] Mattingly, D. (2003, December 16). "Strom Thurmond's Family Confirms Paternity Claim." *CNN Washington Bureau,* http://www.cnn.com/2003/US/12/15/thurmond.paternity/, accessed 08/29/05.

[67] *Plessy v. Ferguson*. 163 U.S. 537 (1896).

Individual Feature 8.2 *Barack Obama, U.S. Senator*

Barack Obama, U.S. senator from Illinois, was born in Honolulu, HI, in 1961 to Ann Dunham, a White woman from Kansas, and Barack Obama, Sr., a Black man from Kenya. His parents named him Barack, meaning blessed. After his parents' divorce, Obama was reared by his White mother and her parents and grandparents, primarily living in Hawaii.

Obama received his undergraduate education at Columbia University, where he studied political science and international relations. In 1985, Obama moved to Chicago where he worked for a nonprofit organization helping to create jobs and improve living conditions in some of Chicago's worst neighborhoods. Obama later entered law school at Harvard, where he was the first Black president of the Harvard Law Review and graduated magna cum laude. After law school, Obama practiced civil rights law, working on key employment discrimination cases in federal and state courts.

In 1996 Obama was elected to the Illinois State Senate where he pursued benefits for the working poor, for people who could not afford health insurance, and for AIDS prevention and care programs. Obama was influential in passage of Illinois' death penalty reform laws because the system was "broken," and many innocent people were on death row.

Obama was elected U.S. senator for Illinois in 2004, and in January 2005, he was sworn in as the third Black U.S. senator in history. As a U.S. senator, Obama is focused on promoting economic growth and bringing good jobs to Illinois, his home state. One of the senate committees on which Obama serves is the Veterans' Affairs Committee, where he is investigating disability pay discrepancies among veterans. In April 2005, *Time* magazine named Obama as one of the 100 most influential Americans. His work for the poor and disenfranchised, to ensure women's rights to mammograms and reproductive freedom, to reduce racial profiling, and advocating for the wrongfully imprisoned, gays and lesbians, veterans, children, and working families, includes key areas of influence to people from many backgrounds and walks of life.

Sources: Obama, B. (2004, July 27). "Transcript of Speech to the Democratic National Convention," http://www.obamaforillinois.com/Obama, B. (1995). *Dreams from My Father: A Story of Race and Inheritance,* New York: Times Books; Obama for Illinois. 2004. http://www.obamaforillinois.com/, accessed 08/02/05.

Regardless of their self- and other identification as being Black, estimates suggest that 70% of the Black population in the United States have some non-Black ancestors. The wide range of skin colors and hair texture attests to the diversity in racial and ethnic background among Blacks. Many well-known Black activists have acknowledged multiracial ancestry, including Martin Luther King, Jr. (whose grandmother was Irish), Malcolm X, W.E.B. DuBois, and Frederick Douglas. Other fairly well-known multiracial Americans include Halle Berry (actor), Lynda Carter (actor), Ann Curry (news anchor), Cameron Diaz (actor), Derek Jeter (athlete), Norah Jones (musician), Alicia Keyes (singer), Barack Obama (politician), Soledad O'Brien (news anchor), Lou Diamond Phillips (actor), Jimmy Smits (actor), and Tiger Woods (athlete). Barack Obama, a U.S. senator from Illinois, is featured in Individual Feature 8.2.

Population

When given the option in the 2000 census, many people celebrated the ability to self-identify, rejecting the category of "other" as an inaccurate reflection of their heritage. Of the 6.8 million people who reported belonging to two or more races in 2000, 2.2 million, or 32%, are Hispanic, compared to 13% of the general population being Hispanic.[68] The great majority of multiracial people are two races (93%), while 6% are three races. The largest to smallest proportions of particular groups reporting membership in more than one race are Native Hawaiian and other Pacific Islanders, American Indians or Alaska Natives, Asians, Blacks, and Whites. Members of these groups, respectively, report proportions of 54%, 40%, 14%, 5%, and 2.5% of the population who are also members of at least one other race.

Multiracial group members tend to be younger than single race people. Forty-two percent of multiracials are under 18, compared with 25% of those reporting a single race. Recall from Chapter 6 that Hispanics are younger than non-Hispanics, and that they are more likely to be multiracial than the general population. Because they are younger than the general population, a greater proportion of multiracials will be entering the future labor force and participating than the one-race population.

People who reported multiple races are more likely to live in California, where nearly 25% of the multiracial people reside. California is the only state with more than one million people in the multiracial population. In all, 40% of multirace people live in the West, 27% in the South, 18% in the Northeast, and 15% in the Midwest.[69]

As interracial relationships increase, the proportion of the population that is multiracial will also increase. The first time that more Americans reported approval of interracial marriage (48%) than disapproval (42%) was in 1991, 24 years after the Supreme Court overruled laws forbidding intermarriage.[70] Prior to 1991, more people disapproved of such marriages than approved of them. Blacks, younger people, those with more education, and people who live in the West tend to view interracial marriage more favorably than Whites, older people, those with less education, and those living in the South, Midwest, and East. While 70% of Blacks approve of interracial marriage, 44% of Whites do. For those under age 30, 64% approve, compared with 61% of those 50 and older disapproving of such marriages. While 70% of college graduates approve of interracial marriage,

---

[68] Jones, N. A., & Smith, A. S. (2001). "The Two or More Races Population: 2000." U.S. Census Bureau, http://www.census.gov/prod/2001pubs/c2kbr01-6.pdf, accessed 08/31/05.

[69] Ibid.

[70] Gallup, G., Jr., & Newport, F. (1991, August). "For First Time, More Americans Approve of Interracial Marriage than Disapprove." *The Gallup Poll Monthly,* pp. 60–63.

66% of those who did not finish high school disapprove. In the West, 60% of people approve of interracial marriage, compared with only 33% in the South.[71]

Relevant Legislation

As with other racial and ethnic groups, Title VII prohibits discrimination against multiracial group members. Executive orders for affirmative action may also apply if a multiracial individual self-identifies as an underutilized minority. No cases involving multiracial individuals were identified from the EEOC Web site, but research evidence suggests they sometimes face negative treatment from members of various racial groups because of being multiracial.[72] They may also experience negative organizational outcomes because one of their racial backgrounds is invisible.[73] Given the importance of identifiability to categorization, stereotyping, and differential treatment, the lack of clear identifiability and ability to clearly categorize multiracial group members may pose unique issues for them.

Amerasians

Amerasians are a distinctive group of multiracial people. Although the term Amerasian formally includes children born of American servicemen and Asian women (e.g., Vietnamese, Japanese, Korean), it is most commonly used in reference to children born of American servicemen and Vietnamese women during the Vietnam War. During the Vietnam War, tens of thousands of Amerasian children were fathered by American servicemen, of various racial and ethnic backgrounds. Most Amerasian children were left in Vietnam when the fathers returned to the United States (or were killed). Because of the stigma associated with being fatherless or being fathered by an American (whose country was at war with Vietnam), Vietnamese Amerasians often experienced extreme discrimination, teasing, and assault by other children, and societal persecution. Referred to as "children of the dust," many were not educated and lived in extreme poverty in Vietnam.

The Vietnamese Homecoming Act of 1987 formalized attempts to bring many Amerasians and their families to the United States. Between 20,000 and 25,000 Amerasians were resettled in the country, but few reunited with

---

[71] Ibid.

[72] See Rockquemore, K. A., & Brunsma, D. L. (2002). *Beyond Black,* Thousand Oaks, CA: Sage.

[73] See Clair, J., Beatty, J., & MacLean, T. L. (2005). "Out of Sight But Not Out of Mind: Managing Invisible Social Identities in the Workplace." *Academy of Management Review,* 30: 78–95; Ragins, B. R. (in press). "Disclosure Disconnects: Antecedents and Consequences of Disclosing Invisible Stigmas across Life Domains." *Academy of Management Review.*

their fathers.[74] Because of lack of education in Vietnam, many resettled Amerasians are illiterate in Vietnamese and English, which impedes their integration into American society. Most live in metropolitan areas around other members of the Vietnamese community, who, as discussed in Chapter 6, are some of the lower earning, least educated groups of Asian Americans.

Individual and Organizational Recommendations

In the following section, individual and organizational recommendations for American Indians and Alaska Natives are first presented, followed by those for multiracial group members.

American Indians and Alaska Natives

In this chapter, we have acknowledged the unique role of American Indians and Alaska Natives to the history and diversity of the United States. Efforts to increase education, participation, and employment of AI/AN by the government and organizations have been somewhat successful. As with any group, increases in education are associated with increases in participation, employment, and earnings.

Most AI/AN now live outside reservation and trust lands, but researchers have found that those who are linked to their traditional culture fare better than those who are not. Thus, it is important to make efforts to continue relationships with one's native traditions and culture.

At an organizational level, conscious support of American Indians and Alaska Natives should be provided, and they should be included in diversity efforts. Although they are a relatively small portion of the population, their representation in certain areas of the country is significant. In addition, their unique place as indigenous people, who once were the only inhabitants of the United States, makes failure to include them in diversity efforts particularly intolerable.

For recruiting, tribal colleges may be a good source of American Indian applicants. As of 1998, there were 27 tribal colleges and three federally charted American Indian colleges in the United States.[75] These schools include Haskell Indian Nations University, the Institute of American Indian Arts, and Northwest Indian College. Nearly all (except the four most recently started schools) are fully

[74] McKelvey, R. S. (1999). *The Dust of Life: America's Children Abandoned in Vietnam,* Seattle, WA: University of Washington Press.

[75] Cunningham, A. F., & Parker, C. (1998). "Tribal Colleges as Community Institutions and Resources." *New Directions for Higher Education,* 102: 45–55.

accredited by the appropriate regional accrediting agencies. In addition to education, these colleges focus on meeting the cultural and social needs of students.

Other universities that have sizable populations of AI/AN are also good sources for recruiting employees. Such schools include the University of New Mexico, New Mexico State University, and the University of Arizona. In 2005, New Mexico State University was recognized for the number of master's degrees awarded to American Indians.[76]

Once AI/AN have been recruited and hired, organizational efforts to retain them are key. Factors that may be exclusionary and discriminatory to AI/AN should be investigated. Barriers unique to the organizational environment and to the specific AI/AN population should be identified and removed. An example of such barriers is English-only rules, as discussed earlier. Organizations should be aware that many Indians view work as one part of other important aspects of life, rather than the most important aspect of life.[77] Rather than imposing work-related values of others upon AI/AN, their values, as with those all racial and ethnic groups, should be acknowledged. In addition, other employees can learn from AI/IN about the importance of life outside of work.

Multiracial Group Members

As the multiracial population increases, efforts to ensure they are treated fairly in organizations are receiving increased focus. Multiracial group members whose multiple group membership is clearly visible may experience pointed disparate treatment specifically due to their multiple group membership. Being asked "What are you?" or being called disparaging slurs related to their multiracial group membership exemplify such pointed discrimination. In addition, those who appear to be members of one group or another group alone (rather than multiracial), may experience many negative outcomes related to the invisible parts of their identity.[78] For example, multiracials who look White may hear negative comments, stereotypes, and disparaging remarks about people of color. They may be fearful of having photos of their family or extended family on their desks at work, or of bringing a family member to an organizational social event. Recall that in the South only 33% of people surveyed approved of interracial marriage; 54% disapproved.

A culture of nondiscrimination would help avoid "inadvertent" discrimination against invisibly multiracial people (as well as gays and lesbians who are not "out" at work). Such a culture would also increase the likelihood that those who are not out would feel comfortable enough to be so. Invisible identities and questions and

---

[76] Frosch, J. (2005). "New Mexico State University Serves American Indian Graduate Students." New Mexico State University News Releases, http://www.nmsu.edu/~ucomm/Releases/2005/august/am_indian_students.htm, accessed 09/04/05.

[77] Massey. (2004). See also Muller. (1998).

[78] See, for example, Ragins, B. R. (in press) and Rockquemore & Brunsma. (2002).

worries about disclosure are stressful to those who bear them.[79] Care should be taken to avoid grouping multiracials with one group to which they have membership (e.g., Blacks, Latinos) while ignoring the other aspects of their identity. As has the U.S. Census Bureau, allow people to define their own group memberships.

Summary

This chapter has considered American Indians and Alaska Natives and multiracial group members as contributors to diversity in organizations. As the original inhabitants of the country and the group recently allowed to self-identify as being a member of two or more races, AI/AN and multiracials are different from the nondominant groups considered in previous chapters. Although they are the original inhabitants of the United States, AI/AN are often overlooked in the study of diversity. The diversity among AI/AN in terms of group membership (e.g., nation), age, and place of residence, and their lower education and employment levels than many groups were discussed.

We next considered the diversity of multiracial people in the United States, an increasingly important and diverse group. Nearly 7 million people self-identify as multiracial, and this number will only increase in the future. Multiracial people are younger than single race people, and numbers (and approval) of interracial relationships and marriage are increasing. As a unique minority group, multiracial people face unusual diversity concerns, including invisibility, and pointed harassment and discrimination based on their multiple identities.

Relevant legislation and research, and focal issues for AI/AN and multiracials were considered. We also considered individual and organizational recommendations for these less-studied, but historically and increasingly important nondominant groups.

Key Terms

Amerasian—a child born of American servicemen and Asian women, in particular Vietnamese, Japanese, and Korean women.

Miscegenation—a mixture of races, *especially* marriage, cohabitation, or sexual intercourse between a White person and a member of another race.[80]

Multiracial—a person who self-identifies as having ancestry including two or more races.

Pakeha—White European New Zealanders.

Passing—usually refers to light-skinned Blacks or others of color pretending to be and being perceived as Whites, also relevant to gays and lesbians who pretend to be and are perceived as being heterosexual, and to others whose nondominant group membership goes unnoticed and undisclosed.

---

[79] Ragins. (in press).

[80] Merriam-Webster Online, http://www.webster.com/cgi-bin/dictionary?book=Dictionary&va=miscegenation&x=12&y=14, accessed 09/01/05.

Questions to Consider

1a. If you are not American Indian or Alaska Native, what has your exposure to them been? Do you know any American Indians and/or Alaska Natives personally? If so, how do you know them? How well do you know them? What stereotypical beliefs about American Indians are you aware of?

1b. If you are American Indian or Alaska Native, how do your work experiences compare with those presented in the chapter?

2a. If you are not multiracial, what has your exposure been to multiracial people? Do you know people who are multiracial? Have you talked with them about being multiracial and about their diversity-related experiences?

2b. If you are multiracial, is being multiracial a salient part of your identity? Did either part of the chapter resonate with you?

3. Homer Plessy of the separate but equal case was seven-eighths White and could have "passed" for White, based on his appearance. What role does the lack of visibility of someone's race or ethnicity play in their treatment, experiences, and identity?

4a. Professional golfer Tiger Woods emphasizes his White, Asian, Black, and American Indian heritage. Were Woods unknown as a professional golfer, what assumptions might be made about his race by (a) a police officer prone to racial profiling, (b) a Black person, (c) an Asian person, (d) a White person, (e) an American Indian?

4b. The chapter lists several other fairly well-known multiracial Americans, including Halle Berry, Lynda Carter, Ann Curry, Cameron Diaz, Derek Jeter, Norah Jones, Alicia Keyes, Soledad O'Brien, Barack Obama, Lou Diamond Phillips, and Jimmy Smits. Are you familiar with any of these people? If so, were you aware that they are multiracial? Were you aware of their particular multiracial heritage? If not, what is your impression of the racial or ethnic group to which each belongs? If they were not famous people, speculate on the racial or ethnic group to which they would be perceived to belong based on their identifiability (e.g., Dworkin & Dworkin) and their experiences based on people's perceptions.

5. What have you learned from this chapter that is most surprising to you?

Actions and Exercises

1. Excluding American Indian schools, find at least five colleges and universities not identified in this chapter that are known for the diversity of their students, particularly American Indian students. What are the demographic characteristics of the student body (e.g., race, ethnicity, sex, and age)? What are the characteristics of the schools (e.g., size of student body, location, and any other relevant factors)?
2. Investigate the demographic characteristics of the student body and the school at the university in which you are studying or studied. Do you know of any AI/AN students who attend or attended school with you?

3. Investigate the history of American Indians in your state and their current status (including population, participation, education levels, income, and poverty rates).
4. Estimates suggest that 70% of Blacks in the United States are of multiracial heritage. If you are not Black, were you aware of this? Begin noticing the variation in skin color, features, and hair texture among Blacks. Choose five Blacks whom you know, with whom you come in contact, or who are well-known people and document the visible variations in their skin tone, features, and hair texture.
5. Visit the EEOC Web site (http://www.eeoc.gov) to investigate how the first case filed by the EEOC involving national origin discrimination against American Indians (*EEOC v. RD's Drive In,* CIV 02 1911 PHX LOA) was resolved.
6. Choose an indigenous people for a particular country (except the United States and New Zealand). Document their original and current population, education level, employment, and participation. How do their education, employment, and participation levels compare to those of the dominant group in that country?

9 Chapter

Sex and Gender

Chapter Objectives

After completing this chapter, readers should understand sex and gender as they relate to diversity in organizations. They should specifically be able to:

- *explain differences in women's and men's participation rates, employment, and income levels.*
- *discuss the role of gender role socialization in men's and women's occupational choices and opportunities.*
- *explain the effects of sex segregation, sex discrimination, and sexual harassment on women's careers and discuss selected cases related to them.*
- *discuss similarities and differences between employment experiences of White women and women of color and White men and women of color.*
- *understand the role of negotiation in male/female salary differences and the feminization of poverty as diversity concerns.*
- *discuss methods that can be used to improve organizational cultures for gender equity.*

Key Facts

In many countries, women comprise more than half the population and about half the workforce.

In the United States, women are 47% of the workforce, but occupy only 4% of the highest-earning positions.

Women working full-time, year-round earn about 70% of the income of men working full-time, year-round.

Nearly 60% of women with children under 5 work outside the home.

The mean income of female college graduates is about $23,000 less than the mean for male college graduates.

Men are about 15% of sexual harassment targets, yet men who complain of harassment are often not taken seriously.

Introduction, Overview, and Brief History[1]

Sex and gender issues are critical aspects of diversity in organizations, affecting women and men from all races, ethnicities, ages, and abilities. Sexual harassment and discrimination, the wage gap in pay, and sex segregation are commonly recognized as concerns for women. Indeed these issues constrain women's progress and opportunities in organizations in a myriad of ways. Even so, although men are significantly less likely to personally experience them, sex discrimination and other gender-based diversity issues also affect men. All men have mothers, wives, daughters, sisters, or friends, making women's concerns personal concerns for many men as well as for the women they care about. Many men with working wives experience firsthand the negative effects of women's lower wages and job rewards on family incomes. Children in single parent homes are very likely to be living with working mothers; pay inequity for working women affects male and female children. Sex discrimination and harassment negatively affect the workplace overall, harming both women and men. Both women and men have prescribed gender roles; for either sex, violations are often met with strong sanctions (consider the man who wishes to work as a child care worker but is perceived as a potential pervert and denied employment because he is male). Women, and increasingly men, experience work and family issues as they cope with work, children, and sometimes parents or other relatives who need care. Men coping with work and family issues often face harsher sanctions than women—the expectation for them is that their work should take priority over family, and they may experience more negative penalties than women who have work and family issues. These and other reasons make sex and gender issues important to both women and men.

Women, who have been called "the 51% minority,"[2] comprise over half of the population and nearly half of the workforce. Despite their nearly equal representation in the workforce, women are overrepresented in lower level, lower-paid jobs and underrepresented in higher-level, higher-paid jobs. Men comprise slightly less than half the population and slightly more than half the workforce. They are overrepresented in higher-level, higher-paid jobs, but underrepresented in lower-level, lower-paid jobs.

Women are inaccurately construed as relatively new entrants to the workforce, even though women have worked throughout history. Women contributed to agricultural labor as well as working in manufacturing industries in the eighteenth through twentieth centuries. In addition, women of color have historically worked outside the home. Slave women worked in plantation homes and in the fields alongside slave men, and then performed their own domestic duties afterwards. As discussed in Chapter 4, Black women continue to participate in the workforce at higher rates than White women.

Women's work has historically been devalued, which plays a key role in sex discrimination and harassment, sex segregation of jobs, and the glass ceiling. Women are frequently viewed as uncommitted workers (because of greater responsibilities for the needs of their families), and as lacking in leadership, management, and decision-making skills—attributes that are desirable in the context

[1] We include a brief history of women's work in this chapter because other chapters include the history of the particular group, and therefore also include a view of sex and gender at work.

[2] Dunn, D. (1999). "Women: The Fifty-One Percent Minority." In A. G. Dworkin & R. J. Dworkin (Eds.), *The Minority Report*, Orlando, FL: Harcourt Brace, pp. 415–435.

of work. In contrast, men are widely construed as providers for their families, committed, capable workers, and as having strong leadership and managerial skills—attributes that are desirable in the work context. Distorted and inaccurate perceptions of the differences between participation rates of men and women and women of color and White women are strong forces in their distinct experiences in the workplace.

Before continuing the investigation of sex and gender issues in the workplace, it is important to clarify differences between the terms. For the most part, one's sex is biological; males have XY chromosomes, while females have XX chromosomes.[3] Title VII specifically prohibits discrimination because of "sex," but the courts have ruled that discrimination because of violating roles associated with one's sex (e.g., gender roles) is also illegal.[4] Gender is socially constructed rather than biological, reflecting what society perceives as appropriate (behaviors, dress, occupation, etc.) for males and females. Because it is socially constructed, what is viewed as appropriate varies somewhat by culture and time. Both sex and gender are important influences on outcomes in organizations.

Relevant Legislation

Legislation particularly relevant to sex and gender at work includes:

- The Equal Pay Act of 1963
- Title VII of the Civil Rights Act of 1964
- Executive orders for affirmative action
- The Pregnancy Discrimination Act of 1978
- EEOC Guidelines on Sexual Harassment of 1980
- The Family and Medical Leave Act of 1993

These acts (and guidelines) were introduced in Chapter 2; in this chapter we provide more details as they relate specifically to sex and gender.[5] A look at the chronology of acts presented provides striking insights as to the status of women and issues they faced in organizations during the time they were passed, and to some extent, in the present. In 1963, the Equal Pay Act attempted to address overt sex-based compensation inequities. In 1964, Title VII was passed prohibiting discrimination against women in employment-related matters, including hiring, firing, promotions, and other employment matters. Executive orders for affirmative action included women, going further than the passive prohibition against discrimination provided in Title VII and requiring certain employers to take active efforts to ensure women had equal opportunity to work. Once women

[3] A small percentage of people have XXY or XYY chromosomes.

[4] See *Ann Hopkins v. Price Waterhouse* Featured Case 9.1 in this chapter and the Babies R Us case in Chapter 11 for examples of cases of discrimination due to gender role violations.

[5] Consistent with Chapter 2, we refer to guidelines issued by the EEOC and to executive orders as "acts."

were working and had some level of protection against discrimination as well as proactive efforts to increase their employment, the next two acts addressed discrimination on the basis of pregnancy and sexual harassment. It is interesting to note that both pregnancy discrimination and sexual harassment were already prohibited by Title VII. That an amendment and formal guidelines were necessary 14 and 16 years later, respectively, indicates these issues continued to be serious, pervasive problems. The Family and Medical Leave Act (FMLA) was passed most recently, attempting to provide some level of job security while allowing women (and men) the ability to take time off for family needs. The FMLA is included as an act relevant to sex and gender at work because family responsibilities disproportionately affect working women and because men who wish to participate in family care are often perceived as violating their gender roles and experience negative organizational outcomes as a result.

The following sections include population, education, employment, and income data for men and women. We then consider several phenomena that are related to sex and gender in organizations: gender-based socialization, sex discrimination, sexual harassment, sex segregation, and the glass ceiling (and other boundaries). A separate section investigates the intersections of gender, race, and ethnicity. Lastly, we consider two unique gender issues (relationships between gender and poverty and gender differences in salary negotiation). While it is impossible to cover all of the issues relevant to sex and gender in organizations, these areas provide a broad representation of the myriad of factors affecting women and men in organizations and their differential organizational experiences.

Population

Females and males comprise 51% and 49%, respectively, of the 282.1 million people in the United States. As shown in Table 9.1, the age distribution of females is different from that of males. At younger ages, boys outnumber girls. Until age 18, there are slightly more than 105 males to females. Between ages 18 and 24, there are approximately equal number of men and women, with a sex ratio of 100.1. In all age-groups afterwards, women outnumber men, with the gap widening with age. Between ages 25 and 64, the years after college to just prior to retirement age, there are 2.9 million more women than men.

The sex ratio has many implications for diversity in organizations. There are more adult women than men as potential employees, and women's longer life expectancies also affect the proportion of older workers who may be female (which may compound multiple effects of diversity). For employers who value the contributions of women workers, treat them fairly, and provide them with opportunities, larger numbers of potential women workers may be an advantage to be seized. For organizations that devalue women workers, more women as potential workers may instead be viewed as a disadvantage.

TABLE 9.1 ***Sex Ratios by Age: 2002 (Males per 100 Females)***

Age Group	Sex Ratio
85 years and over	46.3
75 to 84 years	67.2
65 to 74 years	83.5
55 to 64 years	91.6
45 to 54 years	95.6
35 to 44 years	97.2
30 to 34 years	98.1
25 to 29 years	99.9
18 to 24 years	100.1
5 to 17 years	105.1
Under 5 years	104.1

Source: U.S. Census Bureau, Current Population Survey, March 2002.

EDUCATION

Overall, men in the United States have slightly more higher education than women, although the amount of education varies by education level and age group. As shown in Table 9.2, women are more likely to have a high school degree than men and to have completed some college but less likely to have completed college or obtained advanced degrees. These differences at the higher education levels contribute to women's lower earnings.

For younger adults, women are more likely to have a bachelor's degree than men. About 30% of women and 28% of men aged 25–29 have a bachelor's degree

TABLE 9.2 ***Educational Attainment of the Population (25 Years and Over) by Sex: March 2002 (Numbers in Thousands)***

Educational Attainment	Sex					
	Total		Male		Female	
	Number	Percent	Number	Percent	Number	Percent
Total	182,142	100.0	86,996	100.0	95,146	100.0
Less than 9th grade	12,570	6.9	6,200	7.1	6,370	6.7
9th to 12th grade (no diploma)	16,378	9.0	7,894	9.1	8,484	8.9
High school graduate	58,456	32.1	26,947	31.0	31,509	33.1
Some college or associate degree	46,042	25.3	21,127	24.3	24,915	26.2
Bachelor's degree	32,282	17.7	15,925	18.3	16,357	17.2
Advanced degree	16,414	9.0	8,903	10.2	7,511	7.9

Source: U.S. Census Bureau, Current Population Survey, March 2002, Special Populations Branch, Population Division. Internet Release Date: March 24, 2003.

(not shown), which may reduce future disparities in earnings and participation rates. More education generally means higher earnings and a greater likelihood of participating in the workforce due to the opportunity costs of not working and the ability to afford quality child care, if needed. Unfortunately, higher education does not automatically translate into similarly high earnings for women when compared with men (or people of color, as discussed in earlier chapters). The mean income of women college graduates working full-time, year-round is about the same as the mean income for men with associate's degrees who work full-time, year-round (see Table 9.3). When comparisons are made between White men and White women and people of color, and between those who work full-time year-round versus those with irregular work, disparities in the income to education return are even greater.

Employment Levels, Types, and Income

Participation Rates

Females represent 51% of the population and 47% of the workforce. In 2002, there were 76.7 million men and 67.4 million women participating in the labor force.

As shown in Table 9.4 increases in participation rates are projected for all groups except non-Hispanic Whites.[6] For non-Hispanic Whites, men's participation rates are projected to decline. Clearly, the majority of adult women are employed or looking for work: nearly 60% of all women participate in the labor force and about 94% of the women who want to work are employed.

The number and presence of children influence both men's and women's propensity to work and their earnings at work, although differently. Women without children participate at the same rate of all men (with and without children): 74%. Men are more likely to be employed and to work more hours (and to earn more) if they are fathers. Women who are mothers are less likely to be employed and to work fewer hours if they are employed (and to earn less). These differences are partially due to male and female gender roles. Men are generally perceived as providers; having children means men are expected to work more and earn more to provide for them. Women are generally perceived as caretakers; having children often leads to expectations that women will work fewer hours outside the home (if at any), instead focusing their energies on their families' at home needs. In the past, paying married men "family wages" and requiring women to leave work when they married or became pregnant were common organizational practices. In the present, both men and women, including women

[6] http://www.bls.gov/emp/emplab2002-03.htm, accessed 04/09/04.

TABLE 9.3 ***Mean Income in 2002 by Educational Attainment of Population 18 Years and Over (Percent Female of Male Income)***

		High School				Bachelor's or More	
Year-Round, Full-Time Workers†	**Total**	**Not High School Graduate**	**Graduate, Including GED**	**Some College, no Degree**	**Associate's Degree**	**Bachelor's Degree**	**Master's Degree**
All races male	$54,572	$28,350	$38,841	$47,947	$50,150	$73,139	$85,574
All races female	$37,624	$20,673	$28,496	$33,243	$35,544	$49,909	$58,914
Women's % of men's	69%	73%	73%	69%	71%	68%	69%
Non-Hispanic white female	$39,844	$23,016	$29,675	$35,045	$36,231	$51,283	$58,800
Hispanic women's % of men's	66%	71%	72%	69%	70%	67%	67%
Black female	$32,843	$19,719	$27,111	$29,663	$32,951	$45,367	$54,844
Black women's % of men's	82%	70%	87%	72%	73%	83%	77%
Asian female	$41,006	$20,793	$24,657	$31,751	$35,292	$47,692	$59,890
Asian women's % of men's	71%	95%	70%	71%	84%	74%	75%
Hispanic female (any race)	$28,062	$18,889	$24,058	$27,938	$32,668	$44,475	$65,953*
Hispanic women's % of men's	81%	74%	73%	70%	71%	84%	99%
Income as a Percent of Non-Hispanic White Men's Income							
Non-Hispanic White males	100%	100%	100%	100%	100%	100%	100%
Non-Hispanic White females	66%	71%	72%	69%	70%	67%	67%
All females	63%	64%	69%	66%	69%	65%	67%
Black females	55%	61%	65%	59%	64%	59%	62%
Asian females	68%	64%	60%	63%	68%	62%	68%
Hispanic females	47%	58%	58%	55%	63%	58%	75%

(Continued)

TABLE 9.3 ***(Continued)***

Income of Women of Color as a Percent of Non-Hispanic White Women's Income

		High School				Bachelor's or More	
	Total	Not High School Graduate	Graduate, Including GED	Some College, no Degree	Associate Degree	Bachelor's Degree	Master's Degree
All females	94%	90%	96%	95%	98%	97%	100%
Black females	82%	86%	91%	85%	91%	88%	93%
Asian females	103%	90%	83%	91%	97%	93%	102%
Hispanic females	70%	82%	81%	80%	90%	87%	112%

*Large standard error ($13,004) explains high mean income for Hispanic women with master's degree. Median of $46,255 is more representative.

Note: Percentage calculations are the author's.

Source: Table 8. Income in 2002 by Educational Attainment of the Population 18 Years and Over, by Age, Sex, Race Alone, And Hispanic Origin: 2003. U.S. Census Bureau, www.census.gov/population/socdemo/education/CPS2003/tab08-3.xls, accessed 10/07/05.

† Income for those working less than full-time, year round are lower. See "all workers" categories at same source.

TABLE 9.4 ***2002 Actual and 2012 Projected Participation Rates by Race/Ethnicity and Sex***

	2002		2012 Projection	
	Men	**Women**	**Men**	**Women**
All groups	74.1	59.6	73.1	61.6
White, non-Hispanic	73.8	59.6	72.4	59.4
Black	66.4	62.0	69.1	64.0
Hispanic	80.2	57.1	79.0	58.6
Asian	75.6	57.9	77.3	61.3

Source: http//www.bls.gov/emp/emplab2002-03.htm, accessed 04/09/04.

with small children, work for the financial, emotional, and psychological rewards of working.[7]

In 2000, 19% of all families included employed husbands with wives who did not work outside the home, considerably lower than the 26% of households that were maintained by single mothers.[8] For many of these divorced, never married, or widowed mothers, as the sole or primary source of income for their families, work is not generally an option. Perceptions of single mothers as uncommitted workers do not accurately characterize women who work as providers for their families. In addition, 19% of women past childbearing age do not have children, up from 10% in 1980.[9] For these women, children do not affect their workforce participation, yet because they are women, perceptions that family and child care needs will come before their commitment to work are still likely to negatively affect them at work.

In summary, in contrast to perceptions that women, particularly mothers, do not work outside the home, the majority of women do work, including those with small children. Employers should be careful to avoid basing assumptions about women's ability and willingness to participate in the workforce on whether they currently have or are likely to have children in the future. Women work for the same reasons that men do—to support themselves and, where relevant, their families and children. Chapter 13 considers work and family issues in more detail and provides suggestions for employers to help employees to be successful in both roles.

Misperception: The majority of women with small children leave the workforce to be "stay-at-home" moms.

Reality: Most women, with or without children of any age, work outside the home.

[7] Chafetz, J. S. (1997). "'I Need a (Traditional) Wife!': Employment-Family Conflicts." In D. Dunn (Ed.), *Workplace/Women's Place: An Anthology,* Los Angeles: Roxbury Publishers, pp. 116–124.

[8] Padavic, I., & Reskin, B. (2002). *Women and Men at Work* (2nd edition), Thousand Oaks, CA: Pine Forge Press.

[9] http://www.census.gov/Press-Release/www/2001/cb01-170.html, accessed 11/11/05.

Misperception: Women work to supplement their husbands' incomes.

Reality: Nearly half of all women (48%) are unmarried and 15% of women in married couples earn at least $5,000 more than their husbands earn.[10]

Sex Segregation

Sex segregation, which occurs when members of one sex constitute 70% or more of the incumbents of a job or occupation, characterizes women's occupations, and is a significant contributor to the male/female wage gap. In the United States and many other societies, most jobs are segregated by sex; women tend to work primarily with other women, and men tend to work with other men. A detailed report on sex segregation around the world suggested that half of all workers around the world seek jobs that are at least 80% sex segregated.[11] Well-known female-dominated jobs include secretaries (98.7%), registered nurses (91.9%), and elementary school teachers (82.2%) (Table 9.5).[12] Seventy-two percent of women are employed in four occupational groups: administrative support, professional specialty, service workers, and executive, administrative, and managerial positions. Women are "crowded" into seven occupations that include such low paying jobs as receptionist and cashier. Although "men's" jobs are also segregated by sex, there are seven times as many male-dominated jobs as female-dominated jobs.[13] The laws of supply and demand suggest that the crowding of women into a limited number occupations contributes to women's lower wages. When a large number of women compete for a limited number of positions, this drives down wages and keeps them down.

Occupations that are male dominated include protective services (e.g., police and firefighters), crafts (e.g., carpenters, electricians, and plumbers), and transport (e.g., truck, bus, and taxi drivers).[14] Well-known men's jobs include construction worker, police and firefighter, physician, engineer, and airline pilot. Working in a male-dominated job positively affects one's income (of both men and women in such jobs), while working in a female-dominated job negatively affects one's income (of both men and women in such jobs).

Further complicating the relationship between sex segregation and wages, while working in male-dominated jobs raises women's wages over wages of women who work in female-dominated jobs, women in male-dominated jobs

---

[10] http://www.census.gov/Press-Release/www/2001/cb01-113.html, accessed 11/11/05.

[11] Anker, R. (1998). *Gender and Jobs: Sex Segregation of Occupations in the World,* Geneva: International Labor Organization.

[12] U.S. Department of Labor, 2004.

[13] Padavic, I., & Reskin, B. (2002). *Women and Men at Work* (2nd edition), Chapter 4, footnote 5, p. 95.

[14] Jacobs, J. (1999). "The Sex Segregation of Occupations." In G. N. Powell (Ed.), *The Handbook of Gender and Work,* Thousand Oaks, CA: Sage, pp. 125–141.

TABLE 9.5 ***20 Leading Occupations of Employed Women: Full-time Wage and Salary Workers 2002 Annual Averages (Employment in Thousands)***

Occupation	Total Employed Women	Total Employed Men and Women	Percent Women	Women's Median Usual Weekly Earnings ($)
Total, 16 years and older (all employed women, full-time wage and salary workers)	43,773	100,204	43.7	530
Retail and personal sales workers, including cashiers	1,907	3,519	54.1	326
Secretaries	1,709	1,732	98.7	496
Elementary school teachers	1,677	2,039	82.2	750
Registered nurses	1,597	1,737	91.9	870
Nursing aides, orderlies, and attendants	1,434	1,603	89.5	367
Sales supervisors and proprietors	1,313	3,301	39.8	507
Cashiers	1,036	1,387	74.7	307
Bookkeepers, accounting, and auditing clerks	928	1,011	91.8	500
Accountants and auditors	851	1,424	59.8	734
Investigators and adjusters, except insurance	723	972	74.4	495
Receptionists	688	709	97.0	429
Secondary school teachers	639	1,135	56.3	767
Managers, medicine and health	549	714	76.9	750
Social workers	553	753	73.4	632
Managers, food serving and lodging establishments	487	1,031	47.2	517
Cooks, except short order	486	1,395	34.8	303
General office clerks	486	579	83.4	474
Janitors and cleaners	471	1,548	30.4	336
Administrators, education, and related fields	453	727	62.3	832
Waiters and waitresses	441	624	70.7	311

Note: Median not available where base is less than 50,000 male workers.

Source: U.S. Department of Labor, Bureau of Labor Statistics, Annual Averages 2002.

still earn less than men in male-dominated jobs. In contrast, when men are employed in female-dominated jobs their average earnings are higher than women working in female-dominated jobs. Consider the male-dominated occupation of engineer and the female-dominated occupation of registered nurse. Women engineers earn more than women nurses, but women engineers earn less than men engineers. Male engineers earn more than female engineers and male nurses earn more than female nurses. About 92% of registered nurses are women, who earn 7% less than male nurses.[15] Among dental hygienists (98% female),

[15] Padavic & Reskin. (2002).

women earn 21% less than male hygienists.[16] More details on male/female income disparities are discussed in the following section.

Income

Despite the 40-year existence of the Equal Pay Act and Title VII prohibiting discrimination on the basis of sex, women still earn significantly less than men earn. In the United States, each year during the month of April many women call attention to "Equal Pay Day," noting that it takes over three more months of working for women to earn what men earned in the previous year.[17] The female to male earnings ratio has increased from a low of about 60% in the 1970s to an all-time high of 74% in 1996 and has declined slightly since then. In addition to sex segregation, women's earnings are negatively affected by women's likelihood of working fewer hours per week and year than men work, even when employed "full-time." Clearly, the laws prohibiting discrimination are insufficient to eliminate income disparities between men and women. What other factors exist?

Gender Role Socialization

Gender role socialization is one prominent reason for the persistence of sex discrimination, women's lower wage levels, sex segregation, and other unequal gender treatment. Gender role socialization is the process by which social institutions, including families, friends, organizations, and the media, form and shape expectations of acceptable behaviors for males and females. It affects women's treatment in organizations (by managers and peers), career "choices" and paths, and women's responsibilities outside of work (which are related to organizational progress and success). Socialization neutralizes the effectiveness of antidiscrimination and equal pay legislation by contributing to different career "choices" men and women make as a result of a lifelong socialization. Men and women simply do not work in the same jobs in the same organizations, which severely limits the effectiveness of the Equal Pay Act. Recall from Chapter 2 that the Equal Pay Act requires men and women who work in the same jobs, in the same organization, and who have similar skills, performance, and tenure, to be paid equally. Because of sex segregation, and the role of "choice" in the jobs occupied by men and women, the Equal Pay Act and other laws against pay discrimination are constrained.

[16] Roos, P. A., & Gatta, M. L. (1999). "The Gender Gap in Earnings." In G. N. Powell (Ed.), *The Handbook of Gender and Work,* Thousand Oaks, CA: Sage, pp. 95–123.

[17] http://www.cluw.org/programs-payequity.html, accessed 04/16/04.

Table 9.6 ***Comparison of Average Annual Earnings of Male-Dominated and Female-Dominated Positions in the Same Fields***

Female Dominated	Wages	Male Dominated	Wages
Nurse	49,840	Physician	136,260
Elementary school teacher	44,300	Associate professor, public university	61,500
Dental hygienist	57,790	Dentist	133,350
Legal assistant	40,590	Lawyer	105,890

Source: U.S. Census Bureau, 2003.

What is the role of "choice" in men's and women's work? From early in life, males and females receive clear messages about what "girls" and "boys" do and should do.[18] These messages refer to dress, behavior, occupations, and countless other "choices" people make throughout life. Research indicates that expectant parents who know the sex of their babies before birth speak more softly to girls in the womb than to boys in the womb. Parents of newborns describe girl babies as delicate and soft, while describing boy babies (of the same size) in more masculine, stronger terms.[19]

Through socialization and observation, children learn that acceptable and appropriate jobs for women are elementary school teaching, nursing, and secretarial work—jobs that involve nurturing, care, and support. Research indicates that jobs involving nurturance pay 0.74 per hour less than jobs not requiring nurturance, contributing to the wage gap.[20]

Table 9.6 provides examples of wages of female- and male-dominated jobs in the same industry. The jobs depicted require similar skills, interests, abilities, and often similar work time commitments, but longer training and education, which results in very different outcomes. A few more years investing in training and education would allow some women lifetimes of greater earnings, flexibility, prestige, and stability. Instead, a lifetime of gender role socialization and seeing those similar to themselves in certain jobs may result in young women preparing for female-dominated positions without even considering similar, more lucrative, male-dominated positions as career choices. Many women may not be consciously aware that providing well for one's family and job flexibility are not mutually exclusive, but do take deliberate, conscious thought. Young women may "choose" elementary school teaching because of the anticipated flexibility it provides for

[18] For a thought-provoking discussion of the role of schools in socialization, see Orenstein, P. (2002). "Shortchanging Girls: Gender Socialization in Schools." In P. Dubeck & D. Dunn (Eds.), *Workplace, Women's Place: An Anthology* (2nd edition), Los Angeles: Roxbury Publishers, pp. 38–46.

[19] Smith, D. (2000). *Women at Work: Leadership for the Next Century,* Upper Saddle River, NJ: Prentice-Hall.

[20] England, P., Christopher, K., & Reid, L. L. (1999). "Gender, Race, Ethnicity, and Wages." In I. Browne (Ed.), *Latinas and African American Women at Work,* New York: Russell Sage Foundation, pp. 139–82.

TABLE 9.7 ***Comparison of Average Annual Earnings and Percent Female in the Teaching Profession***

Occupation	% Female	Wages
Elementary school	85	$44,300
Secondary school	52	$45,200
Assistant professor (public/private)	38	$51,500/$55,600
Associate professor (public/private)	25	$61,500/$66,300
Full professor (public/private)	12	$84,100/$101,200

Source: Percent female taken from Dunn, D. (1999). "Women: The Fifty-One Percent Minority." In A. G. Dworkin & R. J. Dworkin (Eds.), *The Minority Report,* Orlando, FL: Harcourt Brace. Average wages taken from U.S. Census Bureau, 2003, Table 294. Average Salaries for College Faculty Members: 2001 to 2003, pp. 415–435; http://www.census.gov/prod/2004pubs/03statab/educ.pdf, accessed 12/08/04.

parenting and family issues. They may be unaware that while elementary school teachers and professors both have the ability to be off with children during summers, professors spend significantly less daily time in the classroom (allowing for time in other roles), and generally earn considerably more money. See Table 9.7 for comparisons of wages between elementary and secondary teachers and college professors.

Girls and boys who deviate from their appropriate gender roles are penalized by parents, teachers, society, and employers. The classic case of *Ann Hopkins v. Price Waterhouse,* described in Featured Case 9.1, is one such case in which a woman was penalized for acting like a man. Although any gender transgression is viewed negatively, for a boy, exhibiting female-typed behaviors (e.g., "sissy") is worse negative than a girl who exhibits male-typed behaviors (e.g., "tomboy"). Girls are discouraged from exhibiting aggression, encouraged to cooperate, and to consider the feelings of others in decision making. Boys are expected to behave aggressively, to "fight it out," and to try to win in most situations. Ironically, greater willingness to cooperate, seek consensus, and reach common goals are assets in today's complex global organizations, yet these skills are less valued because women hold them. In occupational "choices," women who deviate from gender appropriate occupations do so with the opportunity to earn higher wages than they would in female-dominated occupations. In contrast, for a man to deviate from gender-appropriate occupations would be to choose to enter lower-wage, lower-status, female-dominated occupations. While many people would understand a woman's desire to pursue higher status and wages, fewer would understand a man's desire to decline in status and wages.[21]

As well as personal career "choices" that women and men make, managers and decision makers in organizations also make selection and placement decisions

[21] As we discuss later, men in female-dominated positions are rewarded by rapid ascent into management positions.

FEATURED CASE 9.1 *Ann Hopkins v. Price-Waterhouse: Violation of Gender Stereotypes*[22]

In August 1982, 18 years after the passage of Title VII of the Civil Rights Act prohibiting sex discrimination, Ann Hopkins was nominated for partner at Price Waterhouse (PW) accounting and consulting firm. Of the 88 candidates being considered, Ann was the only woman and only seven of the approximately 2,600 PW partners worldwide were women. At the time of her candidacy, Ann had worked for PW for 4 years, demonstrating excellent performance, successfully managing difficult accounts, and billing more hours (e.g., earning more revenue) than any of the other candidates being considered for partner that year. On the other hand, Ann had been counseled for using profanity and being abrasive to subordinates—behaviors that were commonly exhibited by males at PW.

After consideration by the full partners, 47 of the 88 candidates were offered partnerships and 21 were rejected, while Ann and 19 others were put "on hold" for possible consideration the next year. Ann learned that other candidates who had been ranked similarly as she was ranked had been admitted as partners. Even so, Ann continued to work for PW, participating in developmental activities that would ostensibly improve her chances for being made a partner the next year. Thomas Beyer, a partner who had supported her candidacy and considered himself her friend, also told Ann that to increase her chances of obtaining partnership in the future she should "soften her image," "use less profanity," to try to appear "more feminine." He also suggested that she should not drink beer at lunch, wear more jewelry and make-up, style her hair, and not carry a briefcase. In other words, Ann was penalized for acting like a man.

When it became clear that Ann would not be nominated for partnership the following year, she left PW, started a management consulting firm, and sued PW for sex discrimination. After more than 5 years of litigation, the Supreme Court ruled in Ann's favor, awarding back pay and a partnership at PW (which she refused). The Supreme Court stated that for employers to penalize women for behaving aggressively when job requirements necessitate aggressiveness for successful job performance places women in a bind. Such women are "out of a job if they behave aggressively and out of a job if they don't."[23] This influential decision clarified the illegality of using compliance with gender roles in job decisions.

QUESTIONS TO CONSIDER

1. ***How might concerns of 5 years of litigation affect many plaintiffs considering a lawsuit?***
2. ***Instead of telling Hopkins to act more like a woman, what could Beyer have done to address the apparent discrimination against her in the candidacy process?***
3. ***Research suggests that women, minorities, and others who experience organizational discrimination often start their own firms, as Hopkins did. How might those negative organizational experiences be used to make the firms they start be diversity-friendly?***

[22] Details from this case drawn from Gentile, M. C. (1996). *Managerial Excellence through Diversity,* Prospect Heights, IL: Waveland Press; Babcock, L., & Laschever, S. (2003). *Women Don't Ask,* Princeton, NJ: Princeton University Press.

[23] Babcock & Laschever. (2003). p. 111.

based on roles perceived as gender appropriate. A simple example of when such gender steering may occur is when a woman and a man apply for positions at an office without specifying the position of interest. The woman may be given a typing or clerical test, while the man may be interviewed for a management trainee position. Secretaries generally make less money than managers and have considerably fewer opportunities for advancement. At a hotel, an unskilled man may be hired as a valet, for parking cars and delivering luggage, while an unskilled woman may be hired in housekeeping, making beds and cleaning rooms. While both are low-skill, low-status positions, with little opportunity for advancement, the valet stands to make extra money through tips, while the woman may not because many people do not leave tips for hotel maids.

Although illegal under Title VII, gender-specific screening by employers would be difficult to document, prove, or, for the applicant, even to be certain had occurred. Similarly, when current employees make referrals of friends and family for job openings, they may do prescreening based on gender, referring women to jobs seen as "women's jobs" and men to "men's jobs." As no employer is involved in these actions, this type of screening is not illegal, yet it still perpetuates sex segregation and resulting wage inequality.

Sex Discrimination

As discussed in Chapter 2, Title VII of the Civil Rights Act of 1964 prohibits discrimination on the basis of sex in employment-related matters. Although such discrimination has been prohibited for over 40 years, intentional and unintentional discrimination still occurs, with some frequency. In 2003, the EEOC received 24,362 charges of sex-based discrimination and resolved 27,146 charges.[24] More than $98 million was recovered for charging parties and aggrieved individuals (not including litigation awards).[25] The widely publicized case involving sex discrimination by Morgan Stanley, a large financial services firm, was settled in July 2004. The EEOC lawsuit alleged that Morgan Stanley discriminated against women in promotions; compensation; and terms, conditions, and privileges of employment; and retaliated against an employee who complained by terminating her. The lengthy lawsuit was resolved by a 3-year consent decree in which Morgan Stanley agreed to $54 million settlement, including $40 million to affected claimants, $12 million to the terminated complaining party, and $2 million for antidiscrimination and diversity training.[26] The decree also requires

[24] This figure includes charges filed in previous years but resolved in 2003.

[25] http://www.eeoc.gov/types/sex.html, accessed 05/13/04.

[26] EEOC litigation settlement report, July 2004, http://www.eeoc.gov/litigation/settlements/settlement07-04.html, accessed 11/11/05.

Morgan Stanley to monitor implementation and compliance with the decree, providing regular reports on women's status in the company to the EEOC and to an outside monitor.

Disparate treatment on the basis of sex occurs when an applicant or employee, typically a woman, is intentionally treated differently than males are treated. Although such blatant, overt discrimination is less common than in the past, such discrimination is far from obsolete. As an example, the recent EEOC settlement involving the Phoenix Suns professional basketball team and their sports entertainment firm regarding overt sex discrimination through a stated requirement for men applicants is described in Featured Case 9.2.

Disparate or adverse impact against women can occur when an employer's apparently neutral policy or practice negatively affects women's employment opportunities. An example of when adverse impact might occur is with some height and weight requirements. Many such requirements were instituted in the late 1960s and 1970s after passage of Title VII as organizations tried to implement legitimate job requirements. At the time, many job incumbents were White males, and if the average height and weight of current job incumbents was used as a requirement for future employees, this would automatically disadvantage women as a group, who tend to be smaller than men on average, as well as men of Asian, American Indian, or Latino backgrounds, who tend to be smaller than White (and Black) men. While height and weight requirements alone are not discriminatory, employers must ensure that they are truly related to successsul job performance (rather than simply to the normal job incumbents) and that no other nondiscriminatory measure is feasible. Employers may find unintended positive outcomes result from efforts to remove discriminatory barriers to employment of people of different sizes.

Firefighting often comes to mind when people think of jobs in which they would prefer to have larger workers. "I'd prefer a firefighter to be big enough to be able to carry me out of a burning building," captures some of such apparently rational thinking. However, closer consideration calls into question the legitimacy of such thinking. The normal, daily job requirements of firefighters are more likely to include responding to false alarms and paramedic calls than rescues involving carrying someone who is unconscious and dead weight. Given the wide range of adult sizes, it is highly unlikely that any single adult would be able to carry any other adult for a significant distance, without assistance. Further, when considering the need to access small basement or bathroom windows, the benefit of having a smaller-sized firefighter (of any sex) seems apparent.

Another job commonly construed as needing large-sized incumbents is that of police work. "I want a police officer to be strong enough to take down criminals" is a common perspective. Again, when considering the daily job requirements of most police officers (such as directing traffic, writing tickets, completing

Featured Case 9.2 *Phoenix Suns and Sports Magic Sex Discrimination Settlement: A Newspaper Advertisement Seeks "Male" Employees*

More than 40 years after sex discrimination was prohibited by law, companies continue to practice overt discrimination. In a blatantly discriminatory newspaper ad that was published in Phoenix-area newspapers including *Arizona Republic*, the *Mesa Tribune*, and the *New Times*, the Phoenix Suns professional basketball team and Sports Magic Team, sought "males with athletic ability and talent" for half-time and community performances by the "Zoo Crew." The Suns are part of the National Basketball Association and Sports Magic Team is a firm that organizes the Suns' half-time entertainment and promotions by the Zoo Crew.

Prior to the Suns' and Sports Magic's decision to seek only men for the positions, Kathryn Tomlinson had worked as a member of the Zoo Crew, performing acrobatics and other tricks during games, attending community events, and interacting with the public during the 1998–1999 basketball season. After the decision to hire only men, Tomlinson and another woman took their discrimination claim to the EEOC, which took the case. The Phoenix Suns and Sports Magic agreed to pay over $100,000 to settle the discrimination charges. In addition to the monetary settlement, the Phoenix Suns also agreed to strengthen its policies prohibiting sex discrimination, train personnel, establish safeguards to ensure discriminatory advertisements were not disseminated in the future, and to apologize to Tomlinson.

Requirements for a particular sex may be legitimate when sex is a bona fide occupational qualification (BFOQ).[27] Assumptions about physical abilities or customer preferences for a certain sex do not qualify as BFOQs.

Questions to Consider

1. ***Why might the Phoenix Suns and Sports Magic have decided to seek "males with athletic ability and talent"?***
2. ***Is it possible that the organizations involved were unaware of legislation prohibiting sex discrimination? Do you think they considered that their actions might be illegal?***
3. ***What potential benefits might the Suns and Sports Magic have gained by seeking "people" (rather than males) with athletic ability and talent as members of the Zoo Crew?***

Source: EEOC Resolves Sex Discrimination Lawsuit against NBA's Phoenix Suns and Sports Magic for $104,500, The U. S. EEOC, http://www.eeoc.gov/press/10-9-03b.html, accessed 05/13/2004.

paperwork), and their limited use of greater physical strength to subdue suspects (rather than legitimate authority, stun guns, pepper spray, or other nonlethal weapons), the necessity for large size seems less critical. When considering the benefits of having women police officers to interview and assist victims of certain crimes (e.g., child molestation, rape), the benefit of assets and skills other than simply physical strength becomes apparent.

---

[27] See Chapter 2 for a discussion of what constitutes a BFOQ based on sex.

Misperception: Most women are physically unable to perform jobs such as police officer and firefighter.

Reality: Without a partner or special equipment, many men are unable to perform tasks believed to be commonly performed by firefighters and police officers. In addition, most job tasks of police officers and firefighters do not involve strength or size, and certain functions may be performed more successfully by a woman (interviewing rape and child molestation victims) or small person of either sex (crawling into tight spaces).

For firefighting, police work, and other historically male-dominated jobs, a critical look at job requirements can be advantageous for employers as well as female applicants. Pairing male and female officers or those of smaller and larger statures can provide many unintended positive consequences, along with widening the applicant pool to more qualified people. In addition, constraining the applicant pool through unnecessary "job requirements" can result in higher recruitment, selection, and compensation costs to employers. Jobs can be redesigned and equipment replaced to make jobs open to a larger proportion of the workforce, providing benefits to employers, applicants, and society.[28]

In some situations, tests are implemented that constrain the job pool even though some excluded applicants could have performed the job without job redesign or special equipment. In one case, Dial Corporation began using a strength test purportedly to reduce injuries in its Armour Star meat-packing plant in Iowa.[29] The test required repeated lifting of 35 pounds to a height of 65 inches. Although women had successfully performed the job before the test was implemented, only 40% of female applicants passed the test, while nearly all male applicants did. One plaintiff, Paula Liles, successfully performed during the test, but was still rejected because she had to stand on her toes during parts of the test and was told that she was too short (62 inches). The courts ruled that the test was both intentional discrimination against women and disparate impact discrimination that was not justified by business necessity. Liles and the other 51 plaintiffs were to share a $3.4 million settlement that included compensatory and punitive damages. Each plaintiff also received a job offer by Dial, and at least 14 accepted. In response to the judgment, Liles said "I have done physical labor all my life, and I was able to perform the job at Dial. Dial was the highest paying employer in the area, and I felt that I was being rejected because of my sex and my height." The EEOC attorney said that the test was based on "stereotypes rather than actual ability".

---

[28] Padavic & Reskin. (2002).

[29] Dial Ordered to Pay More than $3 Million in EEOC Sex Discrimination Case. http://www.eeoc.gov/press/9-29-05.html, accessed 11/14/05.

Sexual Harassment

As discussed in Chapter 2, sexual harassment is unwelcome conduct of a sexual nature in the workplace and is a form of sex discrimination. The courts have recognized two forms of sexual harassment: quid pro quo and hostile environment. In quid pro quo harassment, managers, supervisors, or others with authority make sexual demands and submission to or rejection of those demands is used as a basis for employment decisions (such as promotion, termination, etc). In hostile environment harassment, unwelcome sexual conduct has the "purpose or effect of unreasonably interfering with job performance, or creating an intimidating, hostile, or offensive working environment."[30] This kind of harassment is most commonly perpetrated by coworkers and peers and is less clear cut and distinct than is quid pro quo harassment. Hostile environment harassment includes such things as jokes, photographs of scantily clad women (or men), and comments that some may view as normal and harmless but others may view as offensive and harassing. The EEOC and researchers suggest that organizations should clarify what constitutes harassment and identify harassing behaviors in regular, mandatory training programs.

Sexual harassment is a common phenomenon for working women around the world. Studies conducted in Australia, Austria, Brazil, Canada, China, Hong Kong, India, Israel, Mexico, New Zealand, Norway, Portugal, Spain, Turkey, the United Kingdom, and various other places found pervasive sexual harassment with common negative individual and organizational outcomes. Estimates suggest that between 25% and 75% of women and 15% of men will be harassed in their work lives.[31] In the U.S. military, between 47% (female officers), 60% (enlisted women), and 96.8% (elite military institutions) of women report having been harassed.[32]

As with other discrimination, most people who are harassed do not sue or file formal complaints when sexually harassed. In the United States, the more than 14,000 new charges of sexual harassment filed with the EEOC each year are but a fraction of the estimated instances of harassment each year.

Briefly scanning the Equal Employment Opportunity Commission Web site provides numerous instances of egregious sexual harassment.[33] In 2004, settlements against franchisees or companies include companies such as Jack in the Box,

---

[30] EEOC Guidelines on Discrimination Because of Sex, 29, C. F. R. Section 1604. 11(a). 1995.

[31] Gutek, B. A., & Koss, M. P. (1993). "Changed Women and Changed Organizations: Consequences of and Coping with Sexual Harassment." *Journal of Vocational Behavior,* 42: 28–48; U.S. Merit Systems Protection Board. (1988). *Sexual Harassment in the Federal Workplace: An Update*. Washington, DC: US Government Printing Office.

[32] Department of Defense. (2004). Report on the Status of Female Members of the Armed Forces.

[33] Equal Employment Opportunity Commission Litigation Settlements—June, July, August, and September, 2004, http://www.eeoc.gov/litigation/settlements/settlement07-04.html.

Jiffy Lube, Priority Staffing, and Brinker International (Chili's locations). Reports include:

- "constant comments about wanting to get into the women's pants . . . remarked on the attractiveness of the women's breasts and buttocks . . . disciplining (complaining party) for cash shortages for which she was not responsible." *EEOC v. Jack in the Box, Inc.*
- "president grabbed their private parts, used vulgar language, and made sexually explicit demands and harassing telephone calls." *EEOC v. Priority Staffing, Inc.*
- "subjected . . . recent high school teenage graduates to sexual harassment . . . (including) propositioning them for dates or sex, groping them, and making lewd comments about their bodies and appearance." *EEOC v. The Oil Shoppe d/b/a Jiffy Lube and Does 1-10 Inclusively.*
- "Invoking the restaurant's sexual harassment policy, the charging parties complained to management 15 times over a 10-month period but the harassment continued . . . In retaliation . . . the assistant manager began to schedule her for work on days when she was unavailable." *EEOC v. Brinker International, Inc., Chili's of MD, Chili's of Bel Air.*

Many of the complaining parties in these and other cases were terminated for complaining or constructively discharged. In addition to the real possibility of job loss, harassment targets experience various negative physical and psychological outcomes, including stress, symptoms of post-traumatic stress disorder, nervousness, and fear. Sexual harassment negatively affects job satisfaction, morale, productivity, turnover, absence, and increases targets' intentions to quit. These negative physical, psychological, and organizational outcomes of sexual harassment have been repeatedly documented in international research.[34] Researchers have also linked sexual harassment to greater conflict in work teams and subsequent lower productivity.[35] Women who are harassed tend to be younger, unmarried, and in lower-status, lower-level jobs than women who are not harassed. Because women's jobs and positions are generally lower in status, power, and authority than men's jobs and positions worldwide, this likely contributes to sexual harassment of women worldwide.

In one study, Barbara Gutek and her colleagues found that sexualization of the work environment, such as sexual jokes, comments, or innuendoes, and a general

---

[34] Fitzgerald, L. F., Drasgow, R., Hulin, C. L., Gelfand, M. J., & Magley, V. J. (1997). "Antecedents and Consequences of Sexual Harassment in Organizations: A Test of an Integrated Model." *Journal of Applied Psychology,* 82: 578–589; Gelfand, M. J., Fitzgerald, L. F., & Drasgow, F. (1995). "The Structure of Sexual Harassment: A Confirmatory Analysis across Cultures and Settings." *Journal of Vocational Behavior,* 47: 167–177; Shaffer, M. A., Joplin, J. R. W., Bell, M. P., Lau, T., & Oguz, C. (2000). "Gender Discrimination and Job-Related Outcomes: A Cross-Cultural Comparison of Working Women in the United States and China." *Journal of Vocational Behavior,* 57 (4): 395–427; Wasti, S. A., Bergman, M. E., Glomb, T. M., & Drasgow, F. (2000). "Test of the Cross-Cultural Generalizability of a Model of Sexual Harassment." *Journal of Applied Psychology,* 85: 766–789.

[35] Raver, J. L., & Gelfand, M. J. (2005). "Beyond the Individual Victim: Linking Sexual Harassment, Team Processes, and Team Performance." *Academy of Management Journal,* 48: 387–400.

lack of professionalism were associated with sexual harassment. Gutek's sample was a broad sample of workers in the city of Los Angeles.[36] Other researchers have also found that the nature of the work environment and expectations are related to sexual harassment; in places where work roles are clear and where workers are generally treated respectfully, sexual harassment is less likely to occur.[37]

Sexual harassment is frequently experienced by women who enter male-dominated fields. Researchers have found that women in blue-collar trade and transit positions, autoworkers, lawyers, police officers, and firefighters experienced more peer harassment than women working in female-dominated fields.[38] In some studies, this harassment and other overt hostility was associated with failure to train new workers, which could then result in failure on the job, termination, or "voluntary" turnover (e.g., quitting due to the hostile environment at work).[39] For those who believe that women are incapable of performing certain male-dominated jobs, women's failure may serve to confirm negative expectations. Such failure may be a result of harassment and lack of training rather than women's incompetence, however. As with any job newcomer of any sex, training and (positive) socialization are critical to success. Lack of training and harassment in *any job* predict failure (for men, women, people of color, etc.) and in certain jobs, lack of training and harassment can be life threatening. Featured Case 9.3 describes a dangerous case of sex-based hostility for a woman truck driver at Fed Ex. Organizational intervention, through education, training, monitoring, and zero tolerance for harassment can help women successfully enter and remain in male-dominated fields, reducing sex segregation and improving the climate for diversity.

Sexual Harassment of Men

Although it is considerably less common, men also experience sexual harassment. The EEOC reports that 14% of its sexual harassment charges are filed by men, most of whom report being harassed by other men.[40] Men who are harassed may be even less willing to complain than are women who are harassed, due to perceptions that they should be flattered if harassed by a woman or that they are

---

[36] Gutek, B. A., Cohen, A. G., & Konrad, A. M. (1990). "Predicting Social-Sexual Behavior at Work: A Contact Hypothesis." *Academy of Management Journal,* 33: 560–577.

[37] O'Hare, E. A., & O'Donohue, W. (1998). "Sexual Harassment: Identifying Risk Factors." *Archives of Sexual Behavior,* 27: 561–580.

[38] Gruber, J. E., & Bjorn, L. (1982). "Blue-Collar Blues: The Sexual Harassment of Women Autoworkers." *Work and Occupations,* 93: 271–298; LaFontaine, E., & Tredeau, L. (1986). "The Frequency, Sources, and Correlates of Sexual Harassment in Traditional Male Occupations." *Sex Roles,* 1(5): 433–442.; Rosenberg, J., Perlstadt, H., & Philips, W. R. (1993). "Now That We Are Here: Discrimination, Disparagement, and Harassment at Work and the Experience of Women Lawyers." *Gender and Society,* 7: 415–433.

[39] See also Padavic & Reskin. (2002).

[40] "EEOC Sues Kraft Foods North America for Same-Sex Harassment of Men," http://www.eeoc.gov/press/10-25-02.html, accessed 01/22/05.

FEATURED CASE 9.3 *Federal Express to Pay over $3.2 Million to Woman Truck Driver*

Marion Shaub of Wrightstown, PA, was the only female tractor-trailer driver at the Middletown, PA, facility of Federal Express. Shaub alleged that she was constantly subjected to antifemale remarks and threats from her male coworkers. After she made numerous complaints about the gender-based hostility and harassment at work, Shaub alleged that the brakes on her truck were sabotaged and that her coworkers refused to help with the loading of her truck. After Shaub was fired in October 2000, she sued Federal Express, under Title VII. In early 2004, a federal jury found Federal Express liable for a sex-based hostile environment and retaliation, awarding Shaub $391,400 in back and front pay, $350,000 in compensatory damages, and $2.5 million in punitive damages. The Civil Rights Act of 1991 allows for punitive damages in cases of intentional discrimination such as that experienced by Shaub.

QUESTIONS TO CONSIDER

1. ***Why might Shaub's coworkers have been so hostile toward her?***
2. ***What signal would Shaub's experiences at Fed Ex send to other women desiring to be truck drivers?***
3. ***What could Federal Express have done to circumvent the harassment prior to Shaub or other women being hired as drivers?***
4. ***Had Shaub (or other people) been injured or killed because her brakes had been sabotaged, what consequences might Fed Ex have faced?***
5. ***What should Fed Ex have done in response to Shaub's initial complaints?***
6. ***What should Fed Ex do to prevent this kind of thing from happening in the future?***

Source: Federal Express to Pay over $3.2 Million to Female Truck Driver for Sex Discrimination, Retaliation, http://www.eeoc.gov/press/2-25-04.html, accessed 05/13/2004.

gay if harassed by a man. Regardless of the sex or sexual orientation of the target or harasser, workplace sexual harassment is illegal.

In 1998, the Supreme Court issued an important decision on same sex harassment, clarifying its illegality. Prior to the Supreme Court's decision, rulings had differed as to whether such harassment was covered under Title VII or whether the sexuality of the harasser was relevant. In 1991, Joseph Oncale worked on an oil platform in the Gulf of Mexico for Sundowner Offshore Services along with seven other men. On several occasions, two of Oncale's supervisors physically assaulted him in a sexual manner, threatened to rape him, and subjected him to humiliating sex-related behavior. When Oncale complained to Sundowner's Safety Compliance clerk, the clerk called him a heterosexist name and characterized the supervisors' behavior as simply "picking on" people, which had occurred to others as well. Oncale said he resigned his position to avoid being raped, and filed a lawsuit against Sundowner.

The first court to hear the case ruled that because both Oncale and the harassers were male, Oncale had no cause of action, and this ruling was confirmed on appeal. The Supreme Court agreed to hear the case in 1997, and in

1998, seven years after the harassment occurred, ruled in Oncale's favor. Prohibitions against discrimination because of sex do not require the parties to be of different sexes. Those who experience sexual harassment, regardless of their sex or that of the perpetrator, have legal rights and recourse. In September 2005, the EEOC won a $765,000 judgment against a chain of movie theaters where young male workers were harassed by their male supervisor, who was a convicted sex offender.[41]

The Glass Ceiling and Other Boundaries

The *glass ceiling* is an invisible barrier that prevents women, people of color, and people with disabilities from progressing beyond a certain level in organizations.[42] The glass ceiling is often perceived or referred to as beginning near top management, including executive positions, however, the ceiling is actually quite low.[43] Relatively few women or minorities advance past first or second level management in organizations, leading researchers to suggest that the term *sticky floors* more accurately reflects this phenomenon. In other words, women are far closer to the bottom rungs of the ladder to the top rather than approaching the ceiling.

In the United States, Canada, the United Kingdom, and most other nations, women rarely reach the executive suite or even middle to upper management. In the United States, despite 40 years in which legislation prohibiting sex discrimination has existed, women comprise nearly 47% of the workforce, but are only 12% of corporate officers, hold about 6% of the highest corporate titles, and hold only 4% of the highest earning positions. In the past few years the number of women in CEO positions in the Fortune 500 companies has consistently been in the single digits.[44] The farther one goes from the first level of management in the organizational hierarchy, the fewer the number of women that are represented, across industries. One exception is Sharon Allen, Chairman of the Board of Deloitte and Touche, discussed in Individual Feature 9.1. Allen is actively involved in Deloitte's diversity initiatives.

Women's persistent overrepresentation in lower-level jobs and underrepresentation in lower-level jobs, in a wide range of industries, cannot be simply attributed to lack of education, qualifications, or desire to advance. Two major employers of

[41] "Carmike Cinemas to Pay $765,000 to Settle Rare Case of Male-on-Male Teen Harassment," http://www.eeoc.gov/press/9-27-05.html, accessed 10/01/05. See also Chapter 11 for a discussion of young workers' experiences with sexual harassment at work.

[42] This chapter considers the effects of the glass ceiling on women; see chapters on Blacks, Latinos, Asians, and people with disabilities for a consideration of its effects on members of these groups.

[43] Hurley, A. E., Fagenson-Eland, E. A., & Sonnenfeld, J. A. (1997). "Does Cream Always Rise to the Top? An Investigation of Career Attainment Determinants." *Organizational Dynamics,* 26(2): 65–71.

[44] http://www.catalystwomen.org/pressroom/press_releases/2000_cote.htm. Catalyst (2000). 2000 Catalyst Census of Women Corporate Officers and Top Earners of the Fortune 500. New York: Catalyst.

INDIVIDUAL FEATURE 9.1 *Sharon Allen, Chairman of the Board of Deloitte & Touche, USA, LLP*

Deloitte & Touche, USA, LLP, is one of a number of member firms of Deloitte Touche Tohmatsu. Deloitte is commonly known as a consulting firm or tax firm, but it also provides audit, advisory, and other services to its clients worldwide. Its clients include more than half of the world's largest companies. In 2004, Deloitte employed 115,000 people in 148 countries and had revenues of $16.4 billion.

When Sharon Allen was named Chairman of the Board of Deloitte & Touche, USA, she became the first woman ever elected a Board Chair and the highest-ranking woman in Deloitte's history. Along the way, she was also the first woman managing partner and first woman to sit on the board in Deloitte's history. A graduate of the University of Idaho, Allen joined Deloitte's Boise office in 1973. She worked in the 60-employee Boise office for 24 years, and there became the first woman managing partner in the company's history. Allen left Boise for Deloitte's Portland office, and then moved to Los Angeles office, as managing partner. She was named Chairman of the Board in May, 2003.

Who is Sharon Allen? How has she done what seems to elude so many executive women? Research on the glass ceiling notes the paucity of women on boards and near absence of women chairing boards. Other research suggests that executive women are less likely to be married and/or to have children than men executives. Allen has done them all. She has served on the board, is now chairman of the board, is still married to her high school sweetheart, and is an actively involved mother, going to soccer games like every other mother. Allen finds that new client relationships can be established "on the sidelines of soccer games" just as well as in the boardroom. In contrast to some perspectives, some executive women can and do "have it all."

During Allen's earlier years with Deloitte, women were overlooked for assignments to work with high-profile clients, in part because women had higher turnover than men. Fearing that the clients would be left in the lurch when this happened, the high-profile accounts that led to promotions were not given to women. Women saw that they were not getting the significant accounts, and left. One of Deloitte's responses was to develop a special program, the "Women's Initiative," to help ensure that women had the opportunity to compete for certain positions and were not overlooked. Allen believes that the Women's Initiative provided her with the visibility to be selected that she might not otherwise have had. She therefore makes it her personal responsibility to help others who might be overlooked. In a 2004 speech at the University of Idaho, where she received an honorary doctorate, Allen said that she considers it her "personal obligation to be a *nag* in ensuring that women are appropriately represented on each short list for succession into important client service and firm leadership positions." At present, Deloitte has the highest percentage of women partners, principals, and directors among similar companies, and plans to increase those numbers.

Allen is a woman whose "work ethic, leadership skills and commitment speak before her gender," yet she realizes the importance of gender and diversity to the success of organizations and corporate boards. She actively supports Deloitte's efforts to increase the diversity of partners and helps develop a corporate culture that allows for family time, which she believes provides Deloitte with a recruiting advantage. "Young people today have an expectation of ensuring they can have balance in their life." Some of Deloitte's benefits to help employees balance work and family include reduced workload, in which high-performing professionals at senior level or higher can reduce their schedules for child or elder care, to pursue an advanced degree, or for other reasons, without affecting their ultimate career potential.

Deloitte has led the Big Four professional services firms with the highest percentage of women partners, principals, and directors for the past 7 years.

Questions to Consider

1. ***Deloitte's Women's Initiative was formed to address their problems with women leaving the company. How likely is it that presumptions about women's turnover (and that of other minority group members) prevent them from getting key assignments and thus contributes to their turnover?***
2. ***Ensuring that women "are appropriately represented on each short list for succession into important client service and firm leadership" positions helps them be able to compete for jobs. How is this similar to affirmative action?***

Source: Cole, Y. (2005, March 11). "Chairman of the Board and Then Some: Deloitte's Sharon L. Allen." *DiversityInc*, 42–50; Benefits information, http://careers.deloitte.com/culture_benefits.aspx; Sharon Allen Chairman of the Board, Deloitte & Touche, USA, LLP, http://www.deloitte.com/dtt/executive_profile/0,1010,sid%253D%2526cid%253D18657,00.html, accessed 05/13/2005.

women, Wal-Mart Stores and Costco, were recently sued by women alleging systematic sex discrimination. Both cases were filed as class action suits and alleged that although women comprise a large percentage of the companies' overall workforce, they were denied management- and executive-level positions and confined to lower-level, lower-paid jobs in the companies.[45] A visit to or review of the overall employee demographic makeup or organization charts of Wal-Mart, Costco, and numerous other retailers will provide anecdotal evidence of their claims. Many women work for these firms, but primarily as cashiers, clerks, and low-level department managers, rather than store managers and executives.

Sociologist Dana Dunn has compiled data from the U.S. Department of Education and the American Association of University Women in a striking example of diminishing representation of women in the field of education. Upon consideration of their personal educational experiences, readers may easily recall the distribution Dunn describes. At the kindergarten level, 99% of the teachers are women; in elementary and secondary schools, 85% and 52%, respectively, are women (see Table 9.7). Among college and university faculty, the highest percentage of women is at the lowest level: assistant professor (38%), followed by associate professor (25%), and full professor (12%).[46] Clearly, the higher one goes in the educational hierarchy (in position, status, and compensation), the fewer the women at the lectern.[47]

Not only are there fewer women in management than would be expected by their proportion of workers, women who are in management also earn less than men in management. A recent troubling report published by the U.S. General

[45] "Discrimination Suit Filed against Costco." *Dallas Morning News*, Wednesday, August 18, 2004, p. 3D.

[46] Dunn. (1999).

[47] Currently Provost at the University of Texas at Arlington, Dunn is among relatively few women in the highest administrative positions in U.S. colleges and universities.

Accounting Office indicated that wages of women in management had declined in seven of the 10 industries in which women were most highly represented.[48] The industries assessed were entertainment and recreation services; communications, finance, insurance, and real estate; business and repair services; other professional services; retail trade; professional medical services; public administration, hospitals, and medical services; and educational services. The former seven industries are private, while the latter three industries are public industries or are highly regulated. These ten industries employ 71% of women workers and 73% of women managers (which itself is evidence of the crowding of women into a few industries), as we discussed earlier. The report investigated changes in wages between 1995 and 2000 and found that in the seven private industries, wages of women managers declined relative to men's wages. These declines were particularly disturbing in that the period measured was a period of income growth and prosperity. In the communications industry, in 1995, women's wages were 0.85 to each $1.00 earned by men. This figure had declined to 0.73/$1.00 by 2000. Researchers suggest that this retrenchment may be in part due to erroneous beliefs that discrimination is no longer a factor, and that conscious efforts to combat discrimination through formal diversity or affirmative action programs are no longer needed.

As discussed in Chapter 4, the term **glass walls** refers to invisible horizontal barriers that constrain women, people of color, and people with disabilities to certain occupations and positions within organizations. Glass walls confine members of these (and other nondominant) groups to staff (supportive) versus line (decision making with profit and loss responsibility) positions. Occupations heavily dominated by women and people of color include human resources, communications, diversity/affirmative action, and public relations, which are positions that rarely advance to the top management level. In contrast, Whites and males dominate areas such as finance, marketing, and operations, from which executives and chief executive officers are most often selected. Glass walls prevent those constrained by them from obtaining breadth of experience and exposure required for advancement.[49]

The term *glass escalator* refers to men's rapid ascent into management and higher-level positions after entering female-dominated occupations. This anomaly may reflect the well-known general preference for men as managers and leaders and the perception of "think manager, think male." Using large-scale data on income, managerial attainment, and career progress, David Maume, of the University of Cincinnati, has documented empirical evidence of the glass ceiling for women and people of color and the glass escalator for White men.[50] Maume found

---

[48] General Accounting Office. (2002). "A New Look through the Glass Ceiling: Where Are the Women?" *The Status of Women in Management in Ten Selected Industries,* Washington, DC: Author.

[49] Smith, D. (2000). *Women at Work: Leadership for the Next Century,* Upper Saddle River, NJ: Prentice-Hall; Lopez, J. A. (1992, March 3). "Study Says Women Face Glass Walls as well as Ceilings." *Wall Street Journal,* B1–B2.

[50] Maume, D. J., Jr. (1999, November). "Glass Ceilings and Glass Escalators: Occupational Segregation and Race and Sex Differences in Managerial Promotions." *Work and Occupations,* 26 (4): 483–509.

that Black men and women and White women waited longer for the managerial promotions they received and that for men, especially White men, the percentage of women in the occupation positively affected men's chances of moving into a supervisory position. After 12 years of working in a female-dominated area, 44%, 17%, 15%, and 7% of White men, Black men, White women, and Black women, respectively, will likely have been promoted into management.[51] Compelling evidence of glass escalators has been found by other U.S. and international researchers.[52]

Sex, Race, and Ethnicity

Previous sections in this chapter have considered women's experiences compared with men's experiences overall. A thorough consideration of sex, race, and ethnicity must also incorporate differences within group, that is, differences between women and men in different racial and ethnic groups (e.g., White women and Latinas). Problems associated with categorizing "women" into one group have been documented by numerous researchers who note that doing so obscures the many important differences between and among women of various racial and ethnic backgrounds and ignores the multiple effects of racism and sexism.[53] Because of the clear dominance of White men in earnings, organizational status, and level, White men and men of color are categorized into a group far less than women are categorized. The following sections consider these issues.

White Women and Women of Color

As members of the dominant racial group, European American women share some workplace advantages with European American men relative to women of color (and, in some regards, relative to men of color). Differences among women exist in education, participation rates, and employment levels, but generally, White women are advantaged relative to women of color. References in the popular press to women of color being advantaged relative to White women because of their double minority status (e.g., racial and sexual minorities) fuel misperceptions. In addition, individuals sometimes claim to know or have heard of a manager who hired or promoted a woman of color for a particular position because of her double minority status. Rather than being a source of double advantage, however, being a woman and a person of color instead multiplies disadvantages stemming from multiple race

[51] Padavic & Reskin. (2002).

[52] For example, Hultin, M. (2003). "Some Take the Glass Escalator, Some Hit the Glass Ceiling?" *Work and Occupations,* 30(1): 30–61; Goldberg, C. B., Finkelstein, L.M., Perry, E. L., & Konrad, A. M. (2004). "Job and Industry Fit: The Effects of Age and Gender Matches on Career Progress Outcomes." *Journal of Organizational Behavior,* 25: 807–829; Williams, C. L. (1992). "The Glass Escalator: Hidden Advantages for Men in Non-Traditional Occupations." *Social Problems,* 39: 253–267.

[53] See Ferdman, B. (1999). "The Color and Culture of Gender in Organizations: Attending to Race and Ethnicity." In G. N. Powell (Ed.), *Handbook of Gender and Work,* Thousand Oaks, CA: Sage, pp. 17–34.

and gender stereotypes, discrimination, and segregation. An organizational analysis of data regarding beneficiaries of affirmative action, organizational status, level, and income, and returns on educational investment would provide hard evidence against the myth of the "two-fer" advantage of being a woman of color for a particular organization. At a societal level, women of color occupy the lowest-paid, lowest-status jobs of any group, including jobs such as housekeepers (both in homes and in hotels/motels), nursing aides, and cashiers. For example, in New Orleans, hotel maids are likely to be African American and Central American (Hispanic) Blacks; in Houston, they are Mexican, Central, or South Americans; in Seattle, many are Asian Americans; in New York and Miami, many maids are Puerto Ricans. Although European American women also work in female-dominated jobs, they are far less likely to be hotel maids than women of color and instead are more likely to be nurses, elementary school teachers, secretaries, or managers.[54] As shown in Table 9.3 (presented earlier), at nearly all education levels, the earnings of women of color are lower than those of non-Hispanic White women.

Misperception: Women of color receive employment preference over White women because of their "two-fer" status, as sexual and racial minorities.

Reality: White women have benefited most from affirmative action programs, are more likely to be in management, and receive higher returns on their educational investments than women of color.[55]

Another common fallacy about differences between White women and women of color, particularly African American women, is that Black women do not work, preferring instead to draw welfare.[56] As shown in Table 9.4 (presented earlier), participation rates of Black women are higher than women of every racial/ethnic group, including White women. Even so, the combination of gender and racial segregation at work creates multiple disadvantages for women of color.[57] In addition to discrimination in hiring and placement, Black women may experience discrimination and harassment based on both race and sex from managers and peers. In a case settled in December 2002, a Chicago-area company agreed to pay four Black female production workers $155,000 in back pay and attorneys' fees. The EEOC alleged that supervisors and coworkers engaged in egregious harassment such as exposing their buttocks and genitals to the plaintiffs, referring to them

[54] Reskin, B. (1999). "Occupational Segregation by Race and Ethnicity among Women Workers." In I. Browne (Ed.), *Latinas and African American Women at Work*, New York: Russell Sage Foundation, pp. 183–204.

[55] Corcoran, M. (1999). "The Economic Progress of African American Women." In I. Browne (Ed.), *Latinas and African American Women at Work*, New York: Russell Sage Foundation, pp. 35–60.

[56] For a discussion, see Murray, C. (1984). *Losing Ground: American Social Policy, 1950–1980*, New York: Basic Books.

[57] Corcoran, M. (1999); Bound, J., & Dresser, L. (1999). "Losing Ground: The Erosion of the Relative Earnings of African American Women during the 1980s." In I. Browne (Ed.), *Latinas and African American Women at Work*, New York: Russell Sage Foundation, pp. 61–104.

using sexually derogatory terms coupled with racist terms, and twice opening the restroom door and throwing water on a Black woman as she used the restroom.[58]

Similarities and differences in participation rates and earnings of women. As shown in Table 9.4, differences in participation rates exist among women of different groups. Black women have the highest rates of participation followed by White, Asian, and Hispanic women, who are least likely to be employed outside the home. Black women's higher participation rates in part reflect their greater likelihood to be single than other women and, when married, the lower earnings of their Black husbands than White men's earnings. Although White women are slightly less likely to work, when employed, they earn more than Black women, who earn more than Hispanic women. Because of the variation in education and employment among Asian American women, some Asian women have higher mean education and earnings than White women, but receive lower returns on their education than White women (e.g., Japanese, Filipino, and Chinese), while others (e.g., Hmong) have lower education and earnings than White, Black, and some Hispanic women.[59] Overall, women of different racial and ethnic groups earn less their coethnic men although this disparity is greatest for White women (in part due to White men's higher earnings than every other group).[60] Sex-based differences by racial/ethnic group are discussed in greater detail in Chapters 4 to 8.

White Men and Men of Color

White men are easily recognized as having higher earnings and being overrepresented in management and executive positions when compared with all women and with all other men. Black, Latino, Asian, American Indian, and other men are considerably less likely to be in management or executive positions and earn significantly less than White men. White men have more formal education than men of color, especially at higher educational levels, however, when education levels are the same, White men still have higher earnings and employment levels (see Chapter 4). Drawing questions on the relationships between education and earnings for people of different backgrounds, Asian men have higher average education levels but still earn less than White men. Differences among men of different racial and ethnic backgrounds are considered further in the respective chapters.

---

[58] EEOC litigation settlement report, December 2002, http://www.eeoc.gov/litigation/settlements/settlement12-02.html, accessed 11/25/04.

[59] Espiritu, Y. L. (1999). "The Refugees and the Refuge: Southeast Asians in the United States." In A. G. Dworkin & R. J. Dworkin (Eds.), *The Minority Report,* Orlando, FL: Harcourt Brace, pp. 343–363; Schoeni, R. F. (1998). "Labor Market Assimilation of Immigrant Women." *Industrial and Labor Relations Review,* 51: 483–504.

[60] England, P. (2002). "The Sex Gap in Pay." In D. Dunn & P. Dubeck (Eds.), *Workplace/Women's Place: An Anthology* (2nd edition), Los Angeles: Roxbury Publishing, pp. 74–87.

Unique Gender Issues

The following section considers two unique gender issues relevant to diversity in organizations: gender and poverty and women's failure to negotiate pay. Numerous other unique gender issues exist, such as gender differences in participation in the second shift (the extra shift of housework and child care disproportionately performed by working women, after they return home from work—see Chapter 13), differences in managerial women's and men's likelihood of being parents, gender differences in health care, and countless others. Space constraints prevent consideration of every issue; readers are encouraged to continue their own exploration of unique gender issues.

Gender and Poverty

Women's lower rates of participation in the workforce, greater amount of part-time work, and the wage gap negatively affect women (and their families) in the present, their lifetime earnings, and their retirement savings and incomes. Women's longer life expectancies, during which time they may deplete lower retirement savings, have long-term implications for women's poverty levels. Worldwide, women earn about 66% of men's earnings and are about 50% more likely to live in poverty than men.[61] In the United States in 2002, 12.1% of all women lived in poverty, compared with 8.7% of men.[62] Many researchers have studied the "feminization of poverty" and its effects on women and children.[63] Readers may be able to easily think of older women whose current financial situation reflects intermittent or no work outside the home, part-time work, or, as is common of women of color, a lifetime of full-time work in lower paying female-dominated jobs, or being paid in cash, with no Social Security contributions by their employers (e.g., private housekeepers). Featured Case 9.4 provides evidence of how employers' perspective of jobs appropriate for men and women disadvantage women and negatively affect their opportunities for employment and earnings.

Negotiating Pay

Another area in which socialization and gender roles negatively affect working women is in salary negotiation. In an eye-opening book, *Women Don't Ask*, Carnegie-Mellon University economist Linda Babcock and Sara Laschever documented women's failure to negotiate pay, promotions, and raises on their jobs.[64]

[61] http://www.un.org/womenwatch/daw/followup/session/presskit/fs1.htm, accessed 03/29/04.

[62] Caiazza, A., Shaw, A., & Werschkul, M. (2004). *The Status of Women in the States, Women's Economic Status in the States: Wide Disparities by Race, Ethnicity, and Region,* Washington, DC: Institute for Women's Policy Research.

[63] The feminization of poverty as a worldwide problem is discussed at http://www.un.org/womenwatch/daw/followup/session/presskit/fs1.htm, accessed 03/29/04. See also Caiazza et al. (2004).

[64] Babcock, L., & Laschever, S. (2003). *Women Don't Ask,* Princeton, NJ: Princeton University Press.

Featured Case 9.4 *Experienced, Licensed Female Delivery Drivers Need Not Apply*

Performance Food Group (PFG), a food service distributor in the Baltimore-Washington area, refused to hire women as delivery drivers.[65] In 2001, PFG hired 44 men and one woman as drivers. The company's Transportation Manager told the lone woman driver that her performance would determine whether any other women would be hired as drivers. Unfortunately for all future women who hoped to be drivers at PFG, the woman had difficulties, and quit in November of 2001. That same month, another woman (who would ultimately become the "charging party") saw PFG's advertised vacancy seeking delivery drivers and applied for the position. Although she had a commercial driver's license, prior delivery experience, and met all posted criteria for the job, the charging party (CP) was told that PFG would not be hiring any women because of a past bad experience with a female driver. The manager instead offered CP a lower paying warehouse position, which she declined and instead took her case to the EEOC.

During the investigation of the case, an e-mail corroborating the company's position about not hiring women drivers surfaced. The e-mail, from the company's president and addressed to the Transportation manager and HR manager, stated that "I think we have experience that tells us female drivers will not work out." The president concluded that making an offer to women for drivers was "inappropriate."

During the course of the lawsuit, PFG extended unconditional job offers to the charging party and six other women applicants. PFG also agreed to develop defined, uniform, and objective job-related qualifications for the driver and helper positions and to implement consistent job application, recordkeeping, and record retention procedures.

In a very similar case, Ameripride Services, a linen supply company with nearly 200 facilities in the United States and Canada, discriminated against women applicants for Customer Service Representative/Route Sales Driver positions in Idaho.[66] Ameripride advertised for applicants for the positions stating that a Class B commercial license was required. The charging party in the case had a Class B license and six years of commercial driving experience and was selected for a second interview. During the second interview, however, the Area Manager discouraged the charging party from pursuing the position, telling her that all the drivers were men and they had a tendency to use foul language. The Area Manager told the charging party that she looked more like a secretary and encouraged her to consider applying for a secretarial position that would open soon. Although the charging party and two other women applicants had superior qualifications, the Area Manager hired a man, who did not have a Class B license or commercial driving experience, for the position.

Sources: EEOC Litigation Settlement Report, June 2004, http://www.eeoc.gov/litigation/settlements/settlement06-04.html, accessed 09/12/05, and EEOC Litigation Settlement Report, June 2005, http://www.eeoc.gov/litigation/settlements/ settlement06-05.html, accessed 10/20/05.

Questions to Consider

1. ***In Featured Case 9.3 involving a lone female driver at Federal Express, the driver, Marion Shaub, alleged that she was subjected to***

---

[65] *EEOC v. Performance Food Group d/b/a Carroll County Foods, Inc.* No. MJG-03-cv-1698 (D. Md. June 3, 2004). At: http://www.eeoc.gov/litigation/settlements/settlement06-04.html, accessed 09/12/05.

[66] *EEOC v. Ameripride Services, Inc.* No. CV-03-065-S-BLW (D. Idaho June 27, 2005). At http://www.eeoc.gov/litigation/settlements/settlement06-05.html, accessed 10/20/05.

antifemale remarks, threats, and sabotage from her male coworkers. Speculate about the manner in which the 44 men hired by PFG may have treated the lone woman, who ultimately quit PFG. How likely is it that she was helped or trained?

2. *The CEO of PFG used one bad experience with a woman driver as a rationale to avoid hiring any other women drivers.*
   a. *How large of a psychological burden might this have placed on the lone woman driver?*
   b. *Of the 44 men hired, is it likely that one of them was unsuccessful—e.g., a "bad experience"? If so, why have different standards been applied for male and female failures?*
3. *PFG had a job description and the complaining party met all job requirements as listed in the job description, yet she was not hired.*
   a. *Speculate on why "male" was not used as a job requirement, as was done in Featured Case 9.2 (Phoenix Suns), since the hiring managers and PFG believed women were incapable of performing the job.*
   b. *What might be the effects of 1) having and 2) using a legitimate job description on employers' recruitment and selection costs?*
4. *The Area Manager of Ameripride told the charging party that she looked more like a secretary and hired a man without a Class B license or commercial driving experience for the position. Had the Area Manager not made these statements to the charging party, how likely is it she would have been suspicious about the reasons she was not hired? How might she have found out that a man who did not meet stated job requirements was hired?*
5. *Use http://www.salary.com or other salary-estimating Web sites to estimate wage differences between a licensed truck driver, a warehouse worker, and a secretary. What is the difference in annual earnings and percentages between these positions? Estimate the differences in lifetime earnings at an annual salary increase rate of 3%. Estimate differences in Social Security and 401k payments that would be matched by PFG employers between the positions over a 30-year career.*

They argue persuasively that this failure is a result of women's lifelong conditioning to graciously accept what is offered, regardless of whether it differs from what they desire or from what is fair and just. Babcock and Laschever report several empirical studies by Babcock and others indicating that women's failure to ask for what they deserve and employers' perspective that women deserve and will settle for less both contribute to the wage gap. They suggest that women should be taught to assert their needs and wishes more and society should learn to accept rather than penalize women who ask for what they want and deserve. Parents, teachers, and other adults can help young women with learning to ask for what they want. Adult women who know that gender differences in asking for what one deserves can be very costly can learn to do what for them may be uncomfortable, but worth the effort. It is also important to consider the possibility that even when women do negotiate, they may face more resistance than men face.[67] In a similar vein, recall from Chapter 4 that White men's initial offers and final negotiated prices were lower for automobiles than prices quoted to other group members.

[67] Belliveau, M. (2005). "An Offer You Should Refuse: Gender Differences in Job Candidate Counteroffers." *Paper presented at Annual Academy of Management Meeting,* Honolulu, HI.

As part of organizational diversity efforts, managers should make concerted efforts to make comparable, fair salary offers to men and women with similar qualifications and skills rather than using the knowledge that women don't or shouldn't ask as rationales to pay them less. There is no long-term benefit from unfair treatment of any group of workers (or customers) in a competitive, increasingly diverse society. Babcock and Laschever propose that paying women less than they deserve can result in women who are dissatisfied and turn over, causing organizations to lose valued workers and experience other costs associated with dysfunctional turnover. Other researchers have also suggested that women leave organizations that treat them unfairly in compensation, advancement, and other areas, although their departures may often be inaccurately attributed to choices related to family and child care needs.

Individual and Organizational Recommendations

Knowledge of sex and gender issues is an important first step for making changes to address them. Everyone should share what they know about gender disparities with friends, family, and coworkers. Lack of knowledge of the long-term, significant, often negative effects of these issues perpetuates adherence to strict gender roles, denial of the continued need for such programs as affirmative action, and failure to effect change. To reduce salary differences due to having less education, individual women should complete college and obtain advanced degrees, if possible. To avoid pay disparities associated with sex segregation, women should make conscious choices of careers that utilize their interests and skills but that also pay well. Men should encourage individual women to do so and provide them with interpersonal social support and intraorganizational support when they are working with such women. Parents can encourage male and female children in their pursuit of nontraditional occupations and interests. Individuals already employed in sex-segregated occupations can make efforts to improve their earnings and opportunities through researching organizations that value women workers, through additional education and training, and possibly through career change or enhancement. What schools, for example, pay elementary school teachers well? How much more does a registered nurse earn compared with a licensed practical nurse or a physician or certified nurse-practitioner rather than a registered nurse? What skills are possessed that are transferable to better paying jobs?

Women and men managers should mentor women employees, helping them gain job and organization appropriate skills for advancement. Both should recognize the value of women's leadership, negotiation, and team-building skills and encourage their display while also encouraging men to learn and apply those skills.[68] Women should be encouraged to use agentic traits, traditionally associated with

[68] Rosener, J. B. (1995). *America's Competitive Secret: Women Managers,* London: Oxford University Press.

men, such as task orientation, assertiveness, and striving for achievement.[69] Women and men should question sexist behaviors, comments, and innuendoes in their personal and organizational lives.

Organizations play powerful roles in influencing sex discrimination and harassment, the glass ceiling, walls, and sticky floors, intrafirm sex segregation and other gender and diversity issues. As with other issues, committed organizational leadership and vigilance are critical in shaping behaviors and ultimately attitudes. One important systemic change that researchers suggest may be effective is formalized pay structures. In their investigation of earnings differences between men and women, Marta Elvira and Mary Graham found that having less formalized pay types (e.g., cash incentive bonuses) resulted in greater salary differences than in more formalized pay types (e.g., merit raises and base salary).[70] They found these differences in a sample of more than 8,000 employees of a large financial services organization. Elvira and Graham suggested that incentive bonuses "may widen the earnings gap between women and men, and have implications for the design of pay structures in organizations."[71] These findings support those of Castilla, discussed in Chapter 7, that indicated the need for careful attention to pay differences over time between dominant and non-dominant group members. Castilla found differences in pay increases and salary growth despite equal performance ratings.

The presence of women in managerial and leadership positions is of particular importance to gender issues at work. Again, the discussion is limited to two areas and readers are encouraged to further investigate other areas of influence.

Curbing Sexual Harassment

Women are 85% of harassment targets and perpetrators in about 7% of harassment cases. Of the men who experience harassment (14 to 15% of cases), most are harassed by *other men.* Thus, both quid pro quo and hostile environment harassment are less likely when there are women in managerial and supervisory roles. Because women are less likely to perpetrate harassment than are men, quid pro quo harassment is less likely when there are significant numbers of women managers. Having women as managers should also reduce hostile environment harassment. Research indicates that women reporting to male supervisors experience more harassment than women working for women managers and that women with male supervisors perceived their employers as being more tolerant of sexual harassment.[72]

[69] Nelson, T. D. (2002). *The Psychology of Prejudice,* Boston, MA: Allyn & Bacon.

[70] Elvira, M. M., & Graham, M. E. (2002). "Not Just a Formality: Pay System Formalization and Sex-Related Earnings Effects." *Organization Science,* 13(6): 601–617.

[71] Ibid, p. 601.

[72] Hulin, C. L., Fitzgerald, L. F., & Drasgow, F. (1996). "Organizational Influences on Sexual Harassment." In M. S. Stockdale (Ed.), *Sexual Harassment in the Workplace,* Vol 5, Thousand Oaks, CA: Sage, pp. 127–150; Piotrkowski, C. S. (1998). "Gender Harassment, Job Satisfaction, and Distress among Employed White and Minority Women." *Journal of Occupational Health Psychology,* 3: 33–43.

Researchers have also found that women and men view hostile environment harassment differently. Certain behaviors that men view as inoffensive, women view as offensive and harassing. These differences suggest that women as managers would view harassing behaviors similar to other, nonmanagerial women. With appropriate support and a zero tolerance policy, managerial women may be well equipped to recognize and curb harassment in their departments and organizations.

The best prescription for sexual harassment may be one of prevention, rather than remedial efforts after harassment has occurred.[73] All employees should receive regular training that clarifies acceptable and unacceptable workplace behavior, reporting channels, and appropriate responses. Sexual harassment training has been shown to increase understanding of what constitutes harassment and reduce uncertainty about what is and what is not harassment.[74] Managers and supervisors should be made aware of their responsibilities in harassment prevention and those who are harassed should not suffer in silence. The organization's sexual harassment policy should be widely and clearly communicated, such that the organization's position on harassment is clear to those who would harass and those who might be harassed. Charges of harassment and informal complaints should be promptly investigated and addressed, with appropriate sanctions as indicated. Chapter 2 provides other details about sexual harassment charges, lawsuits, settlements, and prevention.

Breaking the Glass Ceiling

Several steps are recommended to help remove the glass ceiling. Rather than focusing on helping women "break through" the glass ceiling, which suggests personal failures among women who do not advance, formidable institutional obstacles to women in mid- to upper-management must be dismantled. These barriers include the "old-boys'" network through which information about key positions and assignments is disseminated and employment decisions are made; perceptions that women's leadership styles are inconsistent with management; lip service, but no accountability for advancing women; selection, appraisal, and compensation systems that disadvantage women; cultural discouragement (e.g., environmental cultures that reward face time over performance); and sex discrimination and harassment that serve to remove women from organizations.[75] Executive level

[73] For a discussion of the merits and attributes of a preventive program, see Bell, M. P., Quick, J. C., & Cycycota, C. (2002). "Assessment and Prevention of Sexual Harassment: Creating Healthy Organizations." *International Journal of Selection and Assessment,* 21: 160–167.

[74] Antecol, H., & Cobb-Clark, D. (2003). "Does Sexual Harassment Training Change Attitudes? A View from the Federal Level." *Social Science Quarterly,* 84(4): 826–843.

[75] Mattis, M. C. (2002). "Best Practices for Retaining and Advancing Women Professionals and Managers." In R. C. Burke & D. L. Nelson (Eds.), *Advancing Women's Careers,* Oxford, UK: Blackwell Publishers, pp. 309–332.

women report having to repeatedly outperform men to be considered for high-level positions and having to reestablish credibility with each new assignment.[76] Organizational commitment must precede in-depth organizational analysis of these factors and others unique to the organization that impede women's progress. This analysis must be followed with interventions for change, follow-up, and continued analysis and monitoring.

Women managers may be particularly well equipped to assist in dismantling the glass ceiling. Researchers have found that having more women in management helped other women to advance into top management and that having fewer women in management is related to greater intentions to quit and actual turnover. A few women in power, coupled with men in power who also support gender equity and see value in diversity, may make significant progress.

Summary

Most adult women and men work outside the home, including women with children. Women who work full-time, year-round earn about 70% of the income that men working full-time, year-round earn. Women overall have slightly less education than men, although younger women have more education than men, which should affect the male/female wage gap and workforce participation rates in the future. Men and women work in different occupations, and this segregation contributes to the pay gap. Laws passed since the 1960s have improved women's employment, status, and pay, yet many disparities remain. Organizational efforts to reduce gender inequity and commitment to gender diversity are vital to continued progress.

Key Terms

Coethnic — from the same race or ethnic group.

Gender role socialization — the process by which social institutions, including families, friends, organizations, and the media, form and shape expectations of acceptable behaviors for males and females.

Sex segregation — when members of one sex constitute 70% or more of the incumbents of a job.

Wage gap — differences in wages between groups of workers.

Questions to Consider

1. Are participation rates for women with and without children different from what you would have estimated prior to reading this chapter? Why is the perception that women with children will leave the workforce and are uncommitted workers so prevalent?
2. What is the role of socialization in women's and men's "choices" of occupations and how do these relationships affect sex segregation and the wage gap?

[76] Ragins, B. R., Townsend, B., & Mattis, M. (1998). "Gender Gap in the Executive Suite: CEOs and Female Executives Report on Breaking the Glass Ceiling." *Academy of Management Executive,* 12: 28–42.

3. What are some specific individual and organizational steps that could help reduce sex segregation?
4. How are the participation rates, workplace experiences, income, occupations, and poverty of White women and women of color similar and dissimilar? Why are erroneous perceptions about the similarities and differences among these groups so pervasive?
5. Prior to reading this chapter, had you heard of the "glass escalator"? Are you aware of a situation in which a man is the manager or supervisor of a group of women employees?
6. What can individual women do to reduce the influence of sex and gender discrimination on their careers?
7. What is one thing you learned from this chapter about diversity that is most surprising to you?

Actions and Exercises

1. Interview a person who is employed in a sex-atypical occupation (for example, a male dental hygienist or female professor of business or engineering in a tenure-track position at a college or university). What factors affected his or her career decision? What background experiences and/or educational requirements were needed for his or her to qualify for this particular job? What were the reactions of families, friends, and coworkers? What diversity-related experiences have stood out for him or her at work?
2. Conduct a survey of at least 10 working professionals. How many men versus women negotiated their starting salary? How many were successful in their negotiations? How much, if any, was the increase in salary after the negotiations? When comparing the results for men and women, are any differences apparent?
3. Create an informal organization chart of the organization in which you work or with which you can gather information. Is there evidence of the glass ceiling, walls, and/or escalators in this organization?
4. Construct a table of five jobs that are sex segregated, excluding those listed in Table 9.6, but that have comparable or similar jobs for both sexes. In addition to wages, compile differences in education, training, and/or experience required for those jobs. What factors do you think are responsible for the continued sex segregation of these jobs? What might be done to change the levels of sex segregation in these jobs?
5. Table 9.7 shows large differences in the percent women and wages in the teaching position. These differences are even worse when wages of men and women and public/private teachers in elementary and secondary school positions are compared. Use http://www.census.gov/prod/2004pubs/03statab/educ.pdf (or access a different site where these data are available), Tables 249 (public schools), and 263 (private schools) to make a chart comparing these for men and women for the most current data available. Speculate on why these differences might exist.
6. Begin observing women in organizations. What evidence do you observe of gender and race-based segregation? Where are women clustered? Are women of color in different positions than White women?

10 Chapter

Religion

Chapter Objectives

After completing this chapter, readers should have a greater understanding of religion as an aspect of diversity in organizations. Specifically, readers should:

- *understand the history of religious diversity in the United States.*
- *be able to discuss legislation related to religious diversity and selected EEOC cases involving religious discrimination.*
- *understand relationships between religious organizations and gender diversity among organizational leaders.*
- *discuss ways in which employers can accommodate religious practices of employees and applicants.*
- *examine ways employers may deal with conflicts among employees' different religious beliefs.*

Key Facts

Employers are required to make reasonable accommodations for employees' religious practices, much like reasonable accommodations for people with disabilities.

Harassment of Muslims increased tremendously in the United States after the terrorist attacks of 9/11/2001.

In a similar ratio to the religious leanings of the entire American population, 75% of Arab Americans are Christian.

Women clergy experience a "stained glass ceiling" in religious organizations that is similar to the glass ceiling in other organizations.

Employees may post religious sayings in their workspaces, as long as they are of a size that is reasonable for personal viewing, but posting large religious sayings that target specific groups (e.g., gays) can be grounds for dismissal.

Introduction and Overview

In this chapter, we consider religion as an aspect of diversity. Although religion is one of the specific areas included in Title VII of the Civil Rights Act, it has received considerably less research and media attention when compared with other protected areas. In recent years, religious diversity has grown in importance, partly due to increasing immigration to the United States and to fears of terrorism, which have increased overt discrimination against Muslims or those perceived to be Muslims. In addition to prohibiting religious discrimination, Title VII outlaws harassment and requires employers make reasonable accommodations to allow employees to observe their religious practices.

We begin the chapter with a brief view of the history of religious diversity. We then consider the population representation of religious groups in the United States and legislation related to religion. The standard topical areas of education, earnings, and workforce participation rates are not germane to religious diversity and are not included. Because they often occur concurrently, we consider the relationship between religious discrimination and national origin discrimination in this chapter, also examining misperceptions about Arab Americans and Muslims. Although the diversity of religions in the United States prevents detailed explorations of multiple groups, we do focus on Arabs (most of whom are Christians) and Muslims because of the negativity and hostility toward members of these groups at this time. We also explore misperceptions about religious and sexual orientation diversity, providing suggestions for organizations wishing to provide employees with conflicting beliefs with a discrimination-free workplace.

History of Religious Diversity in the United States

Since the colonies were founded, the United States has been a predominantly Protestant nation and Protestant beliefs have dominated the country's history, courts, and many organizations.[1] The pledge of allegiance includes the phrase "one nation, under God." "In God we trust" is visible on U.S. currency. Elected officials are commonly sworn in with "so help me God." Some of the subgroups of Protestants that have long histories in the United States include Baptists, Methodists, Lutherans, and Presbyterians.

Other religious adherents in the United States have historically been significantly smaller than Protestants, yet they have still played important roles in U.S. history. Such groups include Roman Catholics, Jews,[2] Muslims, Buddhists, and Hindus, among numerous others. The arrival of Irish and French Catholics to the country "curdled the blood" of Protestant colonialists, who viewed Catholicism "as a religious and political threat."[3] The first Jews arrived in the United States

[1] Smith, T. W., & Kim, S. (2005). "The Vanishing Protestant Majority." *Journal for the Scientific Study of Religion,* 44(2): 211–223.

[2] Jews are an ethnic group that experiences religious as well as ethnic discrimination.

[3] Archdeacon, T. J. (1983). *Becoming American,* New York: Free Press, p. 21.

in 1654 from Europe where they had experienced isolation and expulsion.[4] In 1776, 2,500 Jews lived in the United States; by 1870, there were 200,000 Jews, mostly of German origin.[5] Many other religious minorities came to the United States seeking, but not always finding, refuge from religious persecution elsewhere. For example, during certain periods in U.S. history, Jews could not hold political office and Catholics could not practice their faith or hold office, and were heavily taxed.[6] In storefronts, signs notifying Jews and Catholics (and Blacks) that they were unwelcome were common. Along with persecution by Protestants, religious discrimination among nondominant religions themselves existed.

Population and Variations among Beliefs

As in the past, the majority of the U.S. population continues to identify themselves as Christian—about 77%. This figure has declined from 86% in 1990, however.[7] As shown in Table 10.1, the largest single group of Christians is Catholics (24.5%), followed by Baptists (16.3%). Slightly more than 1% of the adults in the United States report being Jewish, and 0.5% each are Muslims and Buddhists.

Because the U.S. population is overwhelmingly Christian, but a nontrivial one quarter is not, the potential for conflict between groups exists. In addition, even though most Americans are Christian, there is diversity of beliefs among Christian organizations, often regarding women's roles, and, as we discuss later, sexual orientation. Religious organizations themselves are some of the most homogenous types of organizations, with primarily male leadership and little racial and ethnic diversity within individual entities. An estimated 1% of Blacks, for example, worship in primarily White religious organizations.[8]

Race, Ethnicity, and Religion

The American Religious Identification survey, conducted by researchers at the City University of New York, provides insightful data on the variation in religious and secular identification by race, ethnicity, age, and sex.[9] Blacks (81%), Whites (77%), Hispanics (75%), and Asians (62%) are most to least likely to

[4] Schaefer, R. T. (2002). *Racial and Ethnic Groups* (8th edition), Princeton, NJ: Prentice-Hall.

[5] Ibid.

[6] Archdeacon. (1983).

[7] American Religious Identification Survey. (2001). The Graduate Center, the City University of New York, http://www.gc.cuny.edu/faculty/research_briefs/aris/key_findings.htm, accessed 10/01/05.

[8] Schaefer. (2002).

[9] American Religious Identification Survey. (2001). The Graduate Center, the City University of New York, http://www.gc.cuny.edu/faculty/research_briefs/aris/key_findings.htm, accessed 09/22/05.

Table 10.1 ***Religious Groups in the United States (Age 18 and Older)***

Christian Groups	
Catholic	24.5%
Baptist	16.3%
Christian (no denomination specified)	6.8%
Methodist/Wesleyan	6.8%
Lutheran	4.6%
Other >1%[*] + Other = or >0.3%[†] + Other <0.3%[‡]	17.5%
Total Christian	76.5%
Other Religious Groups	
Jewish	1.3%
Muslim/Islam	0.5%
Buddhist	0.5%
Other <0.5 and >0.3%[§]	1.2%
Total other religions	3.7%
No Religion Groups	
Agnostic	0.5%
Atheist	0.4%
Those who stated "no religion"	13.2%
Total no religion specified[¶]	14.1%

*Other >1%: Presbyterian, Pentecostal/Charismatic, Protestant, Nondenominational, Episcopalian/Anglican, Mormon/Latter-Day Saints, Churches of Christ.
†Other = or >0.3%: Jehovah's Witness, Seventh-Day Adventist, Assemblies of God, Church of God, Holiness/Holy, Congregational/United Church of Christ, Church of the Nazarene.
‡Others <0.3%: Disciples of Christ, Church of the Brethren, Mennonite, Orthodox (Eastern), Quaker, Reformed/Dutch Reform, and many others.
§Other <0.5 and >0.3%: Hindu, Unitarian, Universalist, Other (examples): Pagan, Wiccan, Spiritualist, Native American, Baha'I, New Age, Sikh, Scientologist, Taoist, Deity, Druid, Eckankar, Santaria, Rastafarian.
¶Smaller representation groups include Humanist, Secular, and others.

Source: Adapted from teaching about religion with a view to diversity, http://www.teachingaboutreligion.org/Demographics/map_demographics.htm, accessed 03/01/05.

regard themselves as religious or very religious. In contrast, Asians (30%), Whites (17%), Hispanics (16%), and Blacks (11%) are most to least likely to view themselves as secular or somewhat secular. Women are more religious than men, with 78% of women reporting being religious or very religious, compared with 72% of men. Older adults are more religious than younger adults; 78% of people ages 35 to 64 are religious or very religious, compared with 70% of those aged 18 to 34. We consider relationships between reported religiosity and attitudes toward sexual minorities later in the chapter.

The American Religious Identification Survey highlights the "multilayered nature of social identity" as it relates to religion, particularly for Hispanics and Jews.[10] The majority of Hispanics (57%) are Catholic, but 22% are Protestant, 12% report no religion, and 5% identify themselves as belonging to some other religion.[11] Common assumptions that Hispanics are Catholic are erroneous for a significant portion of the Hispanic population.

Among American Jews, "Jewish identity" reflects religious, ethnic, and cultural elements, and not everyone who is Jewish identifies with all three elements. Of the population that self-identifies as Jewish, 53% identify with Judaism as a religion, while 47% identify with Judaism because their parents were Jewish, they were raised Jewish, or for some other reason. As discussed in Chapter 7, at one point Jews in the United States were viewed as a separate "race." Overt actions of the government, such as veterans' educational and housing benefits, helped in the "transformation" of Jews to Whites.[12] While 92% of Jews are White, 5% are Hispanic, and 1% each are Black, Asian, and some other race, Jews still experience differential treatment of various forms. In her research on the effects of disclosing invisible stigmas, Belle Rose Ragins of the University of Wisconsin-Milwaukee retells the experience of a Jewish business school professor at a Catholic university:

> My mother told me not to take a job at a Catholic university. She told me they'd fire me once they found out that I'm Jewish. I thought she was so old school, until my first day on the job. The ex-Dean told me that he moved from a neighborhood because "there were too many Jews there." I decided not to tell anyone I was Jewish. But then my colleagues became my friends, and one day I found myself putting up Christmas ornaments before they came over. I was denying who I was in my very own home. So I decided to come out of the "Jewish closet" at work. I found out later that the Provost kept a list of Jewish faculty. He added me to the list.[13,14]

The invisibility of the professor's religion provided the opportunity to let his or her religion remain unknown, yet doing so came with the negative consequence of denying an important aspect of identity. As with people of color and gays and lesbians who "pass," religious minorities suffer the stress and worry that their stigmatized identity may be found out, along with guilt and confusion about the denial. Religious minorities may have common in-group status with those in the majority, such as race, or sex, but at times, religious differences are more salient than areas of commonality.

---

[10] "Religion and Identity: Hispanics and Jews." *American Religious Identification Survey,* http://www.gc.cuny.edu/faculty/research_briefs/aris/religion_identity.htm, accessed 09/22/05. See also Exhibit 13 for race and ethnicity by religion.

[11] Ibid.

[12] Brodkin, K. (1998). *How Jews Became White Folks & What That Says About Race in America,* New Brunswick, NJ: Rutgers University Press.

[13] Ragins, B. R. (In press). "Disclosure Disconnects: Antecedents and Consequences of Disclosing Invisible Stigmas across Life Domains." *Academy of Management Review.*

[14] Leaders of some religious universities (including many Catholic universities) welcome faculty and students of different faiths, believing this enriches the institution and learning.

Legislation

In the United States, laws require that individuals with different beliefs recognize the rights of others to their own religious practices and to a nondiscriminatory workplace. Title VII of the Civil Rights Act of 1964 prohibits employers of 15 people or more from discrimination against employees or applicants in hiring, firing, and other terms and conditions of employment because of their religious beliefs or practices. A person cannot be forced to participate in or prohibited from participating in a religious activity as a condition of employment. Protections from religious discrimination are similar to protections from discrimination on the basis of having a disability and freedom from sexual harassment at work.

Misperception: Inviting a coworker to attend worship services is illegal.

Reality: Pressuring a coworker to attend worship services is illegal.

As under the Americans with Disabilities Act, covered employers should make reasonable accommodations without undue hardship to allow employees to observe their normal religious practices. Reasonable accommodations include such things as flexible scheduling, job reassignments and lateral transfers, and modifying workplace practices when doing so does not pose an undue hardship on the organization's legitimate business interests. Undue hardship varies by employer, and there is no set practice or request that is deemed to be an instance of undue hardship. If, for an individual employer, accommodating an employee's religious beliefs would result in excessive costs of administration, diminished efficiency, or excessive burden to coworkers, a claim of undue hardship would be warranted. What would be considered an excessive cost of administration would differ between a small employer having 30 employees and an organization employing thousands of workers. Similarly, for an organization that operates 24 hours per day, 7 days a week, an accommodation of an employee's request for a particular day off to observe his or her religious practices would be different from a similar request for an organization that was open fewer hours and days per week.

Misperception: A request for Saturdays off to worship is undue hardship for retailers.

Reality: A Saturday Sabbath could be traded for a Sunday workday for organizations that are open 7 days per week.

In one such case in which an accommodation was warranted, Carol Grotts, a practicing Pentecostal, instead experienced religious discrimination.[15] Grotts was

[15] Brinks to Pay $30,000 to Peoria Area Woman for Failure to Accommodate Religious Beliefs, http://www.eeoc.gov/press/1-2-03b.html, accessed 10/07/04.

hired as a relief messenger by Brinks security and was given a standard issue uniform that included pants. Because her religion did not allow her to wear pants, Grotts asked to be allowed to wear culottes (a split skirt) made from the same material, at her expense. Brinks refused and terminated Grotts. After the EEOC filed suit, Brinks rehired her and allowed her to wear the culottes. In addition to a $30,000 settlement and attorneys' fees, Brinks was also required to train all managers about such discrimination and the need to accommodate employees' religious beliefs.

Along with reasonable accommodation, as with sexual harassment, employees have a right to a workplace that is free of religious harassment. Employers are encouraged to have an antiharassment policy that explicitly includes religious harassment and to have an effective procedure for reporting harassment. Employees who report harassment should be assured of a prompt, fair investigation, appropriate consequences where warranted, and freedom from retaliation for having complained.

EEOC Guidelines on Religious Exercise and Religious Expression in the Federal Workplace

Also similar to its guidelines on sexual harassment, the EEOC has issued guidelines on religious exercise and religious expression.[16] The guidelines were written for federal workplaces, but are quite useful to private employers as well, providing recommendations for handling such issues as display of religious materials, wearing religious jewelry, inviting coworkers to religious services, harassment, and accommodations. The focus of the EEOC's guidelines on religious exercise is treating "all employees with the same respect and consideration, regardless of their religion (or lack thereof)."

Charges and Selected Cases under Title VII

In 2004, the EEOC received 2,466 charges alleging religious discrimination and resolved 2,676 charges of such discrimination (including charges from previous years). As with other charges of discrimination, the claimant is unlikely to prevail; 19.2% of resolved charges were merit resolutions. Nonetheless, $6.0 million was recovered for charging parties and other aggrieved individuals.[17]

As shown in Table 10.2, since the terrorist acts of 9/11/2001, settlements with the EEOC for employment discrimination based on religion, ethnic origin, or national origin have increased from pre-9/11 levels, peaking at $48.1 million in 2001. In October 2001, the EEOC issued specific statements regarding such discrimination, reiterating that it was prohibited by Title VII of the Civil Rights

[16] Guidelines on Religious Exercise and Religious Expression in the Federal Workplace, http://clinton2.nara.gov/WH/New/html/19970819-3275.html, accessed 03/24/05.

[17] Religious Discrimination, http://www.eeoc.gov/types/religion.html, accessed 02/28/05.

TABLE 10.2 ***EEOC Settlements for Religious and National Origin Discrimination 1999–2004 in Millions of Dollars***

	1999	2000	2001	2002	2003	2004
Religion monetary settlements	3.1	5.5	14.1	4.3	6.6	6.0
National origin monetary settlements	19.7	15.7	48.1	21.0	21.3	22.3

Source: "Religion-Based Charges FY 1992–2004." *The US Equal Employment Opportunity Commission,* http://www.eeoc.gov/stats/religion.html, accessed 09/22/05.

Act of 1964. Employers and unions were encouraged to be "particularly sensitive" to discrimination against or harassment of persons who are, or are perceived to be, Muslim, Arab, Afghani, Middle Eastern, or South Asian (e.g., Pakistani, Indian, etc.).[18] Despite prohibitions against religious, ethnic, and national origin harassment, cases filed with the EEOC indicate that they still occur, often concurrently. The cases presented below, drawn verbatim from the EEOC Web site, are examples of harassment against members of different religious groups, under varied circumstances.

Selected cases.

- **EEOC v. Pilot Travel Centers LLC[19]**

  No. 2:03-0106 (M.D. Tenn. Apr. 9, 2004)

  The Memphis District Office filed this Title VII action, alleging that a travel center in Cookeville, Tennessee discriminated against a maintenance employee on the basis of religion (Messianic Christian) when it discharged him for refusing to shave his beard, which he wore as part of his religious practices. Defendant's general manager had hired CP and reasonably accommodated him by permitting him to wear his beard despite the company's "no-beard" policy. However, when defendant's regional manager discovered CP working with a beard, he directed the general manager to fire him.

- **EEOC v. DWW Partner's LLP d/b/a Right Honda[20]**

  No. CIV 03-067 PHX VAM (D. Ariz. April 18, 2003)

  The Phoenix District Office alleged in this Title VII lawsuit that defendant, an owner/operator of two car dealerships, subjected charging party, a car salesman

[18] Employment Discrimination Based on Religion, Ethnicity, or Country of Origin. The U.S. Equal Employment Opportunity Commission. http://www.eeoc.gov/facts/fs-relig_ethnic.html, accessed 03/7/05.

[19] EEOC Litigation Settlements—April 2004, http://www.eeoc.gov/litigation/settlements/settlement04-04.html, accessed 12/18/04.

[20] EEOC Litigation Settlements—April 2003, http://www.eeoc.gov/litigation/settlements/settlement04-03.html, accessed 12/19/04.

who is a Jehovah's Witness, to a hostile working environment because of his religious beliefs. As a Jehovah's Witness, charging party does not salute the U.S. flag, say the pledge of allegiance or swear his allegiance to the U.S. or the state of Arizona. Because of his religious beliefs, charging party was regularly harassed by managers and co-workers throughout his five months of employment. The harassment culminated in a verbal and physical assault by two managers which occurred after the men objected to the way charging party brought down the U.S. flag from the dealership's flagpole. After threatening charging party with termination and verbally harassing him because of his religious practices relating to the U.S. flag, two managers grabbed him and one of them placed him into a headlock while the other punched him repeatedly in the shoulders and ribs with his fists. After the assault, charging party quit his job because he feared for his safety. Defendant initially fired the managers involved in the assault but later rehired at least one of them.

- **EEOC v. Sykes Enterprises, Inc.**[21]
  No. 02-M-0957 (OES) (D. Col. Aug. 3, 2004)

  The Denver District Office filed this Title VII lawsuit, alleging that defendant refused to provide charging party a reasonable accommodation for her Christian belief that she could not provide technical support to violent computer games, and then discharged her because of this religious belief. CP had worked for defendant a little over two years when she was assigned to a customer account, GTI, that required her to provide support services for video games with violent depictions that she considered vile and pornographic. CP told her supervisor that the "trash" in the computer was an abomination in the eyes of God and that for moral and ethical reasons she could not support the account. Defendant told CP there were no opening (sic) for technicians on other accounts and that she had to work on the GTI account or be fired. Defendant then fired CP for refusing to work on the account.

- **EEOC v. Poggenpohl, U.S., Inc.**[22]
  No. 03-6190 (LTS) (S.D.N.Y. July 2, 2004)

  In this Title VII case, the New York District Office alleged that a United States subsidiary of a German company that designs high-scale kitchen cabinets subjected charging party, an Egyptian Muslim, to a hostile work environment based on her national origin and religion, and discharged her because she complained about the harassment. CP worked for defendant for 20 years in its

---

[21] EEOC Litigation Settlements—August 2004, http://www.eeoc.gov/litigation/settlements/settlement08-04.html, accessed 12/18/04.

[22] EEOC Litigation Settlements—July 2004, http://www.eeoc.gov/litigation/settlements/settlement07-04.html, accessed 12/18/04.

Middle Eastern location, and in November 1999 became the Operations and Administration manager for the company's midtown Manhattan showroom. During her New York employment, CP was harassed on a daily basis about her Middle Eastern background and Islamic religion by a coworker, and the harassment escalated following the events of September 11, 2001. The coworker cursed and threatened CP, mocked her accent and language, called her names such as "Mrs. Osama bin Laden" and "Mrs. Taliban," and made offensive comments indicating that she wished people from Arab countries "would be killed . . . like the Americans did to the Native Americans." Stating that the offending coworker was one of its best salespersons and brought in a lot of money for the company, defendant's president failed to take prompt or effective action to stop the harassment. Instead, a week after CP wrote a letter to defendant's vice president complaining about the coworker's conduct, defendant discharged CP for violating its no-cursing policy, even though it offered no instance of when she violated the policy, and for poor performance despite her clean work history.

- **EEOC v. Bombardier Aerospace Corp.**[23]
  No. 3-CV-1904-M (N.D. Tex. April 15, 2005)

  The Dallas District Office alleged in this Title VII suit that defendant, a Montreal-based aerospace company that manufactures Lear jets, discriminated against charging party (one of the company's 17 regional sales directors) due to his religion, Mormon, and then fired him in retaliation for complaining about the discrimination. Charging party was hired in May 2001 and received a positive annual performance appraisal in June 2002. In late June or early July 2002, charging party's supervisor learned that he was a Mormon. On July 17, 2002, the head of sales (to whom both charging party and his supervisor reported) told charging party that his Mormon faith hurt his ability to sell jets because he could not drink and smoke with customers. On August 4, 2002, charging party notified the Human Resources Department about the head of sales' comments. Defendant terminated charging party on August 12, 2002, without giving any explanation.

These cases are examples of the many ways that employers' actions can result in illegal religious discrimination, such as by physical appearance requirements, prescribed attire, requiring an employee to work on materials that were objectionable under her religion, stereotypical assumptions, and religion-based assault and threats. Affected employees were from different faiths, including Messianic Christian, Pentecostal, Jehovah's Witness, Mormon, and Egyptian Muslim, and all were protected from discrimination in employment. Each case was resolved by

[23] EEOC Litigation Settlements—April 2005, http://www.eeoc.gov/litigation/settlements/settlement04-05.html, accessed 06/07/05.

a monetary settlement (ranging from $62,400 to $162,500), implementation of policies prohibiting and reporting harassment, training of employees and managers, and other remedies.

ARAB AMERICANS AND MUSLIMS IN THE UNITED STATES

The Arab-American Institute (AAI) estimates that there are 3.5 million Americans with some Arab heritage. Most Arab Americans and Muslims do not support terrorist activities and are law-abiding U.S. citizens. Muslims, followers of Islam, generally eschew violence. Many other contrasts exist between common perceptions about Arab Americans and reality. Eighty percent of Arab Americans are U.S. citizens and only 24% are Muslims.[24] Most Arab Americans are not Muslims and most Muslims are not Arab Americans.[25] Muslims are from various racial and ethnic groups: 34% are Asian, 27% are African American, 15% are White, 10% are Hispanic, and 14% report other racial/ethnic origins.[26] Consistent with other blanket assumptions and generalizations applied to groups, anti-Arab and anti-Muslim stereotypes are often based on erroneous assumptions.

Misperception: Most Arab Americans are Muslim.

Reality: The majority of Arab Americans are Christian.

Racial Profiling against Arabs (or People Who Look as Though They Might Be Arab)

The irrational subheading appropriately depicts the confusion in attitudes and actions associated with profiling. As discussed in previous chapters, profiling is using someone's real or perceived demographic characteristic to single her or him out for scrutiny. As also discussed previously, profiling against African Americans and Latinos is a concern in the United States.[27] Since the 2001 terrorist attacks on the U.S. Pentagon and the World Trade Center, profiling of Arabs, Muslims, and people who look as though they might be either or both has become an increased concern. The term "flying while brown" refers to the numerous instances in which law-abiding Middle Easterners (often long-term residents or

---

[24] Arab American Demographics, http://www.aaiusa.org/demographics.htm, accessed 03/28/05.

[25] "Profile of the U.S. Muslim Population." (2001). *American Religious Identification Survey, Report No. 2, October, 2001.* The Graduate Center, The City University of New York, http://www.gc.cuny.edu/faculty/research_briefs/aris/key_findings.htm, accessed 10/03/05.

[26] American Religious Identification Survey. (2001). The Graduate Center, the City University of New York, Exhibit 13, http://www.gc.cuny.edu/faculty/research_briefs/aris/key_findings.htm, accessed 10/03/05.

[27] Heumann, M., & Cassak, L. (2003). *Good Cop, Bad Cop: Racial Profiling and Competing Views of Justice,* New York: Peter Lang Publishers. See also Bennett, W., Dilulio, J., & Walters, J. (1996). *Body Count,* New York: Simon & Schuster.

U.S. citizens) were repeatedly questioned or removed from planes. Research indicates that Americans of all racial and ethnic backgrounds (including Arab Americans) are uncomfortable with profiling but are also uncomfortable at the thought of boarding a plane with someone Middle Eastern.

As with other forms of discriminatory behavior toward customers, profiling can be expensive and counterproductive. American, Delta, Continental, Northwest, and United Airlines have all been charged with discrimination against customers of Middle Eastern descent. In response to widely reported profiling, the CEO of Delta Airlines insisted that employees' behavior should be based on customers' conduct rather than on their race or national origin.[28]

Feature 10.1 presents questions drawn from the EEOC Web site to help employers and employees avoid religious and national origin discrimination. The focus on discrimination against Muslims, Arabs, and Middle and Southeast Asians reflects the relative frequency of such discrimination in the United States since September 2001.

Work-Related Requirements of Selected Religious Groups

In this section, we consider the attire, prayer, or worship requirements of Muslims, Sikhs, Jews, and Rastafarians that may require accommodation at work. Space constraints prohibit thorough discussion of each possible requirement or each of countless religions practiced. We recommend employers listen to and make attempts to reasonably accommodate the requests of employees and applicants to observe their religious practices.

Many of those who practice Islam pray five times per day and two of the prayers must occur within a specific time period. Washing stations before prayer are needed, as well as a place to kneel and face Mecca. On Fridays, midday prayers are done collectively, and this may require employees take time to go to a local mosque. Muslim women often wear a hijab that may cover the entire head and face, leaving only the eyes exposed, or it may cover only the hair.[29] In 2003, Electrolux, the world's largest producer of appliances and equipment for kitchens, cleaning, and outdoor use, reached a voluntary resolution with the EEOC involving Muslim Somali employees and their ability to pray while at work.[30]

Sikh men, often confused with Muslims, wear distinctly visible religious attire, part of the "articles of faith" as evidence of their religion and to unify them.[31] The five articles of faith are: Kesh (uncut hair, covered by a turban),

[28] Polakow-Suransky, S. (2001, November). "Flying While Brown." *The American Prospect,* 12(20).

[29] Harris, G. (2004), "Religious Diversity and the Workplace," http://www.pluralism.org/research/profiles/display.php?profile=73543, accessed 07/04/05.

[30] EEOC and Electrolux Reach Voluntary Settlement in Class Religious Accommodation Case, http://www.eeoc.gov/press/9-24-03.html, accessed 07/04/05.

[31] Harris. (2004).

ASSIGNMENT #3

FEATURE 10.1 *Questions and Answers about Religious and National Origin Discrimination*

In an attempt to reduce employment discrimination against Muslims or those perceived to be Muslim, the EEOC has developed questions and answers and other guidelines to help applicants, employees, and employers. Immediately following are employer questions and answers. After reading them, read the applicant and employee questions that follow and provide your own suggested answers.

Employer Questions and Answers[32]

Hiring and Other Employment Decisions

Narinder, a South Asian man who wears a Sikh turban, applies for a position as a cashier at XYZ Discount Goods. XYZ fears Narinder's religious attire will make customers uncomfortable. What should XYZ do?

XYZ should not deny Narinder the job due to notions of customer preferences about religious attire. That would be unlawful. It would be the same as refusing to hire Narinder because he is a Sikh.

Harassment

Muhammad, who is Arab American, works for XYZ Motors, a large used car business. Muhammad meets with his manager and complains that Bill, one of his coworkers, regularly calls him names like "camel jockey," "the local terrorist," and "the ayatollah," and has intentionally embarrassed him in front of customers by claiming that he is incompetent. How should the supervisor respond?

Managers and supervisors who learn about objectionable workplace conduct based on religion or national origin are responsible for taking steps to correct the conduct by anyone under their control. Muhammad's manager should relay Muhammad's complaint to the appropriate manager if he does not supervise Bill. If XYZ Motors then determines that Bill has harassed Muhammad, it should take disciplinary action against Bill that is significant enough to ensure that the harassment does not continue.

Religious Accommodation

Three of the 10 Muslim employees in XYZ's 30-person template design division approach their supervisor and ask that they be allowed to use a conference room in an adjacent building for prayer. Until making the request, those employees prayed at their work stations. What should XYZ do?

XYZ should work closely with the employees to find an appropriate accommodation that meets their religious needs without causing an undue hardship for XYZ. Whether a reasonable accommodation would impose undue hardship and therefore not be required depends on the particulars of the business and the requested accommodation.

When the room is needed for business purposes, XYZ can deny its use for personal religious purposes. However, allowing the employees to use the conference room for prayers likely would not impose an undue hardship on XYZ in many other circumstances.

Temporary Assignments

Susan is an experienced clerical worker who wears a hijab (head scarf) in conformance with her Muslim beliefs. XYZ Temps places Susan in a long-term assignment with one of its clients. The client contacts XYZ and requests that it notify Susan that she must remove her hijab while working at the

[32] Questions and Answers about Employer Responsibilities Concerning the Employment of Muslims, Arabs, South Asians, and Sikhs, http://www.eeoc.gov/facts/backlash-employer.html, accessed 03/23/05. Except for formatting and stylistic changes, the questions and answers are verbatim.

front desk, or that XYZ assign another person to Susan's position. According to the client, Susan's religious attire violates its dress code and presents the "wrong image." Should XYZ comply with its client's request?

XYZ Temps may not comply with this client request without violating Title VII. The client would also violate Title VII if it made Susan remove her hijab or changed her duties to keep her out of public view. Therefore, XYZ should strongly advise against this course of action. Notions about customer preference real or perceived do not establish undue hardship, so the client should make an exception to its dress code to let Susan wear her hijab during front desk duty as a religious accommodation. If the client does not withdraw the request, XYZ should place Susan in another assignment at the same rate of pay and decline to assign another worker to the client.

Background Investigations

Anwar, who was born in Egypt, applies for a position as a security guard with XYZ Corp., which contracts to provide security services at government office buildings. Can XYZ require Anwar to undergo a background investigation before he is hired?

XYZ may require Anwar to undergo the same pre-employment security checks that apply to other applicants for the same position. As with its other employment practices, XYZ may not perform background investigations or other screening procedures in a discriminatory manner.

In addition, XYZ may require a security clearance pursuant to a federal statute or Executive Order. Security clearance determinations for positions subject to national security requirements under a federal statute or an Executive Order are not subject to review under the equal employment opportunity statutes.

Applicant and Employee Questions[33]

Hiring and Discharge

I am a South Asian woman from Bangladesh. I applied for a job at a bakery and had a phone interview with the manager. She seemed to like me a lot and she offered me the job over the phone. When I came in to work the first day, she appeared to be startled by my appearance. I have dark skin and wear a hijab. She brusquely stated that she had found someone "better suited to the job" and sent me home. I don't know what to do about this.

Harassment

I am an Arab American man and have been a salesman at a large car retailer for five years. After September 11, my coworkers stopped talking to me, and there has been a lot of tension. One coworker started calling me names like "camel jockey" and "the local terrorist." I used to have a good relationship with my coworkers and enjoyed my job, but now I dread coming to work each day. What can I do about my situation?

Religious Accommodation

I am a computer specialist at a software company downtown. As a devout Muslim, I am required to attend prayer services at my mosque for a short period on Friday afternoons. Obviously this conflicts with my work hours. Can I ask for the time off to attend services?

Questions to Consider

1. *What answers to the three applicant and employee questions listed above would you suggest to the employees in each situation?*
2. *Are you aware of any religious or national origin discrimination that has occurred in a real organization? If so, what happened? Did the affected party file suit?*

[33] Questions and Answers about the Workplace Rights of Muslims, Arabs, South Asians, and Sikhs under the Equal Employment Opportunity Laws, http://www.eeoc.gov/facts/backlash-employee.html.

3. Search the Web site of a newspaper in your city or state for recent instances of religious or national origin harassment against Muslims or those perceived to be Muslim. What happened?

4. Customer preference is not a legal defense for national origin (or any other form of) discrimination. How might national origin (or any other form of) discrimination backfire to alienate customers rather than being the preference of customers? Explain.

Kirpan (a religious sword), Kara (metal bracelet), Kanga (comb), and Kaccha (undershorts). The turban and religious sword are most likely to incite discrimination and discomfort and to need religious accommodation. Sikh women often wear uncut hair covered by scarves or a form of turban.[34]

Practicing Jews may wear a yarmulke (skullcap) constantly.[35] Some Jews wear no clothing that mixes linen and wool, which may require that employers accommodate their use of alternative suppliers for uniforms. Rastafarians wear their hair in dreadlocks, which may require accommodation. Head coverings, dreadlocks, and uncut hair are related to appearance requirements, and are also considered in Chapter 14. Featured Case 10.1 presents unique case of an EEOC settlement involving religious discrimination against an employee's religious tattoo.

Women's Roles in Organized Religion

One important source of diversity of beliefs within and among religions lies in whether to allow women to be ordained as clergy or to otherwise serve in leadership positions. As discussed in Chapter 2, religious organizations are exempted from certain laws prohibiting discrimination. When a religion's doctrines relegate women to subservient roles, and when the organization is strictly religious (and not operating for secular purposes), it is not generally illegal to discriminate against women in hiring, placement, promotion, compensation, or other job-related matters.

The two largest Christian groups in the United States, Catholics and Baptists, do not allow women to serve in the highest leadership positions of their respective churches (priests and ministers, respectively). Some of the other religious groups that bar women from the clergy are the Church of Jesus Christ of the Latter-day Saints, Orthodox Judaism, and the Church of God in Christ.[36]Although they are dissimilar in key beliefs about faith, they are in agreement on women's unsuitability to be clergy.

Despite bans on women clergy in many religious organizations, many other organizations do ordain women. Episcopalian, Presbyterian, and Methodist are some of the organizations that allow women to be ordained. Numbers of ordained

[34] Sikhism at a Glance, http://www.sikhcoalition.org/SikhismGlance.asp, accessed 07/4/05.

[35] Schaefer. (2002).

[36] Schaefer. (2002).

Featured Case 10.1 *Employee Fired for Wearing Religious Tattoo*[37]

BURGER CHAIN TO PAY $150,000 TO RESOLVE EEOC RELIGIOUS DISCRIMINATION SUIT

Suit Says Red Robin Fired Employee for Religious Tattoos, Saying It Wanted "All-American Kid"

SEATTLE—Red Robin Gourmet Burgers, Inc., a casual dining chain with restaurants throughout the country, will pay $150,000 and make substantial policy and procedural changes to settle a religious discrimination lawsuit filed by the U.S. Equal Employment Opportunity Commission (EEOC), the agency announced today. The EEOC had charged the company with refusing to accommodate the religious needs of an employee and then illegally firing him.

The EEOC alleged in its suit, Case No. C04-1291 in U.S. District Court for the Western District of Washington, that Red Robin refused to offer Edward Rangel, a server at the restaurant, any accommodation for his Kemetic religion, an ancient Egyptian faith. As part of his practice, Rangel went through a rite of passage where he received religious inscriptions in the form of tattoos. The inscriptions, less than a quarter-inch wide and encircling his wrists, are a verse from an Egyptian scripture and are written in a liturgical Egyptian language. The inscriptions symbolize his dedication and servitude to his creator and Rangel's beliefs make it a sin to intentionally conceal the religious inscriptions.

Rangel had the religious inscriptions on his wrists when he was hired at the Bellevue, Wash., Red Robin, which has a dress code that prohibits employees from having visible tattoos. The EEOC said that although Rangel worked at Red Robin for approximately six months without a complaint from customers, co-workers or his immediate supervisors, a new manager saw the tattoos and fired Rangel for not concealing them.

Rangel claimed that he had multiple conversations with management, giving "lengthy explanations" about his faith and need for an accommodation. He sought an exemption from the dress code, but Red Robin refused to provide it or any alternatives. In the words of the ex-chief financial officer James McCloskey, if Rangel could not cover his tattoos it "would be better he seek employment elsewhere." At a recent investment meeting, McCloskey stated that the company has "Christian" values and that Red Robin seeks out "that all-American kid" from the suburbs for its server positions, not those with "that urban kind of experience."

Source: Burger Chain to Pay $150,000 to Resolve EEOC Religious Discrimination Suit, http://www.eeoc.gov/press/9-16-05.html, accessed 9/18/05.

women have increased significantly since the 1970s, when women first began to be ordained in sizable numbers. More than one in eight clergy in the United States are now female.[38] However, women clergy are often confined to junior, associate, or copastor positions in smaller, less prestigious congregations, and have lower earnings than men clergy, reflecting a "stained glass ceiling."[39]

[37] Case verbatim from "Burger Chain to Pay $150,000 to Resolve EEOC Religious Discrimination Suit," http://www.eeoc.gov/press/9-16-05.html, accessed 09/18/05.

[38] Women as Clergy: The Status of Women in Society and Religion, http://www.religioustolerance.org/femclrg6.htm, accessed 03/31/05.

[39] Schaefer. (2002); see also Nesbitt, P. (1997). "Clergy Feminization: Controlled Labor or Transformative Change?" *Journal for the Scientific Study of Religion,* 36: 585–598; Sullins, P. (2000). "The Stained Glass Ceiling. Career Attainment for Women Clergy." *Sociology of Religion,* 61(3): 243–267; Purvis, S. B. (1995). *The Stained Glass Ceiling: Churches and Their Women Pastors,* Louisville, KY: Westminster John Knox Press.

In their article entitled "Clergy and the Politics of Gender," Melissa Deckman and her colleagues empirically analyzed attitudinal and behavioral differences between male and female clergy in mainline Protestant organizations.[40] Clear differences between men and women were found: women were more likely to support political and social issues such as abortion, gay rights, and women's rights. Women clergy were significantly more likely to work in race relations programs and domestic violence counseling, to minister to gay people, and to provide support to people living with HIV/AIDS. The researchers proposed that challenges women clergy face "might embolden them to take political action, particularly to fight on behalf of the rights of devalued, disenfranchised minority groups."[41]

Individual Feature 10.1 focuses on Pastor Jacquelyn Donald-Mims, a minister who is concerned with social and economic issues in the community of the multicultural, multiracial church she pastors.

Religion and Sexual Orientation Diversity at Work

As we have discussed, as the U.S. population becomes more diverse in race and origin, religious diversity also increases in importance. At the same time, emphasis on inclusion and on prohibiting discrimination on the basis of sexual orientation in organizations has also intensified. Because many religions in the United States hold that sex outside of marriage and homosexuality are morally wrong, inclusive organizations must attend to the rights of sexual minorities to a nondiscriminatory work environment while not requiring others to profess "valuing" homosexuality or other behaviors contradictory to their religious beliefs. How can both the rights of employees who are sexual minorities and those who strongly believe that homosexuality is immoral be protected? When do attempts at inclusion go too far? When does religious freedom go too far?

Recent research indicates that religious fundamentalism, rather than religiosity alone or membership in any particular religion, is most strongly related to negative attitudes toward sexual (and often racial) minorities.[42] In one study of Christians, Muslims, Jews, and Hindus, people from either of these religions who had strongly fundamentalist beliefs were more negative toward homosexuals than people from those religions who did not have such strong fundamentalist beliefs.[43]

[40] Deckman, M. M., Crawford, S. E. S., Olson, L. R., & Green, J. C. (2003). "Clergy and the Politics of Gender." *Journal for the Scientific Study of Religion,* 42: 621–631.

[41] Ibid, p. 629.

[42] See Altameyer, B., & Hunsberger, B. (1992). "Authoritarianism, Religious Fundamentalism, Quest, and Prejudice." *The International Journal for the Psychology of Religion,* 2(2): 113–133; Duck, R. J., & Hunsberger, B. (1999). "Religious Orientation and Prejudice: The Role of Religious Proscription, Right-Wing Authoritarianism, and Social Desirability." *The International Journal for the Psychology of Religion,* 9(3): 157–179; Laythe, B., Finkel, D., & Kirkpatrick, L. A. (2001). "Predicting Prejudice from Religious Fundamentalism and Right-Wing Authoritarianism: A Multiple-Regression Approach." *Journal for the Scientific Study of Religion,* 40(1): 1–10.

[43] Husberger, B. (1996). "Religious Fundamentalism, Right-Wing Authoritarianism, and Hostility toward Homosexuals in Non-Christian Religious Groups." *International Journal for the Psychology of Religion,* 6(1): 39–49.

Individual Feature 10.1 ***Pastor Jacquelyn Donald-Mims, D. Min., Imani Community Church***

Jacquelyn Donald-Mims founded Imani Community Church in Austin, Texas, in 1995. An African Methodist Episcopal church formally, Imani's objective is to appeal to all with an "interdenominational, multiracial embrace, open to all races, classes, and cultures." In an article entitled "Women Clergy Come into Their Own in Protestant Churches," Donald-Mims writes about women in the ministry. "Christian church tradition worships an inclusive savior but unfortunately has historically denied recognition of women's divine calling. Today, female clergy represent a growing and influential presence," she says.[44] Donald-Mims believes we are witnessing a change in the hierarchy that has traditionally "put men and clergy at the top and women and laity at the bottom."[45] This change is accompanied by upheaval, but also rewards.

One of the rewards of women in the ministry is inclusion. Imani Community Church is a Christian, inclusive church that focuses on those who are "unchurched" and "dechurched" or feel estranged, in Austin's diverse community. Donald-Mims is a member of Austin Area Interreligious Ministries (AAIM), which is an interfaith group of about 150 faith communities, including the various Catholic and Protestant Christian denominations, Buddhist, Hindu, Jewish, Mennonite, Muslim, Scientologist, and Sikh, among many others. She participates in AAIM events designed to focus attention on "long neglected divisions among people of faith." Such divisions include social issues such as racism, classism, and police treatment of minorities, including questionable fatal shootings. Donald-Mims believes that cultural proficiency, embraced by everyone in the community, is important in eradicating stereotypes. Strength emanates from unity of religious leaders, strong and weak. Together, leaders must "speak truth to power," and hold law enforcement and civic leaders accountable for what happens throughout the communities, rather than myopically protecting only their own individual jurisdictions. Along with social issues, Donald-Mims sees helping people deal with economic issues as key aspects of her ministry.

Donald-Mims has earned five degrees, including the Doctor of Ministry degree at United Theological Seminary, Dayton, Ohio; the Master of Divinity at Perkins School of Theology at Southern Methodist University, Dallas; the Master of Theological Studies at University of Dallas; the Master of Business Administration at Georgia State University, Atlanta; and the Bachelor of Science at Tuskegee University in Alabama. Prior to entering the ministry, Donald-Mims had a successful career as a financial manager and executive in a large corporation, where she mentored numerous women and minorities. A dual-career wife and mother, Donald-Mims is married to an intellectual property lawyer and has one son.

Source: http://www.imanichurch.com, accessed 09/21/05; Flynn, E. (2005, July 13). "Uniting in Spirit: Clerics Gather to Address Austin's Racial, Economic Divisions." ***American-Statesman***, http://www.statesman.com/metrostate/content/metro/stories/07/13clergy.html, accessed 09/21/05; Jacquelyn Donald-Mims, personal communication, September 21, 2005.

---

[44] Donald-Mims, J. (2005, February 28). "Women Clergy Come to Their Own in Protestant Churches." Austin Area Interreligious Ministries, http://www.aaimaustin.org/clergy/MimsWomen.htm, accessed 09/21/05.

[45] Donald-Mims has also authored a book about women clergy, entitled *Move over Men: God Calls Women into the Pulpit* (1998), Austin, TX: Devon Publishers.

Misperception: Christians have stronger negative reactions toward sexual minorities than people from other religious groups.

Reality: People from various religious groups who are strong fundamentalists have the most negative reactions toward sexual minorities.

Not everyone who has strongly held religious beliefs will behave negatively toward gays and lesbians, or resist sexual orientation diversity at work, however. Two recent cases exemplify potential conflicts between religious beliefs, sexual orientation, and an organization's diversity practices. In one case, *Peterson v. Hewlett-Packard Co.,* the company was vindicated. In the other case, AT&T Broadband was found liable for religious discrimination.[46]

Religion and Sexual Orientation Conflicts: Two Cases with Different Outcomes

Richard Peterson and Hewlett-Packard.[47] Richard Peterson, a devout Christian, had worked successfully for Hewlett-Packard (HP) for 21 years in HP's Boise, Idaho, office. HP is noted for its diversity efforts, such as same-sex (and heterosexual) partner benefits and a nonharassment policy that includes sexual orientation, among other things. As part of its overall workforce diversity campaign,[48] HP began displaying diversity posters. The posters were photos of HP employees representing different aspects of diversity (e.g., Black, Hispanic, gay, etc.). Peterson objected to the poster that displayed a gay male, and in response to that poster, Peterson posted Bible scriptures condemning homosexuality on his cubicle. The scriptures referred to homosexual acts as an "abomination," and were written in sufficiently large font to be seen by Peterson's coworkers, customers, and others in the office area.

Peterson's supervisors removed the Bible passages because they were inconsistent with HP's nonharassment policy. In at least four discussions with HP management, Peterson acknowledged that he meant for the scriptures to be hurtful and to condemn homosexual behavior. He also claimed that HP's diversity program was intended to target Christian employees. Peterson suggested that he would remove the scriptures if the "gay" posters were moved. When he refused any other compromise, management gave Peterson time off with pay to reconsider. After the paid time off, Peterson returned to work, posted the scriptures again, and was terminated.

Peterson went to the EEOC to complain of religious discrimination, received a right to sue notice, and filed a lawsuit against HP. In his lawsuit, Peterson alleged

[46] Although both cases involve Christians, people from other faiths also may take issue with nonheterosexuals, particularly those with strong fundamentalist beliefs.

[47] http://www.danpinello.com/Peterson.htm, accessed, 03/30/05; "Court Rules for HP in Religious Discrimination Case." *Sacramento Business Journal*. January 7, 2004.

[48] See Organizational Feature 15.2—Hewlett-Packard: Putting Diversity to Work for more details on HP's diversity policies.

that Christians were targeted by HP's diversity policy, that its goals were to change Christians' beliefs to support homosexuality, and that HP was on a crusade to change moral values in Idaho under the guise of diversity. He alleged HP had treated him differently than other employees and failed to reasonably accommodate his religious beliefs. The courts assessed HP's behavior, including a 3-day meeting to deliberately and consciously make decisions about the company's diversity program, and allowing Peterson to post antihomosexual bumper stickers on his car that was regularly parked in the company's parking lot. HP did not forbid Peterson to park his car, but did ask him to exhibit respect for his coworkers.

The district court ruled for HP, noting that the only accommodation that was acceptable to Peterson, removing the posters or allowing his targeted, large font scriptures to remain, required HP to endure undue hardship. Upon appeal, the appeals court also ruled for HP, rejecting Peterson's religious discrimination claims.

Albert Buonanno and AT&T.[49] Albert Buonanno, a devout Catholic, worked for AT&T Broadband in Denver, earning $44,261 per year. Buonanno was described as a model employee, who befriended and helped others, including transgender and gay employees and friends. As part of AT&T's diversity program, in 2001, Buonanno was told that he needed to sign an agreement stating he would "value" fellow employees and their behaviors. Buonanno stated that he could tolerate other religions and love and appreciate other people, but could not "value" homosexuality or other religious beliefs.

Buonanno was fired and sued AT&T under Title VII of the Civil Rights Act, alleging religious discrimination. He asked for compensatory damages to cover his lost wages and contributions to his 401k plan, emotional distress, and interest, and punitive damages (available in cases of intentional discrimination). Judge Krieger's ruling focused on how AT&T handled Buonanno's firing, and she ruled in his favor, awarding all but punitive damages. She acknowledged that although deleting portions of the company handbook could make uniform application of company policies more difficult, a reasonable accommodation could have been made for Buonanno's closely held religious beliefs.[50]

Resolving Conflicts

As these two cases indicate, the courts do assess reasonableness of accommodation requests and undue hardship. People's different beliefs about religion and sexual orientation require careful employer attention to fairness and equity of all parties in a careful balancing act. HP's purposefully designed diversity policy and

[49] Hudson, K. (2004, April 6). "Diversity Suit Loss for Cable Titan." *Denver Post*. http://lgrl.sitestreet.com/news/article.asp?id=1390, accessed 07/01/04.

[50] Ibid.

thoughtful consideration of Richard Peterson's rights allowed HP to prevail in a religious discrimination lawsuit. In contrast, AT&T's failure to carefully consider and reasonably accommodate Buonanno's simple request resulted in its loss in a religious discrimination lawsuit.

Managers and supervisors must avoid being judgmental about those who have strongly held religious beliefs regarding sexual orientation. Employees have the right to their beliefs about homosexuality; they do not have the right to denigrate or harass coworkers based on sexual orientation or for any reason. Even if sexual orientation discrimination is not specifically prohibited by organizational policy, a certain level of respectful behaviors should be required of and toward all employees. In addition, employees with closely held religious beliefs have responsibilities to comply with organizational regulations to the extent that they do not trample the employees' religious rights. Where an organization requires respectful behavior toward each other, employees should comply. In the HP and AT&T cases described, both Christian men had strongly held beliefs. Peterson chose to go against organizational policy in an unreasonable manner. In contrast, Buonanno chose to go against an organizational policy that could have been modified to accommodate his religious beliefs.

An unusual situation involving conflicts between an employee's religious beliefs and job requirements occurred at an Eckerd's drug store in Denton, Texas. In early 2004, Gene Herr, an Eckerd's pharmacist, was fired because he refused to fill a prescription for the "morning-after" contraceptive pill for a woman who had been raped, citing religious grounds. If taken within 72 hours of intercourse, the morning-after pill prevents contraception in most cases. According to news reports, an unnamed rape victim took her prescription for the morning-after pill to the Eckerd's. There, Gene Herr and two unnamed other pharmacists reportedly refused to fill the prescription. Eckerd's has a policy that no pharmacist can refuse to fill a prescription solely on moral or religious grounds and the three pharmacists were fired. Although he had worked for Eckerd's for 5 years, and had refused to fill that prescription for several other women, Herr was reportedly unaware of the policy prior to his termination. Texas law prohibits doctors, nurses, staff, or employees of hospitals or health care centers from being forced to participate in an abortion; however, Eckerd's is neither of those facilities. Herr's attorney has said that the Eckerd's policy violates Title VII's protections from religious discrimination at work. Herr and his attorney were reportedly evaluating whether to file a lawsuit against Eckerd's.[51]

[51] Associated Press. "Denial of Rape Victim's Pills Raises Debate." February 24, 2004, http://www.msnbc.msn.com/id/4359430/, accessed 07/04/05; CNN. "Pharmacist Fired for Denying 'Morning-After' Pill." February 12, 2004, http://www.cnn.com/2004/US/Southwest/02/12/pharmacy.firing.ap/, accessed 07/04/05.

Individual Recommendations

Individuals should be aware of their rights to workplace fairness with respect to religion. Employers should allow employees the ability to observe religious practices, as long as this does not cause undue hardship on the employer. In requesting an accommodation, decide in advance what things would help the employer be able to comply. If a required time to pray is during work hours, plan to make up the time before or after normal hours. Posting religious sayings is not illegal, but such postings should be for one's own edification, rather than to send a message to others. Reasonable sized, nonoffensive language is allowed under EEOC guidelines.

Employees should also carefully watch their own behavior for things that could be construed as discriminatory or unfair. Simple things such as language can be offensive. For example, a statement that someone was "Jewed" down is derogatory and may be offensive to Jews and non-Jews alike.

People should also try not to make assumptions about someone's religious beliefs or practices based on his or her outward appearance, race, or national origin. As with other aspects of diversity, conscious attempts to be aware of and avoid denigrating someone's religion are recommended. Finally, be willing to assess whether your beliefs sufficiently conflict with an organization's legitimate position on certain issues (e.g., the morning-after pill) such that you decide to work elsewhere.

Organizational Recommendations

Although the U.S. population is predominantly Christian, about 74 million people hold other or no religious beliefs. To avoid religious discrimination, organizational leaders should recognize the diversity in religious beliefs in the United States. Implement procedures to ensure that people of various religious groups are treated equitably. Provide a certain number of holidays that employees may use to decide which days they will be away from work. Some employees may choose to be off on Good Friday, while others may take Rosh Hashanah, or days of Ramadan. For most employers, there is sufficient diversity in religious beliefs in the United States to ensure appropriate employee coverage on various holidays.

Employers should also carefully scrutinize appearance requirements that may result in religious discrimination. Is the requirement necessary to the successful operation of the business? Can a reasonable accommodation be made? For most organizations and most religions, different beliefs and certain appearance requirements do not preclude one's ability to perform most jobs.

The interaction between religious diversity and sexual orientation diversity is complex. Some religious doctrines teach that homosexuality is morally wrong, and people with strongly held religious beliefs may hold negative beliefs about nonheterosexual behaviors. However, as was the situation with Albert Buonanno (AT&T case), beliefs that certain behaviors are wrong do not always translate into discriminatory behaviors against others. Rather than trying to change employees' religious beliefs (which may be illegal discrimination against them), leaders should model and require respectful treatment of all applicants, employees, and customers. When organizational policies conflict with employees' religious beliefs, ensure that employees are aware of the policies and that an appropriate accommodation may be available. When employees flagrantly resist legitimate, carefully constructed policies of inclusion and fairness, termination may be warranted.

Summary

In this chapter, we have explored religion as an aspect of diversity. The increasing diversity among religious groups in the United States makes religious diversity a particularly interesting and unique aspect of diversity. Title VII prohibits religious discrimination and requires employers make reasonable accommodations for the religious practices of applicants and employees. We discussed litigation related to religious and national origin discrimination against Arabs and Muslims, or those perceived to be Arab or Muslim. Unique issues to religious diversity, such as the treatment of sexual minorities and the ordination of women, were examined. Recommendations for individuals and employers regarding religious diversity and accommodations were provided.

Key Terms

Invisible stigmas — invisible attributes, characteristics, or experiences that convey an identity that is devalued in some social setting.

Profiling — using someone's real or perceived demographic characteristic to single her or him out for scrutiny.

Sexual minorities — nonheterosexuals, including gay males, lesbians, bisexuals, and transgender people.

Stained glass ceiling — an invisible barrier that keeps women clergy from advancing past associate, junior, and copastor positions and confines them to lower-status religious organizations.

Questions to Consider

1. How is the "stained glass ceiling" similar to and different from the regular "glass ceiling?"
2. Title VII requires that employers make reasonable accommodations without undue hardship for employees' or applicants' religious beliefs. How frequent do you think requests for religious accommodation are?
3. Given that the majority of Arabs in the United States are Christian, why is the perception that they are Muslim so widespread?
4. Of the selected cases from this chapter and others reported on the EEOC Web site, many involved egregious, offensive behavior, including death threats and

physical assaults against people based on their religion. Do most religions espouse such behavior? Do most organizations espouse at work violence against employees? Why were perpetrators of violence often retained in the cases while victims were fired?

5. In the case of Brinks security and the accommodation requested by Carol Grotts to be allowed to wear culottes instead of pants, what factors may have affected the decision not to allow her to wear culottes?
6. In the Eckerd's case, the pharmacist had allegedly refused to fill other women's prescriptions for the morning-after pill but was not fired until he refused to fill the prescription for a rape victim. Why do you think this occurred?
7. This chapter considers profiling against people who look as though they might be Arab. In the Vincent Chin case discussed in Chapter 6, Chin, a Chinese American, was attacked by those who thought he was Japanese. How do mistakes such as these relate to the "identifiability" characterizations of minority groups as proposed by Dworkin and Dworkin in Chapter 3? What signals do mistakes such as these send about the perpetrators of profiling and hate crimes and about hatred itself?
8. What have you learned from this chapter that is most surprising to you?

Actions and Exercises

1. By observation in a service (or outside as people leave), investigate the racial variation in attendance at religious services in the area in which you live. Compare your observed proportions with the racial variation in the area's population. Document your comparisons. What is apparent in this nonscientific study of diversity among members of religious organizations?
2. If you know a woman who is a minister or can locate one, interview her about her experiences related to her position. How did she become a minister? What route did she take? Did she have a male minister as a mentor? What interesting diversity-related stories does she tell?
3. In the Red Robin burger chain case discussed in Featured Case 10.1, the manager reflected desires to hire "all-American." In addition to the religious discrimination that occurred, in what other ways could such a preference be discriminatory? The server, Edward Rangel, had worked at the burger chain for more than 6 months before being fired. Investigate the average turnover rates for fast food restaurants.

11 Chapter

Age

Chapter Objectives

After completing this chapter, readers should understand age as an aspect of diversity in organizations. They should specifically be able to:

- *understand the age distribution and explain what effects recent and projected shifts in this distribution will have on diversity concerns.*
- *define ageism and discuss its meaning for older and younger workers.*
- *explain why younger workers as well as older workers should be included in conceptualizations of age as an aspect of diversity.*
- *discuss misperceptions about the performance and abilities of older and younger workers.*
- *explain age-related legislation and discuss selected cases of employment discrimination against older workers and younger workers.*
- *discuss the effects of discrimination and harassment on young workers and the goals of the EEOC's Youth@Work initiative.*

Key Facts

Age as an aspect of diversity includes older and younger workers.

More people are working after age 65 and fewer younger workers are entering the workforce than in the past.

Although older workers are widely perceived to have lower performance than younger workers, this perception is not supported by research.

Younger workers have higher rates of injury and accidents at work than older workers.

Younger workers are better educated than in the past, yet those who are foreign-born,[1] an increasing proportion of new entrants to the workforce, often have considerably lower education than those who are native born.

[1] The U.S. Census Bureau uses the term *foreign-born* for anyone who was not born in the United States, including legal and illegal immigrants, temporary migrants (e.g., students), and refugees; see footnote 8 at http://www.census.gov/prod/2004pubs/p20-550.pdf. As discussed in Chapters 5 and 6, however, some immigrants arrive with significant education levels.

Introduction and Overview

In this chapter, we consider age as an aspect of diversity, focusing on ageism, age-based misperceptions about the contributions and performance of workers, and the need to value contributions of all workers, regardless of age. Ageism is defined as prejudice, stereotypes, and discrimination directed at a person because of his or her age.[2] As is evident by the definition, ageism is not limited to older workers, contrary to common perceptions. Thus, perspectives and experiences of both younger workers and older workers are included in this chapter. The increasing proportion of older workers, the declining ratio of younger workers entering the workforce, and the greater racial and ethnic diversity of younger workers make both younger and older workers important contributors to an understanding of age diversity in organizations.

Age is a particularly unique aspect of diversity, having unique attributes that differentiate it from such things as race, sex, and ethnicity. First, at some point, those who are young cease to be young and become old and those who are now old were once young.[3] This status change is contrasted with the permanence and stability of race and ethnicity and the limited access to and difficulty of gender change.[4] Although cosmetics, hair dyes, or surgery may provide some help in avoiding the appearance of aging, people's general age range remains fairly apparent to observers and the process of aging remains certain for everyone who lives. This status change also makes age discrimination seem particularly strange when compared with other forms of discrimination. Whites will not become Black, chromosomal men will not become chromosomal women, and American Indians will not become Asians. Those who hold prejudices against and discriminate against other groups will generally not become one of the devalued group; there is no risk of suffering their same fate. With aging, however, unless they die young (which most people would not choose), everyone will become a member of the devalued group. Although this would appear to be impetus to avoid age discrimination, age discrimination is not uncommon.

Second, when compared with perceptions of race, ethnicity, and sex, perceptions of "older" and "younger" are more complex than perceptions of other attributes. When does one become an older worker? At what age does one become older and thus less likely to be hired, trained, or promoted? At what age do employees become old enough such that negative perceptions about younger workers (e.g., irresponsible, lazy) end? At what age do positive perceptions about younger workers (e.g., trainable, energetic) cease and perceptions shift to negative (e.g., too old to learn, set in ways)? Clearly, there are no definitive answers to the questions posed. Perceptions of young, old, younger, and older vary by perceiver, employee/applicant, organization, industry, and position. As much as possible, and where appropriate, in this chapter, the relevant age or age range is explained.

When are younger workers preferred and older workers disadvantaged? Consider the following apparent contradictions. Consistent with general perceptions, in many situations, younger workers are viewed as more desirable than older workers. On the other hand, the great majority of managers, executives, and higher status workers are older, rather than younger workers. Even so, young managers and executives are often highly

---

[2] Nelson, T. D. (2002). *The Psychology of Prejudice,* Boston: Allyn & Bacon.

[3] Ibid, p. 190.

[4] But, for discussions on changes in people's self-reported race or ethnicity over time, see Passel, J., & Berman, P. (1986). "Quality of 1980 Census Data for American Indians." *Social Biology*, 33: 163–182; or, Snipp, C. M. (1989). *American Indians: The First of This Land,* New York: Russell Sage.

pursued and viewed as being on the "fast track." The youngest workers, aged 14 to 17, experience sexual harassment at higher rates than older workers, which may reflect their being targeted because of perceptions of their lack of knowledge and vulnerability. These apparent contradictions may be explained in part by the idea that there is a "prime age." Prime age refers to the age range of the most preferred employees—those who are between 25 and 35, suggesting that this group is favored over both those who are younger and older than that range.[5]

The world's population is aging, and older people are working longer than ever before. Because these older workers often have more corporate memory and experience than others, organizations that fail to recognize the value in providing opportunities for older workers will be disadvantaged. In addition, there are fewer younger workers being added to the workforce than in the past, and there is a bimodal distribution of highly educated young workers and poorly educated young workers. Young workers are the workers of the future, and organizations that fail to recognize the value in providing opportunities for younger workers will also be disadvantaged. In this chapter we consider the value that people of all ages bring to organizations.

Historical Background

During the early and mid-1900s, many employees remained with one employer for most of their adult work lives. The employer/employee relationship was somewhat protective and was often viewed as being familial. Life spans were considerably shorter than they are now, and workers often did not live long enough to work well into their 50s and 60s. During the decade of the 1960s, however, employers' legal refusal to hire older workers and mandatory retirement resulted in outcries and purposeful resistance from older workers. As with many of the civil and employment rights obtained by Blacks, women, and Latinos, older workers have also obtained greater employment rights through vocal and deliberate struggles that contributed to the passage of the Age Discrimination in Employment Act (ADEA) in 1967. Organizations such as the Gray Panthers and the American Association of Retired Persons (AARP) continue to work for equal rights for workers of various ages.[6]

[5] Loretto, W., Duncan, C., & White, P. (2002.) "Ageism and Employment: Controversies, Ambiguities, and Younger People's Perceptions." *Ageing and Society,* 20: 279–302. See also Duncan, C., & Loretto, W. (2004). "Never the Right Age? Gender and Age-Based Discrimination in Employment." *Gender, Work, and Organization,* 11(1): 95–115.

[6] Gray Panthers is a national organization of intergenerational activists dedicated to social change. For information, see http://www.graypanthers.org/graypanthers/info.htm, accessed 01/25/05. AARP is an advocacy and information group focusing on the population that is at least age 50. For information, see http://www.aarp.org, accessed 01/25/05.

Relevant Legislation for Older Workers

The ADEA prohibits employment-related discrimination against employees and applicants who are at least 40 years of age by employers of 20 or more people, including state and local governments, employment agencies, and labor unions. The stated purpose of the ADEA is "to promote employment of older persons based on their ability rather than age (and) to prohibit arbitrary age discrimination in employment,"[7] which acknowledges the effects of age stereotyping on employment opportunities of older workers. Perceptions that older people are unable to perform have greater negative effects on older employees and applicants than actual performance decrements associated with aging.

In 2003, the EEOC received 19,124 age discrimination charges, resolved 17,352 charges (including charges from prior years), and obtained nearly $50 million in settlements for charging parties and other aggrieved parties (see Table 2.1 in Chapter 2). Since inception of the ADEA, most litigants have been White men who had worked in managerial and professional jobs.[8] As with other protected groups, however, those who experience age discrimination are unlikely to sue or to win if they should sue. While 14.7% of charges were resolved with merit, 16.3 % were closed for administrative reasons and 69% of charges were deemed to have no reasonable cause.[9]

Originally, the ADEA prohibited discrimination against persons aged 40 to 65, consistent with the assumption that people retired by age 65. In 1978 the age limit moved to age 70, and in 1986 the upper limit was removed entirely. The removal of the upper age limit reflected the fact that many workers are capable of performing well and still desire or financially need to work past age 70.

The Older Workers Benefit Protection Act (OWBPA) further amended the ADEA in 1990. Because the costs to insure older workers are greater than costs to insure younger workers, the OWBPA allows employers to provide lower benefits for older workers as long as the costs to provide those benefits are the same as the costs to provide (higher) benefits for younger workers. As with requiring reasonable accommodations *without undue hardship* under the ADA (see Chapters 2 and 12), the OWBPA is evidence of lawmakers' goals to protect workers while not unduly burdening employers.

As discussed in Chapter 2, in the United States, it is illegal to discriminate against those at least 40 in favor of those under 40. It is also illegal to discriminate against persons who are considerably over 40 in favor of those who are also over 40,

[7] "The Age Discrimination in Employment Act of 1967." The U.S. Equal Employment Opportunity Commission, http://www.eeoc.gov/policy/adea.html, accessed 01/22/05.

[8] For discussion, see Gregory, R. F. (2002). *Age Discrimination in the American Workplace: Old at a Young Age,* New Brunswick, NJ: Rutgers University Press.

[9] Age Discrimination, the U.S. Equal Employment Opportunity Commission, http://www.eeoc.gov/types/age.html, accessed 01/22/05.

but younger (e.g., preferring 45 year olds over 58 year olds). Intentional age discrimination, disparate impact in layoffs, and hostile environment harassment (e.g., age-related comments, jokes, etc.) are all prohibited, requiring careful attention to decisions, attitudes, and behavior at work. As an example, although the ADEA does not prohibit employers from asking age or date of birth, doing so may create the appearance of age discrimination. Employers are instead advised to ask if applicants are *over 18* or the required age minimum for a particular job. Similarly, employers are advised to ask applicants if they are high school graduates instead of requesting the *date of high school graduation,* which could be used to closely estimate age.

In 2004, the U.S. Supreme Court further solidified the idea that the ADEA is designed specifically to protect older workers from discrimination in employment, even to the detriment of younger workers. In *General Dynamics Land Systems, Inc. v. Cline,* workers who were between 40 and 49 sued General Dynamics because it provided full medical benefits for retirees over 50, but not for those who were older than 40 but not yet 50. After 7 years of litigation and appeals, the Supreme Court ruled for the company, determining that favoring relatively older workers over 40 was allowable under the ADEA. The ruling in *General Dynamics v. Cline* clearly indicates that the ADEA is meant to protect employment rights of older workers. As with any other protected group of workers, however, the ADEA does not forbid disciplining or terminating older workers for cause, including for poor performance. Consistency of treatment is vital, and employers must be certain older workers are treated similarly to (or more favorably than) younger workers to avoid disparate treatment.

When age is a bona fide occupational qualification, failing to hire, discharging, or forcing retirement on certain select types of employees is not illegal. Included are executives, firefighters, law enforcement officers, and others involved in positions involving public safety or transportation. For executives who have reached age 65, and would receive at least $44,000 in retirement earnings, employers may force them to retire. Employers may also set maximum ages for hiring and mandatory retirement ages for firefighters, law enforcement officers, and public safety or transportation personnel (e.g., bus drivers or airline pilots). When employers use age as a BFOQ, the burden of proof that the conditions of business necessity are met rests on the employer. The employer must also demonstrate that substantially everyone who reaches a certain age is limited in the ability to perform the job and distinguishing among those who could perform the job would be impractical.

Selected EEOC Cases Involving Older Age Discrimination Claims

Selected EEOC cases include substantial allegations of egregious age discrimination. These cases involve organizations from various industries and parts of the United States and include forced retirements, age-based slurs, hiring less qualified younger workers, refusing to train older workers, and other overt actions. Consider the following cases:[10]

Forced retirement

- **EEOC v. First National Bank of McGregor**
  No. W-03-CA-011 (W.D. Texas November 15, 2003)

  The Dallas District Office filed this ADEA suit alleging that defendant, a bank, discriminated against charging party, a 68-year-old loan officer, on the basis of her age when it forced her to retire. The loan officer, who had served 45 years at the bank and had never been [sic] received a written reprimand or negative job evaluation, was provided a letter written by the bank president that stated "a decision has been made for you to retire effective March 15, 2001." Charging party, a widow, did not want to retire and could not afford to do so.

Failure to hire more highly qualified older workers while hiring younger, less qualified workers

- **EEOC v. Wells Fargo Financial Texas, Inc., f/k/a Norwest Financial Texas, Inc.**
  No. SA-02-CA-0544 (W.D. Texas October 31, 2003)

  In this ADEA action, the San Antonio District Office alleged that defendant, a financial services company, failed to hire charging party, age 51, and other individuals age 40 and older, into management trainee (credit manager) positions because of their ages. Despite charging party's extensive credentials, defendant told him that his unstable work history disqualified him and then hired a 21-year-old recent college graduate with no experience. In addition, charging party was more qualified than at least seven new hires under age 40. San Antonio also alleged that defendant violated the EEOC's record keeping regulations by failing to keep the job applications, resumes, and other employment forms of applicants who were not hired.

Refusing to hire older workers as management trainees

- **EEOC v. Enterprise Rent-A-Car Company of Texas, Inc.**
  No. A-02-CA-134-SS (W.D. Tex. April 7, 2003)

  The San Antonio District Office alleged in this ADEA lawsuit that defendant, a car rental company with 48 branch offices in the Austin, Texas metropolitan area, refused to hire individuals age 40 and older into Management Trainee positions. Each branch office has one or more Management Trainee positions

---

[10] All cases drawn from the appropriate year and month's settlement summary by accessing http://www.eeoc.gov/litigation/settlements/index.html, accessed 12/18/04.

which are entry level management positions. In 1998, approximately 1100 individuals applied for Management Trainee positions in the Austin area, almost 10% of whom were in the protected age group. Of the 110 candidates hired for trainee positions in 1998, none were age 40 or older.

Preferring a younger (but over 40) worker

- **EEOC v. Maxim Healthcare Services, Inc.**
  No. 6:02-cv-1555-ORL-22DAB (M.D. Fla. April 27, 2004)

  The Miami District Office filed this ADEA action alleging that defendant, a large healthcare company in Florida, promoted charging party, a 64-year-old RN with 40 years of nursing experience, to a clinical supervisor position and then denied her the management-level salary and concomitant benefits that younger supervisors received because of her age. Miami also alleged that although defendant liked CP's skill-level it discharged CP because of her age, retaining her only until it found a younger replacement (age 44) who fit in better with the company's youthful image.

Stereotyping as too old and grumpy

- **EEOC v. KL Shangri-La Owners, L.P., Highgate Hotels, Inc. and Highgate Holdings, Inc., all d/b/a Shangri-La Resort, Inc.**
  No. 03-CIV-077-EA(M) (N.D. Okla. September 10, 2003)

  In this ADEA lawsuit, the Dallas District Office alleged that defendant, a resort comprised of a lodge, several restaurants, conference/meeting centers, and a country club with two 18 hole golf courses, discriminated against charging party, a 58-year-old bartender/cashier, when it denied her a transfer/promotion to a more lucrative bartender/supervisor position (which she had worked on the same seasonal basis in past years) because of her age. Before the denial of the transfer, defendant's General Manager stated that charging party was "too old and grumpy" to work in the bartender/supervisor position and he and another supervisor made other ageist statements. As a result of the discriminatory treatment, charging party was forced to quit her job.

Stating that they really wanted a younger person

- **EEOC v. AT&T, Research Laboratories Division**
  No. 02-cv-3556 (D. N.J. March 6, 2003)

  In this ADEA lawsuit, the Philadelphia District Office alleged that defendant discriminated against charging party, age 50, when it failed to hire him for a Ph.D. Research Statistician position in defendant's Statistics Research Group and instead hired a substantially younger and less qualified individual. Defendant hired a 28-year-old person for the position because, as reflected in an email written by the recruiting official, the company "really wanted a younger person."

Terminated because they were "too seasoned," translated as "too old"

- **EEOC v. Memscap, Inc.**
  No. 03-4323 JF (N.D. Cal. Mar. 18, 2004)

  The Seattle District Office brought this ADEA action, alleging that defendant, a French corporation that designs, manufactures and markets microscopic machines and structures and has a small North American subsidiary headquartered in San Jose, terminated two charging parties because of their ages. CP Michael Tavares (50) and CP Robert Miller (52) were hired for management positions in February and March 2002, respectively, after they had face-to-face interviews with the subsidiary's employees in the San Jose office and a phone interview with defendant's head of sales in North America and its President/CEO. Charging parties first met defendant's management during their training in Grenoble, France the week of March 15, 2002, and a month later they received identical e-mails informing them of their dismissals. The explanation offered by the North American head of sales was that the President/CEO thought charging parties were "too seasoned," and the head of sales agreed with one of the CPs that this meant too old. Further, charging parties were told that their jobs had been eliminated but evidence revealed that defendant sought to fill their jobs immediately after their dismissals.

Legal Protections for Younger Workers

Younger workers are a significant portion of the current and future workforce in the United States, where the legal working age is 14. An estimated 2.8 million 16 and 17 year olds were employed in 2000 and 80% of all teenagers will work at some point during their high school years.[11] Presently in the United States there are no specific federal laws that protect workers who are younger than 40, even though younger age discrimination and stereotyping frequently occur. However, some states in the United States and some other countries do have broad prohibitions against age discrimination based on any (younger or older) age. As with many other areas, local and state laws prohibiting age discrimination vary and at times are more stringent than federal law; employers should focus on avoidance of non-job-related discrimination rather than on compliance with laws.

[11] Nester, R. (2003). "Protecting Young Workers." *Job Safety & Health Quarterly*, 14(2): Winter, 2003, http://www.osha.gov/Publications/JSHQ/Winter2003html/youngwork.htm, accessed 12/29/04.

International Feature 11.1 *Australia's Age Discrimination Act*

In 2004, the Age Discrimination Act (ADA) went into effect in Australia. The Australian ADA is designed to reduce, and ultimately eliminate both younger and older age discrimination. Under Australia's act, age discrimination occurs when an opportunity is denied to a person because of his or her age and age is irrelevant to the person's ability to take advantage of the opportunity. Education, employment, accommodation (housing), and goods, services, or facilities are considered opportunities under the act.

The Australian ADA describes direct and indirect discrimination, which are similar to disparate treatment and disparate impact discrimination in the United States. In direct discrimination, a person is treated less favorably because of his or her age than a person of another age group would be treated under similar circumstances. For example, it is illegal to assume that younger workers will be less mature and responsible than older workers and therefore refuse to hire them. Indirect discrimination occurs when a requirement, condition, or practice used for all parties negatively affects people of a particular age or age group. For example, it is unlawful to require strength and agility tests that disadvantage older applicants or employees when the strength or agility levels are not prerequisites to successful job performance.

All employers, regardless of size, may be found liable for discrimination unless they have taken "all reasonable" steps to reduce liability. Reasonable steps vary by employer, but include implementation of proactive antidiscrimination measures. Complaints under the act are made through Australia's Human Rights and Equal Opportunity Commission (HREC). Complaints must be in writing, are investigated, and the HREC attempts to conciliate disagreements. When agreements are not reached, the complaining party may take the complaint to Australian courts. The HREC also provides education for employers on how to avoid age discrimination.

Source: All About Age Discrimination, http://www.hreoc.gov.au/age/, accessed 03/19/05.

As discussed in International Feature 11.1, Australia's Age Discrimination Act, enacted in 2004, prohibits treating a person unfavorably because of his or her age (or differently than a person of another age group would be treated under similar circumstances).[12] This act covers hiring, terms and conditions of employment, and dismissal. Similar legislation, prohibiting any age discrimination, takes effect in the United Kingdom in December 2006. The state of Michigan's Elliott-Larsen Civil Rights Act prohibits discrimination on the basis of any age and other categories not protected under federal law (such as weight—see Chapter 14). Elliott-Larsen can be used by both younger and older workers who experience age discrimination, but, so far, high-profile cases have involved older, rather than younger workers. In a 2002 case filed under the Elliott-Larsen Civil Rights Act, a class of former Ford managers received a $10.6 million settlement against Ford Motor Company.[13]

[12] All about Age Discrimination, http://www.hreoc.gov.au/age/, accessed 01/20/05.

[13] http://www.aarp.org/research/press/presscurrentnews/cn-2002/Articles/a2003-06-02-nr031402ford.html, accessed 01/23/05.

The AARP represented the plaintiffs in the suit that alleged older managers were discriminated against by Ford's new performance appraisal system allegedly "designed to weed out older workers." The appraisal system forced managers to rank a certain percentage of employees in the lowest tier and being ranked in the lowest tier resulted in loss of bonuses and risk of job loss. Ford has since abandoned that performance management system.

Because there is currently no federal legislation prohibiting younger age discrimination, no specific younger age EEOC cases are available. However, cases involving young workers and their experiences with sexual and gender harassment at work are presented later in the chapter.

Population, Participation Rates, and Employment

As shown in Table 11.1, there are fewer younger people than older people in the population, which creates concerns about the financial stability of the U.S. Social Security system and about the supply of employees as older workers exit the workforce. Between 2000 and 2003, the number of people aged 45 to 64 grew 10%, whereas the number of people under age 24 grew only 2.3%. The median age of the U.S. population as of the 2003 Census Update was 36 years old.

Most people aged 16 and older are employed, with an overall participation rate of more than 66% in 1982 and 1992, and 67.2% projected by 2012 (not shown). Workforce participation peaks between ages 35 and 44, where 81.2% and 85.1% of this group worked in 1982 and 1992, respectively; 86% of people aged 35 to 44 are projected to be working in 2012. After age 44, participation drops steadily, although a greater percentage of older workers are remaining in the workforce now than in the past. In 1982 and 1992, about 16% of workers aged 65 to 74 were still working,

Table 11.1 ***Annual Estimates of the U.S. Population by Selected Age Groups July 2000 and 2003***

Age Range	July 2003	July 2000	Change	% Change
Under 5 years	19,769,279	19,212,312	556,967	2.9%
5 to 13 years	36,752,056	37,037,950	−285,894	−0.8%
14 to 17 years	16,522,171	16,092,356	429,815	2.7%
18 to 24 years	28,899,571	27,311,145	1,588,426	5.8%
Total population under 24	101,943,077	99,653,763	2,289,314	2.3%
25 to 44 years	84,243,194	84,963,775	−720,581	−0.8%
45 to 64 years	68,704,332	62,479,071	6,225,261	10.0%
Total population 25 to 64	152,947,526	147,442,846	5,504,680	3.7%
65 years and over	35,819,174	35,081,145	738,029	2.1%

Source: Table 2: Annual Estimates of the Population by Sex and Selected Age Groups for the United States: April 1, 2000 to July 1, 2003 (NC-EST2003-02). Population Division, U.S. Census Bureau. Release Date: June 14, 2004, http://www.census.gov/popest/national/asrh/NC-EST2003/NC-EST2003-02.pdf, accessed 01/24/05.

but the U.S. Department of Labor projects this rate to be nearly 24% by 2012. The increase in older workers remaining in the workforce reflects changes in technology that lessen the physical demands of work, inflation, increases in costs of medical care, and other economic changes.

Misperception: People over 65 no longer want to work.

Reality: Many people over 65 want to work for personal, psychological, and financial reasons.

The population is also aging in many nations around the world. The AARP reports that with 27.4% of the population at age 50 or over, the U.S. population is younger than that of Japan (38.2%), Germany (35.4%), Italy (36.3%), and Sweden (36.1%).[14] Populations in both developed and developing nations are aging and this draws increased focus on the needs of an older population, including employment.

Bridge Employment and Layoffs

Bridge employment occurs when workers have retired from long-term jobs, but have not fully withdrawn from the workforce.[15] As bridge workers, these midlife workers contribute to organizations and the economy in many ways. Because they are retirees, bridge workers may be more flexible than other workers in terms of scheduling, assignments, compensation and benefits, and other important attributes. Along with flexibility, their expertise and job-knowledge make them valuable contributors. Organizations often hire bridge workers to creatively address worker shortages, to fill needs for part-time workers, and to combat skills losses due to mass retirements and layoffs.

There is considerable discussion about effects of layoffs on older workers, yet younger workers and those with little seniority tend to be hardest hit during economic downturns. During the economic downturn that began in 2001, workers aged 16 to 19 experienced five times the job losses experienced by persons over 25. Workers between 20 and 24 were two times as likely to experience job loss as those over 25.[16] However, younger workers who lost their jobs found comparable employment faster than older workers, taking 18.4 weeks compared with 25.5 weeks for older workers to find comparable employment.[17] This may be partly attributed

[14] AGEing in Europe: Realizing and Promoting the Contributions of Older People, http://www.aarp.org/international/international-report/Articles/a2004-11-11-AGEingEurope.html, accessed 01/24/05.

[15] Kim, S., & Feldman, D. C. (2000). "Working in Retirement: The Antecedents of Bridge Employment and its Consequences for Quality of Life in Retirement." *Academy of Management Journal*, 43: 1195–1210.

[16] Ibid.

[17] Rix, S. E. (2004). "Update on the older worker: 2003." AARP Public Policy Institute. http://research.aarp.org/econ/dd97_worker.pdf, accessed 01/22/05.

to the likelihood that younger workers are employed in lower-level jobs, which are more prevalent (and thus easier to find), than older workers.

Misperception: Compared with younger workers, older workers are often targeted in layoff situations.

Reality: Younger workers are more likely to be laid off, but when laid off they find other employment faster than older workers.

Education

Although there are fewer younger workers as a percentage of the population, younger workers are obtaining more education than previous generations obtained. As shown in Table 11.2, less than 25% of people aged 60 to 64 have a bachelor's degree or more, compared with 28.4% to 31.5% people between 25 and 54 who have that level of education.

As discussed in previous chapters, the racial/ethnic educational gap is decreasing, but Asians and non-Hispanic Whites still obtain more education than Blacks, Latinos, and American Indians. In addition, among young adults, those who are immigrants tend to have considerably lower education levels than those born in the United States.[18] As shown in Figure 11.1, young adults who are immigrants are more than twice as likely to have dropped out of high school as those who were born in the United States.[19]

The foreign-born are also significantly less likely to have obtained a high school diploma or further education than those born in the United States. Because Blacks, Latinos, Asians, and immigrants are increasing as a proportion of the population, many organizational leaders recognize the need to address and attempt to increase education levels of future workers. The PhD Project—an organization focused on increasing education for people of color by increasing the numbers of professors from underrepresented groups—is discussed in Chapter 5.

Research on Employment Experiences of Older Workers

Although there is evidence that in many contexts older workers are preferred over younger workers (e.g., high level or executive management), empirical research also documents negative experiences of older workers in employment situations. Older workers are often perceived as incompetent, unable and

[18] Some immigrants arrive in the United States highly educated, and there is variation in educational attainment among immigrants to the United States.

[19] Sum, A. M. (2003). *Leaving Young Workers Behind,* Special Report. Institute for Youth, Education, and Families. National League of Cities, http://www.nyec.org/youth_report.pdf, accessed 01/02/05.

TABLE 11.2 ***Summary Measures of the Educational Attainment of the Population 25 Years and Over: 2003 by Age Group***

Characteristic	Number in 000s	High School or More	Some College or More	Bachelor's Degree or More
Population	185,183	84.6%	52.5%	27.2%
Age Group				
25 to 29	18,721	86.5%	57.4%	28.4%
30 to 34	20,521	87.6%	58.6%	31.5%
35 to 39	21,284	87.6%	56.5%	28.8%
40 to 44	22,790	88.4%	56.5%	29.1%
45 to 49	21,420	89.3%	57.4%	29.9%
50 to 54	18,814	88.7%	38.9%	31.1%
55 to 59	15,470	86.9%	55.1%	29.0%
60 to 64	11,830	83.0%	47.3%	24.5%
65 to 69	9,438	76.9%	39.1%	19.6%
70 to 74	8,673	72.8%	36.4%	18.5%
Sex				
Men	88,597	84.1%	53.1%	28.9%
Women	96,586	85.0%	51.9%	25.7%
Race and Origin				
White	153,188	85.1%	52.9%	27.6%
Non-Hispanic White	133,488	89.4%	56.4%	30.0%
Black	20,527	80.0%	44.7%	17.3%
Asian	7,691	87.6%	67.4%	49.8%
Hispanic (any race)	21,189	57.0%	29.6%	11.4%

Source: Adapted from Stoops, N. (2004). Table A. Summary Measures of the Educational Attainment of the Population 25 Years and Over 2003. "Educational Attainment in the United States 2003," http://www.census.gov/prod/2004pubs/p20-550.pdf.

unwilling to learn, accident and injury prone, and as having lower performance than younger workers, even though evidence does not support these perceptions.

Mary Kite and her colleagues published a meta-analysis of effect sizes found in studies that included attitudes toward older and younger adults.[20] For 232 effect sizes Kite and her colleagues found that younger adults were consistently rated more favorably than older adults in competence, attractiveness, and behavior. Presentation of information about the targeted adult reduced, but did not eliminate the differences in perceptions of younger versus older adults. Specifically, information on employment history and health status reduced the bias against older adults.

[20] Kite, M. E., Stockdale, G. D., Whitley, B. E. Jr., & Johnson, B. T. (2005). "Attitudes toward Older and Younger Adults: An Updated Meta-Analytic Review." *Journal of Social Issues,* 61: 241–266.

FIGURE 11.1 ***Educational Attainment of Native-Born and Foreign-Born (Immigrant) Young Adults Aged 18 to 24 Who Are out of School (March 2001)***

Education Level	Native Born	Foreign Born
High school dropout	19.5%	45%
High school graduate	45%	32%
13–15 years education	23.8%	14%
16+ years education	11.7%	9%

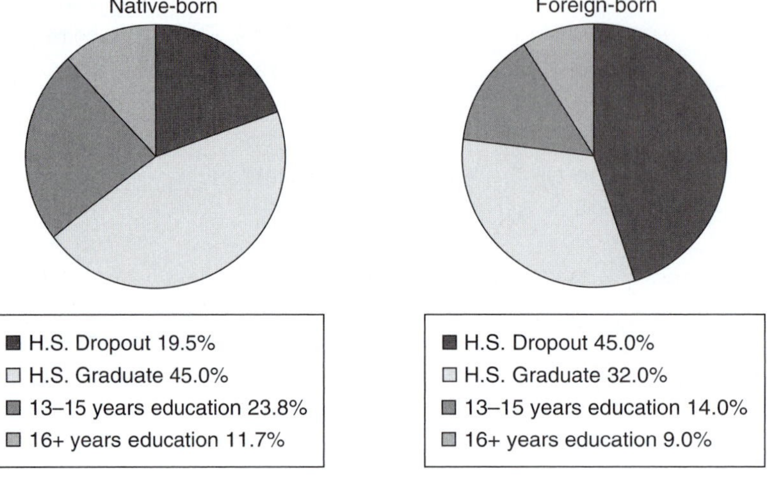

Source: Sum, A. M. (2003). *Leaving Young Workers Behind.* Special Report, Institute for Youth, Education, and Families. National League of Cities.

Rather than attitudes about younger and older workers' competence, Caren Goldberg and her colleagues assessed differences in actual job promotions and salaries based on age and sex of workers and job gender context.[21] Their sample was composed of 232 MBA alumni from a public institution in the northeastern United States. The researchers found complex interactions in which younger workers earned lower salaries, but older workers received fewer promotions. Older men had more salary advantages relative to younger men than older women had relative to younger women. They also found evidence of glass escalators, as men in feminine-typed jobs earned more than those in masculine-typed jobs.

These studies indicate that attitudes about the competence of older and younger workers do not always agree with the promotions and salaries of those workers. Depending on the nature of the job and the organizational context, stereotypical perceptions about workers' competence may or may not result in unfair behaviors toward them.

[21] Goldberg, C. B., Finkelstein, L. M., Perry, E. L., & Konrad, A. M. (2004). "Job and Industry Fit: The Effects of Age and Gender Matches on Career Progress Outcomes." *Journal of Organizational Behavior,* 25: 807–829.

Age, Accidents, and Injuries at Work

Research results on age, accidents, and injuries at work indicate that risks of injury and accidents vary by industry, employee age, and sex. Despite common misperceptions, it is younger and newly hired employees, rather than older and longer tenured employees, who appear to be more likely to have accidents or to be injured at work. The youngest workers, aged 15 to 24, are 75% more likely to be injured at work than people in other age groups.[22] Young men are most likely to be injured. Reasons for this greater risk of injury include lack of experience, training, and supervision, and overconfidence and overenthusiasm on the part of young workers. Proper training and supervision can help reduce the rate of accidents and injury at work for workers of all ages.

Misperception: Older workers are more likely to have accidents and be injured at work than younger workers.

Reality: Younger workers are more likely to have accidents and be injured at work than older workers.

Training and Development

One particular concern for older workers is access to training and development. Older workers are sometimes denied access to training and development opportunities because of two key misperceptions about their time remaining in the workforce and their ability and desire to learn. Because older workers are perceived as being near retirement, many people believe that training older workers is not a good investment of employers' resources. In contrast to this perception, and consistent with changes in perceptions of the benefits of long tenure with one employer, younger workers are more likely to turn over than older workers.

A case settled in November, 2005 involved discrimination against older applicants for an apprenticeship program to become mariners in the U.S. Merchant Marine. The EEOC alleged that applicants who were at least 40 received letters advising them that they "must be between the ages of 18 and 25" to apply for the program. Admissions representatives allegedly coded the applications of many of the older applicants with the notation "too old". After the settlement, the EEOC regional attorney stated that "The age restriction in this case appears to have been based upon the stereotype that older individuals would not succeed in a physically and mentally demanding apprenticeship program."[23]

---

22 http://www.acc.co.nz/injury-prevention/safe-at-work/worksafe/action/hazard-management/people/new-employees/, accessed 01/24/05. See also Salminen, S. (2004). "Have Young Workers More Injuries than Older Ones? An International Literature Review." *Journal of Safety Research,* 35: 513–521.

23 Maritime Training Facility & Union to Pay $625,000 for Age Bias in Apprenticeship Program," http://www.eeoc.gov/press/11-15-05.html, accessed 11/29/05.

The second misperception that older workers are unwilling and unable to learn new technologies is also unsupported by research. Research evidence does indicate that older workers learn *differently* than younger workers, preferring self-paced learning over rote memorization on a rigid time schedule.[24] Despite their inaccuracy, perceptions that they are not good training investments negatively affect the likelihood that older workers will be selected for training at work. Reports from the Department of Labor indicate that people aged 55 to 64 were one-third as likely to receive training as people aged 35 to 44.[25] A study in Hong Kong also found that organizations were more willing to train younger workers than older workers.[26] When workers are older than others in their department or than their managers, they are also less likely to receive training.[27]

Misperception: Older workers will retire soon after being trained; therefore, employers should not invest training dollars in them.

Reality: Younger workers have higher turnover rates than older workers.

Given the relationships between training and development, performance, promotion, and job retention, denying training to older workers can negatively affect them significantly. Since perceptions that older workers are unwilling and unable to learn and are not good training investments are inaccurate, organizations would be well advised to make training and development decisions on criteria other than age.

In contrast to the negative attitudes and beliefs about older workers, some companies purposely hire older employees seeking benefits such as lower turnover and absenteeism, inventory damage and theft, and higher profits. International Feature 11.2 discusses the strategies and experiences of one such company, B&Q hardware.

Older Women at Work

Research suggests that older women experience even more prejudice and discrimination at work than older men. Women are perceived to become old at younger ages than men and being old is viewed more negatively for women than

[24] For a discussion, see Shore, L. M., & Goldberg, C. B. (2005). "Age Discrimination in the Workplace." In R. L. Dipboye & A. Colella (Eds.), *Discrimination at Work: The Psychological and Organizational Bases,* Mahwah, NJ: Lawrence Erlbaum Associates.

[25] Department of Labor report cited in Maurer, T. J., & Rafuse, N. E. (2001). "Learning, not Litigating: Managing Employee Development and Avoiding Claims of Age Discrimination." *Academy of Management Executive,* 15: 110–121.

[26] Heywood, J. S., Ho, L., & Wei, X. (1999). "The Determinants of Hiring Older Workers: Evidence from Hong Kong." *Industrial and Labor Relations Review,* 52: 444–459.

[27] Cleveland, J. N., & Shore, L. M. (1992). "Self- and Supervisory Perspectives on Age and Work Attitudes and Performance." *Journal of Applied Psychology,* 77: 469–484; Shore, L. M., Cleveland, J. N., & Goldberg, C. (2003). "Work Attitudes and Decisions as a Function of Manager Age and Employee Age." *Journal of Applied Psychology,* 88: 529–537.

International Feature 11.2 *B&Q Hardware Stores Finds Hiring Older Workers Profitable*

B&Q PLC is the largest "do-it-yourself" source in the United Kingdom, with over 320 stores and 36,000 employees, many of whom are *older workers,* whom they consider to be persons at least 50 years old. In the late 1980s, B&Q decided to try hiring older workers to help address problems they were having with recruitment and turnover. B&Q was also trying to target different sectors of the population as employees, and the initial response to their recruitment ads was tremendous—600 people applied for the 50 positions advertised. The 2-year performance review of B&Q's Macclesfield store, staffed entirely by people aged 50 and older, was significantly more positive than other stores. In staffing plans, B&Q had allowed for extra training time for the older workers to learn computer technology, but this extra time was not even needed.

Customers had requested employees who could help them with their DIY and decorating needs, and B&Q found knowledgeable plumbers, electricians, and decorators through its recruitment programs targeted at those over 50. These skilled tradespeople have helped B&Q in training other employees as well as growing the nonconsumer side of B&Q's business. Overall, the employees over 50 in the Macclesfield store did extremely well. In comparison with four other stores, the Macclesfield store had more satisfied customers, 18% higher profits, turnover that was six times lower, and absenteeism that was 39% lower.

B&Q has taken other steps to increase employment of older workers, with one of its goals being eliminating age stereotyping from employment. Compulsory retirement has been removed from policies, and workers can shape their hours and work roles as appropriate to their needs. B&Q employs a diversity manager, Sue O'Neill, and has implemented training and development programs for older workers (including fast track management trainee positions).

Hiring older workers is now an important part of B&Q's policies, which, along with age diversity, also include increased diversity in other areas. O'Neill says that the company wants "a workforce where everyone doesn't think and act the same way . . . It's all about diversity—age is just the one diversity issue that affects everyone at some point."

Source: Bradford Metropolitan Borough Council, http://www.britishcouncil.org/diversity/text/age_goodtx.htm, accessed 01/25/05; James, M. (2004, January), "The Value of Experience," *Corporate Sector Review,* 47, http://www.accaglobal.com/publications/corpsecrev/47/1068917.

Questions to Consider

1. ***Given the experience of B&Q with targeted hiring of workers over 50, why do more companies experiencing similar problems with turnover and absenteeism fail to use a similar hiring strategy?***
2. ***This chapter has focused on the need to avoid age bias and discrimination against both younger and older workers.***
   a. ***Given B&Q's success with target hiring of workers over 40, what steps could be taken to ensure younger workers who would also be good workers are not excluded?***
   b. ***What effect might having a mix of workers over 50 along with workers in the 18 to 24 age group have on overall turnover, absenteeism, shortage, and customer satisfaction?***
   c. ***What are some specific steps that an organization might use to best capitalize on a mixed age employee base?***

it is for men.[28] In work and nonwork contexts, older men are sometimes viewed as striking and attractive, while older women are more likely to be viewed as dumpy and unattractive. These general perceptions affect perceptions of older men and women as employees as well. Executives are often men in their mid-50s and 60s, but very few women occupy such positions. One study found that older men were perceived as having more intellectual competence while older women were viewed as being more nurturing.[29] Intellectual competence, but not nurturance, is likely to be associated with executives.

Journalist Christine Craft's story of her experiences with age and sex discrimination in the media are documented in her book *Too Old, Too Ugly, Not Deferential to Men*.[30] More recently, Marny Midkiff, who had worked at the Weather Channel for 16 years, alleged that she was fired because the network wanted younger meteorologists.[31] To bolster her lawsuit, Midkiff showed video excerpts from a staff meeting in which the network's programming chief, Terry Connelly, referred to their female newscasters as "matronly." Ironically, as he spoke, Connelly stood in front of a "diversity" poster.[32]

In another interesting contrast, Organizational Feature 11.1 discusses disparate evidence of L'Oreal's diversity posture regarding older workers. An age-discrimination lawsuit alleges that L'Oreal has engaged in age discrimination and retaliation against a former executive. On the other hand, L'Oreal is the recipient of a best practices award for diversity efforts, including age diversity.

Preferences for younger and male workers most severely disadvantage older women, many of whom may desire (or financially need) to be in the workforce. As considered in Chapter 9, because women generally marry older men, have longer life spans, and are more likely to have spent time outside the workforce (e.g., not contributing to retirement savings or pension growth), older women are considerably more likely to be widowed and impoverished than older men. For example, between ages 55 and 64, 10.3% of women and 8.4% of men live in poverty. For those 65 and older, 12.4% of women and 7.0% of men live in poverty.[33] For older women, employment discrimination may increase their likelihood of being in poverty when they can and want to work.

---

[28] Deutsch, F. M., Zalenski, C. M., & Clark, M. E. (1986). "Is There a Double Standard of Aging?" *Journal of Applied Social Psychology,* 16: 771–785.

[29] Canetto, S. S., Kaminski, P. L., & Felicio, D. M. (1995). "Typical and Optimal Aging in Women and Men: Is There a Double Standard?" *International Journal of Aging and Human Development,* 40: 187–207.

[30] Craft, C. (1988). *Too Old, Too Ugly, Not Deferential to Men,* New York: Prima Publishing of St. Martin's Press.

[31] At the time of the writing of this chapter, the lawsuit had not been decided.

[32] Flint, J. (2005). "A Former Weathercaster Files Charges of Age Bias." CareerJournal.com. *The Wall Street Journal* online, http://www.careerjournal.com/myc/legal/20050118-flint.html, accessed 03/26/05.

[33] Smith, D. (2003). The Older Population in the United States: March 2002, http://www.census.gov/prod/2003pubs/p20-546.pdf, accessed 01/20/05.

ORGANIZATIONAL FEATURE 11.1 *L'Oreal*

"EEOC Sues L'Oreal for Age Discrimination and Retaliation"[34]

"L'Oreal Receives Diversity Best Practices 2004 Global CEO Leadership Award"[35]

These two headlines about L'Oreal's diversity practices are quite disparate. On one hand, the EEOC alleges that L'Oreal has engaged in age discrimination and retaliation. On the other hand, L'Oreal is the recipient of a best practices award for diversity. What are the details behind these headlines that appeared about a year apart?

L'Oreal is the world's largest cosmetics company, with sales of $14 billion in 2003, and employs more than 50,000 people representing 100 nationalities. Women make up one-third of the company's management and 55% of its research and development scientists. L'Oreal USA is the company's largest subsidiary, employing over 8,000 people. Women and minorities comprise 60% and 16% of management, respectively, in L'Oreal USA, which equals or exceeds their representation in many other U.S. companies.

In September 2003, the EEOC announced its filing of a lawsuit against L'Oreal USA, stating that the company had engaged in age discrimination and retaliation against Joyce Head, a woman who had been a senior director at the company. The EEOC alleged that a newly hired vice president of sales told Ms. Head that she was "too old to move to New York," "too old for a VP sales position," and that she needed a makeover "to fit in with L'Oreal's youthful image." According to the EEOC report, Head had sales of $30 million in 2002, and at times had generated 70% of her department's business. Despite her performance, Head was terminated after she reported the VP's negative age comments to L'Oreal's human resources department.

In stark contrast to the EEOC report, in October 2004, L'Oreal was awarded the inaugural Diversity Best Practices 2004 Global CEO Leadership Award. Diversity Best Practices (DBP) is member-based service for companies and government entities to exchange best practices around diversity issues and build diversity management and resources. DBP members include L'Oreal, the recipient of the organization's first award. The award reportedly recognizes the world's most progressive companies and their leaders for embracing diversity in markets, workforces, and communities. L'Oreal was honored for creating a corporate culture that embraces and drives diversity throughout the company. In response to being named the award winner, L'Oreal's CEO stated that the company "fosters and values diversity," including age diversity.

QUESTIONS TO CONSIDER

1. ***What factors may explain the apparent contradiction between the EEOC litigation and the Diversity Business Practices Global Leadership Award received by L'Oreal?***
2. ***How was this case resolved? (Search http://www.eeoc.gov).***
3. ***How might Joyce Head, the former senior director at L'Oreal, view the DBP award received by L'Oreal?***

4a. ***If the award, DBP, and the EEOC's charges are all legitimate, what factors might explain the apparent disconnect between L'Oreal's overall values and the behavior of the newly***

[34] EEOC Sues L'Oreal for Age Discrimination and Retaliation, September 30, 2003, http://www.eeoc.gov/press/9-30-03d.html, accessed 01/22/05.

[35] http://investor.news.com/Engine?Account=cnet&PageName=NEWSREAD&ID=1452930&Ticker=IVIL&SOURCE=NYTU18926102004-1, accessed 01/22/05.

hired vice president of sales who allegedly discriminated against Ms. Head? What could L'Oreal have done in response to Ms. Head's complaints that may have circumvented the lawsuit?

4b. Many companies are recognized for positive diversity efforts while at the same time being charged with discrimination or harassment. What recommendations would you make to help companies deal with these contradictions, both internally with employees and externally, with the media and constituents? Since simply ruling out organizations as potential employers on the basis of lawsuits or bad press is not reasonable, what recommendations would you make for individuals in sorting out in which organizations to seek employment, given contradictions such as these?

Research on Employment Experiences of Younger Workers

In contrast to the large amount of empirical research on the employment experiences of older workers, relatively little comparable work exists about experiences of younger workers.[36] This lack of research may reflect widespread perceptions that younger workers are generally advantaged when compared with older workers. Perceptions that younger workers are irresponsible, disloyal, and immature are also common, however, and a small number of studies have documented reports of younger workers' experiences with age discrimination. Loretto, Duncan, and White found that 35% of their sample felt their age had been a factor, both positive and negative, in their employment experiences. Some of the workers reported that they had gotten a job because of their youth, but then they were paid less than other workers in similar jobs because they were young.[37] In another study, one quarter of the respondents aged 16 to 24 reported having experienced age discrimination.[38]

Anecdotal evidence and reports in the popular press also suggest younger workers experience discrimination based on perceptions that they are unqualified for the positions they hold. Michael Sisler, hired as a bank vice president making $70,000, believed he was fired when management learned he was only 25. Sisler filed a discrimination charge under New Jersey's law prohibiting age discrimination and the case was settled before trial.[39] A 27-year-old attorney reported that in front of a courtroom full of observers and opposing counsel the sitting judge asked if this was "bring your kids to work day" and whether his father would be arguing the case for him.[40] Young college professors report having to dress maturely or wear beards or glasses in attempts to look older than they are.

---

[36] As younger workers are now the new "minority" age group in the workforce, more research may consider their experiences. As an example, see Kwesiga, E. (2005). "Ain't You Too Young to Be the Boss: When Age Discrimination Targets Younger Employees." *Paper presented at the Annual Academy of Management Meeting.* Honolulu, HI.

[37] Loretto, W., Duncan, C., & White, P. (2000). "Ageism and Employment: Controversies, Ambiguities, and Young People's Perceptions." *Ageing and Society,* 20: 279–302.

[38] Age Concern (1998). *Age Discrimination: Make it a thing of the past,* London: Author.

[39] Armour, S. (2003). "Young Workers Say their Age Holds Them Back." *USA Today,* 10/7/2003, http://www.usatoday.com/money/workplace/2003-10-07-reverseage_x.htm, accessed 01/25/05.

[40] Ibid.

Sexual Harassment of Teen Workers and the EEOC's Youth @Work Initiative

In addition to overt age discrimination in hiring, pay, and termination, the high experience rates of younger workers with sexual harassment may be related to their young ages and vulnerability. As considered in Chapters 2 and 9, sexual harassment is a serious problem, with negative consequences for its targets and for the organizations that employ them. The experience of sexual harassment (and other forms of discrimination) may affect young workers' future earnings, work lives, and career decisions in critical ways.

A review of the EEOC Web site provides a disturbing picture of experiences of young workers, in particular, with sexual harassment at work. Well-known companies with EEOC settlements involving young workers include certain locations of Longhorn Steakhouse, Taco Bell, Chili's, Radisson Inn, Church's Chicken, Burger King, and Babies "R" Us, among others. Harassment targets involved included employees as young as 14, summer employees, and students working as part of a class project.

Consider the following egregious cases taken directly from the EEOC Web site:

- **EEOC v. Rare Hospitality Int'l, Inc., d/b/a Longhorn Steakhouse**[41]
  No. 8:02-CV-177OT30-TBM (M.D. Fl. Dec. 30, 2003)

  The Miami District Office filed this Title VII sexual harassment and retaliatory discharge suit against defendant, a national restaurant chain that operates two steak restaurants in Tampa, Florida. The suit alleged that, for nine months, defendant's 36-year-old assistant manager subjected charging party, a 16-year-old student working as a hostess as part of a high school on-the-job training class requirement, to physical and verbal sexual conduct, which included breast grabbing, other inappropriate touching, and remarks about wanting to have sex with her. Two other female employees were subjected to sexually offensive conduct by the assistant manager. Despite charging party's and the other female employees' complaints, the harassment continued. The suit also alleged that in retaliation for complaining to management about the harassment, charging party's hours were reduced and she was eventually terminated.

- **EEOC v. L&L Wings, Inc.**[42]
  No. 5:02-CV-856-BO(3) (E.D.N.C. December 3, 2002)

  The Charlotte District Office alleged in this Title VII lawsuit that defendant, an owner/operator of a chain of retail stores which sell beachwear and accessories,

---

[41] EEOC Litigation Settlements—December 2003, http://www.eeoc.gov/litigation/settlements/settlement12-03.html, accessed 06/07/05.

[42] EEOC Litigation Settlements—December 2002, http://www.eeoc.gov/litigation/settlements/settlement12-02.html, accessed 06/07/05.

subjected four female summer sales associates, ages 16 to 18, to a sexually hostile working environment and discharged one of them because of her sex. The Store Manager and the Assistant Manager repeatedly made comments about the claimants' bodies, questioned them about their sexual activities, touched their legs and buttocks and propositioned them for sex. Two of the claimants quit their jobs after only four days of work due to the harassment and a third was discharged on her fourth day of work. The fourth claimant was employed for less than two months and quit after she was sexually assaulted by the Store Manager.

- **EEOC v. Babies "R" Us, Inc.**[43]

  No. 02-CV-989 (WGB) (D. N.J. January 10, 2003)

  In this Title VII lawsuit, the Philadelphia District Office alleged that defendant subjected charging party, an 18-year-old male sales clerk, to a hostile working environment because of his sex. Throughout his employment, charging party was the target of daily unwelcome and derogatory comments (such as "fag," "faggot" and "happy pants") that mocked him because he did not conform to societal stereotypes of how a male should appear or behave. He was also grabbed and held by co-workers and had his pants forcibly removed. Despite knowledge by defendant's supervisors of the verbal and physical harassment, no action was taken to stop the unlawful conduct. As a result of the ongoing harassment, charging party was forced to quit his job.

As discussed in Chapter 9, sexual harassment of any worker at any age is associated with numerous negative physical and psychological outcomes. Such harassment of young workers has the opportunity to significantly reduce their future outcomes and occupational choices, particularly if the harassment occurs in their first or very early working experiences. The rise in complaints by younger workers about sexual harassment led to the U.S. Equal Employment Opportunity Commission's (EEOC) *Youth@Work initiative,* launched in September 2004, designed to educate young workers on their rights to fair and inclusive work environments. As part of the initiative, the EEOC offers free outreach events at high schools, youth organizations and businesses that hire young workers, providing case scenarios involving discrimination and suggested response strategies. Because some of the EEOC cases involved young people as perpetrators of harassment and harassment targets, education may serve to educate both, neither of whom may have had any sexual harassment, discrimination, or other diversity-related training.

According to the EEOC Vice Chair Naomi C. Earp, one goal of the Youth@Work initiative is to protect and promote equal employment opportunity, thereby creating positive initial employment experiences for young workers, helping them as they "enter and navigate the professional world." Earp explains

[43] EEOC Litigation Settlements—January 2003, http://www.eeoc.gov/litigation/settlements/settlement01-03.html, accessed 09/16/05. Offensive language retained as reported.

that because they are "the next generation of managers, business leaders, and entrepreneurs, young workers will carry the information they learn from our agency with them throughout their professional careers."[44] An understanding of key diversity issues is of particular importance to young workers; not only will education on diversity issues promote fairness and inclusion, but it will also help younger workers reduce the effects of negative diversity concerns (e.g., harassment and discrimination) on their own careers.

Long-Term Consequences of Harassment of Young Workers

Quitting, being fired, or fleeing to another career may shape younger workers' (and people of any age) career paths, earnings, and future in many undesirable ways. Quitting or being fired from one's first job can negatively affect one's ability or desire to seek another position. In addition, other types of discrimination (e.g., hiring discrimination) may result in underemployment (see Chapter 4), and its consequences, such as lower earnings and low or no health benefits, retirement, or vacation. As would be expected, research indicates that young adults who are underemployed experience decrements to their self-esteem, job attitudes, and likelihood of appropriate later employment.[45]

As shown in Table 11.3, along with sexual harassment, two other major factors are included as key to diversity experiences of younger workers: discrimination and gender role socialization (see Chapter 9). These experiences are associated with sex segregation, un- and underemployment, termination, and numerous other negative factors for employees of all ages.[46] These factors are relevant to all workers, but they are particularly significant to the youngest workers. As proposed by the EEOC, young workers' early career experiences related to diversity issues can be strong influences on their current and future behaviors and careers. Given the increasing importance of diversity in organizations, positively affecting future managers, leaders, and employees is critical. The role played by young workers in age and other diversity issues cannot be stressed enough.

Individual Recommendations

Older and younger workers are likely to be aware of stereotypes that exist about people in their age groups. As with all stereotypes, taking steps to combat them does not mean one is at fault or responsible for the existence of stereotypes. Consciously working against stereotypes may enable a person to obtain or keep a job. Since older workers are sometimes assumed to be unwilling and unable to learn, enrolling in and completing training at work and outside of work may be

[44] Equal Employment Opportunity Commission (2004), http://www.eeoc.gov/press/12-15-04.html, accessed 12/21/04.

[45] Winefield, A. H., Winefield, H. R., Tiggemann, M., & Goldney, R. D. (1991). "A Longitudinal Study of the Psychological Effects of Unemployment and Unsatisfactory Employment on Young Adults." *Journal of Applied Psychology,* 76: 424–431.

[46] These concepts were introduced in previous chapters.

TABLE 11.3 ***Relationships between Key Diversity Issues and Career Outcomes for Young Workers***

Diversity Concern	Career Outcome
• Harassment	• Segregation
• Sexual/gender	• Low wages
• Racial	• Low status
• Disability	• Low advancement opportunity
	• Un- and underemployment
	• Termination
	• Constructive discharge
	• Intention to quit/quitting
	• Stress
	• Lowered commitment
• Discrimination	• Segregation
• Sex	• Sex
• Race	• Race
• Disability	• Un- and underemployment
	• Glass ceiling and walls
	• Low wages
	• Lowered motivation
	• Intention to quit/quitting
• Gender role socialization	• Sex segregation
	• Sex appropriate career planning, training (e.g., teaching, firefighting), and job steering
	• Sex stereotyping
	• Sanctions for role violations

useful. When managers or supervisors control access to company-provided training, older workers should make their interests in such training widely known to others who may be more supportive. If tuition reimbursement is available as a company benefit, older workers should utilize it. Tuition reimbursement is not usually limited to younger workers, nor is admission to colleges and universities.

Employees are clearly faced with the dilemma of providing sufficient educational and employment information on resumes without providing information that could result in their being excluded from consideration based on age. The possibility of older age discrimination prior to even being interviewed can be reduced by not putting specific graduation dates on resumes that would allow for estimation of one's age (e.g., such as date of college or high school graduation). On the other hand, putting recently completed training and degree programs with dates may increase perceptions of (and actual) job qualifications.

The categorization of younger workers as irresponsible and lazy may result in access discrimination that prevents them from even being hired. Younger workers may be able to demonstrate responsibility through earning good grades, completing school within a reasonable period, working reliably at previous jobs (e.g., during high school or summers), consistently participating in extracurricular activities, or similar positive behaviors. Once hired, younger workers should make a conscious effort to behave responsibly and maturely at work. Any negative (e.g., immature, irresponsible) behavior may activate preexisting age-based stereotypes more than the same behavior exhibited by an older worker.

Younger workers should not confuse education with company- or job-specific knowledge. They should also not fear asking for advice or seeking a more tenured mentor within an organization. On the other hand, when in management or leadership positions, younger workers should not be fearful of exercising authority and directing workers who are older.

Sexual and gender harassment of young workers is a particularly important concern. As younger workers appear to be unfairly targeted, they must not be afraid to complain, both at work and at home (and school if appropriate), about workplace harassment. The EEOC's Youth@Work initiative provides helpful information on what employees and employers can do to reduce discrimination and harassment of young workers.

Organizational Recommendations

This chapter has documented stereotypes and misperceptions that exist about both older and younger workers. These fallacies lead to discrimination and unfair treatment at work and can reduce organizational functioning. If some managers and supervisors do not want to hire older workers and others do not want to hire younger workers, complex, expensive dysfunctional recruitment and selection consequences could result. The shortage of younger workers and the aging of the population make employment fairness toward both groups of workers critical to employers' ability to attract and retain an adequate supply of workers in the future.

In their article "Learning, not Litigating: Managing Employee Development and Avoiding Claims of Discrimination," Todd Maurer and Nancy Rafuse provided useful prescriptions for employers seeking to avoid discrimination against older workers in training and development.[47] Many of their suggestions are appropriate to help avoid older age discrimination in other areas (e.g., hiring, promotion) as well as against younger employees and applicants.

- Explicitly state age-neutral policies.
- Scrutinize policies and practices for signs of age bias. Have zero tolerance for age bias.

---

[47] Maurer, T. J., & Rafuse, N. E. (2001). "Learning, Not Litigating: Managing Employee Development and Avoiding Claims of Age Discrimination." *Academy of Management Executive*, 15: 110–121.

- Rely on job-relevant criteria, not stereotypical assumptions.
- Train decision makers about age stereotypes and their potential effects on decisions and behavior.

As with race, ethnicity, sex, or other factors, decision makers should not make assumptions about individual workers based on their group memberships. Similar to ways to combat perceptions that women or minorities are not qualified, job-related qualifications of both younger and older hires should be publicized. Acknowledge the young manager's previous experience or relevant educational background. Emphasize the older hire's recent completion of a graduate degree or relevant job experience. Conscious efforts to address stereotypes and adherence to zero tolerance for age-based discrimination are vital.

The importance of fairness to young workers, their future careers, and future influence on diversity issues should provide organizations with sufficient motivation to treat younger workers fairly, even in the absence of legislation requiring it. With or without widespread federal protections against discrimination, young workers should be assured of fair organizational treatment, freedom from harassment and discrimination, and recourse if it does occur.

Summary

In this chapter, we have considered age as an aspect of diversity, including both younger and older workers. Although discrimination against older workers is more common and pervasive, younger workers also experience age-based stereotyping and discrimination. We discussed the ADEA and other legislation related to age discrimination along with worldwide population changes that underscore the need to treat workers from all age groups fairly, even in the absence of legislation. Fewer younger workers are being added to the workforce than in the past and there is more racial and ethnic diversity among younger workers than ever before. Younger workers tend to have more education than older workers, although young foreign-born workers often have less education than workers born in the United States. Older workers are working longer than in the past and now comprise a greater share of the workforce. More than 50% of the U.S. workforce is over age 40, and protected by federal nondiscrimination legislation. We also considered age-based stereotypes, research evidence, and suggestions for age-based fairness for both older and younger workers.

Key Terms

Ageism — prejudice, stereotypes, and discrimination directed at a person because of his or her age.

Bridge employment — when older workers retire from one company, but continue working for the same or other companies, in full- or part-time positions, for a period.

Prime age — between 25 and 35; the age range of the workers often viewed as being most desirable.

Questions to Consider

1. What possible effects could a large proportion of people aged 45 to 64 and smaller proportion of people under 45 in the current workforce have on organizations' ability to attract and retain a competent and motivated workforce? How might younger age and older age discrimination, when combined, affect employers given the shifting age distribution?
2. In addition to the suggestions provided in the chapter, what other things might organizations do to counter age-based stereotypes among employees?
3. How might the lack of broad federal legislation prohibiting younger age discrimination contribute to younger workers' experiences with discrimination and harassment at work?
4. Marny Midkiff's programming chief at the Weather Channel reportedly stood by a diversity poster as he made disparaging age and gender-related comments about the appearance of women anchors. What signal does this send about the Weather Channel's genuine commitment to diversity?
5. In several of the EEOC cases presented, managers clearly stated that applicants were "too old" or that they "wanted a younger person". What factors may make people feel comfortable stating or writing down such preferences compared to overtly stating preferences for a particular race? Is it plausible that the decision makers were unaware that age discrimination is illegal?
6. What have you learned in this chapter that is most surprising to you?

Actions and Exercises

1. Conduct an investigation of age-related employment experiences of your family and friends. Is there evidence of younger or older age favoritism or discrimination or both? Explain.

2a. Conduct an informal census of employees in several places: casual restaurant, bank, department store, university, or other locations where many employees are visible. Document the number of older and younger employees and the positions they appear to hold. Estimate the ages of each person. How do your data fit with what you have read in this chapter? What conclusions did you reach?

2b. Choose two nights to watch television for 30 minutes to 1 hour each. Document the program, commerical type, and the numbers of older and younger characters by sex on the programs and commercials.

2c. What similarities and differences are apparent between the people in questions 2a and 2b ?

3. Conduct research to see what, if any, additional legislation has been passed regarding younger age discrimination in the United States and other countries.

12 Chapter

Physical and Mental Ability

Chapter Objectives

After completing this chapter, readers should have an understanding of physical and mental disability as aspects of diversity. They should specifically be able to:

- *discuss the proportion of people who have disabilities in the United States.*
- *explain purposes of and provisions of the Rehabilitation and Americans with Disabilities Acts.*
- *discuss earnings and employment experiences of people with disabilities.*
- *compare perceptions about people with disabilities with their actual work performance.*
- *describe selected cases involving disability discrimination.*
- *propose reasonable accommodations to enable people with selected impairments to work.*

Key Facts

One in five Americans—about 50 million people—have a disability.

Many people have invisible disabilities.

Although people with disabilities want to work, they are more likely to be unemployed and have lower earnings than people without disabilities.

People with disabilities who have a college degree earn nearly 25% less than similarly educated people without disabilities.

People with disabilities have similar rates of absence and performance as people without disabilities.

Most (70%) workers with disabilities require no accommodations. For those who do, 71% of accommodations cost less than $500 and 20% cost nothing.

Introduction and Overview

The presence of disability is increasing in the United States, now affecting nearly one in five, 49.7 million people. As the U.S. population ages, the proportion of people with a disability is likely to grow.[1] People are working more years than in the past, and the likelihood of acquiring a disability during one's work years is greater than ever. An aging population, greater propensity to acquire a disability with age, and working into more advanced ages make attention to the employment experiences of people with disabilities an increasingly important issue for organizations.

People with disabilities are more likely to be un- or underemployed than any other "minority" group in the United States, in part because of stereotypes and negative perceptions about their employability and abilities.[2] They are believed to be more likely to miss work, to have lower performance, and to require employers to spend considerable money for accommodations. In contrast to these perceptions, people with disabilities have absence, turnover, and performance that are comparable to those without disabilities (and sometimes more favorable). Further, according to the Job Accommodation Network, 70% of workers with disabilities do not require accommodations. If required, accommodations are generally inexpensive; 71% of accommodations cost under $500 and 20% cost nothing.[3] As with other nondominant groups, inaccurate, but commonly held, negative beliefs about people with disabilities result in overt and covert employment discrimination against them.

Although similar in some ways to other aspects of diversity considered thus far, disability has many more complexities. For example, people are generally considered to be immutably male or female, Black, White, or Asian,[4] and there is little public disagreement about whether one even has a sex or race.[5] In comparison, disabilities vary in onset, type, severity, effects on functioning, and permanence, and their existence is sometimes debated by employers and insurance companies. Some disabilities cause periods of lowered functioning at times, but not always (e.g., multiple sclerosis). Some disabilities have few effects on functioning, but are associated with strong negative reactions from others that may affect interactions and acceptance at work (e.g., physical disfigurement, HIV). Certain disabilities are clearly visible (e.g., using a wheelchair), while others are not (such as hearing impairments). A number of disabilities may be completely cured (e.g., cancer), while others are permanent (e.g., paraplegia). With some disabilities, capabilities may not change, while others may decline permanently or improve with therapy (e.g., ability to speak after a stroke).

Although some disabilities are present at birth, many are acquired later; disability has the ability to affect everyone at some point in life. Further, while one may not have a family member who is of a different race, many people have one or more family members with disabilities. Even so, some employment discrimination occurs because people have fears and discomfort about disabilities or illness. Knowledge of a family member's limitations may also be projected onto others with disabilities, even though the disability, level of functioning, and work versus home contexts may be completely different.

[1] Disabilities affect one-fifth of all Americans. December 1997. U.S. Department of Commerce, http://www.census.gov/prod/3/97pubs/cenbr975.pdf, accessed 11/19/04.

[2] Bricout, J. C., & Bentley, K. J. (2000). "Disability Status and Perceptions of Employability by Employers." *Social Work Research,* 24(2): 87–96.

[3] Job Accommodation Network. (1999). *Accommodation Benefit/Cost Data,* Morgantown, WV: Job Accommodation Network of the President's Committee on Employment of People with Disabilities.

[4] A small percentage of people have chromosomal abnormalities and Latinos may be of any race.

[5] Many sociologists, biologists, and psychologists argue persuasively that race is socially constructed, however.

History

Current perceptions of people with disabilities as being incompetent, unable to work, and to be feared are similar to perceptions that have existed throughout history. In ancient times, people with disabilities were viewed as undesirable, defective, or marked. People who could not walk were carried and begged for a living. People with leprosy were banished from villages and towns. The leper colony in Carville, Louisiana, which once served the United States, is now a research facility. Reports of euthanasia of children with physical and mental disabilities in Nazi Germany are chilling.[6] In the 1920s in the United States, offensive advertisements for the photoplay about deformed babies, delivered by the *Black Stork* but not being treated by the doctor or being driven away, were considered amusing.[7] Schools for the blind and deaf separated children with sensory impairments from those without such impairments much as segregated schools separated people by race.[8] Terminology such as "cripple," "deaf and dumb," "crazy," and "retard" reflect commonly held perceptions about the abilities of those with physical or mental disabilities.

As early as 1929, Franklin D. Roosevelt, as president of the United States, attempted to increase opportunities for people with mental and physical disabilities. Roosevelt, a paraplegic due to polio he contracted as an adult, advocated that governments and individuals should play a role in assisting people with disabilities obtain the best assistance and care possible. Ironically, Roosevelt used a wheelchair but had an agreement with the media never to be photographed using it to avoid the appearance that he was handicapped. More recently, people with disabilities are being afforded greater opportunities, in part due to activism, resistance, and legislation prohibiting discrimination and increasing accessibility.

Relevant Legislation

As covered in Chapter 2, two major federal laws exist regarding rights and obligations toward people with disabilities in the workplace, Section 501 of the Rehabilitation Act of 1973 (RA) and Title I of the Americans with Disabilities Act of 1990 (ADA), as amended. The express purpose of the ADA is "to provide a clear and convincing national mandate for the elimination of discrimination against individuals with disabilities, (and to) provide clear,

[6] Shevell, M. I. (1999). "Neurosciences in the Third Reich: From Ivory Tower to Death Camps." *Canadian Journal of Neurological Sciences,* 26: 132–138.

[7] The Black Stork Delivers a Baby, http://www.disabilitymuseum.org/lib/stills/500card.htm; The Black Stork, Movie Advertisement, http://www.disabilitymuseum.org/lib/stills/501card.htm, accessed 11/30/04.

[8] Schools for the blind and deaf were themselves separated by race; Blacks who were blind or deaf went to different schools from Whites so impaired. There were schools for seeing Blacks and blind Blacks, and for deaf Blacks and hearing Blacks.

strong, consistent, enforceable standards for addressing discrimination against individuals with disabilities."[9] One important difference between the acts is that in addition to prohibiting discrimination, the RA requires the federal government to take affirmative action for the hiring, placement, and advancement of people with disabilities, whereas the ADA has no requirements for affirmative action.

Private employers and state and local governments having 15 or more employees for 20 or more weeks per year, employment agencies, and labor unions are prohibited from discrimination against qualified persons in employment matters such as hiring, firing, advancement, compensation, job training, and other terms, conditions, and privileges of employment. Federal sector employees are covered under the RA.[10] Because the acts are substantially similar in purpose and definitions, the remainder of the chapter focuses on the ADA.

Under the ADA, a person with a disability is one who has a physical or mental impairment that substantially limits one or more major life activities, has a record of such impairment, or is regarded as having such impairment. Guidelines issued by the U.S. Code of Federal Regulations clarify these key terms.[11]

A physical or mental impairment is any physiological disorder or condition, cosmetic disfigurement, or anatomical loss affecting at least one of the body's systems, (i.e., neurological, musculoskeletal, sensory, respiratory, cardiovascular, and others). It could also be any mental or psychological disorder, such as mental retardation, organic brain syndrome, emotional or mental illness, and specific learning disabilities. Specifically not included as impairments are such things as substance abuse disorders resulting from current drug use; transvestism, transsexualism, or other sexual behavior disorders; and compulsive gambling, kleptomania, or pyromania. Notice that current drug use, but not previous drug use, is excluded from protection under the ADA, as considered in Feature 12.1.

A person is considered substantially limited when he or she is unable to perform one or more major life activities that most people in the general population can perform. A person who is significantly restricted in the manner or length of performance of major life activities that most people in the population can perform is also viewed as substantially limited. The major life activities are such things as caring for oneself, performing manual tasks, walking, seeing, speaking, hearing, breathing, learning, and working. As is apparent from the

[9] Americans with Disabilities Act, Titles I and V, http://www.eeoc.gov/policy/ada.html, accessed 11/25/04.

[10] http://www.eeoc.gov/types/ada.html, accessed 11/22/04.

[11] Code of Federal Regulations, Title 29, Volume 4, Revised as of July 1, 2002, From the U.S. Government Printing Office via GPO Access, CITE: 29CFR1630.2, pp. 339–342, http://a257.g.akamaitech.net/7/257/2422/14mar20010800/edocket.access.gpo.gov/cfr_2002/julqtr/29cfr1630.2.htm, accessed 11/26/04.

Feature 12.1 *Key Highlights of the ADA*

- Discrimination against someone because of association with, or having a family, business, social, or other relationship with a person with a disability is prohibited.
  - If an employee has a child with spina bifida disability, an employer may not terminate the employee due to fears that the employee will miss work because of the child's illness.
  - If an employee's spouse has AIDS, an employer may not terminate the employee because of the negative reactions and fears expressed by coworkers.
- Interpretations of who is disabled vary, such that one person with certain physical issues may be considered disabled while another person with the same issues is not.
  - Employers should try to avoid making personal judgments about who has a disability and seek expert assistance when needed.
- Applicants or employees should be allowed to make suggestions of what accommodations would allow them to work.
- Employers may not ask applicants about their disabilities; employers may ask all applicants about their ability to perform specific job functions.
  - "Polite" questions about what happened are not advised. If the applicant brings up the disability, focus the conversation on job requirements, as is appropriate for all applicants.
- Medical exams may be required after a conditional job offer has been made, only if job related, and only if exams are required of all applicants entering similar jobs.
- Employees and applicants currently using illegal drugs are not covered by the ADA. Being perceived as a current drug user because of tracks or other evidence of past use may allow for coverage under the ADA if the person is actually drug free.

The Department of Labor has provided useful tips for interacting with people with disabilities.

1. Listen to the person with the disability. Do not make assumptions about what he or she can or cannot do.
2. When speaking with a person with a disability, look at, and talk directly to him or her, not to or through his or her companion. A person who uses a wheelchair may not be able to use his or her legs, but has a fully functioning brain, ears, and eyes.
3. Extend the same courtesies to people with disabilities that you would to anyone else. Feel as comfortable asking, "May I get the door?" or "May I help you with that?" as you would of anyone with or without a disability. Wait until the person answers before you help.
4. If the person has a speech impairment and you are unable to understand what he or she is saying, ask the person to repeat what has been said, rather than pretending that you understand. Learning to listen carefully to and to ask others to repeat or clarify if you do not understand is a good skill, regardless whether you are talking to people with or without speech impairments.
5. Feeling nervousness or discomfort when first meeting or interacting with someone with a disability is not unusual. When first meeting or interacting with someone with a disability think "person," "customer," "new friend," or "new coworker," rather than person with a disability.

Source: Adapted from http://www.dol.gov/odep/pubs/ek99/barriers.htm, accessed 11/29/04.

breadth of these activities, many people who have problems performing these tasks can be deemed to have a disability.

When applicants or employees have, or have a record of having these impairments, they are covered under the ADA. Someone who has a record of being impaired, has a history of or has been erroneously classified as having a substantially limiting impairment is covered. Such a person may have an impairment that in fact does not limit his or her life activities, but is treated as though he or she does.

Perceptions about physical and mental impairment are particularly significant in their attempts to address employment discrimination and are particularly relevant to the study of diversity in organizations. In other words, if someone is perceived as having a disability or as being unable to perform a job because of a disability, regardless of whether this perception is accurate, the person is covered under the ADA. The EEOC's specific wording explains that:

> These parts of the definition reflect a recognition by Congress that stereotyped assumptions about what constitutes a disability and unfounded concerns about the limitations of individuals with disabilities form major discriminatory barriers, not only to those persons presently disabled, but also to those persons either previously disabled, misclassified as previously disabled, or mistakenly perceived to be disabled. To combat the effects of these prevalent misperceptions, the definition of an individual with a disability precludes discrimination against persons who are treated as if they have a substantially limiting impairment, even if in fact they have no such current incapacity.[12] (emphases added)

These strong statements reflect the pervasiveness of perceptions that people with disabilities are incapable of successful work performance along with the recognition that what people believe about others affects how those others are treated, regardless of the accuracy or inaccuracy of these perceptions. This possibility is considered in more detail later in the chapter. Featured Case 12.1 presents a situation in which an experienced applicant with a disability was treated differently than someone without a disability.

How does an organization know if an applicant with a disability is qualified? A qualified person is one who can perform the essential functions of the job in question, with or without a reasonable accommodation. Essential functions are the functions that are the basis for the existence of the job; without having to do these functions, there would be no need for the job. In a human resources context, these are the job functions that are used to focus the recruitment and selection efforts. What are the most important things that the applicant should be able to do?

---

[12] Section 902 Definition of the Term Disability, http://www.eeoc.gov/policy/docs/902cm.html, accessed 11/24/04.

Featured Case 12.1 *A Staffing Company and Its Client Refuse to Hire an Experienced Deaf Applicant*

The ADA prohibits discrimination in hiring by both employers and employment agencies that provide employees to employers. One case involving a temporary staffing employment agency, Mitchell Temporary, and Dakota Pork Industries, a meat processing company, provides evidence of the need for such protections. The complaining party (CP), a deaf woman, applied for positions directly with Dakota Pork and Mitchell Temporary, which provided workers to Dakota Pork. Although she had prior meat processing experience, and both Mitchell and Dakota Pork hired workers during the same period when the CP applied, she was never hired. Also during that same time, Mitchell hired the CP's brother (who did not have a disability) to work at Dakota Pork. He was hired less than an hour after the CP was told there were no jobs available!

The EEOC's suit resulted in financial settlements worth $125,000 for the CP and agreements by both defendants to change their hiring practices. Defendants also agreed to adopt hiring goals for deaf or hearing-impaired applicants.

Questions to Consider

1. *What type of working conditions likely exist in a meat processing plant? What skills do workers there likely possess? How much difficulty do you think Dakota Pork has finding and keeping employees?*

2. *Since Dakota Pork hired the complaining party's brother less than 1 hour after telling the complaining party there were no jobs available, it is possible that they were unaware of the ADA. How likely is this? How likely is it that Mitchell Temporary was unaware of the ADA? Aside from overt discrimination on the basis of the complaining party's disability, why else might the complaining party been told there were no jobs available?*

Source: "Litigation Settlements—August 2004." The U.S. Equal Employment Opportunity Commission, *EEOC v. Mitchell Temporary & Dakota Pork Industries*, http://www.eeoc.gov/litigation/settlements/settlement08-04.html, accessed 12/17/04.

Marginal functions are those that are secondary to the function of the job; the applicant often does them, but if they are not performed, the job would still exist. A qualified applicant or employee must be able to perform the essential, but not marginal functions, with or without a reasonable accommodation. As an example, essential functions of a receptionist would include such things as answering phones and greeting customers. A receptionist might regularly order and drive to pick up a monthly birthday celebration cake, but doing so is not critical to the performance of the receptionist job.

What is a reasonable accommodation and how does one determine if it is reasonable or not? A reasonable accommodation is one that the employer can implement to enable the qualified person to perform essential job functions without causing undue hardship to the employer. If providing an accommodation would require significant difficulty or expense relative to the employer's size, financial resources, and/or nature and structure of the organization, then the employer would face undue hardship and would not have to provide the accommodation. Thus, undue hardship varies by employer; what is reasonable to a large, multinational corporation may be undue hardship to a 50-employee local firm with limited revenues, profits, and employees.

Research indicates that most employees with disabilities do not require accommodations, but of those who do, many of the accommodations (20%) cost nothing, and most (71%) cost $500 or less.[13] As with other equal opportunity legislation, the purpose is to reduce discrimination against, and increase employment opportunities for, persons and groups historically excluded, without unduly burdening employers in doing so. As evident in Feature 12.2, many accommodations result in benefits to employees who were not originally targeted by the accommodation, and are also beneficial to the organization in many ways. By opening our minds to other methods of accomplishing tasks, along with allowing individuals with disabilities to be able to work, organizational effectiveness may be improved in other ways.

An additional point about reasonable accommodations to enable people with disabilities to work is that managers often provide accommodations for people without disabilities, without thought or fanfare. When an employee is a student and wants to work between classes and is allowed to tailor his or her work schedule around classes, this is a reasonable accommodation. If he or she needs time off to study for exams and makes up the time on weekends, this is an accommodation. If an employee is a "night person" and prefers to work between noon and 9 p.m., and the organization allows him or her to do this and provides extra security, this is an accommodation. Providing employees with accommodations (whether they have a disability or not), is often easy, inexpensive, and generates goodwill.

Selected cases

- **EEOC v. Phillips Edison & Co.**

  No. 1:03-CV-02650-WMN (D. Md. June 28, 2004)

  The Baltimore District Office filed this ADA action, alleging that defendant, a commercial real estate company specializing in acquiring retail shopping centers, fired an employee with multiple sclerosis because it feared increased insurance costs. Defendant had initially hired charging party through an employment agency as a temporary administrative assistant. One month after she began work, defendant's Vice President offered her a permanent position to occur automatically after she completed 500 hours under the

[13] Job Accommodation Network. (1999).

FEATURE 12.2 *Examples of Reasonable Accommodations and Estimated Costs*

1. *Circumstances:* An employee had difficulty using a telephone because of a hearing impairment that requires the use of hearing aids.
   Accommodation: A telephone amplifier that works along with the employee's hearing aids is purchased at a cost of $48.00.
2. *Circumstances:* An employee with a learning disability worked in the mail room but had difficulty remembering which streets belong to which zip codes.
   Accommodation: A card system is now filed by street name, alphabetically, with the zip code. This will help the employee increase output. Cost: $150.00.
   Other benefits: This accommodation also improved performance of other employees and reduced misdirected mail by 20% in the first 6 months.
3. *Circumstances:* A large grocery store was considering hiring an applicant with Down syndrome and a mild hearing loss as a stock person. The store manager was concerned that the applicant might not be able to hear the paging loudspeaker system that is used to call stockers to specific areas in the store for work assignments.
   Accommodation: A vibrating personal pager, worn on the wrist or belt, was purchased for the applicant's use. When signaled, the applicant goes immediately to the front office for specific instructions of where to go to do what is needed in the store. Cost: $350.
   Other benefits: Store management is now considering purchasing several vibrating pagers for use by key employees when the loudspeaker is inoperable or when there are many customers in the store, making the loudspeaker difficult for everyone to hear.
4. *Circumstances:* A police officer with dyslexia spent hours completing forms at the end of each day, sometimes missing deadlines.
   Accommodation: The police officer was provided with a tape recorder, which she uses to dictate her reports. The secretary now types this police officer's reports from dictation, and those from the other officers' written reports. Cost of tape recorder: $69.00.
   Other benefits: The tape recorder is so effective that they will be provided to other officers as the budget permits, freeing officers to perform other tasks with the time they would have spent writing reports.
5. *Circumstances:* A person who used a wheelchair could not use his office desk because it was too low and his knees would not go under it.
   Accommodation: The employee brought some scrap wood from home, and the desk was raised with stable wood blocks, allowing a proper amount of space for the wheelchair to fit under it. Cost: $0.
   Other benefits: When the office furniture is replaced, as it is every 3 years, appropriately scaled furniture will be purchased for the employee. Cost: No additional costs for regular furniture replacement.
6. *Circumstances:* An applicant for a housekeeping position at a large hotel chain has a hearing and speaking impairment.
   Accommodation: The applicant was provided with an interpreter who used American Sign Language to conduct the interview. Cost: Free service provided by a local organization.
7. *Circumstances:* An employee with HIV is extremely tired in the afternoons and unable to concentrate.

Accommodation: A futon is put in an empty office and the employee can nap for 20 minutes to an hour, making up the time later in the day. Cost: $100.
Other benefits: Other employees (working students, pregnant women, parents, and older workers) needing a "power" nap also use the futon when it is available and have requested more be added. A "nap room" with multiple futons for power naps will be considered in the next budget cycle.

8. *Circumstances:* An employee with multiple sclerosis is sometimes unable to walk rapidly to weekly meetings in a building across the worksite where he works and is sometimes late for his weekly presentation to upper management.
   Accommodation: Meetings are now scheduled in the conference room in the employee's building. Cost: $0.
   Other benefits: Upper management is now more accessible to employees who work in different buildings and now does more "management by walking around."
9. *Circumstances:* Because one of her arms is considerably shorter than the other one, an applicant for a job at a large retailer had difficulty typing her answers into the computers used for the application process.
   Accommodation: The applicant was given a paper application to write with her preferred writing hand and her answers were scanned into the system. Cost: Nothing.
10. *Circumstances:* A morbidly obese employee is unable to move rapidly from the teller window in a bank's drive-through to the front line to serve walk-in customers.
   Accommodation: Job redesign allows the obese teller to be one of two tellers to work the drive-through during peak hours and to work solely in a front line during other times. Cost: $0.
   Other benefits: This accommodation improves customer service in the drive-through line as customers no longer have to wait for busy tellers to break from the front line to go to the drive-through.

Note: Scenarios 1 to 5 drawn and adapted from Job Accommodation Network, http://www.jan.wvu.edu/media/LowCostSolutions.html, accessed 11/24/04.

contract with the employment agency. CP accepted the job offer and shortly thereafter informed the Vice President that she had MS. After she completed her 500 hours, CP inquired as to why she did not receive a paycheck directly from defendant. Defendant's CEO told her he was going to wait to hire her permanently and that she should continue submitting her time to the temp agency. Thereafter, she heard a recorded phone conversation in which the CEO commented to an investor about increasing healthcare costs and the fact that he had a decent employee who came as a temp seeking full-time employment but had MS, and the difficult ethical issues this presented for a small company. A week later, the CEO fired CP allegedly because of constant tardiness and a backlog of work.[14]

[14] http://www.eeoc.gov/litigation/settlement09-04.html, accessed 12/08/04.

- **EEOC v. Spylen of Denville, Inc., dba Wendy's**
  No. 02-4091 (WHW) (D. N.J March 16, 2004)

  The Philadelphia District Office alleged in this ADA action that defendant subjected charging party to a hostile work environment because of his disability, Down's Syndrome, causing charging party's constructive discharge. Charging party is moderately mentally retarded and is limited in learning, communicating, and caring for himself. The Commission alleged that management staff and coworkers at the Wendy's restaurant where charging party worked repeatedly harassed him because of his disability. Coworkers screamed profanities at charging party and called him "stupid." Charging party was subjected to physical assaults including pushing, shoving, placing a knife against his stomach, putting ice down his clothes, and throwing water in his face. As a result of this harassment charging party was forced to resign.[15]

- **EEOC v. Autoliv A S P, Inc.**
  No. CIV-03-110 (D. Utah April 13, 2005)

  In this ADA complaint, the Phoenix District Office alleged that defendant, a subsidiary of Autoliv, Inc. (a global holding company headquartered in Stockholm, Sweden) that manufactures air bag components, failed to provide a reasonable accommodation to charging party and other similarly-situated employees who attempted to return to work after taking medical leave for disabilities. After about 5 years in a production job at defendant's Ogden, Utah facility, charging party sustained work-related injuries affecting her cervical spine and both elbows. Between August 2000 and September 2001, she underwent multiple surgeries on her cervical spine and elbows. Based on her doctor's restrictions (lifting limited to 10 pounds, no heavy use of right arm, and no overhead work) defendant reassigned her to light duty work, where she remained for about 15 months. In May 2001, defendant adopted a policy that limited light duty assignments to 120 days. The Human Resources Manager told charging party that she could not work in a light duty assignment permanently, but that she could apply for other jobs during the 120-day period. Charging party applied for several vacant jobs for which she was qualified, but was not selected, and was terminated after 120 days, in September 2001. Defendant made no efforts to assist charging party in obtaining a reassignment, and Human Resources managers admitted that employees on light duty were never hired into vacant positions.[16]

[15] EEOC Litigation Settlements—March 2004, http://www.eeoc.gov/litigation/settlements/settlement03-04.html, accessed 07/04/05.

[16] EEOC litigation settlement report—April 2005, http://www.eeoc.gov/litigation/settlements/settlement04-05.html, accessed 07/04/05.

- **EEOC v. Apria Healthcare Group, Inc.**
  No. 04CV00443CAS (D. Mo. March 31, 2005)

  In this ADA suit, the St. Louis District Office charged Apria Healthcare Group, Inc., a provider of home healthcare products and services, with discharging charging party due to her psychiatric disability (bipolar disorder, mixed, rapid cycling). Defendant hired charging party for a temporary position in its St. Louis office and a few months later, in September 2001, converted her to full-time and promoted her to quality assurance coordinator. In late 2001 and early 2002, charging party missed some work because of problems with her medication. On January 9, 2002, charging party's supervisor spoke to her about the absences, and charging party told her she would need an accommodation under the ADA and agreed to obtain a written request from her doctor. The following day, charging party was acutely depressed and suicidal and left the office to go to the hospital. Thereupon her doctor requested a several-week leave of absence. On January 24, 2002, charging party brought her supervisor a release from her psychiatrist. Charging party phoned the supervisor daily, but was not permitted to return to work until February 8. The following week charging party left work early to see her doctor because of her illness (in the release letter, the psychiatrist had explained that his client would need to meet with him once or twice a month as part of her accommodation). Although she called in sick the next day, defendant fired her for "job abandonment."[17]

As is apparent in the cases described, people with disabilities experience varied types of employment discrimination. Employers' attempts to minimize future medical costs by avoiding hiring people with disabilities are prohibited by the ADA, as is harassment of a person with a disability. When an employee acquires a disability through a work-related injury, the employer should provide reasonable accommodations to enable him or her to work. Employee education on reasonable accommodations and the rights of people with disabilities are important ways to avoid discrimination.

Population

U.S. census data report on six different categories of disability: sensory, physical, mental, self-care, go-outside, and employment (work). The areas covered in each disability category are:

- Sensory—having a disability involving sight or hearing.
- Physical—having a condition limiting basic physical activities such as walking, climbing stairs, reaching, lifting, or carrying.

[17] EEOC Litigation Settlements—March 2005, http://www.eeoc.gov/litigation/settlements/settlement03-05.html, accessed 07/04/05.

TABLE 12.1 ***Characteristics of Persons with Disabilities (2000)***

	Total in Millions	Percent
Population 5 years and older	257.17	100.0
With any disability	49.75	19.3
Population 16 to 64 years	178.69	100.0
With any disability	33.15	18.6
Sensory	4.12	2.3
Physical	11.15	6.2
Mental	6.76	3.8
Self-care	3.15	1.8
Going outside the home	11.41	6.4
Employment disability	21.29	11.9

Source: U.S. Census Bureau. Disability Status: 2000. Census 2000 Brief Summary File 3. http://www.census.gov/prod/2003pubs/c2kbr-17.pdf, accessed 10/03/05.

- Mental—having a physical, mental, or emotional condition causing difficulty in learning, remembering, or concentrating.
- Self-care—having a physical, mental, or emotional condition causing difficulty in dressing, bathing, or getting around inside the home.
- Go-outside—having a condition that makes it difficult to go outside the home to shop or visit a doctor.
- Employment (work)—having a condition that affects the ability to work at a job or business.[18]

The population could self-report having none, one, or more of these disabilities. Importantly, for people who did not report an employment disability, having either of the other five disabilities could affect their ability to work or *prospective employers' perceptions about their ability to work,* although they would not be included in the official count for people having an employment disability.

More than 19% of people ages 5 and older have a disability—49.75 million people. As shown in Table 12.1, not all disabilities affect one's ability to work. While 18.6% (33.2 million) of the people ages 16 to 64 have a disability, 11.9% (21.3 million) have conditions that affect their ability to work.[19] With accommodations, many of these people with disabilities would be able to work successfully.

[18] "Disability Status: 2000—Census 2000 Brief." U.S. Census Bureau, http://www.census.gov/prod/2003pubs/c2kbr-17.pdf.

[19] Table 3. Disability Status: 2000 of the Civilian Noninstitutionalized Population of the United States, Regions, States, and for Puerto Rico: 2000, http://www.census.gov/hhes/www/disability/disabstat2k/table3.html, accessed 10/03/05.

TABLE 12.2 ***Education of People Aged 16 to 64 with and without Work Disabilities***

	With a Work Disability	Without a Work Disability	Difference
Less than 12th	25.8%	17.6%	+8.2
H.S. diploma only	37.6%	29.6%	+8.0
AA degree or some college	24.7%	27.6%	−2.9
B.S. or more	11.8%	25.2%	−13.4

Source: Table 1. Selected Characteristics of Civilians 16 to 74 years old with a work disability by educational attainment and sex: 2004. http://www.census.gov/hhes/www/disability/cps/cps104.html, accessed 10/03/2005.

Note: Table 12.2 includes ages 16 to 64 only.

Misperception: People with disabilities prefer to collect disability checks than to work.

Reality: People with disabilities want to work, even though having a disability is a strong predictor of unemployment.

Education and Employment

As shown in Table 12.2, 25.8% of people with a work disability have less than a high school diploma, 37.6% have a high school diploma, 24.7% have an associate's degree or some college, and 11.8% have a bachelor's degree or more. These education levels are lower than the education levels of the U.S. population without a work disability, where fewer people did not finish high school and more people completed college or obtained advanced degrees. Sixteen percent more people with disabilities have a high school degree or less and 16% fewer people with disabilities have completed some college or more. These lower educational levels may reflect barriers faced by people with disabilities in obtaining education.

We first consider employment levels of people in all six categories of disabilities and then focus solely on those who report having a work disability. As shown in Table 12.3, people with none of the six disabilities are considerably more likely to be employed and to work full time year round than people with a disability. People with self-care and mental disabilities are least likely to be employed and to work full time, year round, while those with work disabilities are most likely to be employed. Less than 40% of the people with any of the six disabilities worked full time, year round in 1999.

When comparing earnings and employment of people with and without work disabilities at the same level of education, those with disabilities have lower employment and earnings. Table 12.4 presents 2003 earnings for people with and without disabilities who worked full time, year round. Because people with disabilities are considerably less likely to work full time, year round,

Table 12.3 ***Employment and F/T Year-Round Work for People with and without Any of the Six Disabilities***

% of Population 21 to 64 Years	Employed	Worked Full Time, Year Round in 1999	Difference
With none of the six disabilities	77.2%	57.2%	−20.0%
With any of the six disabilities	56.6%	39.3%	−17.3%
Sensory	49.7%	35.4%	−14.3%
Physical	33.8%	21.7%	−12.1%
Mental	30.4%	16.4%	−14.0%
Self-care	30.9%	12.6%	−18.3%
Going outside the home	45.3%	30.8%	−14.5%
Employment disability	63.1%	44.0%	−19.1%

Source: U.S. Census Bureau. Disability Status: 2000. Census 2000 Brief Summary File 3, http://www.census.gov/prod/2003pubs/c2kbr-17.pdf, accessed 11/22/04.

earnings disparities are actually greater than are apparent. As shown in Table 12.4, for both groups, education increases earnings. People with disabilities earn between 76% (bachelor's or more) and 93% (high school diploma) of the earnings of people without disabilities. At the highest level, mean earnings for people with work disabilities exceed $16,000 more than people without work disabilities.

Table 12.4 ***Comparison of 2003 Year-Round Full-Time Earnings and Employment of Workers with and without Work Disabilities for Persons 16 to 64***

	Mean Earnings without a Work Disability	Mean Earnings with a Work Disability	Difference
12th grade or less, no diploma	$25,281	$20,781	−$4,500
High school graduate	$34,153	$31,726	−$2,427
AA degree or some college	$40,935	$37,415	−$3,520
B.S. degree or more	$69,617	$53,243	−$16,374
Total	$46,609	$37,637	−$8,972
	Unemployment Rate without a Work Disability	**Unemployment Rate with a Work Disability**	**Difference**
12th grade or less, no diploma	12.7%	22.2%	+9.5%
High school graduate	6.8%	14.4%	+7.6%
AA degree or some college	4.9%	16.3%	+11.4%
B.S. degree or more	2.9%	9.9%	+7.0%
Total	5.8%	15.2%	+9.4%

Source: Table 3. Work Experience and Mean Earnings in 2003—Work Disability Status of Civilians 16 to 74 Years Old by Educational Attainment and Sex, http://www.census.gov/hhes/www/disability/cps/cps304.html, accessed 11/22/04; Table 2. Labor Force Status—Work Disability Status of Civilians 16 to 74 Years Old, by Educational Attainment and Sex, http://www.census.gov/hhes/www/disability/cps/cps204.html, accessed 11/22/04.

Note: Table 12.4 includes persons aged 16 to 64 only.

Unemployment rates for people with disabilities are two to three times the unemployment rates of people without disabilities.[20] People with a disability who have at least a college degree are over three times as likely to be unemployed than people who do not have a disability. As educational levels increase, unemployment for people without disabilities declines more than it does for people with disabilities. In other words, obtaining additional education is less helpful in combating unemployment for people with disabilities than to those without disabilities. This phenomenon is similar to differential rates of educational return experienced by people of color compared with Whites.

Employment Experiences of People with Disabilities

The previous section presented education, earnings, and employment differences between people with and without disabilities. Despite the disparities, 10% more of the people with disabilities who are able to work were employed in 2000 than in 1986. Thus, the ADA appears to be having a positive effect on the employment of people with disabilities. According to the census of 2000, about 10.4 million men and 8.2 million women with disabilities were employed. As discussed in Chapter 2, the majority of claims filed under the ADA are deemed to have no reasonable cause. However, many claims are deemed meritorious, and result in settlements and damage awards against small, medium, and large employers. These cases, coupled with the persistent unemployment of people with disabilities, despite their desires and ability to work, provide evidence that discrimination against people with disabilities still occurs. Organizational Feature 12.1 considers experiences of people with several different disabilities when employed or seeking jobs at Wal-Mart.

Intellectual Disabilities

A person is considered to have an intellectual disability when his or her IQ is below 70 to 75; has significant limitations in conceptual, social, and practical skills needed for everyday life; and the disability originated before age 18. An intellectual disability can have characteristics associated with some of those associated with the six disability categories used by the U.S. census. About 2.5 million people in the United States have an intellectual disability, and as with other types of disabilities, intellectual disabilities can impede people's ability to work. Only 31% of people who have intellectual disabilities are employed, although considerably more want to work. Among others appropriate to individual

[20] Recall from Chapter 4 that the unemployment rate does not reflect those who have grown discouraged and stopped looking for work.

Organizational Feature 12.1 *Applicants and Employees with Disabilities at Wal-Mart: Persistent Problems, Expensive Settlements, and Negative Publicity*

Wal-Mart Stores, Inc., America's largest retailer, is at the center of a long-lived, tangled web of litigation, consent decrees, motions for contempt, and settlements involving the EEOC and applicants and employees with disabilities. In 1995, Jeremy Fass and William Darnell, who are both deaf, applied to work at a Tucson Wal-Mart store. They were denied employment, and in 1997, the Arizona Center for Disability Law (ACDL), a nonprofit public interest law firm, and the EEOC filed suit. (See Figure 12.1.) In January 2000, Wal-Mart agreed to the terms of a consent decree regarding Fass and Darnell's case that included

- offering them positions and providing them a sign language interpreter for training and orientation and in other regular meetings.
- paying each young man $66,250 plus profit sharing and reimbursement for out of pocket medical expenses that would have been covered by health insurance benefits had each been hired in 1995.
- providing them corporate service (start) dates of September 1, 1995, payment of their $57,500 attorneys' fees and litigation expenses.
- making corporate-wide changes in the hiring and training of persons who are deaf or hearing impaired.

In the spring of 2001, the EEOC returned to court to file a contempt motion against Wal-Mart. The motion alleged that Wal-Mart had violated terms of the consent decree by not creating alternative training materials for nationwide use by the hearing impaired, by not providing training to management on the ADA, and by refusing to allow the EEOC and the ACDL to visit stores to check for compliance. After reviewing the evidence, a judge agreed awarding more than $750,000 in fines to the ACDL for use in advocacy for employment of people with hearing disabilities.

Figure 12.1 ***Wal-Mart's Disability Troubles***

Entry Date	Caption
January 7, 2000	Wal-Mart settles employment discrimination claim of two applicants who are deaf, also agrees to make corporate wide changes in hiring and training.
May 10, 2001	EEOC files contempt motion against Wal-Mart for violating consent decree in disability bias case.
June 14, 2001	Judge slaps Wal-Mart with major sanctions for violating court order in EEOC disability bias case. Retail giant to pay $750,200 in fines, produce TV ad, reinstate deaf worker, provide ADA training.
June 21, 2001	Wal-Mart violates disabilities act again; EEOC files 16th ADA suit against retail giant.
September 20, 2001	Wal-Mart agrees to air TV ad and pay $427,500 after court finds retailer in contempt of court.
October 23, 2001	Wal-Mart TV ad tells the story of two deaf men's employment discrimination claim against the retail giant.
December 17, 2001	Comprehensive EEOC, Wal-Mart settlement resolves disability lawsuit.

Sources: Wal-Mart TV Ad Tells the Story of Two Deaf Men's Employment Discrimination Claim against the Retail Giant, http://www.eeoc.gov/press/10-23-01.html, accessed 11/26/04; Comprehensive EEOC, Wal-Mart Settlement Resolves Disability Lawsuit, http://www.eeoc.gov/press/12-17-01.html, accessed 11/25/04; Wal-Mart Settles Employment Discrimination Claim of Two Applicants Who are Deaf, also Agrees to Make Corporate Wide Changes in Hiring and Training, http://www.eeoc.gov/press/1-7-00-b.html, accessed 11/26/04; Wal-Mart Violates Disabilities Act Again; EEOC Files sixteenth Suit against Retail Giant, http://www.eeoc.gov/press/6-21-01.html, accessed 11/26/04; Judge Slaps Wal-Mart with Major Sanctions for Violating Court Order in EEOC Disability Bias Case, http://www.eeoc.gov/press/6-14-01.html, accessed 10/03/05.

Wal-Mart was required to reinstate William Darnell, who had been hired but quit because of a lack of assistance with training (given his hearing impairment). Wal-Mart also had to produce and air a television ad about its previous problems with people with disabilities.

Wal-Mart's disability-related difficulties with the EEOC continued with the EEOC's sixteenth ADA suit against Wal-Mart, filed in June 2001. Alice Rehberg was a Wal-Mart People Greeter whose disability made her need to sit periodically. According to the suit, Wal-Mart constructively discharged Rehberg by refusing to allow her to sit periodically, and failing to follow ADA procedures. Notably, in two of the earlier cases mentioned, juries had levied sizable awards against Wal-Mart for intentionally discriminating against an applicant whose arm had been amputated and another applicant who used a wheelchair. Although one award was the most ever awarded for asking an illegal medical question on an application, Wal-Mart's disability and employment problems subsequently worsened.

In September 2001, Wal-Mart consented to pay $427,500 in contempt fines and to air the television ads agreed to in the Fass and Darnell case. The 60-second ads featured Fass and Darnell, and were close captioned for the hearing impaired. They also featured telephone numbers for the EEOC and the ADCL so that viewers who had questions or felt they had experienced discrimination could seek assistance.

The Wal-Mart/EEOC disability saga paused in December 2001, when Wal-Mart agreed to a $6.8 million consent decree to settle the multiple disability lawsuits that were still outstanding. Under the decree, Wal-Mart agreed to

- provide nationwide training on the ADA and job offers.
- abolish a preemployment questionnaire that sought information on disabilities prior to conditional job offers being made.
- institute new or revised selection policies.
- provide priority consideration for hiring those applicants who were qualified, but had been rejected based on medical or disability-related information obtained through the improper questionnaire.

Questions to Consider

1. ***Wal-Mart is the largest retailer in the United States. What role may this size have played in (a) Wal-Mart's persistent issues with disability discrimination and (b) the EEOC's persistence in litigating these cases?***
2. ***Wal-Mart agreed to provide priority consideration for hiring applicants who were qualified to work at Wal-Mart, but had been rejected based on illegal information obtained through their employment questionnaire. What are the likely qualifications required for most jobs in Wal-Mart stores?***
3. ***What might other firms learn from Wal-Mart's experiences regarding application forms, selection decisions, accommodations, management training, and the other human resource management issues discussed in this feature. Have you seen inappropriate questions on employment applications? If so, what kinds?***
4. ***As a large retailer, Wal-Mart may have attendance and turnover problems. How might Wal-Mart address turnover and attendance through hiring of people with disabilities?***

strengths and interests, the EEOC proposes following as examples of jobs that might be appropriate for people with intellectual disabilities to perform: animal caretakers, laundry workers, library assistants, data entry clerks, mail clerks, printers, assemblers, grocery clerks, housekeepers, and automobile detail workers.[21] Along with providing people with intellectual disabilities opportunities to work, the high turnover associated with many of these and similar routine jobs could be reduced if people with intellectual disabilities were given opportunities to work in them. As with all applicants and jobs, it is important to assess job requirements and applicant skills and interests for appropriate fit.

The Glass Ceiling, Walls, and Secondary Job Markets for People with Disabilities

In 1994, the U.S. Glass Ceiling Commission published a comprehensive report on the employment status of people with disabilities.[22] Much like women and minorities, people with disabilities experience a glass ceiling that impedes their advancement beyond certain (low) organizational levels, and tend to be segregated into certain job markets. They are underrepresented in management and professional positions and overrepresented in lower-paid service and operator jobs. White males with disabilities work at higher levels and have higher earnings than women and people of color with disabilities. In particular, women of color who have a disability suffer triple jeopardy, facing obstacles due to race, sex, and disability.

Perceptions of Performance Inadequacies

As is apparent in the cases discussed so far, people with disabilities may experience access and treatment discrimination. Research evidence drawn from rehabilitation counseling, psychology, sociology, management, and legal literatures supports the existence of both forms of discrimination. It appears, however, that much of the discrimination occurs because of people's perceptions that the disability will impede performance.

Misperception: People with disabilities have lower performance than people without disabilities.

Reality: Many disabilities have no effect on job performance.

A study by Adrienne Colella of Tulane University reported that employers' expectations for the work performance of people with disabilities is either the

---

[21] Questions and Answers about Employees with Intellectual Disabilities in the Workplace and the Americans with Disabilities Act, http://www.eeoc.gov/facts/intellectual_disabilities.html, accessed 07/04/05.

[22] Braddock, D., & Bachelder, L. (1994). *The Glass Ceiling and Persons with Disabilities,* Washington, DC: Department of Labor.

same or lower than those of people without disabilities, and the expectations vary by disability type.[23] In one experiment, Colella and her colleagues also found that job-fit affected ratings of people with disabilities as potential task partners. Where the fit was poor, the expectations for performance were lower than where the fit was good.[24] Mary McLaughlin and her colleagues found that for three different disabilities (AIDS, cerebral palsy, and stroke) only concerns about impacts to performance were consistently negatively related to attitude and perceived fairness of accommodations. Concerns about performance were positively related to the propensity to discriminate against the person with a disability.[25] In other words, the type of disability was less important than were the perceptions that the prospective employee would be unable to perform adequately because of having a disability. It is possible that if misperceptions about performance abilities were alleviated, discrimination could also be reduced.

DuPont and Employment of People with Disabilities

DuPont has a long history of hiring people with disabilities and has conducted surveys since 1958 to assess their performance, attendance, and safety records. In the widely cited publication *Equal to the Task II,* DuPont reported findings that workers with disabilities had above average or average ratings of performance, attendance, and safety in 90%, 86%, or 97% of cases, respectively. These ratings were comparable to those of employees without disabilities and are similar to the ratings reported in the study conducted a decade earlier. At DuPont, workers with disabilities have proven themselves "equal to the task" for decades.

In a surprising twist, a disability discrimination case involving DuPont demonstrates the need for widespread vigilance to avoid employer discrimination. The EEOC alleged that DuPont violated the ADA by terminating Laura Barrios, who has severe physical impairments. Despite successfully working for the company for 18 years (with the disability), Barrios was forced to take a lengthy and painful "functional capacity exam" that was not related to her job performance as a secretary in a sedentary position. Although she passed the exam, Barrios was still terminated "due to her alleged inability to walk well

[23] Colella, A. (1994). "Organizational Socialization of Employees with Disabilities. Critical Issues and Implications for Workplace Interventions." *Journal of Occupational Rehabilitation,* 4: 87–106.

[24] Colella, A., DeNisi, A. S., & Varma, A. (1998). "The Impact of Ratee's Disability on Performance Judgments and Choice as Partner: The Role of Disability—Job Fit Stereotypes and Inter Dependence of Rewards." *Journal of Applied Psychology,* 83: 102–111.

[25] McLaughlin, M. E., Bell, M. P., & Stringer, D. Y. (2004). "Stigma and Acceptance of Coworkers with Disabilities: Understudied Aspects of Workforce Diversity." *Group and Organization Management,* 29: 302–333.

enough to evacuate" in case of an emergency. During the trial the human resources manager acknowledged that Barrios could walk to safely evacuate the building, however. A jury verdict found DuPont liable for malicious intentional disability discrimination, and the final award to Barrios was $591,000, which included the maximum allowable $300,000 for punitive damages.[26] Barrios stated, "I tried to prove to them that I could safely evacuate the plant site, but they would not let me prove it. All I wanted was to do my job."[27]

Individual Recommendations

As for other underutilized populations, our first recommendation is for individuals with disabilities wishing to increase their employment opportunities and outcomes to obtain as much education as possible. The Glass Ceiling Commission reports cite research indicating that people with disabilities with higher education levels obtain jobs faster, earn more, and progress farther than those with low education levels.[28] Seek positions in larger firms, and those that have formal diversity and/or affirmative action programs. Organizations with formal programs to hire people with disabilities provide more opportunities and training and development for them. Seek positions well-suited to your interests and abilities. Because perceived job fit reduces discrimination, be aware of accommodations that will enable you to work successfully, and do not be afraid to ask for them, or to seek outside assistance in obtaining them.

People without disabilities should be careful to pursue fairness and equity for people with disabilities. Being aware of the employment obstacles they face and the diversity among them and in their disabilities is one step in improving their opportunities for fairness at work. Not all disabilities are visible, and having one type of disability (e.g., hearing impairment) does not mean one has another type of disability (e.g., mental impairment). Be careful of your speech at all times; common terminology has derogatory marks about many people with disabilities. While most people would try to avoid making racist or sexist remarks openly at work, references to someone as being retarded, cripple, or crazy are not uncommon. Not only could someone with a disability be offended, so also could many others who do not have disabilities.

[26] Judge Upholds Jury Verdict against DuPont for $591,000 in Disability Bias Suit by EEOC, http://www.eeoc.gov/press/6-9-05a.html, accessed 07/08/05.

[27] EEOC Obtains $1.2 Million Jury Verdict against DuPont for Disability Discrimination, http://www.eeoc.gov/press/10-25-04.html, accessed 10/08/05.

[28] Braddock & Bachelder. (1994).

Organizational Recommendations

The U.S. Department of Labor, the National Institute on Disability and Rehabilitation Research, the National Organization on Disability, the Job Accommodation Network, and countless other organizations are available to help employers in their attempts to employ and fully utilize workers with disabilities. Employers may also consult state and local organizations for assistance. First, we consider research on changing negative attitudes. Second we discuss ways in which employers can help applicants and employees with disabilities, focusing on human resource management issues, consistent with the ADA's prohibition of discrimination in all employment-related matters. Lastly, we discuss accommodations for people with disabilities.

Changing Negative Attitudes at Work

What can be done to change the negative attitudes some people have about interacting with, working with, or hiring those with disabilities? Multiple researchers have identified methods to successfully change negative attitudes toward persons with disabilities. In one study, using an established theory of attitude change, the attitudes toward persons with disabilities were changed through behavioral suggestions.[29] These suggestions focused on reducing tension and anxiety often associated with interactions between persons with and without disabilities. In another study, researchers found that providing factual knowledge about people with disabilities improved attitudes toward them.[30] In another study of business leaders with responsibility for hiring, attitudes toward people with disabilities were improved after a one day training seminar.[31] The seminar included a video about hiring people with disabilities, a 3-hour simulation experience, small group discussions, interacting with a panel of persons with disabilities, and listening to employers describe their experiences with hiring workers with disabilities. Training for all employees, including managers, supervisors, executives, and staff, that includes data on the performance, attendance, and safety records of people with disabilities should also be helpful.

Human Resources Needs

Once overall training has been conducted, organizations should ensure all human resources functions are barrier free. First, have a valid, written job description prior to advertising and interviewing for a position, with essential and marginal

---

[29] Evans, J. H. (1976). "Changing Attitudes toward Disabled Persons: An Experimental Study." *Rehabilitation Counseling Bulletin,* 19: 572–579.

[30] Hunt, C. S., & Hunt, B. (2004). "Changing Attitudes toward People with Disabilities: Experimenting with an Educational Intervention." *Journal of Managerial Issues,* 16: 266–281.

[31] Perry, D. C., & Apostal, R. A. (1986), October–December. "Modifying Attitudes of Business Leaders toward Disabled Persons." *Journal of Rehabilitation,* 54(4): 35–38.

functions made clear. Such a job description can help decision makers avoid discrimination against qualified individuals with disabilities, or falling victim to other biases (e.g., similarity error) that may disadvantage people based on their demographic status and reduce organizational effectiveness. To help ensure people with disabilities are treated fairly as applicants and employees, the job description should be used for all phases of the human resources process.

Recruitment. Numerous organizations are available to provide recruitment assistance for organizations seeking to employ workers with disabilities. The Employer Assistance Referral Network (earnworks.com), the Marriott Foundation's Bridges program (see Organizational Focus 12.2), and the Job Accommodation Network are three of many reputable sources. In addition, some career centers at universities provide assistance, particularly if the university is recognized for having large proportions of students with disabilities or being specifically designed to focus on their needs (e.g., the University of Texas at Arlington or Gallaudet University, respectively).

Selection. The job description should be used in selecting applicants who are capable of successful job performance, with or without reasonable accommodations. Having and using a job description can help organizations in selecting appropriately in all situations (not just with applicants with disabilities). Tests and other methods used in selection must be related to successful job performance, and should be required for all applicants—not just those with disabilities. Medical exams can only be required after a conditional job offer is made, only if required for all applicants, and only if necessary for successful job performance.

Compensation and benefits. People with disabilities should be compensated based on the worth of the job, and based on the education, experience, and skills they possess. Disability should not be considered in compensation and disability-based discrimination in compensation is illegal under the ADA.

Training and development. People with disabilities should be given training and development as would those without disabilities. If accommodations are needed to facilitate training, such as for hearing impaired employees, these should be provided. Failure to provide a sign language interpreter for training new hires was one of the problems at Wal-Mart (see Organizational Feature 12.1) that could have been very easily remedied.

Performance evaluation. People with disabilities should have their performance evaluated regularly, as should people without disabilities. Performance standards, for the essential job functions, should be the same as those for people without disabilities. Vague performance standards may disadvantage people with disabilities[32] and are a liability for organizations. On the other hand, some

[32] Braddock & Bachelder. (1994).

Organizational Focus 12.2 *Marriott's Spirit to Serve and Bridges to Employment Program: Helping Employers and People with Disabilities*

Marriott International, Inc. is a leading hospitality company that operates more than 2,600 hotels and resorts, employing over 128,000 people worldwide. For the past several years, Marriott has been recognized by *Working Mother, Latina Style, DiversityInc., Computerworld,* and *Fortune Magazine* as one of the top places to work. Marriott has also been acclaimed as one of the best corporate citizens, Corporation of the Year, and, in 2002, J. W. Marriott, Jr., won the Lifetime Achievement Award for "his exemplary commitment to recognizing and including women, minorities, and people with disabilities in the hospitality industry."

Marriott has been a pioneer in the employment of people with disabilities. In the 1980s, prior to passage of the ADA, Marriott employed adults with Down syndrome as housekeepers at Marriott hotels, paying them $7.00 per hour for 40 hours per week, well above minimum wage at the time.[33] Marriott embraces a "Spirit to serve" philosophy, through which Marriott attempts to make a difference in the lives of others, including other employees, customers, business partners, and the community. This philosophy is reflected in the commitment to the employment of people with disabilities at Marriott and in Marriott's work to facilitate employment of youth with disabilities at other companies around the United States.

The Marriott Foundation for People with Disabilities, a public charity, established the Bridges from School to Work program in 1989 to enhance employment opportunities for youth with disabilities.[34] The Bridges program is guided by three key principles:

- To consistently establish successful employment opportunities, the business needs of employers must take precedence.
- People with disabilities can be employees with capabilities; focusing on their skills and interests is more important than being preoccupied with what they can't do.
- The future needs everyone.

Since the first Bridges program was pilot tested in Maryland in 1990, more than 6,000 young people completing special education programs have been employed by over 1,500 different employers who participate in the program. Bridges now operates in Chicago, San Francisco, the District of Columbia, Los Angeles, Atlanta, and Philadelphia. The Bridges model considers perspectives and needs of employers and youths, job analyses, and the skills, interests, and preparation of youths to make effective job matches.

Bridges establishes strong relationships with prospective and current employers. Through these relationships, fears and negative perceptions about employment of people with disabilities can be allayed, workplaces made more welcoming, and chances for success will be increased. The employers' needs for particular skills are considered paramount, with particular attention being paid to requirements for successful job performance. Potential student participants are identified by school administrators and

[33] The New Workforce. Special Report. *BusinessWeek Online,* March 20, 2000 Issue, http://www.businessweek.com/2000/00_12/b3673022.htm, accessed 11/27/04.

[34] Marriott Foundation for People with Disabilities, http://marriott.com/foundation/facts.mi?WT_Ref=mi_left, accessed 07/03/05.

teachers. Interested students then apply and are considered for participation in the program. Selected students and their parents are trained and coached in the attitudes and behaviors expected at work, appropriate attire, and other important factors that will facilitate success. Importantly, students' interests and skills are assessed, along with a formal review of the students' individual characteristics. These skills, interests, and characteristics are matched with employers' needs, with special attention being paid to needs for accommodation and support. Eighty-nine percent of students who successfully complete the program receive offers of ongoing employment—a figure that likely exceeds other internship-type programs.

Marlee Matlin, an actress and director who is hearing impaired, is one of the well-known participants in Marriott's Bridges program. When she was 21, Matlin received the Best Actress Oscar and attributes some of her success to participation in Bridges. Matlin notes that without the opportunity to participate in Bridges, she doesn't know where she would be. She encourages others to give opportunities to people whom they might not normally consider.

Source: About Bridges. http://marriott.com/foundation/facts.mi?WT_Ref=mi_left, accessed 11/26/04; http://www.marleematlinsite.com/, accessed 11/26/04.

researchers have suggested that people with disabilities receive inflated ratings because of supervisors' desire to be kind.[35] As with people from other underrepresented groups, failure to rate performance accurately, and to provide constructive and developmental feedback keeps employees from improving and advancing. People with disabilities should be rated accurately, and negative feedback provided as appropriate.

Ensure hiring managers and coworkers are trained about stereotypes and misperceptions about people with disabilities. Clarify that performance and absence of those with disabilities are comparable and are sometimes more favorable than that of people without disabilities. Make sure that the job descriptions provided are used in hiring, training, promoting, and evaluating performance of all employees.

Complaint mechanisms. Ensure that there are internal resources, such as an "open door policy" or an ombudsman, which can be used by employees with disabilities who experience discrimination or by others who know that discrimination is occurring. As is evident by what happened to Laura Barrios at DuPont, continued vigilance is needed to ensure workers are treated fairly, even in a company known for supportive behaviors. Although Barrios had worked successfully for nearly two decades, the actions of a few people resulted in her termination. When discrimination occurs, having several avenues for redress can help the individual, peers, and the organization.

[35] Czajka, J. M., & DeNisi, A. S. (1988). "Effects of Emotional Disability and Clear Performance Standards on Performance Ratings." *Academy of Management Journal,* 31: 394–404.

Accommodations

As discussed earlier, most people with disabilities do not require accommodations, and for those who do, most accommodations are inexpensive or cost nothing. In addition, federal tax incentives are often available to fund accommodations, depending on the employer's size and number of employees. The Omnibus Budget Reconciliation Act (1990) provides for credits of up to $5,000 per year for providing accommodations. As tax laws change frequently, seek advice from a tax professional.

SUMMARY

People with disabilities are a valuable, underutilized, and growing portion of the population. Nearly 20% of Americans have a disability, and this proportion is expected to increase as the U.S. population ages and works longer into older age. As are many other groups, people with disabilities are more likely to be un- or underemployed and to have lower earnings than people without disabilities. Access and treatment discrimination against people with disabilities are common problems, but much of this discrimination is based on unfounded perceptions that people with disabilities will be unable to perform effectively or have higher absence than others. In fact, people with disabilities have performance and attendance that is comparable to others. These misperceptions can be changed through concerted efforts. When treated fairly, people with disabilities can help organizations maintain a stable, productive workforce.

KEY TERMS

Essential functions — job functions that are the basis for the existence of the job.

Major life activities — functions such as caring for oneself, performing manual tasks, walking, seeing, speaking, hearing, breathing, learning, and working.

Marginal functions — job functions that are secondary in importance to essential functions.

Physical or mental impairment — any physiological disorder or condition, cosmetic disfigurement, or anatomical loss affecting at least one of the body's systems (i.e., neurological, musculoskeletal, sensory, respiratory, cardiovascular, and others), or any mental or psychological disorder, such as mental retardation, organic brain syndrome, emotional or mental illness, and specific learning disabilities.

Reasonable accommodation — a change that can be implemented to enable a qualified person with a disability to perform essential job functions without unduly burdening the employer.

Substantially limited — unable to perform one or more major life activities that most people in the general population can perform; or significantly restricted in the manner or length of performance of major life activities that most people in the population can perform.

Undue hardship — significant difficulty or expense relative to the employer's size, financial resources, and/or nature and structure of the organization.

Questions to Consider

1. What are *reasonable accommodations*? How does a company determine what is "reasonable" and what is not?
2. What similarities exist between perceptions about the competence of and performance expectations for workers with disabilities and older workers?
3. In the $561,000 DuPont disability discrimination judgment, even if Ms. Barrios had been unable to walk, what steps could have been taken to assist her if the need to evacuate the building arose? Speculate on reasons this case was not resolved before Ms. Barrios was terminated, or after she filed her discrimination charge with the EEOC but before the jury trial.
4. How can recommondations for employment equity for people with disabilities be helpful in ensuring equity for other nondominant group members?

Actions and Exercises

1. Observe people with visible disabilities in your community in one particular place (such as a university, store, restaurant, office, or television commercials). Are you able to observe many people with visible disabilities? Is the proportion of people you observed close to the 20% of the population who have a disability? What does this exercise indicate about invisible disabilities?
2. Conduct library or Internet research on the positive effects of work on people's health and well-being. Discuss the applicability of employment to the health and well-being of people with disabilities.
3. For your own consideration (this does not have to be shared), make a list of at least two common stereotypes about people with disabilities.
   a. If you can, beside each stereotype, write the name of a real person who has a disability who *does not* fit this stereotype. Look first for a friend, family member, or yourself if applicable. If you cannot think of a person whom you know, use a public figure or celebrity.
   b. Beside each stereotype common to people with disabilities, write the name of a real person, preferably one whom you know, who does not have a disability (to your knowledge) and has exhibited the stereotyped characteristic.
   c. How many times did you use a friend, family member, yourself, or a public figure or celebrity for steps a and b?
4. This chapter has several cases in which a person with a disability was clearly qualified to work, and many of the companies involved are those that should have knowledge of the ADA. Choose one of the industries involved and investigate annual turnover and costs of turnover. Speculate on the cost and productivity benefits that might be realized if people with disabilities were sought as applicants and employees.
5. Investigate resources in your community that facilitate employment of people with disabilities. Describe them and their resources, programs, and services.

13 Chapter

Work and Family

Chapter Objectives

After completing this chapter, readers should have a greater understanding of work and family as an aspect of diversity. Readers should be able to:

- *discuss the meanings of family in the United States.*
- *explain changes in workforce participation rates for women with children.*
- *discuss legislation and litigation related to work and family.*
- *compare parental policies in the United States with those in selected other countries.*
- *examine effects of having children on career progress of men and women.*
- *explain why family issues, including low wages, child care, and "the second shift" are relevant to employers and to families.*
- *discuss effects of employer child and elder care assistance on employee satisfaction and turnover.*
- *suggest measures organizations may implement to assist employees to cope with work and family issues.*

[1] Shulman, K. (2000). "The High Cost of Child Care Puts Quality Care Out of Reach for Many Families." Washington, DC: Children's Defense Fund, http://www.childrensdefense.org/earlychildhood/childcare/highcost.pdf, accessed 02/14/05.

[2] U.S. Department of Labor. (2004). "Women in the Labor Force: A Databook." Report 973, Table 6, http://www.bls.gov/cps/wlf-databook.pdf, accessed 12/16/04.

[3] Glover, S. L., & Crooker, K. J. (1995). "Who Appreciates Family Friendly Policies: The Impact of Family-Friendly Policies on Organizational Attachment of Parents and Non-Parents." *Personnel Psychology,* 48(2): 271–288.

Key Facts

The average annual cost of caring for a 4-year-old in an urban city is more than the cost of public college tuition in 49 states.[1]

Since 1975, labor force participation of U.S. women with children under age 18 has increased from 47% to 72%.[2]

On average, working mothers experience a 7% wage penalty per child.

Women spend an average of 17 years caring for children and 18 years caring for aging parents.

About half of employees are not covered by the Family and Medical Leave Act.

Both parents and nonparents are more attached to "family-friendly" organizations.[3]

Over 2.4 million grandparents have primary responsibility for their grandchildren under age 18.

Introduction and Overview

In this chapter, we consider several factors related to work and family, including child and elder care, equal pay, pregnancy discrimination, flexible schedules, paid and unpaid leave for family care, the second shift, and flexible family units. Although these issues do not cover all possible work and family concerns, one or more is relevant to nearly everyone at some point in his or her career. Work and family affect us all.

Many reasons exist for the inclusion of work and family as a diversity concern. Historically, men have been viewed as economic providers and women have been viewed as caretakers of the home. As more women have entered and remained in the workforce, awareness that work and family are not separate and independent spheres has increased. Employers' perceptions about ways that families affect employees' work lives and motivations to work and vice versa are critical in shaping employees' experiences at work. Organizations that assist employees in effectively navigating work and family issues are advantaged in recruitment and retention of people who are currently facing work and family issues as well as those who are not (but likely will be at some point in the future). On the other hand, organizations in which work and family are viewed as enemies negatively affect and often alienate workers with families. Consider the following hostile, irrational statements made to employees:

- In *Trezza v. The Hartford Inc.* (1998), a company official voiced an opinion about working mothers: "I don't see how you can do either job well." A senior vice president complained to the plaintiff about the "incompetence and laziness of women who are also working mothers."
- In *Moore v. Alabama State University* (1997), a supervisor remarked to a pregnant employee while pointing to her extended abdomen: "I was going to put you in charge of the office, but look at you now."
- In *Knussman v. Maryland* (1999, 2001), a state trooper was told he could not take parental leave unless his wife were "in a coma or dead." He was also told that parental leave was for women because "God made women to have babies."[4]

Defining Family

What, exactly, is a family? The U.S. Department of Labor defines a family as "a group of two or more persons who live together and who are related by birth, marriage, or adoption."[5] As we will see, a more appropriate perspective of family would include people who live together and are related by birth, marriage, or adoption, and others in committed, supportive relationships. The narrow definition of family excludes many familial relationships in which two or more people live together (see Chapter 2). It does not include people who live together in a nonmarital, but committed relationship, such as same or opposite sex partners. It also excludes people known as *fictive kin* who live together in a familial-type relationship and are dependent on each other for financial and social support. The narrow definition of family causes concern for many individuals and may require organizations to take specific measures to assist employees in addressing their true work/family needs, regardless of the formal definitions.

[4] All cases drawn from Williams, J., & Segal, N. (2002). "The New Glass Ceiling: Mothers—and Fathers—Sue for Discrimination," http://www.wcl.american.edu/gender/workfamily/chilly_climate0211.pdf, accessed 03/22/05. See also Williams, J. C., & Cooper, H. C. (2004). "The Public Policy of Motherhood." *Journal of Social Issues,* 60(4): 849–865.

[5] U.S. Department of Labor. (2004).

The topic of *work and family* is broad, but the majority of research focuses on issues relating to issues involving working parents, particularly women, and the negative effects of children on women's earnings, career progress, and full-time work status and organizational measures implemented to ameliorate these negative effects. In addition to these areas, we also examine the positive relationships between having children and men's earnings and employment. Increases in the occurrence of grandparents (many of whom are employed) caring for grandchildren are considered as well. Lastly, because of the aging of the U.S. population and employees' increasing likelihood to be responsible for both parents and children, we also investigate caring for elders while also working.

History of Work and Family

The history of work and family is dominated by beliefs that a woman's place is in the home while a man's place is outside the home, earning a living for the family. As a result, in the past, many organizations openly paid men more than the few women who worked were paid, under a "family wage" philosophy. These pay disparities were justified by beliefs that, in contrast to men, women did not have (but were) dependents and were widely accepted until the 1960s.[6] As discussed in Chapter 9, Black women have historically worked outside the home, and much of the outcry about "women working" refers to the increases in middle-class White women's workforce participation.[7] Misperceptions about women's commitment to work have been exacerbated by the failure to include women and men of color in research. The higher participation of Black women when compared with White women (and Latinas) reflects Black women's greater likelihood to be single than other women and, when married, the lower earnings of their Black men compared with other men. For example, 79.2% of Black married women with children under 18 are employed compared with 69.2% of White married women with children under 18. Differences are even more striking for mothers of younger children, where 70.3% of Black married women with children under 3 and 57.4% of married White women with children under 3 are employed.[8] Women work, and perceptions that women do not or should not work do not reflect the reality that women work because they want and need to do so. Representations of women as "stay-at-home moms" simply do not reflect the overwhelming majority of women and mothers. As discussed in Chapter 9, only 17% of married couples consist of an employed husband and a nonworking wife. Economic pressures, the rise in single parenting, and psychological benefits associated with work make women's

[6] Kramer, L. (1991). *The Sociology of Gender,* New York: St. Martin's Press.

[7] Gerstel, N., & McGonagle, K. (2002). "Job Leaves and the Limits of the Family and Medical Leave Act." In P. J. Dubeck & D. Dunn, *Workplace/Women's Place: An Anthology* (2nd edition), Los Angeles: Roxbury Publishers, pp. 205–215.

[8] U.S. Department of Labor. (2004). Report 973, Table 6.

continued participation in the workforce increasingly likely and normal rather than unlikely and abnormal.

Relevant Legislation

Federal legislation particularly relevant to work and family issues includes the Equal Pay Act, Title VII of the Civil Rights Act, the Pregnancy Discrimination Act, and the Family and Medical Leave Act. The Equal Pay Act of 1963 is the oldest equal employment legislation enforced by the EEOC and is significant to working women who have families whom they are completely or partially responsible to support. Title VII is valuable to women, who may experience disparate treatment because of perceptions about their roles as women (and/or as mothers), and to men, who may experience gender discrimination for exercising their responsibilities as fathers or as sons, in caring for elderly parents. The Pregnancy Discrimination Act (PDA) is primarily of interest to women, who may experience pregnancy discrimination, but is also of interest to men, by protecting their pregnant wives or covered partners from being excluded from medical and benefits plans that cover other temporary medical issues. Finally, the Family and Medical Leave Act (FMLA) covers all employees, providing time off, job security, and benefits continuation for one's own illness, illness of a spouse, parent, or child, or for birth, adoption, or placement of a foster child.

Each of the legislative acts has been used by employees in addressing discriminatory organizational treatment. We consider each, and its particular relevance to work and family issues in this section. As in previous chapters, we emphasize that fear of litigation is insufficient to motivate organizations to address and attempt to avoid discrimination. Most aggrieved parties do not approach the EEOC with allegations of discrimination and those who do are unlikely to have their claims deemed meritorious or to prevail in litigation. Even so, the importance of and very real need for these laws are reinforced by the flagrant acts of discrimination and harassment that occur despite the existence of the laws.

Equal Pay Act and Title VII

Title VII and the Equal Pay Act (EPA) are often used concurrently by plaintiffs faced with sex-based pay discrimination in organizations. The EPA addresses only compensation, while Title VII is useful for employment discrimination in all employment-related matters, including compensation.

Litigation settlements indicate the existence of overt sex-based pay discrimination (e.g., disparate treatment), retaliation for complaining about it, and paying men more than women because of presumptions that men have a family to support or are the heads of households. From an employer perspective, having a family is often perceived positively for men and negatively for women. Women are often viewed as being *less* committed to work because of commitments to family, while men are seen as *more* committed to work because of having to provide for a family. When children arrive, employers often expect women to cut back on work hours to care for their growing families and men to work longer and harder to provide for their growing families. In contrast to perceptions, as do men, many women work to financially support themselves and their families and do not decrease commitment to work because of having children and families. Ten million single mothers head households, compared with 2 million single fathers.[9] About 17% of married couple families are composed of working men and unemployed wives. In contrast, 26% of all households in the United States are headed by single women (with or without children), about 24% of married women earn more than their working husbands, and 4.8% of married couple families are composed of working women and unemployed husbands.[10] Despite data to the contrary, perceptions of men as breadwinners and women as unwilling, uncommitted workforce participants persist. As an example, Neil French, a former advertising executive at WPP Group, a large advertising firm, resigned in October 2005, after his statements about the incompatibility of motherhood and being an executive were widely reported in the press. French reportedly said that women were not well-represented as advertising executives because motherhood made them "wimp out" and created distractions that prevented women from succeeding.[11]

Misperception: Most women work only to supplement their husband's income.

Reality: Married or unmarried, most women work to provide for themselves and their families.

As discussed in Chapter 2, the Equal Pay Act has been somewhat successful in reducing male/female pay disparities, but its effectiveness has been limited by sex segregation. Despite the pervasiveness of sex segregation, the Equal Pay Act has been used successfully by many women in their quests for equal pay in jobs that also employed men doing the same or substantially similar jobs. Three such cases brought by the EEOC in the 1990s were against organizations that paid higher wages and benefits to men than to women in the same jobs. Terminology such as "family" and "head-of-household" allowances has been used by organizations engaging in such pay discrimination. Tree of Life Christian Schools agreed to pay almost $100,000 to 19 women who were denied the "family allowances"

---

[9] Fields, J. (2004). America's Families and Living Arrangements: 2003. Current Population Reports, p. 20–553. U.S. Census Bureau, Washington, DC. http://www.census.gov/prod/2004pubs/p20-553.pdf, accessed 12/05/05.

[10] U.S. Department of Labor. (2004).

[11] Lawless, J. (2005, October 21). "Ad Guru Resigns over Comments about Women." *Associated Press.*

given to men. In similar cases, two schools agreed to $48,000 and $80,000 settlements to be paid to female teachers who had been denied "head-of-household" allowances.[12] In a case against a nursing home company, the EEOC alleged that female licensed practical nurses (LPNs) were paid less than male LPNs "based on a presumption that men needed a higher salary to support their families."[13] The $40,000 settlement was divided among 12 women and 1 man whose pay was reduced in an attempt to cover the sex-based discrimination.

Pregnancy Discrimination Act of 1978

Recall that the Pregnancy Discrimination Act (PDA) prohibits employers from discrimination because of pregnancy and related medical conditions but does not require pregnancy-related benefits or leave. Pregnancy discrimination is of most interest to women in child-bearing years, but it is also of interest to men, whose covered wives or partners are provided with protection from pregnancy discrimination under employers' medical plans. Before passage of the PDA, employers commonly required pregnant women to take leaves of absence or resign, openly refused to hire pregnant women, and treated pregnancy differently than other medical conditions in terms of leaves and medical benefits. In 2003, the EEOC received 4,649 charges of pregnancy discrimination and resolved 4,847 charges (including charges from previous years), but charging parties in pregnancy discrimination cases are unlikely to prevail. Only 27.2% of the resolved cases were resolved with merit, compared with 54.2% being judged to have no reasonable cause, and 18.6% being closed for administrative reasons. As is evident by the $57.2 million in monetary benefits awarded to charging parties between 1999 and 2003, however, pregnancy discrimination continues to be a significant issue for working women and covered partners or wives of working men.

Selected pregnancy discrimination cases

- **EEOC v. Berge Ford, Inc. and Auto Care Center, LLC**[14]
  No. CIV 02-943 PHX SRB (D. Ariz. June 10, 2004)

  The Phoenix District Office alleged that a Mesa, Arizona auto dealership and its parent company violated Title VII/PDA when it fired the charging party because she was pregnant. Prior to her termination, CP had been working for Berge Ford for three to four months as a general services technician; her duties included

[12] "Highlights of Equal Pay Act Cases." Fiscal Year 1993, http://www.eeoc.gov/epa/anniversary/epa-highlights.html, accessed 10/22/05. See also Recent Examples of EEOC's Enforcement of Equal Pay in Litigation, http://www.eeoc.gov/epa/litigation.html, accessed 12/05/04.

[13] Ibid.

[14] EEOC Litigation Settlement Reports—June 2004, http://www.eeoc.gov/litigation/settlements/settlement06-04.html, accessed 10/22/05.

cleaning, picking up trash, monitoring the front desk, and driving Berge's customer shuttle. Phoenix alleged that the defendants had no problems with CP's job performance, but when they learned she was pregnant they fired her in fear that she might become ill (since she had been experiencing morning sickness) while driving Berge vehicles and expose defendants to liability.

- **EEOC v. O'Reilly Automotive, Inc., dba O'Reilly Auto Parts**[15]
  No. 03-1347-WEB (D. Kan. June 16, 2004)

  The St. Louis District Office brought this Title VII/PDA case alleging that one of the nation's largest specialty retailers of automotive aftermarket parts, tools, and supplies discharged charging party, an assistant manager at an autoparts store, because she was pregnant. CP's doctor had imposed a 30-pound lifting restriction, and although the store manager and district manager agreed that CP could continue working despite the restriction, defendant's Human Resources staff in its Springfield, Missouri headquarters decided she could not work. After CP exhausted her leave under the Family & Medical Leave Act, she was terminated since she was still pregnant and had lifting restrictions. Defendant had permitted other employees with temporary medical conditions to work even though they had lifting restrictions.

Although the PDA does not require that employers provide leave or medical coverage for pregnancy and related conditions, it does require that employers treat pregnancy similarly to other temporary medical conditions. If the employer provides medical benefits, pregnancy benefits should be at the same level, with the same deductibles, co-pay, and other benefits, as those provided for other medical conditions. Women who are pregnant must be allowed to continue working as long as they are able to perform their jobs. Women who are temporarily unable to perform their jobs must be treated the same as any other employee with a temporary disability.[16]

Because pregnancy is a condition unique to women, disparate treatment on the basis of pregnancy constitutes sex discrimination. In the Berge Ford and O'Reilly Automotive cases just presented, the employers treated pregnant women differently once they became pregnant, even though they had performed their jobs satisfactorily beforehand. In one case, other employees who had lifting restrictions due to other medical conditions (that is, not due to pregnancy) were allowed to continue working. In contrast, the pregnant employee took unpaid family and medical leave, and then was fired. An assistant manager, the woman clearly wished to continue working at O'Reilly Automotive. Even if pregnancy discrimination were not illegal, the HR staff at O'Reilly should have also considered

---

[15] Ibid.

[16] EEOC. "Pregnancy Discrimination," http://www.eeoc.gov/types/pregnancy.html, accessed 10/22/05.

the difficulty in attracting and retaining competent, committed workers such as they apparently had in the pregnant employee whom they terminated. Pregnancy is a temporary, short-lived condition; had the employee's weight restrictions been accommodated, the pregnancy would have soon ended, and her positive employment history could have continued. Multiple studies have found that pregnant women who work for family supportive organizations plan to work later into their pregnancies, to return to work sooner after childbirth, and are more committed to their organizations. The ability to avoid mandatory overtime, length of leave policies, and supportive coworkers and supervisors also play roles in pregnant women's job satisfaction and return to work after childbirth.[17]

The Family and Medical Leave Act of 1993

As discussed in Chapter 2, the FMLA allows employers to take up to 12 weeks unpaid leave when ill, on the birth, adoption, or placement of a foster child, or to care for a sick child, parent, or spouse. When on leave, employees' benefits are continued and they are guaranteed the same or a substantially similar job on returning from the leave. Although this act is positive in many regards, and is an improvement from having no family legislation, the FMLA still fails to meet many of the needs of workers with families. The most obvious inadequacies about the act are that the leave is unpaid, many family members (e.g., parents-in-law, aunts, grandparents, grandchildren) or others in familial-type relationships (e.g., godparents, domestic partners) are not included, and the many people who work for organizations having fewer than 50 employees (about half of working Americans) are not covered. As discussed in International Feature 13.1, family policies in some other developed nations provide considerably more assistance than does the FMLA.

Population, Participation, and Education

The category of work and family includes men and women from all races, ethnic backgrounds, incomes, and ages, making generalizations about population size, participation, employment levels, education, and income impossible. The historical (and somewhat inaccurate) view of women as homemakers alone makes presentation of participation rates of women and mothers one important and easily measured factor, however. Since 1975, labor force participation of all women

[17] Lyness, K. S., Thompson, C. A., Francesco, A. M., & Judiesch, M. K. (1999). "Work and Pregnancy: Individual and Organizational Factors Influencing Organizational Commitment, Time of Maternity Leave, and Return to Work." *Sex Roles,* 41: 485–508; Glass, J., & Riley, L. (1998). "Family Responsive Policies and Employee Retention Following Childbirth." *Social Forces,* 76(4): 1401–1446; Holtzman, M., & Glass, J. (1999). "Explaining Changes in Mothers' Job Satisfaction Following Childbirth." *Work and Occupations,* 26(3): 365–404.

INTERNATIONAL FEATURE 13.1 *Family Policies in the United States and Selected Other Developed Countries*

The United States lags other developed nations considerably in its efforts to help the population manage work and family concerns. The relatively recent implementation of the FMLA (1993) provides only a portion of U.S. workers with a small amount of unpaid time off for family needs, including pregnancy and parenting. Lower wage workers, women, and people of color are more likely to work for smaller organizations that are not covered by the FMLA, to be ineligible because they do not meet the required number of hours worked per year, or to be unable to afford time off without pay.

In the United States, less than half of all working women receive any paid leave during the first 12 weeks after pregnancy and only 7% of employers offer paid paternity leave.[18] In contrast to the United States, many developed countries have long offered mandatory, paid maternity and parental leaves of more than 12 weeks. Since 1973, Sweden has had Parental Benefit Insurance, which provides up to 9 months of maternity or paternity leave at 90% of pay. Canada, Denmark, Finland, the Netherlands, and Norway provide between 15 and 52 weeks of paid maternity and parental leaves. In Norway, mothers may take 42 weeks at full salary or 52 weeks at 80% of salary. Compared with the United States, it appears that some countries view parenting as a social responsibility that benefits everyone and thus provide support for those who parent. Some of those countries responded to very low birth rates by increasing maternity and paternity leaves and benefits; reducing penalties for having children increases the likelihood that citizens will have them. Facilitating women's contributions to the economy benefits everyone as well.

Many countries also offer government subsidized or funded child care for young children, much like public schools in the United States for older children. In Finland, Denmark, Sweden, Belgium, and France, one-third to one-half of all infants and almost all preschool aged children have opportunities to attend publicly supported child care. In contrast, in the United States, 1% of infants and 14% of preschool aged children attend publicly supported child care. In reflection of maternity and parental leave and access to child care, about 90% of mothers in Finland and 60% of mothers of young children in the United States are employed.

In 1942, in response to the need for women workers while men were at war, the U.S. federal government passed the Lanham Act. This act subsidized child care across the country during the war for mothers working in defense industries. After the war ended, however, 2,800 of the 3,000 centers that had been opened were closed, leaving 1.5 million children without services.[19] For most families, child care costs are a significant portion of the family income. A recent Children's Defense Fund Report compared costs of child care for infants and preschool aged children with the costs of attending public colleges in each state. In every state, costs of caring for infants exceeded costs of attending public college in that state. Although costs for caring for older, but still preschool aged children are less than those for infants, they are also quite expensive. In some states,

[18] Gornick, J. C., & Meyers, M. K. (2003). *Families that Work: Policies for Reconciling Parenthood and Employment,* New York: Russell Sage Foundation.

[19] Frohmann, A. (1978). "Day Care and the Regulation of Women's Workforce Participation." *Catalyst,* 1(2): 5–17.

infant care costs were more than double the state's public college tuition. In all but one state (Vermont), the cost of child care for preschool aged children was more than the costs of public school tuition.[20] As examples, in Tucson, annual child care costs for children 12 months and 4 years were $4,965 and $4,352, respectively. In comparison, public college tuition in Arizona averaged $2,158. In Durham, North Carolina, child care costs for children 12 months and 4 years were $6,968 and $5,876, respectively, compared with $1,958 for public college tuition. These significant cost disparities are due in part to state subsidies for college tuition costs, but not for child care.

Questions to Consider

1. ***What is likely the driving force behind social policy regarding parenting and child care in the United States?***
2. ***What factors might make the U.S. policies change to be more supportive?***
3. ***What are some possible reasons for state subsidized public college education but not child care?***

Sources: Martin, G. T., Jr. (1991). "Family, Gender, and Social Policy," In L. Kramer (Ed.), *The Sociology of Gender,* New York: St. Martin's Press, pp. 323–345.

Gornick, J. C., Meyers, M. K., & Ross, K. E. (1998). "Public Policies and the Employment of Mothers: A Cross-National Study." *Social Science Quarterly,* 79(1): 35–54.

with children under age 18 has increased from 47% to 72%.[21] Women with children under age three are also likely to be employed outside the home; over 60% of such women work. Women who are single parents are even more likely to be in the workforce; 79% of such women with children under 18 work outside the home. Single mothers also work more hours than married mothers do.

Education level is an additional factor that affects women's propensity to be in the workforce even if they have very young children. Among mothers of children less than 1 year old, 66.5% of women with college degrees work, and 73.6% of women with graduate or professional degrees (e.g., JD and MD) work, compared with 59% of all women with children less than 1 year old.[22] Women with higher educational levels face higher opportunity costs (such as lost income and promotional and developmental opportunities) of staying home than women with lower educational levels. Census data indicate that while more than 50% of women with less than a high school degree quit their jobs after their first pregnancy, more highly educated women are far less likely to do so.[23] Women with more education are also more financially able to purchase child care and other services that they might themselves provide were they not in the workforce. High education, high career aspirations, and workplace strategies are discussed further in Feature 13.1.

[20] Shulman, K. (2000).

[21] U.S. Department of Labor. (2004).

[22] Bachu, A., & O'Connell, M. (1995). "Fertility of American Women. Current Population Reports." P20-526. U.S. Census Bureau. Washington, DC.

[23] Work and Family Patterns of American Women. (1990). Current Population Reports. Special Studies Series, P-23, No. 165. Table E. U.S. Government Printing Office, Washington, DC.

ASSIGNMENT #4

FEATURE 13.1 ***Education, Career Aspirations, and Work: The Media versus the Data***

A troubling trend of publications and media reports suggest that women, including college-educated and executive women, are less interested in careers than men, preferring instead to be homemakers. Readers may also have personal knowledge of a woman who has left the workforce to be a "stay-at-home mom," which may increase their perceptions that this phenomenon is more frequent than it actually is. What do U.S. census data and large scale empirical studies suggest about women and work?

Women of all education levels participate in the workforce and highly educated women are more likely to be in the workforce than women with less education. Education is also correlated with organizational level; the more education a person has, the more money she or he earns, and the higher organizational position she or he is likely to attain. Relationships between education, earnings, and employment for men and women and people of all backgrounds are clear. Although returns on educational investment differ for men and women, and people of color and Whites, more educated people of all backgrounds earn more and are more likely to be in the workforce than people with similar backgrounds who have less education. Opportunity costs associated with being out of the workforce, inability to use the human capital investments, and ability to afford quality child care if needed make educated women more likely to be in the workforce than to leave the workforce in large numbers, as suggested by the media. Women with lower educations have lower earnings, lower opportunity costs associated with not working, less investment in their education, and less ability to afford quality child care when compared with well-educated women. On the other hand, having a high earning spouse does enable some women (and a few men) to leave the workforce to rear children, which complicates the relationships between parenting, education, earnings, and workforce participation[24] and further confuses observers without access to research and large scale data.

What are the expectations of well-educated women for their future careers, workforce participation, and family roles? Alison Konrad, a professor at the Ivey Business School in Western Ontario has published several empirical studies of women's preferences in job attributes when compared with men. In a longitudinal study of MBAs, Konrad found that while women accurately predicted that family demands would affect them at work more than men, women still desired and pursued fulfilling careers, interesting work, and high salaries. For these women, flexibility and control over hours were important. Konrad suggested that organizations wishing to attract, motivate, and retain such highly qualified workers should add flexibility to their career and job offerings.[25]

QUESTIONS TO CONSIDER

1. ***What employment-related problems for working women may be caused by perceptions that women often stop working to be "stay-at-home moms?"***
2. ***What role does an individual's experience with or personal knowledge of a woman who has left***

[24] Song. (2004).

[25] Konrad, A. M. (2003). "Family Demands and Job Attribute Preferences: A 4-Year Longitudinal Study of Women and Men." *Sex Roles: A Journal of Research,* 49(1/2): 35–46.

the workforce to stay at home play in the perceptions that many or most women do so?

3. ***What specific recommendations would you make for an organization to attract, motivate, and retain women and men with child and elder care issues? How would you convince them that implementing these recommendations was a good idea for the organization?***

Earnings

In this section, we consider differential earnings for men and women who are parents. As discussed earlier, having children creates perceptions that men are more committed to work and that women are less committed to work (and more committed to family). These perceptions are partially driven by gendered views of men as providers and women as caretakers of the home. Whether distorted or realistic, these perceptions are also correlated with lower earnings of women who are parents compared with those who are not and higher earnings of men who are parents compared with men who are not. Multiple studies using data from the National Longitudinal Survey of Youth (NLSY) have found significant gender differences in earnings and promotion based on marital status and the presence of young children. The NLSY began data collection in 1979 using people who were aged 14 to 21 at the time and has continued sampling that population. In one study, using data collected in 1979, 1989, and 1996, researchers found that married men were more likely to have been promoted than single men, but married women were less likely to have been promoted than single women. Further, having preschool-aged children was associated with higher promotion rates for men, but with lower promotion rates for women. Overall, never-married, childless women had the highest rates of promotion.[26]

In a 2001 study, Budig and England found that women with children earned 7% less per child. Because women with more children have fewer years of experience than those with fewer (or no) children, Budig and England controlled for any negative effects that being out of the workforce rearing children would have on wages. Indeed, part-time work, employment breaks, and having accumulated fewer years of job experience helped to explain a portion of the wage penalty, but a 5% wage penalty for mothers remained even after the researchers controlled for those things.[27]

The wage penalty may be partly due to perceptions that mothers are less competent than others. In one study measuring perception of competence of low status groups, mothers were rated similarly to the elderly, blind, retarded, and

[26] Cobb-Clark, D., & Dunlop, Y. (1999). "The Role of Gender in Job Promotions." *Monthly Labor Review,* 122(12): 32–38.

[27] Budig, M. J., & England, P. (2001). "The Wage Penalty for Motherhood." *American Sociological Review,* 66 (April): 204–225.

TABLE 13.1 ***1998 Distribution of Hours Worked per Week by Sex***

Weekly Hours	Women	Men
Total (percentage)	100.00	100.00
35 to 39 hours	12.5	4.2
40 hours	70.7	64.8
41 to 48 hours	7.7	10.4
49 or more hours	9.1	20.5

Source: Bowles, M. (1999). "Women's Earnings: An Overview." *Monthly Labor Review,* 122(12): 13–22.

disabled by working professionals and by college students. In contrast, business women and women without children are perceived as being highly competent.[28] Differences in earnings and rates of promotion may also reflect employers' perceptions about men's and women's home and child care responsibilities as well as differences in actual behaviors of men and women. Overall, men who become fathers increase their time spent at work, while women who become mothers, particularly married women, decrease their time spent at work. As shown in Table 13.1, considerably more men work more than 40 hours while considerably more women work fewer than 40 hours. Nearly three times more women work 35 to 39 hours than men and twice as many men work 49 hours or more than women.

Part-Time Work and Earnings

Part-time work and fewer hours worked in full-time work contribute to lower earnings. Although we have stressed that women, including mothers, do work, more married mothers of dependent children work part-time than single mothers, women without children, and men. For example, while both men and women are most likely to work 40 hour per week jobs, women are more likely to work fewer than 40 hours and men are more likely to work more than 40 hours. Part-time work is one way in which some women address child care needs and greater responsibilities for home and family than men assume. Part-time work is associated with fewer job rewards, lower wages, fewer benefits, and shorter career ladders that are costly to women, however. Some of the disadvantages of part-time work have long-lasting, significantly negative effects. Seventy-three percent of full-time workers have health insurance through their employers, but only 17% of part-time workers do. Sixty-four percent of full-time workers are included in

[28] See Cuddy, A. J. C., Fiske, S. T., & Glick, P. (2004). "When Professionals Become Mothers, Warmth Doesn't Cut the Ice." *Journal of Social Issues,* 60(4): 701–718; Fiske, S. T., Cuddy, A. J. C., Glick, P., & Xu, J. (2002). "A Model of (Often Mixed) Stereotype Content: Competence and Warmth Respectively Follow from Perceived Status and Competition." *Journal of Personality and Social Psychology,* 82(6): 878–902.

pension plans, compared with 21% of part-time workers.[29] Recall from Chapter 9 other factors associated with the feminization of poverty. No fault divorce and limited or no alimony also increase risks of poverty for women and children.

Rather than simply offering part-time work as a means of helping working women cope with family needs, organizations can also address wage, benefits, and promotion disparities, lessening the negative impact on women who decide to work part-time. Further, rather than applying any statistic to individual members of a group, or making assumptions that mothers will want to work part-time, employers should instead consider behaviors of individual employees rather than their sex or marital or parental status in determining raises, promotions, and other rewards.

Along with part-time work, some organizations offer flexible scheduling, paid and unpaid leave, job sharing, telecommuting, referral services, and on-site child care to help employees address work and family needs. Flexible scheduling and leaves are considered in the following sections.

Flexible Schedules

Flexible schedules or "flextime" increase the ability of employees to meet both their work and family needs. Although the specifics depend on each employer's rules, generally, in flex-scheduling, employees may vary their start and stop times on a daily, weekly, monthly, or an as-needed basis, as long as a certain minimum number of hours is worked in a specific time period. For example, flextime may allow workers to start and end the workday earlier or later, such as starting at 6 a.m. and ending at 3 p.m. or starting at 9 a.m. and ending at 6 p.m. In a dual career couple, if both parents used flexible scheduling, one parent could take children to school while the other headed to work early. One parent would arrive at his or her job later in the morning and would then work later in the evening, while the other parent would go to work early and then leave early to pick the children up from school.

Along with regular flexible scheduling (e.g., 6 a.m. to 3 p.m. or 9 a.m. to 6 p.m. as a regular schedule), some companies also allow flexible flex-scheduling. This even more flexible scheduling allows workers to vary start and stop times daily if needed, which provides employees with the ability to deal with day to day emergencies (such as the babysitter's car would not start and the sitter arrives 2 hours late), without unplanned absences or being considered tardy. Tardiness, absenteeism, intentions to quit, and turnover are lower, and job satisfaction is higher in organizations that allow employees flexibility in scheduling.[30]

---

[29] U.S. General Accounting Office. (2000). "Contingent Workers: Incomes and Benefits Lag behind Those of the Rest of the Workforce," HEHS-00-76, http://www.gao.gov/new.items/he00076.pdf, accessed 03/15/05.

[30] Narayanan, V. K., & Nath, R. (1982). "A Field Test of Some Attitudinal and Behavioral Consequences of Flexitime." *Journal of Applied Psychology,* 67: 214–218; Pierce, J. L., & Newstrom, J. W. (1983). "The Design of Flexible Work Schedules and Employee Responses: Relations and Process." *Journal of Occupational Behavior,* 4: 247–262; Glover & Crooker. (1995).

TABLE 13.2 ***Access to Flexible Schedules for Full-Time Wage and Salary Workers by Selected Characteristics, May 2001***

Age	Women with Access to Flexible Work Schedules (%)	Men with Access to Flexible Work Schedules (%)
All ages	27.4	30.0
16 to 24 years	26.4	22.1
25 to 54 years	28.1	31.1
55 years and over	23.3	29.8
Race and Hispanic Origin		
White	28.6	31.0
Black	21.5	20.9
Hispanic origin	21.9	18.4
Marital Status		
Married, spouse present	26.5	32.1
Never married	38.4	26.6
Presence and Age of Children		
With no children under 18	27.0	31.9
With children under 18	27.6	28.7

Source: May 2001 Flexible Schedules and Shift Work Supplement to the Current Population Survey, U.S. Department of Labor, Bureau of Labor Statistics, Table 26 of Women in the Labor Force, a Data Book, Feb. 2004, Report 973.

Flexible scheduling can reduce some of the stress in dealing with work and family issues, but is not a possibility for many jobs, such as those with few or one worker opening a store or other business, teaching, or other place- and time-specific positions in which many people work. As we have discussed, in the United States and much of the world, in most families women assume the larger proportion of family responsibilities than men. Thus, flexible scheduling would most benefit women in their attempts to integrate work and family. Ironically, men are more likely to work in jobs that allow flexible scheduling than women. Consider the female- and male-dominated positions of secretary and executive or professor and elementary school teacher. While the executive may be able to come in late or leave early, the secretary has particular time periods in which she must be at her desk answering phones or greeting clients or customers.[31]

Table 13.2 provides evidence of differences in access to flexible scheduling by gender. Overall, 30.0% of men and 27.4% of women work in jobs with flexible scheduling. White men (31.0%) and women (28.6%) are most likely to have such jobs, while Hispanic (18.4%) and Black men (20.9%) are least likely to work in such jobs.

[31] Because for 97% to 98% of secretaries and receptionists, the term "she" is used in referring to them.

A negative aspect of flexible scheduling comes to the fore when the employer has sole authority to institute flexible scheduling and employees have to comply with these variable, or nonstandard schedules. For these workers, employers do not provide them with a set schedule, and instead schedule them on an as-needed basis, calling them in or sending them home when work demands increase or decrease. Inability to arrange child care in advance can make such a job nearly impossible to hold, further disadvantaging low-wage workers and decreasing the possibility that they will be able to work successfully. When an hourly worker is sent home because of low workload (for example, low customer traffic in a store) she or he is unlikely to obtain a reduced price or a refund for the child care that was arranged.

Unpaid and Paid Leaves

As covered in the previous section, men and Whites are most likely to have access to flexible scheduling to assist them in addressing work and family needs. Access to leave under the FMLA is also differentially available to different populations. The FMLA is applicable to employers having 50 or more employees, and although women and Hispanics are more likely to work for the smallest employers (having 10 or fewer employees), Blacks are more likely to work for larger employers.[32] Gerstel and McGonagle reported that 39% of people making $20,000 or less and 66% of people making $50,000 or more worked for firms that fit FMLA criteria; lower earners were significantly less likely to be working for firms covered by the FMLA. About half of U.S. workers are not covered by the FMLA.[33] As important as questions about which groups of employees are more likely to have access to family leave under the FMLA are questions of whether employees take leave when it is available, and what are the career outcomes for employees who do take leave.

Research indicates that many employees who have access to and need for family leave do not take it even when it is available to them,[34] partly because such leaves are unpaid. In some European countries (for example, Sweden) and in a few states (for example, California), some family or maternity leaves provide all or a portion of employees' salary for certain periods of time. Under the FMLA, however, leaves are unpaid, even though the health emergencies or childbirth that necessitate time off from work make the income associated with work even more important. Organizational Feature 13.1 discusses Bank of America's programs to help employees with work and family needs.

---

[32] Holzer, H. (1998). "Why Do Small Establishments Hire Fewer Blacks Than Larger Ones?" *Journal of Human Resources,* 33(4): 896–915.

[33] Commission on Family and Medical Leave. (1996). A Workable Balance: Report to Congress on Family and Medical Leave Policies, www.dol.gov/dol/esa/public/regs/compliance/whd/fmla/family.htm.

[34] Gerstel, N., & McGonagle, K. (2002). "Job Leaves and the Limits of the Family and Medical Leave Act." In P. Dubeck & D. Dunn (Eds.), *Workplace, Women's Place* (2nd edition), Los Angeles: Roxbury Publishers, pp. 205–215; American Association of University Women, http://www.aauw.org/takeaction/policyissues/familymedical_leave.cfm, accessed 05/10/04.

ORGANIZATIONAL FEATURE 13.1 *Bank of America*

Bank of America has numerous programs to help employees achieve a "healthy balance between work and life," including flexible work arrangements, LifeWorks® consultation and referral source, employee assistance programs, dependent care programs, adoption reimbursement, and paid and unpaid time off. Through its flexible work arrangement options, employees may telecommute, work compressed work weeks, use flexible scheduling, work "select time," and phase in a return to work after leaves. Telecommuting allows employees to work from home, rather than in a Bank of America location. Compressed work weeks condense a full-time work week into fewer days, for example, 40 hours in 4 days instead of 40 hours in 5 days. Flexible scheduling allows employees to start or stop their work days at different times. Select time allows employees to reduce their work schedules and job responsibilities for a specific need. Employees who have been on leaves may phase in their returns to full-time work. In each case, the manager and employee agree on the appropriate flexible work arrangement.

LifeWorks® is a free, confidential resource and referral service offered to help employees cope with and minimize the pressures associated with managing work and family responsibilities. This program offers employees practical advice, consultations, and seminars from experts. Particularly relevant to work and family issues, LifeWorks® is designed to help employees with

- caring for themselves or for older relatives.
- locating quality child care.
- working nontraditional hours.
- adopting a child.

Trained LifeWorks® counselors help employees evaluate their situation, develop a plan of action and provide resources, referrals, and ongoing follow-up with employees.

Dependent care programs help Bank of America employees who have child and elder care needs by providing referrals to quality care facilities. Bank of America also works to increase the availability of quality dependent care providers in the communities it serves. Some of the dependent care assistance offered includes up to $175 monthly reimbursement per child, dependent care reimbursement accounts, inclement weather programs (for when schools are closed unexpectedly), summer camp, and near-site child care centers in certain locations.

Adoption expenses are reimbursed up to $4,000 per adopted child. Paid and unpaid leaves help employees with long- and short-term disabilities, maternity, paternity, adoption, foster care, family care, and personal needs. Bank of America also allows full-time employees to take up to 2 hours per week to work as volunteers in public or private schools (up to grade 12).

QUESTIONS TO CONSIDER

1. ***Bank of America is a large corporation with considerable resources and many employees. What initiatives might be offered by a small firm interested in helping employees achieve a healthy balance between work and life?***
2. ***Are you aware of other organizations that compete with Bank of America for employees that also offer extensive work/family initiatives? How might the work/family policies offered by Bank of America provide them with advantages in resource acquisition and retention?***

Source: http://www.bankofamerica.com/careers/index.cfm?template=benefits_worklife, accessed 03/15/05.

Career Outcomes for Employees Who Take Leaves of Absence

Michael Judiesch and Karen Lyness of Baruch College at the City University of New York investigated the effects of leaves of absence on rewards and promotions of 11,815 managers in a financial services organization. Judiesch and Lyness used human capital theories and gendered organizational theories in developing their hypotheses. **Human capital** theorists argue that while on leaves people fail to accumulate valuable "human capital," such as job knowledge, training, and expertise and this negatively affects their subsequent job performance and thus, their career progress. **Gendered organizational culture** theories suggest that managers reward those who set aside personal and family commitments and are dedicated to their jobs. Both theories suggest that people who take family leave will suffer career penalties as a result of doing so. Only 5% of the nearly 12,000 managers in the study had taken leaves of absence, but those who did take leave were less likely to be promoted subsequently and received lower increases than those who did not take leave. As an example, a 35-year-old manager who had taken a leave of absence would have had a 36% probability of promotion and would have received $7,799 in salary increases. In contrast, managers who had similar qualifications and time on the job but had not taken a leave of absence would have had a 44% probability of promotion and would have received $8,462 in salary increases. Because women are more likely to take leaves of absence than men, women's promotions and earnings are most negatively affected by taking leaves.

THE SECOND SHIFT

The second shift refers to the second 8 hour day of home and child care work performed by most working women after they leave their paid jobs.[35] As discussed earlier in the chapter, most home and child care responsibilities fall upon women, regardless of whether they are single, married, or employed outside the home. Although women's paid employment has increased significantly in the past three decades, men's participation in unpaid household and child care labor has not changed as much in comparison. Thus, women now provide considerable "help" in supporting families financially, but men provide relatively less "help" in performing household and child care duties. One woman interviewed in Laura Kramer's book on the sociology of gender summarized her views on this disparity:

> Well, I fight constantly with my husband . . . about me having to work . . . He does (want me to work), but he's not helping me enough. . . . If you're not going to

[35] Hochschild, A. (1989). *The Second Shift,* New York: Avon Books.

> help me more at home, then *you* go out and get two jobs and I'll stay home and do all the work.[36]

Misperception: Husbands "help" wives by taking care of the home and children.

Reality: When both parents are employed, taking care of the home and children is the responsibility of both men and women.

The actual amount of time men and women spend on housework and child care varies by study and time period, but women consistently spend more time on such tasks than men do. In a study conducted in 1965–1966, working women spent an average of 21 hours and men spent about 2 hours per week on housework. In a 1987 study women reported spending 19.2 hours per week cooking, cleaning, and other housework, while men reported spending about one-third as much time, 6.8 hours. In Hochschild's research for the book, *The Second Shift,* 20% of the men in couples shared housework equally, 70% of men did more than a third, but less than half, and 10% of men did less than a third of the housework. Hochschild reported that the extra hours women work amount to an extra month of 24 hour days each year. Other researchers have found that single men do more housework than married men, while single women do less housework than married women. On dissolution of a marriage, women's household workload declines, while men's workload increases.

In addition to spending more time performing household and child care tasks, women's usual tasks are different from tasks usually performed by men. Similar to the ease involved in listing common men's external jobs (e.g., pilot, firefighter, construction worker) versus common women's jobs (secretary, kindergarten teacher, nurse), most people can easily name men's usual household tasks compared with women's usual household tasks. Jobs that are traditionally performed by men at home include such things as taking out the garbage, mowing the lawn, and washing cars. Women's jobs traditionally include cooking, cleaning, and doing laundry. When comparing frequency, importance, and autonomy associated with these tasks, gender differences are very clear. Women's tasks must be performed regularly (often daily), within a certain time period, or the family suffers; everyone must eat and wear reasonably clean clothes, every day. Men's household jobs are more discretionary; if they are missed or postponed, consequences are far less negative than if women's household jobs are missed. If garbage piles up or the lawn is not mowed for weeks, aside from unhappy neighbors or notices from the city, there are few negative consequences. While men can choose if and when they will take out garbage or mow the lawn, women have little choice in feeding children or

[36] Kramer, L. (1991). "Social Class and Occupational Sex Desegregation." In L. Kramer (Ed.), *The Sociology of Gender,* pp. 288–300.

doing a certain amount of laundry. These gender differences mirror differences at work; jobs commonly occupied by men often involve more autonomy and flexibility than jobs commonly held by women. Lack of autonomy and flexibility contributes to dissatisfaction and stress both at work and home.

Same-Sex Couples in Family Relationships

Important differences exist in the levels of work participation and division of household labor in families with same-sex partners compared with heterosexual partners. In contrast to some married couple families in which women are more likely to work fewer than 40 hours, in most lesbian and gay male couples, both partners work full time. Similarly, researchers have found a more equal division of labor and tasks in most same-sex couples when compared with male/female couples.[37] The sex-based disparities in participation in the second shift are far less common in same-sex couples; both partners are likely to participate in various household roles and tasks without sex-based boundaries and specifications.

A recent study comparing workplace attitudes toward lesbian mothers suggests that stereotypical perceptions of lesbians and views that lesbians are unlikely to be mothers resulted in lesbians being preferred over heterosexual women as employees. This may be partly due to lower expectations that lesbians will get married and stop working to rear children. Lesbians indeed earn more than heterosexual women and lesbian mothers are perceived as being more competent than heterosexual mothers.[38]

Another aspect of same-sex partners that differentiates them from others is the frequent (though declining) lack of organizational recognition and support of the familial relationships of same-sex partners. In some situations, gays and lesbians may not be out at work. In other cases, even when someone is out at work, organizational policies may not include same-sex partner benefits. Lack of such policies negatively affects same-sex partnerships through medical costs if one partner is not covered by another plan, lack of coverage for a surviving partner through pension plans, and inability to take family-leave to care for nonmarital partners.

Men, Work, and Family

Much of this chapter has focused on women, work, and family because women are in fact disproportionately involved in working outside the home while concurrently performing more of the household and child care tasks associated with families. However, increasing numbers of men desire to and do participate in

[37] See Kurdek, L. A. (1993). "The Allocation of Household Labor in Gay, Lesbian, and Heterosexual Married Couples." *Journal of Social Issues,* 49(3): 127–139; Patterson, C. J. (2000). "Family Relationships of Lesbians and Gay Men." *Journal of Marriage and the Family,* 62: 1052–1069.

[38] Peplau, L. A., & Fingerhut, A. (2004). "The Paradox of the Lesbian Worker." *Journal of Social Issues,* 60(4): 719–735.

family and child care. As discussed in the previous section, in gay couples, gender-role stereotypes that prescribe certain responsibilities to men and others to women are significantly less active; both partners participate in housework and child care. In heterosexual couples, husbands contribute more to child care and housework when their wives work full time and when their wives contribute a larger proportion of the family income.[39] More male participation in family and home care is beneficial to husbands, wives, their relationships, and children, who grow up with less rigid gender-role stereotypes.[40]

Misperception: Women are better at family and home care than men.

Reality: Family and home care is learned behavior; participation by men is good for men, women, and children.

Unfortunately, many of the men who participate in caring for their children experience negative reactions from their employers and peers at work for doing so. In conjunction with the "gendered organizations" that value and reward employees who put work first and other things (including family) second, as are women, men who participate in family care are penalized. Stereotypical gender roles and perceptions about what men and women should do create expectations that men should have a wife who takes care of the family responsibilities, freeing men to focus on organizational demands. Some research suggests that men who participate in family care may be more harshly sanctioned than women who do so because women are expected or supposed to care for families while men are not. As increasing numbers of men play and desire to play active roles in childrearing, these negative perceptions of what men "should do" are increasingly untenable.

Men's Earnings and Spousal Employment

As discussed earlier, men who are fathers and husbands do earn more than single, childless men. But, husbands and fathers who actively participate in family care earn less than husbands and fathers who participate less (e.g., whose wives take care of the family). For example, in her article "I Need a (Traditional) Wife" sociologist Janet Chafetz reports on a study that found that men in dual career marriages had significantly lower earnings (about 25%) than men whose wives were not employed.[41] A later study by Stroh and Brett also found that

[39] Coltrane, S. (1996). *Family Man: Fatherhood, Housework, and Gender Equity,* New York: Oxford University Press.

[40] Coltrane. (1996); Chafetz, J. C. (1997). "'I Need a (Traditional) Wife!': Employment Family Conflicts." In D. Dunn (Ed.), *Workplace/Women's Place,* Los Angeles: Roxbury Publishers, pp. 116–124.

[41] Ibid.

fathers in dual-earner marriages earned less than fathers married to stay-at-home wives.[42] Such findings have been interpreted to mean that having an unemployed wife who takes care of the home and children allows a man to focus on and be more successful at work (consistent with the gendered organization thesis). Close inspection reveals that these findings appear to be limited to the very highest earners, and may not be relevant to the overwhelming majority of families and workers. Further, although some men in dual-career marriages do earn less than men whose wives do not work, the causality of earnings and employment of wives is not certain. In other words, some wives may stop working because of high-earning husbands rather than the high earnings resulting from husbands having an unemployed wife who takes care of the home and family needs.

Misperception: Having a working wife negatively affects men's earnings.

Reality: Some men with unemployed wives earn more than men with employed wives, and some men with working wives earn more than men with unemployed wives.

As with many other work, earnings, and employment constructs, there are race/ethnic differences. In a more recent and more complex analysis, economist Younghwan Song found that for Black and Hispanic men, who earn less than White men, having a working wife is not associated with lower earnings.[43] For Black men, earnings were the same, regardless of employment status of the wife. For Latinos, having a working wife was associated with higher earnings—a "working-wife premium" instead of penalty. The difference in whether there was a premium or penalty by race, ethnicity, or occupation resulted from the difference in the distribution of husbands' wages rather than the wife's employment. For higher earning men, who tended to be White, wives were less likely to be employed. When White men were low earners, there was no evidence of a working wife penalty. When Latinos were high earners, similar to high earning Whites (non-Hispanic), there was no evidence of a working wife penalty.

Table 13.3 presents the proportion of income for men and women by race and ethnicity. As apparent in Table 13.3, White men's gender-based earnings advantages exceed the advantages of men of color compared to women of color. While White women working full time, year round earn 66% of White men's earnings, Asian, Black, and Hispanic women earn 71%, 82%, and 81% of the earnings of men in their respective racial/ethnic categories.

[42] Stroh, L. K., & Brett, J. M. (1996). "The Dual-Earner Dad Penalty in Salary Progression." *Human Resource Management,* 35(2): 181–201.

[43] Song, Y. (2004). "The Working Spouse Penalty/Premium Revisited: The Flip-Side of a Backward-Bending Supply Curve of Spouses' Labor." http://idol.union.edu/~songy/WorkingSpouse.pdf, accessed 02/14/05.

TABLE 13.3 ***Male to Female Income Ratio for Full-Time Workers Aged 18 and Older: 2002***

		High School		College		
	Total	Not High School Graduate	Graduate, Including GED	Some College No Degree	Associate's Degree	Bachelor's Degree
All races male	$54,572	$28,350	$38,841	$47,947	$50,150	$73,139
All races female	$37,624	$20,673	$28,496	$33,243	$35,544	$49,909
All women/men ratio	69%	73%	73%	69%	71%	68%
Non-Hispanic White ratio	66%	71%	72%	69%	70%	67%
Black ratio	82%	70%	87%	72%	73%	83%
Asian ratio	71%	95%	70%	71%	84%	74%
Hispanic ratio	81%	74%	73%	70%	71%	84%

Note: Percentage calculations are the author's.

Source: Table 8. Income in 2002 by Educational Attainment of the Population 18 Years and Over, by Age, Sex, Race Alone, And Hispanic Origin: 2003. U.S. Census Bureau, Men's data: http://www.census.gov/population/socdemo/education/CPS2003/tab08-2.xls, accessed 10/05/05. Women's data: http://www.census.gov/population/socdemo/education/CPS2003/tab08-3.xls, accessed 10/05/05.

Broader than the Family: Society, Organizations, and Family Issues

Relationships between society, organizations, and the family are closely intertwined. In her book *The Sociology of Gender,* Laura Kramer described this relationship well:

> ... even if the members of a household reject broader social norms and arrange their own divisions of labor and responsibility, these individuals will find their choices limited to some degree by larger social arrangements outside their control. For example, as long as the average man earns 40% more than the average women, economic factors rather than personal preferences will guide the choice of which parent will take an unpaid parental leave from work. Social policies regarding parental leave, sex disparities in earnings, the practice of mandatory overtime, and the availability of quality child care all inhibit particular families as they try to arrange their lives as best suits their members.[44]

As an example, consider the second shift. That the bulk of responsibility for the second shift falls on women is a reflection of both gender-role socialization and the sex gap in pay. Many researchers suggest that men's failure to equitably contribute to household and child care is partly due to gender-based pay inequities that have broad societal consequences and that are clearly related to diversity in organizations.[45] Researchers also suggest that inequitable contributions to household and child care are related to marital dissatisfaction and divorce and that men's greater earnings give them "power" to limit participation in the second shift, particularly the more onerous tasks.[46] The proportion of the family income contributed by wives is directly related to the amount of housework performed by husbands. In families in which women contribute approximately half the family income, men perform approximately half the household labor.[47] Paula England proposes that women's employment and proportion of earnings contributed to the household income affect the balance of power in marriages. She argues that "the sex gap in pay has profound consequences for the degree of informal democracy in marriages . . . (affecting negotiation) on a wide range of issues, including intimacy, purchasing decisions, the sharing of household work, and geographical moves."[48]

---

[44] Kramer, L. (1991). *The Sociology of Gender,* p. 168. As shown in Table 13.3, the average wage gap for full-time workers is now closer to 30% than in 1991.

[45] See Budig & England. (2001).

[46] Chafetz. (1997). See also Shelton, B. A. (1992). *Women, Men, and Time: Gender Differences in Paid Work, Housework, and Leisure,* Westport, CT: Greenwood Press.

[47] Blair, S. L., & Lichter, D. T. (1991). "Measuring the Division of Household Labor: Gender Segregation of Housework among American Couples." *Journal of Family Issues,* 12: 91–113.

[48] England, P. (1997). "The Sex Gap in Pay." In D. Dunn (Ed.), *Workplace/Women's Place,* Los Angeles: Roxbury Press, pp. 74–87.

When considering the need to take unpaid family leave, gender differences in earnings also play a role. In most married couple families, men earn more than women. Thus, economically, 12 weeks without pay would more negatively affect the family income if the man, rather than the woman, took leave. Even in families that resisted gender-role stereotyping, according to Kramer's arguments, if a child were ill and required a parent to take leave, the lower earning parent, who is more likely to be the woman, would take leave. Further, were family leave available for employees to care for parents-in-law, because of gender disparities in earnings, it is likely that many women would also take unpaid family leave to care for in-laws as well as for their own parents. In this case, the exclusion of parents-in-law from the FMLA reduces the likelihood that the gender-based expectation of women as caregivers would be coupled with women's lower earnings and result in them taking leave to care for parents-in-law. Positively, the exclusion may relieve working women of this responsibility, but may also negatively affect families' incomes and not respect true caregiving desires.

Misperception: Relationships within families are independent of organizations and society.

Reality: Society and organizations significantly affect relationships within families.

Elder Care

Although most research on work and family issues focuses on children and child care issues, elder care is growing in importance as a work and family issue. While people have choices in determining whether to become parents, everyone has or has had parents and other elderly relatives. Indeed, as the U.S. population ages and lifespans increase, more people find themselves caring for both their children and their aging parents; such individuals are called the *sandwich generation*. The National Alliance for Caregiving and American Association of Retired Persons (AARP) estimate that 44 million adults provide unpaid care to another adult and 26 million of them work or have worked while doing so.[49] Similar to child care, women participate in elder care more than men, often caring for their own aging parents as well as for their spouse or partner's parents. Women working full time are four times as likely as men working full time to be primary caregivers to elderly relatives, spending an average of 17 years caring for children

[49] "Adult Caregivers Looking for Elder Care Benefit Packages." 2005, February 11. *Jacksonville Business Journal,* http://www.bizjournals.com/jacksonville/stories/2005/02/14/focus2.html, accessed 10/22/05.

and 18 years aiding aging parents.[50] These years are all or nearly all of a working woman's adult employment years. In response to elder caregiving needs, caregivers come in late, leave early, miss work, take leaves of absence, retire early, or transfer to part-time jobs.[51]

Employees with elder care needs are increasingly requesting assistance from their employers.[52] Elder assistance including care referrals, help with finding and financing in-home care services, and long-term care insurance are offered by major corporations such as Bank of America, Blue Cross/Blue Shield, and Wachovia. Wachovia's progressive program includes the employee's spouse, parents, parents-in-law, grandparents, and grandparents-in-law as eligible dependents.[53] Unlike the FMLA, Wachovia acknowledges people's real responsibilities toward a larger group of elders and loved ones than solely parents.

Parenting Again: Grandparents Caring for Grandchildren

Although older adults are often cared for by their children, they sometimes become *parents again*. This term refers to those grandparents who become responsible for their grandchildren due to teen pregnancy, substance abuse or imprisonment of the parents, child abuse, neglect, abandonment, or death of the child's parents. These grandparents may have legal custody of their grandchildren or they may be caring for the children without having custody. In a staggering figure, at some point, nearly 11% of all grandparents care for their grandchildren for at least 6 months.[54] In the 2000 census, 2.4 million people (1.5 million women and 0.9 million men) indicated they had primary responsibility for coresident grandchildren younger than 18, a significant increase since the 1990 census.[55] More than 1.7 million of these grandparents are between the ages of 30 and 59, key working years. Thirty-nine percent of the grandparents had been caring for their grandchildren for more than 5 years.

The circumstances leading to children being cared for by a grandparent (e.g., incarceration or death of parents) often cause those children to have special emotional, physical, and psychological needs that may negatively affect grandparents at work. These special needs (and other normal needs of children) can be

[50] Martin, G. T., Jr. (1991). "Family, Gender, and Social Policy." In L. Kramer (Ed.), *The Sociology of Gender,* New York: St. Martin's Press, pp. 323–345; "Caregiving in the United States." 2004. National Alliance for Caregiving and American Association of Retired Persons, http://www.caregiving.org/data/04finalreport.pdf, accessed 10/22/05.

[51] Caregiving in the United States. (2004).

[52] Adult Caregivers Looking for Elder Care Benefit Packages. (2005).

[53] Ibid.

[54] Fuller-Thomson, E., Minkler, M., & Driver, D. (1997). "A Profile of Grandparents Raising Grandchildren in the United States." *Gerontologist,* 37(3): 406–411.

[55] Simmons, T., & Dye, J. L. (2003). Grandparents Living with Grandchildren: 2000. U.S. Census Bureau. See also Casper, L., & Bryson, K. R. (1998). Co-resident Grandparents and Their Grandchildren: Grandparent Maintained Families. U.S. Census Bureau. Population Division Working Paper 26.

more disruptive for grandparents than for parents. Grandparents who are caring for grandchildren are not allowed leave under the formal FMLA definition. Grandparents may be forced to take leaves of absence or quit their jobs entirely as a result of parenting again. One study indicated that 40% of grandparents missed or were late to work, or had to leave work suddenly because of grandchildren.[56] These are similar issues to those experienced by working parents, but may be exacerbated the grandparents' lower access to parental assistance, lower tolerance by employers, and lower ability to obtain subsequent employment after job loss than (younger) parents.

Recommendations for Individuals

At some point in their lives, most people are faced with one or more of the work and family issues that have been considered in this chapter. Although societal and organizational constraints affect everyone, educated, conscious choice in decision making about work and family can play an important role in the successful navigation of work and family issues. For example, to help deal with the second shift, Chafetz suggests "reducing standards" for household cleanliness, purchasing services one would normally perform (e.g., laundry, grocery shopping), and refusing to comply with demands of "greedy employers."[57] While reducing standards of cleanliness may be effective in minimizing time spent in housework, buying many services may be unaffordable for most families.

Refusing to comply with demands of employers might prove detrimental to continued employment, but making an educated choice of employers would be a useful strategy. After assessing individual life plans and goals, people should actively seek employment in organizations that offer programs such as flexible scheduling, child and elder care assistance, paid parental leaves, and other family-friendly programs as appropriate to their current or expected needs in the future. If one lives in a nontraditional family, for example, investigating companies that provide benefits for nonmarital partners, leave time when a partner is ill, and other relevant programs is recommended. Women and men wishing for equity in parenting, household, and child care roles can resist gendered notions of who is responsible for what. Attention to equity in the second shift helps parents in other aspects of their lives and helps children develop expectations for equity in relationships.

Because women are often stereotyped as being uncommitted workers and as being likely to leave the workforce when (if) children arrive, women should be

[56] Pruchno, R. (1999). "Raising Grandchildren: The Experience of Black and White Grandmothers." *Gerontologist,* 39: 209–221. For additional research on the characteristics and experiences of custodial grandparents, see Ruiz, D., Zhu, C., & Crowther, M. (2003). "Not on Their Own Again: Psychological, Social, and Health Characteristics of Custodial African American Grandmothers." *Journal of Women and Aging,* 15(2): 167–187.

[57] Chafetz. (1997).

sure that their plans for work and continued development and opportunity at work are known. The misperceptions that women with children do not work that abound can and do negatively affect women who fully intend to continue working despite having children. If one intends to continue working full time, be aware that perceptions may negatively affect one's opportunities and outcomes without concerted, purposeful efforts and deliberate behaviors. Recognize that working while parenting and parenting while working are the norm, rather than the exception. Expectations for a "balance" at all times are not reasonable. During certain periods, work will take precedence over family, while during other periods, family needs will take precedence over work. Realistic expectations, dependable partners, care providers, and backup helpers, along with carefully chosen employers and job assignments make coping with work and family more successful.

If one does decide to temporarily reduce hours, begin working part time or take a leave, make concerted efforts to remain connected to decision makers and key activities at work. Remaining connected will make the return to full-time work easier and more successful.

Recommendations for Organizations

As discussed earlier in the chapter, career and job satisfaction, organizational commitment, returning from maternity leave, absence, and turnover are related to organizational work/family policies. People who work for organizations that are family friendly are more loyal, attached, and committed to their organizations and have greater job satisfaction. Both parents and those without children or experiences work and family conflicts appreciate the organizational support provided by work-family policies. External organizational stakeholders also view work-family policies positively; firms with new initiatives and well-established work-family policies experience increases in share prices.[58] Ultimately, employees, organizations, and society benefit from family-friendly workplaces.

Several practices may be implemented to assist employees in successfully coping with work and family, including:

- Recognize the role that policies and supportive supervisor/manager behavior play; policies without commitment are ineffective.[59]
- When possible, and without penalty, allow employees flexibility in scheduling, work location, part-time work, and choices about overtime and travel.

[58] See Cook, A. (2005, August). "Connecting Work-Family Policies to Supportive Work Environments." *Paper presented at the Annual Meeting of the Academy of Management,* Honolulu; Arthur, M. (2003). "Work-Family Initiatives and Share Price Reaction: An Institutional Perspective." *Academy of Management Journal,* 46: 497–505.

[59] Thompson, C. A., Beauvais, L. L., & Lyness, K. S. (1999). "When Work-Family Benefits are not Enough: The Influence of Work-Family Culture on Benefit Utilization, Organizational Attachment, and Work-Family Conflict." *Journal of Vocational Behavior,* 54: 392–415.

- Limit or eliminate practices of inconsistent scheduling and overtime that prevent employees from being able to obtain child care.
- Provide job guarantees for those taking maternity leave and family leave that exceeds 12 weeks.
- Assist employees who opt for part-time work or leaves of absence in remaining connected to the organization and in returning to full-time work.
- Allow employees to decide which people constitute their family, such as unmarried partners, surrogate children, grandparents, grandchildren, etc., and provide time off, leaves, and other benefits as are provided for legally recognized families.
- Recognize that there is and should be life outside of work for employees, whether single or married, parents, or not.[60]

Consistent with the last recommendation, employers should carefully avoid the assumption that people who do not have families do not have lives outside of work. Employees who are single or do not have children should not be presumed to be more willing to work excessive hours, unreasonable schedules, travel consistently, or perform duties that would not be expected or asked of employees with family needs. All employees (regardless of their family status) could utilize flexible work schedules, leaves, and other benefits primarily associated with families. For example, volunteer commitments, school, and other commitments outside of work may make flexible scheduling be highly desirable among all employees. Organizations should be careful to avoid penalizing workers without families under the assumption that they have no nonwork commitments and interests.

Summary

In contrast to perceptions and reports in the popular press, the majority of women participate in the workforce, including women with children. On average, women work fewer hours when working full time and are more likely to work part time than men. Fewer hours contribute to women's lower wages, but even when hours are controlled for, women earn 7% wage penalty per child. Part-time work has fewer benefits, security, and access to pensions, resulting in long-term negative effects for women. Current issues in work and family include different family relationships, such as same-sex partnerships, grandparents rearing grandchildren, and extended families; employers should let employees determine who makes up "family" for them. Flexible scheduling

[60] See Hamilton, E. A., Gordon, J. R., & Whelan-Berry, K. S. (2005). "We're Busy Too: Understanding the Work-Life Conflict of Never Married Women without Children." *Paper presented at the Annual Meeting of the Academy of Management,* Honolulu.

and family leave can help employees cope with their particular work and family needs, and the availability of flexible scheduling positively affects employees' commitment to their employers and career satisfaction.

Individuals should not have to try to make the impossible choice between work and family. The more organizations are able to assist employees in being effective workers and family members, the better for employees, employers, and society as a whole. Men, women, and organizations should resist gender-role stereotyping. Participation in family care and life outside of work is normal for both sexes and is beneficial to men, women, organizations, and society.

Key Terms

Gendered organizational culture — an organizational culture that rewards employees who are dedicated to their jobs and set aside personal and family commitments for job responsibilities.

Human capital — factors such as education, job knowledge, training, and expertise that positively affect job performance and earnings.

Parents again — grandparents caring for grandchildren, with or without having formal custody.

The sandwich generation — people rearing children while also caring for or assisting with care of their elderly parents.

The second shift — the extra 8 hours of housework and child care performed by parents (usually mothers) after completing their paid employment.

Questions to Consider

1. Why might perceptions that women do not work or are uncommitted workers be so pervasive and persistent? Do you know women who are uncommitted workers? Do you know men who are uncommitted workers? Do you know women and men who are highly committed workers?
2. Negative perceptions about the competence of women who are mothers were evident in research and in the court cases discussed in the chapter. Why might these negative perceptions exist? Why are they ascribed to mothers but not to fathers?
3. In families in which women earn a significant portion of the family income, men participate more in the second shift. What factors may be at work in this phenomenon?
4. What are some specific inadequacies of the FMLA and what are your recommendations to improve its effectiveness and usefulness?
5. In Chapter 9, the feminization of poverty was discussed. How do the negative effects of having children on women's hours of work, earnings, and wages contribute to the feminization of poverty? What are some suggestions for addressing this inequity?
6. Carefully review the comparisons of access to flexible schedules for workers by race, ethnicity, and sex in Table 13.2. What clear differences exist?
7. What are some possible explanations for differences in research findings on the effects of having an employed spouse on men's earnings?
8. What have you learned from this chapter that is most surprising to you?

ACTIONS AND EXERCISES

1. Investigate and document the most current workforce participation rates for men, women, and women with children under 6 and under 18 and for married and single White, Black, Hispanic, and Asian women. Make a table of your findings. What differences are most striking?
2. Interview two working parents with children under 12 (if applicable, answer one set of these questions yourself). Ask questions related to work and family, such as who provides child care after school hours (or all day if required), how having children affects their work, how their employer reacts to child-related absences, etc. What is the age, race, and sex of each interviewee? Compare the answers of both interviewees. Document your findings.
3. If you know a grandparent who is responsible for his or her grandchildren, interview him or her, asking the same questions from #2 above. Document and compare your findings for both parents and the grandparent.
4. Search the EEOC Web site (http://www.eeoc.gov) for recent pregnancy discrimination cases. Summarize the most egregious case and settlement. What kind of organization was involved? How might the situation have been avoided?
5. Investigate several organizations' work-family programs. Include your current employer or an organization for which you'd like to work. How are they similar and different?
6. Prepare a presentation to convince an employer to offer family-friendly programs. Include such things as impacts to absence, turnover, organizational commitment, job satisfaction, and other relevant items.
7. Conduct research (library, Internet, or estimates from users of the relevant services) to make a table with the following information for the city in which you live:
   a. annual costs of care for a child under age 5.
   b. annual costs of care for a school-aged child between 5 and 11 needing after school care and daily summer care or camps.
   c. annual costs for house cleaning every other week.
   d. annual costs for laundry services for a family of four.
   e. annual costs associated with eating out three nights per week at a moderately priced family restaurant.
   f. mean and median annual income for households in the United States or in the city in which you live, if available.
   g. ratio of the sum of items a–e/ item f.

14 Chapter

Weight and Appearance

Chapter Objectives

After completing this chapter, readers should understand weight and appearance as they relate to diversity in organizations. They should specifically be able to:

- *discuss increasing weight levels in the United States and other populations around the world.*
- *understand the U.S. legislation relevant to weight and appearance discrimination.*
- *describe employment experiences of overweight people and gender differences in employment outcomes based on weight and appearance.*
- *explain how weight and appearance are relevant aspects of diversity and consider whether the obese should be a protected class.*
- *discuss legitimate health consequences of obesity and employers' concerns about increased health care and other costs associated with obesity.*
- *discuss how seemingly legitimate appearance requirements may result in illegal discrimination.*
- *develop methods that can be used to increase acceptance of people of varying dimensions, with or without the presence of widespread legislation.*

Key Facts

Two-thirds of the U.S. population is overweight or obese.

Overweight women earn about 20% less than women who are not overweight.

Overweight people are more likely to be absent and have higher medical and benefits related costs than people who are not heavy.

An overweight person is not necessarily in poorer health than someone who is thin.

In most states, people can be fired for being fat.

Attractive people are more likely to be hired and earn more than unattractive people.

Requirements for professional appearance and neatness are generally legal but appearance preferences that discriminate against people from different racial, ethnic, and religious groups are not.

Introduction and Overview

In this chapter, we consider weight and appearance as aspects of diversity. Appearance is the overall umbrella that refers to one's outward form. Weight, height, race, sex, physical disfigurement, beauty, makeup, hairstyle, and attire are some of the attributes of appearance that are important contributors to one's organizational experiences and outcomes. We begin our discussion with and emphasize weight in this chapter because increasing numbers of people in the United States and worldwide are overweight, because of the existence of overwhelmingly negative stereotypes about those who are overweight, and because of the clear relationships between excess weight and health. While some societies value corpulence, for the most part, in the United States, thinness is preferable to being heavy, in a wide variety of contexts. People generally do not want to be fat and some have stated preferences for losing limbs, being run over by a truck, or being mean or stupid instead of being fat.[1] Researchers have found preferences for thinner and dislike for fatter people among adolescents, children, parents, students, practicing managers, medical personnel, and even those who themselves are fat.[2]

Similar to sex, race, and age, weight and appearance are surface-level aspects of diversity. Because their visibility, stereotypical assumptions on the basis of weight and appearance are often immediate and unconscious, as are those based on other visible factors. On the other hand, some aspects of weight and appearance are distinct from other surface-level aspects of diversity. People from every race, ethnicity, sex, age, and ability vary in weight and other physical attributes related to appearance. Another distinction between weight and other surface-level aspects of diversity is that while people are not viewed as being responsible for their race, sex, age, or ethnicity, they are commonly perceived as being responsible for their weight. People may feel guilt and responsibility for their weight and may try to lose excess weight, or, more recently, undergo major, dangerous surgery in attempts to lose weight. Many people also try to change other aspects of their physical appearance through plastic surgery, hair dye, and cosmetics. In contrast, people are far less likely to feel guilty about, responsible for, or try to change their race or sex. These feelings of guilt and personal responsibility may make those who are unattractive or overweight more likely to accept, rather than resist, unfair organizational treatment and discrimination.

Even though overweight crosses demographic lines, people of color, women, older people, and the poor are more likely to be overweight than Whites, men, younger people, and those who are more affluent. Excess weight also has different effects on employment outcomes for people from these different groups. For example, overweight women suffer more negative employment consequences than overweight men.

Those who are overweight are often assumed to be lazy, unmotivated, and lacking discipline—attributes that are undesirable in employment, and many other contexts. Employers' preference for workers who are motivated, disciplined, and not lazy is logical and understandable. However, avoiding applicants who are overweight does not guarantee that those hired will have desirable

[1] National Education Association. (1994); Solovay. (2000). *Tipping the Scales of Justice: Fighting Weight-Based Discrimination,* Amherst, NY: Prometheus Books, p. 57, citing Gaesser. (1996); Staffieri. (1967). "A Study of Social Stereotype of Body Image in Children." *Journal of Personality and Social Psychology,* 7(1): 101–104.

[2] Crandall, C. S. (1991). "Do Heavy-Weight Students Have More Difficulty Paying for College?" *Personality and Social Psychology Bulletin,* 17(6): 606–611; Crandall, C. S., & Biernat, M. (1990). "The Ideology of Anti-Fat Attitudes." *Journal of Applied Social Psychology,* 23: 227–243; Wadden, T. A., & Stunkard, A. J. (1985). "Social and Psychological Consequences of Obesity." *Annals of Internal Medicine,* 103: 1062–1067; Staffieri, J. R. (1967).

attributes, particularly job competence. Even so, because of the negative perceptions about the attributes of overweight people, those who are overweight experience lower selection rates and salaries, placement in positions with little or no customer contact, and more frequent, harsher discipline at work. In addition to negative perceptions about the personal attributes of those who are overweight, excess weight is associated with negative health effects, such as diabetes, hypertension, high cholesterol, and increases in certain types of cancers. These negative health effects are associated with more absence from work and higher medical costs, which, for many, seem to provide legitimate reasons for employment-related discrimination against people who are overweight and create a dilemma for employers. The clear links to absence and medical costs further differentiate weight-related discrimination from discrimination on the basis of race, sex, and age, which is not easily justified based on organizational costs.

In addition to weight, another aspect of appearance that is relevant to diversity is appearance preferences or requirements that disadvantage women, people of color, and persons with visible physical disabilities. While some appearance requirements are legitimate, if improperly applied or ill-conceived, appearance requirements may result in disparate treatment or disparate impact discrimination. Appearance preferences sometimes favor those who are young, physically attractive, slim, White, or those with Caucasian features, and disadvantage those who have other characteristics. As discussed later in the chapter, the retailer Abercrombie and Fitch has been sued by applicants of color alleging such appearance discrimination.[3] Similarly, when organizations require women to wear makeup or dress femininely, this may be illegal gender discrimination. Some questionable requirements and suggestions for organizations to avoid them are considered in this chapter.

Terminology

Weight and appearance share their visibility, stereotypical perceptions about them, their ability to affect people of various backgrounds, and the lack of broad legal protections prohibiting discrimination based on these factors. This chapter discusses these similarities and overlaps, as well as issues solely relevant to weight. As much as possible, weight and appearance are considered separately, as well as together in areas in which they interact. After clarifying terminology and definitions, we begin our discussion with evidence about the population and employment of persons who are overweight, and then follow this with a discussion of relevant legislation. We discuss population first to emphasize the large number of people who are overweight and not protected from weight-based employment discrimination. We then continue as appropriate with the other standard topical areas included in other chapters.

Weight. In this chapter, when referring to specific research or to the population in certain categories, specifically accurate terminology is used. In other cases, the terms overweight, obese, and fat are used somewhat interchangeably. We respectfully use the term *fat* as it is the preferred term of activists, who argue that the terms *overweight* and *obese* assume there is a *normal* weight—an assumption they dispute.[4] Many of the ranges in weight tables were obtained from insurance companies, using middle-class Whites as the standard.[5] What is "normal" for middle-class Whites may be far from "normal" for other groups. Fat activists also argue that contrary

[3] Current events, November 24, 2004, Vol 103, Issue 3, p. 3. "The Look of Abercrombie & Fitch," Dec. 5, 2003, *CBSNEWS.com,* http://www.cbsnews.com/stories/2003/12/05/60minutes/printable587099.shtml, accessed 10/05/2004.

[4] Solovay, S. (2000). *Tipping the Scales of Justice: Fighting Weight-Based Discrimination,* Amherst, NY: Prometheus Books.

[5] Kristen, K. (2002). "Addressing the Problem of Weight Discrimination in Employment." *California Law Review,* 9: 57–109.

Feature 14.1 *Calculating Your Body Mass Index*

The National Institutes of Health (NIH) identifies the following BMI ranges for underweight to obese for those aged 20 or older.

- Underweight = <18.5
- Normal weight = 18.5–24.9
- Overweight = 25–29.9
- Obese = BMI of 30 or greater

To calculate your BMI, use your height and weight and the formula below.

English Formula

Body mass index can be calculated using pounds and inches with this equation

$$\text{BMI} = \frac{\text{Weight in pounds}}{(\text{Height in inches}) \times (\text{Height in inches})} \times 703$$

For example, a person who weighs 220 pounds and is 6 feet 3 inches tall has a BMI of 27.5.

$$\text{BMI} = \frac{220 \text{ pounds}}{(75 \text{ inches}) \times (75 \text{ inches})} \times 703 = 27.5$$

Metric Formula

Body mass index can also be calculated using kilograms and meters (or centimeters).

$$\text{BMI} = \frac{\text{Weight in kilograms}}{(\text{Height in meters}) \times (\text{Height in meters})}$$

or

$$\text{BMI} = \frac{\text{Weight in kilograms}}{(\text{Height in centimeters}) \times (\text{Height in centimeters})} \times 10{,}000$$

For example, a person who weighs 99.79 kilograms and is 1.905 meters (190.50 centimeters) tall has a BMI of 27.5.

$$\text{BMI} = \frac{99.79 \text{ kilograms}}{(1.905 \text{ meters}) \times (1.905 \text{ meters})} = 27.5$$

Source: Centers for Disease Control (2004). Body mass index formula for Adults, http://www.cdc.gov/nccdphp/dnpa/bmi/bmi-adult-formula.htm, accessed 03/26/05.

to common perceptions, being fat and being healthy are not mutually exclusive. Conversely, nor does being thin necessarily mean one is healthy, particularly when this thinness is obtained at the cost of anorexia, bulimia, or smoking.

Even though what is "normal" is debatable and fluid, clarification of criteria commonly used to gauge levels of fat is warranted. Various sources categorize overweight and obesity differently, using percentages of body fat compared with lean muscle mass, weight and height, or weight excess compared with those who are of "normal" weight. The United States' Centers for Disease Control (CDC) define obesity as being 20% above the recommended height and weight for one's sex and morbid obesity as occurring when a person is 100 pounds over the recommended weight for his or her height.[6] With a standard applicable internationally, the World Health Organization (WHO) measures overweight and obesity by the *body mass index* (BMI). As shown in Feature 14.1, the BMI uses weight in kilograms divided by the square of height,

[6] See Roehling, M. V. (1999). "Weight-Based Discrimination in Employment: Psychological and Legal Aspects." *Personnel Psychology,* 52: 969–1016; Kristen, K. (2002). "Addressing the Problem of Weight Discrimination in Employment." *California Law Review,* 9: 57–109; Ziolkowski, S. M. (1994). "The Status of Weight-Based Employment Discrimination under the Americans with Disabilities Act after Cook v. Rhode Island Department of Mental Health, Retardation, and Hospitals." *Boston Law Review,* 74: 667–686.

resulting in respective ranges of BMI for normal, overweight, and obese of 17 to 24.9, 25 to 29.9, and 30 or more. The U. S. National Institutes of Health (NIH) uses slightly different ranges: <18.5, underweight; 18.5 to 24.9, normal weight; 25.0 to 29.9, overweight; 30.0 to 39.9 obese; and, 40 or more, morbidly obese.

As these different criteria show, what determines normal, overweight, obese, and morbidly obese is debatable. On the other hand, the CDC, the WHO, and the NIH all agree that on a continuum, normal, overweight, obese, and morbidly obese represent the least to the most fat with the least to the most negative connotations and health implications. For the average person, exactly where she or he falls on an inexact continuum is not the critical issue. Being fat is negative in employment contexts; being very fat is more negative, yet a prospective employer will not generally be concerned with or consider whether an applicant is specifically overweight or obese in making negative judgments.

Appearance. Researchers use many terms in reference to one's outward form, including appearance, attractiveness, unattractiveness, and beauty. Unlike well-known (although arguable) standards for determining degrees of overweight, standards of beauty are less well-defined. Even so, research suggests that there is agreement on attractiveness and beauty across cultures, periods of time, races, and ethnicities.[7] People tend to agree on what is attractive and believe that attractive people are more intelligent, sociable, and popular (all of which are positive in employment and other contexts). In the United States and in many other societies, weight is closely related to perceptions of attractiveness and appearance, with excess weight often used as a negative qualifier (e.g., "such a pretty face"). Along with our focus on weight, we consider appearance aspects such as physical attractiveness, beauty, height, attire, makeup, hairstyle, beards, and physical disfigurement.

Population

Obesity and overweight are increasing in prevalence in the United States, Mexico, parts of Europe, and in many other places around the world. This increased girth is partially a result of changes in transportation, activities, and quantities and types of food consumed in the twentieth century. Jobs changed from labor intensive to sedentary, and convenience became increasingly important. People began riding more than walking and participating in sedentary work and leisure activities more than active ones (e.g., desk work vs. farming or manual labor, watching television or playing video games vs. playing sports).

[7] See Cleveland, J. N., Stockdale, M., & Murphy, K. R. (2000). "Physical Attractiveness, Interpersonal Relationships, and Romance at Work." In J. N. Cleveland, M. Stockdale, & K. R. Murphy (Eds.), *Women and Men in Organizations: Sex and Gender Issues at Work*, Mahwah, NJ: Lawrence Erlbaum, pp. 67–76; Cunningham, M. R., Roberts, A. R., Barbee, A. P., Druen, P. B., & Wu, C.-H. (1995). "'Their Ideas of Beauty Are, on the Whole, the Same as Ours': Consistency and Variability in the Cross-Cultural Perception of Female Physical Attractiveness." *Journal of Personality and Social Psychology*, 68(2): 261–279; Hamermesh, D. S., & Biddle, J. E. (1994). "Beauty and the Labor Market." *American Economic Review*, 84: 1174–1194; Marin, G. (1984). "Stereotyping Hispanics: The Differential Impact of Research Method, Label, and Degree of Contact." *Intercultural Journal of Intercultural Relations*, 8: 17–27; Shaffer, D. R., Crepaz, N., & Sun, C. R. (2000). "Physical Attractiveness Stereotyping in Cross-Cultural Perspective: Similarities and Differences between Americans and Taiwanese." *Journal of Cross-Cultural Psychology*, 31: 557–582.

During this same period when physical activities began decreasing, people began eating more processed, fried, fatty, and fast foods instead of fresh vegetables, fruits, and home-cooked foods, contributing further to weight gain.

Despite the very real contributions of changes in transportation, work, leisure activities, and food consumption to increases in weight, numerous other factors are associated with weight. Research indicates that weight is controlled by social, behavioral, cultural, physiological, metabolic, and genetic factors.[8] Different people may consume the same amounts of food, but gain or lose different amounts of weight due to their physiological, metabolic, and genetic factors. In one study of 4,500 adoptees who were separated from their biological parents early in life, weight of adoptees was strongly related to weight of biological parents.[9]

Misperception: Overweight people are overweight because they eat too much and exercise too little.

Reality: Strong genetic components are associated with size and weight; the combinations of genetics, eating, and exercise determine one's ultimate size.

Of the 6.5 billion people in the world, more than 1 billion are overweight and at least 300 million people are obese. Between 1995 and 2000, the number of obese adults in the world increased by 50%, from 200 to 300 million. In the United States, about 65% of adults now fall into the combined category of obese and overweight, nearly twice the percentage of those who were overweight just two decades ago. Proportions of the population who are fat vary by race and ethnicity, with 28.6% of African Americans, 21% of Latinos, and 18% of Whites being obese. Women of color are more likely to carry excess weight than Caucasian women, with about 40% of Black, Latina, and American Indian and Alaska Native women being obese.

Obesity affects people in both the developed world and in developing countries; an estimated 115 million people in developing countries are obese. Obesity levels range from lows of about 5% in parts of China, Japan, and Africa to more than 75% in Samoa and other areas of the South Pacific, where fat is viewed as desirable or a sign of wealth by many.[10] Marked increases in overweight and

[8] National Institutes of Health, Clinical Guidelines on the Identification, Evaluation, and Treatment of Overweight and Obesity in Adults; WHO. (2003); Angier, N. (1994). "Researchers Link Obesity in Humans to Flaw in Genes." *New York Times,* A1, A8.

[9] See Stunkard, A. J., Thorkild, I. A., Sorensen, C. H., Teasdale, T. W., Chakraborty, R., Schull, W. J., & Schulsigner, F. (1986). "An Adoption Study of Human Obesity." *The New England Journal of Medicine,* 314(4): 193–198; Stunkard, A. J., Harris, J. R., Pedersen, N. L., & McClearn, G. E. (1990). "The Body-Mass Index of Twins Who Have Been Reared Apart." *The New England Journal of Medicine,* 322(21): 1483–1487.

[10] Brewis, A. A., McGarvey, S. T., Jones, J., & Swinburn, B. A. (1998). "Perceptions of Body Size in Pacific Islanders." *International Journal of Obesity,* 22(2): 185–190; see also Sobal, J., & Stunkard, A. J. (1989). "Socioeconomic Status and Obesity: A Review of the Literature." *Psychological Bulletin,* 105(2): 260–275.

obesity are also occurring in children in parts of the developed and developing world. In the United States, the numbers of obese and overweight youths have more than doubled in the past three decades. In Thailand, for example, the percentage of overweight youngsters increased about 25% in just 2 years.[11] One study in Tianjin, a city in northern China, found one in five children to be overweight, which was attributed to increasing hours spent watching television. Researchers found that 15.8% of those watching TV more than 3 hours per day were obese, compared with 10.8% of children who watched TV for less than 1 hour per day.[12]

Fat children are more likely to have diseases formerly associated with adults, including high blood pressure, high cholesterol, and Type 2 diabetes than children who are not overweight.[13] Increasing numbers of overweight children will lead to more fat adults in the future as those youths age. Seventy to eighty percent of overweight adolescents will be overweight adults, resulting in longer-term, more severe health problems for them.[14] Although increased health problems are indeed important, overweight children view social discrimination as the most immediate consequence of their size.[15]

Education, Employment Levels, Types, and Income

Because men and women from all races, ethnic backgrounds, and ages can be overweight, generalization about their education, employment, and income is difficult. People of various weights will have similar and different education levels, employment levels, types, and income levels. What is clear from numerous studies, however, is that as with members of other nondominant groups, there are fewer fat people at higher levels and disproportionately more fat people at lower levels. Fat people are also more likely to be unemployed and to remain unemployed longer than people who are not fat. They are less likely to be hired than normal weight or thin people are, even when their qualifications are similar.[16] If they are hired, fat people often earn less and are more likely to be assigned to jobs where they are not seen. They receive lower performance evaluations and are more likely to be disciplined than workers who are not fat. All things being equal, fat workers

---

[11] Obesity and Overweight. Fact Sheet 2002. World Health Organization, 2003, http://www.who.int/hpr/NPH/docs/gs_obesity.pdf, accessed 07/14/05.

[12] http://news.xinhuanet.com/english/2004-08/19/content_1825612.htm, accessed 08/19/04; http://www.chinaview.cn, accessed 08/19/04.

[13] "The Surgeon General's Call to Action to Prevent and Decrease Overweight and Obesity." *United States Department of Health and Human Services,* http://www.surgeongeneral.gov/topics/obesity/calltoaction/fact_adolescents.htm, accessed 09/01/04.

[14] WHO. (2003).

[15] The Surgeon General's Call to Action.

[16] Larkin, J. C., & Pines, H. A. (1979). "No Fat Persons Need Apply." *Sociology of Work and Occupations,* 6: 312–327; Pingitore, R., Dugoni, B. L., Tindale, R. S., & Spring, B. (1994). "Bias against Overweight Job Applicants in a Simulated Employment Interview." *Journal of Applied Psychology,* 79: 949–959.

RESEARCH TRANSLATION 14.1 *Fat Women Fare Worse Than Fat Men!*

Multiple studies indicate that fat women experience more negative outcomes than fat men, including two large scale studies conducted in the 1990s. In one study conducted by Gortmaker and colleagues, using over 10,000 randomly selected participants, overweight women had completed fewer years of formal education, had higher rates of poverty, and earned almost $7,000 per year less than slim women.[17] Register and Williams found that young women who were at least 20% over their "ideal" weights earned 12% less than women who were not fat. No effects were found for fat men, however.[18]

Pagan and Davila's 1997 study using the National Longitudinal Survey of Youth indicated that fat women were segregated into lower paying occupations but fat men were more well-represented across occupations. Fat women earned less than thin women, but fat men did not earn less than thin men. Researchers have also found both fat men and fat women to be less likely to be married than their thinner counterparts, although women again fare worse than men (20% less likely vs. 11% less likely to be married).[19]

QUESTIONS TO CONSIDER

1. ***Why are the work-related effects of overweight different for men and women?***
2. ***Researchers have debated whether people are fat because they are poor or are poor because they are fat. How might each affect the other?***

fare worse than those who are not fat, particularly fat women,[20, 21] as discussed in Research Translation 14.1.

In a fascinating, carefully controlled laboratory study, Regina Pingitore and her colleagues found disturbing evidence of weight-based discrimination in hiring.[22] Videotapes of the same professional actors who were made up and dressed to appear normal or overweight were shown to 320 participants who rated the perceived personality attributes of the applicants and their willingness to hire the applicants. The normal weight female applicant was 5 feet 6 ½ inches and 142 pounds, and was dressed and made up to appear to weigh 170 pounds in the overweight video. The normal weight male applicant was about 5 feet 9 inches and weighed 162 pounds, but was dressed and made up to appear to weigh about

[17] Gortmaker, S. L., Must, A., Perrin, J., Sobol, A. M., & Dietz, W. H. (1993). "Social and Economic Consequences of Overweight in Adolescence and Young Adults." *The New England Journal of Medicine,* 329: 1008–1112.

[18] Register, C. A., & Williams, D. R. (1990). "Wage Effects of Obesity among Young Workers." *Social Science Quarterly,* 71(1): 130–141.

[19] Gortmaker et al. (1993).

[20] See Solovay. (2000); Kristen. (2002); Ziolkowski. (1994) for research summaries.

[21] Jasper, C. R., & Klassen, M. L. (1990), "Perceptions of Salespersons' Appearance and Evaluation of Job Performance." *Perceptual and Motor Skills,* 71: 563–566; Bellizzi, J. A., & Hasty, R. W. (1998). "Territory Assignment Decisions and Supervisory Unethical Selling Behavior: The Effects of Obesity and Gender as Moderated by Job-Related Factors." *Journal of Personal Selling and Sales Management,* 18: 35–49; Bellizzi, J. A., & Hasty, R. W. (2000). "Does Successful Work Experience Mitigate Weight and Gender-Based Employment Discrimination in Face-to-Face Industrial Selling?" *Journal of Business and Industrial Marketing,* 15(6): 384–398.

[22] Pingitore et al. (1994).

194 pounds. A professional makeup artist used the size and proportions of actual overweight people, prostheses, and dressed the "applicants" in the appropriately sized (larger) clothing to make them look about 20% overweight. The results indicated that excess weight explained 35% of the variance in decisions to hire or not hire an applicant and overweight female applicants were less likely to be hired than overweight male applicants. Pingitore and her colleagues did not find that fat applicants were more likely to be placed in nonvisible jobs, however.

Effects of Attractiveness of Appearance on Employment and Income

Because attractiveness is broad and covers many factors, it is illogical to attempt to discuss population or education figures for those who are attractive as compared with those who are unattractive. Therefore, in this section, we consider only the effects of attractiveness on employment and income. In contrast to negative perceptions about those who are fat, people often attribute positive attributes to people who are attractive. These stereotypical perceptions translate into employment and income advantages for attractive people.

Numerous researchers have investigated the effects of attractiveness on perceptions of applicant competence and qualifications, hiring decisions, placement, job type, initial salary and salary growth, and promotion and advancement.[23] In both field studies of actual employees and lab studies with simulations, longitudinal and cross-sectional studies, in the United States and other nations, attractive people are advantaged over those who are not attractive or who have average looks. Although the magnitude of effects of attractiveness on the job outcomes varies, overall, attractive people fare considerably better in employment and income than less or unattractive people. In a study published in 2003, researchers Megumi Hosoda, Eugene Stone-Romero, and Gwen Coats reported findings of a meta-analysis of 68 experimental studies that investigated the relationships between physical attractiveness and job-related outcomes. The studies were published between 1975 and 1998 in psychology, management, and economic journals. Their analysis indicated that attractiveness was positively related to hiring, performance evaluations, and promotion, for both men and women. They suggested that although the preference for attractive people had declined in recent studies, providing raters with job-relevant information did not reduce the attractiveness bias.[24]

---

[23] Cash, T. F., Gillen, P., & Burns, S. D. (1977). "Sexism and 'Beautyism' in Personnel Consultant Decision-Making." *Journal of Applied Psychology,* 62: 301–310; Dipboye, R. L., Arvey, R. D., & Terpstra, D. E. (1977). "Sex and Physical Attractiveness of Raters and Applicants as Determinants of Resume Evaluations." *Journal of Applied Psychology,* 63: 288–294; Frieze, I. H., Olson, J. E., & Russell, J. (1991). "Attractiveness and Income for Men and Women in Management." *Journal of Applied Social Psychology,* 21: 1039–1057; Hamermesh, D. S., & Biddle, J. E. (1994). "Beauty and the Labor Market." *American Economic Review,* 84: 1174–1194.

[24] Hosoda, M., Stone-Romero, E. F., & Coats, G. (2003). "The Effects of Physical Attractiveness on Job-Related Outcomes: A Meta-Analysis of Experimental Studies." *Personnel Psychology,* 52: 431–463.

Attractive women may find themselves in a quandary, however. When does attractiveness help and when does it hurt? At what levels and positions is attractiveness positive or negative? Little research has addressed such detailed questions related to attractiveness, but it appears that at lower levels, attractiveness is beneficial for women. In management or for promotional opportunities, being too attractive can backfire, reducing perceptions of competence and qualifications.[25] A lawsuit filed against a Harvard University library is one such example. Desiree Goodwin, a woman with two degrees from Cornell was denied 16 promotions during her tenure at Harvard. In the lawsuit, Goodwin contends she was told that she was viewed as a pretty girl who wore sexy outfits. Goodwin says that she began wearing baggy clothing, but continued to be passed over for other women with less education and experience.[26]

Height is also related to employment outcomes, and has different effects for men and women. Height has been found to positively affect men's likelihood of being hired, but to have limited effect on performance ratings once hired.[27] Another study found that being taller affected starting salaries of men, but not women.[28] In a study of more than 2,000 U.S. participants from the National Longitudinal Study of Youth, Eng Loh found that both men and women who were taller than average had higher earnings; men received greater returns on height than women did.[29] Similar results have been found using other samples.[30] In a comprehensive, strong empirical study published in 2004, Timothy Judge and Daniel Cable found clear relationships between height and workplace success. In four studies with longitudinal samples of 8,590 people, height was significantly related to earnings for both men and women, and advantages for tall people were stable over the course of participants' careers. Judge and Cable concluded that "height clearly matters in the context of workplace success."[31] A British study on the effects of beauty and stature on labor market outcomes is discussed in International Feature 14.1.

---

[25] See Hatfield, E., & Sprecher, S. (1986). *Mirror, Mirror . . . : The Importance Of Looks In Everyday Life*. Albany, NY: State University of New York Press.

[26] Lewis, D. (2005, March 27). "Suit Focuses Attention on Alleged Bias against Beauty, Attire on the Job." http://bostonworks.boston.com/globe/out_field/archive/032705.shtml, accessed 03/27/05.

[27] Hensley, W. E., & Cooper, R. (1987). "Height and Occupational Success: A Review and Critique." *Psychological Reports*, 60: 843–849.

[28] Frieze, I. H., Olson, J. E., & Good, D. C. (1990). "Perceived and Actual Discrimination in the Salaries of Male and Female Managers." *Journal of Applied Social Psychology*, 20: 46–67.

[29] Loh, E. S. (1993). "The Economic Effects of Physical Appearance." *Social Science Quarterly*, 74: 420–438.

[30] Harper, B. (2000). "Beauty, Stature, and the Labour Market: A British Cohort Study." *Oxford Bulletin of Economics and Statistics*, Special Issue, 62: 771–800; Sargent, J. D., & Blanchflower, D. G. (1994). "Obesity and Stature in Adolescence and Earnings in Young Adulthood: Analysis of a British Birth Cohort." *Archives of Pediatrics and Adolescent Medicine*, 148: 681–687.

[31] Judge, T. A., & Cable, D. M. (2004). "The Effect of Physical Height on Workplace Success and Income: A Preliminary Test of a Theoretical Model." *Journal of Applied Psychology*, 89: 428–441.

International Feature 14.1 *Research Translation of Beauty, Stature, and the Labor Market: A British Cohort Study*

The majority of research on the effects of physical attractiveness, weight, and height on labor market outcomes has been conducted in the United States. A study by Professor Barry Harper of London Guildhall University reported findings strikingly similar to those found in U.S. studies. Unattractive, overweight, or short people are penalized in the labor market and effects vary by gender.

Harper's sample was drawn from the National Child Development Study, a longitudinal sample that followed more than 11,000 participants who were born in March 1958. Harper's final sample included 4,160 males and 3,541 females. Their attractiveness at ages 7 and 11 was rated by teachers, who also provided measures of intelligence and sociability—both of which may also affect labor market outcomes. Height and weight was measured by interviewers, except at age 23, when it was self-reported.

Harper found that it was unattractiveness, rather than attractiveness, that affected earnings and likelihood of being employed. Men who were rated as being unattractive at both ages 7 and 11 experienced a 14.9% earnings penalty. Women rated as unattractive at both ages earned 10.9% less than others. The shortest men and women—those in the bottom 10% of the height distribution for their sex earned 4.3% and 5.1% less than those not in the bottom of the distribution. Relatively tall men (about 6 feet) earned nearly 6% more than men of average height, but the tallest men (more than 6 feet) experienced no earnings premium. Taller women of any height did not experience a premium; height benefits accrue to men only. On the other hand, obese women, but not men, were penalized. Obese women in the top 20% of the weight distribution for their sex suffered a 5.3% earnings penalty. Harper also found that unattractive or short people are less likely to be employed than others in the sample. Because he had controlled for differences in productivity, sociability, intelligence, and other factors that may have contributed to earnings differences, Harper concluded that the majority of the earnings penalty experienced by those short, unattractive, or obese resulted from employer discrimination.

Questions to Consider

1. ***How might height affect employers' perceptions about applicants or employees?***
2. ***What specific recommendations would you make to help employers avoid height discrimination?***

Source: Harper, B. (2000). "Beauty, Stature, and the Labour Market: A British Cohort Study." *Oxford Bulletin of Economics and Statistics* (Special Issue), 62: 771–800.

Legislation Relevant to Weight and Appearance

Is it illegal to prefer those who are tall, thin, or attractive over others? In general, it is not, unless doing so also disadvantages people based on other protected attributes (such as race, sex, age, disability, or religion). In this section, we first discuss legislation and some cases related to weight, and then turn to appearance legislation and related cases.

The ADA and Weight

Presently in the United States, no federal legislation prohibits weight discrimination alone; however, in certain cases, such discrimination may be illegal under the Americans with Disabilities Act (ADA). As presented in previous chapters, under the ADA, people who actually have or who are *perceived* to have a disability (regardless of whether this perception is accurate) are protected from employment discrimination. Therefore, if an employer assumes that an applicant's weight will impede his or her ability to perform a job and makes a negative employment decision on the basis of this perception, the applicant could have a claim under the ADA.

Misperception: It is illegal to fire someone because he or she is overweight.

Reality: It is generally not illegal to fire someone because of his or her weight, except in specific cities or states where laws prohibit doing so, or when the person is perceived as having or has a disability. Firing someone simply because she or he is overweight may not be illegal, but is probably not good business sense.

Without need for assumptions by employers, those who are morbidly obese are strictly covered under the ADA. As noted earlier, morbid obesity occurs when a person is two times or 100 pounds over his or her recommended weight for height or has a BMI of 40 or more. Very few people meet these criteria (only about 1% of the U.S. population is morbidly obese), and a person can be extremely obese without meeting the technical criteria for protection under the ADA. Perhaps more important than the relatively small number of people who are morbidly obese is that very few people make weight discrimination claims under discrimination legislation. Whereas women and people of color are not generally ashamed of or feel to blame for their sex or race, those who are overweight may feel ashamed of or at fault for their weight and be more reluctant to address unfair treatment. Further, when overweight people have brought litigation in response to discrimination, the courts have been reluctant to rule in their favor (see Solovay 2000 for discussions). The low risk for litigation, social acceptability of and cost-based rationale for weight-based discrimination make the need for other avenues to reduce weight discrimination even more imperative.

One important case involving weight-based discrimination, *Cook v. Rhode Island Department of Mental Health, Retardation, and Hospitals* (1993), is discussed in Featured Case 14.1.

State and Local Statutes Prohibiting Weight and Appearance Discrimination

In addition to limited protections under the ADA, some cities, states, and localities prohibit weight-based discrimination directly, or as a consequence of prohibitions of appearance-related discrimination. The state of Michigan and cities of

FEATURED CASE 14.1 *Bonnie Cook: Fat, but Clearly Competent*

At 5 feet 2 inches and 320 pounds, Bonnie Cook was morbidly obese when she applied for a position at the Ladd Center of the State of Rhode Island's Department of Mental Health, Retardation, and Hospitals (MHRH). As part of the hiring process, Ms. Cook was given a prehire medical exam, which indicated that although she was morbidly obese, this did not appear to limit her ability to do the job, thus, Cook passed the physical examination. Even so, MHRH refused to hire Cook, stating that her weight would compromise her ability to be able to evacuate patients in emergencies and would make her more likely to become ill, to be absent, and to file workers' compensation claims. Although problematic in and of themselves, these statements were particularly unusual *because Cook had worked successfully for MHRH twice before, from 1978 to 1980 and from 1981 to 1986, when her weight was about the same!* MHRH acknowledged that Cook had been a satisfactory worker when she was previously employed.

Ms. Cook took MHRH and the state of Rhode Island to court for its discriminatory behavior, suing under the Rehabilitation Act of 1973 (the precursor to the ADA). Cook stated that her weight was due to a medical condition, and that she ate properly and exercised. Regardless of Cook's inability to control her weight, the courts saw as more important that MHRH perceived her as having a disability and disregarded her previously demonstrated ability to do the job. The courts ruled in Cook's favor, finding that MHRH's discrimination against Cook was illegal awarding her $100,000 in compensatory damages, and the job for which she had applied.

QUESTIONS TO CONSIDER

1. ***Why do you think MHRH refused to rehire Bonnie Cook after she had successfully worked for them twice before?***
2. ***What might MHRH do to avoid this kind of situation in the future?***

Santa Cruz and San Francisco, CA, Madison, WI, and Washington, DC, are a few of the small number of cities with such prohibitions. These acts use terminology such as "appearance," "height and weight," "personal appearance," "outward appearance," "hair style," "manner of dress," and other broad terms, which should encourage employers to closely scrutinize their appearance requirements. The Human Rights Act of 1977 from Washington, DC, describes *personal appearance* as "the outward appearance of any person, irrespective of sex, with regard to bodily condition or characteristics, manner of style of dress, and manner of style of personal grooming, including, but not limited to hair style and beards."[32] This act and similar acts emphasize that requirements for professionalism and cleanliness are not prohibited when such requirements are necessary for reasonable business purposes and are consistently applied. Michigan's Elliott-Larsen Civil Rights Act forbids employers who have at least one employee from discrimination based on weight (and other areas).[33]

---

[32] http://www.ohr.dc.gov/ohr/cwp/view,a,3,q,491858,ohrNav,|30953|.asp, accessed 10/7/04.

[33] Elliott-Larsen Civil Rights Act, http://www.michigan.gov/documents/act_453_elliott_larsen_8772_7.pdf, accessed 01/20/04.

Should Size Discrimination Be Prohibited by Federal Law?

Some researchers and fat activists have argued persuasively that overt discrimination (in employment, housing, public accommodations, and other areas) and lack of controllability of weight warrant its inclusion as a protected class. This would make weight-based employment discrimination illegal in most circumstances.[34] As discussed in Featured Case 14.2, Jennifer Portnick's claim against Jazzercise was successful because of legislation prohibiting size discrimination. Portnick's attorney, Sandra Solovay, noted that Jennifer was lucky to be living in San Francisco, one of a very few places in which size discrimination is illegal. "On one side of the bridge you can be protected from weight discrimination and on the other side you're vulnerable," speaking of San Francisco and Oakland, two California cities separated by the Bay Bridge.[35] Ziolkowski (1994) has argued that because of the pervasiveness of weight discrimination, the increased risks for health conditions associated with excess weight, and the difficulty in losing weight and maintaining weight loss, it is possible that weight should be a federally protected class, similar to sex, race, ethnicity, and disability.[36] For those who maintain that weight is controllable (unlike sex, race, and age) and therefore deserves no special protection, the issue of whether controllability should be used as disqualifier for protection must be carefully analyzed. Some disabilities, such as cancer due to smoking or paralysis due to reckless driving, could be construed as voluntary, yet persons so disabled are protected from employment discrimination. Further, as with other arguments supportive of diversity in organizations, employers should be encouraged to make job-related decisions on the ability to perform the job in question. Assuming that fat applicants are unfit and unqualified can rule out nearly two-thirds of the population who may also be highly competent employees.

Organizations must also consider the risks of disparate treatment or impact on protected classes as a result of employment actions based on weight, appearance, and perceived attractiveness. Appearance declines and weight gain are more likely as one ages, women of color tend to be heavier than White women, and women tend to carry proportionally more excess weight than men. These and other relationships between appearance, weight, age, and race require that employers pay careful attention to their selection preferences and decisions by emphasizing legitimate job requirements.

---

[34] Solovay, S. (2000). *Tipping the Scales of Justice: Fighting Weight-Based Discrimination,* Amherst, NY: Prometheus Books.

[35] Brown, P. L. (2002, May 8). "240 Pounds, Persistent and Jazzercise's Equal." *New York Times,* http://oldweb.uwp.edu/academic/criminal.justice/fatjazzbkup.html, accessed 07/14/05.

[36] Ziolkowski, S. M. (1994). "The Status of Weight-Based Employment Discrimination under the Americans with Disabilities Act after Cook v. Rhode Island Department of Mental Health, Retardation, and Hospitals." *Boston Law Review,* 74: 667–686.

Featured Case 14.2 *Jennifer Portnick: Clearly Fit, but Not Up to Jazzercise Appearance Standards*

Although 5 feet 8 inches and 240 pounds, Jennifer Portnick's ability to perform high-impact aerobics was not questioned. Portnick exercised 6 days per week and had been doing high-impact aerobics, as a student and a teacher, for 15 years. Portnick performed aerobics so well that her Jazzercise teacher encouraged her to seek Jazzercise certification so that she could teach for the Jazzercise organization. To do so, Portnick had to obtain permission to try out for certification, but, because of her size, Jazzercise management would not allow her to try out. Jazzercise told Portnick that she needed to lose weight and to cut down on carbohydrates. Reflecting the erroneous position that being heavy and being fit are mutually exclusive, Jazzercise management told Portnick that "Jazzercise sells fitness" and that a "Jazzercise applicant must look leaner than the public," among other things.[37]

Portnick sued Jazzercise under San Francisco's May 2000 ordinance that prohibits discrimination on the basis of weight and height. This law is also called the *fat and short law* by critics. The case went to mediation and was settled when Jazzercise changed its mind about the value of a "fit appearance as a standard." In a letter to Portnick, the company stated: "Recent studies document that it may be possible for people of varying weights to be fit."[38]

In addition to one's right to be judged on competence rather than appearance, Portnick's supporters viewed Jazzercise's position as narrow-minded and counterproductive, particularly given the increasing size of the U.S. population. Although overweight people may be self-conscious in a "normal" aerobics class, they may be comfortable and confident in a class taught by a "fat-but-fit" instructor. Instead of Jazzercise, Portnick began teaching aerobics at the YMCA, which viewed her cardiovascular fitness, despite her size, as a tremendous opportunity to reach the sedentary.[39]

Questions to Consider

1. *What are the likely responses to having a large aerobics instructor, such as Jennifer Portnick, from the "normal" weight students at a health club? What are the likely responses to the Jazzercise settlement from the general public?*
2. *Is being "fat and fit" possible? If so, how could this be reconciled with the documented higher costs associated with heavier employees?*
3. *The YMCA viewed Portnick's size as an opportunity to reach the sedentary. How might this opportunity be realized?*

Effects of Weight on Health and on Costs to Employers

A frequent rationale offered for discrimination against overweight workers or applicants is that excess weight is clearly associated with numerous negative health outcomes. Although some overweight people are quite healthy, the correlation between excess weight and various severe health problems is clear.

[37] Fernandez, E. (2002, May 7). "Exercising Her Right to Work: Fitness Instructor Wins Weight-Bias Fight." *San Francisco Chronicle;* Wrong, Y. (2002). "Jazzercise Sued for Weight Bias." *Mercury News,* http://www.mercurynews.com/mld/mercurynews/news/local/2731271.htm.

[38] Brown. (2002).

[39] Ibid.

Table 14.1 ***Mean Costs of Overweight and Obesity at General Motors***

BMI	BMI Category	Percent of Workers	Medical and Drug Costs
18.5–24.9	Normal	25.2	$3,593
25.0–29.9	Overweight	40.4	$3,705
30.0–34.9	Obese	21.8	$5,032
>34.9	Obese, morbidly obese	11.7	$5,965

Source: Adapted from Grossman, R. J. (2004, March). "Countering a Weight Crisis." *HR Magazine,* p. 45.

Being overweight increases the likelihood of one developing Type 2 diabetes and hypertension. Overweight is also associated with certain types of cancers, including those of the colon, breast, prostate, endometrium, and kidney. Carrying excess pounds is associated with arthritis and other joint ailments that contribute to disabilities in adults, to reproductive health problems in women, and to depression. Estimates suggest that overweight will soon surpass smoking as the primary cause of preventable deaths in the United States.

Table 14.1 presents the mean costs of overweight and obesity for employees at General Motors. The negative health effects of excess weight result in increased medical, benefits, and absence costs for other employers as well. Some estimates suggest that obese and overweight workers use nearly 40 million work days and cost employers 15%, 20%, and 55% more in prescription drug, long-term disability, and short-term disability costs, respectively, with greater costs as the weight level increases.[40, 41] As obesity increases among the population worldwide, these costs can only be expected to increase, providing further incentives for many employer-sponsored weight and health management programs. Despite the legitimate reasons for pursuing weight loss, people who exercise and eat properly, yet remain overweight, may be healthier than slim people who do not exercise or eat healthy foods. Fat people who exercise and eat properly may also be healthier than those who lose and regain weight in fruitless "yo-yo" dieting attempts. For most people, losing weight and maintaining weight loss are very difficult, despite ardent, repeated attempts. As anyone who has ever dieted repeatedly can attest, continued attempts to lose weight appear to make weight loss increasingly difficult to achieve and maintain, while also resulting in other negative health effects. Gaesser's book, *Big Fat Lies: The Truth about Weight and Your Health,* provides compelling support for focusing on health, exercise, and avoidance of weight gain rather than on futile attempts to lose weight.[42]

[40] "The Surgeon General's Call to Action to Prevent and Decrease Overweight and Obesity 2001." U.S. Department of Health and Human Services, Washington, DC, http://www.surgeongeneral.gov/topics/obesity/calltoaction/CalltoAction.pdf, accessed 07/03/05.

[41] Wolf, A. M., & Colditz, G. A. (1998). "Current Estimates of the Economic Cost of Obesity in the United States." *Obesity Research,* 6: 97–106.

[42] Gaesser, G. (2000). *Big Fat Lies: The Truth about Your Weight and Your Health,* Carlsbad, CA: Gurze Books.

Misperception: People who diet and lose weight are healthier than those who do not.

Reality: People who repeatedly diet, lose weight, and regain it may be less healthy than people who maintain a stable weight, even if it is a somewhat healthy weight.

Is It the Fat, the Health, or the Stigma of Overweight?

As was the case with Bonnie Cook, employers may argue that those who are fat will be more likely to file workers' compensation claims and to miss work due to illness. Fat people are indeed more likely to miss work than are people who are not fat, and insuring those who are fat is more expensive than is insuring those who are not fat. Those with anorexia and bulimia are also more likely to miss work and, if their conditions are known, more expensive to insure, as are smokers. Persons with cancer and numerous other illnesses are also more likely to be absent and expensive to insure than those without these illnesses. Those who are fat, however, are unique in their experiences with overt hostility, negative comments, and lack of protections from discrimination on the job. Further, unlike anorexia, bulimia, cancers, and many other illnesses that cause employers additional expenses, obesity is clearly visible. Few would question employers' preferences for workers who are energetic, disciplined, and self-controlled. More legitimate questions might ask whether all overweight people are lazy, undisciplined, and have no self-control and whether all thin or normal weight people are energetic, disciplined, and self-controlled. Few would answer affirmatively to these questions. In fact, a recent study indicates that common perceptions about the personality attributes of fat workers—that they are less conscientious, agreeable, and outgoing—were largely inaccurate.[43]

A thin applicant or employee might be thin due to anorexia, bingeing and purging, or smoking, neither of which exemplifies energy, discipline, or self-control. As discussed in Feature 14.2, costs of thinness can also be very high. Further, multiple studies using different populations have found that people who are excessively thin (BMI <18) have higher mortality rates than people who have BMI ranges of 20 to 22.[44] These higher rates of mortality occur after controlling for previous illness, smoking, or being elderly (and associated weight loss).

Misperception: Thinness is always healthier than heaviness.

Reality: Excessive thinness and excessive weight are both unhealthy.

---

[43] Roehling, M. V., Roehling, P. V., & Dunn, H. (2005, August). "The Relationship between Excess Body Weight and Normal Personality Traits: Investigating the Validity of Stereotypes about Overweight Employees." *Paper presented at the Academy of Management Meeting,* Honolulu.

[44] See, for example, Thorogood, M., Appleby, P. N., Key, T. J., & Mann, J. (2003). "Relation between Body Mass Index and Mortality in an Unusually Slim Cohort." *Journal of Epidemiology and Community Health,* 57: 130–133.

Feature 14.2 *Costs of Thinness*

Eating disorders such as anorexia nervosa and bulimia nervosa are increasingly common weight-related health issues that receive less attention than obesity and overweight. Anorexia and bulimia involve disordered eating behavior, such as eating very little for extended periods of time, or eating extreme amounts, in a short period of time, coupled with measures to binge or purge oneself of food consumed. Both anorexia and bulimia are associated with intense fear of weight gain, inappropriate behavior to prevent weight gain, often including misusing laxatives, diuretics, or enemas and accompanied by excessive exercising.

Anorexia is essentially self-starvation. In response to being starved, the body slows down its processes to conserve energy. Negative health effects associated with anorexia include dry, brittle bones (osteoporosis), muscle loss and weakness, hair loss, severe dehydration (sometimes resulting in kidney failure), and disrupted menstrual cycles. Bulimia involves recurrent episodes of binge eating, sometimes accompanied by purging. The binge-eating episodes may last for hours or days, followed by guilt, disgust, and shame. Those suffering from bulimia are likely to be average or above average weight. Negative health effects resulting from bulimia include swelling of the stomach or pancreas, tooth decay (resulting from vomiting), abnormal heart rhythms, and muscle spasms.

Anorexia and bulimia cross racial, ethnic, age, and gender lines; however, young women are significantly more likely to develop them than others. Estimates suggest that between 0.5% and 3.7% of females will suffer from anorexia at some point in life and that between 1.1% and 4.2% will have bulimia at some point. The mortality rate for those with anorexia is 5.6% per decade, or 12 times higher than the death rate due to all causes of death for young women in the population. The most common causes of death due to anorexia are cardiac arrest, electrolyte imbalance, and suicide. In 1983, Karen Carpenter, a popular singer from the 1970s and 1980s, died at 32, after battling anorexia for many years. In 2004, *USA Today* reported that Mary-Kate Olsen sought treatment for anorexia nervosa. Jane Fonda and Sally Field have also reported suffered from bulimia during their careers.

Questions to Consider

1. ***Why do the negative health effects associated with thinness and attempts to be thin receive relatively little attention when compared with obesity?***

2. ***Investigate mortality rates for obese young women. How do these rates compare with young women suffering from anorexia or bulimia?***

Source: Spearing, M. (2001). "Eating Disorders: Facts about Eating Disorders and the Search for Solutions," National Institute of Mental Health, http://www.nimh.nih.gov/publicat/eatingdisorders.cfm, accessed 03/26/05; Soriano, C. G. (2004, June 22). "Mary-Kate Olsen Seeks Treatment for Eating Disorder." *USA Today,* http://www.usatoday.com/life/people/2004-06-22-olsen-treatment_x.htm, accessed 03/26/05.

The widespread dislike for fatness, its clear visibility, its perceived association with many negative personal attributes, and the lack of widespread sanctions for discrimination on the basis of fat all contribute to continued fat discrimination. Research on stigma provides some clues to understanding fat discrimination. Stigma theory suggests that those whose attributes deviate from the typical, normal, or preferred attributes of others in a situation may be *stigmatized* and this stigmatization will result in various negative outcomes.[45] Since two-thirds of the U.S. population is now overweight or obese, the "typical" or "normal" person is no longer thin. Stigmatization appears instead to result from deviance from *preferred attributes* rather than common or normal attributes. As discussed earlier, women suffer more negative consequences for being overweight than do men. Several authors suggest this is partly a response to media images that portray nearly all women as unrealistically thin and ignore larger (normal) sized women,[46] resulting in greater preferences for thin women. Since the images of women's thinness are so pervasive and so strongly equated with beauty, women who deviate from these images and are fat are penalized by society, including employers.

Appearance: Cases and Legislation

When appearance or attractiveness requirements discriminate against non-Whites, women, people with disabilities, or older workers, Title VII, the ADA, or the ADEA may be violated. In prohibiting race, ethnic, sex, religious, age, and disability discrimination, these acts require organizations carefully assess the legality of preferences for certain "looks" or other attributes. The "look" preferred by management at Abercrombie and Fitch was alleged to result in illegal discrimination against women and people of color, as discussed in Organizational Focus 14.1.

Recall that the ADA prohibits discrimination if a person is *perceived as* being limited by a disability, regardless of whether she or he is actually limited by a disability. According to the EEOC, one such case in which appearance preferences resulted in illegal discrimination occurred at a McDonald's in Northport, Alabama. Samantha Robichaud has a cosmetic disfigurement, called a port wine stain, which covers the majority of her face. Ms. Robichaud began working at McDonald's as a cook, but said she accepted that position with the assurance she would have the opportunity to be promoted into management. To obtain such promotions, McDonald's requires employees to be cross-trained and rotated into several of the jobs at the restaurant, including serving customers at the counter. Robichaud worked the front counter for a while, but was removed because of her appearance. She was later told that she would never be able to receive a management position because of her appearance. The EEOC in Birmingham, Alabama, found Robichaud's case to be meritorious and, after failing to reach a conciliation agreement with the restaurant, filed its first suit involving facial disfigurement in Alabama.[47]

Other situations involving questionable appearance requirements concern employers' restrictions against facial hair, preferences for hair color of a person's

---

[45] Goffman, E. (1963). *Stigma: Notes on the Management of Spoiled Identity,* Englewood Cliffs, NJ: Prentice-Hall.

[46] Wolf, N. (1991). *The Beauty Myth,* New York: William Morris & Co.; Goodman, C. (1995). *The Invisible Woman: Confronting Weight Prejudice in America,* Carlsbad, CA: Gurze books.

[47] EEOC Sues McDonald's Restaurant for Disability Bias against Employee with Facial Disfigurement, http://www.eeoc.gov/press/3-7-03.html, accessed 09/29/04.

Organizational Focus 14.1 *Multiple Diversity Concerns at Abercrombie and Fitch*

Abercrombie and Fitch (ANF), an upscale retailer known for its attractive "All-American" salespeople, has been accused of discriminating against applicants who are not blonde, and blue-eyed, even though the company has a stated nondiscrimination policy. While preferring applicants of a certain appearance is not illegal in and of itself, when doing so eliminates nearly all people of a particular race or ethnicity, this can be illegal. According to charges filed by former employees and applicants, and some which have been confirmed by former managers, ANF consciously discriminated against Latinos, Asian Americans, and Blacks in hiring, firing, and job placement. According to formal charges with the EEOC and news reports, actions included people of color being told there were no jobs when jobs were available, being steered to nonvisible jobs (such as stocking), and being fired or transferred and replaced with White employees.

One Latino, Eduardo Gonzalez, applied to work at ANF in a mall near Stanford University, where he was a student. Gonzalez noticed that all the sales staff on duty when he applied were White and said that the manager encouraged him to work in the stock room or in another nonsales position. Gonzalez left ANF and instead was hired at Banana Republic. Asian Americans have also reported suspicious treatment by ANF. Another Stanford student, Anthony Ocampo, a Filipino American, had worked for ANF during the Christmas holidays. When he applied at a different ANF the following summer for a job, Ocampo was reportedly told he wasn't hired because there were already too many Filipinos working there. Jennifer Lu was a student at University of California–Irvine when she worked for ANF. According to Lu, corporate representatives from ANF came to inspect the store, pointed to one of the ANF posters that depicted a White male model, and told the store manager to make the store look like the poster. Soon thereafter, Lu (who had more than 3 years of service) and four other Asian American employees were terminated and an African American was transferred to the night shift at a different store. Class action lawsuits were filed against ANF in California and New Jersey and in a "letter of determination" the Los Angeles office of the EEOC indicated that there was sufficient cause to believe a Latino plaintiff had been discriminated against because of his ethnicity.

Not only has ANF had employment-related diversity problems, it has also had problems related to choice of merchandise, drawing ire from customers. In early 2002, ANF removed T-shirts from its shelves after complaints from customers about "racist fashion." One shirt was particularly offensive, depicting two men with "slanty-eyes" and the words "Wong Brothers Laundry Service—Two Wongs Can Make it White," perpetuating stereotypes of Asians. Customers in downtown San Francisco picketed the stores, and planned boycotts around the country. Although the buyers' decision making in choosing such offensive merchandise is not known, it would appear that a diverse buying team or store-level associates may have recognized the potential for trouble with those particular shirts before they reached the shelves.

Articles about these issues have appeared in the *San Francisco Chronicle*, the *Miami Herald*, the *New York Times*, *Black Enterprise*, in Associate Press reports distributed nationwide, and on CNN and CBS news, generating negative publicity from coast-to-coast. The NAACP Legal Defense and Educational Fund, the Mexican-American Legal Defense and Educational Fund, and the Asian

Pacific American Legal Centers joined forces with the plaintiffs' attorneys in this effort.[48]

ANF's diversity concerns may have negatively affected its ability to market to its target consumers, a point noted in an October 2004 article on young buyers' tastes. According to David Morrison, founder and CEO of a firm that analyzes shopping habits of people from 18 to 35 years old, "to the college-age shopper, Abercrombie is 'so over.'" In Morrison's opinion, "Abercrombie lost it when they became a little 'too white' with their advertising. They lost and alienated a lot of people who didn't see themselves or their friends represented."[49]

Abercrombie and Fitch also lost in the $50 million settlement of the class-action lawsuit in November 2004. In the settlement, ANF agreed to pay $40 million to the over 10,000 estimated affected people and $10 million to monitor compliance attorneys' fees. The consent decree enjoins ANF from discriminating against African Americans, Asian Americans, and Latinos based on their race, color, and national origin; from discriminating against women due to their sex; and from denying promotional opportunities to minorities and women. As part of the settlement, ANF must also implement new policies and programs to prevent future discrimination, hire a vice president of diversity, hire up to 25 diversity recruiters, provide training to all its managers, and "most importantly . . . ensure that its marketing materials will reflect diversity."[50]

In a statement after the settlement, ANF chairman and CEO Mike Jeffries denied engaging in discriminatory practices, stating that they "have, and always have had, no tolerance for discrimination." Jeffries said that ANF decided to settle the suit because a protracted dispute would have been harmful to the company and distracting to managers.[51]

Questions to Consider

1. *Chapters 4 and 5 discuss the "youthfulness" of African Americans and Latinos when compared with Caucasians. Using Census data (http://www.census.gov), document this youthfulness (in raw population or population percentages for persons under age 30) and discuss the potential ramifications of ANF's exclusion of these groups as employees and models.*

2. *How might having buyers from different racial and ethnic backgrounds have circumvented the marketing "blunders" and lost business associated with the offensive merchandise at ANF?*

3. *How may the company's denial of discrimination, even after settling the lawsuit, negatively impact the effectiveness of measures to stop discrimination in hiring and advancement of women and minorities in ANF?*

4. *How does the experience of Asian Americans in California with employment discrimination contrast with the perception of Asian Americans as a group that does not experience employment-related discrimination?*

5. *Choose a retail store in your area or catalog company. Document the racial, ethnic, gender, and estimated age composition of the sales associate in one visit, or models, if a catalog. What diversity-related factors are visible from your report?*

---

[48] Holmes, T. E. (n.d.). "Abercrombie & Fitch's Discrimination Woes," http://www.blackenterprise.com/ExclusivesekOpen.asp?id=387, accessed 09/27/04.

[49] Wellington, E. (2004, October 14). "The Old College Buy: Company Tracks Students' Tastes and Finds Good News for Burt's Bees, Bad News for Nike." Fort Worth Star Telegram, section 8E.

[50] EEOC Agrees to Landmark Resolution of Discrimination Case against Abercrombie & Fitch, http://www.eeoc.gov/press/11-18-04.html, accessed 11/19/2004; Chavez, P. (2004, November 16). "Abercrombie & Fitch to Pay $40 Million to Settle Discrimination Case." *The Mercury News,* http://www.mercurynews.com/mld/mercurynews/news/10189859.htm, accessed 11/18/04.

[51] Chavez. (2004).

Sources: Greenhouse, S. (2003, June 17). "Clothing Chain Accused of Discrimination." *New York Times*; Shannon, P. D. (2003, November 20). The Legal Intelligencer, "Abercrombie & Fitch Accused of 'Whites-Only' Hiring Policy," http://www.law.com/jsp/article.jsp?id=1069170411455, accessed 09/27/04; Chin A. (2002, April 23). "Why Abercrombie and Fitch Still Doesn't Get It," http://www.modelminority.com/modules.php?name=News&file=article&sid=21, accessed 09/27/04; Kong, D. (2002, April 19). "Abercrombie & Fitch Pulls T-shirts, but Asian-Americans Still Protest," http://www.sfgate.com/cgi-bin/article.cgi?file=/news/archive/2002/04/19/state0328EDT0021.DTL, accessed 09/27/04; Lieff Cabraser and Civil Rights Organizations Announce Abercrombie & Fitch Charged with Employment Discrimination in Federal Class Action Lawsuit, http://www.afjustice.com/press_release_01.htm, accessed 09/27/04; Tamara, E. H., "Abercrombie & Fitch's Discrimination Woes," http://www.blackenterprise.com/ExclusivesekOpen.asp?id=387, accessed 09/27/04; Current events, November 24, 2004, Vol 103, Issue 3, p. 3. "The Look of Abercrombie & Fitch," Dec. 5, 2003, *CBSNEWS.com*, http://www.cbsnews.com/stories/2003/12/05/60minutes/printable587099.shtml, accessed 10/05/2004.

ethnic origin, suggestions that women wear makeup or certain hairstyles, and limitations on religious apparel at work. Such requirements may constitute religious, racial, ethnic, or gender discrimination. Restrictions against beards have been challenged by African American men, who sometimes experience a painful condition called pseudofolliculitis barbae or "razor bumps" as a result of shaving.[52] As discussed in Chapter 10, requirements that women wear pants or not wear head coverings can result in religious discrimination, as Brinks security learned. Other companies accused of appearance-related discriminatory conduct include Federal Express, Enterprise Rent-A-Car, Alamo Rent-A-Car, Price Waterhouse, and Jean Louis David Salons,[53] among many others. Blockbuster has recognized diversity programs, but in a case settled in 2005, Blockbuster's dress code that prohibited headwear was deemed to have resulted in religious discrimination against a young Jewish employee who had been forced to remove his yarmulke for the first 2 months of his employment. Along with a monetary settlement, Blockbuster agreed to apologize to the employee, and to train employees about religious discrimination, retaliation, and the right to file a discrimination charge. Blockbuster also agreed to revise its employee handbook and standard operating procedures to provide for exceptions to the dress code to accommodate an employee's religious beliefs.[54] Table 14.2 presents some appearance attributes that may be of concern to employees and relevant legislation.

Individual and Organizational Recommendations

Considerations for Employers: Weight

The increasing numbers of people who are overweight and obese in the United States and around the world, the very real, expensive costs and health risks associated with excess weight, and the discrimination against those who are overweight create an unusual situation for employers. Should overweight people be

[52] Learmonth M., "Saving Face," http://www.metroactive.com/papers/metro/11.14.96/shaving-9646.html, accessed 10/7/04.

[53] For example, see Hwang, S. L. (2003).

[54] *EEOC v. Blockbuster, Inc.* No. CIV 04 2007 PHX FJM (D. Ariz. June 8, 2005.) EEOC Litigation Settlements—June 2005, http://www.eeoc.gov/litigation/settlements/settlement06-05.html, accessed 10/22/05.

TABLE 14.2 ***Appearance Concerns and Relevant Federal Legislation***

Appearance Aspect	Requirement/Issue	Legislation
Hair color	Color of own "ethnic origin"	Title VII: Race
	No gray	ADEA
Hairstyle	Braids, dreadlocks	Title VII: Race
	Length	Title VII: Gender, religion
Makeup	Mandatory to wear	Title VII: Gender
Facial hair	No beards	Title VII: Race, religion
Attire	Restrictions on religious apparel	Title VII: Religion
	Skirt length	Title VII: Gender
Weight	Presumption of performance limitations	ADA
Physical disfigurement	None visible	ADA

denied employment because they are more likely to miss work and are more expensive for organizations to insure? Although weight discrimination is not usually illegal, employers should consider several factors in developing an approach to combat weight-related discrimination. First, employers should consider the legitimacy of health, absence, and cost-related concerns for their specific employee population. Are similar concerns expressed regarding other health issues? Do people with other health issues that are viewed as controllable (e.g., pregnancy, smoking-related lung cancer) experience similar treatment?

Employers should consider the negative consequences of weight discrimination, using the same preventive lenses as used to view other discrimination. Adding size, weight, and appearance to the company's zero-tolerance policy would signal to all employees that discrimination and harassment on the basis of these factors is unacceptable. Fat jokes, comments, and overt discrimination would be strongly sanctioned, as would racist, sexist, or ageist behaviors. Decision makers must be aware that the broad social acceptability of fat discrimination and general dislike for fatness by individuals may make efforts to reduce it more difficult, requiring more concerted, rigorous, and sincere efforts.

Those who are fat report experiencing extreme hostility, rudeness, and harassment by hiring managers, coworkers, and peers. As an example, when he arrived for an interview, one overweight applicant was not spoken to by the interviewing manager. Instead the manager told the secretary to "Get this fat (expletive) out of my office!"[55] Another heavy applicant was forced to stand throughout the interview, for fear he would break the chairs. An article in *Working Woman* magazine reported that a woman who was thinner at the time of a job interview said that on her first day of work she was told she had "put on a lot of weight!" since the interview. Throughout her miserable employment tenure, the woman was

[55] Fraser, L. (1994). "The Office F Word: Job Discrimination against Fat People." *Working Woman,* 53–54(6): 88–91.

told to wear dark clothing, and coached on her appearance, despite successful job performance and an otherwise professional (although fat) appearance.[56] Clearly, these behaviors are unacceptable in any business environment and should not be tolerated. Although fat discrimination is not currently illegal, professional behavior should be mandatory in work, school, and other professional environments.

Finally, because the majority of the U.S. population is overweight or obese, if potential workers are continually screened out due to their weight, recruitment and selection costs could become extremely high. If fat employees are given positions with low visibility, disciplined more harshly, and experience other negative outcomes at work, employer costs related to turnover, absence, and low morale could exceed or rival those related to higher medical and benefits costs for having fat workers. As with other diversity-related issues, employers should focus their decision making and actions on job-related issues and take measures to ensure that fat discrimination that is not job related is minimized. In addition, the social and ethical concerns with hostile treatment toward those who are overweight or obese must not be ignored.

Employers may be able to assist *all workers* with health-related issues by encouraging wellness rather than focusing on weight loss, which may be futile and could perpetuate fat discrimination. Wellness would include healthy behaviors, such as proper eating, exercise, moderate drinking, avoiding smoking, and reducing stress (which contributes to hypertension and weight gain). Employers should offer healthy foods in vending machines and cafeterias, providing bonuses for smoking cessation, regular participation in exercise programs, and other healthy behaviors. Companies could subsidize health club memberships or provide work out equipment and training at work, allowing employees paid breaks at work to exercise. By focusing on health, rather than weight, employers may find a healthier workplace overall, for all employees.

Considerations for Employees: Weight

Whether one is currently thin, "normal" weight, overweight, or obese, the issue of weight as an aspect of diversity has relevance for everyone. We all have the potential to gain weight and experience some of the negative social, employment, and health consequences associated with being heavy. This is particularly true with age, because as people age, the likelihood of growing heavier increases. With age also comes greater likelihood of acquiring a disability, which may also contribute to weight gain. Weight issues and disparate treatment on the basis of weight also reflect intolerance and prejudice to which no one is immune.

When faced with or observing weight-based stereotyping or discrimination, employees should address this with valid information about weight and

[56] Ibid.

the characteristics of those who are overweight. Many people are unaware that weight is a combination of lifestyle choices and genetics and that different metabolic rates may result in some people being heavier than others, regardless of similar activity levels and food consumed. As with many other inaccurate stereotypes, people's beliefs that being fat is solely a result of laziness and lack of discipline may be changed with knowledge. Statements about legitimate health issues as a reason for weight-based discrimination in employment can be countered with statements about other "voluntary" issues discussed in the chapter, such as smoking, or invisible health issues related to other voluntary behaviors that are not so vehemently disdained and acutely obvious.

Those who are overweight should consider and model behaviors of other nondominant groups in the face of overt social and employment discrimination. How have Blacks, women, people with disabilities, and others responded to unfair treatment? Take care to avoid internalizing society's negative beliefs about fat people. Members of other nondominant groups (e.g., women, Blacks, etc.) do not generally feel self-blame and loathing toward their sex or gender. Instead, in response to differential power and treatment, they have sought, and obtained, greater acceptance and understanding of their differences and contributions, and some reduction of discriminatory behaviors. Those who are overweight should also take care to monitor their health; with exercise and proper eating, one may be healthy in spite of excess weight.

Individual and Organizational Recommendations to Minimize Appearance Discrimination

Because there are so many distinct issues related to appearance, broad employer recommendations center on ensuring that employer preferences are job related and that decisions are made only on job-related factors. While requirements for neatness and cleanliness are reasonable and legal, requirements that women wear makeup and carry a purse instead of a briefcase (e.g., Ann Hopkins) are not. Employers should carefully scrutinize appearance preferences and requirements for potential for various types of discrimination. Questions that should be asked include:

- Is the employee or applicant neat? Are his or her clothes ironed, of sufficient length, and an appropriate size?
- Is the employee or applicant's clothing clean?
- Is the requirement necessary to the safe operation of the business?
- Is resistance to the employee or applicant's appearance a situation of race, cultural, ethnic, gender, age, social, or other bias?
- If religious discrimination is a possibility, could the employee's request be reasonably accommodated?

Applicants and employees should be aware that organizations are legally able to prescribe many aspects of appearance at work. Professionalism and uniform appearance alone are not generally illegal, particularly when consistently applied. When no specific racial, ethnic, gender, religious, or disability discrimination results from the appearance requirements, employer rights to a consistent appearance for employees may supersede employees' rights to wear certain clothing. For example, after filing suit and exhausting multiple appeals under Madison, Wisconsin's, policy prohibiting appearance discrimination, an employee learned that her dismissal for wearing an eyebrow ring to her job at Sam's Club was not illegal. Sam's dress code, which specifically prohibited nose rings or other facial jewelry, was deemed to be consistent with the organization's conservative, spartan, "no-frills" approach. When both employees and employers apply logic and reason, many appearance disputes can be avoided.

Summary

In this chapter, we have considered weight and appearance as diversity issues. Weight is a subset of appearance that has many implications for people's organizational experiences. Nearly two-thirds of the U.S. population is overweight or obese, and the prevalence of overweight is increasing around the world. Discrimination against those who are overweight, based on perceptions that overweight people are lazy and unmotivated, negatively affects their employment outcomes. We have examined research documenting discriminatory employment experiences, including differences in rates of employment and unemployment, job assignments, compensation, and performance evaluations of those who are overweight. The lack of widespread legislation prohibiting weight discrimination and the legitimate health costs (some borne by employers) were discussed. Prescriptions for employers and employees seeking to reduce weight discrimination in their organizations were provided.

Many other aspects of appearance, including hairstyle, attire, makeup, height, and physical disfigurement also affect people's organizational experiences. Although employer preferences for certain types of appearance are not necessarily illegal, when ill-conceived or misapplied, such preferences may result in illegal discrimination. Employers should be careful to ensure that appearance requirements are job related and that attractiveness does not overshadow job competence in selection, promotion, retention, and other job-related decision making.

Key Term

Stigma — a negative discrepancy between the real or perceived attributes of an individual and the *expectations for* typical or normal individuals in a particular context.

Questions to Consider

1. What is the perceived relationship between weight and appearance?
2. What are the employment and income-related effects of being overweight for women? For men?

3. The association between excess weight and higher absence and medical and benefits costs is clear. What is the meaning of this relationship for the many individuals who are fat and for organizational policy makers regarding weight discrimination? How should organizations address weight-based discrimination, given these clear, costly associations?
4. Fat is commonly believed to be the result of laziness and gluttony rather than a combination of factors. How do these perceptions affect experiences and treatment of overweight people in organizations? What can be done about these perceptions?
5. What laws are relevant to weight discrimination and appearance discrimination? How might seemingly legitimate appearance requirements result in illegal discrimination? What should organizations do to minimize the likelihood of such discrimination?
6. In 2004, the United States' Department of Health and Human Services (HHS) announced revisions to its policy on obesity, which removed language in its policy manual that stated that obesity was not an illness.[57] How might this action influence other agencies and organizations to change views of obesity and related policies?
7. There are significant, long-term, negative health effects associated with anorexia and bulimia, yet neither receives the attention and focus of excess weight. In Table 14.1, which reports costs associated with weight for GM workers, there is no category for body mass indices that are less than 18.5 (underweight). Why should employers be concerned about the negative health effects associated with under- and overweight?

Actions and Exercises

1. If you are personally overweight or have a close friend/family member who is overweight, consider your or his/her employment or interviewing experiences. Ask yourself or your friend/family member about them. How have they been similar to or different from the experiences of those who are overweight described in this chapter?

2a. Conduct an informal census of employees in several places: fast food restaurant, sit-down restaurant, discount store (e.g., Target, Wal-Mart), department store (e.g., Macy's, Filene's, Marshall Fields), government office, bank, or other locations in which many employees are visible. Document the number of employees and the number of those who appear a little, a lot, and very overweight/obese. What is the race, ethnicity, and sex of the obese workers? Are any of the overweight employees working in positions of power (e.g., managers, supervisors)?

2b. Choose two nights to watch television for 30 minutes to 1 hour each. Document the program, commerical type, and the numbers of overweight/obese or physically unattractive characters on the programs and commercials. What is the race, ethnicity, and sex of those characters/actors?

2c. What similarities and differences are apparent between the people in 2a and 2b above?

[57] HHS Announces Revised Medicare Obesity Coverage Policy, http://www.hhs.gov/news/press/2004pres/20040715.html, accessed 08/19/04.

2d. Refer to the discussion in Chapter 10 about the negative effects of increasing age on women who are television anchors or weathercasters, particularly Marny Midkiff's lawsuit against the Weather Channel. Several male overweight or obese weathercasters have had strong careers, including Al Roker of NBC's Today show (who has undergone a surgical procedure to reduce weight but remains somewhat heavy) and Ira Joe Fisher of the CBS Early Show. Choose several times and broadcasts to watch weather reports. Report on the appearance (including weight, sex, attire, and other appearance attributes) of the weathercasters.

3. Investigate health and medical costs associated with alcoholism, anorexia, bulimia, smoking, and/or another "voluntary" illness. Compare these costs with those associated with obesity.

4. Compare the look allegedly preferred by ANF with the approach used by the United Colors of Benetton to advertising and staffing. What "look" accurately represents the present population of the United States?

5. In the Blockbuster appearance case, the manager was attempting to adhere to the required dress code and may have been unaware of the possibility of religious discrimination. What recommendations would you make to help large organizations with recognized diversity programs to reduce the likelihood of inadvertent discrimination by managers trying to follow procedures?

15 Chapter

Sexual Orientation

LBGT

Chapter Objectives

After completing this chapter, readers should have a greater understanding of sexual orientation as an aspect of diversity. Readers can expect to:

- *have an awareness of the experiences of sexual minorities in organizations, in particular, gays and lesbians.*
- *be aware of similarities and differences between sexual minorities and other nondominant groups.*
- *consider population estimates, education, and income levels of gays and lesbians compared with heterosexual men and women.*
- *examine misperceptions about sexual minorities at work, negative outcomes associated with being closeted, and benefits of full inclusion of sexual minorities.*
- *understand individual and organizational measures that can be employed to include sexual minorities as valued employees, customers, and constituents.*

KEY FACTS

No federal laws currently prohibit sexual orientation discrimination in private workplaces.

Gay males have higher education but lower earnings than heterosexual men, while lesbians have higher education and earnings than heterosexual women.

About 75% of the new HIV/AIDS cases are a result of heterosexual contact or injection drug use.[1]

Since the U.S. military's "don't ask, don't tell" policy was implemented in 1998, more than 6,300 gays and lesbians have been discharged from the military because of their sexual orientation.

[1] Centers for Disease Control. (2005). National Center for HIV/STD and TB Prevention, http://www.cdc.gov/hiv/stats.htm, accessed 05/13/05.

Introduction and Overview

Sexual orientation is an emotionally charged issue, with connotations similar to—yet also very different from—those related to other diversity issues. Experiences of sexual minorities with discrimination, harassment, exclusion, and hate crimes have been similar in many ways to those of other minority groups. Although slavery, near extermination, lynching, and other atrocities against nondominant groups in the United States are significantly different from antigay sentiment and discrimination, certain factors create problems for gays that are not experienced by other nondominant group members. In contrast to sexual minorities, for example, members of other minority groups (e.g., Blacks, women) are not generally viewed as having chosen their group membership. Nor are members of other minority groups commonly faced with the choice of letting others know of their group membership; race, sex, and age range are more likely to be obvious to observers.

One Black lesbian contrasted a critical difference between the difficulties associated with being lesbian to the difficulties of being Black, stating "you don't have to tell your mother you're Black."[2] Whereas many Black (and other minority group) parents discuss race-based prejudice and discrimination with their children from an early age, parents of gays and lesbians may not even be aware that their children are gay. Compared with Blacks and other minority group members whose group status is apparent, gays and lesbians are often unable to learn to deal with heterosexism and homophobia from friends and loved ones. As we will discuss, the invisibility of sexual orientation creates many other difficulties for many who are gay or lesbian. Being in the closet may appear to be easier than risking discrimination, harassment, ostracism, and termination, but it comes with many negative consequences, including stress, anxiety, and continual fear of disclosure.[3]

Terminology

In this chapter, and throughout the book, *sexual orientation,* rather than *sexual preference,* is used. The American Psychological Association defines sexual orientation as a component of sexuality "characterized by enduring emotional, romantic, sexual, and/or affectional attractions to individuals of a particular gender."[4] The three commonly recognized sexual orientations are homosexual, heterosexual, and bisexual. As is apparent by the definition, heterosexuals are included in sexual orientation policies and discussion. As the dominant group, however, they are least likely to experience differential treatment based on their sexual orientation when compared with homosexuals and bisexuals. Thus, we focus on the experiences of the latter groups in this chapter, particularly homosexuals.

Research on sexual orientation often includes people who are gay, lesbian, bisexual, and transgender (GLBT) as a collective; however, many of the individual and organizational experiences of bisexual and, especially, transgender people

---

[2] Correll, S. (1999). "Lesbian and Gay Americans." In A. G. Dworkin & R. J. Dworkin (Eds.), *The Minority Report* (3rd edition), Fort Worth, TX: Harcourt Brace Publishers, pp. 436–456.

[3] Ragins, B. R. (in press). "Disclosure Disconnects: Antecedents and Consequences of Disclosing Invisible Stigmas across Life Domains." *Academy of Management Review.*

[4] Examining the Employment Non-Discrimination Act (ENDA): The Scientists Perspective, http://www.apa.org/pi/lgbc/publications/enda.html, accessed 07/03/05.

are unique.[5] Many concepts that we consider in the chapter do apply to all sexual minorities (e.g., desire for equity and fairness), but when reporting specific research, we will use accurate terminology for the population studied. At times, the term *gays* refers to homosexuals of either sex, and at other times it refers only to homosexual men, for example, in the statement "gays and lesbians." The term *sexual minorities* includes people who are gay, lesbian, bisexual, or transgender.

In a 1972 book, George Weinberg defined homophobia as the fear of homosexuals.[6] More recently, researchers have proposed that heterosexism more commonly affects workplace experiences of sexual minorities than homophobia.[7] Heterosexism is "an ideological system that denies, denigrates, and stigmatizes any nonheterosexual behavior, relationship, identity, or community"[8] and is similar to racism and sexism. Heterosexist organizational policies assume workers are heterosexual, for example. Heterosexist comments suggest gays and lesbians should not "flaunt" their sexual orientation by bringing a same-sex partner to a company event, not recognizing that heterosexuals "flaunt" their sexual orientation by bringing an opposite sex partner to a company event.[9]

History of Gay Rights in the United States

The Stonewall riots of 1969, in Greenwich, New York, are often referred to as the start of the gay rights movement, but the gay rights movement actually started long before 1969. The Society for Human Rights in Chicago, the earliest known gay rights organization, was formed in 1924.[10] In the 1950s, two national gay and lesbian rights organizations were formed—The Mattachine Society, the first national gay rights organization began in 1951 followed by the Daughters of Bilitis, a national lesbian organization founded in 1956. Activism and resistance against sexual orientation discrimination continued through the 1950s and 1960s, which ended with the Stonewall riots in Greenwich Village. In June of 1969, when police

[5] See Lubensky, M. E., Holland, S. L., Wiethoff, C., & Crosby, F. J. (2004). "Diversity and Sexual Orientation: Including and Valuing Sexual Minorities in the Workplace." In M. Stockdale & F. Crosby (Eds.), *The Psychology and Management of Workplace Diversity,* Malden, MA: Blackwell, pp. 206–223; Dietch, E. A., Butz, R. M., & Brief, A. P. (2004). "Out of the Closet and Out of a Job? The Nature, Import, and Causes of Sexual Orientation Discrimination in the Workplace." In R. W. Griffin & A. O'Leary-Kelly (Eds.), *The Dark Side of Organizational Behavior,* San Francisco: Jossey-Bass, a Wiley imprint, pp. 187–234.

[6] Weinberg, G. (1972). *Society and the Healthy Homosexual,* New York: St. Martin's Press.

[7] For example, Herek, G. M. (1984). "Beyond 'Homophobia': A Social Psychological Perspective on Attitudes towards Lesbians and Gay Men." *Journal of Homosexuality,* 10: 1–21. See also Ragins, B. R., & Wiethoff, C. (2005). "Understanding Heterosexism at Work: The Straight Problem." In R. L. Dipboye & A. Colella (Eds.), *Discrimination at Work,* Mahwah, NJ: Lawrence Erlbaum Associates, pp. 177–201.

[8] Herek, G. M. (1993). "The Context of Anti-Gay Violence: Notes on Cultural and Psychological Heterosexism." In L. D. Farnets & D. C. Kimmel (Eds.), *Psychological Perspectives on Lesbian and Gay Male Experiences,* New York: Columbia University Press, pp. 89–107.

[9] See Kaplan, M., & Lucas, J. (1996). "Heterosexism as a Workforce Diversity Issue." In E. Y. Cross & M. B. White (Eds.), *The Diversity Factor: Capturing the Competitive Advantage of a Changing Workforce,* Chicago: Irwin.

[10] The American Gay Rights Movement: A Timeline (2005). Information Please® Database, ©2005 Pearson Education, Inc., http://www.infoplease.com/ipa/A0761909.html, accessed 03/25/05.

raided Stonewall, a gay bar, instead of dispersing as was their normal practice after a raid, patrons resisted and began rioting. Riots and protests continued for 3 days, turning the gay rights movement into a widespread and vocal protest for equality.[11] Hate crimes, overt prejudice, discrimination, and exclusion, and changing attitudes continued to fuel the gay rights movement. As have many other nondominant groups, gays and lesbians have obtained some rights by persistent efforts of many determined activists from all walks of life.

During the same time that activists were fighting for freedom from sexual orientation discrimination, parallels with race, sex, and class discrimination were apparent. In the 1960s and 1970s, some prominent Black leaders vocalized these parallels, calling for unity in the fight against race, sex, class, and sexual orientation discrimination. On the other hand, resistance against and distancing from sexual minorities by some Blacks also occurred.[12]

Population

The wide range in estimates of gays and lesbians in the population reflects difficulties of collecting data on sexual orientation that do not exist in other populations. Recent estimates suggest that 4% to 17% of the nearly 296 million people—between 12 and 50 million people—in the United States are gay or lesbian.[13] Both the lower estimate and the higher estimate reflect significant numbers of people who are gay or lesbian. At 4%, gays and lesbians would be similar to the percentage of Asian Americans in the population; at 17% there would be more gays and lesbians than African Americans and Latinos. With either estimate, or any range in between, sexual minorities are a large proportion of the population, consumers, employees, and applicants.

Education and Income Levels

On average, gays and lesbians have higher education levels than heterosexuals. About a quarter of both gay men and lesbians have college degrees, compared with about 17% for heterosexual men and women.[14] As we have discussed in earlier chapters, education and earnings are highly correlated, and this holds for gays, lesbians, and heterosexuals. However, returns of sexual minorities to

[11] Ibid. See also Schaefer, R. T. (2002). *Racial and Ethnic Groups* (8th edition), Upper Saddle River, NJ: Prentice-Hall.

[12] Boykin, K. (2001). "Blacks in the American Gay Rights Movement," http://www.keithboykin.com/author/blksgrm.html, accessed 03/25/05.

[13] Gonsiorek, J. C., & Weinrich, J. D. (1991). "The Definition and Scope of Sexual Orientation." In J. C. Gonsiorek & J. D. Weinrich (Eds.), *Homosexuality: Research Implications for Public Policy,* Newbury Park, CA: Sage. See also Lubensky et al. (2004).

[14] Black, D., Gates, G., Sanders, S., & Taylor, L. (2000). "Demographics of the Gay and Lesbian Population in the United States: Evidence from Available Systematic Data Sources." *Demography,* 37(2): 139–154.

investment in education are not consistent. While lesbians appear to earn more than comparably educated heterosexual women, gay males earn less than comparably educated heterosexual men.[15]

In one of the first studies investigating earnings differences between gays and lesbians and heterosexuals, Lee Badgett found that gay males earned between 11% and 27% less than heterosexuals. Using a national random sample, Badgett considered people with comparable experience, education, occupation, marital status, and region of residence and did not find statistically significant earnings differences between lesbians and heterosexual women.[16]

More recent studies have further measured the effects of sexual orientation discrimination, finding again that gay males earn less than heterosexual men, but that lesbian women earn more than heterosexual women, in contrast to Badgett's earlier findings. Lesbian and bisexual women's earnings are between 17% and 23% higher than the earnings of heterosexual women.[17] When in partnered relationships, the disparity between lesbians' and heterosexual women's earnings is even greater; lesbians with partners earn considerably more than heterosexual women with partners. This may be due in part to lesbian women's greater attachment to the labor market and to more equitable sharing of household and childrearing responsibilities than in heterosexual couples (see Chapter 13 for further discussion of gender roles in same-sex couples).

On the other hand, gay and bisexual men earn between 30% and 32% less than heterosexual men.[18] Researchers have suggested that this earnings disparity may be due to some gay men being channeled into positions believed appropriate based on their sexual orientation (for example, art designer instead of architect). As we have considered in previous chapters, if these positions are female dominated, the wage disparity is an expected outcome. In one study published in the *Journal of Applied Psychology,* Ragins and Cornwell found that both gays and lesbians who worked with other gays and lesbians had lower earnings than those whose coworkers were primarily heterosexual or equally balanced.[19] They proposed that gays and lesbians may be channeled into jobs deemed appropriate for them or that they may choose work groups with other gays in hopes of finding more supportive coworkers.

Readers may be familiar with reports that gay households have higher earnings than households composed of opposite sex partners. Although the research

---

[15] Ibid.

[16] Badgett, M. V. L. (1995). "The Wage Effects of Sexual Orientation Discrimination." *Industrial and Labor Relations Review,* 48(4): 726–739.

[17] Blanford, J. M. (2003). "The Nexus of Sexual Orientation and Gender in the Determination of Earnings." *Industrial and Labor Relations Review,* 56 (4): 622–643.

[18] Ibid.

[19] Ragins, B. R., & Cornwell, J. M. (2001). "Pink Triangles: Antecedents and Consequences of Perceived Workplace Discrimination against Gay and Lesbian Employees." *Journal of Applied Psychology,* 86: 1244–1261.

Table 15.1 ***Fictitious Example of Earnings for Individual Male and Female Heterosexuals and Homosexuals and in Households***

	All Men	All Women	Gay Male Household	Lesbian Household	Heterosexual Household
Average annual earnings	$20,000	$15,000	$40,000	$30,000	$35,000

reported in this section appears contradictory, closer inspection reveals it is not necessarily so. Male same-sex *households* have earnings that are greater than male/female households; whether gay or straight, men earn more than women. Lesbian household earnings are lower than male/female households because women earn less than men. Without considering differences based on sexual orientation, the influence of men's earnings in households dominates the household earnings differences that appear. As an example, see Table 15.1. This *fictitious* example assumes all men (gay and heterosexual) earn $20,000 per year and that all women earn 75% of that, or $15,000. Simplistically multiplying these fictitious average earnings for men and women by the type of household in which they live demonstrates an example of how these differences *could* occur.

Legislation

Gallup polls indicate that the great majority of Americans believe that gays and lesbians should have equal employment opportunities; only 11% believe that sexual orientation discrimination is acceptable.[20] At the time of this writing, however, no widespread, uniform federal legislation prohibits sexual orientation discrimination in the workplace. Thus, as of 2005, in 35 states, a person can be fired for being (or being perceived as) gay or lesbian.[21] Even fewer states provide protection from employment discrimination for gays and lesbians; in 45 states, someone can be fired for being transgender.

The Human Rights Campaign (HRC), an organization working for lesbian, gay, bisexual, and transgender rights, documents 130 cases of terminations of people who were performing satisfactorily. Reasons given for some terminations were frank—being gay is not acceptable in the organization, the district manager does not like homosexuals, or other such reasons. Other terminations were done under the guise of the employee failing to meet performance standards, having a

[20] "Documenting Discrimination." (2001). Human Rights Campaign, http://www.hrc.org/Content/ContentGroups/Publications1/Documenting_Discrimination/documentingdiscrimination.pdf, accessed 03/25/05.

[21] "The State of the Workplace for Lesbian, Gay, Bisexual, and Transgender Americans 2003." Human Rights Campaign, (2004), http://www.hrc.org/Template.cfm?Section=Get_Informed2&Template=/ContentManagement/ContentDisplay.cfm&ContentID=18678, accessed 03/25/05.

poor attitude, tardiness, or other behaviors for which heterosexual employees were not disciplined. Although legislation has not eliminated sex, race, age, disability, and religious discrimination, not having widespread laws prohibiting sexual orientation discrimination implies that it is acceptable.

Executive Order 11478 (enacted in 1998) prohibits sexual orientation discrimination in federal civilian workplaces, but this has not been extended to other employers. The Employment Non-Discrimination Act (ENDA) proposes to do so, and would prohibit sexual orientation discrimination in all employment matters except in certain circumstances (e.g., religious schools and churches). Many Fortune 500 corporations support ENDA, as do many small and medium-sized organizations.[22] Despite considerable corporate support, widespread individual support, and some political support, the U.S. Congress has failed to pass ENDA as a federal law thus far. Many states and cities have passed legislation prohibiting sexual orientation discrimination, including California, Connecticut, Hawaii, Minnesota, New Jersey, Washington, DC, Wisconsin and numerous others. In the District of Columbia, for example, sexual orientation discrimination is included in the provisions of the Human Rights Act of 1977 that, as covered in Chapter 14, also prohibits discrimination on the basis of personal appearance and other factors not covered in federal laws. Thus, in the District of Columbia, sexual orientation discrimination by employers, employment agencies, and labor unions is prohibited.

In addition, even though Title VII does not cover discrimination on the basis of sexual orientation, it has been used in sexual orientation discrimination in cases of sexual harassment and gender-based stereotyping. As discussed in Chapter 9, early cases of same-sex sexual harassment were not deemed harassment by the courts, but in 1998, in *Oncale v. Sundowner,* the U.S. Supreme Court ruled that harassment may occur between people of the same sex. In cases of gender-based stereotyping, courts have ruled that discrimination because of acting outside of one's gender roles, such as what happened to Ann Hopkins (see Chapter 9) and the young man who was harassed at Babies "R" Us (see Chapter 11), is illegal. In another important case, a gay butler who worked for the MGM Grand hotel experienced virulent verbal and physical harassment and assault because he did not conform to his coworkers' expectations for men. Sexual minorities who experience such discrimination have found relief under Title VII although sexual orientation discrimination alone is not specifically prohibited.

Even in the absence of federal legislation that prohibits sexual orientation discrimination, many employers have incorporated sexual orientation into their nondiscrimination policies. As of the end of 2004, nearly 3,000 employers included sexual orientation in their organizations' nondiscrimination policies. Nearly all

[22] "State of the Workplace for Lesbian, Gay, Bisexual and Transgender Americans 2004." Human Rights Campaign, 2005, http://www.hrc.org/Template.cfm?Section=Get_Informed2&Template=/ContentManagement/ContentDisplay.cfm&ContentID=27214, accessed 07/02/05.

(49) of the Fortune 50, and 410 of the Fortune 500 include sexual orientation in their policies of nondiscrimination.[23] By mid-2005, another 50 companies included sexual orientation, resulting in 92% of the Fortune 500 having such policies.[24] Cracker Barrel's reversal of its overt policy of sexual orientation discrimination is discussed in Organizational Feature 15.1.

Another critical gauge of an organization's stance on sexual orientation discrimination is whether equal benefits for same-sex partners are offered to employees. We consider the issues of partner benefits, HIV/AIDS at work, some of the determinants of attitudes toward gays and lesbians, and the consequences of being out or closeted at work in the following sections.

Partner Benefits

Although many people think of medical benefits when assessing whether an organization's benefits are equitable to same-sex partners, the Human Rights Campaign considers a broader array of benefits that are offered by employers. The HRC Corporate Equality Index surveys companies on their equality of offerings of bereavement leave, family and medical leave, COBRA (legally required) benefits continuation, supplemental life insurance, relocation assistance, adoption assistance, retiree medical coverage, employer-provided life insurance, automatic pension benefits for same-sex partners in the event of an employee's death, and employee discounts. As of April 2005, 83 Fortune 500 companies and 49 other employers offered *all* these benefits to same-sex partners.[25] Far more companies offer at least some of those benefits.

As of December 31, 2004, more than 8,000 organizations, including private employers, state and local governments, colleges and universities, and other employers provided health insurance coverage to employees' domestic partners. In the 10 years between 1995 and 2005, Fortune 500 companies offering domestic partner health benefits increased more than tenfold, up from 21 to 230.[26] Some well-known companies that offer some partner benefits include AMR (American Airlines), Hewlett-Packard, Prudential, Kodak, Merrill Lynch, and Imation. Fears of increased costs associated with offering domestic partner health benefits (especially due to fears about costs associated with HIV/AIDS) are often expressed as reasons for employers to avoid doing so. Evidence suggests that few employees enroll for domestic partner benefits and when they do, costs are generally consistent with any increase in the number of plan participants, instead of being proportionately

[23] Ibid.

[24] As of summer 2005, 460 of the Fortune 500 companies included sexual orientation in their nondiscrimination policies. See http://www.equalityforum.com/fortune500/, accessed 09/23/05.

[25] State of the Workplace for Lesbian, Gay, Bisexual and Transgender Americans 2004.

[26] Ibid.

Organizational Feature 15.1 *Cracker Barrel Reverses Its Antigay Stance but Still Deals with the "Stigma of Discrimination"*

In 1991, Cracker Barrel instituted a policy that called for termination of employees "whose sexual preferences fail to demonstrate normal heterosexual values which have been the foundation of families in our society." The policy, which Cracker Barrel later referred to as a "well-intentioned overreaction to the perceived values" of its customers, set off a storm of negative publicity in the United States. At least 11 workers were fired because of their sexual orientation (e.g., being gay), which is not illegal under federal law nor was it illegal in the states in which the terminations occurred. Some employees' termination slips clearly stated being gay as the reason for dismissal.

Cracker Barrel boycotts were coupled with powerful shareholder activism to result in an official policy change. Ten years of activism, with each year seeing increasing support among shareholders for a policy change finally worked. The New York City Employees Retirement System (NYCERS), controlling 189,000 shares of Cracker Barrel's stock, was the most vocal and powerful shareholder pressing for a change. NYCERS and other shareholders resulted in 58% of its outstanding shares supporting a nondiscrimination policy. In late 2002, Cracker Barrel's board voted to add *sexual orientation* to its nondiscrimination policy. The official Web site of Cracker Barrel now says that, "Cracker Barrel will not tolerate any form of discrimination, harassment, or retaliation affecting its employees or applicants due to race, color, religion, sex, sexual orientation, national origin, age, marital status, medical condition, or disability."[27] The site also includes prohibition of discrimination against guests (customers) or would-be guests on the basis of similar factors, including sexual orientation.

Cracker Barrel's other diversity troubles include more than 100 allegations of discrimination against African American customers. Black customers have reported excessive wait times, racial slurs, being seated in smoking sections with other Black customers, despite having requested nonsmoking and despite nonsmoking tables being vacant, and being followed around the store. A Justice Department inquiry included interviews of 150 employees, 80% of whom said they had experienced or witnessed discriminatory treatment of Black customers and suggested this behavior was directed, participated in, or condoned by management.[28] The department found evidence of discriminatory conduct in about 50 stores in seven states. In May 2004, although admitting to no wrongdoing, CBRL agreed to an $8.7 million settlement. CBRL also agreed to improve its employee diversity training and to create a new department to investigate discrimination complaints, among other changes.

In a June 2005 Associated Press article, Daryl Herrschaft of the Human Rights Campaign noted that "Cracker Barrel has come a long way, but they still have a long way to go." The article also noted that the stigma of discrimination can "hobble a company for years."

[27] Cracker Barrel Corporate Site, http://www.crackerbarrel.com/about-outreach.cfm?doc_id=740, accessed 11/30/05.

[28] "Justice Department Settles Race Discrimination Lawsuit against Cracker Barrel Restaurant Chain." (2004, May 03). U.S. Attorney's Office, Northern District of Georgia, http://www.usdoj.gov/usao/gan/text_version/press_textversion/05-03-04.html, accessed 07/03/04.

Questions to Consider

1. *What similarities and differences exist between the race and sexual orientation concerns at Cracker Barrel?*
2. *What kinds of factors likely exist in an organization in which customer, applicant, and employee discrimination occurs?*
3. *What does the Cracker Barrel Web site say about its new "Pleasing People" goal?*

Sources: Human Rights Campaign, http://www.hrc.org/Content/ContentGroups/News_Releases/20021/HRC_Praises_Cracker_Barrels_Decision_to_Prohibit_Discrimination_Based_on_Sexual_Orientation.htm, accessed 07/03/05; French, R. (2005, June 21). "Cracker Barrel Fights Stigma of Discrimination." *Associated Press*, Detroit News, http://www.detnews.com/2005/business/0506/21/C03-221878.htm, accessed 07/03/05; Schmidt, J., & Copeland, L. (2004, May 7). "Cracker Barrel Customer Says Bias was 'Flagrant'." *USA Today*, http://www.usatoday.com/money/companies/2004-05-07-cracker-barrel_x.htm, accessed 07/03/05.

higher. On average, less than 2% of the entire employee population enrolls for partner benefits when they are offered.[29] Low enrollment rates are partly because in same-sex partnerships, both partners are likely to be employed and may already have medical coverage through their own employers. Privacy concerns probably also contribute to low enrollment rates for domestic partner benefits. When same-sex partners do sign up for benefits, they tend to be younger than other enrollees (which reduces insurance costs), less likely to enroll minor children (who are expensive to insure), and less likely to later have high costs associated with pregnancy, childbirth, and insurance for newborn and young children.

Misperception: Offering same-sex partner benefits adds considerable health insurance costs to employers, especially due to risks of AIDS.

Reality: Adding same-sex benefits increases costs to employers between 1% and 3%; costs are proportionate to any increase in plan participants.

As discussed in Organizational Feature 15.2, Hewlett-Packard has offered domestic partner benefits to its employees since 1997 as part of its efforts to create an inclusive environment and to attract and retain top talent. Not offering partner and family benefits to a subset of the employee population sends a message to employees. Family life and well-being of heterosexuals (but not homosexuals) are important to the organization. Retirement and income security are important for heterosexual employees and their dependents and survivors, but not for homosexuals and their dependents and survivors.

HIV/AIDS at Work: Unnecessary and Unfounded Fears

Fears of excessive costs due to HIV/AIDS are also sometimes specifically expressed as a rationale for not offering domestic partner benefits. The fear of contracting HIV/AIDS may also affect many people's resistance to working with or employing

[29] See Human Rights Campaign Foundation for further discussion.

Organizational Feature 15.2 *Hewlett-Packard: Putting Diversity to Work*

The Hewlett-Packard Web site says that the company believes that "diversity and inclusion are key drivers of creativity, innovation, and invention." Some of the inclusive practices that HP has implemented to support the company in its goals are:

- nondiscrimination policy
- electronic job posting
- harassment-free work environment
- domestic partner benefits
- employee network groups
- flexible work hours
- safe and pleasant work environment

HP's nondiscrimination policy includes a commitment not to discriminate against applicants or employees on the basis of race, color, religion, sex, and disability. It also includes nondiscrimination on the basis of sexual orientation and gender identity/expression, which sets it apart from many organizations. Sexual orientation and gender identity/expression are also included in its nonharassment policies.

HP has offered domestic partner benefits to its employees since 1997. According to HP's chairman, "The extension of benefits to domestic partners continues HP's ongoing efforts to create an inclusive environment" and also enhances HP's ability to attract and retain top talent.[30] Under the policy, domestic partners may be the same sex or opposite sex. To qualify for most benefits, the employee must submit a declaration of domestic partnership. The domestic partnership must be a committed relationship that has lasted for at least 6 months. Partners must live together and share financial responsibility for the household. If criteria are met, medical, dental, retiree medical, long-term care, and life insurance are available. Because the Family and Medical Leave Act does not cover unmarried partners, HP's plan allows for 12 weeks unpaid leaves of absence to care for a domestic partner with a serious health condition, with job security, as would be offered under the FMLA to married partners. Children of domestic partners are eligible for HP's employee scholarship program.

If a domestic partnership ends, HP must be notified within 30 days and the former domestic partner (and his or her dependents) must be removed from the benefits plans. A 6-month waiting period is required before a new domestic partner becomes eligible for benefits.

Questions to Consider

1. *One important purpose of company Web sites is to communicate positive information about the company. How might the seven inclusive practices listed above affect applicants who are gay, lesbian, or transgender? How might the practices affect working parents?*

2. *Electronic job posting can be viewed as a means to ensure that every applicant has a fair chance, based on his or her qualifications, to be considered for a job. How might electronic job posting be viewed positively by workers from all backgrounds?*

3. *How do the requirements for coverage for domestic partners, such as length of the relationship, compare with requirements for benefits for married couples? Do companies usually require a waiting period after dissolution of a marriage (divorce) before a new spouse can become eligible for benefits? What factors may have influenced the inclusion of these stipulations?*

[30] State of the Workplace for Lesbian, Gay, Bisexual and Transgender Americans 2004.

4. Why do you think that HP offers domestic partner benefits to opposite sex partners as well as same-sex partners?

Source: http://www.hp.com/hpinfo/, accessed 03/29/05; Human Rights Campaign, 2005. Hewlett-Packard Co.—Domestic Partner Benefits Program.

gay males, but there are two fallacies associated with both fears. First, although HIV/AIDS is strongly perceived as a gay male disease, it simply is not. Currently, in the United States and other countries, less than one quarter of the new AIDS cases are a result of male-to-male sexual contact.[31] Second, the risk of contracting HIV/AIDS while at work is very small.

Misperception: HIV/AIDS is a gay male disease.

Reality: About 75% of the new HIV/AIDS cases are a result of heterosexual contact or injection drug use; less than 25% are a result of male-to-male sexual contact.[32]

Importantly, employers should take specific steps to alleviate unfounded fears of transmission through education: HIV/AIDS is not spread through casual contact, such as those behaviors that occur at work. For people working in the medical profession, where blood and bodily fluids are handled, safe-handling procedures minimize the risk of transmission. Everyone can and should take steps to minimize transmission of HIV/AIDS, but transmission at work is very unlikely.

Misperception: Working with someone with AIDS puts people at high risk of transmission.

Reality: HIV/AIDS is transmitted through sharing of blood and bodily fluids, primarily through unprotected sex or the sharing of needles in intravenous drug use. In most occupations, the risk of transmission of HIV/AIDS is very, very small.

Employees and managers should be trained regarding HIV/AIDS and the law. Coworkers who refuse to work with someone who has, is perceived as having, or is associated with someone who has HIV/AIDS can be fired. HIV/AIDS is a protected disability under the Americans with Disabilities Act (ADA), and employers are prohibited from discriminating against people with HIV/AIDS. In one such case, Cirque du Soleil agreed to a $600,000 settlement for discriminating against an employee who was HIV positive.[33] The charging party, Matthew Cusick, was awarded the $300,000 maximum punitive damages allowable under the ADA, $200,000 in lost wages, $60,000 in front pay, and $40,000 in attorneys' fees.

---

[31] Centers for Disease Control. 2005.

[32] Ibid.

[33] Cirque du Soleil to Pay $600,000 for Disability Discrimination Against Performer. August 22, 2004. http://www.eeoc.gov/press/4-22-04.html, accessed 11/03/05.

The settlement also required Cirque du Soleil to appoint an EEOC officer to oversee its annual training on the laws enforced by the EEOC, with an emphasis on HIV/disability discrimination.

In another case, Lambda Legal reached a settlement with a company accused of firing an employee who was HIV-positive.[34] When he was hired, the employee, Joey Saavedra, told his direct supervisor he was HIV-positive. When higher management learned he was HIV-positive, Saavedra was fired, even though his supervisor wanted to retain him. In announcing the settlement of the lawsuit, Lambda Legal stated that "Employers must come to understand that discriminating against someone with HIV is bad for business and against the law."[35]

Gays in the Military: Don't Ask, Don't Tell, Don't Pursue, Don't Harass

The U.S. military is a unique organization. It employs 1.4 million people who are more diverse in race, ethnicity, and sex than ever before.[36] Diversity in sexual orientation in the military remains controversial, however. The official U.S. military policy regarding gays, lesbians, and bisexuals (GLB)—"don't ask, don't tell, don't pursue, don't harass"—has been referred to as the "only federal law that mandates firing someone because they are gay."[37] This policy excludes GLB who are open about their sexual orientation from military service. The policy, commonly known only as "don't ask, don't tell" policy was passed in 1993 under President Clinton. President Clinton's initial plans to repeal the ban on gays in the military were met with such virulent resistance that the "don't ask, don't tell" policy was passed as a compromise, of sorts.

An estimated 2.5% of military personnel are believed to be gay male (2%) or lesbian (5%).[38] Since the "don't ask, don't tell" policy was implemented, more than 10,000 gays and lesbians have been discharged from the U.S. military, at an estimated cost of between $250 million and $1.2 billion.[39] These discharge rates are higher than before the implementation of the new policy, indicating that pursuit does indeed occur. The number of people discharged began declining with the start of the war in Iraq, however. In 2003, 770 were discharged, down from 907 in 2002, and 1,273 in 2001. Although the declines in discharges are a positive

---

[34] Lambda Legal is an organization that works to achieve full recognition of the civil rights of sexual minorities and people with HIV through "impact litigation, education, and public policy work.

[35] http://www.lambdalegal.org/cgi-bin/iowa/news/press.html?record=1702, accessed 12/01/05.

[36] Segal, D. R., & Segal, M. W. (2004). "America's Military Population." *Population Bulletin,* 59(4): 1–44. Population Reference Bureau. Washington, DC.

[37] "Documenting Courage: Veterans Speak Out." 2004. Human Rights Campaign, Service Members Legal Defense Network, and American Veterans for Equal Rights, http://www.hrc.org/Content/ContentGroups/Documenting_Courage/Stories2/Documenting_Courage__Veterans_Speak_Out2.htm, accessed 07/05/05.

[38] Segal & Segal. (2004).

[39] Documenting Courage: Veterans Speak Out. 2004.

signal, a loss of 770 competent service personnel is still significant. Further, if reductions in discharges are solely the result of low wartime enlistments, this does not bode well for discharges during times of peace.

Media reports and discharge testimony indicate that many of those discharged were successfully and dependably performing in key positions, such as linguists and nuclear warfare experts. These discharges represent a tremendous loss of investment in training, education, and key skills of military personnel.[40] Individuals who are discharged are disproportionately enlisted personnel; of the 6,300 discharged between 1998 and 2003, only 75 were officers.[41] Women, particularly those aged 18 to 25, are also more likely to be discharged when compared with men. Though women make up about 15% of the military, 29% of those discharged under the policy are women. Some reports suggest women are discharged after "witch hunts" and for refusing men's sexual advances. A recent publication entitled "Documenting Courage: Gay, Lesbian, Bisexual and Transgender Veterans Speak Out" describes experiences of GLBT veterans, including "witch hunts," and how one veteran suffered in silence after a gay military friend committed suicide.[42] Their accounts of discrimination, revoked security clearances, and fear of being discharged, while at the same time striving to serve the country are compelling.

Fears of reduced cohesion, reduced enlistment of heterosexuals, and violations of the right to privacy of heterosexual personnel are given as reasons for barring gays and lesbians from the military.[43] Evidence does not support the legitimacy of these fears, however. Many gays serve openly in units that disagree with the "don't ask, don't tell" policy with the full knowledge of their commanders. The FBI, CIA, NASA, and the Secret Service, as well as numerous foreign militaries have lifted bans on service of gays and lesbians, without ill effects.[44] Police forces in large cities have used advertisements in gay publications to recruit for officers.[45] As discussed in Individual Feature 15.1, Lupe Valdez, a lesbian and sheriff of Dallas County, Texas, has served successfully in the military and law enforcement.

Determinants of Attitudes toward Gays and Lesbians

Several determinants have been found to be consistently related to attitudes toward sexual minorities: sex, education, marital status, and religious fundamentalism. Those who are more highly educated, unmarried, female, and less religious

---

[40] Ibid.

[41] Fouhy, B. (2004, June 21). "Military Discharged 770 Last Year for Being Gay: Hundreds Held High Level Job Specialties that Required Years of Training." *San Diego Union Tribune,* http://www.signonsandiego.com/uniontrib/20040621/news_1n21troops.html.

[42] Documenting Courage: Veterans Speak Out. 2004.

[43] See Segal & Segal. (2004).

[44] The State of the Workplace for Lesbian, Gay, Bisexual, and Transgender Americans, 2003. See also Belkin, A. (2003). "Don't ask, Don't Tell: Is the Gay Military Ban Based on Military Necessity?" *Parameters,* 33(2): 107–119.

[45] Correll, S. J. (1999). "Lesbian and Gay Americans." In A. G. Dworkin & R. J. Dworkin (Eds.), *The Minority Report* (3rd edition), Fort Worth: Harcourt Brace Publishers, pp. 436–456.

Individual Feature 15.1 *Lupe Valdez, Sheriff, Dallas County, Texas*

"There's a new sheriff in town."[46] Lupe Valdez was elected the sheriff of Dallas County, Texas, in November 2004 by a margin of nearly 18,000 votes of 658,000 cast. In Dallas County, the sheriff is the only countywide law enforcement official. With a salary of more than $130,000 and 1,322 deputies to manage, Valdez is a powerful law enforcement figure in one of the largest counties in Texas. She is bilingual, with a master's degree in criminology and criminal justice from the University of Texas at Arlington. Her election was notable for many reasons.

Valdez was the first woman ever elected as Dallas County Sheriff. In a state noted for Republican governors and presidents, Valdez is a Democrat—the first Democrat elected county sheriff in 25 years. She is also Latina, and grew up picking crops from Texas to Michigan. Valdez and her family often slept and ate in the car to save money and to avoid being turned away at hotels and restaurants. The family eventually settled in her mother's hometown of San Antonio. There, Valdez recalls seeing a fellow student hit with a ruler for speaking Spanish in school. Valdez attended college in Oklahoma and later was a captain in the U.S. Army Reserves, serving as an officer in the military police and army intelligence. She was an agent for the U.S. Customs Service until she retired to run for sheriff.

Perhaps most notably in an election year in which same-sex marriage was a hot issue, Valdez is a lesbian. In what appeared to be an act of desperation, one of her opponents complained that Valdez would be committed to a "gay agenda" because she had gotten an endorsement from the Gay and Lesbian Victory fund. Rather than any agenda, Valdez ran a campaign that emphasized integrity, which was quite effective after years of scandals had plagued the sheriff's office. Apparently, voters were more concerned with integrity and job qualification than with Valdez being a lesbian. In response to charges that she would promote a "gay agenda," Valdez emphasizes that her job as sheriff provides no opportunity to influence legislation. Although she has always been open about her sexual orientation, Valdez notes that "it has nothing to do with being sheriff." It does, according to one author, say a lot "about the new politics of sexual orientation in Texas."[47]

As the story unfolds, having Valdez as sheriff may also positively influence other diversity issues. In November 2005, a year after she was elected, Valdez suspended one of her top commanders for referring to hurricane evacuees as "knuckle draggers" and "knee walkers" in a staff meeting. The evacuees were being housed in various Dallas-area facilities as the result of two hurricanes in August and September of 2005. After the comments, the commander was suspended for 20 days, which will cost him the equivalent of one month's salary ($7,153), and ordered to attend diversity training. The suspended commander wrote to Valdez that he was "embarrassed" at having failed as a "leader and a role model." He also has met with and personally apologized to each staff member who attended the meeting where the offensive comments were made and assured Sheriff Valdez that "there would be no further conduct of this sort."

Sources: Blumenthal, R. (2004, November 10). "An Improbable Victor Becomes a Texas Sheriff." *The New York Times*. Section A, Column 1, National Desk, p. 16; Olsson, K. (2005, January). "The Gay Non-Issue." *Texas Monthly*. p. 82; http://lupevaldez.com/events.php, accessed 07/03/05.

Trahan, J. (2005, November 11). "Sheriff commander denigrated evacuees." *Dallas Morning News*. Metro, p. 1B.

[46] http://lupevaldez.com/events.php, accessed 07/03/05.

[47] Olsson, K. (2005, January). "The Gay Non-Issue." *Texas Monthly*. p. 82.

have more favorable attitudes than others. Race is an inconsistent predictor of attitudes toward sexual minorities. Some researchers have found that African Americans have more negative attitudes about homosexuality than Whites; other researchers have found that attitudes of Whites and Blacks toward homosexuality were similar when differences in religiosity were controlled.[48] Heterosexual men have more negative attitudes toward gays and lesbians, particularly toward gay men. People who believe that sexual orientation is biologically determined, rather than a choice, have more favorable attitudes toward gays and lesbians.[49]

Out at Work?

Many gays and lesbians expect—and often receive—discrimination, harassment, or termination if they are open at work about their sexual orientation.[50] In contrast to women and many people of color as minority groups, sexual minorities have the option of disclosing or not disclosing their sexual orientation.[51] By not disclosing (e.g., "passing"), sexual minorities can avoid some of the negative consequences associated with being out at work. At some point in their work lives, many gays pass as a strategy to avoid discrimination.[52] Not disclosing, however, is also associated with negative consequences that rival those of passing. Being continually on guard at work, efforts to avoid letting information about one's sexual orientation "slip" in conversation, or constructing heterosexual (imaginary) partners is extremely taxing and guilt inducing. Researchers have suggested this requires "a great deal of psychological effort and perpetual vigilance."[53] As a result, gays and lesbians may distance themselves from coworkers, resulting in dysfunctional team and communication processes.[54] When passing, gays and lesbians are likely to hear many negative comments and stereotypes about members of their group, as do other invisible minorities.

---

[48] Herek, G. M., & Capitanio, J. P. (1996). "'Some of My Best Friends': Intergroup Contact, Concealable Stigma, and Heterosexuals' Attitudes toward Gay Men and Lesbians." *Personality and Social Psychology Bulletin,* 22: 412–424. See also Herek, G. M., & Capitanio, J. P. (1995). "Black Heterosexuals' Attitudes toward Lesbians and Gay Men in the United States." *Journal of Sex Research,* 32(2): 95–106.

[49] Wood, P. B., & Bartkowski, J. P. (2004). "Attribution Style and Public Policy Attitudes toward Gay Rights." *Social Science Quarterly,* 85: 58–74.

[50] See Levine, M. P., & Leonard, R. (1984). "Discrimination against Lesbians in the Work Force." *Signs: Journal of Women in Culture and Society,* 9: 700–710; Kronenberger, G. K. (1991). "Out of the Closet." *Personnel Journal,* 70: 40–44; Graham M. A. (1986). "Out of the Closet and into the Courtroom." *Employment Relations Today,* 13: 167–173; Ragins, B. R., & Cornwell, J. M. (2001). "Pink Triangles: Antecedents and Consequences of Perceived Workplace Discrimination against Gay and Lesbian Employees." *Journal of Applied Psychology,* 86: 1244–1261.

[51] Ragins, B. R. (in press).

[52] See Woods, J. D. (1993). *The Corporate Closet: The Professional Lives of Gay Men in America,* New York: The Free Press.

[53] Dietch, E.A., Butz, R. M., Brief, A. P. (2004). "Out of the Closet and Out of a Job? The Nature, Import, and Causes of Sexual Orientation Discrimination in the Workplace." In R. W. Griffin & A. O-Leary-Kelly (Eds.), *The Dark Side of Organizational Behavior,* San Francisco: Jossey-Bass, pp. 187–234. For a discussion of specific strategies gays and lesbians may use to avoid concealment, see also Chrobot-Mason, D., Button, S. B., & DiClementi, J. D. (2001). "Sexual Identity Management Strategies: An Exploration of Antecedents and Consequences." *Sex Roles,* 45: 321–336.

[54] Chrobot-Mason, D., et al. (2001).

INDIVIDUAL FEATURE 15.2 *Pascal Lepine, President of Atypic Multimedia Marketing and the Chambre du Commerce Gaie Du Quebec*

Pascal Lepine is president of the successful multimedia marketing firm, Atypic, and of the Chambre du Commerce Gaie Du Quebec in Montreal. Atypical himself, Lepine, at 28, is viewed as a role model for young gays entering the workforce. When Lepine entered the workforce, he was dismayed to find no gay role models and now is doing his part to ensure young gays entering the workforce do have gay role models.

Lepine believes that networking is the key to running a successful business, and thus he and the Chambre du Commerce Gaie Du Quebec have partnered with McGill University to help gay and lesbian students as they start their careers. Chamber members network with students as prospective employers; students network with members. McGill's director of career and placement students, Gregg Blachford, who is also gay, holds career workshops for gay and lesbian students. Blachford encourages students to be open about their sexual orientation; being open helps one build supportive networks of other gays and lesbians. Being closeted takes work and erodes confidence because of fear of slipping up and being found out. Both Lepine and Blachford view gayness as an advantage. Perhaps most importantly, they believe being gay helps people be more positive toward diversity. "Sometimes, when you've been marginalized in society, you're more open to others who are marginal. You're open to diversity and seeing the negative effects of discrimination against others."

Source: Whittaker, S. (2005, April 18). "Coming Out, Moving Up." *The Gazette* (Montreal). Bottom Line, p. B2.

QUESTIONS TO CONSIDER

1. ***Do you agree with the perspective that gays and lesbians are more likely to embrace diversity and others who have been marginalized? Why or why not?***

Misperception: Most people can tell who is gay or lesbian just by looking.

Reality: Sexual orientation cannot be determined by someone's outward appearance.

In one study on relationships between being out at work and job-related psychological outcomes, Nancy Day and Patricia Schoenrade found that employees who were open at work about their sex orientation had higher affective commitment and job satisfaction, and viewed top management as being more supportive. Employees who were out had lower role ambiguity, role conflict, and conflict between work and home.[55] Other researchers have found that perceptions of workplace discrimination were negatively related to likelihood of being out at work. People who perceived sexual orientation discrimination existed in their workplace had more negative job attitudes, lower satisfaction, and perceived they had less opportunity for promotion.[56] As discussed in Individual Feature 15.2, some gays

[55] Day, N. E., & Schoenrade, P. (1997). "Staying in the Closet versus Coming Out: Relationships between Communication about Sexual Orientation and Work Attitudes." *Personnel Psychology,* 50 (1): 147–163.

[56] Ragins & Cornwell. (2001).

recommend being open about one's sexual orientation at work, building supportive networks, and serving as role models for others.

Individual Recommendations

Although we have considered many negative aspects of discrimination and unfair treatment toward sexual minorities, many positive ones were also considered. As with other nondominant group members, sexual minorities should take active roles in their employment searches and careers to minimize discrimination and unfairness, and to maximize positive outcomes. In job seeking, determine which organizations include sexual orientation in their nondiscrimination policies and offer equality in partner benefits. Such overt inclusive actions make strong statements about organizational commitment to fairness for sexual minorities. This information is usually available on company Web sites or through organizations such as the Human Rights Campaign.[57] Each year, the HRC publishes thorough reports of inclusive organizations, their benefits offerings, whether they include sexual minorities in their nondiscrimination policies, and other information useful to people concerned about fairness for sexual minorities.

Sexual minorities should consider using referrals from friends and allies. Referrals are excellent sources of job information; as insiders, referrals know whether the company culture is supportive or hostile toward sexual minorities. Gay males should carefully assess their initial starting salaries and salary increases throughout their careers. Being active, knowledgeable, and willing to seek other employment options when faced with unfair treatment is a good idea for everyone. Make conscious career choices and resist being channeled into jobs that others perceive as appropriate for gay males, unless these occupational choices agree with personal career interests.

Organizational Recommendations[58]

Including sexual orientation in an organization's nondiscrimination policy and offering equality in benefits for domestic partners are two important aspects of supporting sexual orientation diversity. As we have discussed, multiple studies have found that a supportive climate, including nondiscrimination policies, and top management support are related to increased commitment and job satisfaction

[57] http://www.hrc.org.

[58] See also discussion described in Chapter 13 on allowing individuals to choose who constitutes their family.

of sexual minorities.[59] Organizations with supportive climates may experience many of the positive outcomes proposed by Cox and Blake, including cost, resource acquisition, creativity, and marketing. Losing valuable employees due to discrimination is an unnecessary cost. Being known for fairness to sexual minorities can help in attracting and retaining valued employees. For creativity, when energy (e.g., "perpetual vigilance") spent worrying about concealing one's sexual orientation on the job can be spent on productive work, many individual and organizational benefits ensue. For marketing advantages, gays and lesbians have higher average education levels than heterosexuals, strong buying power, and are responsive to organizational fairness efforts. Market researchers estimate a $610 billion buying power for GLBT in 2005.[60] Many heterosexual allies of GLBT will also choose to patronize companies that emphasize fairness to sexual minorities.

Negative outcomes are possible as well, however. While overt racism, sexism, and ageism are less widespread than in the past, overt heterosexism is fairly common. Some employee resistance can be circumvented through training and education and discipline and termination of those who would persist in discrimination. Misperceptions about "special rights" being afforded to sexual minorities should be dispelled, as should fears about the risks of transmission of HIV/AIDS. One relevant question about whether gays and lesbians should be afforded equal rights in organizations has to do with whether their sexual orientation affects their job performance. Does one's sexual orientation affect one's job performance? Objectively, it does not, but one way in which sexual orientation may affect performance is through causing worry about being discriminated against, ostracized, fired, or "outed" at work, similar to with other invisible minorities.[61] Removing those fears through organizational policies of nondiscrimination based on sexual orientation would reduce those impediments to performance.

Management or coworker preferences for apparently heterosexual employees do not justify discrimination and it should not be tolerated. Although care must also be taken not to trample on belief systems of other employees, as occurred in the *Albert Buonanno v. AT&T* case discussed in Chapter 10, there is no reason to believe that different belief systems among employees should be allowed to disrupt carefully constructed policies of inclusion and non-discrimination. For organizations concerned with fairness and equity for all employees, carefully created, widely communicated policies of inclusion and zero tolerance for discrimination, as existed in the *Peterson v. Hewlett-Packard Co.* case, are upheld by the courts.

---

[59] Day, N. E., & Schoenrade, P. (2000). "The Relationship among Reported Disclosure of Sexual Orientation, Anti-Discrimination Policies, Top Management Support, and Work Attitudes of Gay and Lesbian Employees." *Personnel Review,* 29: 346–363; Burton, S. B. (2001). "Organizational Efforts to Affirm Sexual Diversity: A Cross-Level Examination." *Journal of Applied Psychology,* 86(1), 17–28.

[60] Gay Buying Power Projected at $610 billion in 2005. (2005, January 31). Witeck-Combs Communications.

[61] Examining the Employment Non-Discrimination Act (ENDA): The Scientists Perspective, http://www.apa.org/pi/lgbc/publications/enda.html, accessed 07/03/05.

Resistance to measures to reduce sexual orientation discrimination may also come from external customers and stakeholders. As discussed in Chapter 1, Disney is one organization that faced vociferous, lengthy boycotts as a result of its nondiscriminatory position toward gays and lesbians. In June 2005, the 16 million member Southern Baptist Convention voted to end its 8-year boycott of Disney because it offered same-sex partner benefits. A similar boycott by the Mississippi-based American Family Association was lifted earlier in 2005.[62] In developing and implementing policies related to sexual orientation, leaders should be prepared for resistance and committed to their plans. Organizational leaders must make decisions and organizational policies based on belief systems, mission, and long-term goals.

Summary

Sexual orientation as an aspect of diversity is increasing in importance. Gays and lesbians are estimated to be between 4% and 17% of the U.S. population; the large difference in estimates reflects the difficulties associated with collecting data on sexual orientation. Employment discrimination against sexual minorities is not prohibited by federal law, and overt discrimination against gays and lesbians is not uncommon. The lack of federal protections for gays and lesbians may signal that sexual orientation discrimination is acceptable. The U.S. military's "don't ask, don't tell" policy was offered as a compromise to eliminating the ban on gays in the military, but it has resulted in more discharges after the implementation of the policy than before it was implemented. Many organizations do include sexual orientation in their nondiscrimination policies and offer equal benefits to domestic partners. The Human Rights Campaign regularly assesses organizations' progress toward equal treatment for sexual minorities, and more organizations are offering equal benefits and including sexual orientation in their nondiscrimination policies than ever before.

Key Terms

Heterosexism — attitudes and behaviors denigrating and stigmatizing to nonheterosexuals.

Homophobia — the fear of being around homosexuals.

Passing — refers to gays and lesbians who pretend to be and are perceived as being heterosexual, to light-skinned Blacks or others of color pretending to be and being perceived as Whites, and to others whose nondominant group membership goes unnoticed and undisclosed.

Sexual minorities — nonheterosexuals, including gay males, lesbians, bisexuals, and transgender people.

[62] Southern Baptists End Disney Boycott, http://www.cnn.com/2005/US/06/23/baptists.disney.ap/, accessed 07/04/05.

Sexual orientation — a component of sexuality characterized by enduring emotional, romantic, sexual, and/or affectional attractions to individuals of a particular gender.

Questions to Consider

1. Some states and cities have legislation prohibiting discrimination based on sexual orientation, weight, appearance, and other factors that are not covered under federal legislation. What factors may affect the passage of such legislation in some areas, but not in others? Is sexual orientation discrimination prohibited in the city or state in which you live?
2. How might the reduction in the number of discharges during war times affect perceptions about the stated policy on gays and lesbians in the military?
3. When the U.S. armed forces were first integrated there was tremendous opposition, but integration has been accomplished. How similar and different is the opposition to open service of gays and lesbians in the military to integrated service of Blacks and Whites?
4. What is the official policy on partner benefits and sexual orientation discrimination in the organization in which you work or are interested in working?
5. How is the invisibility of sexual orientation similar to or different from the invisibility of religion?
6. In Chapter 10, Melissa Deckman and her colleagues proposed that women clergy might be more likely to advance the causes of devalued, disenfranchised minority groups. In Individual Feature 15.2, Pascal Lepine similarly proposes that gays and lesbians may also be more open to others who have also been marginalized in society. In what kinds of situations have devalued, disenfranchised, and marginalized groups in the United States supported each others' causes? In what situations have they undermined or resisted each others' causes?
7. What have you learned from this chapter that is most surprising to you?

Actions and Exercises

1. Conduct research to identify at least two people who are gay or lesbian who are not politicians, actors, or entertainers, but who are somewhat public figures. How difficult was it to find these two people? What did you learn about them?
2. Investigate the number of states in which sexual orientation discrimination is currently illegal in the United States.
3. If you are not gay, interview a close friend or relative who is gay about his or her experiences at work. If you are gay, how do your experiences compare with those reported in the chapter?

SECTION III

Global Vision

16 Chapter

International Diversity and Facing the Future

Chapter Objectives

After completing this chapter readers will:

- *have an understanding of the overarching issue of dominant and nondominant groups and the need for equity and fairness as key to diversity around the world.*
- *be able to discuss inequity on the basis of sex and gender, disability, sexual orientation, and poverty as common diversity concerns in many countries.*
- *understand how to analyze historical and current factors to help identify and assess the specific diversity issues in a country.*
- *be able to make specific recommendations for individuals, organizations, and society for fostering diversity.*
- *understand why the diversity of the U.S. population, the globalization of the world, and increased competitiveness make attending to diversity in the United States and including the contributions of its entire population imperative, rather than optional.*

Key Facts

Diversity issues are relevant to work and organizations in countries around the world.

Workforces in many nations are changing due to changes in birth and mortality rates, immigration, age distributions, external pressures, and competition.

The status of women, people with disabilities, sexual minorities, and people living in poverty are key diversity concerns in nations around the world.

Diversity in organizations is an aspect of societal changes and is increased or impeded by individual, organizational, and societal factors.

Past and present diversity issues in the United States make its urgent attention to diversity vital to future success and competitiveness.

Introduction and Overview

In the first chapter of this book, diversity was defined as real or perceived differences among people that affect their interactions and relationships.[1] Using this foundation and the focus of differences among the U.S. population, the following 14 chapters covered legislation; key theories; experiences of Blacks, Latinos, Asians, Whites, American Indians, Alaska Natives, and multiracial group members; sex and gender; religion; age; physical and mental ability; work and family; religion; weight, obesity, and appearance; and sexual orientation as specific aspects of diversity. These focal areas were chosen because they are the issues that are currently most important in the United States. These racial and ethnic groups and women have the longest and continued histories of discrimination and are covered by civil rights laws. The United States is also where most of the furor about *increasing* diversity began and is the source of most of the published diversity research. Admittedly, despite including an "international feature" in many chapters and reporting research conducted outside the United States, this book has been largely written from a U.S. perspective, at least until the present chapter.

In this chapter, we explore *diversity* from an international view, recognizing that the term diversity is often perceived as being appropriate from a Western, even U.S. viewpoint. Researchers and scholars outside the United States have emphasized the limited relevance of U.S. diversity issues to other countries.[2] Yet, diversity as "real or perceived differences among people that affect their interactions and relationships," is quite appropriate in an international context. Internationally, the existence of discrimination, dominance, marginalization, and colonization of people based on race, ethnicity, gender, religion, sexual orientation, and numerous other factors attest to this relevance. When viewed as issues of power, dominance, discrimination, and control of resources, the rationale for viewing diversity (regardless of the chosen terminology) as a universal concept becomes clearer. As we investigate diversity from an international view, we continue from the perspective that diversity is increasingly inevitable and is valuable to individuals, organizations, and society worldwide.

Misperception: Diversity is a U.S. concept.

Reality: When viewed as concerns of nondominant and dominant groups, power, discrimination, and control of resources, the universality of diversity issues is clear.

Why is diversity important worldwide? The current and potential workforce in many nations is changing considerably as a result of changes in birth and mortality rates, immigration, age distributions, advances in health care, external pressures, and competition. As in the United States, in Canada, the United Kingdom, and Mexico, workforce growth is small when compared with growth in previous periods. In Spain, Italy, Germany, France, Japan, and South Africa, declines in the population of working adults are projected for 2010 through 2050. The need to allow, or, indeed, encourage active, full workforce participation is particularly vital in these countries.

Further, although the majority of the laws, cases, and examples in earlier chapters are from

[1] Dobbs, M. F. (1996). "Managing Diversity: Lessons from the Private Sector." *Public Personnel Management,* 25 (Sept): 351–368.

[2] See, for example, Jones, D., Pringle, J., & Shepherd, D. (2000). "'Managing Diversity' Meets Aotearoa/New Zealand." *Personnel Review,* 29(3): 364–380.

the United States, the overall premise of the book has relevance everywhere. Similarly, many of the focal items in each chapter have substantial similarities regardless of where they occur. For example, sex and gender strongly influence one's education, workforce participation, income, treatment, occupation, and status within organizations in Australia, China, England, Japan, New Zealand, Pakistan, the United States, and most places that one could name. Work and family considerations, including availability and cost of child care, social policies, income, and institutional support are also important to people wherever they live and work. Differences in people's religious beliefs affect them everywhere and employer discrimination based on religion occurs in many countries. While the specific racial and ethnic groups vary from country to country, numerous similarities, such as wage discrimination, un- and underemployment, and occupational segregation exist for nondominant racial and ethnic groups in many countries. In many places, there are employment-related laws that focus on diversity issues (for example, equal employment for women, minority, or disenfranchised groups—even though who is targeted varies by country).

On the other hand, despite the global importance of diversity issues and the similarities among certain phenomena, within each different region there are numerous unique issues and concerns. These unique issues are based on the region's historical, cultural, religious, and other differences that must be considered. For example, in Saudi Arabia, religious beliefs severely impede women's workforce participation. In Japan, most women hold temporary jobs, rather than lifetime jobs that are common for Japanese men. India has caste-based differences in which the majority of its population is disadvantaged due to their caste position rather than to their individual abilities and competencies.[3] Burakumin people in Japan experience extreme discrimination in a similar caste system. The sheer size of the world and the numbers of countries, each with distinct diversity concerns, make a comprehensive view of worldwide diversity a near impossible and quite irrational undertaking. Even so, there is value in understanding issues that are common around the world.

Each of the previous chapters about a particular nondominant group has provided details about the group's historical background in the United States, recognizing that history affects group members' current status and opportunities. Because this chapter considers international aspects of diversity, it is not possible to include historical conditions for multiple groups in every country as was done in previous chapters for U.S. groups. Despite this, knowing that historical, cultural, legal, and country-specific concerns affect diversity everywhere will increase readers' ability to address and value diversity, regardless of context. When country- or region-specific knowledge is needed, readers will be more equipped to investigate, understand, and apply ways to best incorporate the diversity of the particular area. We recognize that a "Western" view of diversity is not at all appropriate to every culture; indeed a United States view of diversity is not appropriate for Canada, nor is a Canadian view of diversity appropriate for the United States, although both are Western countries. However, what is appropriate is recognition that different diversity issues affect individuals and, thus, organizations differently around the world. Diversity issues should be investigated within the context of where they occur.

[3] The Chinese Executive MBA class of 2005 at the University of Texas at Arlington provided unique insights into some of these areas.

FIGURE 16.1 ***Considerations Useful for Identifying Specific Diversity Issues in a Country***

- Identifiability, power, discrimination, and group awareness[4]
- Distribution of wealth
- Employment, unemployment, and underemployment
- Participation rates
- Occupational levels, types, and representation in management and executive positions
- Income and earnings distributions
- Literacy
- Educational attainment
- Return on educational investment
- Residential and employment segregation
- Poverty rates
- Health and longevity
- Incarceration rates
- Legal protections

Figure 16.1 presents some of the considerations useful in determining the dominant and nondominant groups and areas of diversity concerns in areas around the world. While not every consideration is relevant to each group in every area, analyses of these factors should help identify areas of potential differences worldwide.

We begin our exploration of international diversity with discrimination and differential treatment as worldwide phenomena, and then consider sex and gender, disabilities, sexual orientation, and poverty as being important to diversity around the world. In much of the chapter, we use research drawn from the International Labour Organization (ILO), an international organization designed to help workers in 178 member states. Members of the ILO include such developing and developed countries as Albania, Australia, Austria, Bahrain, Cambodia, Canada, Finland, France, Hungary, Kenya, Nicaragua, St. Lucia, Swaziland, Switzerland, the United Kingdom, the United States, and Zambia. We next consider facing the future and make recommendations for change, providing suggestions for improving opportunities for equity and fairness for all workers as the twenty-first century continues. As much as possible, we try to avoid ethnocentrism, recognizing the variance in the dominant and nondominant, the colonized and colonizers, and other important distinctions worldwide.

Coming full circle, the chapter (and book) ends with a return to the factors unique to the diversity situation in the United States, emphasizing the urgency of attention to diversity in the United States, given the distinctive history and great diversity among its inhabitants as compared with other countries. The history of slavery, borders open to immigration, religious freedom, and often expressed welcome of diverse people (e.g., "e pluribus unum," "the melting pot," and Ellis Island) makes the United States potentially more diverse and generates more potential division but also

[4] From Dworkin, A. G., & Dworkin, R. J. (1999). *The Minority Report* (3rd edition), Orlando, FL: Harcourt Brace Publishers, pp. 11–27.

more opportunities than in many other more countries. While other countries have had slavery or indentured servitude, near annihilation of indigenous people, and subordination of women, none has had the unique combination of diversity factors that the United States has had and continues to have. Given this past history and continued diversity the population, discrimination, exclusion, and limiting contributions of an increasingly diverse population are no longer options if the United States is to compete in an increasingly global world without boundaries. Thus, recommendations for the United States are considered in the final section of the chapter and book.

Discrimination and Differential Treatment as Worldwide Phenomena

The ILO's Declaration on Fundamental Principles and Rights at Work is viewed as a "commitment by governments, employers' and workers' organizations to uphold basic human values—values that are vital to our social and economic lives."[5] One of the four values addressed in the ILO's declaration is the elimination of workplace discrimination. As discussed throughout the book, discrimination is a formidable impediment to diversity in organizations. The ILO's posture on people's rights to freedom from employment discrimination clarifies the existence of discrimination and differential treatment worldwide. Targets vary by region, but discrimination exists everywhere. Regarding the universality of worldwide employment discrimination, the ILO states:

> Discrimination in one form or another occurs in the world of work every day, throughout the world . . . Literally millions of people in the world are denied jobs, confined to certain occupations or offered lower pay simply because of their sex, their religion or the colour of their skin, irrespective of their capabilities or the requirements of the job.[6]

Needs to eradicate discrimination and to take other conscious efforts to include and value perspectives of all workers have been consistent themes in this book. According to the ILO, eradicating discrimination would benefit individuals, organizations, the economy, and society. As such, many countries have instituted antidiscrimination or equal opportunity legislation, as shown in Table 16.1.[7] The emotional, psychological, and economic rewards of workplace

[5] International Labour Organization. (2003). "Declaration on Fundamental Principles and Rights at Work," http://www.ilo.org/dyn/declaris/DECLARATIONWEB.INDEXPAGE, accessed 08/24/05.

[6] Ibid.

[7] Table 16.1 provides a limited summary of laws in selected areas. Readers are encouraged to investigate the laws in specific countries of interest.

TABLE 16.1 ***Various Equal Employment Opportunity in Selected Countries****

Country	Act(s)	Provisions
Argentina	Anti-Discrimination Act, No 23.592, 1988	Prohibits sex discrimination. Sanctions any person who impedes, obstructs, limits, or in any way undermines constitutional rights or guarantees on the basis of sex.
Australia	Disability Discrimination Act; Sex Discrimination Act, as amended; Equal Opportunity for Women Act; various others	Prohibit discrimination on the basis of age, criminal record, disability, sex (including pregnancy, potential pregnancies), sexual orientation, same-sex couples, various others.
Canada	Canadian Human Rights Act; various others	Prohibits discrimination based on race and color, national or ethnic origin, religion, age, sex, sexual orientation, marital or family status, physical and mental ability, and other areas. An act requiring equal pay for men and women in same jobs also exists.
France	Constitution, Penal Code of 1994	Criminalizes discrimination based on race, religion, or ethnicity.
Germany	Various laws	Prohibit sex discrimination, harassment, unequal pay, pregnancy, and maternity discrimination.
Hungary	Act CXXV 362/2004 of 22 December 2003. Equal Treatment and Promotion of Equal Opportunities	Prohibits direct or indirect negative discrimination, harassment, unlawful segregation, and retribution based on sex, racial origin, color, nationality, national or ethnic origin, mother tongue, disability, state of health, religious or ideological conviction, family status, motherhood (pregnancy) or fatherhood, sexual orientation, sexual identity, age, social origin, financial status, among other protected areas.
South Africa	Employment Equity Act (amended)	Applies to a broad spectrum of employers, prohibits "unfair discrimination," and requires affirmative action; covers Africans, coloreds, Indians, people with disabilities, and women.
United Kingdom	Equal Pay Directive; Equal Treatment Directive; various others	Prohibits discrimination on the basis of age, race, sex, pregnancy, parental status, marital or family status, among other protected areas.

*The language of the legislation may vary, and all protected areas are not listed. In addition to employment related laws, many laws refer to housing, accommodation, and other areas.

fairness for individuals are apparent. For organizations, as reiterated in the chapters, diversity can provide benefits related to cost, resource acquisition, marketing, creativity, problem solving, and system flexibility. Avoidance of lawsuits, boycotts, and lost business are also positive for organizations, wherever they are. For society, the benefits of eliminating discrimination and valuing diversity are immense, extending to reduction of worldwide poverty, increased life spans, and stronger economies, among other countless positive outcomes. Again turning to the ILO, we see that people who have the opportunity to work, contribute, and receive fair treatment and remuneration become "creators of life and communities . . . caregivers and receivers . . . workers, consumers, and entrepreneurs . . . savers, investors, producers and employers . . . inventors and generators of knowledge . . . as citizens and organizers."[8] On a societal level, these outcomes are lasting and sustaining.

Having argued that diversity is indeed a worldwide phenomenon, we now consider three of the topics from the preceding chapters specifically from a global perspective: sex and gender, disabilities, and sexual orientation. In addition, we investigate poverty and class as worldwide diversity concerns, recognizing the unique contribution of discrimination and differential treatment to poverty in countries around the world.

Sex and Gender: The Status of Women around the World

Volumes of research from various disciplines attest to women's low occupational status worldwide. Females often receive less education than males, and, as discussed throughout the book, education is closely associated with earnings and likelihood of being employed. In part as a consequence of lower education, women are less likely to be employed, and when employed they tend to earn less than men, worldwide. On the other hand, even with similar or more education, women's earnings and status worldwide are lower than men's. In many countries, fewer employment opportunities result in women spending more time (rather than less) pursuing education. The opportunity to work is less of a lure for women to leave school. With more, less, or equal amounts of education, discrimination and segregation contribute to women's lower occupational status and earnings worldwide.

Population and Participation Rates

There are 1.2 billion women workers in the world and women are participating in the workforce at higher rates than ever before. This increased participation is due to economies' needs for more workers, lower birthrates, and to changes in

[8] "Working out of Poverty." (2003). Report of the Director-General, International Labour Conference, 91st session, p. 23.

attitudes toward women's employment and social policies toward childcare. These factors, coupled with men's declining participation rates, result in women making up a larger proportion of the worldwide workforce than at any time in the past. In some countries, women now participate at about 80% of the rates that men participate. However, in other areas, such as the Middle East, Arabia, North Africa, and South Asia, women participate at about 40% or less of the rate that men participate.[9]

Sexual Harassment, Segregation, Discrimination, and Other Inequities

Sex discrimination and harassment, sex segregation, wage inequity, and the glass ceiling are eerily common problems faced around the world.[10] Women work fewer hours than men or not at all, and are more likely to be in poverty than men. Sex segregation of jobs is common and women are considerably less likely to be in high status or managerial positions than their proportions in the population and workforce participation would suggest. Women's concentration in low status, often powerless, positions contributes to the prevalence of sexual harassment worldwide. Researchers have found evidence of sexual harassment in Australia, Austria, Belgium, Brazil, Canada, China, Denmark, France, Italy, Japan, Mexico, the Netherlands, New Zealand, Northern Ireland, Norway, Spain, Sweden, and the United Kingdom.[11] In multiple studies of working women, Louise Fitzgerald and her colleagues have found that sexual harassment is similar in structure, type, and negative consequences for women, regardless of where the harassment occurs.[12] As we have discussed, sexual harassment results in negative physical, psychological, career, and financial consequences for those who are harassed, as well as having high costs for organizations in which they work. Absence and turnover, lowered productivity, reduced creativity, and damaged reputations are among a few of the organizational costs.

---

[9] International Labor Organization. (2005). "Women's Employment: Global Trends and ILO responses," http://www.ilo.org/dyn/gender/docs/RES/399/F1503666968/Womens%20Employment%20-%20Global%20Trends%20and%20ILO%20Respon.pdf, accessed 04/11/05.

[10] Shaffer, M. A., Joplin, J. R. W., Bell, M. P., Oguz, C., & Lau, T. (2000). "Gender Discrimination and Job-Related Outcomes: A Cross-Cultural Comparison of Working Women in the United States and China." *Journal of Vocational Behavior,* 57: 395–427; Muli, K. (1995). "Help Me Balance the Load: Gender Discrimination in Kenya." In J. Peters & A. Wolper (Eds.), *Women's Rights, Human Rights: International Feminist Perspectives,* London: Routledge, pp. 78–81.

[11] Fitzgerald, L. F., & Hesson-McInnis, M. (1989). "The Dimensions of Sexual Harassment: A Structural Analysis." *Journal of Vocational Behavior,* 35: 309–326; Gelfand, M. J., Fitzgerald, L. F., & Drasgow, F. (1995). "The Structure of Sexual Harassment: A Confirmatory Factor Analysis across Cultures and Settings." *Journal of Vocational Behavior,* 47: 164–177. For reports on research evidence of sexual harassment in North American and European countries, see Gruber, J. E. (1997). "An Epidemiology of Sexual Harassment: Evidence from North America and Europe." In W. O'Donohue (Ed.), *Sexual Harassment,* Boston: Allyn & Bacon, pp. 84–98.

[12] See, for example, Shaffer, M. A., Joplin, J. R. W., Bell, M. P., Oguz, C., & Lau, T. (2000). "Gender Discrimination and Job-Related Outcomes: A Cross-Cultural Comparison of Working Women in the United States and China." *Journal of Vocational Behavior,* 57: 395–427; Wasti, S. A., Bergman, M. E., Glomb, T. M., & Drasgow, F. (2000). "Test of the Cross-Cultural Generalizability of a Model of Sexual Harassment." *Journal of Applied Psychology,* 85(5): 766–778.

Wage Inequity and the Glass Ceiling

The glass ceiling phenomenon discussed in Chapter 9 exists in developed and developing countries. In industrialized nations, women occupy at most 10% of the highest positions. In Canada, for example, 10% of executives are women, compared with 43% in middle management. In the United Kingdom, women occupy 9.6% of executive positions. In terms of the wage gap, women working full time in the United States earn about 75% of men's earnings, in Russia the ratio is about 72%, while in France and Australia, women earn between 80% and 90% of men's earnings. Worldwide, women earn 66% of men's earnings.[13]

One of the contributors to women's lack of advancement is people's perception that characteristics associated with successful managers are those associated with men, rather than women. The "think manager, think male" phenomenon was first identified by Virginia Schein in 1973. In the more than three decades since then, researchers have confirmed the existence of this perception in the United States as well as in Germany, Britain, Japan, and China.[14] More recently, American men continue to perceive men as having requisite managerial characteristics, while women now view both men and women as having characteristics of successful managers. In China and Japan, however, both men and women view men, but not women, as likely to have qualities associated with successful managers.

People with Disabilities

The ILO includes people with disabilities as part of those "marginalized," "disadvantaged," or "vulnerable" groups in society—terms that are also relevant to other nondominant groups.[15] As members of a marginalized, disadvantaged, and vulnerable group, workers with disabilities around the world face issues with un- and underemployment, lower wages, misperceptions about competence, and overt and covert employment discrimination. The proportion of people with a disability has increased due to longer life spans, yet new types of illnesses (e.g., HIV/AIDS), landmines, substance abuse, and illnesses associated with child labor. While some countries prohibit employment discrimination on the basis of disability, many do not. We consider the population and participation of people with disabilities and disability legislation in the following sections.

[13] International Labour Organization. (2005).

[14] See Schein, V. E. (1973). "The Relationship between Sex Role Stereotypes and Requisite Management Characteristics." *Journal of Applied Psychology,* 57: 95–100; Heilman, M. E., Block, C. J., Martell, R. F., & Simon, M. C. (1989). "Has Anything Changed? Current Characterizations of Men, Women, and Managers." *Journal of Applied Psychology,* 74: 935–943; Schein, V. E., Mueller, R., Lituchy, T., & Liu, J. (1996). "Think Manager—Think Male: A Global Phenomenon?" *Journal of Organizational Behavior,* 17: 33–41.

[15] "Disability and Poverty Reduction Strategies." (2002). Working Paper. The Disability Programme, InFocus Programme on Skills, Knowledge, and Employability. International Labour Office: Geneva, http://www.ilo.org/public/english/employment/skills/disability/download/discpaper.pdf, accessed 08/24/05.

Population and Participation

Estimates from the International Labour Organization and the World Health Organization suggest that more than 600 million people worldwide have disabilities and 386 million of them are of working age.[16] Greater un- and underemployment and lower earnings of people with disabilities when compared with people without disabilities are common worldwide. When compared with other marginalized groups, the position of people with disabilities is even more extreme, and requires specific attention, recognizing their uniquely marginalized roles.[17]

Legislation

The ILO views employment fairness toward people with disabilities as "a human rights issue," with the right to decent work being one of those basic human rights. The ILO has carefully compared laws in Canada, France, Germany, the Netherlands, New Zealand, Sweden, the United Kingdom, and the United States. In countries in which the laws are more carefully designed and monitored (e.g., through controlling hiring, conditions of employment, and dismissal of workers with disabilities), there is more employment equity than in countries that use the "laissez-faire" approaches. The United States, New Zealand, and the United Kingdom use the latter, less strict, and thus less successful, approaches.[18] In contrast, Germany, France, and Sweden use recruitment grants, public subsidies, and special incentives to promote employment of people with disabilities. Strategies to improve job retention for people with disabilities are helpful to employers in controlling escalating costs of payments to workers with disabilities who are out of the workforce. By encouraging and assisting workers with disabilities to return to the workforce, both employers and individuals benefit.[19]

The ILO issued recommendations for employment of people with disabilities and for managing disability in the workplace in 1983 and 2001. The recommendations promote equal opportunity and employment for people with disabilities through training and development, funding and disseminating research, and writing policy guidelines and manuals for employers. Employers wishing to begin active hiring of and efforts to retain people with disabilities may consult the International Labour Organization and their local governments for recommendations.

[16] "Managing Disability in the Workplace." (2002). International Labour Office: Geneva, http://www.ilo.org/public/english/employment/skills/disability/download/codeeng.pdf, accessed 08/24/05.

[17] Disability and Poverty Reduction Strategies. (2002).

[18] International Labour Organization. (1998). "Worker Disability Problems Rising in Industrialized Countries." Press Releases, http://www.ilo.org/public/english/bureau/inf/pr/1998/19.htm, accessed 08/24/05.

[19] Managing Disability in the Workplace. (2002).

Sexual Orientation

Gays and lesbians face discrimination and harassment in much of the world. Discrimination against sexual minorities is exacerbated by religions that view homosexuality as being particularly abhorrent and that justify extreme means to curb homosexual behavior. In July 2005, two Iranian teens were hanged in a public square because of their sexual orientation. Reports suggest that more than 4,000 lesbians and gay men have been executed in Iran since 1979.[20] One study in Lithuania, Latvia, and Estonia documented discrimination against sexual minorities in the workplace, in service organizations, and in religious institutions such that many respondents reported desires to move to other countries.[21]

Legislation Prohibiting Sexual Orientation Discrimination

Because many sexual minorities face discrimination and harassment in various situations, many remain closeted. In response to or fear of employer discrimination, many sexual minorities remain closeted or work in informal labor markets. Although no federal legislation in the United States prohibits employment discrimination based on sexual orientation, several countries do have such laws, including Canada, Denmark, Finland, France, Hungary, Iceland, Ireland, Israel, the Netherlands, New Zealand, Norway, Slovenia, South Africa, Spain, and Sweden and other countries. Strength of the laws and entities targeted varies, with some limited to federal governments, or to public or private organizations. Without genuine commitment, however, laws do little to help those experiencing discrimination.

Poverty

The ILO condemns persistent poverty as a "moral indictment of our times."

> For individuals, poverty is a vicious cycle of poor health, reduced working capacity, low productivity, and shortened life expectancy . . . it leads to the trap of inadequate schooling, low skills, insecure income, early parenthood, ill health, and an early death.[22]

As discussed in Feature 16.1, a sobering indictment of poverty in the United States occurred in New Orleans, Louisiana, in the aftermath of the 2005 Hurricane

---

[20] Ireland, D. (2005). "Iran Executes Two Gay Teenagers." http://direland.typepad.com/direland/2005/07/iran_executes_2.html, accessed 09/07/05.

[21] Platovas, E., & Simonko, V. (2002). *Sexual Orientation Discrimination in Lithuania, Latvia, and Estonia,* Lithuanian Gay League Publisher.

[22] Working out of Poverty. (2003). Report of the Director-General, International Labour Conference, 91st session. p. 1 http://www.ilo.org/public/english/bureau/exrel/mdg/briefs/woop_summ.pdf, accessed 11/09/05.

Feature 16.1 *Poverty as a Diversity Concern*

Poverty is a specific area of emphasis for the International Labour Organization, which argues that poverty remains widespread in the developing world and some transition countries.[23] It is not limited to developing and transition countries, however—it is deep and widespread in some developed nations as well. The horror of the unnecessary loss of lives as a result of the 2005 Hurricane Katrina in the southeastern United States awakened the country to long-denied and ignored, yet long-lasting and stable distinctions based on class, poverty, and race. Around the world, the U.S. aura of wealth, affluence, and the illusion of equal opportunity for all grew dim while the consequences of persistent poverty, discrimination, and inequity were illuminated. In New Orleans, a city known for Mardi Gras, good times, and decadence, 26.9% of the population lived in persistent poverty even as the U.S. poverty rate was 12.7%. In 2004, the average poverty threshold for a family of four was $19,307, for a family of three it was $15,067, and $12,334 for a family of two.[24] Many affected by the disaster were working poor, employed in restaurants, hotels, and casinos, or driving cabs, trolleys, and limousines for affluent tourists, partygoers, and conventioneers.

Despite mandatory evacuation orders, persistent poverty left tens of thousands of people, largely Blacks, unable to flee the natural disaster, and vulnerable to its destruction. Without cars, credit cards, or money to rent hotels out of town, the persistently poor went to the Louisiana Superdome (a large sports facility) and Convention Center for shelter. After the hurricane and in the midst of unprecedented flooding, their persistent poverty left these victims vulnerable to further, man-made destruction of insensitivity and neglect.

Poverty, discrimination, and societal and governmental neglect contributed to the tortuous deaths of people in New Orleans in the Superdome, the Convention Center, hospitals, nursing homes, and attics around the city. New Orleans is not alone, however. The poor and disenfranchised live in projects in communities near toxic waste dumps in Chicago, Memphis, and Cleveland; cancer-causing refineries in Baton Rouge and Houston; and in flood prone areas of Tucson, Dallas, and New Orleans, and struggle to make ends meet.[25] Every day, in cities all around the United States, poverty, persistent segregation, poor housing, and separate and unequal schools contribute to preventable disease, violence, and suicide.[26] Those affected are disproportionately Black, Latino, American Indian, and Asian, although poor Whites experience many similar negative outcomes. In the United States, poverty rates for these groups, respectively, were 24.7%, 21.9%, 24.3%, 9.8%, and 8.6% in 2004.[27]

Although income and earnings requirements that constitute "poverty" vary by locale, being poor has similar consequences worldwide—from poor health to inadequate schooling to early death in Africa, Brazil, England, India, Mexico—everywhere

[23] Working out of Poverty. (2003). p. 22.

[24] U.S. Census Bureau. (2005). http://www.census.gov/Press-Release/www/releases/archives/income_wealth/005647.html, accessed 09/11/05.

[25] Ash, M., & Fetter, T. R. (2004). "Who Lives on the Wrong Side of the Environmental Tracks? Evidence from the EPA's Risk-Screening Environmental Indicators Model." *Social Science Quarterly,* 85: 441–462.

[26] See, for example, Barnes, S. L. (2005). *The Cost of Being Poor: A Comparative Study of Life in Poor Urban neighborhoods in Gary, Indiana,* Albany, NY: State University of New York Press.

[27] U.S. Census Bureau. "Poverty," http://www.census.gov/hhes/www/poverty/poverty.html, accessed 09/09/05. Figures for American Indians drawn from U.S. Department of Commerce, http://www.census.gov/Press-Release/www/2002/cb02-124.html, accessed 09/09/05.

one would venture to look. Favelas, barrios, projects, shanty towns, and slums are where the impoverished can be found. Although who is impoverished varies by where one is in the world, persistent poverty is a universal diversity concern. An "underlying feature" of this persistent poverty is "discrimination based on race, caste, ethnic origin, skin colour, religion, gender, sexual orientation, health status and disability."[28]

In France, the motto of "liberte, egalite, fraternite," meaning "liberty, equality, fraternity" has little meaning to French youths of North African descent. In France, there is ostensibly no distinction on the basis of race, religion, or ethnicity, yet North Africans in France, many of whom are Muslim, experience overt discrimination, un- and underemployment, and high rates of poverty.[29] Overall unemployment in France is 9.2%, but among those who are foreign born, it is 14%, after controlling for differences in education. For university graduates the unemployment rate is about 5%, but for North African university graduates it is 26.5%.[30] Name-based employment discrimination against and racial profiling of those of North African descent have been documented.

Michel Wierviorka, a sociologist who studies political violence, noted the similarities between the French riots and the 1992 riots in Los Angeles, California, in the aftermath of the Rodney King beating that was captured on videotape. "Riots occur when there is a strong feeling of injustice. Remember Los Angeles . . . It didn't start with the Rodney King beating; it started when the jury said the police were not guilty."[31] France has a long history of discrimination against immigrants and resistance toward immigration, and the failure to include descendants of immigrants brought to France when their labor was needed. This injustice and denial of the associated problems led to the rioting in late 2005.

Questions to Consider

1. ***Given education and opportunity, why is it easier for Whites in the United States to escape poverty and discrimination than it is for people of color?***
2. ***Why is it easier for men to avoid or escape poverty than it is for women?***
3. ***The ILO proposes that discrimination is an underlying feature of poverty. How are discrimination in employment and poverty related for workers around the world? Discuss.***
4. ***In this and previous chapters, the un- and underemployment of nondominant group members were documented. How do such un- and underemployment negatively affect the productivity of a country?***

Katrina and in France in late 2005 as a result of the widespread rioting of French youths of North African origin in response to discrimination, unemployment, and widespread poverty. In the United States, many tend to blame those who are in poverty for their situations, failing to acknowledge the role of discrimination and systemic exclusion, blaming instead personal failures and

[28] Working out of Poverty, p. 68.

[29] Hundley, T. (2005). "Uprising in France springs from sense of discrimination." Chicago Tribune. http://www.kansascity.com/mld/kansascity/news/world/13115428.htm, accessed 11/09/05.

[30] "French Muslims face job discrimination." 11/02/05. http://news.bbc.co.uk/2/hi/europe/4399748.stm.

[31] Hundley, T. (2005).

laziness—poor people could do better if they simply tried.[32] In France, Nikolas Sarkozy, the country's interior minister, referred to the young men responsible for the rioting in a word that translates as "scum." Similar to the myth of meritocracy that allows people to believe they alone have earned their wealth, affluence, and positions, many place the predicament of the poor or otherwise disadvantaged squarely on their choices. In contrast, the ILO gives a positive perspective of the character of the impoverished, suggesting that people living in persistent poverty

> draw from enormous reservoirs of courage, ingenuity, persistence, and mutual support to keep on the treadmill of survival. Simply coping with poverty demonstrates the resilience and creativity of the human spirit. . . . Imagine where their efforts could take them with the support and possibilities to move up a ladder of opportunity. Our common responsibility is to help put it there.[33]

Misperception: Most people who live in persistent poverty are lazy and unmotivated.

Reality: Most people living in poverty survive through enormous courage, persistence, and resilience.

Valuing, pursuing, and embracing diversity can help place a ladder of opportunity at the feet of those previously ignored but who have enormous reservoirs of skills and assets, be they poor, minority group members, women, sexual minorities, people with disabilities, or other nondominant group members. At the same time, valuing, pursuing, and embracing diversity can be a ladder of opportunity for organizations and society.

Facing the Future: The Broad Reach of Diversity in Organizations

As we become an increasingly diverse world population, the diversity of organizations should also be increasing. Organizations themselves are diverse in size, structure, earnings, design, and purpose. Included are schools, churches, governments, nonprofits, retailers, service providers, co-ops, farms, and countless entities in which people earn a living and interact with others. Success, or failure, of organizations will be greatly influenced by the ability to attract, retain, and maximize the contributions of people from all backgrounds and from around the world. It will be influenced by the ability to market to diverse customers, to engage diverse constituents, and to encourage full participation of every worker and potential worker.

[32] For example, see Cozzaredi, C., Tagler, M. J., & Wilkinson, A. V. (2001). "Attitudes toward the Poor and Attributions for Poverty." *Journal of Social Issues,* 57(2): 207–228.

[33] Working out of Poverty. (2003). p. 1.

As the world becomes more globally connected, discrimination, harassment, and exclusion based on race, ethnicity, sexual orientation, religion, age, family status, physical or mental ability, weight, appearance, and other irrelevant factors will be increasingly unwise, unprofitable, and unacceptable. At the same time, as the world's population becomes more diverse, this diversity will bring new challenges, threats, and opportunities. Included are the propensity to stereotype and discriminate, to hoard rather than to help, and to fight for resources believed to be scarce. Rather than stereotyping, hoarding, and fighting, those who understand the value in diversity would expect that inclusion of the ideas and input of more and more diverse contributors would result in more resources to be shared. Organizations and their leaders should welcome the challenges of diversity, minimize the threats, and capitalize on the opportunities resulting from diversity.

Attending to "diversity in organizations" is necessary, but not sufficient to increase organizational diversity. Organizations cannot be separated from individuals and society, nor can individuals and society be separated from organizations. Diversity among individuals in the population should result in diversity in organizations. Without conscious efforts to ensure that it does, however, historical evidence and the current status of many groups clearly indicates that it will not. The ideas proposed by Cox and Blake, which have been central to the discussion of why diversity should be valued and pursued, are only part of the picture. When organizations pursue diversity solely to obtain cost, resource acquisition, marketing, creativity, problem solving, system flexibility, and other advantages this will help some individuals improve their circumstances. Indeed, for these individuals, an organization's self-interested pursuit of diversity is personally helpful. And, if sufficient numbers of individuals in a group are helped, the group's overall position will improve to some extent. However, these are surface and shallow changes, incapable of long-term, sustainable progress. For long-term change to occur, a fundamental shift in views of the value in diversity and the reasons to pursue it must occur. Rather than seeing diversity solely as a means of gaining competitive advantage, this shift would require changed views of ourselves, our prejudices and biases, our personal attitudes, and our behaviors. It involves willingness to pursue and to advance societal changes that will reduce widespread inequity among people of the world. Diversity in organizations is but one aspect of such societal changes.

Recommendations for Change at a Societal Level

Governments of many countries have implemented legislation prohibiting discrimination against and encouraging the employment of nondominant groups. The legislation in the United States has been examined in previous chapters. Similar legislation prohibiting discrimination exists in such countries as Australia,

Canada, China, England, India, Mexico, New Zealand, South Africa, Sweden, and numerous others. Some are more successful than others in reducing disparities, but clearly more needs to be done. The persistence of discrimination, segregation, and exclusion even in countries having legislation make obvious the insufficiency of legislation. However, without legislation, circumstances would likely be even worse. At a minimum, laws are required to signal the need to pursue equity for all people. Strong measures are needed, rather than "laissez-faire" approaches that have no consequences for continued disparity nor incentives to comply.

In addition to legislation, governmental actions to improve the education of nondominant groups are needed. Education is an important part of preparedness for equity, and without education, inequity is certain to persist. Governments must work to ensure all residents have a certain minimum level of education in quality, safe schools. The digital divide between Whites and people of color, and rich and poor, must be eliminated. Everyone should have access to computers and the power of the Internet as part of the education process. As much as possible, to improve the opportunities of women to work, family policies should be implemented. Rather than viewing child care and rearing as an individual or personal responsibility and societal burden, children should be seen as the future of a society.

Organizational Feature 16.1 considers the Bill Gates and Melinda French Gates Foundation's efforts to reduce education gaps and the digital divide for Latinos and Blacks in the United States and to improve lives of those in poverty in the United States and worldwide. One goal of the foundation is reducing "inequities that divide our world." *Time* Magazine named Bill and Melinda Gates "Persons of the Year" for 2005 for these and other philanthropic efforts.

Recommendations for Change at an Organizational Level

In this section, we synthesize and expand upon some of the recommendations from previous chapters that were suggested to help organizations in their pursuit of a diverse workforce, along with suggesting some additional recommendations. Although diversity issues relevant to a variety of formal organizations in a variety of aspects were considered (e.g., customer discrimination in restaurants or stores) the recommendations in this section focus on formal organizations as employers. They are based on problems considered in the previous chapters and are drawn from human resources and diversity literatures and that are generally applicable to many organizations worldwide. Some of the recommendations are in the form of questions, recognizing the differences inherent in organizations' human resources practices. Answering these questions, and formulating more that are relevant to one's specific organization in its specific industry and locations will improve one's opportunity for success. The specific situation for a particular organization and location affect the recommendations for any particular organization. What is the

Organizational Feature 16.1 *Bill Gates and Melinda French Gates Foundation: Committed to Making a Difference*

Bill Gates is most well-known as the founder of one of the most powerful corporations in the world, Microsoft. Not only is Microsoft an immense financial success, Microsoft products have completely changed the amount of information that is available, the way information is shared, how knowledge is obtained and disseminated, and countless other aspects of life in the world today. The Bill and Melinda French Gates Foundation, established in 2000, and its partners are also making tremendous efforts to address many of the world's problems including some that are directly related to the present and future of diversity in organizations—education gaps among Hispanics and African Americans and the information divide.

The foundation's education program helps to ensure that more students are college ready, to reduce drop-out rates, and to improve the quality of education for those who do graduate. For various reasons, some graduates remain ill-equipped to obtain jobs that will support a family or to succeed in college. A particular focus of the program is low-income Hispanics and African Americans, who are less likely to graduate from high school and who are more likely to attend substandard schools. The foundation also provides scholarships for low-income students in Washington state low-income minority students in all states, and outstanding scholars and leaders throughout the world to pursue graduate degrees at Cambridge University. Through the Gates Millennium Scholars program, $1 billion over 20 years will provide college scholarships for over 20,000 talented, low-income minority students.

To help bridge the information divide, the foundation has been working with partners throughout the country to install nearly 50,000 computers in 11,000 libraries. In 1997, only 20% of public libraries had Internet access. Now, more than 95% of libraries do, making Internet access available to everyone, regardless of race, ethnicity, or income. Access to the Internet and learning about computers makes jobs and educational opportunities available to many people who do not have computers or Internet access in their homes. "Equality of access" is now a reality for anyone who can get to a library.

The Bill and Melinda Gates Foundation also works to improve health in some of the world's poorest nations by investing in research to prevent HIV/AIDS, TB, malaria, and to improve childhood immunizations and maternal and reproductive health. So far, half a million children's lives have been saved through immunizations. In the Pacific Northwest, the foundation works to help at-risk families, to reduce homelessness, and improve the likelihood that those who were once homeless will become self-sufficient through job training, abuse prevention, and education.

Bill and Melinda Gates believe that today's problems are solvable and are working to make a difference and to encourage others to do likewise. Reducing "inequities that divide our world" is a worthwhile goal embraced by the Bill and Melinda Gates Foundation.

Source: Bill and Melinda Gates Foundation. http://www.gatesfoundation.org/default.htm, accessed 07/15/05.

population of employees, applicant pool, customers, clients, and constituents? What are their key concerns with respect to diversity? What legislation exists in the particular location? Is there evidence of discrimination that needs attention, even in the absence of legislation?

Diversity Training and Diversity Education

In a study selected as the best published research in Human Resources in 2001, Marc Bendick, Mary Lou Egan, and Suzanne Lofhjelm provided a list of nine benchmarks for the most comprehensive organizational development approaches to diversity training.[34] Their survey of diversity training providers throughout the United States indicated diversity programs that are successful in the long-term:

1. have strong support from top management
2. are complemented by human resource practices
3. are tailored to each organization (rather than off-the-shelf, mass marketed programs)
4. are conducted by managerial or organization development professionals
5. enroll all levels of employees (as non-supervisory employees and peers often perpetrate discriminatory or harassing behaviors)
6. discuss discrimination as a general process (e.g., stereotyping, exclusion, and in-group bias)
7. explicitly address individual behavior (rather than focusing solely on attitudes, such programs help people learn how to behave and not behave in situations)
8. are linked to the organization's central operating goals
9. impact the organizational culture (such that discrimination, harassment, and exclusion are discordant with norms, values, and rewards of the organization)

Bendick et al. estimated that only 25% of training providers use such a comprehensive organizational development approach. Organizational development programs require a longer commitment and more resources than most of the diversity programs that currently exist in organizations. As the scope and depth of efforts increase, so too does their effectiveness in bringing about organizational diversity change. Committed organizations recognize the long-term value of investing resources in such a manner.

Although Bendick and his colleagues used the term diversity *training,* addressing discrimination as a general process and addressing behavior (rather than solely attitudes) are more representative of aspects of diversity *learning* or diversity *education.* Management research suggests that training is short term

[34] Bendick, M., Jr., Egan, M. L., & Lofhjelm, S. M. (2001). "Workforce Diversity Training: From Anti-Discrimination Compliance to Organizational Development." *Human Resource Planning,* 4(2): 10–24.

and with an immediate focus. Education and development, on the other hand, have a long-term focus.[35] Diversity education includes comprehensive diversity training and development efforts that investigate the historical background and current status of specific groups, focuses on discrimination as general processes and addresses individual attitudes and behavior. Education on the historical background and current status of groups increases understanding of the sources of and continuing need for diversity programs. Many people are simply unaware of the pervasiveness of discrimination, harassment and exclusion, the glass ceiling, and inequity experienced by people of color, women, working parents, sexual minorities, older people, and people with disabilities. Many are unaware of the multiple group memberships that everyone has and how these multiple group memberships affect everyone at some point. An educational perspective, coupled with the now commonly acknowledged reasons to value diversity, will be more effective than a training perspective.

Diversity education, management commitment, changes in human resource practices, and links to organizational goals can be expected to bring about more knowledge-based behavioral change for individuals and corporate cultural change. We consider management commitment and human resource practices in detail in the following sections.

Management Commitment to Diversity in Organizations

Diversity literature documents miserable failures of ill-conceived diversity initiatives, training programs, and other "diversity" measures. Prior to embarking upon diversity efforts, top management commitment is imperative. One step as a result of this commitment would involve the appointment of a key leader at the executive level who is responsible for and has the authority to make changes. Some of his or her responsibilities would include such things as assessing the organization's diversity climate, developing and implementing organization-specific diversity objectives and goals, then measuring progress against them, and addressing concerns, comments, and suggestions by employees, customers, and constituents. This person would also ensure diversity is linked to the organization's central operating goals and to decision-makers' performance measurement.

In addition to a key diversity executive with power to effect change, genuine commitment from other executives is also required for success. When leaders view diversity as an imperative, whether due to competitive advantages or moral and ethical concerns, diversity is more likely. However, not only is *top* management commitment to diversity an imperative, commitment from *all* management in an organization is also required. Without the commitment of managers and supervisors throughout an organization, diversity efforts will not be successful.

---

[35] Bohlander, G. W. & Snell, S. (2004). *Managing Human Resources* (13th edition). Mason, OH: Thomson South-Western.

Senior managers and executives, middle managers, first-line managers, assistant managers, and supervisors all play important roles in ensuring all employees have an opportunity to work and contribute to organizational success. As the first lines of decision making, first-level managers and supervisors have the power to obstruct or facilitate diversity among employees. They are the ones who make fair selection decisions, encourage working parents to have a healthy balance, facilitate employees in their quests to learn multiple languages, provide reasonable accommodations for applicants with disabilities and for those with specific religious preferences, and so on. First-line, mid-level, and executive-level management all foster or impede diversity.

Diversity-supportive behaviors of all levels of management are observed by employees, and employees are most likely to come into contact with low-level managers on a regular basis. How do such managers behave regarding diversity in the organization? Are they sincere about eradicating sexual, racial, and other harassment? Do they make sexist, racist, ageist, heterosexist, and other "-ist" comments and decisions? Are business meetings held in inappropriate or questionable locations (e.g., strip bars, Hooters, etc.)? Are older workers given or denied training opportunities? Performance of diversity-supportive aspects of managers' jobs should be rated along with other job criteria. The adage that "If it's not measured, it doesn't matter" is particularly true for diversity efforts.

Changes in Human Resource Practices

Job criteria and selection team. To facilitate diversity in the selection process, management and human resources should start with clear job criteria—what competencies are desired of a successful candidate? How will these competencies be identified and compared among candidates? Are the desired competencies clearly related to successful job performance (e.g., valid)? What is the demographic makeup of the recruitment and selection team? What measures are in place to ensure all candidates are viewed fairly? Are there posthiring analyses of candidate demographic backgrounds and hiring ratios to observe potential unfairness? As discussed throughout the book, applicants may not even be aware of discrimination or unfairness and are unlikely to sue. Although avoiding lawsuits is not a sufficient rationale for pursuing diversity, taking these steps will increase the likelihood of a diverse employee population, which should be the real stimulus.

Recruiting. What efforts can be taken to ensure that qualified applicants from a variety of backgrounds are in the pool of candidates? Schools with high representations of candidates that are diverse in race, ethnicity, sexual orientation, physical (and, as appropriate, mental) ability are good places to begin. Referrals from employees who are members of the target population are likely to be demographically similar to those making the referral—provide incentives for referrals who are hired and retained.

Advertising in publications geared toward certain groups, for example, *Latina Style, Ebony,* and the *AARP Magazine* would increase the pool of Hispanics, Blacks, and older applicants in the United States. For companies outside the United States, seek appropriate country-specific outlets that target different groups.

Selection. Once the pool of qualified applicants is generated, concerted efforts must be made to ensure that certain candidates are not unfairly eliminated as the selection process continues. In attempting to increase diversity among university faculty, for example, is research in areas related to race, ethnicity, gender, and diversity devalued because it is not considered to be "mainstream?" Is rigor in such publications discounted because of the research topic? In diversity efforts in a corporate organization, are candidates recruited at historically Black universities (HBCUs) or American Indian universities deemed to be less qualified than those from other universities? What steps can be taken to reduce these misperceptions? Are the schools for recruiting accredited by recognized bodies? Has this been publicized to employees involved in hiring and selecting and to the employee population as a whole?

Are managers and employees aware of ingrained preferential treatment toward certain groups that has to be deliberately counteracted? Do misperceptions exist about the qualifications of nondominant and dominant group members? If either or both are perceived as having been hired due to non-job-related qualifications (e.g., being a person of color or being White; being a woman or being a man), how might publicizing qualifications of all hires reduce such misperceptions? After hiring, are nondominant employees held to different standards (higher or lower) than dominant candidates? What mechanisms are in place to determine whether differential standards exist and to address and remove them if they do? Is the performance of all employees regularly and fairly assessed? Are poor performers advised and counseled to facilitate improvement? Is there evidence of "the norm to be kind" when evaluating employees with disabilities?[36] If employees are not given negative performance feedback when warranted, they will not be able to improve. If performance is unfairly scrutinized, this will not go unnoticed by employees and will serve to depress motivation and increase dissatisfaction and turnover.

Training and development. Are all employees provided opportunities to participate in job-related training and development? Are older workers steered away from training? By participation in training and development, workers prepare for advancement opportunities.

[36] Colella, A., & Stone, D. L. (2005). In R. L. Dipboye & A. Colella (Eds.), *Discrimination at Work: The Psychological and Organizational Bases.* Mahwah, NJ: Lawrence Erlbaum, pp. 227–253.

Researchers propose that "training in basic supervisory skills for inexperienced supervisors often reduces inconsistencies in policies, failures of communication, and interpersonal conflicts – changes that disproportionately aid members of groups traditionally experiencing discrimination but (that) improve the working environment for other employees as well."[37] Training in performance evaluation and compensation administration (to use job-related criteria) would also be helpful for all employees. Some of the cases presented in earlier chapters provide clear examples of how managers' apparent lack of basic supervisory skills (e.g., appropriate selection and promotional criteria) and of key laws related to employment resulted in discrimination.

Are all workers provided substantive diversity learning (e.g., training and education) opportunities? Research indicates that poorly designed or implemented diversity training can have negative consequences, such as backlash and unmet expectations. Are diversity learning programs high-quality, well-implemented, and relevant? Do such programs include short-term as well as long-term, educational efforts? Diversity training is not a "quick-fix" to long-term issues, particularly given institutional and systemic sexism, racism, ageism, and other "isms." People need help unlearning and divesting themselves of stereotypical beliefs about others. Do diversity learning programs help to eradicate stereotypes?

Do programs include sound data on the hiring, retention, promotion, and advancement of all groups? If there is fear associated with dissemination of such data, that fear suggests inadequate attention to diversity. Is there something to hide? Do employees resist attending diversity-learning programs or do they understand their importance? Is there tolerance for joking and kidding in sexual harassment training? Are managers and supervisors periodically updated with changes in EEOC guidelines and regulations?

Mentoring. Mentoring is valuable in helping dominant and nondominant group members succeed in organizations. Dominant group members are advantaged with similarity to leaders and executives—forming mentoring relationships without organizational assistance is simpler for them than for nondominant group members. Successful mentoring programs pair a protégée with a mentor who is genuinely interested in seeing the protégée grow and advance. Dominant group members tend to have greater access to social networks who share valuable job- and organization-related information. A formal mentoring program can provide access to such networks to nondominant group members also.

Promotion and advancement. Promotion and advancement rates of employees should be regularly monitored. Are promotion rates for nondominant and

---

[37] Bendick et al. (2001). p. 18.

dominant group members similar? Since measures to recruit, select, and train and develop will be carefully monitored to ensure fairness and equity, both nondominant and dominant group members would ideally experience similar rates of advancement. If they do not, reasons for differential rates should be investigated. Are women assumed to be less interested in advancement opportunities because of perceptions they are more focused on their families? Are groups with strong family ties believed to be unwilling to relocate for promotional opportunities due to their strong family ties? Are men with children viewed as more committed workers, and thus advantaged because of (and regardless of the veracity of) that perception?

Affinity groups. Many organizations sponsor affinity groups, groups in which people who are similar in some regard formally and informally gather as employees. American Airlines, for example, has affinity groups for Blacks, Latinos, gays and lesbians, and other nondominant group members. Shell has affinity groups for women, Latinos, Blacks, and Asians, and other groups. Verizon and Lockheed have similar groups. The existence of affinity groups in an organization may signal support and commitment to diversity to employees and constituents. Affinity groups that are social in nature should not be confused with formal mentoring programs that provide more instrumental support and assist nondominant groups in actual career progress.

Equitable benefits. Offerings of same-sex and domestic partner benefits is an important signal to gay and lesbian employees. Although this is a recommendation that is particularly important to gays and lesbians, such an offering sends a strong signal to heterosexual employees about the value the organization places on diversity and its sincerity in pursuit of it. In addition, domestic partner benefits are also useful to heterosexuals who are in committed relationships, but who remain unmarried.

Although organizations are not required to provide benefits for any employee, inclusion of all employees in benefits offerings indicates that all are valued. In addition to same-sex and domestic partner benefits, are employees allowed to indicate who is part of their family? Are care-giving responsibilities toward grandchildren, grandparents, and fictive (but no less important) kin recognized? Fears of excessive costs associated with recognizing different family members are similar to fears of hiring women in child-bearing years, or of hiring workers with disabilities—largely unfounded. As discussed in Chapter 15, costs associated with offering domestic partner benefits are similar to any increase in plan participants. Costs of offering such benefits will likely be offset by reduced turnover costs, lower resource acquisition costs, greater commitment and productivity, and intangible benefits resulting from treating employees equitably.

Other Employment Considerations

The preceding sections have considered ways in which organizations can work to increase the diversity among employees. The recommendations are in no way exhaustive, and management is encouraged to investigate their particular organization, and to assess its diversity strengths and weaknesses when developing an organization-specific plan. Are women fairly represented in various levels, but people of color not represented? Are men of color well-represented, but women underrepresented? Are certain groups overrepresented in technical fields and underrepresented elsewhere? A commitment to diversity will ensure that the appropriate questions are asked, answers evaluated, and steps taken to continue to work toward fairness and equity for all applicants and employees.

Diversity for Service Providers

The previous sections of recommendations focused on organizations as employers. We now consider organizations in other roles, particularly service providers, dealing with diverse customers and clients. Previous chapters provided evidence of disparate treatment of customers, such as assuming Black customers had stolen merchandise they had paid for or following them in stores, expecting them to steal. Customers of color have also reported being ignored in stores, while Whites are offered help in finding merchandise, and excessive wait times for restaurant service. Hotels, restaurants, retailers, colleges, and universities have also treated certain customer groups unfairly. While certain large and expensive lawsuits occurred in the United States (e.g., Denny's, Shoney's, Eddie Bauer, and Dillard's), as we have discussed in previous chapters, most customers do not sue. Costs associated with lost business and goodwill are more likely and more expensive than lawsuits, judgments, and settlements.

As institutions with strong societal influence, service providers must take a strong and proactive stand for diversity. Employees at all levels should receive education on common biases and stereotypes they may hold against members of certain groups. Customer complaints should be taken seriously and addressed. Mystery shoppers (diners, hotel guests, students, etc.) can provide valuable information on treatment of customers of different backgrounds. Are all customers greeted pleasantly when they enter an establishment? Are Black and female customers quoted higher prices for goods than White males? Are certain customers routinely seated in the least desirable tables in restaurants? In hospitals and nursing homes, are there multilingual and multicultural doctors, nurses, social workers, clergy, and counselors who are aware of cultural differences in beliefs about medical treatment, life, and death?

Law enforcement agencies. Law enforcement agencies play critical roles in diversity concerns. Hiring and retention of women and those who are bilingual (to reach large populations of non-English speakers) are employee-related concerns. Racial profiling is a customer and societal concern. As we have discussed, racial profiling of Black, Latino, Asian, and, in some areas, American Indian young men is a widespread problem in the United States. When men of color are disproportionately stopped and searched based on perceptions they are more likely to have done something criminal, indeed, they are more likely to be arrested than those who are not stopped and searched. When arrests are used as screening mechanisms for certain jobs, racial profiling takes an expensive, long-lasting, life-changing toll. To avoid discrimination, many employers require that convictions for crime, rather than arrests, be used as the deciding factor for exclusion. Using convictions is an attempt to reduce the effect of biased arrests, but the pool of people convicted is drawn from those arrested. Further, poor and minority group members are more likely to be convicted when arrested, and to receive harsher sentences.[38] Focusing on convictions does not address one contributor to the higher arrest and conviction rates of Blacks and Latinos: racial profiling. Committed law enforcement agencies must get to the heart of that matter. The public, of all racial and ethnic backgrounds, must demand that they do.

Colleges and universities. Because they are training grounds for future employees, managers, and leaders, colleges and universities are in a unique position to shape the future of diversity in organizations and society. Diversity should be an integral part of every college student's curriculum, and graduate student's curriculum as well, to equip them as future managers and leaders in a diverse society. As discussed in the book, many researchers have documented the ways in which exposure to diverse classmates and to diversity curricula benefits students. Diversity should be included as a critical and required part of every student's education. Diversity issues are relevant to each one of us, throughout our lives and careers. Students need to understand the historical background relevant to diversity concerns, the current status of dominant and nondominant groups, legislation, why stereotyping occurs and how to avoid it, and why diversity learning is important to individual and organizational success.

What measures are taken to build diversity learning into curricula? The book chosen for Syracuse University's 2005 shared-reading selection required summer reading for all incoming freshman was *Life on the Color Line,* by Gregory Howard Williams, president of City College of New York. In it, Williams details his experience of learning he was Black, after living life as White. At the start of the semester, Syracuse hosted a panel session for incoming freshmen, their parents, and other members of the community to discuss the

[38] See Beckett, K., & Sasson, T. (2004). *The Politics of Injustice: Crime and Punishment in America* (2nd edition), Thousand Oaks, CA: Sage; Dees, M. (with S. Fiffer). (1991). *A Season for Justice: The Life and Times of Civil Rights Lawyer Morris Dees,* New York: Scribners.

book. Discussants included representatives from Syracuse University's Lesbian, Gay, Bisexual and Transgender Center, the Team against Bias, the Office of Multicultural Affairs, and the counseling center, reflecting Syracuse's attempts at inclusiveness.[39]

Learning occurs outside of college classrooms as well. Are minority students assumed to need "remedial" coursework simply because of their racial or ethnic group? For students of any race or ethnicity who do need remedial coursework, does needing such coursework indicate need to improve the schools that they have attended, improving opportunities for others in the future? Are gay and lesbian students harassed and ostracized or welcomed and embraced? Is service-learning facilitated? The University of California at San Diego's "Principles of Community" express its commitment to diversity at the institution, stating:

- We acknowledge that our society carries historical and divisive biases based on race, ethnicity, gender, age, disability, sexual orientation, religion, and political beliefs. Therefore, we seek to foster understanding and tolerance among individuals and groups, and we promote awareness through education and constructive strategies for resolving conflict.
- We reject acts of discrimination based on race, ethnicity, gender, age, disability, sexual orientation, religion, and political beliefs, and we will confront and appropriately respond to such acts.
- We affirm the right to freedom of expression at UCSD. We promote open expression of our individuality and our diversity within the bounds of courtesy, sensitivity, confidentiality and respect.
- We are committed to the highest standards of civility and decency toward all. We are committed to promoting and supporting a community where all people can work and learn together in an atmosphere free of abusive or demeaning treatment.
- We are committed to the enforcement of policies that promote the fulfillment of these principles.[40]

This policy communicates the organization's position on understanding and appreciation of differences, education, rejection of and appropriate sanctions for discrimination, and commitment to the principles of community. A similar, carefully crafted and organizationally appropriate policy would be invaluable to organizations sincere about fostering diversity among its community of employees, customers, and constituents. Such a policy would be widely communicated, documented, understood, and genuinely pursued (rather than lip service).

[39] Snyder, M. (2005). "SU Selects 'Life on the Color Line' for First-Year Shared Reading," http://alumni.syr.edu/FullStories/Issue8-05-15.htm, accessed 09/11/05.

[40] The UCSD Principles of Community, http://www.ucsd.edu/principles/, accessed 09/10/05.

For the 80% of the U.S. population who do not receive college degrees, inclusion of diversity in their educational process (e.g., high school level) would exponentially increase the beneficial outcomes.

The Role of the Media

The media must take an active stance against promulgation of stereotypes that work to impede diversity and to harm society. Selling a story and generating high ratings are simply less important in the overall scheme. If responsible journalism is a priority, the programming will still sell. As with efforts that organizations take to ensure diversity among employees, the media must make sincere and concerted efforts to foster diversity. The first step is working to eradicate discriminatory news reports, television and movies, and commercials. Another step would include inclusive programming and discontinue programming that fosters stereotyping and bias. While entertainment is one goal of programming, critical analysis and thought can assist the media in promoting and support diversity and equity.

Recommendations for Change at an Individual Level

Blacks, Latinos, Asians, American Indians and Alaska Natives, multiracial group members, and other non-Whites, women, people with disabilities, those who are overweight or obese, sexual minorities, and religious minorities are the nondominant group members that we have discussed in the United States. The Maori in New Zealand, Asians in Britain, the Burakumin in Japan, ethnic Chinese in Indonesia, Blacks and coloreds in South Africa, Koreans in Japan, North Africans in France, women, people with disabilities, sexual minorities, immigrants, and the "untouchables" in India are some of the numerous nondominant groups who experience discrimination and differential treatment in countries around the world. Racism, sexism, heterosexism, ableism, classism, and other "isms" are alive and well, however, there are some things that individuals can do to minimize the negative effects of such discrimination. As proposed in many chapters, whenever possible, individuals should work to obtain as much education and learn as much as possible. As much as possible, work to be prepared to seize every opportunity when it arises—education, multiple language fluency, and job flexibility are just some of the ways in which one can work to circumvent discrimination.

Although race, sex, and often class segregation of jobs is prevalent around the world, nondominant group members should try to avoid segregated jobs and occupations. Investigate the diversity posture of an organization during the job search process. Is there evidence of the glass ceiling and walls? Are nondominant group members confined to staff, rather than line, jobs? Are nondominant group members represented at all levels of the organization? Find and talk with people who work there. What is the diversity climate of the organization *truly* like?

Don't deny one's identity and individuality, and don't be fearful of being viewed as a "token" or "affirmative action" hire. Such perceptions reflect on the perceiver, rather than on the perceived. Be careful to avoid internalizing low expectations. Reject stereotypes about one's own and others' group members. Avoid the temptation to accept perceptions about oneself and others based on group memberships. Resist discrimination against other nondominant group members—work for fairness for everyone, even when doing so does not appear to be a personal issue. Do not assume that all dominant group members are against diversity; many allies exist among dominant group members.

In addition to seizing opportunities when available, work to make opportunities for oneself and others. As are increasing numbers of nondominant group members, consider starting a business and let it be a beacon, modeling diversity support and providing opportunities for others. Seek a mentor, and serve as a mentor. Ask what one person can do to make a difference, and then do it. Do not be a passive observer or complainer—take action to make a difference about what you can when it is possible. Activism can help give one a sense of power while also helping to change situations.

Dominant group members should recognize unearned advantages. Be aware of one's membership in many groups and the fluidity of some group memberships (e.g., age, physical and mental ability). Recognize the value in and pursue diversity, working to foster it and resisting stereotyping and discrimination. Don't be afraid that it's "us" against "them" competing for a slice of a small and finite pie. Instead, view the value in diversity as fostering more and greater opportunities for everyone, but only when everyone has the opportunity to contribute. In an increasingly global community, "us" is everyone, and without the contributions of everyone, long-term success for anyone is at risk.

Capitalizing on the Strength of Diversity in the United States

At the beginning of this chapter, we considered the idea that *diversity* is not a U.S.-specific concept. Indeed this perspective was strongly and persuasively argued. At this point, however, a discussion of the unique diversity challenges in the United States is appropriate. Unique to the United States are: the annihilation and banishment to reservations of American Indians, the enslavement of and continued discrimination against Blacks, the targeted anti-Chinese legislation and sentiment, and long-lasting purposeful restriction of citizenship only to "White men," the internment of Japanese, the relative paucity of women in the political system and complete absence of women in the highest elected offices (e.g., president and vice president) when compared with other nations (e.g., England, India), the peculiar love of the benefits of immigrant labor but stated disdain for illegal immigration, and many other diversity factors. The diversity in the United States is uniquely its own, even though many aspects (e.g., gender issues, sexual orientation, disability, and poverty) are similar in many ways to that of many other countries. Although other countries have some level of racial, ethnic, religious, and other diversity, the exceptional history of the United States and its stated posture as a welcoming place for diversity makes its present position distinct from all others. Indeed, people seeking refuge from racial, ethnic, religious, and other persecution, and seeking opportunities often turn to the United States. As such, and given the increasing globalization of the world, the United States is in a particularly unique and precarious position with respect to diversity. It is unique in that no other nation has its diversity history and posture. It is precarious in that if its diverse population is not given opportunities to contribute, the United States may be left behind in an increasingly competitive and global world.

The United States no longer has the "luxury" of ignoring, excluding, devaluing, failing to adequately educate, and segregating large populations of workers. If women are to continue to be 51% of the population, and women live longer than men, as "minorities" grow to become the majority, as older workers are needing and desiring to work longer, as more people acquire and live longer with disabilities, as religious diversity increases, and as more people work and have families, all potential workers must be encouraged to bring their contributions to the country's success. The United States needs women as scientists, engineers, computer programmers, and truck drivers, rather than only as kindergarten teachers, nurses, and secretaries—limited to a few job categories and competing for low wages in these limited categories. It needs Blacks, Latinos, and American Indians as scientists, engineers, programmers, managers, and entrepreneurs, rather than only as custodial workers, laborers, hotel housekeepers, and construction workers, or, worse still, as having twice the unemployment rate of Whites, and many having given up looking for work. The United States needs workers with disabilities to be allowed to work—their stability, their education, their willingness to work must not be ignored. It needs all workers to have the opportunity to obtain at least a high school education, rather than having large proportions of the fastest growing groups remain uneducated. The United States needs a population that is multilingual rather than one in which many people are monolingual and resist languages other than English. It needs older workers who are willing and able to work to continue to provide their technical and managerial expertise, and sexual minorities to feel comfortable being "out" in the workplace rather than worrying about being "out-ed" and thus failing to contribute as they otherwise would.

In sum, the United States simply cannot afford to have potential contributors prevented from or limited in their contributions in an increasingly competitive world. As the boundaries of the world grow increasingly blurry, as mergers, acquisitions, cross-cultural relationships, and international business are the norm, intranational in-fighting and discrimination are increasingly absurd. Case Study 16.1

Case Study 16.1 *Fictitious Country A and Fictitious Country B*

Fictitious Country A and Fictitious Country B are competing in a globally competitive marketplace for employees, customers, goods and services, and stakeholders, among other things. Both countries have diverse population bases, comprising men, women, various racial and ethnic groups, nationalities, gays, lesbians, transgenders, bisexuals, various religious groups, older and younger workers, and people with physical and mental disabilities, among other aspects of diversity. Country A has implemented concerted efforts to provide employment opportunities for people from diverse backgrounds and is vigilant about monitoring their opportunities, promotion and advancement, termination, and other employment outcomes and attributes. Country A provides quality education for its diverse population, encourages multiple language fluency, and helps women remain in the workforce by providing quality, affordable, safe child and elder care. Older workers are encouraged to remain in the workforce if they wish, and their expertise, knowledge, and stability are valued and utilized. Provisions are made for those who wish to retire, but to work part-time, such that their needs and employers needs remain met. Needs of workers with disabilities are also accommodated, thus they participate in the workforce at high rates, rather than being confined to no or part-time work and forced to rely on disability benefits for survival.

Country A works to ensure job-related decisions in organizations are made on job-related attributes rather than stereotypes, statistical discrimination, in-group–out-group biases, fears, and other erroneous information. Executives, managers, leaders, employees, and stakeholders recognize the contributions of diverse employees to organizational advantages in cost, resource acquisition, marketing, creativity, problem solving, and system flexibility. They also acknowledge value in retained (rather than lost) business, avoidance of lawsuits and boycotts, and in higher stock prices stemming from proactive, purposeful diversity efforts. Individuals in Country A view diversity as contributing to their individual creativity, perspective taking, social awareness, and acceptance of differences. They value and pursue multiple language fluency and differences among their peers. The population of Country A views pursuit of diversity as contributing to the country's ability to compete in an increasingly global world, through greater creativity and innovation, new ideas, flexibility, and ability to put the talents of the entire population to work.

In contrast, Country B has some legislation regarding nondominant group members, but is less than vigilant in ensuring it is enforced. Perceptions that certain groups are unqualified and lazy, and that this is the reason they do not succeed, are widespread. In Country B, there are limited provisions to assist workers with families, and few to ensure that the entire population (and future workforce) is educated and skilled. Poverty is viewed as a personal shortcoming. Certain groups are viewed as less worthy of benefits and security than others and are encouraged to be invisible about their identity. Others are viewed as being uninterested in or unable to succeed in the highest-level decision-making jobs and are confined to a narrow set of low-level positions. Many groups in Country B are not allowed or encouraged to advance beyond a certain level or to enter certain occupations. Harassment and exclusion are not uncommon in organizations in Country B. Many other aspects of life in Country B ensure that much of the population is limited in its contributions and intellectual growth.

What is the expected result of future competitiveness of Country A, in which all potential workers are educated, skilled, have the ability to grow, learn, and apply their skills, and decisions about employment, promotion, advancement, and retention are truly based on merit and performance? What is the expected result of future competitiveness of Country B in which subsets of potential workers are educated, skilled, and have the opportunity to grow, learn, and apply their skills, but other subsets (who are increasingly large proportions of the population) are not, and decisions about employment, promotion, advancement, and retention are based on factors such as race, sex, national origin, religion, age, sexual orientation, and other characteristics not related to ability and performance? What is the expected result of this scenario for the long-term competitiveness of Country A and Country B in an increasingly competitive, global world?

presents a fictitious scenario of competitiveness in a country that fosters participation of its entire population compared with one that does not.

In addition to the organizational, societal, and individual recommendations presented earlier, what else can be done to encourage diversity? Attention to the pursuit of diversity should be increased, rather than decreased. The playing field is not level—indeed there has been significant retrenchment in the last two decades. The education, employment, opportunities, and earning power of many nondominant groups have actually declined given resistance to diversity measures. Religious and sexual orientation harassment have increased, as have racial profiling, hate crimes, and hostility toward the poor. Intellectual leaders and a government with a view to the country's future must work to educate the population that diversity is not about "us" versus "them" and a finite set of resources. Rather, by embracing diversity, and pursuing education, equity, fairness, and opportunities for all, the contributions of 300 million potential contributors create an infinite set of possibilities.

Summary

This chapter has considered three focal areas: international diversity, facing the future and recommendations for change, and the imperative of attention to diversity in the United States. For international diversity, we discussed the university relevance of *diversity* around the world, specifically, sex and gender, people with disabilities, sexual orientation, and poverty. In facing the future and recommendations for change, we explored the relationships between individual, organizational, and societal diversity, emphasizing that they are all intertwined. In the final section, we considered the unique position of the United States and its particular need and opportunity to embrace and foster diversity in organizations, given the diversity of the U.S. population.

We conclude with hopes that readers have learned a great deal about diversity in organizations, its relevance to individuals and society, and are inspired to pursue diversity—perhaps for competitive advantage, but more importantly, as a moral imperative. When everyone, regardless of race, sex, ethnicity, age, sexual orientation, physical and mental ability, family status, or other non-job-related attributes, has opportunities to work in a variety of jobs, to obtain promotions and advancement at work, to shop without being followed and drive without being profiled, and to obtain education, housing, loans, service in restaurants, and other "normal" privileges, individuals, organizations, and societies will be more able to contribute to the well-being of us all in the world in which we live.

Key Terms

Affinity groups — informal social organizations at work comprising demographically or otherwise similar members.

Diversity education — comprehensive diversity training and development efforts that provide historical background and current status of specific groups, focuses on discrimination as a general process and addresses individual attitudes and behavior.

Questions to Consider

1. Aside from those discussed in the chapter (sex and gender, workers with disabilities, sexual orientation, and poverty), what other areas exist that are of universal relevance to diversity in organizations, regardless of one's location in the world?
2. What can dominant group members in each society do to foster diversity? What can the nondominant do? What can you do?
3. Figure 16.1 provides some of the considerations useful in identifying specific diversity areas in a country. What other considerations would you add to the list?
4. Why is diversity a particularly important concern for the United States?

Actions and Exercises

1. Choose a country other than the United States. Document the key diversity concerns for that country. Which groups are dominant and nondominant? What are the participation rates, earnings, and employment differences among the groups? What legislation regarding those groups exists in the country? How is diversity in the country you chose similar to or different from diversity in the United States?
2. Assume you are starting a business in that country. Upon which diversity-related factors would you place most emphasis or be most concerned, based on the information you obtained in item 1?

INDEX

A

I

J

K

L

M

Q

R

S

T

U

W

Z